Kirk Haselden

Microsoft SQL Server 2005

Integration Services

Microsoft SQL Server 2005 Integration Services

International Standard Book Number: 0-672-32781-3

Library of Congress Catalog Card Number: 2005937212

Printed in the United States of America

First Printing: June 2006

09 08 07   4

Trademarks

All terms mentioned in this book that are known to be trademarks or service marks have been appropriately capitalized. Sams Publishing cannot attest to the accuracy of this information. Use of a term in this book should not be regarded as affecting the validity of any trademark or service mark.

Warning and Disclaimer

Every effort has been made to make this book as complete and as accurate as possible, but no warranty or fitness is implied. The information provided is on an "as is" basis. The author(s) and the publisher shall have neither liability nor responsibility to any person or entity with respect to any loss or damages arising from the information contained in this book.

Bulk Sales

Sams Publishing offers excellent discounts on this book when ordered in quantity for bulk purchases or special sales. For more information, please contact

U.S. Corporate and Government Sales
1-800-382-3419
corpsales@pearsontechgroup.com

For sales outside of the U.S., please contact

International Sales
international@pearsoned.com

Editor-in-Chief
Karen Gettman

Acquisitions Editor
Neil Rowe

Development Editor
Mark Renfrow

Managing Editor
Patrick Kanouse

Project Editor
Seth Kerney

Copy Editor
Karen Annett

Indexer
Heather McNeill

Proofreader
Tracy Donhardt

Technical Editor
Matt David

Publishing Coordinator
Cindy Teeters

Interior Designer
Gary Adair

Cover Designer
Gary Adair

Contents at a Glance

Table of Contents

PART III: Control Flow Services

PART IV: Management Services

Foreword

Microsoft SQL Server 7.0 and SQL Server 2000 both contained a component called Data Transformation Services (DTS). DTS was an ETL tool. If you don't already know that ETL means Extract, Transform and Load, this might not be the book for you. But if you do care about ETL, have challenging ETL problems, and have SQL Server 2005, this most likely is the book for you! This book is about SQL Server 2005 Integration Services, the successor to DTS.

It took a unique team to build SQL Server 2005 Integration Services. If I had told you in 2000 when we started the Integration Services project that we would assemble a team of almost 30 people at Microsoft who were utterly passionate about ETL, you would have been skeptical. Through the leadership of Kamal Hathi, Donald Farmer, Eduardo Alvarez-Godinez, and your author Kirk Haselden, we did just that.

When we began planning "Yukon" (which became SQL Server 2005), we knew that our customers were facing ever larger and more challenging ETL problems. Years ago, data warehousing and business intelligence were "local" problems; or perhaps better said as "solutions to local problems."—the sales warehouse sourced answers to questions in the sales department, and marketing had its own warehouse. True performance management, the evolution of business intelligence, however, requires a complete company view. Customers want to load far more data than in the past, and they want to do so far more frequently.

We knew it was time to reinvent our ETL tool. We wanted to increase performance by at least an order of magnitude. We wanted to incorporate best-of-class ease of use, unparalleled programmability, and a very high level of out-of-the-box functionality. We truly sought to reinvent our ETL offering. Thinking about who in our industry really knew how to push a lot of processing against a lot of data, I sought out programmers and architects from the compiler team. We were lucky to find Mike Blaszczak, who had made key contributions to MFC, and who is one of the best programmers in the world. Mike in turn knew Kirk, and brought him into the team early on. In just a few years, Kirk became the Development Manager for Integration Services, and with his team, brought it to market.

This makes Kirk an ever-so appropriate guide for you in your exploration and use of Integration Services. He of course has a deep understanding of SSIS at every level—we expect that from a Development Manager. Beyond that, he has a love for users and customers that translates into a clear writing style and an enjoyable read. In each chapter, Kirk motivates you, teaches you, and delivers insight only a "Dev Manager" would possess. Pay attention to the notes in various chapters: This is where you get to see into the mind of the developer. Also, pay attention to the quotes that open each chapter—I can verify many of these, I was there to hear them, and they are often entertaining.

One of the ways in which SSIS improves on DTS is in manageability. The "configuration" is a new concept in SSIS. Configurations allow ETL developers to put some of the metadata of their package on the outside of the package, so that administrators can tweak them at deployment time. Chapter 14, "Configuring and Deploying Solutions," covers this in detail. Chapter 23, "Data Flow Task Internals and Tuning," covers optimization and tuning. SSIS can handle enterprise ETL needs, and this chapter gives you the insight and details you need to run your SSIS packages at their fullest performance.

Another area of difference between DTS and SSIS is extensibility. Chapter 24, "Building Custom Tasks," covers the development of custom tasks. Chapter 25, "Building Custom Data Flow Components," covers the development of custom components. The companion website at www.samspublishing.com includes all of the source code that Kirk develops in these chapters. I'm personally looking forward to using his source component to pull EXIF information out of JPEG files: Kirk is an avid photographer and has used real-world examples throughout the book.

It's been a privilege to work with Kirk for several years. I hope to work with him for years to come. He worked hard on this book because he loves SSIS and its customers. I hope you enjoy his work and profit from this book.

Bill Baker

May 2006, Redmond, WA

About the Author

Kirk Haselden is the Development Manager on the Integration Services team. Kirk has been with Microsoft for 10 years in various groups, including Hardware, eHome, and five years in the SQL Server group developing Integration Services. Kirk is primarily responsible for the design and implementation of the Integration Services runtime. Before Microsoft, Kirk worked for various small to midsized software companies writing educational, dental, and online software.

Dedication

To Christine, Lindsey, Tyson, Amanda, Jenny, and Sarah.

Acknowledgments

Over the years, I've probably read hundreds of acknowledgments in books just like this one. Only now do I fully comprehend the depth of gratitude all those authors were expressing. Writing a technical reference is an extremely challenging undertaking. It takes an enormous amount of time, patience, and persistence while impacting everyone near and dear to the author.

I'd like to thank my loving, supportive, and patient bride Christine who has done so much to make this book possible. Thanks for all the meals delivered to my desk, the supportive words, and immense patience. You are a wonderful eternal partner. I could not have done this without you. Thanks to my children, Lindsey, Tyson, Amanda, Jennifer, and Sarah, who sacrificed six months of "quality time" with their father while I was distracted with writing. I look forward to catching up on the Father/Son and Daddy/Daughter dates.

To Matt David, my technical editor, thanks for reading every line and for reviewing the code. You are an amazingly talented and professional developer. To Sergei Ivanov, who has been so instrumental in this book and in the development of Integration Services, thanks for your help forming the ideas and writing the sample profile transform. To Mike Blaszczak, thanks for your friendship and mentoring. Thanks for your insight and guidance into how to write a technical book. To Ashvini Sharma, thanks for your constant words of support and encouragement, especially toward the end. To the rest of the Integration Services team, thanks for such a cool product without which there would be no need for a book.

Thanks to Scott Turner, Mark Durley, and Gunther Beersaerts for your ad hoc chapter reviews and feedback.

To the folks at Sams, Neil Rowe, Mark Renfrow, and Karen Annett, thanks for your patience and hard work. Karen, thanks for the copy editing; it always amazed me how accurate and consistent your suggested changes were.

Thanks to Kamal Hathi, Bill Baker, and Tom Casey, my managers and general managers, for giving me support and a little extra space as I wrote. Thanks to Euan Garden for the long hours of white board discussions that started it all. Thanks to Richard Waymire for your friendship, peer mentoring, and asking me to write this book.

Thanks to Scott Stout for your friendship and support and Craig Osterloh for saving me from the precipice of a tax accounting career.

Finally, thanks to mom and dad for not stopping at five.

We Want to Hear from You!

As the reader of this book, *you* are our most important critic and commentator. We value your opinion and want to know what we're doing right, what we could do better, what areas you'd like to see us publish in, and any other words of wisdom you're willing to pass our way.

As an associate publisher for Sams Publishing, I welcome your comments. You can email or write me directly to let me know what you did or didn't like about this book—as well as what we can do to make our books better.

Please note that I cannot help you with technical problems related to the topic of this book. We do have a User Services group, however, where I will forward specific technical questions related to the book.

When you write, please be sure to include this book's title and author as well as your name, email address, and phone number. I will carefully review your comments and share them with the author and editors who worked on the book.

Email: feedback@samspublishing.com

Mail: Paul Boger
         Publisher
         Sams Publishing
         800 East 96th Street
         Indianapolis, IN 46240 USA

For more information about this book or another Sams Publishing title, visit our website at www.samspublishing.com. Type the ISBN (excluding hyphens) or the title of a book in the Search field to find the page you're looking for.

PART I

Getting Started

IN THIS PART

Welcome to SQL Server Integration Services 2005

"I SAVED THE SHOT WITH MY FACE!"—MARK DURLEY

This chapter is a brief introduction to Integration Services, its origins, its history, and a high-level view of what Integration Services is and how it can be used.

What Is SQL Server Integration Services?

Depending on whom you ask, you might get different answers to that question ranging from descriptions such as a data import/export wizard, to an ETL tool, to a control flow engine, to an application platform, or to a high-performance data transformation pipeline. All are correct because Integration Services is a set of utilities, applications, designers, components, and services all wrapped up into one powerful software application suite. SQL Server Integration Services (SSIS) is many things to many people.

Data Import/Export Wizard

One of the most popular features of Integration Services is the Import/Export Wizard, which makes it very easy to move data from a source location such as a flat file or database table to a flat file, table, or other destination. The Import/Export

Wizard was the first utility developed back in the SQL Server 7.0 time frame and contin-ues today as an important utility in the Database Administrator's toolbox.

ETL Tool

ETL is an acronym for Extract, Transform, and Load and describes the processes that take place in data warehousing environments for extracting data from source transaction systems, transforming, cleaning, deduplicating, and conforming the data and finally loading it into cubes or other analysis destinations. Although Data Transformation Services (DTS), Integration Services' predecessor application, was considered a valuable tool for doing ETL, Integration Services is where true Enterprise ETL became available in SQL Server.

Control Flow Engine

The processes involved in moving data from location to location and transforming it along the way are not restricted to only processing data. Integration Services provides a control flow for performing work that is tangentially related to the actual processing that happens in data flow. Examples include downloading and renaming files, dropping and creating tables, rebuilding indexes, performing backups, and any other number of tasks. Integration Services provides a full-featured control flow to support such activities.

Application Platform

Developers can create applications that use Integration Services as a platform, embedding the engines within their application using the provided object models. As a developer, you can embed the Integration Services engines and components within your applica-tions using the object models.

High Performance Data Transformation Data Pipeline

That's a mouthful and really incorporates two ideas: high performance and data pipelin-ing. The Data Flow Task is a high-performance tool because you can use it to perform complex data transformations on very large datasets for incredibly performant processing. The pipeline concept means that you can process data from multiple heterogeneous data sources, through multiple parallel sequential transformations, into multiple heteroge-neous data destinations, making it possible to process data found in differing formats and on differing media in one common "sandbox" location.

A Short Integration Services History

Integration Services is the successor to Data Transformation Services (DTS). DTS had humble beginnings. It was started on a shoestring budget with very few resources. Its first incarnation was a proof-of-concept transformation, which later became known as the data pump. The proof of concept caught the attention of some folks around Microsoft and it was given some funding.

The first release of DTS shipped with SQL Server 7.0 to receptive users. The alternatives at the time were either very difficult to work with, very expensive, or both. Many DBAs were forced to write custom transformation software, which was inflexible and difficult to maintain. Some tools had limitations, such as the need for source and destination schemas to match exactly, direct dependence on a particular database product, and/or no transformation capabilities. Many wrote custom parsing and transformation applications. For example, many companies are only now converting from hand-coded flat file parsers, SQL Scripts, and transformation code to a standard platform such as Integration Services.

The first release of DTS addressed several of these issues and simplified life for a lot of people. By using OLEDB for its data access layer, DTS could access various data sources with little or no custom coding. DTS was also affordable because it shipped "in the box" with SQL Server. Users had access to all the power of more expensive products, yet incurred no additional cost for their ETL tools. This was obviously a benefit to IT shops trying to stretch their budgets. DTS was a flexible product that was easy to use. There were also a number of standard tasks in the box, including the Transform Data, Execute Process, Active X Script, Execute SQL, and Bulk Insert Tasks.

SQL Server 8.0 added even more functionality by adding more tasks. The Execute Package, FTP, and MSMQ Tasks added incremental improvements across the product. However, users experienced some frustration with DTS when attempting to work with large datasets and some of the other limitations inherent in a script-based tool. The time was ripe to create a truly enterprise-ready integration tool.

Bill Baker, the general manager of Business Intelligence in SQL Server, made the investment in the ETL and Integration space. He brought together some very talented folks such as Gert Draper, Euan Garden, Mike Blaszczak, Ted Lee, Jag Bhalla, and numerous other individuals who formulated the ideas behind the Data Flow Task and the next version of Integration Services. Over a period of five years, the development time frame for SQL Server 2005, the DTS team completely redesigned and rewrote DTS to become what is now Integration Services.

What's New? (Or, This Is Not Your Father's DTS!)

A popular answer to this question is "Everything." Integration Services is the successor to Data Transformation Services (DTS), so there are some similarities, but because it is a complete rewrite, there is very little code from DTS remaining in Integration Services. In some ways, it is easier to list what is the same than to list everything that's different.

If you are familiar with DTS, you'll quickly grasp the control flow concepts. In DTS, the control flow and data flow were all on the same design surface. Integration Services provides a separate design surface for control flow and data flow. The separation makes it easier to understand and organize complex packages. Big gains were made in the data flow functionality. Where DTS has the Datapump, Integration Services has the Data Flow Task or Pipeline. The Datapump supported only one source, transform, and destination. DTS transformations are limited in scope, number, and performance. Integration Services Data Flow Tasks can perform extremely complex and advanced data processing within one pipeline.

Integration Services still has tasks, but they have been cloistered to some extent because the package pointer is no longer passed to them and through various mechanisms, the Integration Services runtime ensures that tasks do not access their own package during execution.

The DTS concept of a Step has been expanded to what is now called a Taskhost. The Step participated in the task execution scheduling. The Taskhost schedules the task execution and much, much more.

Integration Services still has the concept of precedence constraints. However, they have been made smarter by adding expressions to the precedence equation and multiple precedence constraints can be OR'ed so that if any one of multiple precedence constraints pointing to the same task is satisfied, the task can execute.

Connections still exist in Integration Services, but they are now called connection managers. In DTS, given certain conditions, a connection would serialize workflow. Connection managers generate a new connection every time you call AcquireConnection, so there is no connection conflict. Every task gets its own physical connection.

Logging still exists but has been expanded and updated. Variables are more important and flexible than their DTS counterparts and the designer is much more comprehensive and powerful. Debugging support is now available in the form of breakpoints, watches, and call stacks. Eventing has been enhanced to make it possible to handle them inside the package with event handlers.

As you can see, Integration Services carried forward, improved, and augmented many of the concepts found in DTS while adding a few new tasks and many more transformations.

How This Book Is Organized

This book is organized into six parts starting from basic introductory or conceptual discussions and steadily transitioning to more advanced topics. The first parts are appropriate for those seeking a high-level overview of Integration Services. The middle parts are appropriate for users such as Database Administrators, ETL developers, and data architects. The last part is appropriate for those interested in writing custom components or simply better understanding how Integration Services works "under the cover."

- **Part 1**—Getting Started covers how to set up the sample packages and sources, setting up Integration Services, and how to migrate packages from DTS.

- **Part 2**—Integration Services Basics and Concepts is a conceptual and practical guide to understanding and using the product. This is a high-level overview of important concepts.

- **Part 3**—Control Flow Services covers the stock tasks and other control flow features of Integration Services.

- **Part 4**—Management Services covers the features that support the day-to-day management of Integration Services solutions.

- **Part 5**—The Data Flow Task focuses on exploring the capabilities of the Data Flow Task and components.

- **Part 6**—Programming Integration Services teaches you how to build components that plug into Integration Services.

Each chapter was written to stand alone as much as possible. Although some topics naturally rely on other previously discussed concepts, great effort was made to write the chapters so that each could be read independently. Also, most of the topics are reinforced with samples. Samples are an important part of this book and should be studied carefully if you want to fully understand Integration Services.

Each chapter begins with a quote. Many books do this. Some with erudite quotes that make your head swim with visions of celestial ponderings. These quotes are a little more down to earth and most of them have been collected over the period during which Integration Services was developed. Many of the quotes are from key individuals on the team, some are simply humorous, and still others should give you some insight into the day-to-day life on the Integration Services team. They are offered to you as simple entertainment.

The Sample Projects

In the provided samples, numerous sample solutions with packages illustrate the discussed concepts. In addition, custom task and custom component projects are provided that you can study to better understand how to write custom components for Integration Services. The custom tasks, components, and utilities provided are as follows:

- `SampleTask`—A very rudimentary task discussed in Chapter 24, "Building Custom Tasks."

- `StarterTask`—A custom task project with a full task UI you can use to start your own custom task project.

- `HTTPTask`—A custom task for downloading files via HTTP. This is a very simple task with no UI.

- `ExpressionTask`—A custom task for evaluating expressions using the Integration Services Expression Evaluator engine.

- `CryptoTask`—A fully functional task for encrypting and decrypting text files using the Rijndael algorithm.

- `ImageFileSrc`—A Data Flow Source Adapter for reading image file information from JPG files.

- `DataProfiler`—A Data Flow transform for profiling data.

- `SQLClientDest`—A Data Flow Destination Adapter for writing data flow data to SQL Server using the ADO.NET SQL Client provider.

- `ODBCDest`—A Data Flow Destination Adapter for writing data flow data to SQL Server using the SQL Server ODBC Client provider.

- `ConfigEdit`—A simple utility for editing configurations in a package.

- `ConfigBatch`—A utility for adding, modifying, or deleting a configuration from multiple packages in a batch.

By purchasing this book, you have license to use and freely distribute these components. You can also modify the components in any way you want for sale or redistribution. In the event that you do use this code, a small attribution to this book and the author would be appreciated.

Setting Up Integration Services

"WE DON'T BELIEVE IN CD-ROM TECHNOLOGY."—CHAD EVANS

Installing IS

This chapter is a quick introduction to setting up Integration Services (IS) and the samples found at www.samspublishing.com. Helpful resources are provided that you can reference when you want to extend your studies beyond what's covered here. In addition, some common pitfalls are discussed that you should avoid for a smooth setup experience. This chapter is a quick-start setup guide. This chapter is not thorough enough to provide all the details and should not be considered a replacement for reading the setup documentation that comes on the setup disks. Most importantly, take the time to read the readme page in the root folder of the setup disk called ReadmeSQL2005.htm. Simply stated, many setup problems and questions can be avoided by reading this document.

CAUTION

Before attempting any setup, be certain that all beta and CTP installations have been completely removed from your machine. Your best bet is to wipe the machine clean and rebuild. If you are installing Microsoft SQL Server to a production server machine, rebuilding the machine is highly recommended.

Setting Up Integration Services

To get started with setup, go to the root of the installation disk and run Setup.exe. Figure 2.1 shows the End User License Agreement (EULA) dialog box that opens. Make sure you read this and understand it completely.

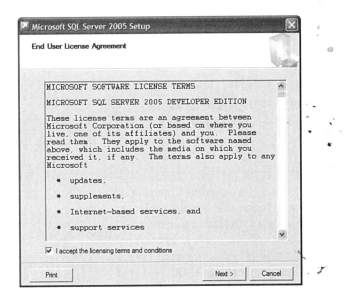

FIGURE 2.1   The first dialog box shows the End User License Agreement.

Click the Next button until you arrive at the dialog box shown in Figure 2.2.

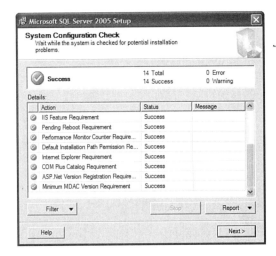

FIGURE 2.2   The System Configuration Check checks your system before installing.

This dialog box checks various settings and components on your system to ensure that they are available and correctly configured. If all the rows show a status of Success, you can move on to the next steps. If not, the Filter and Report buttons can help you isolate the problem and report it. Clicking the Next button takes you to the dialog box shown in Figure 2.3.

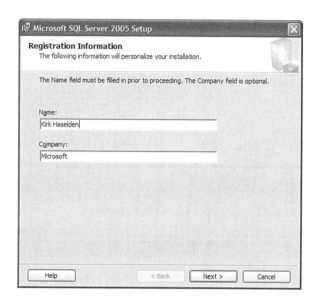

FIGURE 2.3   Enter your registration information.

Enter your name and company name and click the Next button to see the dialog box shown in Figure 2.4.

For this example, only SQL Server, Integration Services, and Workstation Components are selected. You, however, can select any combination you want, but make sure you have SQL Server Database Services, Integration Services, and Workstation Components, Books Online and Development Tools installed for working through the samples in this book. To better understand what each check box means, click the Advanced button to see the dialog box shown in Figure 2.5.

The Advanced button shows you the details behind each feature check box and whether it is installed by default. One thing you might notice is that the Sample Databases are not installed by default. Many of the samples in this book use the AdventureWorks database, so make sure you install it. Also, if you want to do any work with legacy Data Transformation Services (DTS) packages, ensure that the Legacy Components under the Client Components node are set to be installed. If you don't install Legacy Components, DTS packages will not run. This is covered in more detail Chapter 3, "Migrating from DTS."

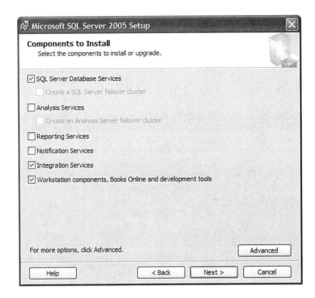

FIGURE 2.4   Choose the components you want to install.

FIGURE 2.5   Use the Advanced button to double-check what's getting installed.

TIP

Northwind and Pubs sample databases are not installed by default. If you want to have those sample databases, you can download them. The website address is http://www.microsoft.com/downloads/details.aspx?FamilyId=06616212-0356-46A0-8DA2-EEBC53A68034&displaylang=en. If you don't want to type in this monstrous URL, you can go to the downloads section of Microsoft.com and search for "pubs database."

Surface Area Configuration

As you might already know, security was a high priority for this release of SQL Server. Each individual in the SQL Server organization spent an enormous amount of time on security-related efforts. One thing that became clear during the security reviews and planning was that too many features in SQL Server were enabled by default. An effort was launched in the SQL Server organization to correct this and was called, appropriately enough, "Off By Default." One result of these efforts is the Surface Area Configuration Wizard.

To open the Surface Area Configuration Wizard, select Microsoft SQL Server 2005, Configuration Tools, SQL Server Surface Area Configuration from the Start menu. Figure 2.6 shows the Surface Area Configuration Wizard.

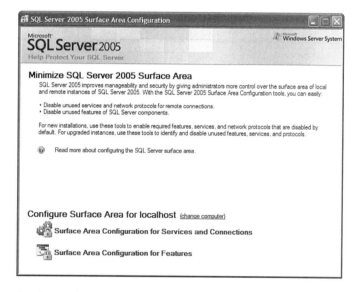

FIGURE 2.6   Configure the security surface area of your server.

You can choose one of two types of settings, as listed at the bottom of the screen shown in Figure 2.6 and discussed in the following sections.

- Surface Area Configuration for Services and Connections
- Surface Area Configuration for Features

Surface Area Configuration for Services and Connections

Let's first take a look at the configurations for services and connections. Ensure that the Integration Services service is running and the startup type is Automatic. Also, be aware of the Remote Connections setting in the Database Engine node. It's often the source of problems with connecting remotely. In general, you should be aware of all the features and settings that are impacted by this wizard. You might be scratching your head trying to figure out why something won't work until you realize it's off by default—more than a few users have been bitten by this! Figure 2.7 shows the Surface Area Configuration for Services and Connections dialog box.

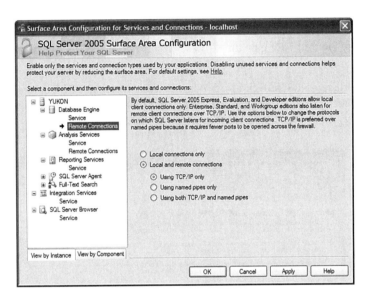

FIGURE 2.7   Configure services and connections that are off by default.

> **NOTE**
>
> Occasionally, Integration Services fails to establish connections to SQL Server, even when on the same machine as the server. In case SQL Server Integration Services (SSIS) fails to connect, check the SAC Enable Remote Connection setting.

Surface Area Configuration for Features

As you can see in Figure 2.8, the Surface Area Configuration for Features dialog box allows you to turn off potentially vulnerable features in the Database Engine, Analysis Services, and Reporting Services.

Again, you should become familiar with those features that have been disabled. You should get a descriptive error alerting you to the fact that the features are turned off. In the absence of such an error, a good first step is to double check the Surface Area Configuration Wizard to see if the feature you're trying to use is enabled.

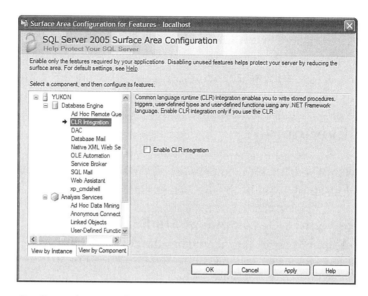

FIGURE 2.8   Configure features that are off by default.

Setting Up Book Samples

A number of sample packages and other projects are referenced heavily in this book. You can copy these samples to your hard drive so that you can learn by playing. After downloading the sample files from www.samspublishing.com, locate the folder at the root called SAMPLES. In Windows Explorer, simply drag that folder to a location on your machine's hard drive.

At the root of the SAMPLES folder is a file called README.TXT. It explains how to set up your machine so that the packages run without having to change them in any way. Here are the instructions as found in the readme file:

Each sample is kept in a folder named in similar convention to the chapter folders. Chapter folders are named 'C' followed by the chapter number and simple name. Sample folders are named 'S' followed by the chapter number and simple name of their corresponding chapter. For example, samples for Chapter 12, C12-Variables, are in a folder called S12-Variables.

To run the samples, create the following environment variables at the command prompt:

SET SSISSAMPLESROOT=D:\SSISBOOK\SAMPLES

This is the root folder where the samples are stored.

SET SSISSAMPLESERVER=MYMACHINE\SS2K5RTM

This is the name of the server where the sample database is attached.

SET SSISSAMPLESWORKINGFOLDER=D:\SSISBOOK\SCRATCH

This is where packages put any temporary files they create.

Don't append a '\' to the end of these paths. All the packages append it as part of their configurations.

Each package in the samples has an environment variable configuration that uses these environment variables to build paths to the scripts and other resources. After you have this set up correctly, each of the packages should run without modification.

Where Is Everything?

Integration Services isn't just one application, but a collection of components, utilities, engines, and wizards. You'll want to know where these are, so the following sections provide a list of the most useful files and where to find them.

Business Intelligence Development Studio

The Business Intelligence Development Studio is the designer and development environment for all Business Intelligence applications. You can find a link to it in the Microsoft SQL Server 2005 menu tree on the Start menu.

Management Studio

Management Studio is the management interface for accessing the SQL Server services, including SQL Server, Analysis Services Server, Reporting Services Server, and Integration Services Server. It is in the same location as the Business Intelligence Development Studio. Figure 2.9 shows the SQL Server 2005 menu.

FIGURE 2.9   Most SQL Server applications can be started from the Start menu.

Import/Export Wizard

Not all SQL Server applications can be started from the Start menu. The Import/Export Wizard is what you use to quickly generate Integration Services packages for moving data from one location to another. It is not on the Start menu. To make it easier to find, put it on the Start menu or, a favorite, the Quick Launch toolbar on the taskbar. To find it, open Windows Explorer and go to the location where you installed SQL Server. It should be in Program Files under the Microsoft SQL Server\90\DTS\Binn folder. The filename is DTSWizard.exe. Right-click on this file in Windows Explorer and drag it to the taskbar. When the shortcut menu appears, click Create Shortcut Here.

Migration Wizard

The Migration Wizard is what you use to migrate DTS packages to IS packages. It's not on the Start menu either. You can find it in the same location as the Import/Export Wizard and the name is DTSMigrationWizard.exe. You can place it on the Quick Launch toolbar right next to the Import/Export Wizard.

DTExec, DTUtil

These two command-line utilities are for executing (DTExec) and managing, moving, and deleting (DTUtil) packages. They are also in the same folder as the Import/Export Wizard. Setup automatically creates a path entry to this folder so these utilities will always be available on the command line.

DTExecUI

DTExecUI is the package execution utility with a graphical user interface (GUI). You can use it to build command lines for DTExec, execute packages directly, and pass parameters to the package. If you double-click a package file in Windows Explorer, DTExecUI appears. Setup puts DTExecUI.exe in the Program Files folder under Microsoft SQL Server\90\Tools\Binn\VSShell\Common7\IDE.

Helpful Resources

Integration Services is a large and complex product. There is much to learn. Fortunately, there are multiple resources you can reference in addition to this book. The following sections provide links to additional resources you can check out.

SQL Server 2005 Setup and Upgrade Forum

If you have questions or run into problems with setup or when migrating, a Microsoft web-based forum is dedicated to helping you. The forum address is http://forums.microsoft.com/MSDN/ShowForum.aspx?ForumID=95&SiteID=1.

Books Online

Books Online is a great resource that documents everything in SQL Server. It is a reference, so it's not always easy to follow, but if you want code samples or API references, it's a great place to go.

You can locate it by clicking the Start menu and selecting Programs, Microsoft SQL Server 2005, Documentation and Tutorials, SQL Server Books Online. You can then perform a search for Integration Services and start your meander.

SQLIS.COM

This is the community site for Integration Services started and supported by Darren Green and Allan Mitchell, Microsoft SQL Server MVPs. Here, you'll find a veritable feast of information from articles to coding practices to custom components.

The website address is http://www.sqlis.com.

MSDN

MSDN has a web page dedicated to Integration Services with links to whitepapers, articles, blogs, partners, and other resources.

The web page address is http://msdn.microsoft.com/SQL/bi/integration/default.aspx.

The SQL Server Integration Services Forum

The forum is a great resource and perhaps the first place to go with general SSIS questions.

The web page address is
http://forums.microsoft.com/msdn/showforum.aspx?forumid=80&siteid=1.

Summary

You should now have everything installed and ready to move forward with the samples. You have some resources to reference if you run into problems. Make sure you read the setup documentation, especially the readme file for any late-breaking issues. Now you can get started with Integration Services. In the next chapter, you'll create a simple package to become familiar with Integration Services basics. If you're familiar with Integration Services already, you can safely skip it. If not, it's a great way to get started.

Migrating from DTS

"WHAT HAVE YOU DONE WITH MY DTS?!"—DARREN GREEN

The Scope of Things

When presenting Integration Services (IS) to current or former Data Transformation Services (DTS) users, one of the first things they want to know is how Integration Services will affect their current packages. The questions come in different forms, such as the following: Will it break my current packages? Can I run IS side by side with DTS? Can I continue to use my DTS packages while building new IS packages? or Can I upgrade my DTS packages to IS packages? But, essentially, what people are asking is, "What's the migration story?"

> **CAUTION**
>
> If you have DTS packages, please read this chapter thoroughly before you begin installing SQL Server 2005. It is possible that you could lose access to your existing packages if you're not careful.

Some of the answers are simple; some are complex. For the most part, the story is pretty positive and much of the difficulty with upgrading is related to the decisions you must make about when and how to do the migration. You also have some good options for retaining your current investment in DTS packages.

This chapter explains the available resources for performing migrations and some of the problems you might encounter. By the end of the chapter, you should have answers to the previous questions and a better idea how to proceed with your upgrade and migration.

NOTE

If you have never used DTS or you have no existing DTS packages, you can safely skip this chapter.

SSIS Is Not DTS

The first thing everyone should clearly understand is that DTS and SQL Server Integration Services (SSIS) are completely different applications. If you were to draw rudimentary system views of DTS and SSIS on a whiteboard, it might be difficult to tell them apart, depending on how you draw them. There are still transforms, tasks, precedence constraints, connections, and variables, and the purpose for the products are closely related. But that's where the similarities end.

There is very little code shared between the two products. The architectures are very different. The scope of Integration Services is largely expanded to be a true enterprise-level Integration and Extract, Transform, and Load (ETL) platform. The data integration and transformation features in Integration Services are hugely improved and the application itself provides a more robust environment for true ETL. In short, anyone reading this should clearly understand that although Integration Services was designed upon ideas developed in DTS, it is a wholly different product.

The Scope of Differences

This section briefly covers some of the more pronounced differences between Integration Services and Data Transformation Services. Many improvements or additional features in IS were not found in DTS. For example, the designer has been vastly improved and there are a large number of new tasks and transforms. But, because this chapter is about migrating existing DTS solutions, the discussion is constrained to those feature differences that are specifically problematic when migrating. Table 3.1 shows the list of the four most problematic feature differences.

TABLE 3.1   Major Feature Differences Between DTS and SSIS

Feature	DTS Solution	SSIS Solution	Description
Data transformation	Limited transforms and ActiveX script with the pump	Numerous stock transformations, error outputs, and easy extensibility with custom components in the Data Flow Task	DTS transforms were limited and ActiveX was slow. ActiveX transformations cannot be migrated.

TABLE 3.1   Continued

Feature	DTS Solution	SSIS Solution	Description
Control flow looping	ActiveX scripting using DTS object model	Built-in Loop container objects with stock enumerators	DTS had no built-in looping constructs and users were forced to hack the object model with ActiveX scripts. ActiveX looping code cannot be migrated.
Package initialization and configuration	Dynamic Properties Task and ActiveX Script Task	Package configurations and property expressions	The Dynamic Properties Task and ActiveX Script Task traversed the package object model to config-ure other tasks. SSIS no longer allows tasks access to the object model.
Custom behavior in packages	The ActiveX Script Task was used extensively to provide not only task behavior, but DTS runtime behavior.	The Script Task can only be used to provide task functionality and cannot access the object model or other tasks.	This is a specific instance of a general problem, which is that tasks accessing the object model are difficult to support and upgrade.

As you can see from Table 3.1, most of the problems arise from the differences between the Pump Task and the Data Flow Task, using ActiveX and allowing tasks to access the object model in promiscuous ways. The Integration Services Data Flow Task is a whole different class of integration and transformation tool, with its own object model and new set of transformations and adapters. The differences are too numerous to list here. ActiveX scripting was a great tool for one-off, simple work. However, because it is inter-preted, ActiveX scripting can be quite slow and doesn't scale well. Finally, DTS lets tasks modify the object model of an executing package, which created numerous problems, not the least of which was how to seamlessly migrate packages if the object model changes. Microsoft decided to eliminate task object model access altogether for these and many other similar reasons. Because of these and other differences, you take a one-time migration hit with the expectation that by eliminating the previously mentioned barriers to migration, future upgrades will be much easier.

Good News

Now, for the good news: Microsoft took great care to provide viable and reasonable migration paths for existing DTS packages. You, as the DTS user, have the ultimate control for how and when you migrate to Integration Services. As you'll see in the following sections, you have options for upgrading, migrating, embedding, sharing, calling, and/or running side by side with DTS packages so that you can continue to use your existing investment in DTS while migrating to Integration Services according to your requirements. Also, the upgrade process, no matter how you approach it, is noninvasive and keeps your packages intact.

Available Migration Resources

Knowing that the changes in architecture and features would essentially break a large number of customers, the Integration Services team developed a set of tools and features that you can use to simplify migration. These tools can be used exclusively or in combination with each other, depending on the approach you take, as discussed in the next section.

WHO IS JIM HOWEY?

Jim is the Program Manager (PM) on the Integration Services team who was largely responsible for, among other things, championing the cause of you, the DTS 2000 user who needs to upgrade packages. In any project of scale and complexity, there are always several priorities that compete for attention and resources. Jim constantly pushed, at times against determined opposition from the author and others, for a better DTS 2000 migration experience. It is largely through his efforts and sturdy determinism that the flexible and substantial options presented here are available. Jim managed the Upgrade Advisor, Migration Wizard, Execute DTS 2000 Package Task, and the SQL Server DTS 2000 Designer Components that make it possible to edit DTS packages in the Execute DTS 2000 Package Task.

So, the next time you successfully upgrade a DTS package or edit one in the Execute DTS 2000 Package Task UI, think of Jim.

Upgrade Advisor

The Upgrade Advisor is a tool that interrogates your servers and builds a report that lists any potential problems you might have when migrating to SQL Server 2005. Running the Upgrade Advisor should be the first thing you do when you're considering an upgrade.

Running the Upgrade Advisor

When you first place the SQL Server setup disk into your machine, there should be a splash screen that appears with several links on it. Figure 3.1 shows the splash screen with the link to install the Upgrade Advisor highlighted.

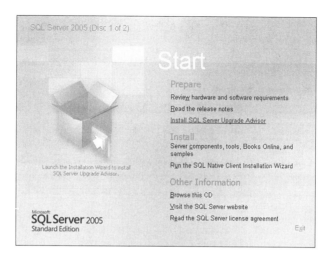

FIGURE 3.1   Install the SQL Server Upgrade Advisor from the Setup Splash Screen.

TIP

Some users have reported trouble getting the splash screen to show up. You can install the Upgrade Advisor from the disk directly. Under the redist folder, there is an Upgrade Adviser folder with an msi file called SQLUASetup.msi. Right-click on the msi file and select Install to install the Upgrade Advisor.

After you've stepped through the setup and have the Upgrade Advisor installed, you can launch it from the SQL Server 2005 Start menu. Figure 3.2 shows the Upgrade Advisor start page. Some links are provided for finding out more about upgrading. The bottom two links are the most interesting. The first link, Launch Upgrade Advisor Analysis Wizard, lets you perform the actual upgrade analysis. The second link, Launch Upgrade Advisor Report Viewer, lets you view reports generated from previous runs of the Upgrade Advisor.

Click the link to launch the Upgrade Advisor Analysis Wizard. Figure 3.3 shows the first page in the wizard, which tells you the steps you'll take in the wizard.

Click the Next button to see the page shown in Figure 3.4. Type in the name of the server and click Detect; the wizard autodetects what SQL Server 2000 components are installed on the server.

For the purposes of this exercise, you are only interested in getting advice about upgrading your DTS packages, so leave only the Data Transformation Services check box checked. Click the Next button, and input your credentials to attach to the server and the instances you want to scan. You can select multiple instances. Click the Next button again to see the dialog box shown in Figure 3.5.

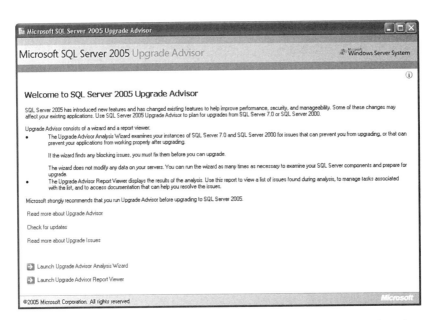

FIGURE 3.2   The Upgrade Advisor lets you view reports or run the Upgrade Advisor Analysis Wizard.

FIGURE 3.3   The Upgrade Advisor Analysis Wizard start page details the steps you'll follow.

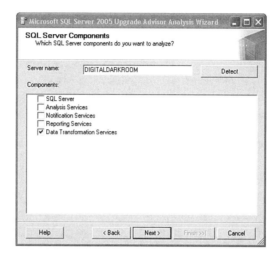

FIGURE 3.4   The wizard autodetects SQL Server 2000 components.

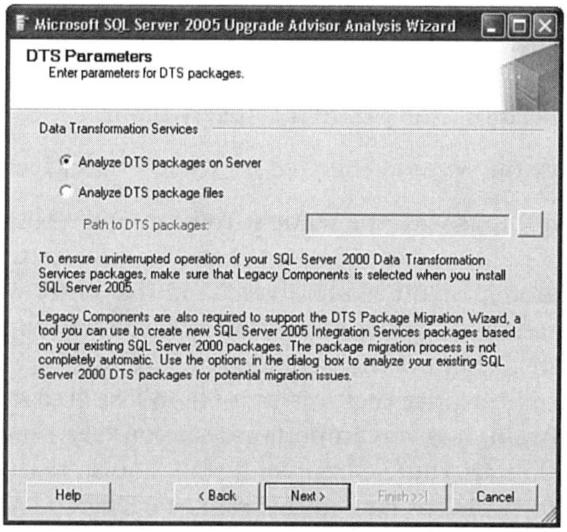

FIGURE 3.5   The wizard allows you to scan packages on the server or file system.

The wizard mentions the Package Migration Wizard, which is covered later. When you select packages on the server, all packages on the server are scanned. There is no way to scan a subset of the packages. Click the Next button and the wizard shows you a summary of the settings. Click the Run button and the wizard starts scanning and analyzing the packages on the server and instances you've selected. Figure 3.6 shows the dialog box shown after the wizard has completed the analysis.

FIGURE 3.6   The wizard generates a report after performing the analysis.

After the wizard has completed the analysis, it writes out the report to the SQL Server 2005 Upgrade Advisor Reports folder under your My Documents folder. You can save these reports to another location and review them later if you want. However, if you leave the report in the same location, the wizard may overwrite it.

Figure 3.7 shows a report the wizard generated for the DTS packages on the test server.

You can do a number of things with the reports. You can open existing reports, filter line items by issues or component, and even export them. Pay close attention to the When to Fix column. If it says Before, you'll need to understand that entry well, and possibly take action on it before upgrading. To get more information about each issue, click on the issue in the report. Figure 3.7 shows the expanded description for Meta Data Services packages after clicking on it. Notice that it is possible to lose access to the packages stored in Meta Data Services. Again, it is very important that you take time to scan and analyze your packages **before** you start your SQL Server installation so that you know about the preinstallation tasks before it is too late. In this case, the Upgrade Advisor is telling the user to move any packages stored in Meta Data Services to SQL Server or save them to the file system before installing SQL Server because they will no longer be accessible after installing SQL Server 2005. Certainly, this is something you'd want to handle before installing.

CAUTION

Make sure you run the Upgrade Advisor Analysis Wizard before you install SQL Server 2005. It will forecast the problems you might experience when upgrading so you can make informed decisions on how to proceed.

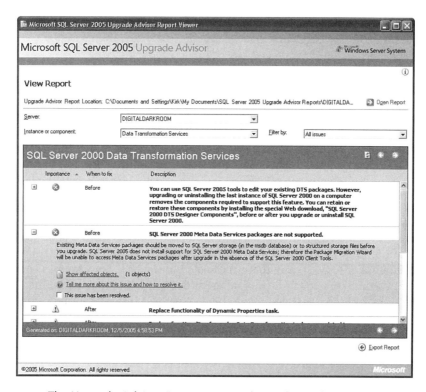

FIGURE 3.7   The Upgrade Advisor Report Viewer shows the analysis results.

The Execute DTS 2000 Package Task

The Execute DTS 2000 Package Task is a thing of beauty for anyone who needs to use their DTS packages in Integration Services. It provides the entire DTS 2000 package editing environment inside the Business Intelligence Development Studio and a way to execute DTS packages from an Integration Services package. This task is provided to help bridge the gap when migrating from Data Transformation Services to Integration Services. Because the architecture of Integration Services is so different from DTS, few legacy DTS packages will successfully migrate and run in Integration Services. This task provides a "half" migration step so that legacy packages can be run side by side with newer Integration Services packages. Even limited interaction between the two is possible using outer variables such that existing investment in DTS packages is not lost when upgrading to Integration Services. For more information about this task, see Chapter 8, " The Stock Tasks."

Migration Wizard

The Migration Wizard is a way to convert your DTS packages to Integration Services packages. It is a "best efforts" migration, meaning it attempts to migrate the biggest parts of packages, such as tasks and variables. However, in the event that it fails to successfully migrate a package, it migrates those parts of the package that it can and wraps the rest in an Execute DTS 2000 Package Task.

When Package Migration Fails

Many DTS packages will successfully migrate, but most will not. What could cause package migration to fail? The list in Table 3.1 is a good place to start. For example, the DTS Data Transformation Task and the Integration Services Data Flow Task are not compatible and their features don't map to one another. Custom tasks won't migrate because they depend on the DTS object model. The Multiphase Pump and Dynamic Properties Task migration will fail because they have no counterpart tasks in IS and you will probably need to fix up ActiveX Script Tasks, especially if they access the DTS object model.

Because the object models are so different, the package and task properties have changed, and there are so many different package configurations, the odds are against a thoroughly clean migration. Even IS tasks that map well to their DTS counterparts will sometimes fail migration because of some setting that isn't related to the task. For example, the IS packages might be stored on a machine in a different domain without access to the same files or servers. The simple fact that you move the package to a different location can break it. The takeaway here is that there is no free ride. You might get lucky and have great success with migrating a few packages. But, as a general rule, most migrations will be a fairly labor-intensive operation. Fortunately, as discussed in the following section, you have options.

Individual Components and Settings

When it comes to migrating packages, the success or failure of the package migration really boils down to what tasks and connections are in the DTS package. Also, a DTS package is more than a set of tasks. It's a combination of tasks, transforms, logging, and other package settings. A number of DTS-compatible components and settings in Integration Services seem to migrate pretty well with little or no user intervention. In addition, some components and settings don't migrate at all or somewhere in between. Following is a list of DTS components and settings with a very rough expectation of how often each will successfully migrate. The success probability is based on estimates on a number of factors, including the author's own tests, the number of differences between DTS and IS components, the complexity of the component, and wizard support. Notice that none of the success probabilities are estimated at 100%. This is because there are simply too many points of failure when migrating to be sure that any component will succeed all the time.

CAUTION

The estimates given here for probability of success are the author's. They are strictly based on his experience. You can use them to sanity check the effort it will take to migrate your packages, but please don't rely on these numbers for any substantial commitments. Only by testing in your environment with a representative subset of your packages can you accurately gauge what your migration effort will be.

Migrating Tasks   There seem to be three categories of DTS tasks. The first category is tasks that migrate straight across with few complications and if they don't run successfully the first time, a tweak or two usually fixes any lingering issues. Table 3.2 shows the tasks in this category listed with the IS task to which they migrate.

TABLE 3.2   Tasks with High Probability of Migration Success

DTS Task	IS Task	Success Probability
File Transfer Protocol	File Transfer Protocol	90%
Execute SQL	Execute SQL	95%
Execute Process	Execute Process	95%
Copy SQL Server Objects	Transfer SQL Server Objects	90%
Send Mail	Send Mail (New SMTP Info)	95%
Bulk Insert	Bulk Insert	70%
Execute Package	Execute DTS 2000 Package	90%
Message Queue	Message Queue	80%
Transfer Error Messages	Transfer Error Messages	95%
Transfer Databases	Transfer Database (one for each database)	85%
Transfer Master Stored Procedures	Transfer Master Stored Procedures	95%
Transfer Jobs	Transfer Jobs	95%
Transfer Logs	Transfer Logs	95%

The second category contains those tasks that might migrate successfully, but often fail because they are either too complex to migrate or they do something that is no longer supported. The ActiveX Script Task often fails to migrate because it contains code that attempts to access the DTS Object Model. The Data Pump Task fails if it is too complex or contains ActiveX Script. The Data Driven Query does not migrate, but the Migration Wizard wraps it in its own DTS package and calls the package from the Execute DTS 2000 Package Task.

TABLE 3.3   Tasks with Low Probability of Migration Success

DTS Task	IS Task	Success Probability
ActiveX Script	ActiveX Script	40%
Transform Data	Data Flow	40%
Data Driven Query	Execute DTS 2000 Package	40%

The third and final category of tasks is those that simply will not migrate because they are designed to work against a different API or there is no compatible Integration Services task. For example, the Dynamic Properties Task is built upon the premise that it can traverse the package hierarchy and modify other task properties directly. This won't work for two reasons:

- The runtime doesn't allow promiscuous package access any longer.

- Even if it did allow such access, the object model has changed.

TABLE 3.4   Tasks That Will Not Migrate Successfully

DTS Task	IS Task	Success Probability
Analysis Services	Analysis Services Processing	0%
Dynamic Properties	ActiveX	0%
Data Mining Prediction	Data Mining Query	0%

Migrating Connections   Connections are important in DTS and if the connection doesn't migrate successfully, you've got a broken package just the same as if the task didn't successfully migrate. The good news is that the OLEDB connections, the most common connections in DTS packages, have a very high migration success rate because the settings for the IS OLEDB Connection Manager are identical to its DTS counterpart.

TABLE 3.5   Various Connection Managers and Their Probability to Successfully Migrate

DTS Connection	IS Connection Manager	Success Probability
OLEDB	OLEDB : OLEDB Provider	99%
Access	OLEDB : Jet 4.0 Provider	95%
Excel	OLEDB : Jet 4.0 Provider	95%
Dbase 5	OLEDB : Jet 4.0 Provider	N/A
HTML File	OLEDB : SQL Native	0%
Paradox	OLEDB : Jet 4.0 Provider	N/A
Text File (Source)	Flat File	0%*
Text File (Dest)	Flat File	0%*
ODBC	OLEDB : MSDASQL Provider	30%

*The Text File connections migrate to the Flat File Connection Manager, but they will never be complete until you open them in the new package and finish their configuration.

Migrating Settings   The package has a number of settings that impact how the package should run. The Migration Wizard generally ignores these settings. For example, it ignores all the package properties, with the exception of Global Variables. So properties like Package Priority Class, Logging Settings, Fail Package on First Error, Write Completion Status to Event Log, Use Transactions, and so on do not get migrated or in any way affect the properties of the destination IS package. The message here is: Even if your package appears to successfully migrate and you get no errors from the Migration Wizard or the new IS package, this is no guarantee that the package will behave exactly as it did when running under the DTS environment. If you want to retain the values for these properties or the behavior they represent, you need to manually review the package settings and make appropriate settings in the IS package. The Migration Wizard does not do it for you.

Where to Launch the Migration Wizard

You can launch the Migration Wizard from the Business Intelligence Development Studio by right-clicking on the SSIS Packages node in an Integration Services project and selecting the Migrate DTS 2000 Package menu option. You can also launch it from SQL Server Management Studio by right-clicking on the Data Transformation Services node of the Legacy branch in the Management node of SQL Server 2000 servers. The Migration Wizard is a standalone executable, so it can also be launched outside of the designer. On most machines, the Migration Wizard is in the \Program Files\Microsoft SQL Server\90\DTS\Binn\ directory and is named DTSMigrationWizard.exe.

> **CAUTION**
>
> The Migration Wizard generally fails to migrate a task if the task is missing any settings or if it cannot make a connection. To increase the likelihood of migration success, double check your packages before migrating them to ensure that all the tasks and connections are correctly configured and the servers they reference are online.

Some Migration Considerations

When upgrading, SQL Server setup performs some installs and uninstalls of which you should be aware. The following are some key points you should understand before migrating your packages.

SQL Server Instances and Enterprise Manager

When upgrading to SQL Server 2005, SQL Server 2005 setup uninstalls certain deprecated components. Based on how you do your installs, it's possible that the Enterprise Manager environment will get uninstalled and take the package designer with it—essentially leaving your legacy DTS packages stranded with no way to edit them. To avoid this situation, you have a number of options, which are discussed in the following sections.

> **NOTE**
>
> When upgrading to SQL Server 2005, all packages stored in the SQL Server 2000 instance in the msdb.dbo.sysdtspackages table get migrated to a table by the same name in the SQL Server 2005 instance. So, the packages are not deleted or lost.

Installing an Instance

If you install SQL Server 2005 as an instance side by side with your SQL Server 2000 instances, all the SQL Server 2000 tools remain intact and you'll have access to the packages for editing and so forth. All packages that are scheduled to run with DTSRun and/or Agent continue to execute without issue.

Leaving One SQL Server 2000 Instance

This option is very similar to the previous one. Except instead of installing SQL Server 2005 as a different instance, you upgrade all SQL Server 2000 instances to SQL Server 2005 except one—leaving the tools intact. So long as there is a SQL Server 2000 instance on a machine, all the SQL Server 2000 tools you have used remain intact.

Upgrading and Installing Designer Components

When you select Integration Services for installation, setup also installs support for DTS packages, including the DTS runtime and DTS package enumeration in SQL Server Management Studio. This happens as part of the SQL Server 2005 installation, but only the runtime components are installed, not the designer components.

For the design time components, Microsoft has created a special distribution called the Microsoft SQL Server 2005 DTS Designer Components. The Designer Components distribution replaces the components that get uninstalled when you upgrade your last instance of SQL Server 2000. If you want to upgrade all your SQL Server 2000 instances, this is the best and only option for recovering the DTS designer. To download the designer components, go to the download section of Microsoft.com and search for Knowledge Base article 339810.

Meta Data Services

Meta Data Services has been deprecated and is no longer supported as a package store. SQL Server 2005 does not install or use the Repository, so you cannot enumerate or open packages stored there. You can still access packages stored in Meta Data Services using DTSRUN, but not using the designer tools. The SQL Server 2000 Data Transformation Services (DTS) designer and the dtsrun.exe utility continue to support DTS packages that were saved to Meta Data Services.

SQL Server 2005 Integration Services supports the Repository only in the Upgrade Advisor and the Package Migration Wizard, and only if SQL Server 2000, the SQL Server 2000 tools, or the Repository redistributable files are installed on the local computer. When the Repository files are present, the Upgrade Advisor can scan and the Package Migration Wizard can migrate DTS packages that were saved to Meta Data Services. When the Repository files are not present, the Upgrade Advisor can only scan and the Package Migration Wizard can only migrate DTS packages that were saved to SQL Server or to structured storage files.

The Integration Services Execute DTS 2000 Package Task cannot execute a DTS package that was saved to Meta Data Services. As a workaround, when the Repository files are present, you can create a DTS package that uses an Execute Package Task to execute the Meta Data Services package, save this new parent package to SQL Server or as a structured storage file, and execute the parent package from the Execute DTS 2000 Package Task.

CAUTION
_____

If you have packages stored in Meta Data Services, it is recommended that you move them to SQL Server or structured storage files before upgrading to make it easier to migrate them later. They will remain safe and unchanged through the upgrade.

Migrating Packages with Passwords

If the DTS packages that you need to migrate have been protected with passwords, you need to know the passwords to migrate them. The passwords are not retained, nor does the Migration Wizard change the package protection setting on the resulting IS package. You need to manually modify the IS package to enable passwords again.

Where Are My Packages?

One thing you should understand is that regardless of how you upgrade to SQL Server 2005—whether you install side by side with a separate instance, upgrade the last instance, or retain the last SQL Server 2000 instance—SQL Server setup keeps your packages intact. Depending on how you upgrade, the packages can be found in a different location.

File System

Packages remain on the file system undisturbed. You can migrate them with the Package Migration Wizard or load them up in the Execute DTS 2000 Package Task.

Install Instance

If you install SQL Server 2005 as an instance side by side with your SQL Server 2000 instances and you were storing your packages in SQL Server, you will still have the Enterprise Manager environment intact so the packages will be where they have always been, in the Local Packages node of the Data Transformation Services tree of Enterprise Manager. Figure 3.8 shows DTS packages stored there.

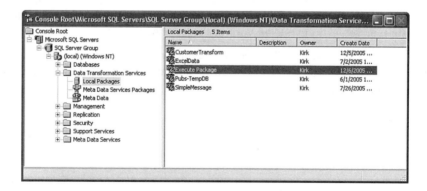

FIGURE 3.8   DTS packages remain in local packages.

Because Management Studio can enumerate packages in SQL Server 2000 instances, you can also find the DTS packages in the Object Explorer in Management Studio under the

Management tree, Legacy, Data Transformation Services node. Figure 3.9 shows the packages in the Legacy node.

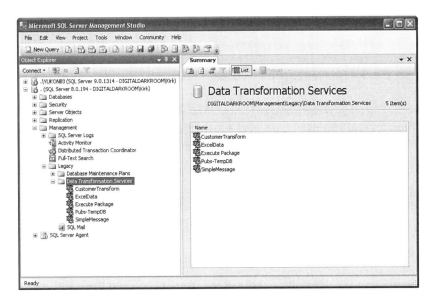

FIGURE 3.9   DTS packages remain in the Legacy node.

Summary

You have several options available for migrating to Integration Services. The Upgrade Advisor tells you what to expect when you migrate, the Migration Wizard gets you started on migrating packages, and the Execute DTS 2000 Packages Task allows you to embed DTS packages into Integration Services packages. You can choose to keep all your DTS packages and run side by side with Integration Services while slowly migrating packages at your leisure, or you can migrate all your packages at once.

For more information, see the MSDN article "Migrating Data Transformation Services Packages" on MSDN at http://msdn2.microsoft.com/ and search for "Migrating Data Transformation Services Packages."

Building a Package— Quick Start

"IT'S EASY IF YOU'RE IGNORANT."— JIM HOWEY

This chapter is a quick, get-your-hands-dirty, introduction to Integration Services and walks you through the creation of a new package. The package you'll build uses many of the important features of Integration Services, including the Data Flow Task, Foreach Loop, variables, and transforms.

Quick Start

If you're like most people, when you get a new product, you like to see it in action as soon as possible. You want to just load it up and try it out. This chapter is about getting you into Integration Services as quickly as possible without worrying about all the details of how to do it and with no particular claims to thoroughness or depth of coverage. If you are familiar with Integration Services, you might want to skip this chapter or quickly read through it to catch the high points. If you have used Data Transformation Services in the past, you should work through this chapter to see how things have changed. If you're new to Integration Services and you've never used Data Transformation Services, this chapter is essential to establishing a context on which to build a solid understanding of Integration Services.

The Scenario

You want to build a process that will do rudimentary reporting on sales numbers. The report you'll build is a yearly summary but could easily apply to any periodic sales depending on the query you use to retrieve the sales data. You also want to have the numbers sent to you via email. More complex scenarios are possible, but this scenario is representative of the kinds of things you can do in Integration Services and yet is still pretty easy to follow.

> **NOTE**
>
> Make sure you have Integration Services set up with the AdventureWorks sample database installed and attached.

Creating a New Integration Services Project

The first thing you'll need to do is create a project. Projects are like workspaces and provide a way to manage your packages.

1. From the Start menu, select Microsoft SQL Server 2005, Microsoft Business Intelligence Development Studio.

2. When the Business Intelligence Development Studio appears, select New, Project from the File menu.

3. In the Project Types window, select Business Intelligence Projects.

4. In the Templates window, select Integration Services Project.

5. In the Name field, type Quickstart.

6. In the Location field, type (or select using the Browse button) the folder where you want to create your project. When you've completed entering the information, your screen should look similar to Figure 4.1.

7. Click the OK button.

The first thing you'll do is get the package started. In Integration Services, the package is the main container. You build up the package by dropping tasks on it and configuring them.

Starting the Package

1. Show the Toolbox by pressing [Ctrl+Alt+X] or by clicking the View menu and then clicking Toolbox.

2. Drag and drop a Data Flow Task from the Toolbox onto the main designer window with the tab labeled Control Flow.

3. Rename the Data Flow Task to "Get Sales Data" by clicking on it once to select it and then clicking on the name.

4. Click the Format menu and select Autosize to size the Data Flow Task to the name. Figure 4.2 shows the Toolbox, the resulting Data Flow Task, and the Control Flow designer so far.

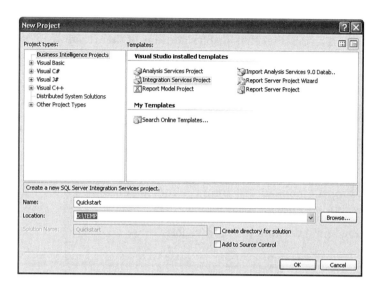

FIGURE 4.1   Create a new Integration Services project with the New Project dialog box.

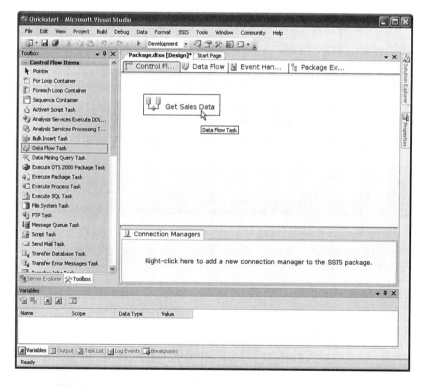

FIGURE 4.2   Build the package by dropping tasks onto the control flow.

Adding the Foreach Loop

The Foreach Loop is a container that enables portions of the workflow to be executed multiple times as it enumerates items in a collection. The values of the items in the collection can be passed as parameters to the workflow so that the workflow inside of the Foreach Loop is effectively controlled by the collection. In the scenario, the Foreach Loop only iterates once because there is only one row in the collection of rows.

1. Drag and drop a Foreach Loop Container from the Toolbox onto the same designer window.

2. Rename the Foreach Loop to "Send Mail With Results."

3. Drag and drop a Send Mail Task from the Toolbox onto the Foreach Loop so that it appears within the Foreach Loop.

4. Rename the Send Mail Task to "Send Report."

5. Click the Format menu and choose Autosize to resize the Send Mail Task.

6. Click the Data Flow Task you renamed to "Get Sales Data."

7. There should be a small, dangling arrow extending from the bottom of the Data Flow Task. Drag the arrow to the Foreach Loop title bar and drop it to create a precedence constraint.

8. From the Format menu, select Autolayout and then Diagram.

9. From the Tools menu, select Options. In the Options dialog box, select the Business Intelligence Designers node, then select Integration Services Designers, and then select General. Under Accessibility, select Show Precedence Constraint Labels. Click the OK button. Your package should now look similar to the package shown in Figure 4.3.

Adding the Variables

You use variables in Integration Services to store values. In this scenario, you'll use variables to store sales numbers. You'll also define the Results variable to hold an ADO recordset object.

1. If the Variables window is not visible, right-click on the designer window and select Variables.

2. In the Variables window, click the icon in the upper-left corner to create a new variable.

3. Call it TopSales2004. Make sure the type is Int32.

4. Create another variable and call it SubTotal2004. Make sure the type is Int32.

5. Create a third variable and call it AvgSales2004. Make sure the type is Int32.

6. Create a fourth variable in the same way and call it Results. Choose Object as the data type.

7. In the Variables window, click the icon in the upper-right corner to show the Choose Variable Columns dialog box. Put a check in the Namespace check box to show the Namespace column in the Variables window.

8. For each of the variables you just created, change the namespace to SAMPLES.

9. Click the File menu, and then click Save All or press [Ctrl+Shift+S] to save the entire project.

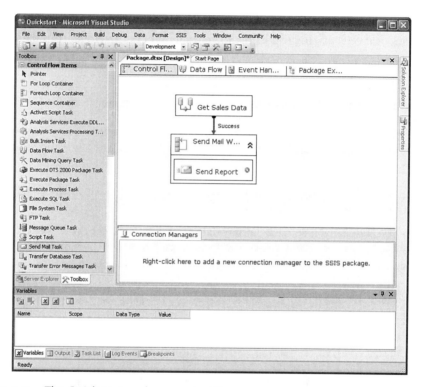

FIGURE 4.3   The Quickstart package control flow.

Figure 4.4 shows the Variables window after creating the variables.

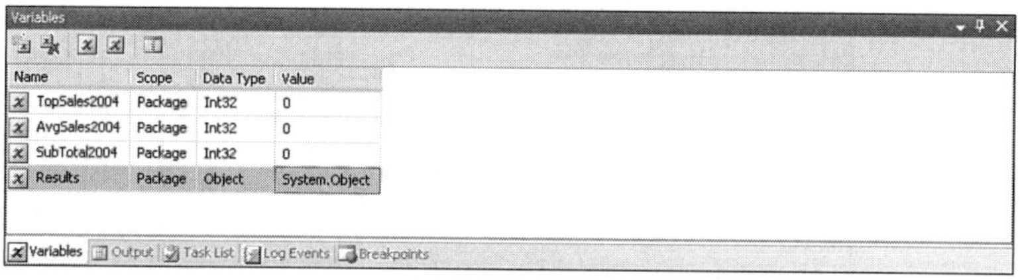

FIGURE 4.4   The Variables window shows all variables in the package.

Configuring the Data Flow

The Data Flow Task is a high-performance, data-processing engine. In this scenario, you'll be using it to summarize annual sales data from the AdventureWorks sample database. You'll store the resulting summarized data in a row that you'll later use in the Foreach Loop.

The OLE DB Source

The OLE DB Source Adapterretrieves rows from an OLE DB connection and places the row data into the Data Flow Task. The Data Flow Task uses adapters to access data in different formats and locations, making it possible to centrally process heterogeneous data.

1. Double-click the Data Flow Task or click on the Data Flow tab at the top of the designer.

2. From the Toolbox, drag and drop an OLE DB Source Adapter from the Data Flow Sources group of components.

3. Rename it to "Retrieve Fiscal Sales per Person."

4. Double-click on it.

5. When the Editor dialog box opens, click the New button to open the Configure OLE DB Connection Manager dialog box.

6. Click the New button to create a new data connection. Select the server on which the AdventureWorks database is installed. Figure 4.5 shows the Connection Manager dialog box.

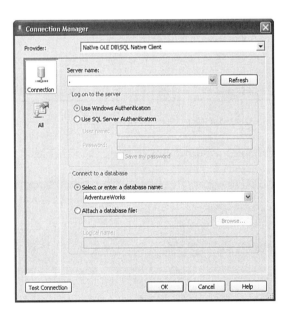

FIGURE 4.5   Create a new connection manager with the Connection Manager dialog box.

7. Click the OK button twice to return to the OLE DB Source Editor dialog box.

8. In the Data Access Mode field, select SQL command.

9. In the SQL Command Text field, type in the query to retrieve the sales data. Figure 4.6 shows the OLE DB Source Editor dialog box correctly configured with this query.

```
SELECT "2004" FROM Sales.vSalesPersonSalesByFiscalYears
```

10. Click the Columns tab on the left of the dialog box.

11. Ensure that the check box next to the column named 2004 is checked.

12. Click the OK button.

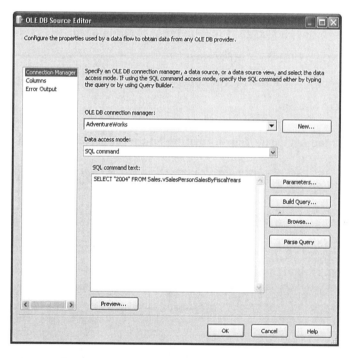

FIGURE 4.6   Retrieve data from a database table or view using a SQL command.

The Aggregate Transform   The Aggregate transform is used to perform one or more aggregations on the data in the Data Flow task. It supports simple aggregations such as average and sum and more complex operations such as group-by and count distinct.

1. Drag an Aggregate component onto the data flow.

2. Rename it to Figure Sum, Avg, and Max.

3. Click the OLE DB Source you just configured.

4. Drag the green (on the left) data flow output to the Aggregate component and drop it.

5. Double-click on the Aggregate transform.

6. Check the 2004 column in the Available Input Columns window.

7. In the Input Column column, select the 2004 column.

8. For the Output Alias, type in 2004Total.

9. For the Operation, choose Sum.

10. On the next row, choose 2004 for the Input Column again.

11. For the Output Alias, type in 2004Avg.

12. For the Operation, choose Average.

13. On the third row, choose 2004 for the Input Column again.

14. Type in 2004Max for the Output Alias.

15. For the Operation, choose Maximum.

16. Click the OK button.

Figure 4.7 shows the Aggregate Transformation Editor properly configured.

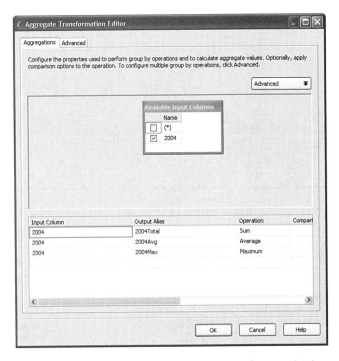

FIGURE 4.7   The Aggregate Transformation Editor can perform multiple aggregations per column.

The Data Conversion Transform   Integration Services is very type aware and will fail if you attempt to set the value of a variable or column of one type with a different type. But the columns you're retrieving from the tables are of type Currency. So you need to convert the types. You'll use a Data Conversion transform to do this.

1. Drag a Data Conversion transform to the data flow.

2. Click on the Aggregate transform you just configured and drag its output to the Data Conversion transform.

3. Double-click on the Data Conversion transform.

4. Select all three columns in the Available Input Columns window.

5. For each column, name the Output Alias and Data Type, as shown in Figure 4.8.

6. Click the OK button.

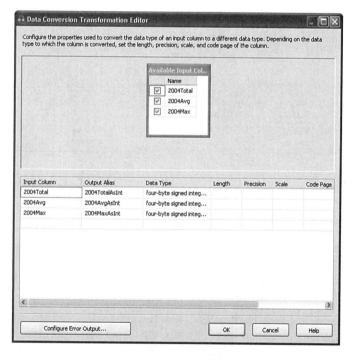

FIGURE 4.8   The Data Conversion transform can change the data type of a column.

The Recordset Destination   The Recordset Destination will take the row that you've built using the Aggregate transform and place it into an ADO.NET recordset.

1. Drag a Recordset Destination to the data flow.

2. Click on the Data Conversion transform and drag the green output to the Recordset Destination.

3. Double-click on the Recordset Destination.

4. In the VariableName property, type in "Results," which is the name of the variable of type `Object` you created earlier.

5. Click the Input Columns tab and check the columns you named with the AsInt suffix. There should be three: 2004TotalAsInt, 2004AvgAsInt, and 2004MaxAsInt.

6. Click the OK button.

Figure 4.9 shows the resulting editor for the Recordset Destination.

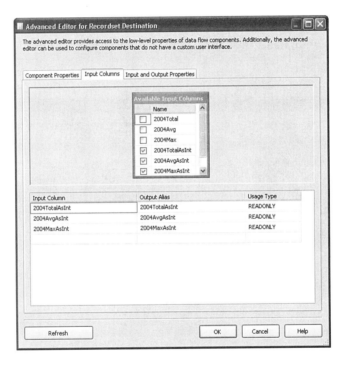

FIGURE 4.9   The Recordset Destination transform creates an ADO recordset.

Now, the Data Flow Task is built. It will retrieve the 2004 sales numbers and then find the sum, average, and maximum sales. Then, using the Data Conversion transform, you modify the type of the aggregated results to be integers instead of type `Currency`, which will make it a little easier for you in the control flow. Finally, put the resulting row in a recordset. Figure 4.10 shows the resulting data flow.

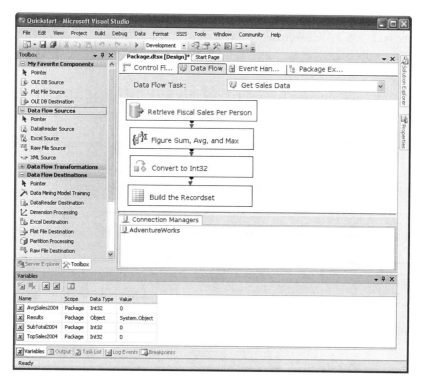

FIGURE 4.10   The sales report data flow.

Configuring the Foreach Loop

The Foreach Loop provides a way to iterate over a collection and assign the values in the collection to variables. In this case, there is only one row in the recordset and so the loop only iterates once. You'll assign the values from each column in the row to a variable. Later, you'll use the variables to build the very rudimentary report. You'll do this in two steps. First, you'll configure the enumerator so it can find the recordset. Then, you'll configure the variable mappings so it can correctly place the column values from the row into the variables.

Configuring the Enumerator   In this step, you tell the Foreach ADO Enumerator what variable is holding the recordset. At package execution time, the Foreach ADO Enumerator finds the variable, retrieves the recordset, and iterates through it.

1. Select the Control Flow designer by clicking the Control Flow tab.

2. Double-click on the Foreach Loop.

3. In the left pane of the Foreach Loop Editor, select the Collection node.

4. In the Enumerator property in the upper-right grid, select the Foreach ADO Enumerator.

5. For the ADO Object Source Variable selection, select the User::Results variable. That's where you stored the recordset object.

6. Ensure that the Rows in the First Table option is selected, which is the default.

Figure 4.11 shows the resulting Foreach Loop Editor with the Foreach ADO Enumerator properly configured.

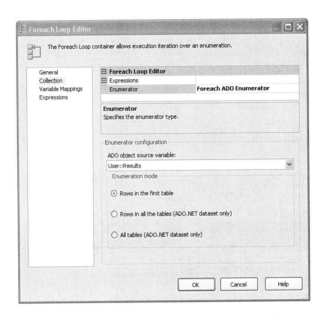

FIGURE 4.11   The Foreach ADO Enumerator iterates over rows in a recordset.

Configuring the Variable Mappings   The variable mappings are how Foreach Enumerators know where to place the values they extract from collections. In this case, the mappings are between the variables in the package and the columns in the recordset.

1. In the left pane of the Foreach Loop Editor, select the Variable Mappings node.

2. Click on the first row in the grid on the right and select User::SubTotal2004 as the variable.

3. Ensure that zero is the index (which is the default).

4. Click on the second row and select User::AvgSales2004.

5. Set the index to 1. The index is the zero-based column index.

6. Click on the third row and select User::TopSales2004.

7. Set the index to 2.

8. Figure 4.12 shows the resulting Variable Mappings dialog box.

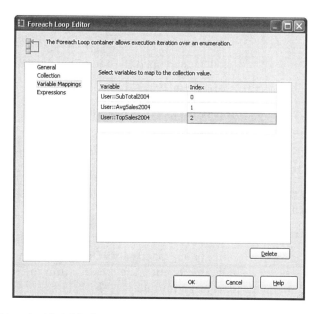

FIGURE 4.12   Use the Variable Mappings node to map values from collections into variables.

Configuring the Send Mail Task

Now, it's time to send mail with the numbers you've generated. Notice that the Send Report (Send Mail Task) has a red x icon. That's an indication that there were errors when the task was checked and that it needs to be configured. Figure 4.13 shows the error that's causing the problem.

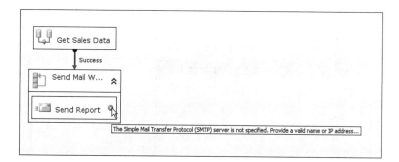

FIGURE 4.13   The Send Mail Task must have a valid SMTP connection manager.

You haven't set up an SMTP connection for the task or set up the actual message that you'll send. You'll do that in the following section.

The SMTP Connection Manager and Other Properties   The SMTP Task, like other components, uses a connection manager for making connections to server resources. The

SMTP Task uses an SMTP Connection Manager, which you'll need to set up with the SMTP server name.

1. Double-click on the Send Mail Task to open the Send Mail Task Editor.

2. In the left pane, select the Mail node.

3. In the SmtpConnection property, select New Connection.

4. In the SMTP Connection Manager Editor dialog box, type the name of the SMTP server in the SMTP Server text box. For example, it could be smtp.yourdomain.com. Click the OK button.

5. In the right pane of the Send Mail Task Editor, enter the appropriate addresses for the From and To properties.

6. Enter a subject for the Subject property.

7. Ensure that the MessageSourceType property lists Direct Input (which is the default). This tells the task that you'll directly enter the message into the MessageSource property, which you'll add in just a minute.

Figure 4.14 shows the resulting SMTP Connection Manager Editor and Send Mail Task Editor.

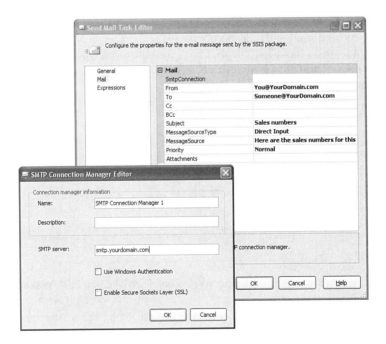

FIGURE 4.14   Specify the mail properties in the Mail node of the SMTP Task.

The Message Source   The message source is the actual content of the email. You generate the message based on the results of the data flow as stored in the variables you populated with the Foreach Loop. To do this, you use a feature called property expressions.
Property expressions are a way to associate an expression with a property. In this case,
you'll build an expression that will generate the text for the message body.

1. With the Send Mail Task Editor still open, click on the Expressions node in the left
   pane.

2. On the right, there is a grid with one element called Expressions.

3. Click on the Expressions entry, and then click on the button with the ellipsis.

4. The Property Expressions Editor dialog box opens, which is shown in Figure 4.15.

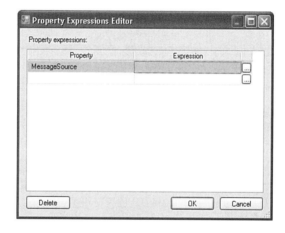

FIGURE 4.15   Use the Property Expressions Editor to manage expressions.

5. In the Property column, choose MessageSource. This tells the designer that the
   expression you're about to add should be associated with the MessageSource property.

6. Click on the ellipsis button in the Expression column.

7. The Expression Builder appears.

   In the Expression field, type in the following expression:

```
"Here are the sales numbers for this year
" + "Average Per Salesperson        " + (DT_WSTR, 20) @[SAMPLES::AvgSales2004] + "
" + "Total Sales                     " + (DT_WSTR, 20) @[SAMPLES::SubTotal2004] + "
" + "Top Salesperson Sales           " + (DT_WSTR, 20)@[SAMPLES::TopSales2004]
```

8. Click the Evaluate Expression button. It should correctly evaluate with zero for the sales numbers.

Figure 4.16 shows the resulting Expression Builder.

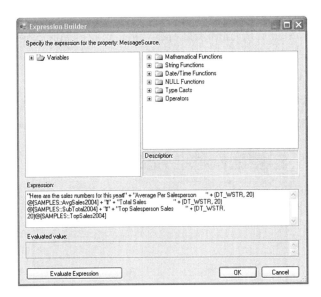

FIGURE 4.16   Use the Expression Builder to build property expressions.

9. Click the OK button three times to return to the designer.

You should now be ready to run the package. Click the little green triangle that looks like a Play button on the main toolbar, or you can simply press the F5 button. The package should execute in a few seconds and send email to the email address you've specified in the To field of the SMTP Task with the sales summary data. Figure 4.17 shows the designer Progress tab after the package has successfully completed. The Progress tab shows the progress of the package as it is executing.

When you are finished running the package, click the Stop button, the square blue button next to the Play button, to reset the designer to design mode.

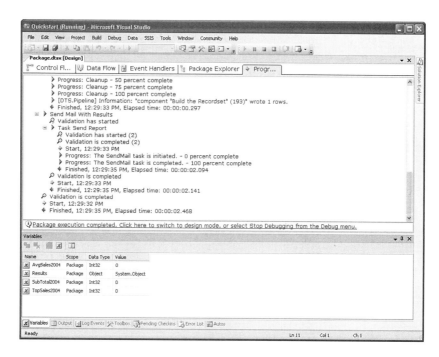

FIGURE 4.17   Use the Progress tab to view the package as it executes.

Summary

If you have trouble getting this to work or just don't want to walk through all the steps,
there is a copy of the package in the samples under the S04-Quickstart folder. At any rate,
if you're new to Integration Services, you should spend a little time with this sample. Try
changing a few settings and see how it affects the package. Try building more features
into the package as well. It's a good package because it cuts a broad swath through some
of the more important features in the product. If you understand how this package works,
you'll have a pretty good understanding of the fundamentals of Integration Services as a
whole.

PART II

Integration Services Basics and Concepts

IN THIS PART

The Business Intelligence Development Studio

"PEOPLE ARE GOING TO BE BLOWN AWAY BY THIS!"—ALLAN MITCHELL

This chapter is an in-depth exploration of the Business Intelligence Development Studio (BIDS). Although those familiar with Visual Studio will feel at home in BIDS, this chapter covers the Integration Services–specific features in detail and should be helpful for those who have never used Visual Studio as well as old pros.

The Business Intelligence Development Studio, generically known as the designer or BIDS for short, is a full-featured development environment for building business intelligence solutions. It is built on the mature Visual Studio infrastructure that provides a powerful, flexible, and easy-to-learn environment for Integration Services, Analysis Services, Reporting Services, Visual C++, Visual Basic, and other products, making it possible to truly build and maintain all your business intelligence solutions in one development environment.

> **TIP**
>
> This chapter is best read while in front of the computer so you can follow along, trying the different settings as they are explained.

The designer is a complex piece of software with many options and features that cannot be covered in complete detail here. However, this chapter attempts to cover those settings, features, and options that you're most likely to use when building Integration Services solutions. On occasion, some features are covered that are right next to others that aren't mentioned at all. Also, many of the user interface elements are merely touched upon because they are covered in more detail in other parts of the book. It might not be clear to you how to use all the features you'll discover in this chapter or even what the features do. But, that's OK for now. At least you'll know where to find them later.

If you are already familiar with Visual Studio, this chapter assists you in quickly getting acquainted with the SSIS-specific features. If you're unfamiliar with the Visual Studio environment, this chapter is a good introduction to how to get around, but is not a general Visual Studio introduction. A lot of Visual Studio content is available that might be helpful to you and can be found in Books Online with simple searches or in other references more focused on Visual Studio.

This chapter is basically a meandering walk through the designer, a tour if you will. Even though it comes fairly early in the book, the features are not explained in detail here. The idea is to cover the basic designer elements so you can get acquainted with the environ-ment quickly while also describing some of the more esoteric and hard-to-find features. By the time you're finished with this chapter, you should feel comfortable in the Visual Studio environment and have a good idea how to navigate to the Integration Services features, even if you don't fully understand what they do yet. You should read through this chapter quickly when you first start learning Integration Services. Later, when you have more experience with the product, revisit this chapter to pick up the pieces you don't catch the first time around.

> **NOTE**
>
> Examples in this chapter assume you have installed the AdventureWorks sample data-base. If you haven't installed it yet, please see Chapter 2, "Setting Up Integration Services."

Getting Started

Chapter 4, "Building a Package—Quick Start," was a really quick introduction to creating a project and building a package. It's now time to take a step back, walk through the designer a little slower, and learn more about it as you go. When you open the designer, it should look similar to Figure 5.1.

The Start Page and Community Menu

First notice the "Getting Started" pane of the Start Page. This helpful list of links takes you to various getting started Books Online topics, such as overviews, concepts, and tuto-rials. There is a wealth of details to be found there. The Recent Projects pane of the Start Page gives you quick-and-easy access to the last set of projects you've been editing. The MSDN: SQL Server pane provides live and current links to SQL Server–related Internet content that is constantly updated as new content becomes available.

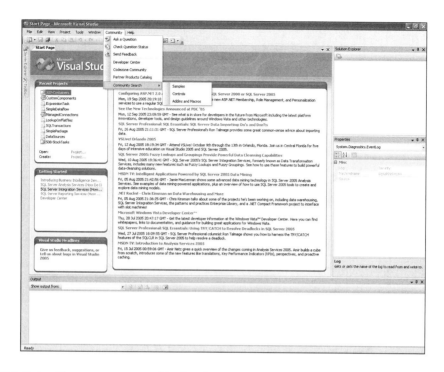

FIGURE 5.1   You can get started in the designer in many ways.

NOTE
_____

If the Start Page isn't visible, you can open it using the View menu. Select View on the menu bar, click Other Windows, and then click Start Page.

The Community menu is your link to the Visual Studio community. These links take you to the MSDN forum. For example, the Check Question Status menu item takes you to the MSDN web page that shows you all the forums and threads in which you've participated. This is a quick way to get to the support forums screen shown in Figure 5.2.

Microsoft MVPs, employees, and other knowledgeable users visit these forums regularly and are very helpful. It's the first place you should go when you can't find the answer to a problem on your own.

A New Solution

To create a new Integration Services solution, click the File menu, click New, and then click Project. This opens the New Project dialog box shown in Figure 5.3.

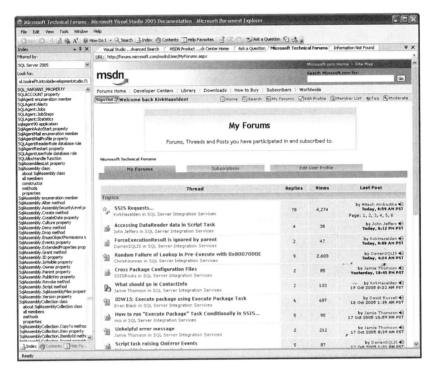

FIGURE 5.2   Use the Community menu items to quickly access the forums.

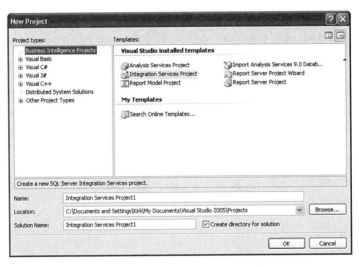

FIGURE 5.3   Create projects using the New Project dialog box.

When creating a new project, if there is no solution open, the designer creates a new solution automatically. As you can see from Figure 5.3, you can create a multitude of project types. To create an Integration Services type, select Integration Services Project, and then choose the name and location for the project and the solution name. If there is a solution open already, you are given the choice of adding the new project to the open solution or creating a new solution.

TIP

Because solutions typically contain multiple projects of different types, it's a good practice to name the project specific to its function and the solution according to the overall nature of the projects it contains.

The Integration Services Options

After you've created an Integration Services solution and you have the package open, a number of important changes occur in the designer. The most obvious changes are that certain menus become available and some windows open. Following is a discussion of some important changes that result when creating an SSIS project. As you work through this chapter, important Integration Services–specific features are pointed out, but also try to keep an eye open for how the environment adjusts as you make suggested changes. This simple exercise can save you some later frustration and put you further down the learning curve by simply being extra observant.

The SSIS Menu

With the Integration Services project and a package open, a new SSIS menu becomes available between the Data and Tools menus on the main menu. The SSIS menu has the following menu items:

- **Logging**—Set up logging options
- **Package Configurations**—Create and manage package configurations
- **Digital Signing**—Sign packages
- **Variables**—Show the Variables window
- **Work Offline**—Toggle offline mode

CAUTION

If you select the Work Offline menu item, be aware that in some cases, you might get errors. For example, if you are building a data flow and you attempt to access the Columns tab in the component user interface of an OLEDB connection, you receive the following error:

```
Error at Data Flow Task [OLE DB Source [1]]: An error occurred due to no
connection. A connection is required when requesting metadata.
```

If you get this error, ensure the Work Offline setting is disabled.

- **Log Events**—Show the Log Events window

- **New Connection**—Create a new connection manager

CAUTION

Keep this in mind if you ever attempt to access a menu and it's not there. In Visual Studio, the available menu options often vary depending on the currently selected designer window or the object selected within the window.

This menu only shows all menu items when the Package Designer pane is selected. If you click on one of the other windows such as the properties grid, the only option available is Work Offline. The SSIS menu and some additional menu items are also accessible by right-clicking on the package workflow designer surface. Figure 5.4 shows that menu.

FIGURE 5.4   The SSIS menu is available by right-clicking on the control flow designer.

The additional interesting menu items include the editing options for Cut, Copy, and Paste. An additional option is available to add an annotation, which is a way of adding comments and is a good way to document the package.

The Edit Breakpoints menu item is how you add and remove debugging breakpoints. Figure 5.5 shows the Edit Breakpoints dialog box that opens when you choose to edit breakpoints.

The Toolboxes

The toolboxes are where the tasks and data flow components are accessible. Two Visual Studio toolboxes are unique to Integration Services. Figure 5.6 shows the toolbox for the control flow with tasks in it. You can control which tasks are visible in the toolbox by adding and deleting items from it.

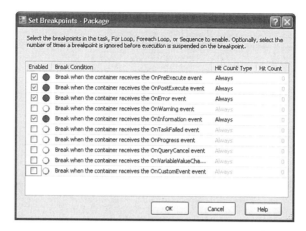

FIGURE 5.5   The Edit Breakpoints dialog box lets you set and remove breakpoints.

TIP

You can also select the List View option to turn off List View mode in the toolbox. If you liked the DTS look with only icons, that might appeal to you. That option turns off the text portion of the tool and only shows the icon.

To delete an item from the toolbox, simply select it, and then press the Delete key. This does not uninstall the component from the machine, it simply removes it from the toolbox so that it is no longer visible.

To add an item to the toolbox, right-click on the toolbox anywhere and select the Choose Items option.

The Choose Toolbox Items dialog box opens, as shown in Figure 5.7. If you happen to accidentally delete an item from the toolbox, simply open this dialog box, put a check next to the item you deleted, and click OK. It then reappears in the toolbox. You can also remove items from the toolbox by deselecting the item in this dialog box. As you can see, the dialog box has tabs that organize the components into subgroups. For Integration Services, the three tabs of interest are the SSIS Data Flow Items, the SSIS Control Flow Items, and the Maintenance Tasks.

The Designers

This topic has the potential to be confusing; this book uses the term "designer" to describe the overall Visual Studio environment. It also uses "designer" to describe the windows in which you build packages. The context of the discussion should help you know which designer is intended. Figure 5.8 shows the designers as they appear just after creating a new empty package.

FIGURE 5.6   The Control Flow Items toolbox contains all currently selected tasks.

NOTE

Seasoned DTS users might be caught off guard by the separation between the design time environment (BIDS) and the management environment, SQL Server Management Studio. Microsoft has received more than one panicked email in which a customer wonders why the design environment was removed from the management environment and wondered how Microsoft expects anyone to create packages without it. In DTS, the design environment was embedded in the management environment, Enterprise Manager. But for SQL Server 2005, Microsoft made a distinction between design and management activities to reflect the separation of responsibilities that exist in many enterprise environments. BIDS is targeted at developers who are creating packages, cubes, reports, or, in other words, developing solutions. Management Studio is targeted at database administrators and operators. See Chapter 17, "SQL Server Management Studio," for more about that environment.

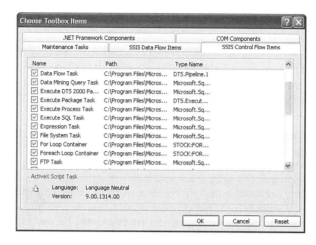

FIGURE 5.7   The Choose Toolbox Items dialog box allows you to add tasks to the toolbox.

FIGURE 5.8   The designers are the windows in which you build the package.

The Control Flow Designer

Clicking on the first tab to the left takes you to the Control Flow designer, where you create tasks, precedence constraints, and connections. You can think of this designer as the top-level package view because it shows the package at the highest level of detail. It's also true to its name and shows the flow of control from task to task.

NAMING BEST PRACTICE

When I was growing up, my mother used to always tell me to "Clean up as you go, so you don't end up with messes like this!" Now I'm a dad and I find myself telling my kids this a lot. As it turns out, this advice also works well with building packages. When you're building a package, it can get pretty messy, pretty fast. To avoid creating a big messy package, keep this rule in mind.

"When you drop it, name it."

This means that whenever you drop an object on a designer surface, create a new connection manager, or do anything else that results in the creation of a new package object, give it a name and a description. You will best understand the purpose for the object you are creating at the time when you create it. Although this takes a bit of extra time, it is immensely better than the alternatives, such as scratching your head at 2:00 a.m. wondering why you created that connection manager or trying to wrap up a project by doing a commenting pass on packages you wrote months before.

Use a naming convention. Be verbose in your descriptions. Whatever conventions you choose to follow, make sure you follow them consistently and "Clean up as you go."

Drop a Data Flow Task onto the Control Flow designer surface. Drop a Script Task as well. Notice the dangling pointer beneath the task. That's a precedence constraint and is called a dangling connector. Drag it from one task and drop it onto another to create a precedence constraint between the two tasks. The precedence constraint controls the order in which the two tasks execute. Drag one more Data Flow Task onto the Control Flow designer so you have some tasks to work with on the other designers.

NOTE

Often, you might have the need to create a proof-of-concept package or might just need temporary placeholder tasks while you "sketch out" the design of a package, but you don't always know what tasks you'll need or even how you want the final package to be structured. In other cases, you might need a common starting point from which to begin the package, but you don't need the starting point to do anything. For example, you might want to execute a different part of the package depending on some condition. In these cases, it would be nice to have a placeholder or dummy task.

The Script Task is just such a task. By default, the Script Task returns success and does nothing else. Later, you can replace it with other tasks or modify it to add execution value. So, in addition to being a powerful customization option, it's helpful to think of the Script Task as a placeholder task.

To open the editor for a given task, simply double-click on it or right-click and select Edit from the context menu.

The Connections Tray

Below the Control Flow designer, there is a tabbed window called the Connection Managers window or Connections Tray. This is where you create, manage, and delete connections and it's available in the Control Flow, Data Flow, and Event Handler designers. To create a new connection manager, right-click on the Connections Tray and select the type of connection you want to create from the context menu shown in Figure 5.9.

FIGURE 5.9   The Connection Managers menu allows you to create new connection managers.

If the type of connection you want to create isn't directly available to you in this menu, you can choose the New Connection option, which opens the Add SSIS Connection Manager dialog box shown in Figure 5.10.

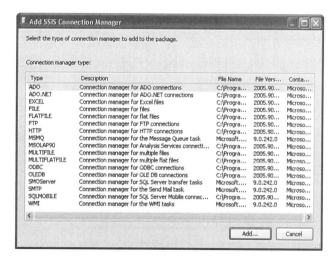

FIGURE 5.10   The Add SSIS Connection Manager dialog box shows all available connection manager types.

The Add SSIS Connection Manager dialog box shows all the connection manager types that are installed on the working machine. To create a connection manager from this dialog box, click the Connection Manager type you want to create, and click the Add button. The creation dialog box for the type of connection manager you chose opens.

The Data Flow Designer

Now let's take a look at the Data Flow designer. If you haven't dropped two Data Flow Tasks onto the Control Flow designer, do so now. To get to the Data Flow designer, you can either double-click on the Data Flow Task or click on the Data Flow tab.

TIP
_____

Double-clicking the Data Flow Task is the preferred way to get to its designer, because it always takes you to the correct designer. If you have more than one Data Flow Task in the package, clicking on the Data Flow tab takes you to the Data Flow designer for the currently selected Data Flow Task, which might not always be the one you want to edit. Also, if there is a task selected and it's not a Data Flow Task, when you click on the Data Flow tab, the Data Flow designer for the Data Flow Task that was created first opens. So, it's easiest to just double-click on the Data Flow Task you want to edit.

Figure 5.11 shows the Data Flow designer. Notice that there are two available to edit, "Data Flow Task" and "Data Flow Task 1." Having two illustrates how the Data Flow designer supports more than one Data Flow Task per package. You can select which task you want to edit in the drop down at the top of the designer window.

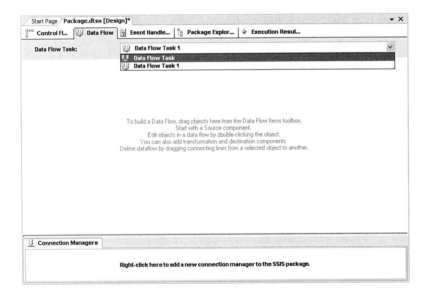

FIGURE 5.11   The Data Flow Task designer allows you to choose which task to edit.

After you're in the Data Flow designer, drag an OLEDB Source component onto the designer and double-click it. This opens the OLEDB Source Editor. Create a connection manager by clicking on the New button and point the connection manager at any server you have running. Select the Table or View data access mode (default), and then select any table, such as the CompanyAddresses table from the AdventureWorks sample database. Click the Columns tab on the left and the columns should be correctly mapped from the input table to the output.

Customizing the Toolbox

With the Data Flow tab selected, turn your attention to the toolbox. Notice that it looks similar to the Control Flow toolbox, but has different components in it. It functions the same way and you can change the contents in the same way as the Control Flow toolbox. However, you can customize the toolbox in a few more ways. If you right-click on the toolbox, the context menu shown in Figure 5.12 appears. Along with the Choose Items menu item previously mentioned, a few more options are worth noting here.

FIGURE 5.12   You can modify the toolbox using the context menu.

The Reset Toolbox option is an easy way to reset the toolbox to the entire set of components installed on the machine. So, if you've deleted a bunch of components or reorganized them in a way that doesn't make sense to you, it's a simple way to return to the default toolbox setup. It's fairly expensive to do, however, and takes quite a while to complete. So, only do this if you're prepared to wait a while.

The usual editing commands, Cut, Copy, and Paste are available for moving items around too. So, you can cut or copy a component and paste it somewhere else in the toolbox. You can also rename components, and so forth.

Figure 5.13 shows a sample Data Flow toolbox. Notice at the top there is a tab called "My Favorite Components."

The toolbox supports creating your own tabs. This might be useful to you if you only typically use a small number of the components or tasks and are always searching for those items. You can create your own tab with only those items you use the most and make them much easier to find. To create your own tab, select the Add Tab menu item from the context menu.

FIGURE 5.13   The toolbox is customizable.

TIP

The thumbtack in the upper-right corner of the toolbox is available on all the docking windows, such as the toolbox, Solution Explorer, and properties windows. Clicking on that button toggles the Autohide state of the window. If you toggle the Autohide state off, you can also drag these windows away from the main window edge and they become free (nondocking) standing windows.

Data Flow Component Context Menus

In the Data Flow designer, if you right-click on one of the components, a context menu appears. Figure 5.14 shows the context menu for the OLE DB Source component.

FIGURE 5.14   Data flow components have a context menu.

There are the standard editing options and the Show Advanced Editor menu item. The
Advanced Editor provides a way to edit component properties that are not normally
exposed through their custom interfaces. For example, column types are not visible in the
standard UI for the OLE DB Source, but they are visible in the Advanced Editor. Figure
5.15 shows the Advanced Editor.

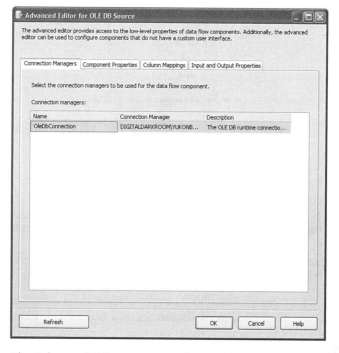

FIGURE 5.15   The Advanced Editor exposes advanced component settings.

The Autosize menu item is a quick-and-easy way to change the size of the task or component to match the size of the name. To see it work, simply change the name to be much
longer or shorter and select the option in the context menu; the task or component box
will be sized to fit the text.

<u>**TIP**</u>

Another useful formatting command is the Autolayout menu under the Format main menu. Select this option to have the designer organize the components on the designer. This is useful when your package gets a little visually unruly and you need to quickly reformat it. To get there, select the Format menu, and then select the Autolayout menu option.

Control Flow Component Context Menus

Tasks also have a context menu, as shown in Figure 5.16. The Task context menu has a few interesting menu choices. The Execute Task menu item executes the task individually. Only the task that was selected when you open the menu will execute.

<u>**NOTE**</u>

The context menu for containers also contains a menu option called Execute Task. That is a misnomer and in SP1 will likely be changed to Execute Container. Selecting this menu option will, of course, execute the container and its children only.

FIGURE 5.16   The Task context menu is a quick way to access common features.

The Edit Breakpoints menu item opens the same dialog box shown previously; however, the difference is that the breakpoints are set on the task and not on the package.

The Group menu item creates a visual grouping container. If you select multiple tasks or containers and select this option, the designer creates a grouping container around all the selected objects. To remove a group without deleting its contents, right-click on the title bar for the group container and select Ungroup.

NOTE

The grouping container has the same look and feel as other containers, such as the Sequence or Foreach Loop. It contains other containers and tasks and you can collapse and expand it. However, it is not a true runtime container and does not provide the same services as true runtime containers, such as variable and logging scope. It only exists in the designer environment and does not affect execution.

The Zoom option is also available on the main menu under the View menu tree. This option lets you change the size of the objects in the designer. This is useful when you need to see more of the package simultaneously. Or, if you want to show the package in a demonstration, it's helpful to make the tasks larger for easier viewing.

Figure 5.17 shows the designer panning feature. In the lower-right corner of the designer, there is a small black cross with arrows. It is only visible if the package view is larger than the designer surface. If you click on that small button, it shows a view window with the contents of the entire package called the Navigator window. You can use the Navigator to quickly move or pan to different parts of large packages. The Navigator is available in all the box and line designers. To see it work, make the designer window small enough so that a task or component is outside the visible design surface.

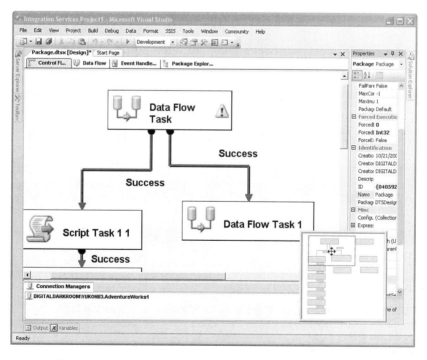

FIGURE 5.17 Panning makes package navigation simple.

Error and Warning Indicators

When tasks and components have errors or warnings, the designers indicate that to the user by placing small icons in the task and component. Figure 5.18 shows the Execute SQL Task after it has just been dropped onto the designer surface. Moving the mouse over the icon shows the error or warning.

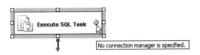

FIGURE 5.18   Tasks with errors have a small, red, letter X icon.

Figure 5.19 shows the Send Mail Task with a warning. Tasks and components raise warnings in various cases. For example, if a task has a setting that could possibly result in a failure or if there is some noncritical setting missing, it should raise a warning. In this case, the Send Mail Task raised a warning because there was no subject provided.

FIGURE 5.19   Tasks with warnings have a small, yellow, exclamation icon.

Data Flow Paths and Viewers

To show you some of the Data Flow designer features, you need to build a data flow. The following instructions show you how to build a data flow that builds a contact list for all employees in the AdventureWorks table with a name that starts with the letter *M* and puts it into a flat file. Alternately, you can open the S05-BIDS solution in the samples folder, which has this package already created.

Setting Up the OLE DB Source   In this step, you'll set up the Data Flow Task and the OLE DB Source Adapter. Part of the setup for the OLE DB Source is creating an OLE DB Connection Manager as well.

1. Delete all the tasks or create a new package.

2. Drop a Data Flow Task onto the Control Flow designer.

3. Double-click on the Data Flow Task.

4. Drop an OLE DB Source Adapter onto the Data Flow designer.

5. Double-click on the OLE DB Source Adapter to bring up the UI.

6. On the Connection Manager tab, create a new OLE DB Connection Manager by clicking the New button.

7. In the Configure OLE DB Connection Manager dialog box, click the New button.

8. For the server name, select the local server where you've installed the AdventureWorks sample database.

9. For the database, select the AdventureWorks sample database.

10. Click the Test Connection button to ensure you've got a valid connection.

11. Click the OK button in the two dialog boxes to return to the OLE DB Source Editor.

12. Ensure the Data Access mode is set to SQL Command.

13. Type the following query into the SQL Command text, as shown in Figure 5.20:

```
SELECT    EmployeeID, FirstName, LastName, JobTitle, Phone, EmailAddress,
AddressLine1, AddressLine2, City, StateProvinceName, PostalCode
FROM        HumanResources.vEmployee
WHERE FirstName LIKE 'M%'
```

14. You can click the Preview button if you want to see the rows that result from the query.

15. Now, select the Columns tab in the upper-left corner. This dialog box establishes which columns will be used in the data flow. For now, don't worry about the Error Output tab.

16. Click the OK button.

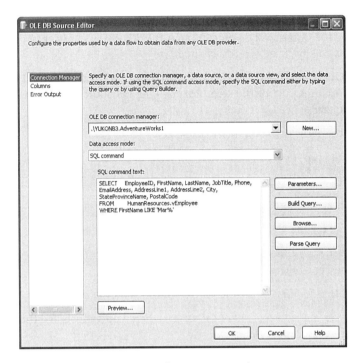

FIGURE 5.20   Use the OLE DB Source Editor to set up the source.

Setting Up the Flat File Destination Adapter   Now, you can set up the Flat File Destination Adapter. While still in the Data Flow designer, complete the following steps:

1. Drop a Flat File Destination component onto the designer.

2. Drag the dangling green connector from the OLE DB Source and drop it onto the Flat File Destination.

3. Double-click on the Flat File Destination.

4. Click the New button to create a new Flat File Connection Manager.

5. Choose the format you want to use, such as delimited.

6. Click the OK button.

7. The next dialog box is the Flat File Connection Manager Editor. Click the Browse button to find the folder to create the new flat file or type the filename in directly, for example, `D:\TEMP\EmployeeContacts.txt`.

8. Click on the option to set column names in the first data row.

9. Figure 5.21 shows the General tab of the Flat File Connection Manager Editor after it has been set up.

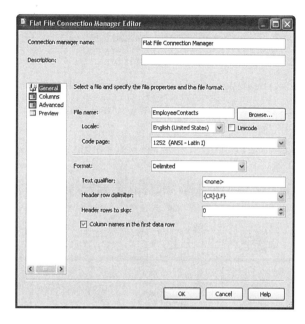

FIGURE 5.21   Use the Flat File Connection Manager UI to specify the output flat file.

10. Click the Columns tab.

11. Click the OK button.

12. You should be back to the Flat File Destination Editor.

13. Click the Mappings tab and check that the component correctly maps all the columns.

14. Click the OK button.

Setting Up the Data Flow Path   The package should now be configured to extract the employees whose first names start with the letter *M* and you're now at a state at which you can examine data flow paths and viewers more closely. Figure 5.22 shows the Metadata tab of the Data Flow Path Editor dialog box. To open this dialog box, double-click on the path between the OLE DB Source and the Flat File Destination and click on the Metadata tab.

With the Data Flow Path Editor open, click the General tab if it isn't already selected. A number of interesting settings and properties are available on this tab.

- **Name**—The name is useful for documentation. Used well, it can document what data is going across the path. This path is named Employee Contact List.

- **ID**—The ID is the unique identification number used to represent the path in the Data Flow Task. The Data Flow Task often shows the ID in errors that are related to the data flow path.

- **PathAnnotation**—This setting controls the value the designer will use as the annotation for the path. There are four options available:

  - **Never**—The designer shows no annotation.

  - **AsNeeded**—The designer shows the annotations transforms provide.

  - **SourceName**—The designer shows the source transform name as the annotation.

  - **PathName**—The designer shows the name of the path as the annotation.

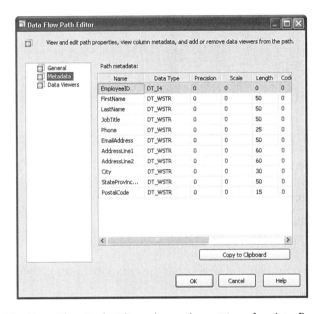

FIGURE 5.22   The Data Flow Path Editor shows the settings for data flow paths.

Figure 5.23 shows the data flow path with the PathName option selected. By changing the Name property, you can also change the annotation value that the designer displays.

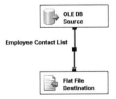

FIGURE 5.23   The annotation can describe the data flowing through it.

Setting Up the Data Flow Viewers   One of the more powerful debugging and troubleshooting features in the Data Flow Task is available in this dialog box on the Data Viewers tab. As data flows through the Data Flow task and across the data flow path, it would be nice if you could actually see the data as it flows. That's what Data Viewers do. They allow you to view the data as it flows through the Data Flow Task.

Click the Data Viewers tab and click the Add button to show the Configure Data Viewer dialog box shown in Figure 5.24.

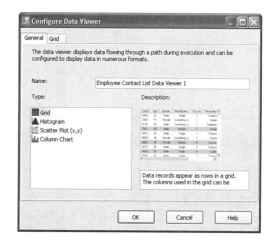

FIGURE 5.24   Create and configure Data Viewers in the Configure Data Viewer dialog box.

There are two tabs in this dialog box. Use the General tab for creating new Data Viewers. Use the Grid tab to configure the Grid Data viewer. Each Data Viewer type has a configuration tab with the same name as the type that you use for further configuring of the viewer. As you change the viewer type selection on the General tab, the name of the second tab changes as well. For this exercise, you'll create two viewers:

1. From the Data Viewer dialog box, select the viewer type "Grid."

2. Click the OK button.

3. Click the Add button again.

4. Select the Column Chart type.

5. Select the Column Chart tab.

6. Select the PostalCode column.

7. Click the OK button twice to get back to the Data Flow designer.

Now, you're all set to see Data Viewers in action.

Running the Package   Press the F5 button or click the Start Debugging button to start the package running. The Data Viewers should appear immediately. Data Viewers are essentially breakpoints in the data flow. They temporarily stop the data from moving through the Data Flow Task to give you the opportunity to view it before it rushes off to the destination. You can look at the data as long as you want. The Data Flow Task waits until you allow it to continue. To tell the Data Flow Task to continue, use the buttons on the viewers. Figure 5.25 shows the Data Viewers as they appeared in the sample package.

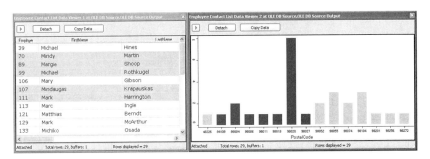

FIGURE 5.25   Data Viewers allow you to interactively view data as it flows through the Data Flow Task.

As you can see from Figure 5.25, there are three buttons on each of the Data Viewers. The Copy Data button allows you to copy the viewed data to the Clipboard. To allow the Data Flow Task to continue, press the small button with the triangle. This button tells the Data Flow Task to continue until it displays the next set of values in the viewer. Then it stops again. In this way, it's possible for you to view all the data that moves through the path on which the viewer has been created. You use the Detach button when you no longer want to view the data. Clicking it temporarily detaches the viewer from the flow and does not stop the Data Flow Task until the next time you run the package.

Viewers Interact   One of the interesting aspects of Data Viewers is that they interact. Figure 5.25 shows some of the data points selected. To do this, simply drag the mouse over the data points. Selecting rows in the Grid view also selects columns in the Column Chart view. The interactive nature of Data Viewers makes it possible to do real-time analysis or to simply spot-check the data. Certainly, it aids you in better understanding the shape of the data. In the example given, it's possible to quickly discover and retrieve which employees live within the 98020 ZIP Code.

The Progress or Execution Results View
When you execute a package, one of the changes that happens in the environment is a new designer window appears. It isn't that obvious because it only shows up as a tab at the top of the designers along with the Control Flow and Data Flow tabs. While the package is running, the tab is named the Progress view and is updated with important information as the package is executing. When the package is complete and you select the Stop Debugging button or [Shift+F5], the tab name changes to Execution Results and retains all the progress information from the package execution.

If your package fails for some reason, this is a good place to start looking for the cause. Any errors and warnings that the package raised during execution show up here as well as some other interesting information, such as execution order and duration. Figure 5.26 shows the Execution Results view as it appears after running the DataViewers sample package.

FIGURE 5.26   The Progress or Execution Results view shows important information.

The Package Explorer View
The Package Explorer view is another way to view your package. It shows the entire package, both Control Flow and Data Flow, in one unified view. This is useful for getting to objects fast and, in some cases, such as for log providers, it is the only place where certain settings can be edited. Figure 5.27 shows the Package Explorer view for the DataViewers sample package.

The Event Handlers Designer
The Event Handlers designer is the way you edit event handlers. Event handlers are package containers that Integration Services executes when an object in the package raises an event. The Event Handler designer is practically identical to the Control Flow designer. You can create tasks and variables in this designer. The only difference is that the control flow you create in these designers is only conditionally executed when the associated event is fired.

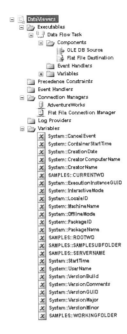

FIGURE 5.27   The Package Explorer view is a quick way to access the entire package.

The Log Events Window

Figure 5.28 shows the Log Events window with output from the execution of the DataViewers sample package. This window shows the same data that is output to logs and can be configured in the same way as log providers are configured.

To see the log events in the designer with the Log Events window, click the main View menu, click Other Windows, and then click Log Events. This shows the Log Events viewer. If you run the package now, with the default settings, nothing shows in this window. That's because you still need to enable logging, which is disabled by default for performance reasons.

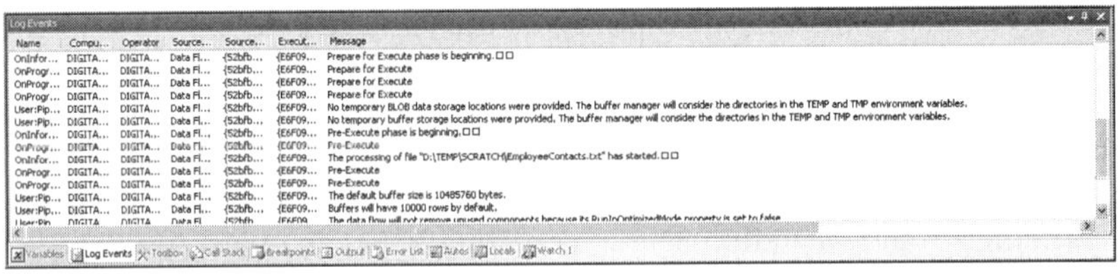

FIGURE 5.28   The Log Events window shows log output during execution.

To enable logging events, right-click on the Control Flow designer, and then click Logging. Figure 5.29 shows the Configure SSIS Logs dialog box. Notice that the check boxes in the left pane are both selected. This turns on logging for those containers. The default for these is unchecked. On the right side of the dialog box are the events that are available from the container. In this example, all log events are selected, but you can be selective and only choose those log events in which you are interested.

TIP

If the Log Events window isn't visible while your package is executing, you'll need to open it as explained previously. The set of visible windows during design time is different than the set visible while executing a package.

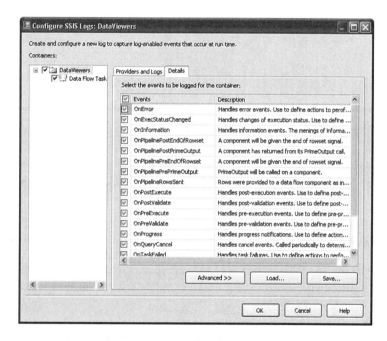

FIGURE 5.29   Use the Configure SSIS Logs dialog box to turn on logging.

The Configure SSIS Logs dialog box is also where you create and delete log providers. Click the Providers and Logs tab and you'll see the dialog box shown in Figure 5.30.

To create a new log provider, select the type of log provider you want to create and click the Add button. In Figure 5.30, a log provider is created that logs to SQL Server. The configuration, in this case, is a connection manager to a SQL Server database. The Configuration setting takes different connections depending on the type of log provider. For example, text file log providers require a file connection manager, whereas Windows Event Log log providers don't require any configuration because they log to the local Windows Event Log system.

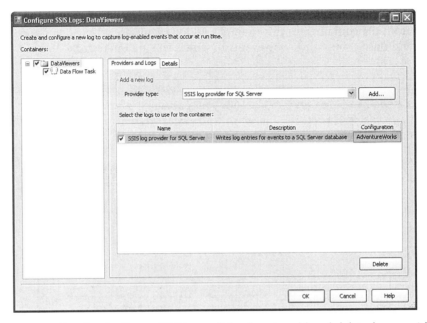

FIGURE 5.30   Use the Configure SSIS Logs dialog box to add and delete log providers.

Package Configurations

Package configurations are a way to change the settings in the package without modifying the package directly. All the sample packages that accompany this book use configurations to make it easy to load and run packages on your machine. To get to the Package Configurations dialog box shown in Figure 5.31, right-click on the Control Flow designer and select Package Configurations.

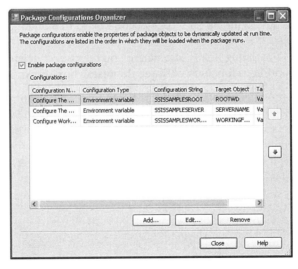

FIGURE 5.31   Edit package configurations with the Package Configurations dialog box.

The Package Configurations dialog box is a wizard that walks you through the process of creating a configuration. To start the wizard, click the Add button.

At this point, this chapter has covered those features of the Business Intelligence Development Studio that are specific to and created for Integration Services. Most of these features exist only in BIDS and are not found in the standard Visual Studio environment that ships with Visual C# or any other language.

Visual Studio Standard Options

One of the reasons that Visual Studio is such a great platform is that it provides so many commonly required features for individuals, ISVs, shareware developers, or corporations that develop tools. The options and features about to be described are all provided as part of the Visual Studio Industry Partners platform. This is a publicly available SDK you can download free of charge from MSDN. The Business Intelligence team created the Business Intelligence Development Studio essentially as a premier partner with Visual Studio using the same SDK as third parties. For more information about this program, see MSDN at http://msdn.microsoft.com/vstudio/extend/vsipoverview/default.aspx.

What follows is a quick run through of the Visual Studio features as they apply to Integration Services. It's a testament to the flexibility and time-proven design of Visual Studio that the generalized features found in Visual Studio apply so well to specific domains such as Integration Services. Whole books have been written about Visual Studio, so this section covers those Visual Studio features that are specific to or useful for Integration Services.

The Solution Explorer

To get started, look at the place where most Integration Services work begins, the Solution Explorer. For such a simple tree view, there are a remarkable number of things you can accomplish using the Solution Explorer. To start out, make sure you open the sample solution for this chapter, S05-BIDS.

Notice that there are three projects in the solution. There is an Integration Services project named BIDS and two other projects. One is an Analysis Services project named DummyASProject; the other is an Integration Services project named DummyISProject. The dummy projects have been added to illustrate the nature of solutions and to provide a little more with which to work while discussing the Solution Explorer.

TIP

If you only have one project in the solution, by default the solution node is hidden. Likely, this is to eliminate the confusion that can result from having two root nodes. Also, the menu items for solutions are redundant if there is no more than one project in a solution. To always view the solution node, click Tools from the top menu, and then click Options. In the Options dialog box, select the Projects and Solutions tab and then the General node. Select the Always Show Solution check box and the solution node will be visible even when you only have one project.

Figure 5.32 shows the solution in the Solution Explorer.

FIGURE 5.32   The Solution Explorer is the central solution management window.

The Solution Explorer Context Menu

As in other places in BIDS, a lot of the solution and project features are accessed with context menus. Figure 5.33 shows the context menu for the sample solution. This menu contains many of the same menu items as the main File menu, but is better focused around managing the solution. It also contains many of the same options as the Project context menu you'll see in a moment. The Solution Explorer context menu is provided for convenience. When you select one of the solution build menu options, for example, it simply traverses the tree of projects and calls the corresponding project build options on each contained project.

FIGURE 5.33   The Solution Explorer context menu provides quick access to solution management features.

Build   Several build options are available in the Solution Explorer context menu. These are mostly self-explanatory, but it's worthwhile to understand some of the finer details of what these options do. The build options include the following:

- **Build Solution**—Calls Build on all projects

- **Rebuild Solution**—Calls Rebuild on all projects

- **Deploy Solution**—Deploys each project according to its project settings

- **Clean Solution**—Calls Clean on all projects

- **Batch Build**—Opens the Batch Build dialog box for selecting which projects and configurations to selectively build

- **Configuration Manager**—Opens the Configuration Manager dialog box for creating new project configurations

- **Project Dependencies**—Opens the Project Dependencies dialog box to create dependency relationships between projects

- **Project Build Order**—Shows the build order of projects

NOTE

Depending on the load and build state of your solution, some of the context menu options might not be available.

The Build Solution option traverses the tree of projects and builds each project. What happens when the project builds is wholly dependent upon the project type and its settings, which are discussed shortly. What is interesting here is how Visual Studio decides the order in which to build the projects. That's where the Project Dependencies and Project Build Order menu items come in. Figure 5.34 shows the Project Dependencies dialog box that opens when you select the Project Dependencies menu option. This dialog box allows you to describe to Visual Studio which projects depend on others. For example, you might have a custom task you're building in the same solution as the package you use to debug it. To ensure that the task is compiled and registered before the package attempts to run, you use the Project Dependencies dialog box to specify that the Integration Services project is dependent on the custom task project.

The Build Order tab shows the build order that results from the dependencies. In the previous example, because the Integration Services project is dependent on the custom task project, the custom task project builds before the Integration Services project. In many cases, project build order isn't important. But if you ever have a project that depends on the successful output of another project in the same solution, ensure that the project dependencies reflect that relationship.

FIGURE 5.34   The Project Dependencies dialog box controls the project build order.

Set Startup Projects   The Startup Projects dialog box allows you to configure which projects start when you start debugging by clicking the Start Debugging button on the Standard toolbar, when pressing the F5 button, or when choosing Start Debugging from the Debug menu. To open this dialog box, click the Set Startup Projects menu option from the Solution Explorer context menu. Figure 5.35 shows the dialog settings for the BIDS solution.

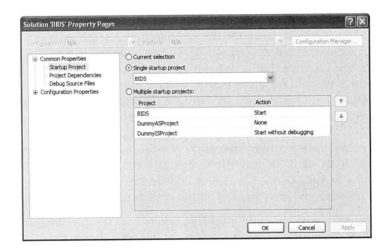

FIGURE 5.35   The Startup Projects dialog box helps you flexibly debug projects.

In Figure 5.35, the Startup Projects dialog box is configured to start the DummyISProject without debugging and to start the DataViewers.dtsx package in the debugger.

CAUTION

This can be a little disconcerting if you're not aware of what's happening. The DummyISProject pops up a command window with the output from DTExec.exe and shows a message box. When you launch a package without debugging, it executes the package using the package execution utility named DTExec.exe.

This is useful in cases in which you need to have one process running that another process uses. Often, this can come in handy when debugging a custom component or when you have a custom user interface for accessing a server system. You can set up one project to execute the user interface without the debugger while the other project is running the server within the debugging environment. Although these types of debugging scenarios are fairly rare, when you really need this kind of debugging support, it is invaluable.

The Project Context Menu

Figure 5.36 shows the Project context menu, which contains many commonly used menu options used to manage projects. These same options are also available from the main Project menu. One of the first things you'll likely notice is that there are a few of the same options that are on the Solution Explorer context menu. This is because the Solution Explorer context menu options call down to each of the projects and some project types have different behaviors for the different menu selections.

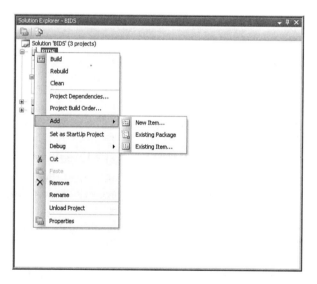

FIGURE 5.36   The Project context menu contains many commonly used options.

Build, Rebuild, and Clean   Because packages don't compile like code projects, the Build, Rebuild, and Clean menu options operate a bit different than they do for projects like C# or Visual Basic. The Integration Services Build option copies all the packages in the project to a certain folder and if deployment is enabled for the project, it also copies some deployment-related files to a certain folder. Rebuild overwrites the binaries previously placed in the locations where Build placed them and Clean removes them from those locations. How these Build functions behave is largely dependent on the settings in the Project Properties dialog box. To configure these settings and where these files go, open the Project Options dialog box shown in Figure 5.37 by selecting Properties in the project's context menu.

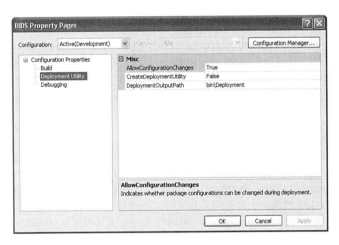

FIGURE 5.37   The Project Properties dialog box lets you control build behavior.

Properties

The Project Properties dialog box has three tabs. The first tab is the Build tab. The only setting on this tab is the OutputPath. This path tells Visual Studio where to place the package when you build the project. The default path is "bin". With this setting, Visual Studio creates a folder named "bin" below the project's home directory. So, if your project is at C:\Solutions\BIDS, the default setting is to place the packages in the project in the C:\Solutions\BIDS\bin folder. You can also specify the fully qualified path of a folder and Visual Studio dutifully places the package in the specified directory.

The second tab contains the settings that control if and where the deployment utility and files get created. The Deployment Utility tab in the project's Property Pages dialog box has three settings. AllowConfigurationChanges allows the person who runs the deployment utility to change configuration settings when installing on the destination machine. CreateDeploymentUtility turns on the feature when building. DeploymentOutputPath lets you configure where the designer drops the deployed files. Like the OutputPath on the Build tab, DeploymentOutputPath is relative to the location of the project. The default folder is bin\Deployment.

The third tab, Debugging, controls the settings related to debugging your packages:

- **RunInOptimizedMode**—Turns on the Data Flow Task optimized mode, which attempts to improve performance by removing unused columns, outputs, and components from the data flow.

- **InteractiveMode**—Indicates if interactive features, such as dialog boxes should be enabled. For example, the Script Task uses this setting to determine if it should pop up error messages when there is an error while running the task's script.

- **Run64BitRuntime**—Uses the 64-bit runtime if it is available.

- **StartAction**—Indicates what to do when debugging is started. Typically, this is set to ExecutePackage; however, if you're writing a custom client that programmatically creates or loads a package, you can set this to Program.

- **StartApplication**—Indicates the application to launch when debugging. If you've selected Program for the StartAction, this is where you need to specify the application to run.

- **StartObjectID**—Specifies the package to execute.

- **CmdLineArguments**—Specifies the command-line arguments to pass to the package.

Unload Project   Unload Project does just what it says. It unloads the project and closes all the files it contains. At first sight, this probably doesn't seem too useful. But there are some advantages to unloading projects, for example, if you have a lot of projects in one solution, unloading projects makes the solution load faster. To reload a project, you simply right-click on the project and select Reload from the context menu.

Set as StartUp Project   This menu item is a shortcut to the setting you make in the Set Startup Projects dialog box mentioned previously. If you select this option, the startup project listed in that dialog box changes accordingly.

The SSIS Packages Node Context Menu

Figure 5.38 shows the SSIS Packages context menu. This is an important menu for managing packages in the Visual Studio environment. It provides an easy way to create new or add existing packages to the project.

FIGURE 5.38   The SSIS Packages context menu provides several ways to add packages to the project.

Each of these options results in a new package being added to the project. The first option is New SSIS Package to create a new package. Select this option and the new package is created and opened in the designer for you. The SSIS Import and Export Wizard option opens the Import/Export Wizard and generates a package. The Migrate DTS 2000 Package option launches the DTS 2000 Migration Wizard, which can generate one or many packages. Finally, the Add Existing Package option allows you to select packages to add to the project that are stored in SQL Server, the file system, or the SSIS Package Store.

Data Sources and Data Source Views

Data sources are small files that contain information about how to connect to a server and some metadata; they are essentially a connection string saved to a file. Data Source Views are objects that allow you to create a view on a source of data. You create both by right-clicking and selecting the single create option. For Data Sources, select New Data Source. To create a new Data Source View, select New Data Source View.

The Individual Package Context Menu

By now, you should be getting the idea that context menus are really powerful and that there are a lot of them in Visual Studio. You might find little use for the menu bar menus after you've grown accustomed to context menus.

The final context menu covered here is the one found when you right-click on an individual package. Figure 5.39 shows that context menu.

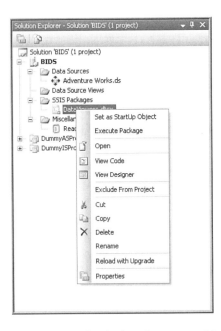

FIGURE 5.39   The context menu on individual packages provides important package-specific options.

Set as Startup Object   This menu item is project specific and tells BIDS which package you want to execute when debugging. This is useful when your Integration Services project has more than one package.

Execute Package   This is a quick way to execute a package and is especially useful if you have used the Set as Startup Object option to set a different package as the default to run when debugging. If this menu option didn't exist, you'd have to change the startup object setting every time you wanted to run a different package than the currently selected startup object.

View Code   This menu item opens an XML viewer with the contents of the package. This is useful when you want to edit the settings in the package directly instead of through the designer view.

CAUTION

Microsoft does not support editing the package directly in this fashion. However, studying a package in Code View can yield some interesting and helpful information. If you ever use Code View to make changes to your package, you should make sure that you back up the package first. It is extremely easy to break a package in Code View and should not be attempted unless you know what you are doing.

View Designer   This menu item opens the package in the designer.

Exclude from Project   This option removes the package from the project, but doesn't delete the package file from the file system. To include the package in the project again, you can select the Add Existing Package option from the Project context menu.

Editing Menu Options   These options do as they say, but be careful. The Delete option not only removes the package from the project, it deletes the package file from the file system.

Reload with Upgrade   This option loads the package, but sets a special property on the package that instructs Integration Services to attempt to upgrade any tasks that are referenced in the package to newer versions of the component if available.

These are the important features of the Solution Explorer. Not all of them are covered here, so take a few minutes and look around the Solution Explorer some more. Right-click on everything in the Solution Explorer window. See if you can find some context menus or other features that aren't mentioned here. You'll want to get to know the Solution Explorer well because it's where almost all project-level management starts.

The Properties Window

The Properties window is another Visual Studio idiom that provides a lot of power to the Integration Services designer. With the Properties window, you can quickly see and modify the values for properties on any object in the package. This is important because packages are very declarative, or, in other words, a package's execution time behavior is dependent on its design time settings. By default, the Properties window is positioned on the right side of the designer. If it isn't open yet, right-click on any task, variable, or package, and select Properties.

Figure 5.40 shows the Properties window for the sample package called BIDS in the sample solution for this chapter. There are a lot of properties there and as you select different objects in the designer, the set of properties changes.

FIGURE 5.40   The Properties window shows properties for package objects.

Variables Window

The Variables window is where you create, modify, and delete package variables. Figure 5.41 shows the Variables window with the default settings.

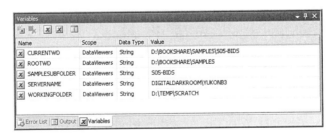

FIGURE 5.41   The Variables window shows a variable's name, scope, namespace, type, and value.

Along the top of the Variables window are five icons for managing variables. The following is a list of the icons and their purpose in order from left to right.

- **Create New Variable**—Creates a new user variable.

- **Delete Variable**—Deletes an existing variable.

- **Show System Variables**—Shows/Hides variables in the System namespace. There are quite a few system variables and they can be overwhelming. This button allows you to simplify the variable view a bit.

- **Show User Variables**—Shows all user variables in the entire package, not just those in scope.

- **Choose Variable Columns**—Allows you to change the columns that are visible in the Variables window. This is how you make a variable's namespace visible or hide other properties, such as scope or data type.

Figure 5.42 shows the Column Picker dialog box for the Variables window.

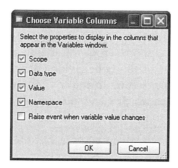

FIGURE 5.42   Use the Column Picker dialog box to modify the visible columns.

The File Menu

Although you are likely familiar with the File menu, two menu choices are worth exploring in more detail. They are the Save Package As and the Save Copy of Package As menu options. These two menu items don't behave exactly as you might expect.

Save Package As

Save Package As allows you to change the name of the package, but it also affects a few other things that are not so obvious:

- The designer leaves a copy of the package with the old name in the same folder.

- The designer provides the option to change the name of the package object as well. This changes the package name that you see in the properties grid.

- The source control history is lost for the package in Source Safe.

None of these side effects of changing a package name is severe or detrimental, but it is good to understand them so you're not surprised when it happens. For example, you might rename your package several times and then, upon viewing the package folder and finding more than one package, become confused as to which package is the current one. Just be aware of this behavior and you should be able to avoid such confusion.

Save Copy of Package As

This menu option is a deployment shortcut. It allows you to save the package to a location other than the solution folder. When you select this menu item, a dialog box opens that lets you save directly to the Integration Services package store, SQL Server, or the file system.

CAUTION

This menu option can be a little hard to find because it is only visible when there is a package loaded and you have selected one of its designers.

Options Dialog Box

A wealth of settings can be found in the Options dialog box. To get there, click Tools on the main menu, and then click Options. From this dialog box, you can change the look and feel of the designer, alter file-handling behavior, change fonts, set up key mappings, and control just about every other setting in the environment. If you haven't looked around this dialog box before, it's worth a few minutes to just select each node and familiarize yourself with the settings found there.

There are too many settings to cover them all here, but there are a few Integration Services settings worth mentioning.

Business Intelligence Designers

These settings control the Analysis Services and Integration Services designers. Under the Integration Services node, there are three subnodes.

General On the General tab are the settings for digital signatures for ensuring that packages are signed. There is also a setting for people who have color differentiation problems. The Show Precedence Constraint Labels check box enables labels to show whether a constraint is for success, failure, or completion. Figure 5.43 shows precedence constraints with this setting enabled.

FIGURE 5.43 Show Precedence Constraint Labels clearly show constraints.

Auto Connect   Figure 5.44 shows the Options dialog box with the Control Flow Auto Connect tab selected. This dialog box allows you to configure how the designer adds tasks to the design surface when you double-click on it in the toolbox. This is really handy when you build packages quickly, such as when building a lot of packages, or if you just can't stand building packages from left to right. The Data Flow Auto Connect dialog box serves the same purpose, but for the Data Flow Task.

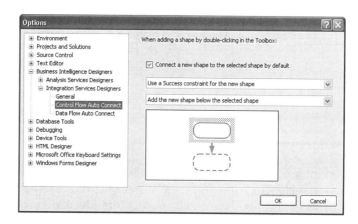

FIGURE 5.44   Auto Connect lets you decide the default visual layout for components.

Environment   On the Environment tab, there is a Fonts and Colors subtab. Selecting this tab shows a dialog box with some hard-to-find font settings. With the Fonts and Colors subtab selected, select the Show Settings For drop down and select Business Intelligence Designers. Play with these settings a bit and watch where the fonts change in the designer.

Debugging Windows

Occasionally, a package will have a bug or behave differently than designed, making it necessary to debug it. The following windows provide a view into the package that would otherwise be difficult or impossible to obtain. Wise use of these windows can make debugging packages much simpler. Often, by simply setting a breakpoint and watching the value of a variable, you can quickly find the reason behind package problems. Get to know these windows well.

The Breakpoints Window

The Breakpoints window shows all the breakpoints in the package and you can configure the window to show different properties using the Columns selection menu. Figure 5.45 shows the Breakpoints window with one breakpoint set. There are seven buttons at the top of the window for modifying the existing breakpoints.

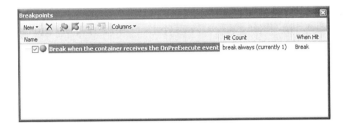

FIGURE 5.45   The Breakpoints window helps to manage package breakpoints.

CAUTION

The New button does not function in Integration Services. It's provided to support creating new breakpoints in code-based projects and currently cannot be used to create breakpoints in packages.

The Breakpoints window is the only debugging window that is visible while in design mode. The remaining debugging windows are only available while executing a package. To open these windows, select the Debug menu option from the main menu and then select the window you want to open from the Windows menu.

The Watch Window

The Watch window is useful for viewing values of objects as they change during execution. Currently, the Integration Services designer only supports viewing variables in the Watch window. You can view the value of a variable by dragging it from the Variables window and dropping it on the Watch window. Figure 5.46 shows the Watch window with the system variable CreationName added. This is the only way the designer provides a way to view the value of variables during execution.

FIGURE 5.46   The Watch window lets you view variable values at execution time.

CAUTION

Often, users attempt to view the value of a variable in the Properties window during execution. Because the designer creates a separate instance of the package for execution, the values displayed in the Properties window reflect the package state at design time and never change. The values of the variable in the separate instance of the package can only be viewed through the Watch window or the Locals window.

The Locals Window

The Locals window shows all local-scoped variables and some key properties of the currently selected container. Figure 5.47 shows the Locals window for a package that is currently suspended after hitting a breakpoint on a Script Task. Notice that there are three variables in the User namespace: `User::ScriptTaskScopeVariable`, `User::SequenceScopeVariable`, and `User::PackageScopeVariable`. Each of these was created at different variable scopes, as indicated by the names. If a variable is not in scope for a task or container, it will not show up in the Locals window. This is useful when trying to understand why a task is unable to find a variable or when you just want to see all the variables in a snapshot. Why would you use the Watch window instead of the Locals window then? The Watch window shows you the value for a variable at any time during the execution of the package, not just when it's in scope. It's also easier to focus on the value of a variable in the Watch window than in the Locals window.

FIGURE 5.47   The Locals window lets you view key values and variables in scope.

The Call Stack Window

The Call Stack window shows you how the package arrived at its current execution location. This debugging window is useful when you have a hierarchy of containers and you need to see how the package flows through that hierarchy. For flat packages, packages without much hierarchical structure, the Call Stack doesn't provide much value. However, if you have multiple embedded containers, this window can help you better understand your package.

Figure 5.48 shows the Call Stack window next to the package it documents. Notice that the package is at the bottom of the call stack. This will always be true. The stack grows up from the bottom in reverse order from the execution order. Notice that the Script Task is at the top of the call stack because it is the task that was executing when the designer hit a breakpoint. The Language column typically shows the language used to develop the particular function call. Because Integration Services isn't a language, this column is empty.

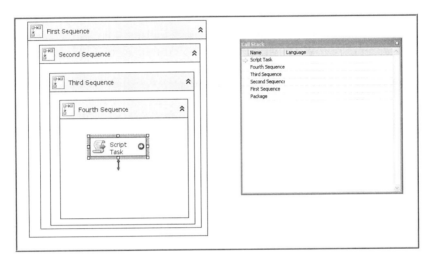

FIGURE 5.48   The Call Stack window shows the execution order of containers.

Diagnostic Windows

The diagnostic windows are useful for troubleshooting packages or to simply understand how a package works. These are the first windows you should consult when trying to fix a package that fails validation or execution. They contain most of the information that the package exposes about its execution, errors, warnings, information events, execution times, planning, and so on.

The Error List Window

The Error List window provides a quick way to see the errors, warnings, and information events produced by the current package. Figure 5.49 shows the Error List window after loading a package containing an unconfigured FTP Task and an invalid configuration. The buttons at the top of the window let you filter which type of message you want to see. If you only want to see errors, you can toggle the warnings and messages off by simply clicking on the corresponding buttons.

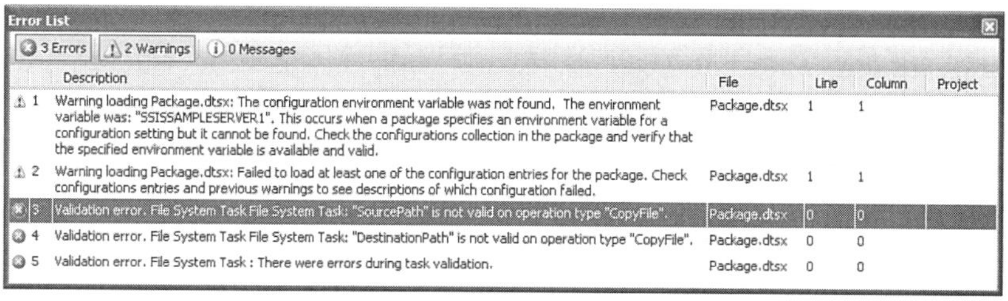

FIGURE 5.49   The Error List window shows errors, warnings, and messages.

There are a couple of hidden features in the Error List window of which you should be aware. First, if there is a dialog box for the task that generated an error and you double-click on the error, the designer opens the task dialog box for you. This makes it really handy when building a package, especially large packages, to quickly find and correct the error.

Second, if you right-click on the errors, warnings, or messages, you can choose the Show Help option from the context menu. This menu option displays more information about the error, warning, or message in your default browser. At the time of this writing, there were very few of the messages documented in this way. The plan is to gradually add additional documentation as the message is better understood and as more documentation becomes available. This feature makes it possible to continually update the documentation for a given message and even add links to other sources of information, such as magazine articles, Knowledge Base articles, or MSDN resources.

The Output Window

The Output window is a favorite window in the designer. It provides a relevant and continuous flow of information as the package executes. The information is a combination of diagnostic messages, package status, and debugging information. Figure 5.50 shows the Output window with an example of the kind of information it provides.

FIGURE 5.50   The Output window shows package diagnostic information.

Figure 5.50 also shows the buttons and options at the top of the window. The drop down allows you to select the type of output you want to view. The second button from the right with the small, red x clears all content and the button on the far right allows you to toggle word wrap, making it easier to see very long messages.

The Task List Window

The Task List window, shown in Figure 5.51, isn't really a diagnostic window, but it can be used to track a list of things you need to do. Don't confuse "Task" with SSIS tasks. This is the more generic term that means "things to do."

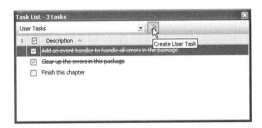

FIGURE 5.51   The Task List window helps you organize your remaining work items.

Two controls are at the top of the Task List window. The drop down lets you choose whether to view comments or user tasks. The button with the check mark creates a new task. To delete a task, right-click on it, and select Delete.

The Server Explorer Window

Visual Studio provides access to servers with the Server Explorer window. To see this window, select the View menu and then select Server Explorer. The Server Explorer window lets you create new databases, explore SQL Server and other servers, view Windows System event logs, traverse the Windows Management Instrumentation class hierarchy, manage MSMQ Queues, view performance counters, and view the services control panel. It's one more way that the Visual Studio simplifies access to your system. Figure 5.52 shows the Server Explorer window.

> **NOTE**
>
> The Server Explorer window is not available in all editions of Visual Studio 2005. Also, in some editions of Visual Studio 2005, the Server Explorer window is called the Data Explorer or Database Explorer. You must have Visual Studio 2005 installed to get some Server Explorer features, such as the Management Classes node.

FIGURE 5.52   The Server Explorer window lets you access server-related settings.

Summary

This chapter covered a lot of information—and it only covered Integration Services–specific features! The Visual Studio Development Environment is feature rich and sometimes a bit complex. It is well worth the time to explore all the menu items, windows, settings, and dialog boxes to get a feel for where everything is. Hopefully, this little meandering tour through the designer gives you a quick start on developing packages. As mentioned at the beginning of this chapter, read though this chapter again after you've had a chance to work with Integration Services a bit. You'll find that some things that didn't make sense at first will become clear the more you understand Integration Services.

The Building Blocks of Integration Services

"THIS IS LIKE LEGO MINDSTORMS PROGRAMMING."—TYSON HASELDEN

This chapter is a conceptual introduction to Integration Services and sets the stage for later, more technical chapters. It is a gentle introduction to Integration Services concepts. Old Data Transformation Services (DTS) hands will benefit from the discussion as it relates to the updated DTS feature set. Those who have never used DTS will benefit because it gives a high-level view of all the components and a simple introduction to important Integration Services objects and how they interact.

The Building Blocks of Integration Services

At its heart, Integration Services (IS) is a collection of components or objects. It is sometimes called an object model, but that can be confusing. It's helpful to just think of IS as a bunch of components with defined relationships between them and each of the components playing a role. Arguably, the most important component in IS is the package.

Almost everything you do in Integrations Services happens in or is related to the package because it is the fundamental organizing unit in IS. So, it's important that you understand the package and the components that make up a package. Tasks are another key component because they are the verbs of IS. Without tasks, your packages wouldn't do anything. Other important components in IS include connection managers, log providers, containers, precedence constraints, variables, transforms, and adapters. This chapter discusses the roles each of these components plays and how each interacts with the others. This chapter provides a high-level view, whereas later chapters cover these objects in more detail.

The Package and Other Objects

Packages are to Integration Services users what the canvas is to an artist or the field to the farmer. It's the basic starting point for everything you do and the foundation upon which Integration Services solutions are built. The first thing people do when designing a solution in IS is to create a package. After you create a package, you can add other objects to it, gradually building it up into a solution. After you've built your package, you can execute it using one of the tools that ships with Integration Services, such as the designer, dtexec, or dtexecui. So, in a way, building packages is like building custom software or an application.

In very basic terms, the package is the object that contains all the other objects. The tasks are the objects that cause things to happen, such as moving a file from here to there or pulling data from one location and putting it in another.

Connection managers describe the location of resources outside the package boundaries. Tasks and other components use connection managers to access those outside resources. There are connection managers for describing the location of a file or how to connect to a database among others.

Variables are objects used for holding data or communicating information from one component to another inside the package. For example, one task might place a date in a variable and another task might use that date for naming a file.

Containers are objects that contain other containers or tasks. They give structure and scope to packages and the objects within them. Containers can be executed like tasks. When executed, containers also execute the objects within them, their children.

Precedence constraints are objects that dictate the order of execution of containers and tasks, given certain constraints, such as the success or failure of the previous task or if a variable has a certain value.

Log providers are the objects responsible for outputting log information to a particular destination. For example, there is a SQL Server log provider and a flat-file log provider. Log providers have names based on the log destination format they support. Take all these different objects, put them together, set their properties, and you'll have a package that does something like populate a dimension table, deduplicate a customer list, or back up a database.

People use the name package to describe different things, all of them related to the basic building block of Integration Services. A package could be the actual object you create when you first start building a new solution. It could be a disk file that holds the persisted state of the package object, a collection of packages that are all children of one package, or the part of the package that's visible in the designer. Mostly though, when this book uses the term package, it refers to a collection of objects together with the package object that makes up the solution, as shown in Figure 6.1.

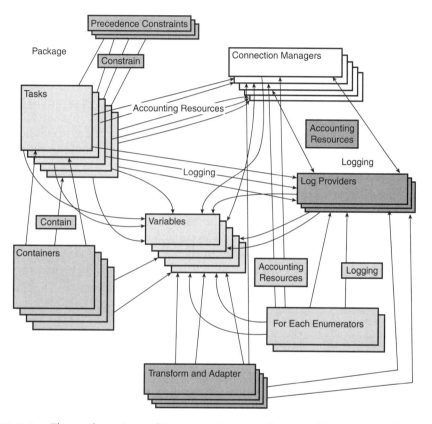

FIGURE 6.1   The package is an object containing a collection of interrelated objects.

Tasks

Tasks do the work of packages. They determine a package's behavior and each task has a well-defined function that it performs. Many stock tasks ship with IS, including the FTP Task for using the FTP protocol to move files from and to remote machines, the SQL Task for executing SQL, a Web Services Task for invoking web methods, and others. Perhaps the most important stock task is the Data Flow Task. Its function is to move and transform high volumes of data at high speed. Tasks are pluggable extensions, which means third parties, not just Microsoft, can easily write custom tasks that can plug in to the IS environment.

Variables

Figure 6.1 illustrates how central and important variables are in packages. You use them to communicate between the different objects because the objects you see in Figure 6.1 are isolated from one another by the Integration Services architecture. One task cannot see another. In other words, one task cannot directly communicate with another so they must communicate through variables. This separation is designed to isolate the various objects, especially tasks, yielding better security, usability, manageability, and robustness. Without this isolation, it would be possible for tasks to gain access to other objects and manipulate their properties at any given time. In some cases, this is harmless, but in many cases, it is fatal to the package. Interaction between objects is also difficult to discover. If it were possible to write packages that were self-modifying, it would be very difficult to upgrade or migrate them in future versions. For example, suppose you wrote a package in which one task was designed to execute another task. There would be no way for IS to detect that relationship between the two tasks. Further, it would be difficult for the user to discover that as well, especially if the design was buried in the bowels of that task's code.

Variables, on the other hand, are designed to be the communication mechanism between objects. The IS runtime guards them to prohibit variable value data corruption that can occur with multiple simultaneous data access. IS variables are also hardened to avoid some of the other technical issues that occur in such a simultaneous multiaccess object model environment. IS variables can contain various types of data, including integers, strings, or even other objects.

Connection Managers

Connection managers are objects that provide other components with a link to the world outside of the package. Their name is perhaps a misnomer, because they don't always provide a connection. Some connection managers only provide the name of a file or a web address. Others provide more information than just a connection. For example, the Flat File Connection Manager provides a filename as well as information about the format of the flat file. Connection managers serve as a barrier between packages and the environment. That barrier is useful in all environments, but is especially useful in cases when the environment changes. For example, when moving a package from one machine to the next, connection managers provide a central location for updating the package to point to new locations on the destination machine. Without connection managers, tasks and other objects must provide properties to the user for specifying where to find resources such as files and web pages. It's much easier to modify the connections than to find all the objects that access those resources and modify each of them directly. Connection managers are also pluggable extensions. Although at the time of this writing, there are already more than 15 different types of connection managers, Microsoft realized that the industry changes and new data access technologies would emerge over time. Microsoft also realized that they hadn't built a connection manager for every existing type of data access technology and so made it simple to augment the stock offerings with custom connection managers.

Log Providers

Log providers are an important part of the IS logging infrastructure. Every IS object has access to the logging infrastructure. The problem is that not every user wants to send their log entries to the same format or destination. Some prefer the Extensible Markup Language (XML), others prefer flat files, and still others would rather send their logs to a table in SQL Server. Still, others might want to log to a destination that IS doesn't yet support. This is why Microsoft created log providers. Log providers are, yet again, pluggable components that are responsible for taking log entries sent by components in the package and writing them to the particular destination and medium they support. For example, a stock XML log provider writes log entries to an XML file. Tasks and other components are not aware of the destination to which they send their log entries. They just send their logs to the IS runtime and the runtime routes the log to the configured log providers. The log providers then take the log entries and convert them to the correct format and save the log entries based on how they are configured. It's also possible to log to more than one location at a time using two different log providers simultaneously on the same package. And, if you want to log to a location, format, or medium that isn't supported, you can write your own log provider. Log providers use connection managers to describe the destination of their log entries.

Containers

Containers are like the skeleton of packages. They organize the package into smaller chunks while providing transaction scope, variable scope, execution scope, looping functions, debugging breakpoints, error routing, and logging scope. The package is a container. There are loop containers that allow workflow to execute multiple times. The ForEach Loop allows the workflow to execute once for each item in a collection. The For Loop allows the workflow to execute until an expression evaluates to false. The sequence container helps to better organize packages. Each task has its very own container called the TaskHost that is, for the most part, transparent to the user. There is also an EventHandler container that the runtime executes when a task or other component raises an event.

Precedence Constraints

Precedence constraints are the traffic lights of IS. You use them to control which tasks execute and when or if a task should even execute at all. In the designer, they take the form of an arrow line from one task to another. Precedence constraints can minimally be defined to cause a task to execute when another succeeds, fails, or completes. They can also be configured to use complex expressions that reference IS variables to determine if workflow should execute. This flexibility provides an enormous number of options for conditionally branching within the package at execution time. In a way, precedence constraints are like If statements in structured coding that check Boolean expressions to determine if a certain piece of code should execute.

The Data Flow Task, Adapters, and Transforms

The Data Flow Task is arguably the most important task in the IS box. It is the task you'll use for virtually all data processing in IS. Because data comes in many forms and can be quite complex, the Data Flow Task reflects that complexity. Although most tasks are fairly flat, meaning they are simple objects with simple properties, the Data Flow Task has its own object model, or collection of objects. You can even write custom components that plug in to the Data Flow Task.

Data comes in different forms and is found on different media. The problem we face when trying to use that data is how to get it all into some common format and a common location so we can manipulate it. The Data Flow Task addresses these problems. By providing what are called adapters, it addresses the problem of how to access data on various types of media. The other problem, the common location problem, is addressed with buffers. Buffers are memory locations that hold data as it moves through the Data Flow Task. The shape of the buffer is described in the buffer metadata definition and reflects the data that flows out of adapters and transforms. Figure 6.2 shows a conceptual view of these different components and their relationships to each other.

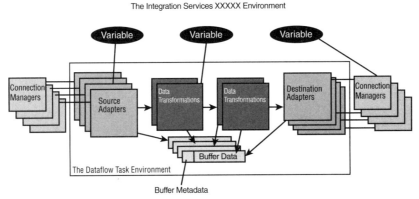

FIGURE 6.2   The Data Flow Task has an object model with adapters and transforms.

Data Flow Adapters

Adapters perform the following three functions:

- Communicate with connection managers

- Provide an abstraction between different data access mechanisms

- Move data into or out of data flow buffers

Communicating with Connection Managers

This function is rather vague because the relationship is different for different adapters. For example, the OLEDB Source Adapter uses OLEDB connection managers in a way that you'd expect. It calls the AcquireConnection method on the OLEDB connection manager and the connection manager returns an OLEDB connection object.

The flat-file adapter uses connections in a different way, however. When it calls the AcquireConnection method on the Flat File Connection Manager, it gets a string containing the fully qualified filename of the flat file. The Flat File Connection Manager also does some additional work. It discovers the types and lengths of the columns in the flat file. It's factored this way because other components that need to access flat files also need that column information. If the function to discover flat-file column types and lengths was in the Flat File Source Adapter, other objects that use the Flat File Connection Manager would also have to include the same code. Factoring the functionality to the various roles helps eliminate duplicated functionality throughout the object model and componentry.

Providing an Abstraction Between Different Data Access Mechanisms

Each of the transforms in a given Data Flow Task must have data passed to them that is both uniform and well described. This isn't something connection managers can provide. Connection managers don't know about the Data Flow Tasks buffers. It's too detailed and connection managers just aren't that specific to any given component. Also, connection managers don't actually retrieve data, they mostly just point to where the data can be found. For example, the Flat File Connection Manager can be used to point to XML files, binary files, or even other package files, but it doesn't provide a mechanism to actually retrieve data from those files. What's needed is a component that knows the details of the source system—and that knows how to get at the data there. This is what adapters do. They know the mechanics of accessing data in source and destination systems.

Moving Data into or out of Data Flow Buffers

So, the adapter is capable of accessing the data on systems, but it must also discover the format or shape of that data and place the data in a common format for the transforms to operate on it. For source adapters, this involves discovering the format of the data on the source system and telling the Data Flow Task how the buffer should be structured to optimally hold the data. It also involves converting that data into a consistent and well-described form that the transforms can consume. Source adapters retrieve rows of data from the source system and place those rows into the buffer. For destination adapters, the process is essentially the same, but in reverse. So, adapters are the components that accomplish the function of converting data from/to the common buffer format into/from the storage or various other media formats.

Data Flow Transforms

Transforms, as their name implies, transform data. Each transform has a specific function, such as the Sort, Aggregate, or Lookup transforms. Each takes as input the output of another transform or adapter. Each has an output that is defined by the data that it releases. As this book moves into more detailed discussions, you'll see that there are classes of transforms that are defined by the way the data flows through them. For example, it's possible to have a transform that takes many inputs and has only one output. It's also possible to have a transform that doesn't release any data to its output until it has received all the data at its inputs. For this discussion, it's enough to understand that these transforms interact through outputs and inputs. One transform is not aware of any of the other transforms around it. It is only aware of its inputs and outputs. Here again, the components are isolated to eliminate dependencies and to create a more robust and predictable system.

Data Flow Versus Workflow—Fundamental Differences

In many ways, the data flow in the Data Flow Task looks like workflow in the runtime. Boxes represent functionality. Lines represent relationships between the boxes. Components in the Data Flow Task use connections, log data to log providers, and so forth. But, when you get past simple visual comparisons at the boxes and lines level, you'll see they are quite different. This is why Microsoft makes the distinction in the designer and object models. Following are the main differences between data flow and workflow:

- Execution model

- Connecting lines

- Functional gamut

Execution Model

Data flow and workflow components execute differently. The duration of a given task's execution time is a fraction of the total duration of the execution time of the package it runs within. The IS runtime starts a task and waits for it to complete before scheduling the tasks constrained by that task. So, for the simple package in Figure 6.3, the Data Flow Task won't execute until the Preparation SQL Task has finished successfully. The total package execution duration can closely be approximated by adding together the execution duration times from each of the individual tasks. The execution time for workflow boils down to the following formula: $E = \sum e + s$, where E is the total time it takes to execute a package, $\sum e$ is the sum of the execution duration times of all tasks on one logical thread, and s is the package startup and shutdown duration. Of course, this is complicated when there is more than one logically parallel executing thread. Then, the execution duration of the package is the execution duration of the longest logical thread duration. The point is that execution duration for workflow is an additive operation derived from combining the execution durations of the tasks. In addition, tasks on the same logical thread don't run at the same time.

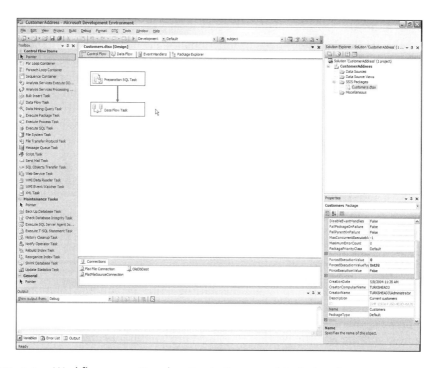

FIGURE 6.3   Workflow execution duration is the sum of task duration.

Estimating the total execution duration of a Data Flow Task is a little more complicated, but conceptually it is driven by the amount of data running through the Data Flow Task and the types of transforms in the Data Flow Task. A logical data flow thread is what you get if, graphically, you were to draw a single line from a source adapter, through each succeeding transform, until you get to the destination adapter. The significant difference is that it's possible for all adapters and transforms on one logical thread to be active at the same time.

You wouldn't use these methods for estimating package or Data Flow Task execution durations. There are better ways to do that, such as running the data flow with a subset of data and then multiplying that execution duration by the scale of the full set of data. The point is that tasks in the same logical thread do not run at the same time. Transforms run simultaneously even if on the same logical thread.

Connecting Lines

Tasks have precedence constraints. Transforms have paths. Those connecting lines look a lot alike, but they're very different. Precedence constraints as described previously do little but determine if the next task can execute. Paths actually represent outputs of transforms and the metadata associated with those outputs. Precedence constraints control task execution; paths show where the data flows.

Functional Gamut

Functional gamut refers to the breadth of functionality a component can provide. The functional gamut of tasks is virtually unlimited. Tasks can be written to do just about anything any piece of software can do. Witness the stock tasks that ship with IS that vary from the Script Task, which, in itself, represents the key to unlock the full power of .Net software development, to the Data Flow Task. The Windows Management Instrumentation (WMI) and Web Services Tasks are other good examples of the range of different tasks you can write that use various emerging technologies.

Transforms, on the other hand, are very specific to processing data and are strictly bound to the architecture of the Data Flow Task. This isn't to say that it is a deficit for transforms, but merely to point out that tasks and transforms are quite different. The beauty of these differences is that both are supported within one framework and both are equally extensible through pluggable architectures.

Summary

The package is the main object in IS and the starting point for building solutions. You build IS solutions by adding other IS components to the package and establishing relationships between them. There is a fundamental difference between the way the package does data flow and the way the package does workflow. Adding IS objects to a package, you can create solutions that in many ways resemble software applications but are specifically targeted to solving a particular problem.

Grouping Control Flow with Containers

"IF I DON'T KNOW IT, IT'S NOT KNOWLEDGE."—MIKE BLASZCZAK

Containers are an important object in Integration Services packages. Visually, they provide separation and organization of the control flow. Under the covers, they are central to the functioning of packages. This chapter details the important role containers play in making packages simpler, better structured, more manageable, and consistent.

Containers are objects in Integration Services that contain other containers, forming a hierarchy of parent and child containers. Containers give structure to packages and provide services such as property expressions, breakpoints, transaction, variable, logging, and execution scope. Looping containers provide iterative workflow execution, whereas the Sequence container makes it possible to organize packages into subparts. Each task has its very own specialized container called the Taskhost that is, for the most part, transparent to the user. There is also an EventHandler container that the runtime can execute in response to a task or other component raising an event. Finally, as you might expect, packages are containers. Containers are central to all Integration Services workflow and understanding how they function is central to understanding Integration Services workflow.

CAUTION

The properties discussed here are those visible in the Business Intelligence Development Studio and are not all the properties found on containers. Some properties are not used at design time or by package developers.

The Container Concept

Containers are new in Integration Services. Data Transformation Services (DTS) had something called a Step object that was similar to the Taskhost, but not as encompassing. In Integration Services, the container concept is much more developed and prevalent throughout the object model.

Organizing

Containers are not a new concept. If you think of the containers in your home, you can probably come up with several different types. There are food containers, drawers, book shelves, and cabinets. All of these share a common purpose, which is to organize your stuff. Containers in Integration Services serve the same purpose. They organize the objects in the package.

Reducing Complexity

Containers make it possible to divide your package into subgroups. The average human brain can only comprehend five to seven different concepts or objects simultaneously. When confronted with a package that has 10 or 20 tasks, most people cannot describe what the package does without first studying the package for some length of time. However, when packages are subdivided into smaller parts, using containers, it is much easier to comprehend them. This is especially true if the containers are accurately labeled with names that describe the container's overall function.

Figure 7.1 shows how a typical workflow might look without containers. As you can see, it's complex and hard to understand. There is very little indication, other than the task icons and task names, what each of the tasks do or how they relate to each other. The person viewing the package must make the conceptual leap between all the various tasks and containers shown in the designer and what their overall purpose is. Grouping and labeling tasks and containers reduces the necessity for such conceptual leaps by abstracting the details of the package and makes packages much easier to comprehend at a glance.

Figure 7.2 shows how containers can help to reduce complexity by grouping tasks together based on their function or relationship to each other. The Foreach Loop actually makes it possible to eliminate and reuse tasks. Note that these two packages are not identical. For example, the Foreach Loop executes the tasks it contains serially, whereas the first package shown in Figure 7.1 executes them in parallel. If it was important to execute the FTP and other tasks in parallel, they could still be placed in a Sequence container for better organization.

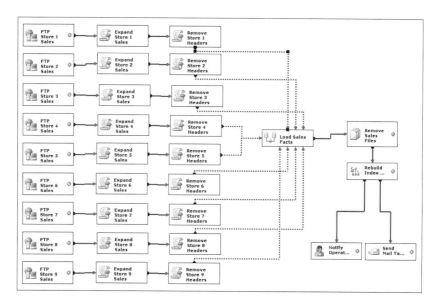

FIGURE 7.1   Package workflow can often become complex.

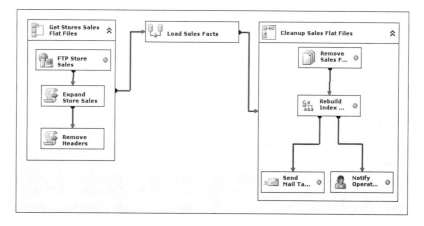

FIGURE 7.2   Containers organize related workflow into one location.

Figure 7.3 shows how the containers can be collapsed to take up less space in the designer. As you can see, it's much easier to understand the three-step package in Figure 7.3 than it is to understand the 32-step package in Figure 7.1. Combining related workflow into containers removes complexity and makes it possible to view the package as a set of high-level steps.

FIGURE 7.3   Collapsing containers makes packages simpler.

Structuring Solutions

Another benefit of containers is the ability to structure your package in such a way that it better reflects the high-level processes of your solution. For example, it's often desirable to build more than one optional execution path for the workflow based on some external constraint, such as the day of the week or month. You might want to perform some basic workflow daily, but then on the first day of the month, you might also want to do additional work. Although it's possible to do this without containers using annotations or placement, it's easier to separate the workflow into logical groupings in a visual way with containers. Figure 7.4 shows how containers can be used to structure packages into conditional parts that represent an overall process view.

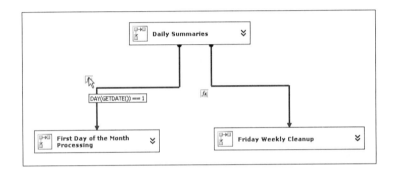

FIGURE 7.4   You can easily structure packages to visually represent a process.

Scoping

Scoping is a term used to describe the visibility or availability of an object in a given context. This is the meaning of scoping in Integrations Services as well and is a function of containers. Containers define the scope of transactions, variables, execution, configurations, logging, connections, and events. In other words, depending on in which container the given object is created, it is visible to different parts of the package. As you might expect, scoping takes on slightly different meanings and is implemented in different ways for each of the object types. The following few paragraphs explain how scoping affects each of the workflow features.

SCOPING IN DTS

Scoping actually existed in DTS as well, it just wasn't as obvious. The name Global Variable actually hints at scope. The difference is that in IS, the concept of scope is formalized to a greater extent with the introduction of containers. The IS equivalent of DTS global variables is those variables found at package scope. Although, that's not "true" global scope, it is the equivalent to DTS global variables. True global scope variables would be variables that are available to multiple packages—something the Microsoft team hopes to make available in a near-future release.

Transaction Scope

Containers expose the properties needed to configure transactions. If the container is configured to support a transaction, it begins the transaction when executed and either commits or rolls back the transaction, based on the container execution results, when it completes execution. Generally speaking, if the container execution succeeds, the container commits the transaction and if it fails, it rolls back the transaction.

Configuration Scope

Currently, only package containers expose configurations. Microsoft didn't see any compelling reason to extend the scope of configurations inside the package. So currently, configurations are only scoped at the package level.

LocaleID

LocaleID is, perhaps, self-explanatory. It is the ID of the locale that is used for all data operations in a given container. How the LocaleID property works and how it is scoped by containers is, perhaps, not so clear. LocaleID is inherited from the parent container to the child. By default, the package LocaleID adopts the system LocaleID and all children containers in the package inherit their LocaleID from their parents. However, you can override the LocaleID for a given container and all children of that container then inherit the new LocaleID. LocaleID affects how data conversions are performed. For example, the format of dates varies from locale to locale. For those tasks that perform locale-sensitive operations, such as data conversion or formatting operations, the LocaleID is important.

Variable Scope

Variable scope is mostly about visibility. For example, if a variable is defined at package scope, all objects in the entire package have access to the variable. Local scope variables, those defined closer to a task, are visible to the task and hide variables with the same qualified name at global scope. Chapter 12, "The Venerable Variable," covers variable scoping in detail.

Execution Scope

Typically, you might not think of scope relating to execution, but in Integration Services, the notion applies quite well. For example, in the designer it's possible to execute only portions of a package. If several tasks are in a container, right-clicking on the container and selecting Execute Task executes the entire container. Also, disabling a container disables all its child containers and tasks. Because containers are hierarchical, executing the parent executes the workflow it contains subject to the constraints within the container. This is true for all containers from the package to the Taskhost.

Connection Scope

Currently, connections are only scoped to the package level and visible to the entire package.

NOTE

Since the early releases of Integration Services, many users have commented to Microsoft that they want to see connections participate in scoping to simplify packages and provide more global connections "above packages" and to bring them closer to the object that's using them "down into packages," or on all containers. Currently, Microsoft is considering these options.

Logging Scope

Logging settings are configured in two package locations. Log providers are those components responsible for outputting log entries to different formats. Log providers have package scope and represent the actual objects that perform the logging. However, you configure log options on all containers. Log options are simple settings on containers that control the columns and log-entry types as they flow through the Integration Services object model to the log providers to be written out to the log destination. This design makes it possible to finely control the logging output from containers. For example, it's possible to log only errors from one portion of a package within a given Sequence container, while logging progress, errors, warnings, and information events from another container. The notion of scoping comes from the fact that logs destined to arrive at the same log table or output file can be filtered differently depending on the scope of the log settings. Logging is explained in detail in Chapter 11, "Logging and the Stock Log Providers."

Event Handler Scope

Each container has a collection of event handlers. Event handlers are containers that the runtime contingently executes when a task or other component fires an event. Each container can have event handlers associated with it that are dedicated to handling a given event just for that container. For the purposes of this discussion, it's enough to understand that event handlers are specific to, or in other words, associated with, only one container. Each container can have multiple event handlers associated with it, but an event handler has only one parent container.

Common Container Properties

So, what makes a container a container? What are the characteristics that make a sequence a container but not, for example, a connection manager? The most distinguishing characteristic of containers is the fact that they are capable of executing. Containers also have a unique set of properties that are provided for controlling their design time and execution time behavior. The following sections list the properties that all containers share, which distinguish them from all other objects in the package.

Identification

The identification properties are not unique to containers; almost all objects have them. But, because they are important, they are discussed here for completeness. Package writers and the Integration Services engines use these properties for identifying containers.

- Name—This is the name the designer displays in the container header. The designer enforces unique names for containers.

- Description—This is a free-form description of the container. It should contain a description of the container and its function. Integration Services does not use this property for any purpose. So, it can be freely modified without concern for causing problems or breaking the package.

- ID—This is a type GUID unique identifier. Integration Services uses this property extensively and it should not be modified. It cannot be changed through the designer, with one exception described in the following note.

NOTE

When creating new packages, it's a good practice to use package templates with default settings already defined, adding these to existing Integration Services projects. However, if you do this, you need to change the ID property of the package to avoid confusing packages in logs, and so on. The designer has a special feature for changing the ID of a package. Click on the ID property in the property grid and an option to Generate a New ID is available in a drop-down list. Use this to change the ID of the package and eliminate possible package confusion whenever you create a new package from an existing one.

Execution

There are times, for example, when debugging a package, when it's very useful to be able to simulate certain conditions. The following properties allow the package writer to use brute-force techniques to coerce the package to behave in a certain way during execution. They make it possible to force the package to execute certain precedence constraints, ignore return values or error counts, and so forth. However, you should exercise care when using these properties. With certain exceptions, these properties should not be used in production environments.

- DelayValidation—For a container, validation happens three times: once when the package is opened, once when the package executes, and once right before the container executes. DelayValidation is a brute-force way to eliminate all but the last validation. The reasoning behind this is fairly complex, but it boils down to the fact that not all containers are ready to validate when loaded or when the package is validated and executed. Successful execution for some containers is dependent on something changing in the package before they execute. For those containers, validation will fail at all times except right before they execute. A variable value might get set by a preceding task, for example. `DelayValidation` makes it possible to put off validation until the very last instant.

- `Disable`—`Disable` is a powerful way to make a container or task disappear without actually deleting it. For example, this property is useful for isolating portions of the package when debugging it to find out why a particular variable is getting changed, and so on. `Disable` is not intended to be used in production packages and should never be used to manage control flow.

- `DisableEventHandlers`—This property simply turns off event handlers, making it possible to eliminate event handlers from the execution equation.

- `FailPackageOnFailure`—This property is self-descriptive. It forces the containing package to fail if the container fails. Without this property, the conditions whereby packages would fail would be severely limited because errors are not automatically considered failures. This property must be set to `TRUE` if you want the container failure to signal a checkpoint restart.

- `FailParentOnFailure`—Similar to `FailPackageOnFailure`, this property can be used to create cascading container failures. Refining the use of this property, it's possible to finely control which failures cause the package to fail.

- `MaximumErrorCount`—This property sets how many errors a container must accumulate before the container execution fails.

Forced Execution

This group of properties allows the package writer to access the values returned from a container or task after execution. Tasks return two values when they complete execution:

- `ExecutionResult`—Whether the task succeeded, failed, or was canceled

- `ExecutionValue`—An arbitrary, task-specific value

Some tasks support the `ExecutionValue` property. For example, the Execute SQL Task returns the number of rows the SQL query affected. These forced execution properties are truly brute-force methods for manipulating a package. In fact, with the following properties, it's possible to force a value to be generated regardless of whether the task supports the `ExecutionValue` property. Sometimes, `ForcedExecutionValue` is used in conjunction with expressions to generate new variable values. The same caveat applies to these properties as the previous ones. Use them with care.

- `ForcedExecutionValueType`—Specifies the type of the value found in `ExecValueVariable`.

- `ForcedExecutionValue`—Holds the value to place into the execution value variable.

- `ForceExecutionValue`—Toggles the `ForceExecutionValue` on or off. When set to `TRUE`, the value in `ForcedExecutionValue` is placed in the variable specified in `ExecValueVariable`.

- ExecValueVariable—Contains the name or ID of the variable to contain the forced execution value.

- ForcedExecutionResult—Holds the value to return instead of the real Execution Result. Using this property, you can force the container to appear as though it succeeded or failed regardless of the actual execution result. It also supports setting the result to "completed." Although not a result that tasks return, this value matches the precedence constraint for both success and failure constraints. To turn this feature off, set the property to "none."

NOTE

It's important to note that the task or container must still pass validation before executing for these properties to take effect. If the task or container fails validation, the package does not execute and the package doesn't use or even reference these properties.

Transactions

The following properties control the nature of the transaction the container creates:

- IsolationLevel—IsolationLevel specifies the safety level of a transaction. This value controls what one database client will see when accessing data concurrently with other clients. The settings range from viewing only fully committed data to viewing data that might turn out to be incorrect because a concurrent transaction might roll back. This setting represents the trade-off between performance and assurance of data correctness. The least performant setting, Isolated, is the safest, whereas the most performant, Read Uncommitted, is the most likely to return false data.

- TransactionOption—The TransactionOption property controls how the container enlists in the transaction. There are three possible settings:

  - Not Supported—When not supported, the container does not attempt to enlist in or start a transaction.

  - Supported—When supported, the container attempts to enlist in any existing transaction in its scope. If there is no transaction in its scope, it does not attempt to create a transaction. In-scope transactions are those started in a parent or an ancestor container.

  - Required—Required is the same as Supported, except if there is no transaction available in scope, the container begins a new transaction.

Properties in the Miscellaneous Category

The following two properties are in no particular grouping, but control important container settings:

- LoggingMode—LoggingMode is inherited from the parent container. Three settings are available for this property: Enabled, Disabled, and UseParentSetting. Enabled and Disabled make it easy to turn logging on or off, while still retaining all the logging settings for the container. UseParentSetting simply instructs the container to inherit the parent LoggingMode settings and is the default.

- Expressions—Expressions are the property expressions for the container. The Expressions property is available on all containers and hosts. To read more about expressions, see Chapter 9, "Using Expressions."

Designer Groupings—the Noncontainers

Before going further, this section briefly covers the designer object known as a designer grouping. Designer groupings are a designer-only feature that allows you to group tasks and containers visually, but without any object model or runtime implications. There is no designer grouping in the Integration Services object model, but yet, if you were to create one in the designer, it looks an awful lot like a container. This is why it is called the noncontainer. Figure 7.5 shows a designer grouping.

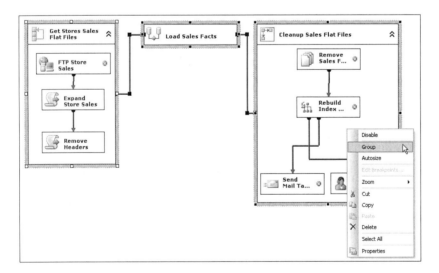

FIGURE 7.5   Designer groupings are a designer-only feature.

The Task and the Taskhost Container

By now, you should have a pretty good idea how containers look and act. Each container shares some properties with the other container types, yet provides some unique behavior. Containers, including the `Package`, `Event Handler`, and `Loop` containers, are essentially derivations of the `Sequence` container; they all execute a series of tasks in some order dictated by precedence constraints. The `Taskhost` is somewhat different. It always contains exactly one task.

The `Taskhost` is a very dedicated sort of container. `Taskhost`s live and die with the tasks they contain. Every instance of a task has a `Taskhost` surrounding it, servicing it, protecting it, and controlling it. When the task is deleted, the `Taskhost` goes with it. Yet, when viewed within the designer, the task is all you see, whereas the `Taskhost` is mostly invisible.

Properties Collection

In the bowels of the `Taskhost` code is a bit of logic that interrogates the task to discover what properties the task has. The `Taskhost` then builds a collection of property objects for each of the properties on the task. The properties collection is called the properties provider. This is how the designer discovers properties on the task. It's how property expressions and configurations are able to modify the values of task properties. If you ever write code to embed Integration Services into your application, using the properties provider is the easiest way to set property values on tasks. Figure 7.6 is a conceptual illustration of the relationship between tasks and `Taskhost`s.

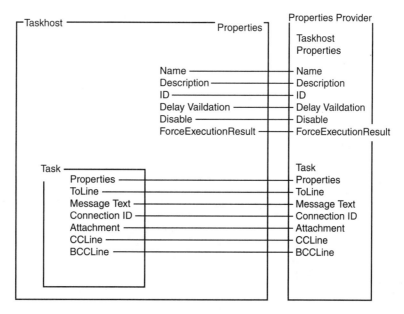

FIGURE 7.6   `Taskhost`s have property object collections.

Persistence

Tasks can be written so that they save and load their own property values. However, for tasks with simple typed properties, the `Taskhost` can save and load the properties for the task, relieving the custom task writer from the chore of writing persistence code. Custom task writers need only create properties on their tasks and the Taskhost takes care of the rest through the properties provider and supporting persistence logic.

Package Paths and Configurations

When you create a configuration that changes the value of a property on a task, you're using the Taskhost. Each configuration has a value and a path, called a package path. The path is submitted to the package that parses it up to the portion of the package path that points to a child container or property. This process is repeated until the final object in the package path is found. If the package path points to a property on a task, the Taskhost sets the task property to the value in the configuration.

Debugging Features

Many of the logging features are implemented at the container level as follows.

Breakpoints

The ability to add breakpoints to tasks is one of the more powerful features available in Integration Services and is made possible by the Taskhost. Tasks set up custom breakpoints when the runtime calls their Initialize method by adding them to a special breakpoints collection. During package execution, the Taskhost interacts with the task to indicate when a breakpoint is hit and when the task should continue to execute.

A set of default breakpoints are available on every task as well. The Taskhost exposes these breakpoints by default, even for custom tasks that don't support breakpoints. Figure 7.7 illustrates how the Taskhost provides breakpoints for these standard events, even when the task doesn't support them.

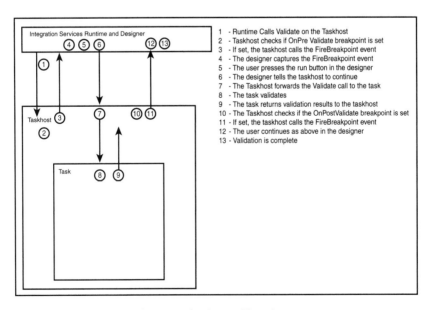

FIGURE 7.7   Taskhosts provide a standard set of breakpoints.

Disabling Control Flow

Occasionally when you're debugging a package, it's nice to remove tasks and simplify and eliminate some of the noise from the package to better understand what's happening, or what's going wrong. But, chances are, you've put a lot of work into the settings for each task. Deleting them means you'd have to add and reconfigure them all over again. It would be nice if you could just simulate deleting the tasks until you can troubleshoot the package, and then just turn them all back on again. This is the idea behind disabling tasks. Figure 7.8 illustrates how the Taskhost implements disabling.

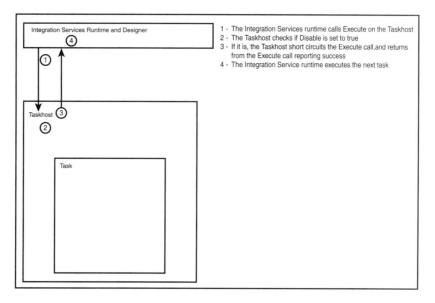

FIGURE 7.8   Taskhosts implement disabling of tasks.

Custom Registration

Tasks can create their own custom breakpoints and Log events.

Breakpoints

As noted in the "Debugging Features" section, tasks can provide custom breakpoints. When the user creates a task by either dropping it onto the designer or programmatically and if the task supports it, the runtime provides a method to add additional custom breakpoints to the standard ones. Although it's not necessary to support custom breakpoints, for complex or long-running tasks, it provides a way for package writers to easily peek into the behavior of the task as it is running. Custom breakpoints are covered in greater detail in Chapters 24, "Building Custom Tasks."

Log Events   The Taskhost provides default logging that logs the Execute, Validate, and other events. Tasks can also send information to the logs. Figure 7.9 shows the Configure SSIS Logs dialog box in the designer. Using this dialog box, package writers can filter events and the information they want to log for each event. Each item in the list (shown in Figure 7.9) is a log event.

To make it possible for package writers to filter custom events, it's necessary for tasks to describe to the Taskhost what custom log events they will log. To do this, the Taskhost checks to see if the task supports custom logging and then retrieves from the task the names and descriptions of all the custom log events the task will log. In Figure 7.9, the custom log events are FTPOperation and FTPConnectingToServer.

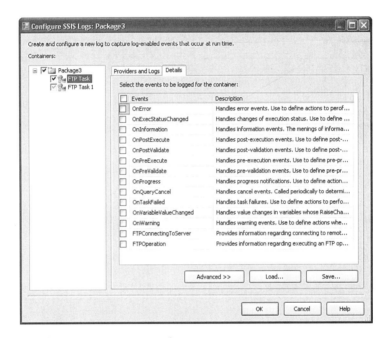

FIGURE 7.9   Tasks can support custom log events.

Custom Events   Like custom log events, tasks can also describe custom execution events they may raise. This makes it possible to create event handler containers for custom events in the same way that you can create event handlers for stock events like OnPreExecute and OnVariableValueChanged. In this way, it's actually possible to build Integration Services workflow that executes as a direct result of an arbitrary event raised from a custom task.

Contact Information and Graceful Load Failover

Graceful load failover and contact information are two features aimed at reducing the occurrence of loading problems or, at least, simplifying their resolution. Graceful load failover is what the object model does when a component that is referenced in a package is not installed on the machine. When the package attempts to load a component such as a transform or a task, it checks to see if it succeeded. If not, it captures the failure and emits an error but continues to load the remainder of the package.

Contact information is a feature that allows components to describe themselves. Look at the XML for any package with stock tasks in it and you'll see the contact information for the task as part of the task's XML. If the task fails to load, the `Taskhost` retrieves the contact information for the component and builds an error with the contact information embedded. The following is the contact information property node for the Execute SQL Task:

```
<DTS:Property DTS:Name="TaskContact">
 Execute SQL Task; Microsoft Corporation; Microsoft SQL Server v9;
 © 2004 Microsoft Corporation; All Rights Reserved;
 http://www.microsoft.com/sql/support/default.asp;1
</DTS:Property>
```

Because of the graceful load failover feature, the package still successfully loads, but the `Taskhost` emits an error and creates a placeholder task in the place of the missing or uninstalled task. The designer shows the placeholder task in the same location in the package as where the uninstalled task was, and the `Taskhost` retrieves the contact information for the task and displays it as part of the error. This allows the package user a way to find out what task is missing and how to correct it. It also presents the user with an opportunity to correct the package by either deleting the task and repairing it or reinstalling the missing task.

NOTE

Although contact information is simply a string and can contain any information you want to supply, Microsoft recommends that the following format be used for contact information:

Task Name;Company Name;Product Name;Copyright;Component Webpage

---

To see graceful load failover and contact information work, try this:

1. Build a package with an Execute SQL Task.

2. You don't need to modify it, just drag and drop it on the designer for a new package.

3. Save the package and close it.

4. Open the package by right-clicking on it in the Solution Explorer and selecting View Code.

5. Find the SQL Task node.

6. Change the creation name of the SQL Task node in some way to make it invalid. For example, you could add two periods where there should be one.

7. Save the package in the Code View.

8. Restart the designer.

9. Now, attempt to load the package into the designer again.

The package looks the same. The task is there, but you should also receive an error message telling you that there were errors loading the task and that the package didn't load successfully. What's happening under the covers? In this case, the Taskhost gets as much information about the task as possible and creates something that looks like the SQL Task. Try to run the package and it fails, but, at least, now with graceful load failover, you know that there was a SQL Task there and that it's invalid. The error looks similar to the following with some of the specifics such as package name and so on changed:

```
Error    1    Error loading FactCheck.dtsx: Error loading a task. The
contact information for the task is "Execute SQL Task; Microsoft
Corporation; Microsoft SQL Server v9; © 2004 Microsoft Corporation; All
Rights Reserved;http://www.microsoft.com/sql/support/default.asp;1". This
happens when loading a task fails.
```

NOTE

Graceful load failover is only implemented for tasks and data flow components. Contact information is implemented for tasks, Foreach Enumerators, log providers, connection managers, and data flow components.

Isolation

The Taskhost isolates the task. This means that it only provides as much information to the task as is absolutely necessary, but no more. This isolation keeps the task from doing things such as traversing the package object model and making changes to other objects and tasks. Likely, the benefits of isolating tasks are not immediately obvious to the new Integration Services user. After all, DTS allowed tasks access to the object model of the package. What's so bad about that?

The problems with that are legion as follows. Tasks that modify the object model

- Cannot be migrated or upgraded

- Cannot be sandboxed or otherwise executed in alternative locations

- Can modify other tasks or objects and cause bugs that are difficult to debug and fix

- Can break execution time behavior of the runtime

- Can create race conditions that the runtime cannot detect or resolve

- Can access variables unsafely causing inconsistent or incorrect values

- Might cause crashes or other severe behavior due to invalid object access

- Might cause memory corruption or leaks by breaking COM reference counting, apartment, or Managed/Native code interop rules

The point here is the guiding philosophy from the start of Integration Services and that tasks should not be in the business of controlling workflow or anything like it. Tasks do the work; the runtime provides management, scheduling, variable access, cancellation, and all the rest. Tasks should only be provided as much information as is needed for them to successfully execute and communicate their status to the outside world, the object model, and they do that through the Taskhost. Basically, the Taskhost provides a way to ensure that tasks "keep their hands to themselves" in the Integration Services runtime sandbox.

Sensitive Data Protection

Another service Taskhosts provide is sensitive data protection. Some tasks have properties that contain sensitive data such as passwords. Integration Services provides overarching security settings for protecting sensitive data and the Taskhost supports those settings. To enable this, tasks mark their sensitive properties with a Sensitive=1 attribute when saving. The Taskhost detects this setting and applies the appropriate action in memory, either stripping out the value or encrypting it based on the global security setting, and then writing it out to the package file.

In summary, the Taskhost is a virtually invisible container that performs much of the work that makes tasks easy to develop, configure, and maintain. It provides default behavior for tasks; prevents tasks from doing harmful operations; and provides configurations, property expressions, properties discovery, and many other crucial features on behalf of tasks.

The Simple Sequence Container

The Sequence container is very simple and perhaps often overlooked. To be sure, not everyone or every situation requires its use, but the Sequence container has some valuable purposes. You can use the Sequence container to simply divide up packages into smaller, more comprehensible pieces. This was covered in the general container discussion previously, but applies specifically to the Sequence container because it does not offer any additional functionality.

So, let's look at a case in which the Sequence container can be useful. You might want to perform multiple, discrete operations, yet ensure that they either all succeed or fail together. For example, you might want to execute multiple SQL scripts in sequence. The Sequence container is ideal for this because it, like other containers, allows you to create a distributed transaction with a lifetime that begins when the Sequence container begins executing and either commits or rolls back when the Sequence container returns. The Sequence container commits the transaction if it completes successfully and it rolls back the transaction if it fails execution.

The SequenceContainers package in the S07-Containers sample solution illustrates container transactions. Figure 7.10 shows the Sequence container from the sample package. The sample package creates a table and inserts some values into the new table. However, if any of the tasks fail, you want the actions from the previous tasks to roll back. With the Sequence container, this is simply a matter of configuring the TransactionOption property to have the value Required, which forces a transaction if one does not already exist on the parent container of the Sequence container.

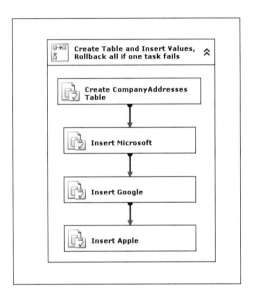

FIGURE 7.10   Sequence containers support transactions.

The package has a Sequence container with four Execute SQL Tasks. The first task creates a table named CompanyAddresses having a column called ID with the UNIQUE constraint. The next three tasks insert rows into the table. The last task, Insert Apple, attempts to insert a row for Apple with a nonunique ID. The TransactionOption property for the Sequence container is set to Required to ensure that if a transaction has not already been started in the parent of the Sequence container, it starts a new one. If you open the package and run it, the last task, the Insert Apple Execute SQL Task, should fail, causing the transaction for the entire Sequence container to roll back and undo the actions of the previous tasks, including the insertions and table creation. This sample demonstrates one of the powerful features of containers, called user-defined transaction scope. Try changing some of the settings for this package and see how it affects the transaction. You can also change the ID for the Apple company (in the task's query property) to a unique value and it correctly inserts all rows and commits the entire transaction.

Another use of the Sequence container is to build exceptional workflow. A common request is to conditionally execute a task in the workflow, but to continue executing the remainder of the workflow even if the conditional task doesn't execute. Because the Sequence container makes it simple to build smaller units of execution inside the package, this request is easy. Figure 7.11 shows the sample package after being executed. Notice that Task 2, the conditional task, didn't execute, but Task 3 executed anyway. This is because Task 3 executes dependent on the successful completion of the Sequence container, not the exceptional class. Although there are other solutions to this problem, they can be quite difficult to set up. This method is simple to set up and easy to understand.

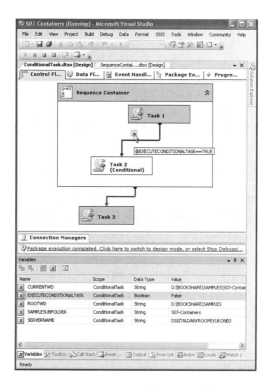

FIGURE 7.11   Sequence containers create smaller units of execution.

To see this package in action, open the ConditionalTask package in the S07-Containers sample solution. To see the package execute all three tasks, change the variable named EXECUTECONDITIONALTASK to be TRUE and run the package again.

Although the Sequence container is not as powerful as the looping containers and doesn't get used as much as other containers, it has its place and value. Use the Sequence container to document and reduce complex packages and you'll start to really appreciate its simple elegance.

The Looping Containers

There are two looping containers in Integration Services. The For Loop is the simpler of the two and iterates over workflow based on expressions. This container is useful when you need to iterate a certain number of times or until a certain condition exists. The Foreach Loop is the more complex and makes it possible to iterate over workflow for each item in a collection. This container is useful when you have a list of inputs that you want to apply to the same workflow.

The Foreach Loop and For Loop support transactions in the same way as the Sequence container. They commit all operations if the container completes successfully and roll back all operations if not.

The LoopContainers package in the S07-Containers sample solution illustrates this with a Foreach Loop that performs the same function as the SequenceContainers package. The Foreach Loop has a Foreach Item Enumerator with the values to be entered into the table. The last item has a nonunique ID that causes the insert to fail and, consequently, all the inserts to roll back. The difference is, because the table is created outside the Foreach Loop, it's not in the transaction and remains even when the transaction gets rolled back. To read more about the looping containers, see Chapter 13, "Looping and Foreach Enumerators," where they're covered in detail.

The Package Container

We come now to the Package container. The package is to the Integration Services user what the canvas is to the artist. It is the starting point upon which you build solutions. It's not just a container either. Most of the settings that impact the contents and execution of the package are found on the Package container. Get to know the package properties better and you'll increase your understanding of workflow in Integration Services.

Packages are essentially souped-up Sequence containers. In fact, if you were to look at the code for the Package container, you'd see that the code that is run when the package executes is the same code that is run when a Sequence container executes. The difference is that packages are treated differently internally. They are considered the top-level container and represent the outermost structure of packages. They also have a lot more properties and collections of objects than do the Sequence containers. The following are collections found only on the Package container.

- Connections—All the connection managers

- Configurations—All configurations

- LogProviders—All configured log provider objects

- ExtendedProperties—A collection of variable-like objects for package clients to store values

The first three have already been discussed in some detail, and later chapters cover these collections in even greater detail. However, the final collection, ExtendedProperties, hasn't yet been discussed. This collection is a place where clients of the package can store data and is interesting because it's the only property or collection on the package, or any other container for that matter, that the object model persists but doesn't use. The object model provides this collection so that third-party developers or object model clients can have a place to store private data related to a package and that remains with the package, but is not modified or lost when saving or loading. This is how the designer stores the layout information for a package.

If you open a package created in the designer in Source View, the `ExtendedProperties` are visible at the very beginning of the package. There is a package variable node that looks similar to the following:

```
<DTS:PackageVariable>
 <DTS:Property DTS:Name="PackageVariableValue" DTS:DataType="8">

&lt;Package xmlns:xsd="http://www.w3.org/2001/XMLSchema"
➥xmlns:xsi="http://www.w3.org/2001/XMLSchema-instance"
➥xmlns:dwd="http://schemas.microsoft.com/DataWarehouse/Designer/
➥1.0"&gt;&lt;dwd:
DtsControlFlowDiagram&gt;&lt;dwd:BoundingTop&gt;1468&lt;➥
/dwd:BoundingTop&gt;&lt;dwd:Layout&gt;&lt;dds&gt;
More of the same…
</DTS:PackageVariable>
```

This is the substantially shortened layout portion of the package. The designer stores all the information about where the objects are located and saves it all into an XML document. The designer then stores the XML document in an `ExtendedProperty`.

The `ExtendedProperties` collection isn't exposed through the designer. It's only available to object model clients. But, it's included in this discussion to help further differentiate packages from other containers and to emphasize their extended role as the outermost containers.

NOTE

In the "how products evolve" category, the node for `ExtendedProperties` is called `PackageVariable` even though the collection is called `ExtendedProperties` and the object is called `ExtendedProperty`. Originally, the collection was called `PackageVariables`, but people were confused by this. Some thought that `PackageVariables` were just variables at package scope. The node name remained `PackageVariable` so as not to break packages that were written before the change and Microsoft never revisited the issue to make the persisted node consistent with the name of the objects.

Important Package Properties

In addition, several properties are unique to the package. Many of these properties are covered in detail in other chapters. However, some brief introductory discussion is in order.

PackageType

This property should have been called `WhichDesignerCreatedThisPackage`, but that would have been a little long! So, it's called `PackageType`. It's actually a holdover property from DTS and is an enumerated value. There are six possible values as follows:

- `Default`—This value is what is used if the client doesn't change it. For example, if you create a package through the object model, the type is the default.

- `Wizard`—This value indicates that the Import/Export wizard created the package.

- `Designer`—This value indicates that the package was created with the DTS designer. If a package has this value, it was likely migrated from a DTS 2000 package.

- `Replication`—Replication used DTS for some purposes and still does. This setting is rare, but if a package has this value, it was likely migrated from a DTS 2000 package.

- `Designer90`—This value indicates that the package was created in the Integration Services 2005 designer. Each future designer will have a unique value with an incremented postfix version identifier.

- `DBMaint`—This value indicates that the package was created in the Database Maintenance utility in SQL Server Management Studio.

Changing these values is not advised, especially for the DBMaint types because DBMaint is a scaled-down Integration Services designer and usually fails to load packages it did not create.

CreatorName
This is the NetBIOS username of the individual who created the package. It is set when the user creates the package and Integration Services never changes it again. It's OK to change this at any time. Integration Services never uses this property.

CreatorComputerName
The is the NetBIOS computer name of the computer used to create the package. It is set when the package is created and Integration Services never changes it again. It's also OK to change this at any time.

CreationDate
This is the date when the package was created. Integration Services does not use this value in any way and it can be changed at any time.

MaxConcurrentExecutables
This property has confused and confounded newby and experienced Integration Services users alike. It's a simple concept, but the name is confusing. Basically, this is the number of threads the runtime execution engine uses to execute executables. The default is four. The maximum is 128. If you set the number higher than 128, the engine automatically uses 128. If you set it to zero, the engine automatically uses four threads. Finally, if you set the value to -1, the number of threads used is the number of processors on the machine plus two. So, if there are four processors and you set `MaxConcurrentExecutables` to -1, the runtime execution engine uses six threads. Also, don't confuse this number with the Data Flow Task's `EngineThreads` property. That property is a hint to the Data Flow Task how many threads it should use.

PackagePriorityClass
This is another holdover from DTS. It changes the priority the runtime engine uses for its threads.

VersionMajor
This is the first of three values you can use for versioning your package.

VersionMinor
This is the minor version and can be used anytime you make minor changes to the package.

VersionBuild
The designer increments this value every time you build the project in which the package is found. You can change any of the version number properties at any time without a problem. Integration Services does not use these properties other than incrementing the VersionBuild value.

VersionComments
This property can be used for any comments you might have about the current or past versions. It's provided to give you a way to document the changes to the package at certain milestones.

VersionGUID
The Integration Services runtime changes this value every time you save the package. It is read-only and should not be modified.

Summary

Containers are a way of organizing packages, but they also do a lot of the work in the workflow. Many of the features of Integration Services are provided in the context of containers to the extent that if you don't understand containers, it's difficult to understand workflow as well. Taskhost containers provide much of the default behavior for tasks and make building custom tasks much easier. Sequences simplify packages and loops encourage package part reuse and smaller packages. Use containers wisely and your packages will be easier to build, understand, and maintain.

PART III

Control Flow Services

IN THIS PART

The Stock Tasks

"SO, IT'S JUST NOT AS FUN TO TWIRL YOUR OWN."—ROB YOUNG

This chapter is an introduction to the stock tasks, the standard tasks that ship with Integration Services. Integration Services ships with many tasks that provide a wide range of functionality based on a broad set of technologies. This chapter provides a general explanation of each task, highlighting their more notable features, their purpose, how to set them up, some tips and tricks, as well as some of their less-documented properties. The preceding chapter, Chapter 7, "Grouping Control Flow with Containers," covered in detail the common properties and behavior for all tasks. If you haven't read that chapter, it would be worthwhile to review it before proceeding here, because this chapter references those commonalities. In the interest of brevity and to make this chapter manageable, this chapter only covers the stock tasks.

Some sample packages are provided to help you understand stock task basics: how to set up the tasks, how they work, and when to use them. Although not earth-shattering, each package gives you a quick template to draw from when building your own packages. With Integration Services, one thing is clear; solutions and packages can be quite complex, but, in the end, they're really just combinations of very simple elements. The packages in the sample solution are intended to give you a quick start to setting up tasks. Later chapters focus on combining these tasks into solutions. As you read about each of the tasks in this chapter, open the sample package and tinker with it a bit. That's the quickest way to learn how to set up and use each of the stock tasks.

Common Task Conventions

Although each of the stock tasks provides unique functionality, there are also some similarities between them. Microsoft made great efforts to ensure that the stock tasks adhered to certain conventions. This section covers what those conventions are, why they are important, and how to use them. All the stock tasks use these conventions to some extent, so after you understand the conventions, you can easily find your way around unfamiliar tasks as well.

Task User Interface

This section describes the standardized user interface supported by each of the stock tasks.

Task UI Sections

Figure 8.1 shows the four main sections of the stock task user interface (UI). These areas exist in all the stock task UIs. The following sections describe each of the areas.

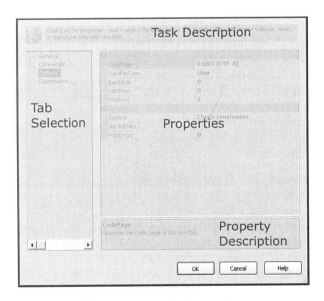

FIGURE 8.1   The stock task UI is separated into four main areas.

Task Description   The task description at the top of the task UI is provided to describe how the task functions and how it can be used. Don't confuse this with the Description task property. This description is the generic description of the task, whereas the Description property on all tasks is a place where package writers can document things such as how the task is configured for that particular package, and so on.

Tab Selection   The Tab Selection window allows you to view different properties windows. Every task has at least two tabs, the General tab and the Expressions tab.

Properties   The Properties window is where you make all the settings on the task. The properties shown here are a subset of the properties shown in the properties grid in the package designer when you select the task in the package. The task UI categorizes the properties into tabs so they're a little easier to find and edit. Although it's possible to edit these properties in the property grid of the designer, the task UI combines like properties together so they're easier to understand, find, and use.

Property Description   The property description describes the property that is currently selected in the Properties window. Changing the selection in the Properties window changes the description shown here. The property description helps clarify the purpose of the task property.

UNUSED PROPERTIES HIDDEN

The set of properties that are visible in the properties grid is not always the same. On almost all tasks, there are one or two key properties that when changed, the list of available properties also changes. Usually, the property is called Operation. In this chapter, these properties are called key settings. For example, the File System Task has some operations that only require one connection. If one of those operations is selected, for example, Delete File, there is only one connection property visible. It's important to set these key properties first so that the other related properties become visible. Originally, this was not the case. All the properties, even those that did not apply to the current operation, were visible simultaneously. The properties are now hidden when not needed because usability studies found that it was confusing for users to have those properties visible, even if they were disabled.

Access Methods

Many of the tasks provide different methods for providing a value for a property. By default, the package writer directly enters the value for a property in the task UI or the designer. For some properties, it's useful to retrieve the value from some other source. The options are as follows:

- **Direct Input**—The package writer directly enters the value into the task's user interface or it is configured somehow. Essentially, this tells the task that the correct value will be set on the property and the task need only retrieve the value to use it.

- **File Connection**—The file connection access method tells the task that it must attempt to open the named file and read the contents to retrieve the value for the property. For example, the SQL Task has the option to open a text file and read the contents of the file to retrieve the T-SQL script.

- **Variable**—This access method indicates to the task that the value for the property will be found in the named variable.

There is no formula for choosing which properties support multiple access methods, but some elements make it more likely. If one of the following is true, the property likely supports multiple access methods:

- The object on which the task operates can be stored in different locations, such as SQL Server or the file system, as in the Execute Package Task.

- The property points to a file system folder.

- The property value can be a very long string, such as the SQL script for the SQL Task.

CONNECTION FIX UP

Stock tasks appear to reference connection managers by name because the task displays the selected connection manager name. However, stock tasks actually store the ID of the connection manager and look up the connection manager by ID. This is so that if the connection manager name changes, the reference isn't broken.

Standard Tabs

The Standard tabs exist on every stock task UI.

The General Tab

The General tab, for most tasks, has two properties, the name and description for the task. The Name property is visible as the task name in the package designer. It can also be changed by selecting the task and clicking on the name and directly editing it there or by changing it in the task UI.

The Description property is useful for storing information about how the task is configured and any other information that can be useful for maintaining the task long term. There is no arbitrary limit to how long the description text can be.

The Expressions Tab

The Expressions tab is for entering property expressions. Property expressions allow a property value to be set by an associated expression. For more information about property expressions, see Chapter 9, "Using Expressions."

Task Groups

This chapter has grouped the stock tasks into rough categories to help you quickly grasp the breadth and depth of the task offering. Try not to get too caught up in the groupings. In some cases, these groupings represent architectural or structural similarities to other tasks in the same grouping, but, for the most part, they are for convenience only. Those similarities are noted as necessary in the individual task discussions.

The Workflow Tasks

The workflow tasks are used to accomplish simple and common workflow so they are commonly used in most packages. DTS users will likely be most familiar with these tasks because many of them are rewritten incarnations of DTS tasks, with the exception of the WMI Data Reader, WMI Event Watcher, File System, Execute DTS 2000 Package, and Web Services Tasks that are new in Integration Services. Workflow tasks perform the mundane grunt work of packages, such as moving files, checking for storage space, or sending email, and they form the backbone of any Extract, Transform, and Load (ETL) or other data integration workflow.

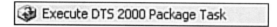

Execute DTS 2000 Package Task

The Execute DTS 2000 Package Task is briefly discussed in Chapter 3, "Migrating from DTS," as are the reasons it ships with Integration Services. To review, this task is provided to help bridge the path when migrating from Data Transformation Services to Integration Services. Because the architecture of Integration Services is so different from DTS, few legacy DTS packages will successfully migrate and run in Integration Services. This task provides a "half" migration step so that legacy packages can be run side by side with newer Integration Services packages. Even limited interaction between the two is possible such that existing investment in DTS packages is not lost when upgrading to Integration Services.

The Execute DTS 2000 Package Task is installed as part of the legacy components. To ensure you will have this task available, select the Legacy Components option in the advanced section of SQL Server setup. Figure 8.2 shows the proper selection to make. This option installs the task and the Data Transformation Services components. If you do not have this task available, you can run SQL Server setup again and select this option to install it.

If you want to have the user interface available, you must install SQL Server side by side with an existing install of SQL Server 2000 with DTS installed.

You need to have a DTS 2000 package already built before you can use this task. Alternatively, you can refer to the tip later in this chapter about creating a new DTS package inside the hosted DTS designer. The package can reside in any of the DTS supported locations, such as SQL Server or in a DTS structured storage file. Also, packages can be embedded in an Execute DTS 2000 Package Task in an Integration Services package.

Setting Up the Execute DTS 2000 Package Task

Figure 8.3 shows the task user interface for the Execute DTS 2000 Package Task with the default settings. Drop the task onto the designer and double-click it to bring up the task UI. You might notice that the task UI resembles the task UI for the DTS Execute Package Task. The two are functionally very similar.

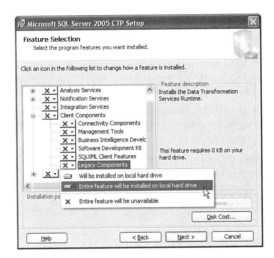

FIGURE 8.2   Install the legacy components to ensure the task is available.

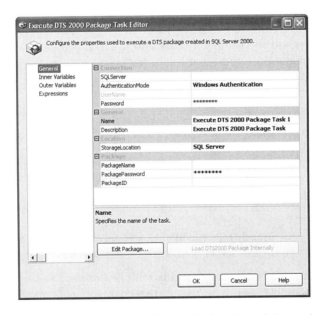

FIGURE 8.3   The task UI allows you to configure the location of the package.

SQL Server Packages   The StorageLocation property describes from where DTS should load the package. It is the key setting because some of the other available properties change based on this selection. So, you'll want to set this property before setting any of the others.

Setting the StorageLocation property to SQL Server indicates that the package is stored in a SQL Server 2000 instance and the SQLServer property holds the name of the SQL

Server 2000 instance. After you've set the server name, you can click on the ellipsis button in the PackageName property and browse the available packages on the specified server in the Select Package dialog box shown in Figure 8.4. After you've selected a package and closed the Select Package dialog box, the PackageName and PackageID properties should be populated with the name and ID of the package you've selected.

FIGURE 8.4   The Select Package dialog box allows you to browse available packages.

<u>NOTE</u>

The available properties for Meta Data Services are the same as for SQL Server.

Structured Storage File   Selecting Structured Storage for the StorageLocation property changes the available properties to those shown in Figure 8.5.

Instead of specifying server connection information, you need only to specify the fully qualified filename of the structured storage file on the file system. The file must have the .dts extension for the Browse dialog box to recognize it as a DTS package.

Embedded in Task   This is an interesting option because it removes all notions of a separate package. When set, the DTS package is embedded inside the IS package. To use this setting, you must first select the package from another location, such as Meta Data Services, SQL Server, or from a structured storage file as described previously. When the package is selected, the Load DTS 2000 Package Internally button is enabled. Clicking on that button then embeds the DTS package inside of the IS parent package. You can continue to edit the package at will and it's possible to subsequently save the package to a different location as well. Embedding packages in this way makes it easier to move the parent and child packages together and eliminates connectivity issues with legacy systems containing the DTS child package. The only drawback here is that, depending on the size

and number of the embedded packages, your parent package disk size can grow substantially larger.

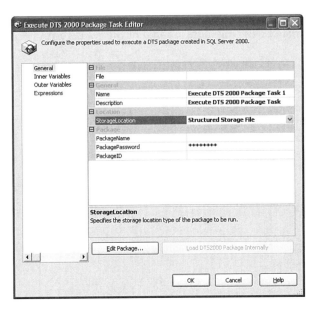

FIGURE 8.5   Structured Storage packages require a filename.

Inner Variables   If you're familiar with the way inner and outer variables work in the
Execute Package Task in DTS, you already know how they work for this task. Inner variables are a way of adding a variable to the child packages' global variables. The value for
inner variables is statically defined in the UI. At execution time, the Execute DTS 2000
Package Task creates a new variable at package scope on the child package with the static
value specified. The variable is only temporary and is not visible to the child package at
design time.

Outer Variables   Outer variables are important for allowing legacy DTS packages to integrate well with IS packages. Outer variables allow the parent package to pass in an IS variable that can be used in the DTS environment. To see outer variables in action, open the
package called ExecDTS2KPackage.dtsx in the S08-StockTasks sample solution. It uses an
outer variable to pass in a message that the child DTS package displays in a message box.

Custom Breakpoints
Two custom breakpoints are available for this task:

- Before loading the target package
- Before executing the target package

Task-Specific Peculiarities or Nonstandard Settings

This task is fairly complex because, after all, it's essentially the DTS 2000 tasks, designer, and other features all wrapped up and embedded into one IS task. The Edit Package button allows you to open the package in the DTS 2000 designer where you have full access to virtually every feature in the DTS 2000 designer.

TIP

Creating a new DTS package with the Execute DTS 2000 Package Task is possible. If you have an existing package, you can simply open it and save it to a different name. If you don't have an existing DTS package available, you can create one by creating a temporary file and opening it as though it was a DTS package and then save it to a different name. Here are the steps:

1. Create a target text file without any content and give it a `.dts` extension. Call it `target.dts`.

2. Open the `target.dts` file in the DTS designer of the Execute DTS 2000 Package Task.

3. Save it as a package with another name. This is necessary because the DTS designer has the current file opened for edit.

4. Change the Package to Execute property in the Execute DTS 2000 Package Task to point to your new DTS package.

One reason you might want to do this is if you're refactoring existing packages. Perhaps there is some logic in one part of a DTS package you want to remove and replace with an SSIS package and you want to retain the other parts of the package. Or, perhaps you want to separate an existing DTS package into multiple packages. This is a quick-and-easy way to create new DTS packages for such purposes.

File System Task

The File System Task is used to copy, create, delete, rename, move, rename, and attribute files and directories in the file system.

THE FILE SYSTEM TASK ORIGINS

The File System Task is new in Integration Services, sort of. In DTS, you used the FTP Task to move files around. In keeping with the one-task, one-purpose mantra of Integration Services, the file system behavior of the FTP Task was separated into its own dedicated task. The File System Task was actually designed, specified, and coded on a round-trip train ride between Seattle and Chicago.

The developer who wrote the task was taking a train trip home for a visit in Chicago, but wanted to work while on the train so he wouldn't have to take vacation. We knew we were planning to write something like the File System Task, so he took a laptop. Two weeks later, when he returned, the File System Task arrived as well.

The Operation property is a key setting for this task and changing it changes the setting of other available properties. There are nine available operations. Some operations require a source and destination, as Table 8.1 shows.

TABLE 8.1   Connection Managers Required per Operation

Requires a Source Connection Manager Only	Requires a Source and Destination Connection Manager
Create Directory	Copy File
Delete Directory	Move Directory
Delete Directory Content	Move File
Delete File	Rename File
Set Attributes	

Setting Up the File System Task

To see a simple package that uses the File System Task, open the package called FileSystem.dtsx in the S08-StockTasks sample solution. It copies and renames a file and then deletes it with a subsequent File System Task.

Figure 8.6 shows the setup for copying the file. Notice that the specified operation is Copy File and that the task references two file connection managers. The SourceConnection specifies the connection manager the task will use to find the file to copy. The DestinationConnection specifies the connection manager the task will use to determine where to copy the file and what to name it. Doing the copy this way is similar to using the Copy command in the command prompt:

```
copy c:\filename.txt c:\newlocation\newfilename.txt
```

USING FLAT FILE CONNECTIONS IN THE FILE SYSTEM TASK

The File System Task creates a file connection manager by default when you select New Connection from the Connection Manager list in the task UI. However, it also supports using Flat File Connection Managers to locate files. The Flat File Connection Manager provides a lot of information about the flat file to IS components, but the File System Task can also use a Flat File Connection Manager as a simple file connection manager as well. If you already have a Flat File Connection Manager that points to a file on which you need to perform some file operation, you can reuse it instead of creating a new file connection manager and eliminate a connection manager in the Connections Tray.

Send Mail Task

The Send Mail Task makes it possible to generate and send email from the package. This is helpful for alerting you to certain events such as package completion or errors.

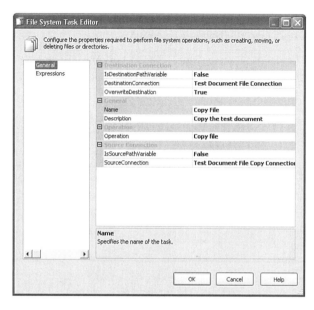

FIGURE 8.6   The File System Task can copy and rename files in the same operation.

To use the Send Mail Task, you need to have access to an SMTP server. Most SMTP addresses are in the form smtp.domain.extension and look similar to SMTP.MyDomain.org.

Setting Up the Send Mail Task

If you're familiar with common email programs, the Send Mail Task will seem quite familiar. The four properties that need to have values are the SMTP Connection Manager, a From email address, a To email address, and a message in the MessageSource property. Figure 8.7 shows some pseudosettings for the Send Mail Task.

The SmtpConnection property holds the name of the SMTP Connection Manager the Send Mail Task uses to communicate with the SMTP server. The To property holds the address of the email recipient and can contain multiple email addresses. The To property must contain a valid email address. The optional CC and BCC properties can also contain multiple email addresses. The Subject property is not required, but should be included and contains a description of the contents of the email. The Priority property sets the priority of the email, which some email clients use to prioritize email. The Attachments property contains a list of fully qualified filenames of files to attach to the email.

The MessageSourceType property directs the task from where it should retrieve the message body. Three options are available for this setting:

- **Direct Input**—If the MessageSourceType is set to Direct Input, the MessageSource property contains the text that is sent as the body of the email.

- **File Connection**—If the MessageSourceType property is set to File Connection, the MessageSource property contains the name of the file connection manager. The

Send Mail Task opens the file to which that file connection manager points and reads the contents into the body of the email.

- **Variable**—If the `MessageSourceType` is set to Variable, the `MessageSource` property contains the name of a variable. The Send Mail Task inserts the value of the variable into the body of the email.

FIGURE 8.7   The Send Mail Task uses the SMTP protocol to send email.

FIGURE 8.8   The SMTP Connection Manager holds the address to the SMTP server.

Custom Breakpoints

One custom breakpoint is available for this task:

- Before sending mail

FTP Task

The FTP Task is used to move files between local and remote machines using the File Transfer Protocol. It's a dependable and secure way to noninteractively download or upload files. Although newer technologies have come along, the FTP Task is the old standby that will likely remain relevant for years to come. Other operations, such as creating local or remote folders and deleting local and remote files and folders are also available with the FTP Task.

The FTP Task is installed with Integration Services and you don't need to do anything special to make it available. For the remote operations, the FTP Task communicates with a remote server, so you need to have access to an FTP server for all remote operations.

Setting Up the FTP Task

To see a simple package that uses the FTP Task, open the package called `FTP.dtsx` in the S08-StockTasks sample solution. It downloads a command-line utility called `soon.exe` that's useful for generating AT execution schedules.

The first thing to do when setting up the FTP Task is to configure the FTP connection. Figure 8.9 shows the General tab of the FTP task UI where you set the `FtpConnection` property. If you don't already have an FTP Connection Manager, you can create one by selecting New Connection from the drop down.

The FTP Connection Manager holds the address for the FTP server. Figure 8.10 shows the UI for the FTP Connection Manager. The most important setting on the connection manager is the FTP server name. The User Name and Credentials are also needed if your server doesn't support anonymous access. The Server Port default is port number 21. Likely, you should not have to change that. The Passive setting is useful in environments with a firewall. Passive mode is considered safer because it ensures the FTP Task initiates all communication rather than from the FTP server or other outside program. The Retries setting configures the number of times the FTP Connection Manager retries to establish a connection before giving up. The Timeout setting configures how long the FTP connection waits before giving up on a connection attempt. The Chunk Size setting configures how much data is transported in one FTP packet. The Test Connection button causes the FTP Connection Manager to attempt a connection with the server and shows a message box with the results.

FIGURE 8.9   Configure the FTP connection on the FTP Task General tab.

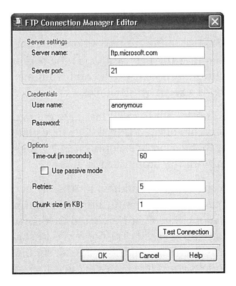

FIGURE 8.10   Configure the FTP Connection Manager.

The file transfer settings are on the File Transfer tab shown in Figure 8.11. The key setting for the FTP Task is the `Operation` property. Begin by setting the Operation so that the other properties will be available. In the sample package, the FTP Task is configured to download a utility from the Microsoft.com FTP site.

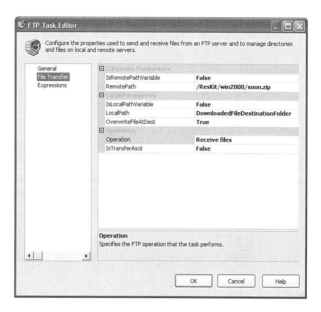

FIGURE 8.11   Configure the file transfer settings on the File Transfer tab.

TIP

It is strongly recommend that you do not use the FTP Task for local file operations; rather, you should use the File System Task because it is better suited to local file system operations. Also, it can be confusing when viewing a package with an FTP Task that isn't doing an FTP operation. The local operations will likely not be supported in future versions. They are artifacts left over from earlier FTP Task designs and do not present any advantages over using the File System Task.

Wildcards Supported

The FTP Task supports wildcards for remote operations but not for local operations. The `*` character can be used to indicate entire names. For example, in the sample FTP package, you could change the `RemotePath` to `/ResKit/win2000/*.zip` to download all zip files in the remote directory. When the `RemotePath` is changed to `/ResKit/win2000/T*.zip`, the FTP Task downloads all the utilities that start with the letter 'T,' including `tracedmp.zip`, `toolhelp.zip`, `timethis.zip`, and so on.

The ? character can be used for more surgical file filtering. This is useful in cases in which your files are named with a particular naming convention. For example, you might have a naming convention in which the number of letters in the name is always constant, but certain parts of the name change. You might have a group of files named with the prefix of "Cases" and the suffix of the date such that you have filenames that look like this:

Cases02042004, Cases05222005, Cases10032005

To only retrieve the files from October, 2005, you can use the ? character to define the RemotePath as follows:

"/Cases/Cases10??2005"

Message Queue Task

The MSMQ Task is useful for transferring information between packages or other MSMQ client applications and synchronizing workflows. MSMQ is very versatile and can be used for many purposes, some of which are included in the following list:

- Synchronizing multiple package execution
- Transferring data processed by one package to another package waiting on the queue
- Communicating via MSMQ between DTS packages and SSIS packages when using the Use2000Format option
- Synchronizing workflows within the same package
- Temporarily storing data to be processed on subsequent package runs

If you're not familiar with MSMQ, many excellent references are available. Unfortunately, the scope of this book doesn't allow for great detail about MSMQ here.

To use the MSMQ Task, you must be sure Message Queuing is installed on the machine on which the package with the MSMQ Task will run. To install Message Queuing, launch the Add/Remove Programs Control Panel and select Add/Remove Windows Components.

Figure 8.12 shows the Windows Components Wizard dialog box you use to install Message Queuing. Click the Message Queuing option if it isn't already selected, and then click the Next button to complete the installation.

To use the sample packages, you'll also need to create a queue. You can do that by launching the Computer Management console shown in Figure 8.13. Right-click on the Private Queues node, click New, and then click Private Queue. Name the private queue SSISSAMPLEQUEUE. Notice also that the Label column at the upper-right of the window shows the path to the queue. This is the path that you'll enter into the Path property of the MSMQ Connection Manager. Also notice the Number of Messages column. MSMQ has the option of leaving messages in the queue. As you'll see in the sample package, this can be useful when you want to have more than one MSMQ client, like the MSMQ Task, reading from the queue.

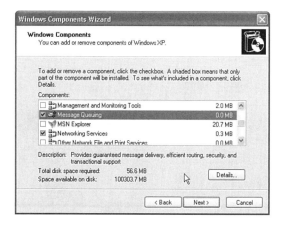

FIGURE 8.12   Use Add/Remove Windows Components to install Message Queuing.

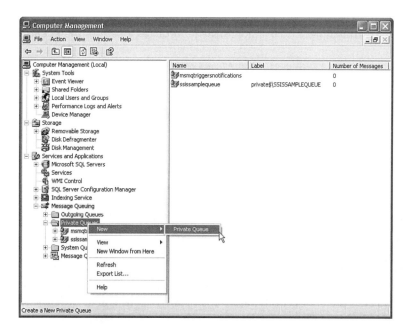

FIGURE 8.13   Use the Computer Management Control Panel to create queues.

Setting Up the MSMQ Task

The MSMQ Task has two primary modes, Send and Receive. You set the mode in the task UI on the General tab in the Message property. Two options are provided: Send Message and Receive Message. The default is Send Message. Changing the Message property changes the Send tab to the Receive tab with all the appropriate properties for configuring the task to receive from the queue.

Send Mode   In Send mode, the MSMQ Task places data in the queue to be retrieved by another MSMQ client at some future time. To set the task to Send mode, set the Message property on the General tab to Send Message. This is the key setting for the MSMQ Task. After being set, you need to create an MSMQ Connection Manager. Select the MSMQConnection property and select New connection. The MSMQ Connection Manager UI is displayed, as shown in Figure 8.14.

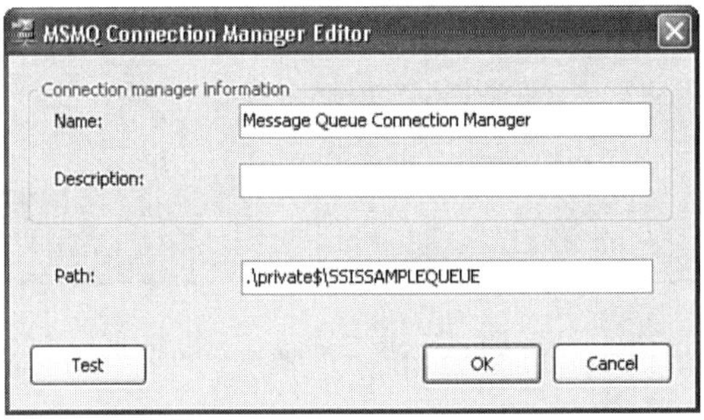

FIGURE 8.14   The MSMQ Connection Manager requires a path to the queue.

The MSMQ Connection Manager requires one setting, the path. The path is what tells the MSMQ Task where to access the queue. You build a path with the computer name and queue name. Following are some examples of a path:

MyComputerName\PRIVATE$\MyQueueName

MyComputerName\MyQueueName

.\PRIVATE$\MyQueueName

.\MyQueueName

The final two paths use the shorthand '.' to indicate that the queue is on the local computer. Figure 8.14 shows the MSMQ Connection Manager UI using a private path to point to a queue on the local computer. A private queue is not registered with directory services and so isn't visible to other machines. Private queues are typically more performant due to reduced overhead. After you've entered the path, you can click on the Test button to check if the connection manager is correctly configured. After the MSMQ Connection Manager is set up, you can set up the rest of the task.

Send mode has three options for where to retrieve the message, as shown in Figure 8.15:

- **Data File**—The data comes from a file
- **Variable**—The data comes from a package variable
- **String**—The message is directly entered into the task

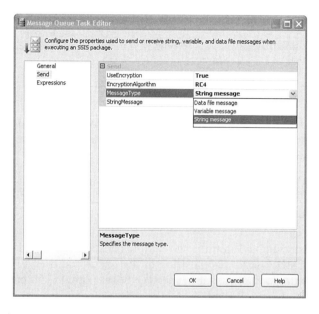

FIGURE 8.15   The MSMQ Task supports three message types.

Receive   When in Receive mode, the MSMQ Task needs an MSMQ Connection Manager as well. MSMQ Connection Managers can be shared between multiple MSMQ Tasks if needed without issue. Figure 8.16 shows the MSMQ Task when in Receive mode and the MessageType options drop down.

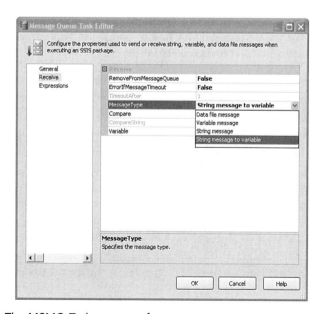

FIGURE 8.16   The MSMQ Task supports four message types.

Figure 8.16 shows the four message type options for Receive mode:

- **Data File**—You can retrieve the message as a file. This message type also has more options for how to handle the received file.

- **Variable**—You can apply a filter so that the MSMQ Task only retrieves values from variables in certain packages.

- **String**—The MSMQ Task retrieves a string, and if configured to do so, compares the string to determine if it matches a pattern. If so, it returns. This is useful in work-flow synchronization scenarios.

- **String to Variable**—The MSMQ Task retrieves the string and places it in the variable specified in the Variable property. This is the way the MSMQ Task is used in the sample packages.

In the S08-StockTasks sample solution, two sample packages use the MSMQ Task. One package uses an MSMQ Task to place a string in the queue and then two other MSMQ Tasks retrieve the string and display it in message boxes. The second package also waits on the queue for the string and displays it and then cleans up the queue.

This sample shows a number of ways the MSMQ Task can be used:

- As a multipackage synchronization mechanism, the second package waits until the MSMQ Task in the first package sends the string to the queue. The string need not be intrinsically meaningful. It can just be a globally unique identifier (GUID) or other unique string as a way to indicate it's OK for the dependent package to continue executing.

- As an interpackage synchronization mechanism, the subsequent tasks in the same package wait for the sending MSMQ Task to complete. This shows how MSMQ Tasks can be used instead of precedence constraints.

- As an interpackage communication mechanism, the MSMQ Task can send meaning-ful information or data to other tasks in the same package.

- As an intrapackage communication mechanism, the MSMQ Task can send meaning-ful information or data to other tasks in another package running in a different package, even on another machine.

- As a queue cleanup mechanism, the MSMQ Task can remove the message from the queue.

To run the packages, load both into the designer. Select the `MSMQ2.dtsx` package so that it shows in the designer. From the Debug menu, select the Start Without Debugging menu item or press [Ctrl+F5]. This starts the package running in a separate process so you can see both packages running simultaneously. Then, start the `MSMQ.dtsx` package by pressing [F5].

There is a short wait so you can see the impact it has on the tasks in the package. Note that the Receive MSMQ Tasks start, but don't complete. They are waiting for the queue to fill with the string that the Send MSMQ Task is about to send. The other package also has an MSMQ Receive Task that is waiting for data to become available in the queue. The Script Task waits for approximately five seconds and then sends a string to the queue; you should see three message boxes displaying that string. The final MSMQ Task, Clear MSMQ String, removes the string from the queue. These packages are very instructive; try changing around the settings a bit to see how the different tasks interact with the other packages and with each other.

Custom Breakpoints

Two custom breakpoints are available for this task:

- Before sending the message
- Before receiving the message

The WMI Tasks

Windows Management Instrumentation (WMI) is a powerful and comprehensive standards-based management technology for Microsoft Windows operating systems. WMI is an implementation of the Distributed Management Task Force's (DMTF) Web-Based Enterprise Management (WBEM) initiative. WBEM is a set of open, industry-defined specifications for managing and controlling enterprise-computing environments. Using WMI, you can manage, control, and monitor your entire enterprise inventory of hardware, configurations, networks, servers, services, and applications.

You interact with WMI via the scripting language called WMI Query Language (WQL), which is a subset of ANSI SQL with some modifications to support WMI requirements. For the most part, the limitations are in the level of complexity the WQL parser supports certain keywords. WQL provides similar flexibility and power in the management space that SQL does in the database space, allowing the client to finely control the information retrieved from WMI. Keywords such as SELECT, WHERE, and HAVING will be familiar to SQL users. There are other WQL keywords with which the average SQL user will likely be unfamiliar, such as REFERENCES OF, ASSOCIATORS OF, KEYSONLY, and __CLASS. For more detailed coverage of WMI and WQL, search Microsoft MSDN and TechNet.

WMI is a collection of objects that represent settings and properties of everything in, around, and connected to your network. Things like disk drives, applications, services, BIOS settings, and removable media are all represented in WMI by instances of classes. You can build web pages that track your network and all the machines on it. You can write applications that can control machines remotely, alert you to problems with the network, and so on. And now, with the WMI tasks, you can build network and machine awareness and interaction into your packages.

There are three types of queries in WMI:

- **Data queries**—These queries are used to retrieve information about the information about instances of classes. This is how you retrieve information about local or remote machines. For example, you can detect if a service is running on a machine. The WMI Data Reader Task supports this type of query.

- **Event queries**—These queries are used to register to receive event notifications. For example, you can set thresholds for certain events, such as low memory or when hard drive space is exhausted. The WMI Event Watcher Task supports this type of query.

- **Schema queries**—These queries are used to retrieve information about classes rather than instances of classes. Integration Services does not support this type of query explicitly.

WQL queries are generally composed of four elements, as shown in Table 8.2.

TABLE 8.2 **WQL Syntax and Reserved Words**

WQL Clause	Description
SELECT	Describes what information you want back from your query. Similar to standard SQL, the * character is a wildcard meaning return all elements in the set that match the WHERE clause.
FROM	Specifies the type of event to listen for or the class to query.
WITHIN	Defines the polling interval in seconds. With this clause, there's a trade-off: longer intervals improve performance, but fire less frequently.
WHERE	Defines the criteria to use for filtering the query.

Using WMI—Tools and Documentation

WMI provides so much information. There are few data points or properties on your network or machines that you cannot get from WMI. The problem is how to wade through all the classes and instances and namespaces to get at the one piece of information you want. What you need is tools, and Microsoft provides a wealth of tools, resources, and documentation if you know where to look. There are helpful references and tools on the Microsoft download site at http://www.microsoft.com/downloads. Search for "WMI Extensions" to find the Visual Studio Server Explorer plug-in that you can use to traverse the WMI object tree. There is a tool called WMI Browser that is useful for learning more about WMI namespaces and classes and building queries. To download WMI Browser, do a search for "WMI Browser" on the Microsoft download website. The Scriptomatic tool included in the sample files available at www.samspublishing.com in the TOOLS folder is very useful for learning more about the namespaces and classes on your machine or for generating and testing scripts and queries you can use in your code, web pages, or packages. WBEMTest, available in the WMI SDK and also downloadable from the Microsoft download site, is another utility that is useful for doing ad hoc queries and searching for specific classes. Finally, a command-line tool is available on all Windows XP machines called WMIC. You can use it to explore WMI namespaces, classes, and properties. These tools make it much easier to browse, explore, and, most importantly, discover information that's stashed away in the bowels of WMI.

One last resource that should not go unmentioned is Alain Lissoir's excellent WMI-focused website: http://www.lissware.net. Alain is the program manager for WMI technologies at Microsoft and has written prodigiously about WMI. This site contains many boilerplate scripts, pointers to other resources, lots of samples, links to other web pages, and tools. If you're going to be using the WMI tasks, this is one website you should definitely bookmark.

The WMI tasks are installed by default with Integration Services. WMI is also available on all the operating systems SQL Server supports, so there should be no issues with using the WMI taskspoints or properties on your network or machines that on any of those platforms.

The WMI Connection Manager

The first thing you'll needpoints or properties on your network or machines that to do when setting up the WMI tasks is create a connection manager. Figure 8.17 shows the connection manager UI.

FIGURE 8.17   The WMI Connection Manager requires a server name and namespace.

If you're accessing the local machine, the default server name is "\\localhost". You can access another machine on your network by typing in its NetBIOS name.

COMPUTER NAMES IN WQL QUERIES

Computer names in WQL are typically specified using the computer's NetBIOS name:

\\bipm-r9-01

However, DNS names and IP addresses can also be used: bipm-r9-01.Microsoft.com or an IP address:

192.168.1.1.

The namespace is the WMI namespace in which you're interested. WMI namespaces are a way to logically group classes and instances of classes that relate to a particular managed environment. The default namespace for the WMI Connection Manager is \root\cimv2. CIMV2 stands for Common Information Model, Version 2. The CIMV2 namespace includes various classes for managing windows machines. To see the namespaces on your machine, start the Computer Management Control Panel, right-click on the WMI Control node under Services and Applications, and click Properties. Figure 8.18 shows the typical list of namespaces for a Windows XP system.

FIGURE 8.18   The Computer Management Control Panel displays WMI namespaces.

Table 8.3 shows a few of the more interesting and useful namespaces. This list is not exhaustive and will vary from machine to machine, so the list of namespaces you see on your machines will likely vary.

TABLE 8.3 Interesting WMI Namespaces

Class	Description
Root	The lowest level namespace in the WMI hierarchy
CIMV2	The default namespace for the WMI Connection Manager; contains classes that you use to manage the host system
Directory	The Groups directory–related namespaces
SECURITY	The namespace containing WMI security management classes
Microsoft\SqlServer\ComputerManagement	The namespace containing SQL Server–related classes for discovering information about SQL Server, including instance names, server protocol, version, security certificate, registered SQL Server services, process ID, descriptions, and even file locations
MSAPPS11	The namespace used to discover information about Microsoft Office applications, such as where files are stored, default file locations, startup folder, and registered OLEDB and ADO.NET providers
CIMV2\Applications\MicrosoftIE	The namespace containing classes for discovering Microsoft Internet Explorer and other Internet settings, such as cache, security, and connection settings

If you don't choose to connect to the WMI server with Windows authentication, the User Name and Password properties must be entered. These properties are also useful when connecting to a server that is on a different domain.

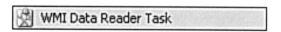

WMI Data Reader Task

The WMI Data Reader Task is useful for retrieving information about everything on or connected to your network. There are too many WMI classes to enumerate here; however, Table 8.5 lists the important classes and properties you might want to query. The WMI documentation lists more, and tools such as the WMI Browser can help you explore the enormous repository of information WMI provides.

Setting Up the WMI Task

After you've created a WMI Connection Manager, you'll need to set a few more properties. Figure 8.19 shows the WMI Data Reader Task UI.

FIGURE 8.19   The WMI Data Reader Task returns data about a system.

The WMI Data Reader Task provides settings for controlling the WQL to use, where the WQL will be found, where to place the results, and in what form you want the results to be returned. Table 8.4 lists these settings and their options.

TABLE 8.4   Settings for the WMI Data Reader Task

Setting	Options	Description
WqlQuerySourceType	Direct Input, File Connection, Variable	Describes from where the WQL source will come.
WqlSource	The WQL source, variable name, or file connection manager name	Contains the source WQL that will be used for the WQL query if Direct Input is specified. Otherwise, this contains the name of the variable that contains the query or the file connection manager that points to a file with the query.
OutputType	Data table, property name and value, property value	Specifies what data should be returned, all data in a table, just the property/name pairs, or the values only. If table is specified, the output type is a table object. The other two options return a string.

TABLE 8.4   Continued

Setting	Options	Description
OverwriteDestination	Append to Destination, Overwrite Destination, Keep Original	Specifies if data at the destination should be appended to, overwritten, or protected. The task will only append the results if the destination is a file.
DestinationType	Variable, file connection	Specifies where the results will be placed.
Destination	File connection manager or variable name	Depending on the DestinationType, contains the file connection manager that points to a file to contain the results or to a variable to contain the results.

Finding Information About Services   The Win32_Service WMI class in the CIMV2 namespace provides information about services installed on a machine. The WMIDataReader.dtsx package in the S08-StockTasks sample solution uses the following query to display the name, display name, and description of all the services installed on your machine with names that begin with the letter *M*.

```
SELECT Name, DisplayName, Description FROM Win32_Service  WHERE Name > "M" AND Name
< "N"
```

Then, the package uses a Script Task to display the returned properties and their values in a message box. There is also some disabled workflow in that package for enumerating the files in a folder. Try modifying the query slightly to get different results. For example, instead of returning just the Name, DisplayName, and Description, you could return all properties using the * wildcard like the following:

```
SELECT * FROM Win32_Service WHERE Name > "M" AND Name < "N"
```

Table 8.5 shows some useful classes in the CIMV2 namespace you can use to test different queries. To see the properties on these classes, insert the class name into a SELECT statement, as follows:

```
SELECT * FROM <<CLASSNAME>>
```

Likely, this will generate a large resultset, so you might want to qualify the SELECT statement with a WHERE clause, as shown previously. Name is always a valid property on WMI classes. After you see the properties on one or two classes, you can further refine your select statement to only show the properties you want to see.

TABLE 8.5   Useful WMI Classes and Descriptions

Class	Description
Win32_Service	Starts, stops, or pauses services, as well as obtains status information
Win32_Processor	Provides information about processors, including name, speed, bus speed, L2CacheSize, and architecture
Win32_LogicalMemoryConfiguration	Provides information about the amount of physical and virtual memory and available virtual memory
Win32_LogicalDisk	Discovers information about disk drives, including size, FreeSpace, Name, and so on
Win32_NetworkAdapter-Configuration	Discovers IP addresses, status, and MAC addresses of network connections
Win32_PerfFormattedData_PerfOS_Processor	Obtains performance data on the processor, which is useful when trying to gauge processor load
Win32_TimeZone	Provides information about the time zone
Win32_SystemUsers	Enumerates all users of a machine
Win32_SystemDevices	Enumerates all devices on a machine
Win32_OperatingSystem	Provides access to the version and serial numbers of Windows

TARGETED QUERIES MORE PERFORMANT

Targeted queries can cut down the amount of data that is returned. This is an important consideration for scripts that run over the network. WMI can be very verbose, so it's important to refine your query to only retrieve the information you need. The sample package calculates the number of bytes returned from the query and displays it with the returned string. Tweak the query and watch the amount of data fluctuate. Less targeted queries like SELECT * FROM Win32_Service or SELECT * FROM Win32_SystemDevices can return enormous amounts of information.

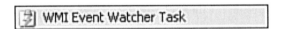

WMI Event Watcher Task

WMI also provides an eventing infrastructure for clients who want to be alerted to certain events as they happen. The Event Watcher Task provides a way for Integration Services to subscribe to WMI events in the package and to execute workflow either in the main package body or in event handlers based on the results of the event.

Setting Up the WMI Event Watcher Task

WMI is a very large, powerful, and complex technology. There is simply not enough space here to do it justice. So, this section concentrates on a simple but useful example, watching for a file to appear in a folder. To get started, you need to pick an existing connection manager or create one, as shown in the previous WMI Data Reader Task discussion. Table 8.6 shows the important settings for the WMI Event Watcher Task.

TABLE 8.6   Settings for the WMI Event Watcher Task

Setting	Options	Description
WqlQuerySourceType	Direct Input, File Connection, Variable	Describes from where the WQL source will come.
WqlQuerySource	The WQL source, variable name, or file connection manager name	Contains the source WQL that will be used for the WQL query if Direct Input is specified. Otherwise, this contains the name of the variable that contains the query or the file connection manager that points to a file with the query.
ActionAtEvent, ActionAtTimeout	Log event or timeout, log event or timeout, and fire SSIS event	Specifies what the task should do when the event is received. The SSIS event can be handled by an event handler in the package.
AfterEvent, AfterTimeout	Return with failure, return with success, watch for event again	Specifies what the task should do after receiving the watched event or timing out.
NumberOfEvents	Enter an integer value; 0 is interpreted as 1	Specifies how many times to watch for the event. The task returns after receiving the event the number of times specified. If 1, the task returns after seeing the event once. If 10, the task returns after seeing the event 10 times.
Timeout	Enter an integer value	Specifies the number of seconds to wait before timing out.

Figure 8.20 shows the WMI Event Watcher Task configured to watch for a file to be created in the D:\Temp directory.

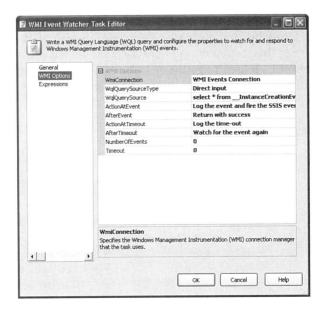

FIGURE 8.20   The WMI Event Watcher can listen for system events.

The query for this task is as follows:

```
SELECT * FROM __InstanceCreationEvent WITHIN 10 WHERE Targetinstance ISA
➡"CIM_DirectoryContainsFile" and TargetInstance.GroupComponent=
➡"Win32_Directory.Name=\"d:\\\\temp\""
```

The preceding WQL script has several parts that are worth mentioning.

- The SELECT statement—WMI uses a format called instances to return WMI data to a requesting client. Unlike SQL, which is record-based, WQL works against instances. Instances are populated occurrences of CIM classes. Properties that a class defines contain data and the WQL can filter on that data.

- __InstanceCreationEvent—There are many instance events. Some of the more important are __InstanceCreationEvent, __InstanceDeletionEvent, and __InstanceModificationEvent. These events are created when an instance of a class representing some system entity such as a file, directory, or hardware has been created, modified, or deleted.

- WITHIN 10—This tells the WMI subsystem how often to poll for the event in seconds. Shortening this increases the frequency of polling, giving you more up-to-date events while creating more network traffic. Lengthening this value means less bandwidth but less up-to-date events. Tune this based on your requirements. Generally, 10 seconds is considered very short. Settings of minutes or hours are possible and useful for tasks you need to do only two or three times a day.

- WHERE Targetinstance—This is the WHERE clause to filter on certain attributes of the instance that is creating the event. In this case, you only want the event if it's being generated by an instance of a CIM_DirectoryContainsFile class and the directory is the one specified.

The WMIEventWatcher.dtsx package in the S08-StockTasks sample solution uses the preceding query to watch a directory for any new files that get created there. To see this package in action, load it and then modify the SAMPLES::TEMPDRIVE and SAMPLES::TEMP-FOLDER to point to the location where you want to drop files. Run the package and drop a file or create a new one in the directory you specify. The task returns when it receives the event.

WMI Event Watcher Task Peculiarities
The WMI Event Watcher Task generates custom events that can be handled by event handlers. To see this, select the WMI Event Watcher Task and then click the Event Handlers tab. Next, click on the Event Handler drop down. Notice that there are two nonstandard events listed there: WMIEventWatcherEventOccurred and WMIEventWatcherEventTimedOut.

Another interesting peculiarity with the WMI Event Watcher Task is that it can execute once, multiple times, or forever depending on how you configure it. It's possible to configure it to raise the event each time it receives the WMI event and then continue executing.

Web Services Task
Web services is a technology designed to aid in the distribution and sharing of information by connecting disparate, standalone, and remote systems. There are web services that provide monetary exchange rates, credit card validation, stock quotes, weather information, nucleotide sequences, measurement and temperature conversions, document searches and delivery, web searches, and many more. The Web Services Task makes it possible to tap into these and other web services resources.

The WebService.dtsx package in the S08-StockTasks sample solution uses a web service to retrieve the stock price for a given company. This is a simple example of the kinds of web services that are available.

The Web Services Task is installed with Integration Services and it should not need any additional settings or configuration. You do, of course, need an Internet connection to use it.

Setting Up the Web Services Task
To set up the Web Services Task, first create an HTTP connection. Figure 8.21 shows the HTTP Connection Manager UI with the correct URL specified for the delayed stock quote

service. The URL for the connection should point to the web services URL, which typically takes the following form:

```
http://ws.domain.com/servicename/servicename.asmx?wsdl
```

This web service does not require credentials or a certificate. If you're using a proxy that
requires credentials, you can enter those on the Proxy tab.

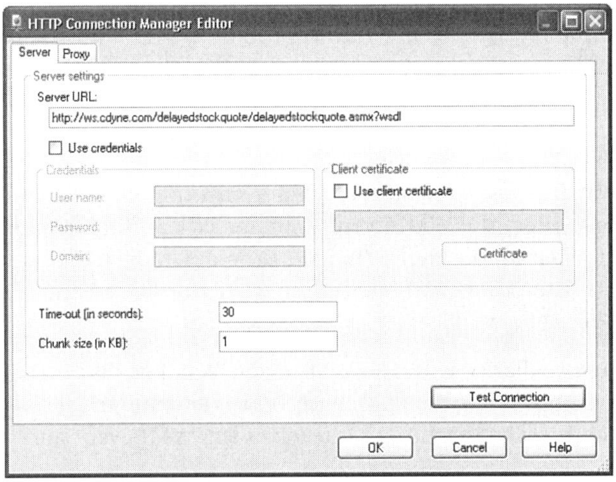

FIGURE 8.21   The Web Services Task requires an HTTP Connection Manager.

To ensure that the package can correctly find the WSDL files, the WSDLFile property has a
property expression that builds the path to the files in the SAMPLES folder. The property
expression that builds the path to the stock quote web service is as follows:

```
@[SAMPLES::ROOTWD] + "\\SampleData\\StockQuotes.wsdl"
```

If you've correctly configured the ROOTWD variable with the environment variable configuration, the package finds the WSDL automatically.

Initially Retrieving the WSDL File
A button on the Web Services Task UI on the General tab allows you to download the
WSDL file. To enable the Download WSDL button, type the fully qualified name that you
want to use for the file in the WSDLFile property and press the Enter button. This enables
the Download WSDL button. If the OverwriteWSDLFile property is set to TRUE, clicking
the DownloadWSDL button downloads the WSDL file to the location you specified in the
WSDLFile property.

After you enter the WSDLFile and HTTP connection, as shown in Figure 8.22, you need to
give input on the Input tab. The contents of the Input tab change based on the web
methods available for the web service. A web service can provide more than one service,
so the service property allows you to select which service you want to use.

FIGURE 8.22   Specify the HTTP Connection Manager and WSDL on the General tab.

In the delayed stock quote example shown in Figure 8.23, only one is available, the DelayedStockQuote service. Four methods are available for this service. The sample uses the GetQuote method. As the method changes, the method selection also changes to reflect the parameters required for the method you've selected. In the sample, MSFT is entered to see how flat the Microsoft stock curve is. This web service requires a zero for the LicenseKey for trial users.

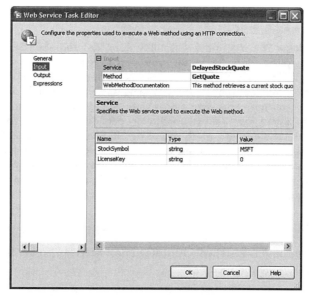

FIGURE 8.23   Specify the service, method, and parameters on the Input tab.

The Output tab provides a way to store the results of the Web Method invocation to a file or an SSIS variable. If the output type is set to Variable, the second property is named Variable and allows you to either pick an existing SSIS variable or create a new one to hold the results. If the output type is File Connection, the second property is named File and allows you to select an existing file connection or create a new one.

When executed, the sample package executes the Web Services Task, retrieves the quote, loads it into a variable called SAMPLES::STOCKQUOTE, and then uses a Script Task to parse the returned XML stored in the variable to get the quote.

Passing Parameters

The Web Services Task does not provide a way to dynamically provide parameters for the web method via variables or property expressions. This was an unfortunate oversight by Microsoft and will likely be fixed in the next service pack. For the immediate future, parameters must be entered directly.

Execute Package Task

The Execute Package Task is conceptually very simple. Its primary purpose is to execute other packages. However, this simplicity belies the importance of the task because it can be used to reduce complexity and simplify solutions. In any complex system, the key to understanding the entire system is to understand its constituent parts in decreasingly complex chunks. Likewise, the Execute Package Task can be used to break down complex packages into simpler, more comprehensible packages, thus reducing the overall complexity of the entire system.

REUSING PACKAGE PIECES

The Execute Package Task is also the reusability story for Integration Services 2005. Often, you'll have pieces of packages that you want to reuse over and over again in different packages. For example, you might have a pattern that names files with a naming convention and you want to use that same pattern in multiple packages. You could copy and paste those "package pieces" into all the packages where you need that pattern, but then, if you later want to update any part of the pattern, you'd have to modify it in all the locations into which you pasted it. The more manageable solution is to place those package pieces you want to reuse into a standalone package. Then, you can execute the package containing the pattern with the Execute Package Task wherever you would have pasted the package pieces. Need to update the pattern? Just change the package where it is stored, and all the packages that call it will then be updated as well.

The Execute Package Task is installed with Integration Services. To use this task, you need only have a child package to execute.

Setting Up the Execute Package Task

The key setting for this task is the Location property on the Package tab. The Execute Package Task can execute packages stored in SQL Server 2005 instances or on the file system. Select the location from which to load the package. If you select File System, you'll need to create a File Connection Manager to point to the package file. If you select SQL Server, use an existing OLEDB Connection Manager or create a new one to load it. The Password property can be used to store the password for the child package if it has been saved with one of the Encrypt with Password package-protection options.

CAUTION

Microsoft felt it was important to protect the sensitive data often stored in packages and decided to only perform SQL Server operations when using an encrypted channel. Integration Services does not support saving packages to SQL Server 2000 because it does not provide connections with an encrypted channel. Therefore, if you attempt to connect to a SQL Server 2000 instance, it fails with the following error:

```
An OLE DB error 0x80004005 (Client unable to establish connection) occurred
while enumerating packages. A SQL statement was issued and failed.
```

This can be fairly difficult to diagnose, especially if you're running instances of SQL Server 2000 or earlier versions on the same machine. If you see this error while attempting to enumerate the packages on the server, double-check that the instance you're pointing to is indeed a SQL Server 2005 instance.

Figure 8.24 shows the Execute Package Task UI open with the Select Package dialog box open. The packages shown in the Select Package dialog box are stored in SQL Server in MSDB in the sysdtspackages90 table.

You can also execute maintenance plan packages with the Execute Package Task. These are packages you create in the Database Maintenance Editor in SQL Server Management Studio. The Select Package dialog box shows the Maintenance Plan packages as well, which are also stored in the sysdtspackages90 table.

VARIABLES AND THE EXECUTE PACKAGE TASK

When using the Execute Package Task, the child package might need to use a variable from the parent package. Although conceptually this is quite simple, all variables that are visible to the Execute Package Task in the parent package are visible to the package that it executes. In reality, it's a little more complicated. Several factors create problems when using parent package variables in child packages. Validation is problematic for those components in the child package that validate that the variable is available at validation time because the subpackage doesn't always have access to the parent package's variables during validation. Also, child packages that reference parent package variables will not successfully run as standalone packages because the parent variable won't be available, ever.

In most cases, the solution to these problems is to use parent package configurations. Simply put, parent package configurations configure a child package variable with the value from a parent package variable. For more information, see Chapter 14, "Configuring and Deploying Solutions."

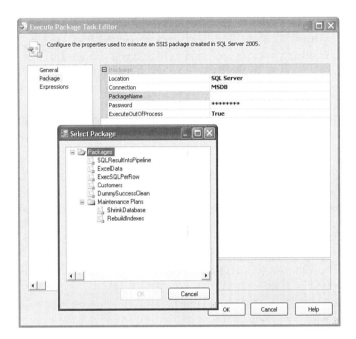

FIGURE 8.24   You can execute packages on the file system as well as in MSDB.

TIP

You should be careful how you set up your package-protection options. If you set the parent package-protection option to Do Not Save Sensitive and the child package-protection option is one of the two Save with Password options, the parent package will be unable to execute the child package. This is because the parent package stores the password of the child package as part of the Execute Package Task information. But, with the Do Not Save Sensitive package-protection option, which is the default, the parent package will lose the password and will be unable to open the child package successfully. Other interesting and problematic settings are also possible, such as when executing packages stored with a user key, and so on. Pay close attention to the package-protection option. If the parent package cannot open the child package, chances are you've got a conflicting package-protection option setting.

Executing Out of Process

The ExecuteOutOfProcess property tells IS to run the package in a host process outside of the parent package process. When run out of process, the package is hosted in dtshost.exe. While running a package out of process, you might see one or more dtshost.exe processes in the Windows Task Manager.

The advantage of running out of process is more available memory for the package. All packages running in the same process must share the same 2GB of memory on 32-bit systems. Running out of process, the full 2GB of memory is available for the single package.

The decision about whether to execute the child package in process or out of process should really be made based on whether you're using child packages to reduce complexity as described previously or to gain some memory space for the child packages. If you're using child packages to better structure your solution and eliminate complexity, executing in process is likely the better choice. However, if your child packages are memory intensive, for example, they contain Data Flow Tasks that perform memory-intense operations, such as sorts, aggregations, or lookups, running out of process might be the right choice.

CAUTION

If you have multiple Execute Package Tasks in a package, you have the option of running the package without the debugging environment of the Business Intelligence Development Studio if you don't need to set breakpoints or use watches. A lot is going on in the designer when you debug a package. The designer launches debugging windows and manages breakpoints, for example. For each child package, the designer creates another window to display the child package. This increases the load on the designer and slows it down. You can execute the package without debugging by using the Start Without Debugging menu item or by pressing [Ctrl+F5]. This executes the package using dtexec instead and eliminates much of the designer overhead.

The `ExecPackage.dtsx` sample package in the S08-StockTasks sample solution executes a child package stored in the `SAMPLES\SampleData` folder called `SimplePackage.dtsx`. The child package shows a string that it receives via a parent package configuration. The parent package references the child package with a file connection manager with a property expression that builds the folder and package file name. Note that the value of the `SAMPLES::ParentVariableValue` variable is "default," but when the Script Task shows the value of that variable, it has changed to whatever the value of the `SAMPLES::ParentVariable` is when you execute the parent package. Change the value of the `SAMPLES::ParentVariable` and watch the value change in the message box. This is a simple example of how to set up the Execute Package Task and use parent package configurations to pass in parent package variables such as parameters to the child package.

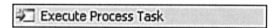

Execute Process Task

The Execute Process Task provides a way for the package to launch a process, pass parameters to the process, and return the results to the package. Although it can be used to launch applications with a graphical user interface, it is generally used to execute batch files or command-line utilities such as the command-based script host `cscript.exe` because packages typically run in the back office without any human intervention. The stock tasks covered here generally provide the gamut of features required for a large percentage of workflow and ETL processing requirements, but occasionally it's nice to have a way to use system utilities to accomplish tasks that IS doesn't directly support. The Execute Process Task provides the simple means to do this while capturing the results for use in the package.

Setting Up the Execute Process Task

This is one of the simpler tasks to configure because it's really just a matter of entering the same commands that you'd type on the command line were you to execute the utility there. The twist is that the task provides a way to enter the parameters, working directory, and arguments separately from the executable. This gives some flexibility for entering the parameters and makes it possible to use property expressions to populate the settings.

The standard and error output results of the utility can be captured in IS variables by specifying a variable of type string in the StandardOutputVariable and StandardErrorVariable properties. This way, whatever output you would normally see from the utility in the command prompt gets captured in the variables you specify. If the utility fails, chances are the error output will contain information about the failure. If the program requires input, it can also be provided via the StandardInputVariable property. If the utility you're launching takes input from the command-line prompt, this property can be used to provide it. For example, some utilities take the output of one command-line utility and process it; findstr is a good example of this.

The task also has a way of detecting whether the command line succeeded. Most command-line utilities return an error level of zero for success and numbers greater than zero for failure, but you can't count on that. A few even document what their error levels are, but generally you're left to guess. The following simple batch file shows the error level for a utility given different inputs and can be found in the Samples\Script folder in the sample files available at www.samspublishing.com.

```
@ECHO OFF
%1 %2
ECHO =======================
ECHO The Error level was : %errorlevel%
ECHO =======================
```

Type this into a .bat or .cmd file named ErrorLevelBatchFile.bat and then launch it, passing the name of the utility and a parameter similar to the following:

```
ErrorLevelBatchFile Dir X:\
```

There isn't an X: drive on the example machine, so the batch file prints out:

```
The system cannot find the path specified.
.
=======================
The Error level was : 1
=======================
```

This is a quick-and-dirty way to find out what the success and some of the failure error levels are for StandardOutputVariable and a command-line utility. Obviously, if the utility adequately documents the error levels, that's even better.

The Sample Package

Figure 8.25 shows the Execute Process Task as it is configured in the sample package provided in the S08 sample solution. The sample uses a utility that is available on Windows called systeminfo.exe. When diagnosing problems with packages, it's often helpful to have information about the machine on which the package was executed. This information can be sent to logs as part of the error-handling processing for failed packages or tasks or just as part of the regular preexecution processing for all packages as a sort of package execution header. The systeminfo utility does a quick job of gathering information about the machine that includes germane points, such as operating system details, chipset, BIOS, hot fixes installed, virtual and available memory statistics, domain and user details, as well as other important system information.

FIGURE 8.25   The Execute Process Task executes command-line utilities.

The sample package executes the systeminfo utility and then captures the results in a variable called SYSTEMINFOOUTPUT. The next Execute Process Task passes those results into the findstr utility, which filters the input to find the registered owner and organization entries returned from the systeminfo utility and captures the results in the variable called FINDSTROUTPUT. Then, using a Script Task, the package logs the information to the configured log text file and shows the information in a message box. Make sure you have the SSISSAMPLESWORKINGFOLDER environment variable correct. The folder to which it points is where the log file will be created.

This pattern can be reused in your packages to capture machine information that's useful for postmortem analysis of failed packages or simply to document where packages are running. It's a nice way to get information because it's real time and will always be up to date and accurate, even if the package is executed on different machines. One way to use it in your packages is to create an `OnPreExecute` event handler with an Execute Package Task that calls this package.

Also, you can adjust the package to suit your needs. Perhaps you don't want all the information that systeminfo provides so you can change the findstr command to include more or different information or simply eliminate it altogether and log all the information. If you do incorporate the package into your packages, make sure you remove the line of code in the Script Task that shows the message box and configure the child package to use the parent package log settings. Using this pattern, all your packages can self-document the environment on which they're running.

> **TIP**
>
> The sample package illustrates one way you can link multiple Execute Package Tasks together to accomplish functionality on par with that provided by a custom task or Script Task. If you're thinking of using a Script Task to accomplish something, look around to see if there isn't a command-line utility that already does what you want. In general, the less coding you have in your package, the easier it will be to understand and manage.

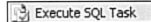

The Execute SQL Task

The Execute SQL Task, or SQL Task for short, provides a way to execute SQL script or stored procedures against SQL Server or other databases. The SQL Task is commonly used to build tables, query data or metadata, execute DDL commands, and to insert and delete data in preparation for other data operations like the bulk insert or Data Flow Tasks. The SQL Task can pass input and output parameters to SQL script and stored procedures and capture the results in variables.

> **CAUTION**
>
> The Execute SQL Task does not support every type of query available in the source database. For example, OPENROWSET BULK statements that execute without error in SQL Server Management Studio will fail with an error in the SQL Task.

You need to have access to either a database or an Excel file to use the SQL Task, which connects to databases or other data sources through various connection manager types.

Setting Up the Execute SQL Task

Figure 8.26 shows the settings for the SQL Task in the `ExecSQL.dtsx` sample package in the S08 sample solution that does a simple join between two tables in the AdventureWorks sample database.

2008 VSAHA
State Tournament

ONE DAY PASS

DATE:

Adult (18+) $2
Child (8-17) $1
Host: Middlebury

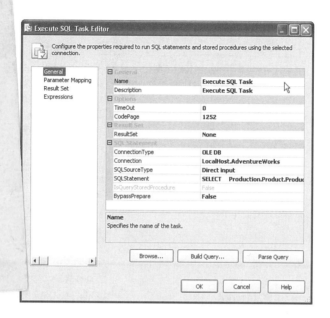

FIGURE 8.26   The Execute SQL Task General tab is where you input the SQL script.

The General tab contains the most commonly used and mandatory settings. This is where you input the SQL script and other important properties. Table 8.7 details the important settings on the General tab.

TABLE 8.7   The General Tab Settings

Setting	Options	Description
TimeOut	0—Infinite	
N—Number of seconds to wait before the task will time out	This is the timeout for the query and is passed into the connection when executing the statement. The timeout applies to the query, not the execution time of the task.	
ResultSet	Single Row, Full Result Set, XML, None	This controls how the query results get returned.
Connection Type	OLEDB, ADO.NET, ODBC, ADO, EXCEL, SQLMOBILE	This specifies what connection manager type to use.

TABLE 8.7   Continued

Setting	Options	Description
`Connection`	Create New, select an existing connection manager	This is a key setting in which you specify which connection manager the task should use. Some settings in the task will be impacted by this setting. For example, `IsQueryStoredProcedure` is only enabled when ADO connection types are selected.
`SQLSourceType`	Direct Input, File Connection, Variable	This is a key setting and specifies where the SQL query or stored procedure will come from. If File Connection, the SQL Task will open the file and read the query from it.
SQLStatement	SQL script	This contains the SQL or the name of the stored procedure and any parameter markers if needed.
File Connection	Name of file connection	If the SQLSourceType is File Connection, this setting becomes available and points to which file connection to use for opening the SQL script file.
`BypassPrepare`	True, False	This setting is only available for OLEDB connections and provides the option to bypass the prepare phase and directly execute the query. Prepared execution is an optimization that attempts to reduce the overhead of compiling the script by reusing existing compiled execution plans. In SQL Server 2000 and 2005, direct execution attempts to reuse existing plans so the benefits of preparation are reduced. However, if you will be executing the SQL Task within a loop, setting `BypassPrepare` to `FALSE` (default) can improve performance.

TIP

If you're attempting to retrieve the resultset from the SQL Task in managed code, it will likely be an exercise in frustration because the SQL Task has some portions written in native code, particularly those parts that deal with native data access layers like OLEDB and ODBC and will return native ADO recordsets when using those native connection types. If you want to have a managed dataset returned, use the ADO.NET Connection Manager type, which returns a managed type and can be manipulated easily in the Script Task or other component written in managed code.

The Browse button allows you to search for a SQL script file to open. When you select a file with SQL script using this method, the SQL Task UI opens the file and retrieves the entire contents into the SQLStatement property. Consequently, this method only works when opening files with nothing but valid SQL script or if you modify the script after reading it in to make it correct.

The Build Query button opens the query designer. Figure 8.27 shows the query designer with the query from the ExecSQL.dtsx sample package. In this environment, you can add tables, draw relationships between them for joins, choose columns to select, and test your queries.

FIGURE 8.27   The query designer makes it easy to build SQL queries.

The Parse Query button is a quick way to check that the query is valid. This button is only useful if the connection type is OLEDB and BypassPrepare is set to FALSE because the feature uses the prepare function of OLEDB to perform the parse. The parse does not have side effects. In other words, it only parses the statement; it does not execute it.

It's possible to successfully run the SQL Task with only the General tab settings configured and, in some cases, such as when you're creating tables or inserting data, it is sufficient. However, if you want to retrieve rows of data or pass in parameters to queries or stored procedures, you need to configure the other tabs as well.

Mapping Parameters

Mapping parameters has been a stumbling block for many users. It can be confusing. The biggest problem is the format. Depending on the connection manager type the SQL Task uses, the format of the parameters changes. Another problem is that there are some elements of the query that can be parameterized and some that cannot and it's not always clear how to distinguish between the two.

ANSI-SQL allows only certain elements to be parameterized. Metadata structures such as column names and table names cannot be parameterized, only those elements that are the equivalent of constants. If you attempt to parameterize a query, you might get an error similar to the following:

```
Error: 0xC002F210 at Execute SQL Task, SQL Task: Executing the query "SELECT * INTO
➥[TableNameParameter] FROM ?" failed with the following error: "Syntax
➥error or access violation". Possible failure reasons: Problems with the
➥query, "ResultSet" property not set correctly, parameters not set
➥correctly, or connection not established correctly.
```

Chances are good that you've attempted to parameterize an element that is not supported by SQL. Integration Services provides two ways of performing parameter substitution. The first is the traditional method using parameter markers, such as the ? character to mark where the parameter should be inserted, which is limited by the ANSI-SQL substitution rules noted previously. For those cases in which you want more flexibility in building queries, you can use property expressions to perform the parameter substitutions, building the query as a string. The SQL Task does no parsing of the query. It simply passes the query string and the parameters, if provided, along to the data access layer underlying the connection manager. Therefore, the formats for parameters are based on the connection type. The formats for each connection manager type are detailed in Table 8.8.

TABLE 8.8   Connection Managers and Substitution Parameters for Queries

Connection Manager Type	Parameter Marker	Parameter Name	Example Query	Example Parameter Name
OLEDB	?	0 1 ...	SELECT Name FROM People WHERE Name LIKE ?	0

TABLE 8.8   Continued

Connection Manager Type	Parameter Marker	Parameter Name	Example Query	Example Parameter Name

ADO.NET	@Varname	@Varname	`SELECT Name`
			`FROM people`
			`WHERE Name`
			`LIKE @Name`
				@Name

ADO	?	@Param1
		@Param2 ...
			`SELECT Name`
			`From People`
			`WHERE Name LIKE ?`
				@Param1

ODBC	?	1
		2 ...
			`SELECT Name`
			`FROM People`
			`WHERE Name Like ?`
				1

The sample package `ExecSQL.dtsx` in the S08-StockTasks solution shows how to set up the SQL Task for each of the connection types in Table 8.8. As you can see, the way you set up the parameter replacements for each of the different connection manager types is quite different. Notice that all the data access layers except ADO.NET use '?' as the parameter marker and that the OLEDB parameter names start with 0 as the first name, whereas ODBC starts with 1. This is why people get confused. Hopefully, this scheme is simplified in the next release of the SQL Task. For calling stored procedures, the setup is almost identical with the exceptions that for ADO.NET connection types, you do not specify the parameter markers in the query and you set the `IsQueryStoredProcedure` property to `TRUE`.

The sample package queries the AdventureWorks sample database using replacement parameters stored in the `SAMPLES::DESCRIPTIONMATCH` and `SAMPLES::NAMEMATCH` variables. The results are placed into a collection that the `Foreach Loop` enumerates and the values are placed in the `SYSTEM::PRODUCTNAME` and `SYSTEM::PRODUCTDESCRIPTION` local variables, which the Script Task picks up and displays in a message box. This sample package is not intended to demonstrate best practices, but rather to illustrate how to configure the SQL Task to use parameters with the different connection manager types. You can change the values of the input variables and otherwise modify the package to learn a little more about how parameterized queries work in the SQL Task.

RETAIN SAME CONNECTION

This is probably a good time to talk about the `RetainSameConnection` property on connection managers. The reason connection managers are called that instead of just connections is because they do a little more than just return a physical connection as they did in DTS. The problem with that design was that tasks in the workflow that used the same connection would be serialized. The advantage to this design is that objects like temp tables and SQL transactions whose lifetimes are bound to the lifetime of the connection will live as long as the connection is active. For DTS, the connection might stay alive for the duration of the package.

With Integration Services Connection Managers, you can have it both ways. By default, the connection manager generates a new physical connection on each `AcquireConnection` call. The benefit is that multiple tasks and components can use the same connection manager without worrying about serializing the workflow. This also frees some space in the Connections window of the designer. However, when the need arises, it's still possible to emulate DTS behavior and retain the same connection for the life of the package by setting the `RetainSameConnection` property to `TRUE`. See Chapter 25 for an example of how to use this property to create and use a SQL transaction across multiple tasks.

CAUTION

You should be aware that the default transaction isolation level for the SQL Task is serializable. This level creates the greatest isolation from other transactions and is the safest. However, this is different than the DTS default, which was Read Committed, which is more performant but not as safe. The decision to make the default serializable was in the interest of defaulting to the safest level. If you experience performance degradation in your queries from what you saw in DTS, you might try changing this setting to see the benefits.

The Scripting Tasks

The Script Task is very important because it provides flexibility, quick extensibility, and a compromise option for gaps in functionality left between stock tasks and custom tasks. Scripting tasks provide a way to implement a custom task without the effort and discipline of building a full-fledged component. The Script Task takes care of the details so that you can concentrate on writing only the necessary code to accomplish the work at hand.

Former DTS users know that the Script Task in DTS was used frequently, in almost every package and was often employed to implement loops and configure the package. This is not the case in Integration Services. Most work you need to do in a workflow can be accomplished using IS features, such as configurations, deployment, property expressions, and stock tasks, or through a combination of those features. So, the Script Task is now generally used to implement what are essentially package-bound custom tasks.

This chapter covers the stock tasks, so we've included a Script Task entry for completeness and consistency; however, the Script Task is quite complex and too important to attempt coverage here. For detailed coverage of the Script Task, see Chapter 15, "Using the Script Task."

ActiveX Script Task

The ActiveX Script Task

The ActiveX Script Task remains essentially the same as it existed in DTS. It has been provided as a backward-compatibility option but should under very few circumstances be used for new development because it will be deprecated in the very near future. Script running in this task is interpreted and, therefore, much slower than comparable code running in the new Script Task. When the Migration Wizard attempts to migrate DTS packages that contain ActiveX Script Tasks, it creates an ActiveX Script Task as a target where it can store the script from the task in the DTS package. This should not be considered an encouragement to use it, however. You should eliminate the ActiveX Task from your migrated packages as soon as possible.

The Data-Processing Tasks

The tasks in this group transform and/or move data in some way. The data-processing tasks are special and deserve their own grouping if for no other reason than to distinguish the Data Flow Task, which is arguably the most important feature in this release of Integration Services. Several chapters of this book focus exclusively on the Data Flow Task, so it is not covered in detail here. See Chapters 19 through 23 for more information about the Data Flow Task.

Bulk Insert Task

Bulk Insert Task

The Bulk Insert Task is provided as a way to quickly load large amounts of data from flat files into SQL Server. The Bulk Insert Task provides a simple way to insert data using the BULK INSERT T-SQL command. The SSIS Bulk Insert Task is provided as a backward-compatibility feature to ease migration into SSIS from DTS. It will likely be deprecated in coming versions.

No Longer Preferred

In DTS, using the Bulk Insert Task was the preferred way to do large bulk loads because it takes advantage of the performance gains using the T-SQL BULK INSERT command. With Integration Services, however, it is recommended to use the Data Flow Task. The Data Flow Task has numerous advantages over the Bulk Insert Task, which has rigid limitations on how it can consume and insert data. The Data Flow Task can bulk load data with comparable performance, especially if using the SQL Server Destination Adapter, while providing much more flexibility.

The SQL Server Destination Adapter and Bulk Insert   What's the connection? The SQL Server Destination Adapter uses the same interface into SQL Server as the Bulk Insert Task. So, although you get the same performance as you do with the Bulk Insert Task, with the Data Flow Task and the SQL Server Destination Adapter, you also get a whole lot more flexibility.

The following is a list of considerations to be aware of when using the Bulk Insert Task versus the Data Flow Task:

- The Bulk Insert Task can only transfer data from text CSV or similarly formatted flat files, whereas the Data Flow Task can transfer data from many source systems.

- Only members of the sysadmin or bulkadmin fixed server roles can run a package containing the Bulk Insert Task. Because the SQL Server Destination Adapter also uses the bulk insert API, its use is constrained by the same requirements. Other adapters also have similar security constraints but can output to multiple target systems.

- The Bulk Insert Task can only insert data into SQL Server tables, whereas the Data Flow Task can output to multiple target systems.

- For maximum control, you should use format files. (You can generate format files using the BCP utility.) The Data Flow Task does not use format files.

- The Bulk Insert Task does not have metadata or format discovery features like the Data Flow Task.

- The Bulk Insert Task has some limitations when importing empty double quoted fields, whereas the Data Flow Task does not.

- Only views in which all columns refer to the same base table can be bulk loaded. The Data Flow Task has no such limitations.

THE BULK INSERT TASK INSIDE

The Bulk Insert Task is a wrapper task around the T-SQL Bulk Insert statement. The task generates the Bulk Insert statement from the properties set on the task and then sends it to the server where it will be executed. Therefore, all the limitations that apply to the Bulk Insert T-SQL statement also apply to the Bulk Insert Task.

Because the Data Flow Task replaces the features provided by the Bulk Insert Task, it is recommended to use the Data Flow Task for bulk-loading scenarios. The Data Flow Task is easier to set up, just as performant for straight bulk inserts, and more flexible.

XML Task

The XML Task provides a way to perform various operations on XML and XML documents. The XML Task can validate the XML against an XML Schema Definition (XSD) or

Document Type Definition (DTD), apply an XSL transformation, retrieve element or attribute values with XPath, merge two different XML documents together, show differences between XML documents, and perform patch operations.

The XML Task is installed with the rest of Integration Services and does not have any special requirements or external dependencies to properly function.

Setting Up the XML Task

The sample package XML.dtsx in the S08-StockTasks solution performs an XSL transformation on a package you select or configure. It finds the executables, connection managers, and variables in the package and generates a very simple HTML report with a list of these package contents. The XSLT file itself is quite simple and should serve, with a little effort, as a starting point for anyone wanting to build an autodocumentation or metadata feature for their packages. The package shows how to set up the XML Task to perform an XSLT operation. If placed in a Foreach Loop with a ForeachFile Enumerator pointing to your package store, it would be possible to build reports for all of your packages with one package run.

Figure 8.28 shows the XML Task from the sample package with the OperationType "XSLT" selected. The XML Task uses three connection managers. The first is the file connection manager named PackageToReportOn. As the name implies, it points to the folder where the package is stored that will be processed with the XSLT. The second connection manager is the file connection manager named ReportHTMLFile, which points to the temporary location to store the resulting HTML report. The third connection manager is the file connection manager with the name XSLT File, which points to the location of the XSLT to apply to the package to generate the report.

CAUTION

Make sure you've defined the SSISSAMPLESWORKING environment variable to point to a temporary folder for the resulting HTML file. The package uses property expressions to build the fully qualified file path.

Task-Specific Peculiarities or Nonstandard Settings

The key setting for the XML Task is the OperationType. In fact, the visible property set changes quite drastically depending on which operation type you select. The other settings that can be a little confusing are the SecondOperandType and SecondOperand. These two properties express the information needed for all operations. For example, for the Merge operation, the second operand is the file to be merged with the primary file. For the XSLT operation, the second operand is the XSLT file, and so on. Table 8.9 lists the second operands and their function.

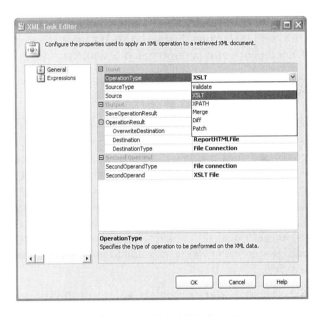

FIGURE 8.28   The XML Task performs multiple XML functions.

TABLE 8.9   Second Operands and Their Function

Operation Type	Second Operand Function
Merge	Provides the XML file or text to be merged with the primary XML (specified by the Source property)
Diff	Provides the XML file or text to be compared with the primary XML
Patch	Provides the Diffgram document to be merged with the primary XML
XSLT	Provides the XSLT document to be used to transform the primary XML
XPath	Provides the XPath query to be used to retrieve nodes or text from the primary XML
Validate	Provides the DTD or XSD to be used to validate the primary XML

The XML Task is fairly flexible and can be used in many ways to process or retrieve information from XML files or text. The XML can be stored in a variable, in a file, or directly entered into the source property.

TIP

A common complaint about the XML Task is that it cannot "pipeline" operations or perform multiple serial operations on XML. But, this is not true. Actually, this is one of the reasons the XML Task supports storing the XML in a variable. To efficiently apply multiple operations to one XML document, you can simply output the XML text to a variable and then use the same variable as the input for the next XML Task.

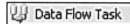

Data Flow Task

The Data Flow Task supports one to many simultaneous and heterogeneous source connections to data from different source systems and media types. This data can be routed through one or more transformations executing in parallel out to zero to many different destination systems and media types. The Data Flow Task is the heart of Integration Services, where the bulk of the data processing, integration, and transformation happens.

The Data Flow Task is extremely important and several chapters are dedicated to describing it. Like the Script Task, this chapter included a Data Flow Task entry for completeness and consistency; however, the Data Flow Task is quite complex and too important to attempt coverage here. For detailed coverage of the Data Flow Task, see Chapters 18 through 23.

Summary

Integration Services ships with many useful tasks. Microsoft tried to make the task user interfaces and working models similar across tasks so that they're easier to learn and use consistently. The array of stock tasks is impressive and powerful. Yet, if the offering still doesn't cover your needs, the Script Task is available to quickly and easily implement your own task behavior. Further, you have the ability to easily build your own custom task if you want.

Using Expressions

"IT'S IMPOSSIBLE TO OVERSTATE JUST HOW POWERFUL EXPRESSIONS CAN BE IN AN SSIS SOLUTION. GOTTA BE MY FAVORITE FEATURE OF SSIS, I RECKON."—JAMIE THOMSON

Package expressions are a feature that allows simple expressions to be used in various parts of a package. They are a very important feature of Integration Services because they simplify packages by facilitating surgical, intelligent, dynamic, and subtle adjustments to the flow and settings of the package. Understanding how to use expressions is critical to creating effective packages and getting the most from Integration Services. This chapter is a gentle introduction to package expressions. Appendix B, "Expression Syntax and Cookbook," covers more detailed descriptions of expression evaluator functions and syntax.

The expression syntax is a combination of operators and math, string, and T-SQL like functions. See Appendix B for a listing of the expression functions and operators. Expressions can use package variables and can perform useful functions, such as concatenating strings, calculating dates, building unique filenames, or generating unique numbers. Package expressions can be found on virtually every object in Integration Services, but how they are used and when they are evaluated is different depending on where the expression is found. There are several types of package expressions, as follows:

- Property expressions
- Data flow property expressions

- Variable expressions

- Precedence constraint expressions

- For Loop expressions

- Data flow transformation expressions

Expression Basics

Package expressions provide a straightforward way to express a computation. The expression can be as simple as the sum of two numbers, as mundane as parsing a string to remove prefixes, suffixes, and spaces, or as complex as determining the total miles to award frequent fliers based on their frequent flier plans. Complex expressions are combinations of ever simpler expressions, and simple expressions are combinations of functions, literals, casts, operators, variables, and columns.

For example, the expression 1 + @Count is a simple expression constructed from a combination of a literal, the number 1, the operator +, and the variable Count indicated by the @ character. This expression tells the Expression Evaluator to add the literal 1 and the value of the variable Count.

More complex expressions can be built up from simple expressions. For example, the following expression builds a string with the current date and then appends the .csv file extension to create a filename:

```
RIGHT("0" + (DT_STR, 2, 1253)  MONTH( GETDATE()), 2) +
RIGHT("0" + (DT_STR, 2, 1253) DAY( GETDATE()), 2) +
(DT_STR, 4, 1253)  YEAR( GETDATE()  ) +
".csv"
```

This expression gets the date using the GETDATE() function, and prepends a zero to the month and day parts of the date. This is so that if the month or day is one digit, it has a zero prefixed to make a string like "02" or "09." However, if the month is already a two-digit number, the prepended zero is ignored because the RIGHT() function only takes the last two characters. The year is always a four-digit number and is returned as is. All date parts are dates and so they need to be converted to strings with the DT_STR cast. Chapter 22, "Advanced Data Flow Transformations," covers casting in detail, but for now, you should understand that the Expression Evaluator strictly applies type to all operations. All values must be explicitly cast to the type expected by functions if the two differ, or when using operators between two different types, one of the values must be cast to the type of the other.

Expression Functions

Four types of functions are available in this release of Integration Services:

- Mathematical—These include numeric functions and power functions.

- String—These include functions for parsing, finding, casing, and arranging strings.

- Date/Time—These include functions for getting whole dates or parts of dates.

- Null—These are special functions for dealing with the value NULL.

Literals

Literals are actual values that you directly input into the expression. There are Boolean, numeric, and string literals. Numeric and string literals are things like the number 1036, the string "War and Peace," and the float 7.35. Boolean literals can be expressed as the nonquoted and non–case sensitive strings TRUE and FALSE.

Casts

Casts are a way to coerce values of one type into another type. A text string like "10-03-1963" is obviously a date to any human, but to a computer, it's just text. Casting allows you to convert such strings into dates, numbers into strings, strings into floats, TRUE to a Boolean, and other such operations.

The Expression Evaluator is type sensitive because it's tightly bound to the way we do things in the Data Flow Task and is designed to be efficient, performant, and predictable. Casts minimize the guesswork the Expression Evaluator needs to do when confronted with two differing types. This also makes it easier to read an expression and know exactly what the resulting value and type will be.

Operators

Expression operators can be categorized into the following types (with example):

- Simple arithmetic: * (Multiplication)

- Logical: || (Logical OR)

- Bitwise or Binary: ! (Unary logical NOT)

- Grouping: ( ) (Parentheses)

- String: + (String concatenation)

- Comparison: == (Equal to)

- Assignment: = (Only available in For Loop Container expressions)

Variables

Variables can be referenced in expressions as long as they are in scope. For more about variables and variable scope, see Chapter 12, "The Venerable Variable." Variables are set apart in expressions by prefixing them with the @ character. All expression operations, casts, and functions can be used with variables.

Columns

In the SQL Server 2005 release, two data flow components support expressions. The derived column and conditional split transforms operate on columns on a row-by-row basis. In these transforms, the expression for a given column is evaluated for each row and a resulting operation is performed. To use the value of a specific column in the current row in an expression, you reference the column name separated by square brackets like this: [Column Name].

Property Expressions

Property expressions are as the name implies—expressions on properties. It is a way to have the value of a property automatically set to the result of an expression.

Suppose you want a property on a task to have the value of 42. You could simply set the property value directly by typing it into the task's user interface or into the property grid in the designer. Property expressions allow you to assign an expression to that property, for example 11+31. From that time forward, the value of the property is the result of the expression in the property—not the value you set. It is still 42, but the value of the property is actually the result of the expression, not a static value typed into the property directly. In addition, variables can be referenced in expressions. Because variable values can be set in so many ways—for example, configurations, other tasks, or the package writer—expressions can be applied in virtually unlimited ways to affect the execution of packages based on dynamic input from external influences. If you set a value of a property or variable, but the package seems to be using a different value, check to see if there are any property expressions for the variable or property because the current designer does not provide any indication where property expressions exist.

A Simple Example

Property expressions are easiest to understand when you see them in action. You can put property expressions to work in a simple example. You'll create an expression on the Send Mail Task that will generate the Subject line for the email that will reflect the execution time of a given package.

1. Start up the IS designer and create a new package.

2. Drag and drop a Send Mail Task onto the designer.

3. Right-click on the task, and select Properties from the shortcut menu.

4. In the Properties grid, click the Expressions property. An ellipsis button becomes visible.

5. Click the ellipsis button to open the Property Expressions Editor shown in Figure 9.1.

This is one way to access property expressions to a package.

TIP

On all stock tasks, you can also access the Property Expressions Editor from the task
user interface on the Expressions tab.

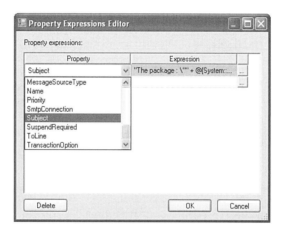

FIGURE 9.1   The Property Expressions Editor is used for adding property expressions.

Notice that there are two columns. The Property column allows you to select the property
you want to associate with an expression. The Expression column allows you to enter the
associated expression. There is also an ellipsis button next to the Expression field.
Although you can type or paste the expression directly into the field, select a property
and click on the ellipsis button to launch the Expression Builder dialog box shown in
Figure 9.2.

FIGURE 9.2   The Expression Builder dialog box simplifies expression building.

The Expression Builder dialog box has four main areas. The upper-left area is the Variables pane that lists all the variables in scope with the object where you are creating the property expression, in this case the Send Mail Task. The upper-right area is the Functions pane that shows all the available functions and operators for use in expressions. You can drag variables and functions from the Variables and Functions panes and drop them in the large window in the center of the Expression Builder, which is the Expression edit box. You can also directly modify the expression in the center Expression window.

When you finish your expression, you can click on the Evaluate Expression button to test your expression. If your expression is valid, the results of the expression show in the Evaluated Value box. If your expression has errors, an error dialog box opens with detailed errors.

Type in the following expression and click the Evaluate Expression button.

```
"The following package : " + @[System::PackageName] +
", started at : " +  (DT_WSTR, 20)@[System::StartTime]
```

If you correctly typed in the expression, you should get a result similar to the following:

```
The following package : SimpleExpression, started at : 7/1/2006 5:20:26 PM
```

If you want to see this in action, complete the rest of the properties on the Send Mail Task so that it successfully sends mail and executes the package. The email will have the updated Subject line with the time you ran the package. From this example, you can see how simple it is to add property expressions to your packages.

   Sample: This package is also available in the samples in the Chapter 9 subdirectory.

Accessing Property Expressions for Other Object Types

The pattern for adding property expressions is the same for containers, connection managers, log providers, and Foreach Enumerators as it is for tasks. However, where you access the property expressions for log providers and Foreach Enumerators is a little different.

Property expressions for log providers are only available in the Package Explorer tab. To add or edit property expressions for log providers, you must first add a log provider to the package. See Chapter 11, "Logging and the Stock Log Providers," for more information on setting up log providers. Select the Package Explorer tab at the top of the designer and then open the Log Providers node. Right-click on the log provider for which you want to add an expression and select Properties. You can click the ellipsis button for the expressions property to access the Property Expressions Editor, as shown in Figure 9.3.

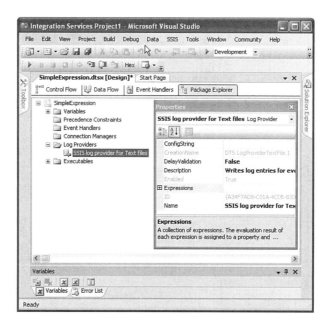

FIGURE 9.3   Property expressions for log providers are available in the properties grid for the log provider in the package explorer.

If you need to access the property expressions on Foreach Enumerators, open the Foreach Loop Editor by double-clicking on it. Click on the Collection tab and then select the expressions property as with other object types. Figure 9.4 shows the Collection tab in the Foreach Loop Editor with the expressions property selected.

> **CAUTION**
>
> In the left pane of the Foreach Loop Editor, there is also an Expressions tab. This tab allows you access to the Property Expressions Editor for the ForEach Loop, not the Foreach Enumerator. It's the same Property Expressions Editor you would get via the property grid for the ForEach Loop. It can be a bit confusing, but just remember that the property expressions for the Foreach Enumerator are only available on the Collection tab.

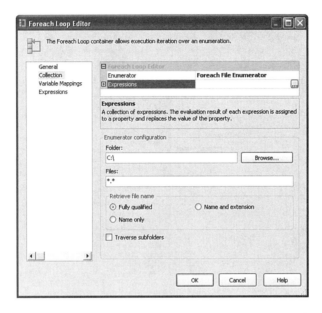

FIGURE 9.4   Property expressions for Foreach Enumerators are available in the properties grid on the Collection tab in the Foreach Loop Editor.

Data Flow Property Expressions

Although property expressions can be added to virtually all writable properties of containers, connection managers, log providers, Foreach Enumerators, and tasks, property expressions can only be added to a limited set of properties on certain data flow components. This feature was added very late and so it is limited to only a few components.

Table 9.1 lists the data flow components and their properties that can have expressions.

TABLE 9.1   Expressionable Data Flow Components

Component	Property	Description
XML Source	XMLData	Dynamically modifies the data processed
XML Source	XMLSchemaDefinition	Dynamically changes to reflect the XMLData
Fuzzy Grouping	MaxMemoryUsage	Allows flexibility for different load scenarios
Fuzzy Lookup	MaxMemoryUsage	Allows flexibility for different load scenarios
OLEDB Command	SqlCommand	Enables dynamically changing the dataset returned
PercentSampling	SamplingValue	Allows percent sampled to change or be turned off (set to 0)

TABLE 9.1   Continued

Component	Property	Description
Row Sampling	SamplingValue	Allows percent sampled to change or be turned off (set to 0)
Sort	MaximumThreads	Allows you to tune sort for varying loads, and so on
Unpivot	PivotKeyValue	Changes pivot results
Pivot	PivotKeyValue	Changes pivot results
Flat File Destination	Header	Allows flexible header modifications
SS Mobile Dest	TableName	Easily configures destination table to target
SQL Dest	Timeout	Allows you to change the timeout and is useful for debugging when server may not be available
Data Reader Source	SqlCommand	Dynamically modifies the data returned
Derived Column	Friendly Expression	Dynamically modifies the expression used to create data for column

Adding Data Flow Property Expressions

Data flow property expressions are handled the same as other tasks, but there is a twist. Because the Data Flow Task contains subcomponents, the properties on subcomponents are exposed as if they are properties of the Data Flow Task. The property name for subcomponents is exposed in the following form:

[Component Name].[Input|Output Name].[Column Name].[Property]

- **[Component Name]**—This is the name you see in the component when you look at the component in the data flow designer.

- **[Input|Output Name]**—This is the name of the input or output on which the column is found.

- **[Column Name]**—This is the column on which the property is found.

- **[Property]**—This is the property associated with the expression.

The derived column component happens to be one of the components that supports expressions on one of its properties. If you were to view the properties for the Data Flow Task, you would see a property similar to the one shown in Figure 9.5.

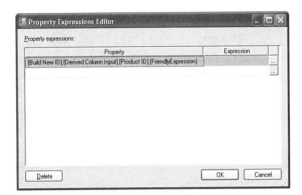

FIGURE 9.5   The four-part name for data flow component properties is shown in the Property Expressions Editor.

The four-part name is composed of the following elements:

- **[Build New ID]**—The name of the component

- **[Derived Column Input]**—The input name

- **[Product ID]**—The column ID

- **[Friendly Expression]**—The property name

PROPERTY EXPRESSIONS IN THE PIPELINE

Late in the Yukon development cycle, "property expressions in the pipeline" was a phrase that often caused grief and acrimony on the Integration Services team. In the beta 2 time frame, property expressions were quickly becoming an important feature in the runtime. We were beginning to see their power and real benefits. Adding property expressions to data flow components was fraught with technical challenges. Twice we attempted to find a design that would work in the data flow environment and failed. Each attempt resulted in long, painful, and sometimes contentious meetings with no satisfactory conclusions or workable designs. As we got closer and closer to beta 3 (June CTP), there were several bugs and customer requests that might easily be resolved if we just had "property expressions in the pipeline." One day, I approached Matt David, the technical lead for the Data Flow Task and started a discussion around the problem. Matt said, "I've been thinking about this a bit" or something similar. Sergei Ivanov walked over and said, "Did I hear someone say 'property expressions in the pipeline?'" Matt proposed his solution, and Sergei suggested options for how to make it work without modifying the user interface. This was very important at this time because we were, after all, trying to stabilize for beta 3. There was a bit of magic in the air that day. As we talked, Cim Ryan, the test lead for the Data Flow Task happened by and overheard someone say "property expressions in the pipeline" and hovered around the office, just to see what the crazy developers were up to. Before long, half the development team and many of the testers were sitting in Matt's office working out the details of how to make it work. Finally, we had worked out the issues and struck on a design that met all the requirements. A little talk with others on the team to get approval and "property expressions in the pipeline" became the last major feature added to Integration Services 2005.

Variable Expressions

It's sometimes useful to reference a variable that has a value that is the result of an expression. Variables can contain values that you or a task sets, but they can also contain expressions and return the result of the expression instead of their value.

For example, suppose you need to use an expression to generate a folder name, filename, or date in a certain format, and you need to use the same expression in multiple locations in your package. You could copy the expression and paste it into all the locations you need it. But then, if it ever needs to change, you must change it in each of those locations. That's really a headache and just bad practice. It would be nice if you could build the expression in one place and then use it in all the locations throughout the package where you need it. Then, managing the expression would be simple because you would only need to change it in one place.

You can use variable expressions for this. Create the variable with an expression and then you can reference the variable in the other locations through property expressions. If you're familiar with the concept of macros in other languages and applications, this is very similar. For a more detailed discussion of this approach, please see Chapter 22, which demonstrates variable expressions and how to use them in detail.

There are two properties on IS variables related to expressions. The `EvaluateAsExpression` property is a Boolean that tells the variable to return the results of an expression instead of the value in the variables `Value` property. The second property related to expressions is the `Expression` property. This property contains the actual expression to be evaluated. When the `EvaluateAsExpression` property is set to `TRUE`, the variable returns the result of the expression whenever you get its value. If `EvaluateAsExpression` is set to `FALSE`, the variable simply returns the value in the variable's `Value` property.

Precedence Constraint Expressions

Precedence constraints control the workflow of packages. They do this by determining if some constraint is met, and if so it "fires." In other words, it tells the runtime engine that it's OK to execute the next executable in the workflow to which that precedence constraint points. In DTS, options for constraints were limited to whether the previous task succeeded, failed, or just completed. Although useful in the general case, at times it would be helpful to include other factors into the equation. Precedence constraint expressions give package writers virtually unlimited flexibility to make the precedence constraint fire based on any condition in the package environment by allowing the precedence constraint to factor the result of an expression into the constraint.

Figure 9.6 shows the Precedence Constraint Editor in which you enter the expressions. Notice there are a few options for how expressions can be used. Four options are available in the Evaluation Operation drop down. The Constraint option ignores expressions and only fires if the Value constraint is met. The Expression option ignores the Value constraint and only fires if the expression evaluates to `TRUE`. The Expression and Constraint option only fires if both the Value constraint is satisfied and the expression evaluates to TRUE. The Expression or Constraint option fires if either the Value or Expression constraints are met.

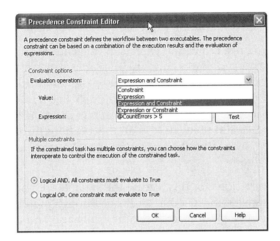

FIGURE 9.6   The Precedence Constraint Editor allows you to enter expressions.

Expressions on precedence constraints are useful in those cases in which you want to control what workflow gets executed based on criteria other than the success or failure of previous workflow. The following are some examples when this might be useful:

- You want to control which workflow executes by passing in a command-line configuration.

- You want to configure workflow with other configurations.

- You want to determine which workflow executes during the package's execution.

- You want to only execute a workflow if a variable has a certain value or is not empty.

These are just a few examples of how expressions can be useful on precedence constraints.

For Loop **Expressions**

The For Loop is a container with three expressions that control the number of times the loop executes. The InitExpression is the first expression to be evaluated on the For Loop and is only evaluated once at the very beginning. It is evaluated before any workflow in the loop is executed and you use it to initialize a variable that will be used in the other expressions. You can also use it to initialize a variable that might be used in the workflow of the loop.

The EvalExpression is the second expression evaluated when the loop first starts and is evaluated before each iteration of the loop. The EvalExpression is the terminating case. If it evaluates to TRUE, the loop executes again. If it evaluates to FALSE, the loop terminates.

The `AssignExpression` is used to increment, decrement, or otherwise modify the variable used in the `EvalExpression`. This expression is evaluated for each iteration of the loop as well, but at the bottom of the workflow, or, in other words, after the workflow has executed. Figure 9.7 illustrates the order in which the expressions are evaluated.

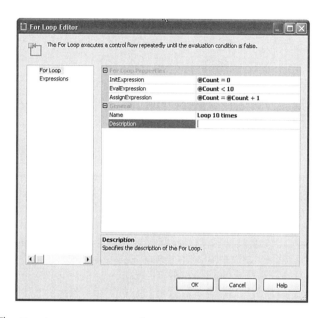

FIGURE 9.7   The `For Loop` uses expressions.

Summary

Two data flow components rely on expressions. The Derived Column and the Conditional Split transforms use expressions to determine how they should handle data. These components are covered in detail in Chapter 20, "The Stock Data Flow Components."

Expressions are important in Integration Services. This chapter has shown the power and flexibility package expressions bring to the table. Take some time to learn expressions well and it will pay off in simple, manageable, and powerful packages. The total number of operations and functions in expressions is fairly limited, which makes it easy to quickly get up to speed. Yet, when combined with variables and placed strategically within your package, expressions provide a simple and elegant way to control packages.

The Stock Connection Managers

"IF IT'S NOT SCOTTISH, IT'S CRAP!"
—BILL BAKER

Connection Manager Concepts

Connection managers are a new object type in Integration Services. They are fundamentally different from Data Transformation Services Connection objects, yet very similar in function. There are also a lot more connection managers because of a fundamental shift in the way connections are used in Integration Services. This chapter explains the concepts behind connection managers and then describes each of the stock connection managers.

Connection Managers

Integration Services has an object called a connection manager. The name should give you a hint about what it does. It manages connections, or, more accurately, it creates connections to resources based on its property settings and delivers the connection to the object that asks for it by calling the `AcquireConnection` method. So, connection managers are essentially connection factories. OLEDB connection managers create OLEDB connections, WMI connection managers create WMI connections, and so forth. To generate or "build" a new connection, components call `AcquireConnection` on the connection manager.

NOTE

DTS users will note that this is a departure from DTS connection design. DTS connections were not connection factories. They were more like connection wrappers and were only capable of generating and holding one physical connection.

In Integration Services, if you want to access resources, you create a connection manager. The reasons for this design are not always apparent at first, and some benefits won't be fully realized until later versions of Integration Services take full advantage of the design, but the following are some of the immediate benefits:

- It's much easier to identify what resources the package references if they are all centralized in the Connections window at the bottom of the Control Flow Designer than if the connection strings and filenames are spread throughout the package as values for component properties.

- It's easier to manage connection managers than hard-coded strings.

- It is easier to configure connection managers than properties on tasks and data flow components.

- Connection managers can be copied and pasted.

- Connection managers can be extended with custom types.

- Connection managers can be used by more than one component.

- Connection managers make it possible to do impact analysis.

- Connection managers relieve tasks from the burden of validating connection strings.

MICROSOFT PRACTICING WHAT IT PREACHES?

Astute readers and users of Integration Services will note that there are some cases in which stock components don't adhere to the standard of using connection managers for accessing resources. For example, the raw source adapter only supports directly typing in the source filename or retrieving it from a variable. The reasons for this are varied and have to do with trying to pull together an overall philosophy for a product while building the product simultaneously.

These exceptions should be corrected in future releases.

Categories of Connection Managers

In the client/server, two-tier world, people typically think of a connection as a link or contract between the client and the server over a network that can be used to access resources on the server. Integration Services supports this type of connection but extends the idea to include access to resources other than servers.

Depending on the resources to which the connection manager provides access, the type of object or value returned from the `AcquireConnection` call is different. For example, the OLEDB Connection Manager returns a pointer to an instance of an OLEDB Session object, the File Connection Manager returns a simple string, and the WMI Connection Manager returns an instance of a .NET object called `System.Management.ManagementScope`. The current collection of stock connection managers can be classified into three categories, as follows:

- Database connections that use the various data access layers and often support distributed transactions, such as ODBC, OLEDB, MSMQ, and ADO.NET

- Network connections to resources found on the Internet, such as FTP, HTTP, and web services

- File-system resources, such as flat files, text files, and folders

NOTE

If you're familiar with Data Transformation Services, you'll recognize this is a fundamental shift in philosophy. DTS packages had only the first type of connection.

Database Connection Managers (ADO.NET, OLEDB, ODBC, and Others)

At the low level, database connections are the starting point for accessing resources. Typically, pointers to objects or opaque numbers function as a handle, and the client code uses the pointer or handle to access even more information and perform more functions. For this class of connection managers, every call to `AcquireConnection` creates a new physical connection. This makes it possible for multiple tasks or other clients to use one connection manager and still have different connections to a database.

TIP

This category of connection managers has a property in common called `RetainSameConnection`. `RetainSameConnection` tells the connection manager to keep the connection it creates the first time a client calls its `AcquireConnection` method until the package completes. It gives out that same physical connection every time a client component calls `AcquireConnection`.

This is useful if you need to maintain a SQL transaction across multiple clients, you want to simulate DTS behavior, or you want to retain a temporary table for use by multiple clients.

Network Connection Managers (FTP, HTTP, WMI, and Others)

This category of connection managers each returns something different. Most of these return an object that the calling task or component must know how to use. For example, the FTP Connection Manager returns a special FTP object with properties such as `ServerName`, `ServerPassword`, `Retries`, `PassiveMode`, and other related FTP settings.

File System Connection Managers (File, MultiFlatFile, and Others)

File system connection managers are a bit odd. They don't return a pointer or handle. They return a string that points to a given file on the file system. The MultiFile and MultiFlatFile Connection Managers support wildcards and lists of files so that more than one filename can be returned by calling `AcquireConnection`.

Creating Connection Managers

Connection managers can be created in a variety of ways. The most common way is perhaps through the Connection Managers window in the designer below the Control and Data Flow windows. If you right-click on the Connection Managers window, a context menu opens with a few menu options for creating some of the more common connection managers. If you want to create a connection manager type that isn't listed on the context menu, select New Connection, which opens the Add SSIS Connection Manager dialog box shown in Figure 10.1.

FIGURE 10.1   Use the Add SSIS Connection Manager dialog box for creating a new connection manager.

Connection managers can also be created in the various editors for components. For example, the WMI Data Reader Task Editor (shown in Figure 10.2) has the option to create a new WMI Connection Manager in the Connection Manager selections. This is a common way to create connection managers for those components that need them and vastly simplifies package creation because you can configure tasks and other components all in the same location, on the task or component editor.

Also, many components provide a button for creating a new connection manager. Figure 10.3 shows the button for this purpose in the OLEDB Source Editor.

FIGURE 10.2   Creating a new WMI Connection Manager from the WMI Data Reader Task Editor dialog box.

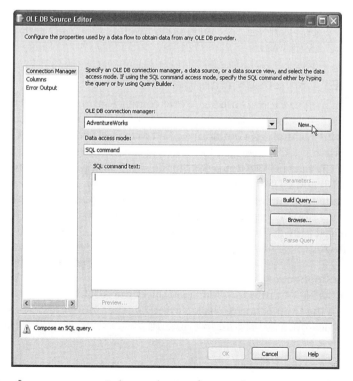

FIGURE 10.3   Some components have a button for creating new connection managers.

Stock Connection Managers

Integration Services ships with a number of stock connection managers. In general, Microsoft developed connection managers that were needed to support the components and tasks they were creating, so the list is fairly long. The following sections contain a brief introduction to and a brief discussion about each of the stock connection managers.

> ## NOTE
> Connection managers are one of the component types in Integration Services that are extensible, meaning third parties can also create custom connection managers. Therefore, by the time you read this, the list of available connection managers might have grown even longer.

The ADO Connection Manager

The ActiveX Data Objects (ADO) Connection Manager is for accessing ADO objects, such as a recordset, and is provided for custom tasks written using VB6 or that support legacy applications that use ADO. You should not use this connection manager unless you need to support legacy applications or components.

Setting Up the Connection Manager

The configuration steps for the ADO Connection Manager are the same as for the OLEDB Connection Manager. Please see "The OLEDB Connection Manager" section later in this chapter for more information.

The ADO.NET Connection Manager

This connection manager type is used to create connections to a broad class of data access providers called managed providers. They are called managed providers because they were written using .NET technology, commonly called managed code. The ADO.NET Connection Manager is the most flexible of all the database connection managers because it also supports the new managed provider model while still providing backward compatibility with OLEDB and ODBC with the managed provider for OLEDB providers. ADO.NET is gaining great momentum of availability and support. Currently, there are a limited but steadily increasing number of native ADO.NET managed providers. The combination of emerging managed providers and OLEDB support make ADO.NET broadly useful and a preferred connection type for your packages.

Setting Up the Connection Manager

To set up the ADO.NET Connection Manager, select the ADO.NET option from the context menu in the Connection Managers window. The Configure ADO.NET Connection Manager dialog box opens, as shown in Figure 10.4.

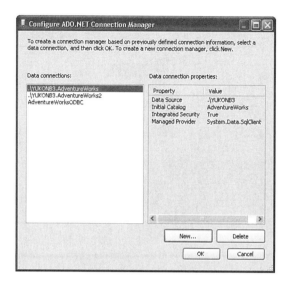

FIGURE 10.4   Use the Configure ADO.NET Connection Manager dialog box to create a new ADO.NET Connection Manager.

TIP

The designer keeps track of connections you've previously created and places those in the left pane of the Configure Connection Manager dialog box. These are tracked in the Registry. On most machines, the designer stores them in the following Registry key.

TIP

HKCU\Software\Microsoft\VisualStudio\8.0\Packages\{GUID}\Settings\Data\Connections

Regardless of the connection type, the settings are cached in this location. Information about ADO.NET, ODBC, and OLEDB connections you've previously created is saved here to make it easier to re-create similar connections. Because these are stored in the Current User key, they are only visible to you or someone logged in under your account. They are not part of the project or solution.

Figure 10.5 shows the Connection Manager dialog box that opens when you click on the New button in Figure 10.4. This is where you tell the connection manager which ADO.NET provider to use, specify the server name, and give credentials. Essentially, this is where you build connection strings.

Figure 10.6 shows the All tab of the Connection Manager dialog box.

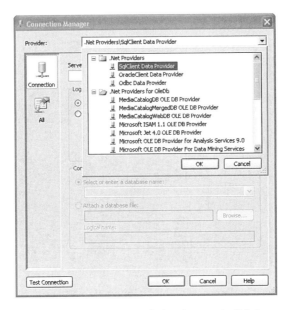

FIGURE 10.5   Use the Connection Manager dialog box to build the connection string.

The Connection Manager dialog box gives you ultimate control over the settings for the connection. For example, you can turn on MultipleActiveResultSets (MARS), choose the network library, change the packet size and the connection timeout, modify the pooling behavior, turn on encryption, and specify the initial catalog. These are all things you can do in the connection string directly as well.

> **NOTE**
>
> The All tab displays all the connection string settings for the connection manager. Those settings that are displayed in bold have been modified and show up in the connection string. Those setting shown in nonbold fonts use the default setting and do not appear as part of the connection string.

The Excel Connection Manager

The Excel Connection Manager is provided as a simple way to access Excel spreadsheets. The connection manager is an alternative to the more complex setup of the OLEDB Connection Manager using the Jet OLE DB Provider. In many cases, the Excel Connection Manager is all you'll need and the ease of configuration makes it a cinch to set up. If you need to have finer control of the Excel range and so forth, the OLEDB Connection Manager is a better option.

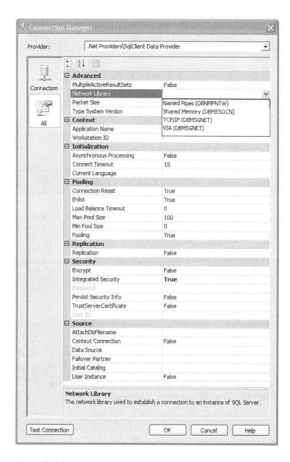

FIGURE 10.6   Use the All tab to set advanced connection string settings.

Setting Up the Connection Manager

Setting up the Excel Connection Manager is quite simple. Figure 10.7 shows the Excel Connection Manager dialog box. Choose the correct Excel version and then browse to the file. If the first row in the spreadsheet has column names, you can select the First Row Has Column Names check box, which comes in handy when working in the Data Flow Task.

Peculiarities

The Excel Connection Manager doesn't have a Test Connection button. Using the OLEDB Connection Manager for accessing Excel files, you can get the satisfaction of clicking the Test button and getting the success message. Because there is no Test Connection button, there is no way to get errors until actually running the package or task that uses it. For example, if you choose the wrong Excel version, you won't know until you actually run a package containing a component that uses the connection manager.

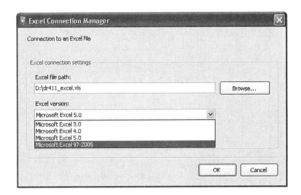

FIGURE 10.7   Use the Excel Connection Manager to access Excel spreadsheets.

Also, the Excel Connection Manager doesn't allow you to select Excel ranges. Although you can hack the connection string to do so, it's just easier to use the OLEDB Connection Manager if you need to select a range.

THE EXCEL CONNECTION MANAGER AND OLEDB

The Excel Connection Manager is actually a slightly modified OLEDB Connection Manager with a different user interface. The IS team felt that it would be useful to have a simple answer for how to connect to Excel spreadsheets. Unfortunately, making it simpler meant eliminating some of the control. Fortunately, the OLEDB Connection Manager is available for situations in which you need more control.

Following are the steps to set up the OLEDB Connection Manager to access Excel files.

1. Create a new OLE DB Connection Manager.

2. In the Native OLE DB provider list, select the Microsoft Jet 4.0 OLE DB provider.

3. For the Database filename, browse and select an Excel file.

4. Click the All tab.

5. In the Extended Properties property, type in Excel 8.0.

TIP

Also, if you're struggling to get the data out correctly, you might want to try the IMEX=1 setting in the Extended Properties property as well. This tells the driver to read all "intermixed" columns as text. A typical Extended Properties value might be:

Excel 8.0;IMEX=1;HDR=Yes

If you use the connection in the Data Flow Task, you can convert the columns as needed using the Data Conversion transform.

If you use the connection manager in the Data Flow Task with an OLEDB or Excel source adapter, the adapter designer allows you to select the table (Excel Worksheet) in a drop-down list. If you want to use the connection manager in the SQL Task, you can use a query to retrieve the data. The query takes the following form:

```
SELECT * FROM [SheetName$FromCellName:ToCellName]
```

So, a typical `select` statement might be:

```
SELECT * FROM [NewContacts$A51:K1005]
```

to retrieve the columns from A through K, rows 51 to 1005. Or simply

```
SELECT * FROM [NewContact]
```

to retrieve all the available populated rows and columns.

> **NOTE**
>
> You can find more information about this in the Knowledge Base article 257819 at http://support.microsoft.com.

The File Connection Manager

The File Connection Manager is for specifying the name of one file or file system folder. As you can imagine, the File System Task depends on the File Connection Manager heavily, but other components and tasks use this connection manager as well.

Setting Up the Connection Manager

Setup for this connection manager is simple. Specify the usage type and the file or folder name. The usage type only affects validation. When the task or component that is configured to use the File Connection Manager validates, it can also validate that the usage type is correct on the File Connection Manager. The File Connection Manager supports fully qualified file and folder paths as well as UNC paths. Figure 10.8 shows the File Connection Manager Editor.

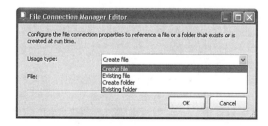

FIGURE 10.8   Use the File Connection Manager Editor to access files and folders.

Validation

The File Connection Manager validates when the package validates. If the usage type is "Existing File" or "Existing Folder" and the file or folder is not available, the File Connection Manager fails validation.

> **TIP**
>
> Sometimes, a file is only available after the package has partially run. For example, you might FTP some files from a server and then want to access them later in the package. In this case, the File Connection Manager fails validation because the file isn't available. To make this scenario work, you can use the `DelayValidation` property to postpone validation until the very last moment.

The Flat File Connection Manager

Like the File Connection Manager, the Flat File Connection Manager is also for specifying the name of one file. However, it also provides flat-file column information for clients. The Flat File Source Adapter relies heavily on this connection manager to define the file type, columns, and column names for flat files.

Setting Up the Connection Manager: General

To create a new Flat File Connection Manager, right-click on the Connection Manager window and select the New Flat File Connection Manager option from the context menu. The Flat File Connection Manager Editor shown in Figure 10.9 opens with the General tab selected.

FIGURE 10.9   Use the General tab to specify the location of the flat file.

The General tab is where you specify the flat file location, locale, code page, and other critical file-level settings. The following sections provide a description of each of these settings.

Filename   This is the fully qualified name of the file you want to load.

Locale   The Locale drop-down box lets you select the locale the source connection and adapter will use. The locale setting affects the way Integration Services converts string data. For example, it influences date-to-string conversions. IS would convert the date Monday, May 17, 2004, to the short-date format 17/5/04 in the English/New Zealand locale but 04/5/17 in the English/South Africa locale. The Flat File Connection Manager locale defaults to the default locale of the machine on which the designer is running. If you change the locale, the Flat File Connection Manager Editor attempts to make life a little easier and selects the default code page for that locale.

Code Page   The code page isn't bound by the locale setting, however, and you can select any code page using the Code Page drop down. Also, if you check the Unicode check box, the editor disables the Code Page options because they're not needed for Unicode.

Format   Three formats are available: Delimited, Fixed Width, and Ragged Right.

- **Delimited**—The columns have some delimiter, such as a semicolon, tab, or comma. Comma separated value (CSV) files are an example of delimited data.

- **Fixed Width**—The data is aligned into columns whose width is the same for all rows.

- **Ragged Right**—The same as fixed width with one exception: Each row is delimited, by default, with a CR/LF combination but can be configured to use other delimiting characters. Ragged-right flat files are a little more flexible because the last column can be of different widths.

Text Qualifier   Often, a string contains a character that can be confused for a delimiter. For example, if you specify the format as delimited and the delimiter as a comma, any comma found within a string is interpreted as a delimiter and confuses the flat file parser. The text qualifier specifies what character the file uses to indicate the beginning and end of a string. Typically, the character is a double quote or single quote, but other characters can be used as well.

Header Row Delimiter   Some flat files, particularly those from legacy systems such as mainframes and so on, use a different delimiter for the header row than for the rest of the rows. This setting lets you specify the delimiter. If it is the same as for regular rows, specify that. The default is {CR}{LF}.

Header Rows to Skip   Some flat files have extra data at the top of the file, such as borders made of the '_' or '=' characters, file creation date, owners, source of origin systems, and so on. These rows of information typically do not conform to the same format as the rest of the data in the flat file and, thus, confuse the flat file parser. You can use the Header Rows to Skip setting to essentially ignore such rows.

Column Names in the First Data Row   This check box specifies that the first row contains the names of the columns and essentially ignores the row when retrieving the actual data rows. However, when clients access the Flat File Connection Manager, they can use the names. For example, the Flat File Source Adapter uses these names in its designers to label columns. If this option is selected, the Flat File Adapter starts at the second row when counting the number of header rows to skip. For example, if you set Header Rows to Skip to 2 and check the Column Names in the First Data Row option, the Flat File Source Adapter skips a total of three rows when retrieving data from the flat file.

Setting Up the Connection Manager: Columns

After you set the source file and format, you can set up the columns by clicking on the Columns tab. Depending on the format you selected, the Columns dialog box is different.

Delimited   If you select Delimited format, the Columns dialog box appears as shown in Figure 10.10.

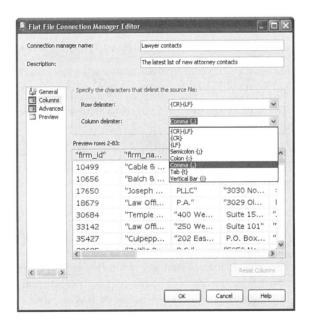

FIGURE 10.10   The Columns dialog box shows columns based on the settings on the General tab.

Notice that you specify the delimiter on this tab in the Column Delimiter drop down. If the delimiter you're using isn't available in the drop down, you can directly type in the delimiter character. The default delimiter is the comma. You can also change the row delimiter. This is the character or character combination the flat file parser uses to determine the end of a row.

Even though it is called a row delimiter, it is really just the last column delimiter. The Flat File Connection Manager only counts columns. If the row delimiter comes in the wrong order, the Flat File Connection Manager does not reset its read position to the start of the next row and the columns are read out of sync.

Fixed Width   If you selected Fixed Width format, the Columns dialog box appears as shown in Figure 10.11.

FIGURE 10.11   Use the Columns dialog box to set the row and column widths.

The first step to configuring the fixed width columns is to set the row width. You can set the row width by directly typing it, if you know it, into the Row Width Edit box, or by dragging the red row width line to the end of the first row. Next, to establish each column width, click on the ruler control at the start of each column. This sets the column width for each column. You can delete a column width line by either double-clicking it or right-clicking it and selecting Delete from the context menu.

Be careful with fixed-width flat files. If one column is missing for one row, the rest of the rows will be offset and you'll end up with things like state abbreviations in zip code columns. Fixed-width flat files are an extremely fast way to import data, but if they are not formatted correctly, the flat file parser will get confused.

Ragged Right   The setup for ragged right columns is identical to fixed width except, instead of setting the row width, you set the row delimiter in the Row Delimiter drop down. The default is the {CR}{LF} character combination.

Setting Up the Connection Manager: Advanced

The Advanced tab lets you add new or delete existing columns, modify the settings for each column, and suggests column lengths. Figure 10.12 shows the Advanced tab of the Connection Manager dialog box.

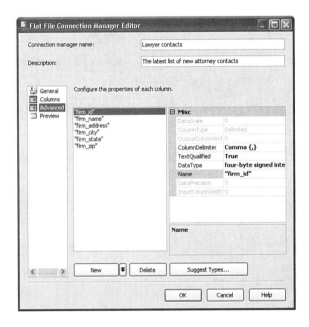

FIGURE 10.12   Use the Advanced tab to directly set column properties.

The Suggest Types button is a handy feature that tells the Flat File Connection Manager to attempt an educated guess at the type and other attributes of each column. Because flat files are text, the Flat File Source Adapter considers all columns as text, even those columns that are obviously numbers to a human viewer. The default width of each column is also 50. There are a lot of good reasons to change these settings. Columns that are wider than necessary slow down the Data Flow Task and generate larger files. You'd also like to have columns that are dates treated as dates, integers treated as integers, and so forth. The Suggest Types button does a pretty good job of figuring out what the type of a given column is, but occasionally it gets the type wrong. For those cases, you can manually modify the column types using the column property grid on the right side of the dialog box.

Figure 10.13 shows the Suggest Column Types dialog box with the default settings.

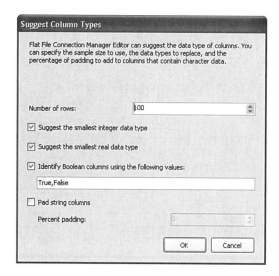

FIGURE 10.13   The Suggest Column Types dialog box lets you configure how column metadata is suggested.

The Number of Rows setting tells the type discovery algorithm how many rows to use when discovering types. For very large files, you might want to increase this number so that the sample rows are statistically significant. It's possible that the first 100 rows for one column appear as numbers. For example, the Zip Code column might be all numbers for the first half of the file because they're all U.S. ZIP Codes. Further into the file, the column might contain ZIP Codes for other countries that contain letters. The type discovery algorithm incorrectly guesses the ZIP Code column type in this case.

The Suggest the Smallest Integer Data Type and Suggest the Smallest Real Data Type settings instructs the algorithm to use the smallest integer or real type that holds the maximum value found in the column up to the number of rows specified in the Number of Rows setting. For example, if the value of the largest integer found in a column was 42, this setting instructs the algorithm to select a 1-byte integer, but if the value of the largest integer found was 342, a 2-byte integer would be required because a 1-byte integer can only hold values up to 255.

The Identify Boolean Columns Using the Following Values setting tells the algorithm to set the type of a column to Boolean if it contains the strings specified. The defaults are TRUE and FALSE but could also be TREU and FALSCHE.

The Pad String Columns setting adds spaces to the columns up to the percentage specified. This is useful in cases in which you're concerned that a column might not be large enough to hold the longest values or to allow for potential column width growth.

Setting Up the Connection Manager: Preview
After setting the column properties, you're ready to look at the data preview in Figure 10.14.

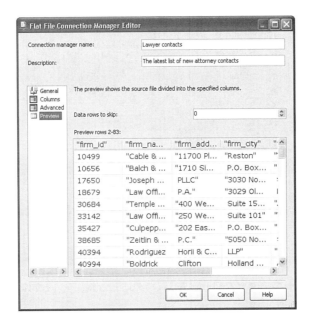

FIGURE 10.14   Use the Preview tab to view the data columns.

This tab doesn't provide much functionality other than some peace of mind that you've got all the settings right. Use the Data Rows to Skip setting to specify how many rows to skip after the header. Note that this is different than the Header Rows to Skip setting. The total rows skipped are the sum of the number of header rows and data rows skipped.

The FTP Connection Manager

The FTP Connection Manager provides a connection to an FTP server but also provides all the FTP-related functionality for Integration Services. For example, when the FTP Task downloads a file, the actual work occurs in the FTP connection. Uploading files, creating and deleting folders, enumerating lists of files on the FTP server, and so on all happen within the FTP Connection Manager. The reason that the FTP Connection Manager contains all the FTP functionality instead of the FTP Task is because the IS team wanted to enable custom task writers to be able to use FTP. If the code for accessing FTP servers were in the FTP Task, this would not be possible.

Setting Up the Connection Manager

Figure 10.15 shows the FTP Connection Manager Editor. Passive mode instructs the FTP Connection Manager to only allow FTP responses to requests it sends. In some cases, this setting enables FTP connections through corporate firewalls that won't otherwise succeed.

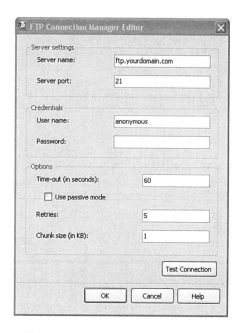

FIGURE 10.15   Use the FTP Connection Manager to connect to a remote FTP server.

The HTTP Connection Manager

The HTTP Connection Manager implements the full HTTP functionality for Integration Services. The IS team created the HTTP Connection Manager to support the Web Services Task, but other tasks can use it as well. See Chapter 24, "Building Custom Tasks," for a custom task that uses this connection manager.

Setting Up the Connection Manager

Figure 10.16 shows the HTTP Connection Manager Editor.

> **NOTE**
>
> If you specify the root without an explicit filename, the HTTP Connection Manager operates on the default page. To target specific files or pages, you'll need to add their path and name as follows: http://support.microsoft.com/kb/257819

There are two tabs on the dialog box. On the Server tab, you specify the settings to connect to the HTTP server. The Server URL is the full URL to the file you want to access. For HTTP pages that require credentials or a certificate for authentication, you can provide them here. If you check the Use Client Certificate check box, the dialog box enables the Certificate button. Click the Certificate button to choose the certificate from the Select Certificate dialog box shown in Figure 10.17.

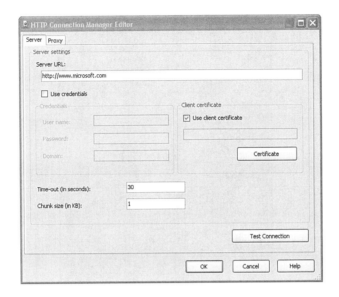

FIGURE 10.16   Use the HTTP Connection Manager to connect to a website.

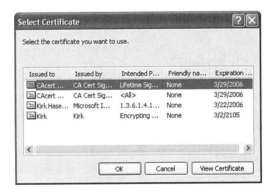

FIGURE 10.17   Select the certificate using the Select Certificate dialog box.

On the Proxy tab, you can configure settings for working with a proxy. The Proxy tab is shown in Figure 10.18.

The Proxy URL specifies the address for the proxy, which is typically on Port 8080. Some proxy software configurations require that you log in. The Credentials settings allow you to enter your credentials so you can do so. The Proxy Bypass list is provided as a way to bypass the proxy for certain, typically internal, addresses.

TIP

The HTTP Connection Manager returns a native COM object when clients call its `AcquireConnection` method. This makes it difficult to use it in the Script Task.

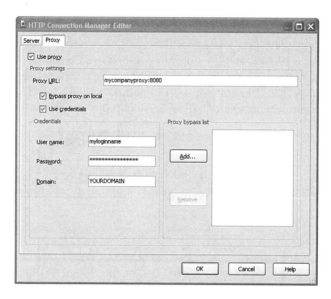

FIGURE 10.18   Use the Proxy tab to configure proxy settings.

The MSMQ Connection Manager

The MSMQ Connection Manager provides a way to centrally configure settings for accessing an MSMQ queue. Multiple MSMQ Tasks in the same package can use the same MSMQ Connection Manager to access the same queue. This connection manager returns an instance of a .NET object defined in System.Messaging called appropriately enough, MessageQueue. The MSMQ Task knows how to use this object to access features and services of MSMQ. Figure 10.19 shows the MSMQ Connection Manager Editor. For more on how to set up this connection manager, see the MSMQ Task discussion in Chapter 8, "The Stock Tasks."

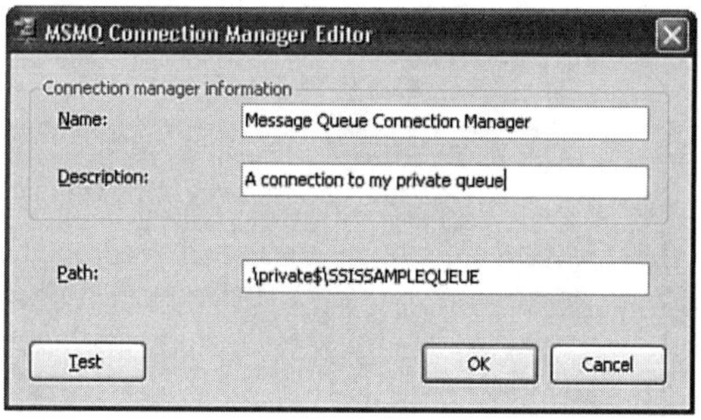

FIGURE 10.19   Use the MSMQ Connection Manager to connect to MSMQ.

The Microsoft Analysis Services Connection Manager

The Analysis Services Connection Manager is how Analysis Services Tasks connect to Analysis Services servers. Figure 10.20 shows the Add Analysis Services Connection Manager Editor. An interesting feature of this connection manager type is that it can connect to an existing Analysis Services project in the same solution to populate cubes as well as an Analysis Services server. The connection to an Analysis Services project is only valid in the designer.

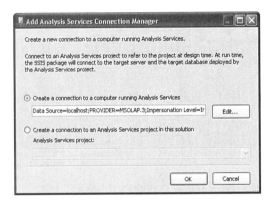

FIGURE 10.20   Use the OLAP90 Connection Manager to connect to Analysis Services.

Setting Up the Connection Manager

To set up this connection manager, you can type in the connection string for the Analysis Services server directly, or you can click the Edit button, which opens the Connection Manager dialog box for Analysis Services shown in Figure 10.21.

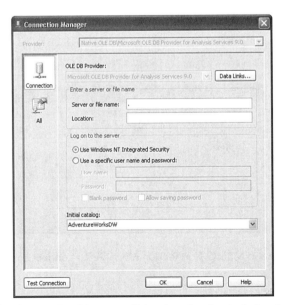

FIGURE 10.21   The Connection Manager dialog box for Analysis Services automatically selects the OLEDB provider for Analysis Services.

If you choose to create a connection to an Analysis Services project in the same solution, the designer populates the Analysis Services project drop down with the AS projects in the solution.

The MultiFile Connection Manager

The MultiFile Connection Manager makes it possible to access multiple files from the same connection manager in succession. The MultiFile Connection Manager supports file-name lists as well as wildcard names. Although most operations on multiple files can be done with the Foreach Loop using the ForEach File Enumerator, there are occasions when it's convenient to retrieve more than one file within the same execution of a task. The MultiFile Connection Manager returns the fully qualified name of a different file each time a client task or component calls AcquireConnection until it returns all the filenames, and then it returns NULL.

Setting Up the Connection Manager

Figure 10.22 shows the Add File Connection Manager dialog box with some files already selected. To add more, click the Add button. To remove a file or files, select the files and click the Remove button. The Edit button lets you select a new file to replace the currently selected file.

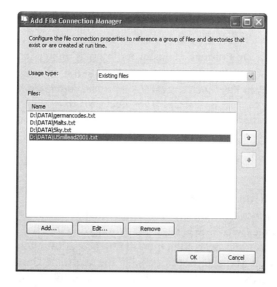

FIGURE 10.22   Use the MultiFile Connection Manager dialog box to easily select multiple files.

After you've selected the files, the ConnectionString property contains the list of strings separated by the pipe (|) character. For example, the list of files selected in Figure 10.22 is represented in the ConnectionString as:

```
D:\data\USmillead2001.txt|D:\data\germancodes.txt|D:\data\Malts.txt|D:\data\Sky.txt
```

You can also use the ? and * wildcards to specify files. The dialog box doesn't provide a way to build a connection string with wildcards, so you have to directly enter them into the ConnectionString in the property grid. For example, to access all the .txt files in the D:\data folder, type the following into the ConnectionString property:

D:\data*.txt

The MultiFlatFile Connection Manager

The MultiFlatFile Connection Manager is useful for building Data Flow Tasks that need to process more than one flat file. The Flat File Source Adapter is designed to take advantage of the MultiFlatFile Connection Manager. The Flat File Source Adapter attempts to acquire the name of another flat file to process and continues to do so until no more flat files are available before setting the end-of-file flag on the data flow. This capability comes in handy for efficiently processing data contained in multiple flat files.

CAUTION

Each flat file must have the exact same schema for this to work.

MULTIFLATFILE CONNECTION MANAGER USEFUL IN COMMON SCENARIOS

Donald Farmer, the Group Program Manager for Integration Services, explained:

One important scenario that this enables is the aggregation of data across several flat files. In many cases, data files, such as cash register files, equipment, or server logs, are split into several files for FTP or transfer from local sites to a central warehouse. Calculating aggregates across these files normally requires a staging table. But with this feature, the multiple files can be aggregated (or sorted) as if they came from a single file.

Setting Up the Connection Manager

The setup for this connection manager is virtually identical to the way you set up the Flat File Connection Manager with one exception: When you click the Browse button for the MultiFlatFile Connection Manager, the Open dialog box allows you to multiselect files. The Flat File Connection Manager does not. Like the MultiFile Connection Manager, you can also use the wildcards ? and * to implicitly select multiple files.

The ODBC Connection Manager

The ODBC Connection Manager is provided to support the long-established ODBC data access standard and the multitude of ODBC drivers.

NOTE

Integration Services ships with an ADO.NET Source Adapter for the Data Flow Task that may be used to access ODBC sources through ADO.NET ODBC providers, but not an ODBC Destination Adapter. Hopefully, an ODBC Destination will be available soon.

Setting Up the Connection Manager

The key to setting up ODBC Connection Managers is the DSN. DSN is short for Data Source Name. Data Source Names provide a way to connect to a database through an ODBC driver and contain information such as the database name, database driver, directory, UserID, and password. After you have a DSN for a particular database, you can simply select that DSN whenever you create a connection to the database.

There are three types of DSNs:

- **System DSN**—Can be used by anyone who has access to the machine.

- **User DSN**—Created for a given user.

- **File DSN**—Information is stored in a text file with the .DSN extension.

TIP

System and User DSNs are stored in the Registry. System DSNs are stored in the HKLM key under SOFTWARE\ODBC\ODBC.INI.

User DSNs are stored in the HKCU key under SOFTWARE\ODBC\ODBC.INI.

Although they can be stored anywhere in the file system, file DSNs are typically stored in the %Program Files%\Common\ODBC\Data Sources folder.

Installed ODBC drivers are stored in HKLM under SOFTWARE\ODBC\ODBCINST.INI.

You can create new ODBC DSNs with the ODBC Data Source Administrator Control Panel applet shown in Figure 10.23.

To get to this dialog box, select Administrative Tools from the Start menu or go to the Control Panel, Administrative Tools and select the Data Sources (ODBC) Control Panel application.

You can also create file and system DSNs using the ODBC Connection Manager dialog box. To get there, right-click on the Connection Managers window, and then select New Connection. Then, select ODBC for the Connection Manager type, and click the Add button. The Configure ODBC Connection Manager shows a list of available DSNs, if any have already been created on the machine. You can select one of the existing DSNs in the list or create a new one with the New button.

Figure 10.24 shows the Connection Manager dialog box for ODBC. You have the option of choosing an existing user or system DSN or creating a new one. To create a new one, you select the Use Connection String option and click the Build button.

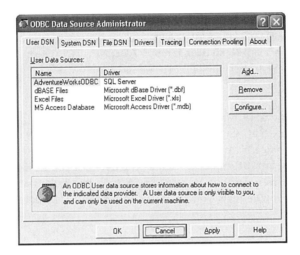

FIGURE 10.23   Use the ODBC Data Source Administrator to create new DSNs.

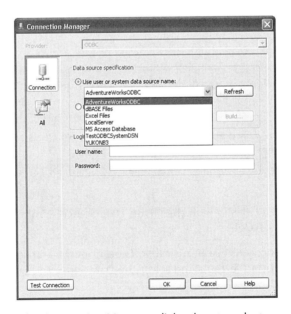

FIGURE 10.24   Use the Connection Manager dialog box to select or create a DSN.

Figure 10.25 shows the Select Data Source dialog box that opens.

When you select the data source, the connection string it contains is placed in the connection string for the connection manager you are currently creating.

FIGURE 10.25   Use the Select Data Source dialog box to choose a file data source.

The OLEDB Connection Manager

The OLEDB Connection Manager is for accessing data using OLEDB data access components. OLEDB is the default access method for Integration Services and is currently the most predominant data access method. Many important data access drivers are OLEDB providers. With the advent of managed providers, however, this will likely change in the near future.

Setting Up the Connection Manager

To set up the OLEDB Connection Manager, select it from the context menu in the Connection Managers window. Figure 10.26 shows the OLEDB Connection Manager dialog box with the provider list showing the SQL Native Client selected. After you've selected the provider you want to use, specify the server and database name.

The OLEDB Connection Manager dialog box also lets you specify a connection to a database in a database file. When the connection manager attempts to connect to the database in the file, it first attaches it to the local server.

NOTE

The connection manager does not detach the database, even after the package has completed execution or if you close the designer.

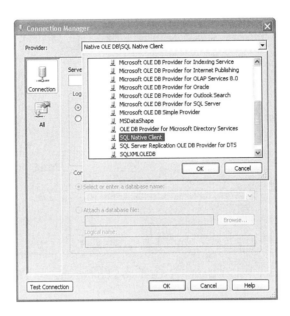

FIGURE 10.26   Select the provider from the OLEDB Connection Manager dialog box.

A WORD ABOUT SQL NATIVE CLIENT

MDAC (including the SQL Server ODBC driver) is now an OS system component. MDAC will continue to be serviced and released only with OS and OS service packs moving forward. MDAC drivers and providers will remain at the SQL Server 2000 feature level, but can be used to connect to SQL Server 2005 although will not be able to take advantage of new functionality. Microsoft SQL Server Native Client (SQL Native Client or SQLNCLI) contains the SQL OLE DB provider and SQL ODBC driver in one native dynamic link library (DLL), supporting applications using native-code APIs (ODBC, OLEDB, and ADO) to Microsoft SQL Server. You should use SQL Native Client rather than Microsoft Data Access Components (MDAC) to create new applications or enhance existing applications that need to take advantage of new SQL Server 2005 features such as Multiple Active Result Sets (MARS), Query Notifications, User-Defined Types (UDT), and XML data type support.

To use SQLSVR32.dll, use "DRIVER=SQL Server;..." in your connection string.

To use SQLNCLI.dll, use "DRIVER=SQL Native Client;..." in your connection string.

For more information, see http://msdn.microsoft.com/data/sqlnative/default.aspx

The SMOServer Connection Manager

SMO is the acronym for SQL Management Objects and is the new API for managing SQL Server objects, such as databases, tables, and logins. The SMO Connection Manager is pretty simple and provides a way to use SMO objects in the control flow.

Setting Up the Connection Manager

To create a new SMOServer Connection Manager, select the SMOServer connection type from the Add SSIS Connection Manager dialog box. Figure 10.27 shows the SMO Connection Manager Editor.

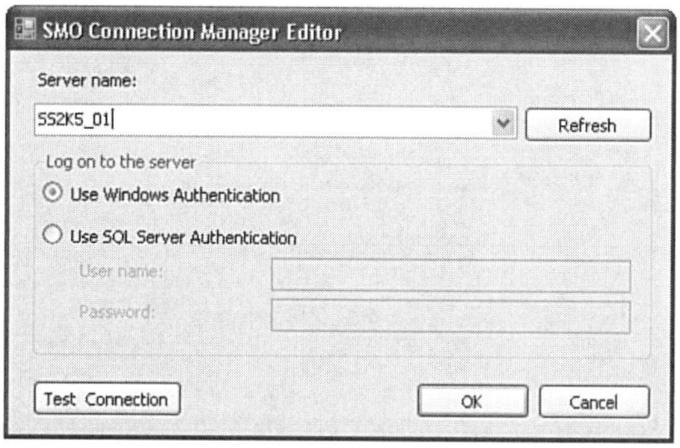

FIGURE 10.27   Use the SMO Connection Manager Editor to access SQL Server objects.

For the server name, enter the name or instance name of the server you need to access. Select the authentication method you want to use and you're done.

The SMO Connection Manager returns a `Microsoft.SqlServer.Management.Smo.Server` object when clients call its `AcquireConnection` method.

> **TIP**
>
> The `Microsoft.SqlServer.Management.Smo.Server` object is a managed object, so you can easily use it in the Script Task if needed.

The SMTP Connection Manager

The SMTP Connection Manager provides a central location for specifying an SMTP server address. The Send Mail Task is based on SMTP and uses this connection manager.

Setting Up the Connection Manager

The SMTP Connection Manager is probably as simple as they come. Whatever you specify for the SMTP server string is what it returns from its `AcquireConnection` method as the connection string. Figure 10.28 shows the SMTP Connection Manager Editor.

The WMI Connection Manager

The WMI Connection Manager provides a way to specify a connection to the WMI service on a machine. WMI is the acronym for Windows Management Instrumentation and provides a powerful set of tools and features for discovering, describing, and querying network resources. The two WMI tasks use the WMI Connection Manager. This connection manager returns an instance of a .NET object defined in `System.Management` called

ManagementScope. The WMI Tasks know how to use this object to access other features
and services of WMI.

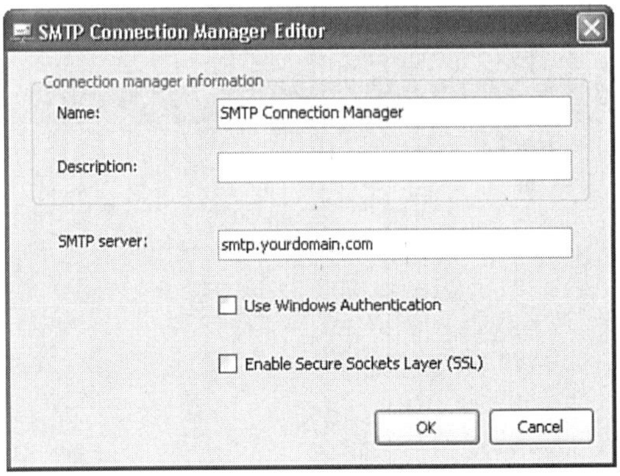

FIGURE 10.28   Use the SMTP Connection Manager Editor to specify the SMTP server
name.

Setting Up the Connection Manager

Figure 10.29 shows the WMI Connection Manager Editor with the default server name
and namespace. Most of the work you will do with WMI will be in the default namespace. The server name might change if you are attempting to query remote machines. To
find out more about WMI and how to use it in Integration Services, see Chapter 8.

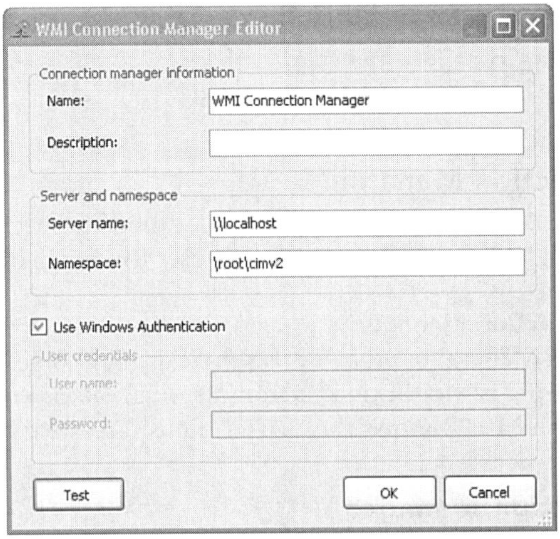

FIGURE 10.29   Use the WMI Connection Manager Editor to connect to the WMI service.

Data Sources and Data Source Views

Data sources and Data Source Views are not connection manager types, but they are closely related to connection managers and often used in the same ways.

Introduction to Data Sources and Data Source Views

Data sources are a way to specify a connection that can be shared between packages, machines, and even project types. Data sources are similar to Data Source Names or DSN files. They are files with a .DS extension and contain the connection string to a server. Integration Services, Reporting Services, and Analysis Services all support data sources. One limitation of connection managers is that if you create one in a package, they are specific to that package only and cannot be shared with other packages or projects. Data sources, on the other hand, might be shared, giving several distinct advantages that should be considered by anyone wanting to make their packages more manageable.

- Data sources can be a common link between different project types. If you're using the same server for AS and IS, it's possible that you might also only need one data source to represent that connection. Fewer files means fewer locations to change as your system evolves.

- Modifying one file, the data source, modifies all connections that use that data source. With connection managers, if you don't configure them, you must modify each and every connection manager every time something about the connection string changes. In this way, data sources are very similar to configurations. They're a central location that can configure or modify package behavior without modifying the package directly.

- Data sources are machine resident, and can be used as recommended in Chapter 14, "Configuring and Deploying Solutions." Data sources remain on a machine and packages deployed to the machine environment can automatically reference the machine resident data source.

Data Source Views (DSVs) use data sources. DSVs are objects that provide an abstraction layer between the underlying source data and the client application and provide a way to cache and reduce the complexity of the source data and metadata. For example, you can configure a DSV to only show tables that are important for a given solution by eliminating those that aren't necessary or related. So when you open the editor for an OLEDB Connection Manager created from a Data Source View, only those tables in the Data Source View show up in the Tables drop down. You can filter and generate data in DSVs. DSVs can be updated to reflect changes in the data source and speed up offline use in some cases by providing metadata to work against when the server isn't available. The following are some other ways you can use DSVs:

- Contain metadata from one or more underlying sources.

- Contain calculated columns that do not exist in the underlying data source.

- Contain relationships between objects that do not exist in the underlying data source.

- Contain queries that do not exist in the underlying data source.

- Can generate new metadata for building an underlying relational store.

- Can reference more than one data source, making it possible to present one unified view of multiple sources.

- Make it possible to easily alter underlying data store because client applications bind to the Data Source View instead of directly to the underlying data.

- Multiple Data Source Views can be created per data source so the DSV can provide different views into the same server; you can essentially isolate the parts of a database or databases of interest and only see specific tables of interest.

Data Source Views (DSV) can be hard to conceptualize, so let's take a look at one example of how you can use them. Suppose you want to create an application on your existing complex Online Transaction Processing (OLTP) system that requires some relationships and calculated columns. The OLTP database administrators are unwilling to make any changes to the production tables, not even to create a view. Also, you're only familiar with the tables that relate to your particular application and want to only view those tables in your IS projects.

The DSV can act as an abstraction layer. You can implement the changes, create a simplified "view" of the complex OLTP system by selecting only those tables you need to reference, and build the calculated columns and relationships between them in the DSV. The client application can reference the DSV and experience the benefits of the changes without needing to change the source system directly.

DSVs also allow you to efficiently explore, test, and experiment with data in an ad hoc, trial-and-error way. As part of preliminary system discovery, people often create test databases that are scaled down, smaller copies of production systems. Creating these test databases can be tedious and time consuming. You can quickly simulate such an environment by pointing the DSV at your system database, selecting the subset of tables with which you want to work, enter filtering queries to decrease the size of the data set, and generate new data. These are the kinds of benefits you can get from DSVs.

Setting Up Data Sources

To create a new data source, right-click the Data Sources node of your Integration Services project and select New Data Source. The Data Source Wizard appears. The first dialog box is the welcome screen. Click the Next button to see the Data Source Wizard shown in Figure 10.30.

The Data Source Wizard gives you an option to create a data source from an existing or new connection or based on another object. If you select the Create a Data Source Based on Another Object radio button, the wizard lets you select data sources in the current solution or based on an Analysis Services project in the current solution. Figure 10.31 shows the Data Source Wizard with those options.

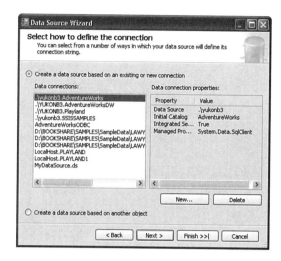

FIGURE 10.30   Create a data source with the Data Source Wizard.

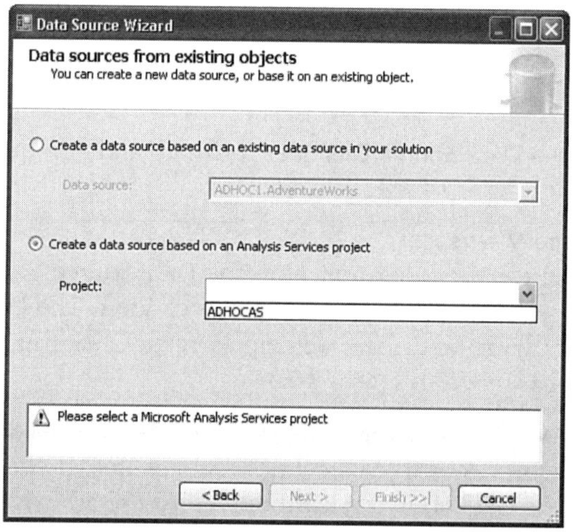

FIGURE 10.31   Create a data source from an existing object.

If you want to use an existing connection, you can click on one in the Data Connections list. For a new data source, click the New button and the Connection Manager dialog box opens where you can build the connection string. That's pretty much all there is to creating a data source. After you've created a new data source, you can double-click on it in the Connections window or in the Solution Explorer to edit it in the Data Source Designer, as shown in Figure 10.32.

There is an option in the Data Source Designer to maintain a reference to another object in the solution. This is another way to create a data source from another data source or that references an Analysis Services project in the same solution.

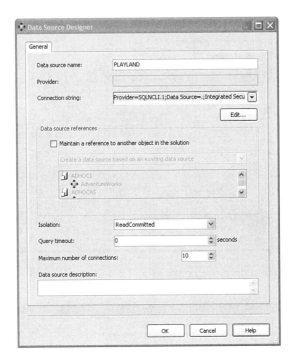

FIGURE 10.32   Use the Data Source Designer to create and edit data sources.

Setting Up Data Source Views

To create a new Data Source View, right-click on the Data Source Views node of your Integration Services project and select New Data Source View. The Data Source View Wizard opens. The first dialog box is the welcome screen. Click the Next button to see the Data Source View Wizard shown in Figure 10.33.

The Data Source View Wizard gives you an option to create a Data Source View from existing relational data sources or to create a new data source. If you click the New Data Source button, the Create Data Source Wizard opens. To use an existing data source, select it in the pane on the left and click the Next button. The next dialog box in the wizard lets you select the tables to load into the DSV. Figure 10.34 shows the selections with the "dbo.dim" filter.

Because databases can have many tables, the filter provides a way to narrow down the list, for example, only the dimension tables. Click the Greater Than button and the dialog box moves the tables that are selected into the Included Objects list. Click the Add Related Tables to add tables that have primary key/foreign key relationships with the tables you've selected. Click the Next button and the dialog box shows a summary view of the tables you've selected. Click the Finish button and the Data Source View Designer opens. Figure 10.35 shows the Data Source View Designer with the Data Source View menu open.

FIGURE 10.33   Create a Data Source View with the Data Source View Wizard.

FIGURE 10.34   Select the tables to load into the DSV.

At this point, you should have a pretty good idea what DSVs are. You can explore the Data Source View main menu and the other features of Data Source Views for a better understanding, and so on. Also, Books Online covers Data Source Views in detail. Indeed, an entire book could be written on Data Source Views alone. Before leaving the subject, let's look at how to create a connection manager that uses a DSV in an Integration Services package.

If you've already created a DSV, create a new package with a Data Flow Task. Drop an OLE DB Source Adapter onto the data flow and open the editor. Figure 10.36 shows the available OLEDB Connection Manager selections.

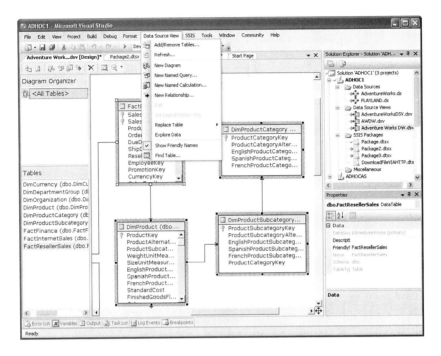

FIGURE 10.35   Data Source Views have their own designer.

FIGURE 10.36   OLE DB Source Adapters can use DSVs.

There are two data sources named AdventureWorks and PLAYLAND. There is also an OLEDB Connection Manager named LocalHost.PLAYLAND available. Under the AdventureWorks Data Source, there are three DSVs available: AdventureWorksDSV, AWDW, and AdventureWorks DW. If you've created named queries in any of the DSVs, they will become available for selection in the Data Access mode. Figure 10.37 shows the OLE DB Source Editor after selecting the AdventureWorks DW DSV and then selected the named query named ProductCustomerProfile. The Named Query generates four columns: ProductKey, YearlyIncome, EnglishProductName, and EnglishOccupation that will be available to components that are downstream of the OLE DB Source Adapter in the data flow. With this setup, you can modify or rename columns, filter rows, and even create new columns without affecting the source system.

Summary

Integration Services provides a wealth of resources for accessing data from various sources in various forms. The connection managers make it possible to access resources in a consistent and central location, making it easy to manage and configure packages. There are three categories of connection managers. Those that connect to data servers, those that connect to network services and those that return file system paths for accessing folders and files. Data sources and Data Source Views are two new technologies that make it easy to abstract the details of source data from the querying clients.

Logging and the Stock Log Providers

"I'VE GOT SOME GOOD IDEAS ABOUT LOGGING."—SERGEI IVANOV

The Basics

One of the most important features of Integration Services is logging. Logging is one of the ways people troubleshoot their processes. You can use logging to watch the progress of packages. Logging can alert you to errors that would otherwise be hard to diagnose or locate. In many ways, logging is indispensable in the production environment, so it is important to have a powerful and flexible logging infrastructure.

Logging in Integration Services is all that and more. The package writer can configure log entries to be written to zero, one, or many different locations simultaneously. Different tasks can log to different locations and use different filters. You can log to several different formats, including text, XML, and SQL. You can also view log entries in the Designer Log Events window as you test packages.

A single log message is called a log entry. Log entries come from a variety of sources, including the SSIS infrastructure, stock tasks, and custom logging. You can set up log filters to eliminate whole or parts of log entries. Filters can be saved to a file and later reloaded in other packages, making it easy to get consistent logging across packages.

A single type of log is called a log event, which components register so that the runtime can configure and filter them. A single log entry is, therefore, an instance of a log event. Log entries are often confused with package events. This is probably because the runtime registers a log event for every package event, and creates a new log entry every time a package raises a package event. However, the two should be distinguished. Package events result from substantial occurrences inside a package and for every package event, the runtime generates a log entry. However, this is only part of what ultimately ends up in an IS log. Components can also log any useful information at any time through the IS logging infrastructure, without limitations. As you'll see later, you can also implement custom logging.

Log providers are Integration Services components that perform the actual output. There are several types of log providers, each responsible for outputting the package log entries to a specific format. For example, the XML Log Provider takes all the log entries the Integration Services runtime sends its way and writes them out to an XML file. The Text Log Provider writes all the log entries to a text file, and so forth.

Quickstart

To get started, let's do some simple logging. This will give you a good feel for where things are and a chance to try it before getting into all the details.

Default Logging

Open the designer (BIDS) and create a new Integration Services project. Before adding any tasks or modifying the package in any way, go ahead and run it. Not much happens in the package, right? The point here is that, by default, all packages log their start and finish results into the Windows Event Viewer. There's no way to turn this off.

Open up the Windows Event Viewer under Administrative Tools on the Start menu. There should be two events logged from the SQLISPackage: the package started and finished events. Figure 11.1 shows the Event Viewer on the sample machine with the two events from the package. To see the details, double-click on one of the events.

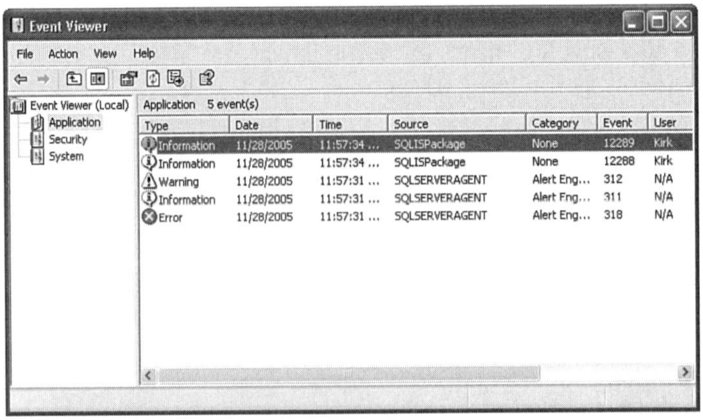

FIGURE 11.1   Packages automatically log start and finish events to the Windows event log.

<u>**NOTE**</u>

In many cases, individuals do not configure any logging on their packages, but later regret it because they have no way to determine which packages are still being used in their system or even how often the packages get executed.

Configuring Package Logging

Now, let's add a little more logging to the package. Drop a Script Task onto the package, right-click on the Control Flow designer, and select Logging. The Configure SSIS Logs dialog box opens, as shown in Figure 11.2.

<u>**TIP**</u>

Make sure you select [Shift+F5] to stop debugging or click the square Stop Debugging toolbar button to enable the Logging menu option. If you're still in debug mode, the designer disables the logging options menu.

Let's configure the package to log to a trace file. Notice the package (Logging) and Script Task nodes in Figure 11.2. Selecting the container in this tree indicates that you want to enable logging for that container. In the designer, put a check mark in the check box for the package and the Script Task. Checking the nodes in this way doesn't fully configure logging; you still need to set up the log destinations and filtering. To do that, click on the package node and select the SQL Profiler type from the Provider Types drop down. Click the Add button. This adds a new SQL Profiler log provider to the package. Next, you need to configure the log provider. This log provider needs a file connection manager, so click on the configuration and the drop down will have a New Connection option. Select that option to create a file connection manager that points to a trace file somewhere on your file system. Make sure the log provider is checked and then click on the Script Task node in the left window. Notice that the dialog box hides the option to create and delete log providers because instances of log providers can only be created at the package level. With the Script Task node selected, make sure that the log provider has a check mark next to it. Your dialog box should look similar to Figure 11.2.

You now have the log providers set up and both the package and the task are configured to send logs to the profiler log provider. Next, let's configure the filters for each of the containers. Click the Details tab on the top of the dialog box next to the Providers and Logs tab. This is where you filter log events. Each selection you make here is specific to the container you have selected in the left window such that the set of selected log events with the Script Task node selected might be different than the set of selected log events for the package. For this example, all the events for both containers are selected. The check box next to the Events label in the header toggles all the events.

Figure 11.3 shows the Details view of the Configure SSIS Logs dialog box.

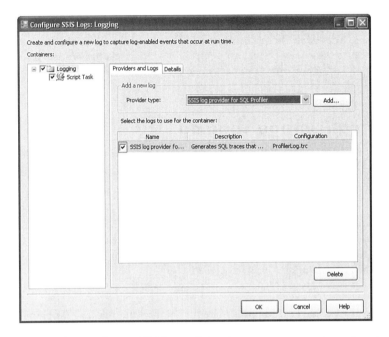

FIGURE 11.2   Use the Configure SSIS Logs dialog box to set up package logging.

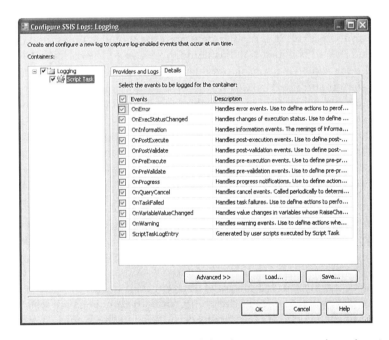

FIGURE 11.3   Use the Configure SSIS Logs dialog box to set up package logging.

Also, notice that there is an additional log event for the Script Task node called `ScriptTaskLogEntry`. That's because the Script Task registers the additional log event type. To create log entries of this type, double-click on the Script Task. Select the Script node in the left window and click on the Design Script button. Delete the code comments that say "Add your code here," and in its place, add the following line:

```
Dts.Log("This is a test log entry", 0, Nothing)
```

Now, you are all set up for logging. You have created a SQL Profiler log provider in the package, configured the package and Script Task to log to the SQL profiler trace file, selected the events you want logged from the package and the Script Task, and even added some custom logging from the Script Task. If you run the package now, it will create a few log entries in the trace file you specified in the file connection manager. To view the log, open SQL Profiler from the main SQL Server Start menu under Performance Tools. In SQL Profiler, select File from the main menu and select Open, Trace File or [Ctrl+O] and select the file you previously specified in the file connection manager. Figure 11.4 shows the trace file that was created.

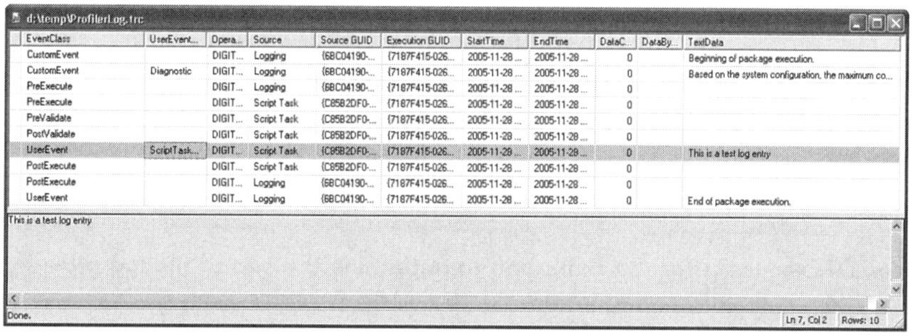

FIGURE 11.4   SQL Profiler shows the log with the custom log entry.

This should give you a pretty good idea how to configure logging. There's also a sample package called `Logging.dtsx` in the `\Samples\S11-Logging` sample folder. The package is fairly simple but illustrates how you can configure logging in a package so that different tasks log to different destinations each having its own filter. Try changing the logging settings and filters a bit and see how it affects the logs.

NOTE

The log providers use connection managers to determine where to create the logs. The connection managers each have an expression to build the `ConnectionString` and point to the temporary working folder. Look at the `SAMPLES::WORKINGFOLDER` variable to find where the package creates the log files.

The Stock Log Providers

As with other SSIS pluggable components, Microsoft provides some stock log providers that cover a broad range of logging requirements. There are no dedicated designers for log providers like there are for tasks and components, but the designer does provide a way to edit the filter and output settings generically. Because each log provider supports a different output format, each requires a slightly different configuration. Following is a description of each log provider and how to configure it.

Windows Event Log Provider

The Windows Event Log Provider writes logs to the Windows event log and so it doesn't require a connection manager at all. This has been confusing to some users who attempt to create a connection manager or otherwise enter some value for the configuration in the Logging Configuration dialog box. For this log provider, it is safe to ignore the configuration.

TIP

To set up a log provider for a package you run with DTExec, you use the /Logger switch. Normally, the /Logger switch expects two parameters within quotes: the name of the log provider to use and the configstring argument within the quotes. Because the event log doesn't require a configuration, you would think the command line would look similar to this:

```
DTExec … /LOGGER "DTS.LogProviderEventLog.1"
```

However, DTExec looks for the semicolon to determine the end of the log provider name. So, to successfully configure the Windows Log Provider using DTExec, use the following format with the semicolon appended to the name inside the quotes and a dummy configuration.

```
DTExec … /LOGGER "DTS.LogProviderEventLog.1;Foo"
```

Text File Log Provider

The Text File Log Provider writes out log entries to comma separated values in text files. The files generated with the Text File Log Provider are amenable to viewing in Excel or consumed in the Data Flow Task, which makes it simple to have a postprocessing Data Flow Task that does analysis on the logs. The LoadTxtLog.dtsx sample package in the S11-Logging solution shows how to set up the Data Flow Task to consume a text log file. There is a little trick to getting the header just right because of the "#Fields:" string the text provider inserts. This package consumes the text log file that the Logging.dtsx sample package generates, so be sure to run the Logging.dtsx sample package before running the LoadTxtLog.dtsx sample package.

XML Log Provider

You configure the XML Log Provider the same as you do the Text File Log Provider. The difference is, of course, that the XML Log Provider creates an XML file. Figure 11.5 shows the XML log file generated from the sample package.

FIGURE 11.5   View XML logs in any browser.

The advantage to the XML format is that the logs can be consumed by any XML-aware system without concern for compatibility with the Integration Services logging schema. You can also use XML utilities such as XSL transforms to convert logs to HTML reports.

SQL Server Log Provider

The SQL Server Log Provider adds log entries to the system table called sysdtslog90 and requires an OLEDB connection to an instance of SQL Server and containing the target database name. If the sysdtslog90 table does not exist in the destination database, the SQL Server Log Provider creates it. The default database is MSDB.

The advantage of this logging method is that you can use the full querying power of SQL Server to process the logs. It's a good choice as your default log provider.

SQL Profiler Log Provider

As you saw previously, the SQL Profiler Log Provider requires a file connection manager and outputs the log entries in native SQL Profiler format. Logging to SQL Profiler makes it possible to correlate the log entries from the package to other activities that you want to view in SQL Profiler, such as queries, stored procedures, and so forth while helping you analyze the impact package runs have on system performance.

Designer Log Events Viewer—The "Virtual Log Provider"

Occasionally, it's nice to be able to see the logs in the designer as you are developing packages. The Designer Log Events window isn't a log provider, but it functions in much the same way as log providers do. It only displays log entries according to the filter settings in the Logging Configuration dialog box. It is something like a virtual log provider as the package writes none of the log entries to disk anywhere. Figure 11.6 shows the Log Events window after executing the `Logging.dtsx` sample package.

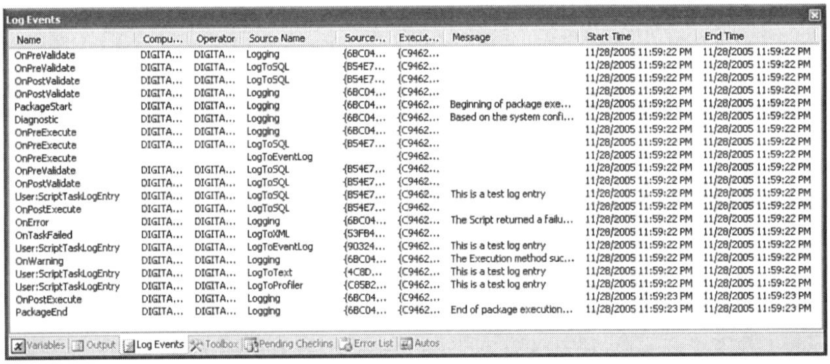

FIGURE 11.6   The Log Events window shows log events inside the designer.

The advantage of this logging method is that you don't actually have to configure a log file or SQL connection. Simply enabling logging on containers is sufficient. As the package matures and you better understand how the logging requirements apply to the package, you can configure one of the other log providers as appropriate. This window can be used to quickly determine which combination of filters to use to get just the right logging coverage.

TIP

DTExec.exe also provides a similar function using the /consolelog parameter.

Logging Providers and Logging Options

You're probably already starting to get a good picture of the architecture that underlies logging in Integration Services. As you can see from the preceding text, log providers are associated with the package and logging options are somehow associated with containers. This section quickly describes how log providers and logging options work together to help you better understand logging overall.

As described earlier, log providers are components that take log entries as input and send them to a destination. With any pluggable component architecture, there are contracts or agreements between the component and the architecture it plugs into. In the case of Integration Services logging, the agreement is that the runtime will manage the exclusion or inclusion of log entries, channeling the log entries to the right log provider, configuring and storing log entry and column filtering. The log providers agree to actually put the log entries somewhere. Log providers know nothing about filtering and the runtime knows nothing about how to write out a log event to a file or anywhere else for that matter. Log providers and the runtime are partners in the agreement, each relying on the other to do its part.

Log Providers

The runtime supports having multiple log providers in one package. In fact, it's possible to have more than one instance of the same log provider associated with the same package. Because components can also be associated with more than one log provider, it's also possible to support logging to multiple destinations simultaneously, even from the same component. The package has a collection of log providers. This is why in the Configure Logging dialog box, the option to create and delete log providers is only visible when you select the package node.

Logging Options

The runtime portion of the agreement is to filter, channel, and store the logging settings and does it through what are called logging options. A logging option is an object. On each container, including the Package, Sequence, Loops, and Taskhost, there is a collection of logging options objects that contain the settings you create in the Configure Logging dialog box. This is why in the Configure Logging dialog box, there is an option to create filters on all containers.

> **NOTE**
>
> The logging options have the ability to filter log entries exclusively or inclusively. However, the Configure Logging dialog box hides that detail from you.

There is also a property on containers called LoggingMode. This property has three states: Enabled, Disabled, and UseParentSetting.

- `Enabled`—Enable all logging from the container. This is the default.

- `Disabled`—Disable all logging from the container, but retain logging options.

- `UseParentSetting`—Use the `LoggingMode` and logging options from the parent. This setting is helpful when you have established a filter at the package or other parent container level that you want to use throughout the package. You can create your filters once and then set the rest of the container `LoggingMode` properties to `UseParentSetting`. Then, you only need configure logging in one place, even if you need to modify it later.

CAUTION

The `UseParentSetting` is helpful as noted, but can cause unexpected behavior. Depending on the method you use to filter log events, it is possible that certain log events that a child task exposes will be unexpectedly filtered because the log event isn't supported by the parent. For example, the Script Task supports the `ScriptTaskLogEntry` log event. But, the package doesn't. The `ScriptTaskLogEntry` event will be filtered out if the Script Task's `LoggingMode` is set to `UseParentSetting` and the parent is using Inclusive filtering. The Configure Logging dialog box uses inclusive filtering, meaning only those log events that have been selected will be allowed to be logged. Because the child log event is not visible at the parent, it cannot be included and will, therefore, be unavailable.

Logging Schema

The logging schema contains the fields shown in Table 11.1.

TABLE 11.1   Integration Services Logging Schema

Element	Description
Computer	The name of the computer on which the log event occurred.
Operator	The identity of the user who launched the package.
SourceName	The name of the container or task in which the log event occurred.
SourceID	The GUID ID of the container in which the log event occurred.
ExecutionID	The GUID of the package execution instance. The ExecutionID is uniquely generated for every package execution.
MessageText	The message associated with the log entry.
DataCode	The log event-specific code that indicates the content of the DataBytes field.
DataBytes	A byte array specific to the log entry. The meaning of this field varies by log entry. It is typically used as a log payload and can contain data or text.
StartTime	The time the log event started.
EndTime	The time the log event completed.

Log Events

The following is a list of log events you might see in your logs and a description of each. The stock log events are those log events that the IS runtime registers and logs whenever there is an event of the same name. These log events will always be available for all containers. Table 11.2 shows those log events.

TABLE 11.2   Stock Log Events

Event Log Entry	Description
OnError	Writes a log entry when an error occurs
OnExecStatusChanged	Writes a log entry when the execution status of the executable changes
OnInformation	Writes a log entry during the validation and execution of an executable to report information
OnPostExecute	Writes a log entry immediately after the executable has finished running
OnPostValidate	Writes a log entry when the validation of the executable finishes
OnPreExecute	Writes a log entry immediately before the executable runs
OnPreValidate	Writes a log entry when the validation of the executable starts
OnProgress	Writes a log entry when measurable progress is made by the executable
OnQueryCancel	Writes a log entry at any juncture in the task processing where it is feasible to cancel execution
OnTaskFailed	Writes a log entry when a task fails
OnVariableValueChanged	Writes a log entry when the value of a variable changes
OnWarning	Writes a log entry when a warning occurs

The stock task log events are those log events that IS stock tasks register and log. These log events are only available in and logged from the specific tasks noted. Table 11.3 shows the stock task log events.

TABLE 11.3   Stock Task Log Events

Task Name	Log Event Name	Description
Execute SQL	ExecutingQuery	Logs entry with the query
Bulk Insert	Begin	Logs when task begins insert
Bulk Insert	End	Logs when task completes insert

TABLE 11.3   Continued

Task Name	Log Event Name	Description
Bulk Insert	TaskInfo	Logs the bulk insert task information, such as row delimiters, column delimiters, format file path, source connection, destination connection, destination table name, and data file type
Data Flow	BufferSizeTuning	Logs when the Data Flow Task changes the buffer size and it is different from the default values and includes buffer size and reasons for the change
Data Flow	BufferLeak	Logs when a transform holds onto buffer references and should be releasing them; useful for building custom transforms
Data Flow	ExecutionPlan	Logs the execution plan
Data Flow	ExecutionTrees	Logs the input the Data Flow Task scheduler was given when forming the execution plan
Data Flow	Initialization	Logs Data Flow Task initialization information, such as Buffer Size, Buffer Row Size, and Not Optimized Mode
Execute DTS 2000 Package	TaskBegin	Logs when the DTS package starts executing
Execute DTS 2000 Package	TaskEnd	Logs when the DTS package completes executing
Execute DTS 2000 Package	TaskInfo	Logs information about the DTS 2000 Package, such as the package name and package location
Execute DTS 2000 Package	TaskResult	Logs the result of the task

TABLE 11.3   Continued

Task Name	Log Event Name	Description
Execute Process	ExecutingProcess	Logs information about the process, such as the executable name, working directory, window style, and so on
Execute Process	Variable Routing	Logs the name of the variables where the task will store Standard Input, Standard Output, and Standard Error
File System	Operation	Logs the operation the task performed, including copy, delete, create directory, and so on
FTP	ConnectingToServer	Logs when the task attempts to connect to the FTP server
FTP	Operation	Logs the operation the task performed, including get, put, create directory, and so on
MSMQ	AfterOpen	Logs after the queue is opened for reading
MSMQ	BeforeOpen	Logs before the queue is opened for reading
MSMQ	BeginReceive	Logs before receiving the message
MSMQ	BeginSend	Logs before sending the message
MSMQ	EndReceive	Logs after receiving the message
MSMQ	EndSend	Logs after sending the message
MSMQ	TaskInfo	Logs task information, such as the queue type, queue path, use DTS 2000 format, encryption enabled, encryption algorithm, message type, and so on
MSMQ	TaskTimeOut	Logs when a timeout occurs while receiving a message

TABLE 11.3   Continued

Task Name	Log Event Name	Description
Script	LogEntry	User-generated log entries. Can be logged anytime with any description and content
Send Mail	TaskBegin	Logs when task begins sending
Send Mail	TaskEnd	Logs when sending completed
Send Mail	TaskInfo	Logs information about the task, such as To, From, CC, Subject, Priority, and so on
Transfer Database	DestSQLServer	Logs the destination server instance name
Transfer Database	SourceDB	Logs the source database name
Transfer Database	SourceSQLServer	Logs the source server instance name
All Transfer Tasks	FinishedTransferringObjects	Logs when task completes transfer of error messages
All Transfer Tasks	StartTransferringObjects	Logs when task starts to transfer error messages
Web Services	WSTaskBegin	Logs before executing web methods
Web Services	WSTaskEnd	Logs after executing web methods
Web Services	WSTaskInfo	Logs task information, such as connection name, service name, output type, output location, and web method
WMI Data Reader	Operation	Logs the WMI query used to retrieve data
WMI Event Watcher	EventOccurred	Logs when the event the task was waiting for occurred
WMI Event Watcher	EventTimedOut	Logs when the task is waiting for an event and times out
XML	Operation	Logs the operation the task will perform, including diff, merge, patch, XSLT, XPath, and Validate

Custom Logging

Integration Services logging is flexible and there are several options for logging destinations. However, with the standard facilities, logging might not always be as surgical as you'd like. Also, as you've seen previously, you can only create log events that the components support. There are several methods to augment and enhance the standard logging events and infrastructure. What follows is a description of two of those methods.

Using the Script Task and Script Component

This is by far the easiest and simplest way to do custom logging. In the previous quick-start sample, this method was used to add a custom log entry as well as the sample packages for this chapter. For most cases, this method is the best choice for custom logging.

In the Script Task, the code to write to the log is as follows:

```
Dts.Log(messageText as String, dataCode as Integer, dataBytes() as Byte )
```

And you log the message similar to the following:

```
Dts.Log("This is a log entry message", 42, nothing)
```

You log in the Script transform the same way with the exception that you need to omit the "Dts." prefix. You'd write the log in the script component as follows:

```
Log("This is a script component message", 42, nothing)
```

The dataCode is caller dependent and can be any integer. These log entries show up with the name ScriptLogEntry, so if you plan to parse the logs later and you want to find a particular custom log entry, give it a unique ID to differentiate it from the others.

Using the SQL Task

An even more flexible way to do custom logging is to use the SQL Task. This approach has its advantages and disadvantages.

The disadvantages to using the SQL Task are as follows:

- Log entries can only be sent to SQL Server. None of the other logging destinations are possible.

- It is more complicated to set up and manage.

- It doesn't respond to changes you make in the designer for log settings.

The advantages to using the SQL Task are as follows:

- Log entries can conform to Integration Services logging schema and show up in the sysdtslog90 table.

- Log entries don't have to conform to Integration Services logging schema and can thus be expanded, simplified, or enhanced.

- Log entries can conform to legacy or third-party schema for log reporting, dash-boarding, or monitoring applications.

The sample package `CustomLogging.dtsx` in the S11-Logging solution creates a simple table in the ISSAMPLES sample database called CustomLog with the following statement:

```
USE [SSISSAMPLES]
GO
if OBJECT_ID('CustomLog') IS NULL
CREATE TABLE CustomLog (
  username varchar(50),
  packagename varchar(50),
  machinename varchar(50),
  packageID varchar(50),
  starttime datetime
);
GO
```

This is there just for purposes of the sample to create the table. It's not necessary, of course, if the table already exists in a production environment.

The second SQL Task has the following `INSERT` statement:

```
INSERT INTO CustomLog VALUES(?,?,?,?,?);
  /* username    varchar(50),
     packagename varchar(50),
     machinename varchar(50),
     packageID   varchar(50),
     starttime   date */
```

Next, some of the system variables are mapped to the query using parameter mappings. Figure 11.7 shows the Parameter Mapping tab of the Execute SQL Task Editor. This creates a new row with the values of the system variables listed and generates a nice table that tracks executed packages, their names, IDs, where they were executed, and at what time. This log schema doesn't include anything you don't get with the IS log schema, but it's easy to see how you could change the sample to implement your own that conforms to your custom schema.

Put this SQL Task in the package at package scope to log simple information about the run of the package. Now, whenever you run the package, it enters a log into the PackageRun table, as shown in Figure 11.7. You can use this pattern to log any information you want in any schema you want inside a package without constraints.

FIGURE 11.7   Use parameter mappings to include package information in your logs.

Summary

Existing log events cover a lot of ground and the IS logging infrastructure generously handles the general logging case, but it's a broad brush and doesn't always get as detailed as you'd like. There are situations in which there is no way to log specific information. For example, you might want to log the parameters to event handlers, the LocaleID of a specific container, or task execution values. This logging mechanism can be used for those and just about any other type of custom logging you'd like at any time during the execution of the package and is great for one off, surgical logging of custom data that the existing log infrastructure doesn't support. If you ever run into a situation in which you wished something got logged, but it didn't, this method might fill in the gaps.

The Venerable Variable

"IT'S REALLY EASY IF YOU'RE IGNORANT."—JAMES HOWEY

In each succeeding version of DTS, variables have taken on a more important and central role in packages. This is certainly true of Integration Services (IS). In IS, variables have become absolutely essential. Variables are the primary method of communication between all components and make it possible to create packages that are more dynamic and configurable. This chapter discusses important concepts about variables and how to use them.

A common guideline in any traditional coding or development environment, "Hard-coding strings is bad," holds true for IS as well. Specifying the location of a file or the name of a table by directly typing it into a property should be avoided because it's difficult to manage and update packages written that way. Variables should be used extensively within the package for all settings. Following are some examples of how components use variables:

- Tasks use variables to store results that can be used in other components.

- Foreach Enumerators use variables to store the values of the current item being enumerated.

- Source adapters use variables to specify which table to reference.

- Variables are the primary method of dynamically building settings in expressions.

- The Script Task can use variables as input parameters.
- The SQL Task uses variables as parameters in queries and stored procedures.
- Event handlers have system variables that hold the value of the event parameters.
- The For Loop uses variables to determine when the loop should terminate.

Because variables have an expanded role and set of features, have grown in importance, and come in different flavors, this chapter is dedicated to thoroughly describing them.

So, what is an Integration Services variable? Simply put, IS variables are objects that store values and that other objects such as tasks and transforms use to store data temporarily.

NOTE

Variables were known as "Global Variables" in DTS. The reason Microsoft dropped the "Global" moniker is because variables in IS have scope and are not always visible to the entire package. Although you can still create variables at the package level (global) in IS, variables can now be created at different scopes throughout the package on containers.

Important Variable Concepts—Properties, Scope, Type, and Namespace

Variables in Integration Services function much like variables in structured programming—they store values temporarily. However, in Integration Services, they are also objects, and therefore have properties and behaviors. This section drills down a little more on variable properties and behavior.

Variable Properties

For an object that simply serves as a temporary storage location for other objects, the variable is a fairly complex thing. There are a few properties that you'd expect, such as Name, Value, and Type. However, there are others that might be a little unexpected, such as RaiseChangedEvent, EvaluateAsExpression, and QualifiedName. So, the following list takes a look at each of these properties and their purpose.

- **Name**—Variables are one of the few objects in IS that actually enforce naming rules. Connections are the other. For other objects, such as tasks, it's not so important to have unique names because they're not referenced within the package by other objects. However, variables are referenced by other components and if IS didn't enforce unique names for them, it would be very easy to break a package. Suppose you have a package with a task that uses a variable with the name vServer and the task uses the variable to indicate which server contains a table it references to look up information. Later, someone else edits the package and creates a new variable with the same name but with a different server name. Execute the package and it is possible that the task will reference the new variable and attempt to access the wrong server, failing to find the table. Enforcing unique variable names ensures that variables referenced by name will not get confused.

- **ID**—The ID is a globally unique identifier, commonly called globally unique identifiers (GUIDs). This property is read-only.

- **Description**—This property is for documenting information about the variable. You can put descriptive information about what the variable is for, how it is used, from where its value comes, and so on.

- **CreationName**—This property does not serve a purpose for variables and should be ignored. CreationName is a property that is found on all named objects. Only extensible objects actually use this property. Others, such as variables and precedence constraints, do not. The designer hides this property because it is only useful to object model client applications, such as Business Intelligence Development Studio.

- **ValueType**—This property exposes the type of the value the variable holds. Type is more important in IS than it was in DTS. IS is type safe. This means IS won't allow changes to a variable's type while a package is executing. This helps to eliminate pathological package errors caused by type mismatches. Failing at the type change event makes failures more obvious at the location that causes them, instead of later when the type change causes the error.

- **Value**—This property holds the stored value. It can be any type as described in Table 12.1.

- **ReadOnly**—This Boolean property affects the Value property. If set to TRUE, the Value property is read-only during execution. This property can be changed at design time.

- **QualifiedName**—Variables now have namespaces and this string property exposes the name of the variable together with its namespace in the proper format, which is: [Namespace::]Name. If there is no namespace given to the variable, only the name shows.

- **RaiseChangedEvent**—This Boolean property controls the VariableValueChangedEvent. If set to TRUE, the variable raises the event whenever its value changes.

- **Scope**—This read-only string property reflects the container on which the variable was created. It is shown as a property of variables in the designer, but it's actually not found on the variable object. It is synthesized by the designer and shown in the properties window to help users better see where the variable is defined.

- **SystemVariable**—This Boolean read-only property is only true for system variables. System variables are variables that IS creates to communicate information about the environment to components in the package.

- **EvaluateAsExpression**—This Boolean property controls how the expression property is used. If set to TRUE, the variable returns the result of the expression as its value. If set to FALSE, the expression is ignored.

- **Expression**—This string property holds an IS expression.

Variable Scope

Variable scope is a feature that provides a way to create variables in a location close to where packages use them. You build packages around a structure of containers and each container creates a pocket of functionality. This is good because it is generally easier to understand and manage packages built this way. For more on this, see Chapter 7, "Grouping Control Flow with Containers."

In very simple terms, variable scope is about visibility and safety. If a variable is out of scope, it's not visible. This means that fewer objects have access to the variable, which means that there are fewer opportunities for the variable to be accidentally modified. In small packages, this isn't usually a problem. But the problem is magnified as packages grow more complex.

Scoping variables allows you to better organize them and eliminates complexity. For example, if you define a lot of variables at the package level, they are all shown together in a cluttered view. It can be quite time consuming and frustrating to search through large lists of variables to find the one you want, especially when opening selection boxes in the component user interfaces. By scoping variables throughout the package in locations that are closest to where they are used, it is easier to find variables that apply to that part of a package without having to filter through all the unrelated variables.

The following are the variable scoping rules in IS:

- A variable created on a container is visible to all its children containers.

- A variable defined on a container "hides" a variable with the same qualified name on that container's parent or grandparent and all ancestors.

- A variable defined on a container is not visible to that container's ancestor, sibling, or children of sibling containers. For a variable to be visible to a component, it must be created on that component or on an ancestor of that container.

- A variable that is visible to an Execute Package Task is visible to the package it executes.

Variable Inheritance

As the simple conceptual model of variables in a package in Figure 12.1 shows, variables created at the package level are visible to the rest of the package. Variables created at the level of the task, on the Taskhost, are only visible to the task. Variables created on a parent container are visible to all its children. Notice that as you get closer to the tasks, the number of variables in scope increases if there are variables created on parent containers.

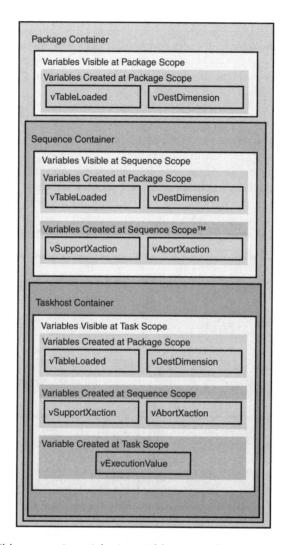

FIGURE 12.1   Children containers inherit variables created on ancestors.

Variable Hiding

A side effect of variable scope is variable hiding, which is what happens when a variable is created with the same name as another variable at higher scope. This effectively hides the variable at higher scope from all containers at or below the level of the new variable. Generally, it's not a good idea to name variables the same. But there are rare times when it is useful. It is because of variable hiding that it is possible to hide parent package variables in child packages. If lower scope variables didn't hide higher scope variables, it would be possible to break a child package by adding a variable with a differently typed value but the same name at outer scope. It would be possible for a component to confuse the two and possibly retrieve the wrong one.

CAUTION
_____

Although it is supported, there are very few good reasons for creating locally scoped variables with the same name as globally scoped ones. Unless you have a really good reason, you should avoid doing this. One of the situations in which it is useful to do this is discussed in the section "Parent Package Configurations."

Sibling Container Variables Not in the Same Scope

This is where variable scoping becomes quite powerful because this aspect of scoping is what allows the variables to be localized to subparts of the package where they are used. Figure 12.2 shows a simple conceptual model of a package with two tasks. Notice that there are four variables in the package. Two are found on the package and the other two in the tasks. Task1 has a variable created in its scope called vExecutionValue. Yet it's not visible to Task2. Likewise, vScriptSource, the variable defined in Task2's scope, is not visible to Task1.

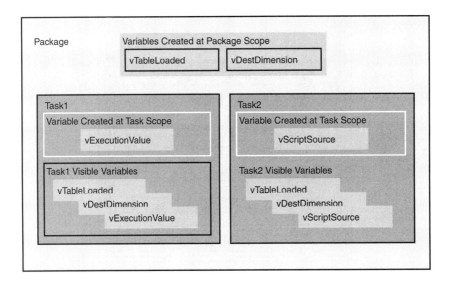

FIGURE 12.2   Variables on sibling containers are not in the same scope.

The Execute Package Task Scoping Wrinkle

When you create solutions, you'll ideally create packages that factor along certain functions, and then call out to those packages when you need their function so that you only implement the function once. This is smart package design because it eliminates duplicated effort and if there is an issue with the package, you only need to change it in one place.

When you build packages this way, you'll occasionally need to pass information back to the parent package. Perhaps you want to pass back status on the child package or perhaps you use the child package to get information about the machine it's running on and you need a way to get that information back to the parent package. This is simple in IS because child packages follow the same variable scoping rules as containers. The interesting wrinkle here is that the Execute Package Task is considered the parent of the child package. So, because of the rule that variables visible on a parent container are visible to all its children, the variables visible to the Execute Package Task are visible to the child package it is configured to execute as well.

Parent Package Configurations

You might experience a problem when using variables from parent packages if you try to run the child package separately. The reason is because the child package attempts to reference the parent variable and it isn't available. You have at least two options for debugging packages that reference parent package variables:

- Create a temporary variable in the child package with the same name. Using a temporary variable with the same name is useful when the child package is under development. Later, when the package is complete, you can delete the temporary variables and the child package will then reference the parent's variables.

- Use a parent package configuration. Parent package configurations are a more permanent solution, but only work when you want to set a child package variable to the value of the parent package variable. For a full discussion about parent package configurations, see Chapter 14, "Configuring and Deploying Solutions." That chapter covers parent package configurations in detail. It is mentioned here because it is one way to simplify the variable story when creating child packages. You'll still need to define variables in the child package but they won't be temporary and the child package will always reference them.

Variable Type

Variables are capable of holding various types of values. The designer shows the available variable data types as managed data types. It's a little more complicated than that, however. IS variables are actually implemented as COM objects, and they are essentially COM VARIANTs. The designer exposes the available types as managed types. Also, the Data Flow Task uses a wider set of types to reflect the broader type set that SQL Server and other databases provide. Table 12.1 lists those types and how they map to one another.

TABLE 12.1   Variable Type Mappings

Variable Data Type	Variant Data Type	Data Flow Data Type	Description
Boolean	VT_BOOL	DT_BOOL	A Boolean value; TRUE equals -1; FALSE equals 0
Byte	VT_UI1	DT_UI1	A 1-byte, unsigned integer
Char	VT_UI2	DT_UI2	A single character

TABLE 12.1   Continued

Variable Data Type	Variant Data Type	Data Flow Data Type	Description
DateTime	VT_DATE	DT_DBTIMESTAMP	A time stamp structure that consists of year, month, hour, minute, second, and fraction
DBNull	VT_NULL	Not supported in data flow expressions	A null value
Double	VT_R8	DT_R8	A double-precision, floating-point value
Int16	VT_I2	DT_I2	A 2-byte, signed integer
Int32	VT_I4	DT_I4	A 4-byte, signed integer
Int64	VT_I8	DT_I8	An 8-byte, signed integer
Object	Depends on how the object is marshaled	Not supported in data flow expressions	An object
Sbyte	VT_I1	DT_I1	A 1-byte, signed integer
Single	VT_R4	DT_R4	A single-precision, floating-point value
String	VT_BSTR	DT_WSTR	A null-terminated Unicode character string with a maximum length of 4,000 characters
UInt32	VT_UI4	DT_UI4	A 4-byte, unsigned integer
UInt64	VT_UI8	DT_UI8	An 8-byte, unsigned integer

Variable Namespaces

Variable namespaces have been the source of some confusion in the past. They shouldn't be. It's a very simple concept. Think of people names. In many cultures, there is the notion of a first and last name. In western cultures, the first name is how most people refer to a person—it's the casual or "nickname." The last name is used to indicate family, clan, or other affiliation and is generally more formal. First names are commonly used in everyday interactions, but last names are important because they imply grouping and can have other important benefits such as familial association, might even imply some history, and give finer distinction to an individual. In eastern cultures, such as Japan, your family name is your first name and your familiar name is your last. But, the rule still holds true that people call you by your first name because Japanese are typically more formal than your average American and they still use their first names. The point is that few people struggle with first/last name issues even though they're much more complicated than variable namespaces in Integration Services.

Variable namespaces are like last names for variables. They're used for grouping variables. Even if you live in Washington State, part of your family lives in Kansas, part in the UK, and part in the Carolinas, you're all part of a family. Namespaces are a way to identify variables as having something in common.

Namespaces are also a way to distinguish variables from one another. There are many Kirks, Treys, and Rushabhs in the world. Well, there are a lot of people with those names anyway. Add a last name like Haselden, and you've got a pretty good chance that you've got an original name. Add some scoping, for example, all the Kirk Haseldens in Washington State or Trey Johnsons in Florida, and you've narrowed matters down substantially.

Namespaces are sometimes confused for variable scoping as well. In the early days, the designer actually named variables with a namespace that was the name of the container. That was confusing because it made it appear that namespaces and scoping were related somehow. They're absolutely independent. Now the User default namespace is used to differentiate User-created variables from System-created variables. But, that's just the default namespace. You are free to use any namespace you want with the exception of the System namespace. Only IS can use this namespace for system-created variables. Nonqualified variable names are not guaranteed to be unique. So it is possible to create two variables with the same name if their namespaces are different.

Variables with a namespace can still be accessed without appending the namespace. For example, suppose you create a variable called Samples::vADORecordSet. You can still use the nonqualified name vADORecordSet to access the variable, or you can use the qualified name Samples::vADORecordSet. Both are legal. However, especially in organizations in which more than one individual builds packages, it is safer to use the qualified name. If someone else modifies the package or subpackage and adds a variable by the same name, it's possible that they will introduce bugs or otherwise break the package because there is no guaranteed order of retrieval for variables. Using the qualified name, you will ensure that you always get the variable you ask for.

These are a few cases in which namespaces are useful. Most of them boil down to protecting or creating a pocket in which any name can be used without concern for conflicting with other variable names. One case in which namespaces could be used is for wizards. Imagine you've come up with an idea for a wizard that will build a bit of workflow or data flow and insert it into an existing package. Part of the wizard requirements are that it creates variables for the components to use. If there were no namespaces, you'd have to concern yourself with how to name the variables so that they don't conflict with variables that already exist in the package. With namespaces, you don't need to worry. Simply use a namespace that is related to your wizard, something such as your company name or the wizard name like CommonPatternWizard or AcmeCompany. Any variable you create will now be unique throughout the package. As an observant reader, you'll note that it's possible to pick a namespace that is already being used in the package. But, the probability of conflicts is drastically reduced.

Another way to use namespaces to your advantage is to quickly find all the variables within the namespace. The designer allows you to sort the variables by clicking on the column heading. If your package is complex with many variables spread throughout, you can click on the Show All Variables in the Package button and then click on the Namespace column heading to quickly yield a list of all the variables in a given namespace.

TIP

The Namespace column of the Variables window is not visible by default. Click the upper-right button in the Variables window to open the Choose Variable Columns dialog box and select the Namespace option.

System Variables

System variables are a special type of variable that the IS runtime creates to expose information that would otherwise be inaccessible. For example, the very first system variable the IS team created was the System::PackageName variable. It's created at package scope, so it is visible to the contents of the entire package, and, of course, it exposes the package name. Not all system variables are found at package scope, however, and some serve different purposes than just exposing properties on containers. There are basically four classes of system variables as follows:

- System variables that contain the value of properties on objects—These are by far the most common and include System::PackageName and are read-only.

- System variables that support functionality—For example, the System::CancelEvent contains the system event that will be signaled if the package is attempting to terminate. Tasks can read this event to determine if the package is canceling execution and therefore should terminate prematurely.

- System variables that contain parameters from events—When an IS component fires an event, it also passes parameters as part of the event. The package can contain an event handler to handle the event inside the package. The control flow inside the event handler needs access to those parameters. So, the IS runtime places the values of those parameters into system variables that are scoped to the event handler for the event. For example, the OnError event handler has eight system variables. Three of them are common to all event handlers. They are System::SourceName, System::SourceID, and System::SourceDescription. These system variables contain the name, ID, and description of the component that fired the event. The other system variables on the OnError event handler, with one exception, hold the values of the parameters to the event. For example, the error code is in the System::ErrorCode variable and the error description is in the System::ErrorDescription. The one remaining variable is the System::Propagate variable.

- System variables that control package functions—There is only one of these in SQL Server 2005. It's called the System::Propagate variable. It is only found on event handlers and its purpose is to control the propagation of an event up to parent containers. If set to TRUE, which is the default, after the event handler executes, the event is propagated up to the parent container. To propagate the event means that the IS runtime executes the event handler by the same name on the parent container with the same parameter system variable values as the current event handler. System::Propagate is exposed as a system variable this way to inform the runtime engine to propagate the event. Propagating events in this way is useful in cases in which you want to attempt handling the same event in more than just the local event handler. One case is to set the propagate variable based on success or failure of the current event handler. For example, if the event handler succeeds, it can set System::Propagate to FALSE. If it fails, the event propagates up to the parent's event handler where it can be handled in a more general way, for example logging an error or attempting a different workflow.

The System namespace is read-only and cannot be changed. By default, system variables are hidden in the designer to help simplify the variables tray. You can click on the Show System Variables button at the upper-left of the Variables window to make them visible.

Creating and Using Variables

To get to the Variables window, right-click on the designer surface and select Variables. You can find the same menu item on the SSIS main menu tree. Like other windows in the VS environment, the Variables window is dockable and you can move it, collapse it, and, if you're on a multiscreen monitor, move it to your second monitor.

Figure 12.3 shows the buttons that are visible at the upper-left of the Variables window. You use these buttons to create, delete, and sort the variables. The first button on the left is the Add Variable button. The next button is the Delete Variable button. The next button toggles system variables. When you click the Show System Variables button, the designer makes all the system variables in the scope visible. The next button is the Show All User Variables button. This button shows you all the variables in the entire package that are not system variables. Finally, the Choose Columns button allows you to choose which properties of variables will show up as columns in the window.

To change a variable, select the one you want to change and press the F4 key or select View from the main menu and click Properties Window. The Properties window is where you make all your changes to variable properties or you can change the variable values within the Variables window directly. There is no special editor for them.

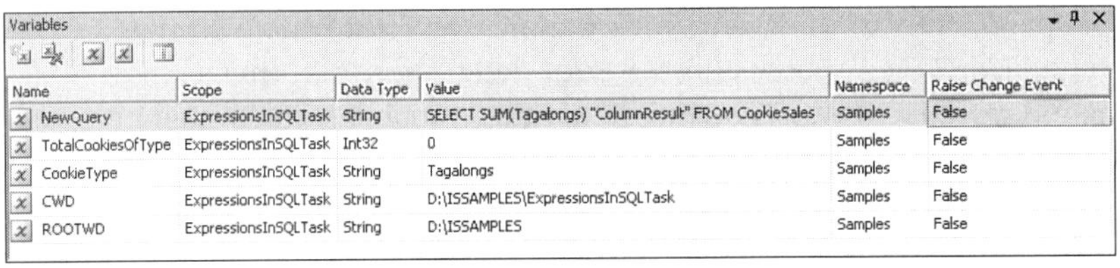

Name	Scope	Data Type	Value	Namespace	Raise Change Event
NewQuery	ExpressionsInSQLTask	String	SELECT SUM(Tagalongs) "ColumnResult" FROM CookieSales	Samples	False
TotalCookiesOfType	ExpressionsInSQLTask	Int32	0	Samples	False
CookieType	ExpressionsInSQLTask	String	Tagalongs	Samples	False
CWD	ExpressionsInSQLTask	String	D:\ISSAMPLES\ExpressionsInSQLTask	Samples	False
ROOTWD	ExpressionsInSQLTask	String	D:\ISSAMPLES	Samples	False

FIGURE 12.3   The Variables window is configurable.

Execution Time Behavior

Variables behave a little differently depending on whether the package is executing. During design time, a variable's type can change; variables can be created, deleted, and renamed; namespaces can be changed; and so on. However, during execution, only the value of the variable can change and the IS runtime does not allow variable creation, deletion, or type change either. The reason for this policy is to make packages more robust and declarative. One of the design guidelines that underlies this decision is that packages should be completed and validated at design time, which makes it easier to detect problems in the package and detect when parts are missing, and so forth.

Of course, variable values can be changed during execution, but not their type. Another way of putting it is variables are type safe during execution. Because the values in variables are often used in expressions or to populate the values of properties on other IS objects and because the properties on those objects are strictly typed, it is dangerous to allow a variable's type to change during package execution. Because assigning a value of a variable with one value type to a property with another type can fail, it is possible to break a well-tested package by simply modifying a package to assign a value of a different type to a variable as it is executing. Therefore, the package prohibits all attempts to assign values to variables that will change the variable type and will emit an error. Whatever type to which they've been configured during design time, variables retain that type during execution.

Variables also cannot hold instances of Integration Services object model objects. For example, a task would not be allowed to set a variable value to point to itself and then later use the Script Task to modify the values of that task. IS variables detect whenever an attempt is made to place an IS object into the value of the variable and will emit an error. The only exception to this rule is Foreach Enumerators. Because of the various ways they can be created and populated, Microsoft felt that there needed to be a little more flexibility in how Foreach Enumerators can be created. This makes certain usage patterns possible; for example, it is possible to populate a ForEachItem Enumerator with a Script Task.

Variable Tips and Tricks

Variables can be used in a variety of ways to simplify your packages. The following section describes some of the more common things people do with variables.

EvaluateAsExpression in SQL Task with Parameters

You might want to use the EvaluateAsExpression feature of variables to simplify the SQL script in the Execute SQL Task. The feature is particularly useful for SQL queries that take parameters.

The SQL Task provides a way to substitute variables as parameters in queries. It's called *parameter mapping*; however, that feature is limited to only certain parts of the query. For example, some OLEDB providers do not allow parameters to be used for column names. The ExpressionsInSQLTask sample shows how you can use the EvaluateAsExpression property on variables to work around this limitation.

The ExpressionsInSQLTask package has three tasks. The first task is a SQL Task and it creates a table in the ISSAMPLES database and populates it with data. The second task is also a SQL Task. It uses a query retrieved from a variable to determine the total number of a particular type of cookie sold. The variable uses the EvaluateAsExpression property to build the query. During execution, the expression returns which column to query based on the CookieType variable. The third task is a Script Task that merely pops up a message box with the total. This is a simple example of how you can use the EvaluateAsExpression property of variables and expressions to prebuild or otherwise preprocess variable values before returning the value to the caller. To see the value change, you can change the CookieType value to one of the following cookie names: DoubleDutch, LemonCoolers, AllAbouts, ThinMints, Samoas, Tagalongs, DoSiDos, and Trefoils.

If you study this package, it should give you some ideas how to use variables and the EvaluateAsExpression property to simplify your packages or to work around infrastructure limitations.

Hiding Parent Variables in Subpackages

Child packages often require the values of variables found in their parent package and typically access those values by directly referencing variables found in the parent package. This can be problematic when designing or executing the child package standalone because parent package variables are only available to the child package when the child package is running as a child. To resolve these issues, it's possible to create variables in the child package with the same names as the parent package variables. Then, when you're done designing and debugging the child package, you can remove the temporary variables. When the package is executed as a child package, it will reference the parent variables.

Storing Objects in Variables

Variables hold things like filenames, numbers, table names, and other integral and string value types. However, variables can also contain objects, or more accurately, they can contain pointers. This means that you can create an object such as a collection of names, a .NET object or a COM object and store its memory location in the variable. Other Integration Services components can then access that object by getting the variable value and using it to access the object. This is especially useful for building collections that will later be consumed by a Foreach Enumerator. For example, you can build a collection of database names in the SQL Task. Later, you can iterate over each of them in the ForEach Loop with workflow to back up each of the databases. See Chapter 13, "Looping and Foreach Enumerators," for more information about this.

Summary

Variables are very important in Integration Services. They are the way components communicate with each other. Variables provide a temporary location for storing data or objects. Variables also provide a way to preprocess settings before actually being used in the package. Variables are type safe but their value can be modified during execution if the new value is not of a different type than the current type of the variable. System variables are a special type of variable that exposes system settings and property values to components in the package and are usually read-only.

Looping and Foreach Enumerators

"IT'S ALWAYS EMPTY, AT LEAST WITH RESPECT TO BEING FULL."—KAMAL HATHI

Integration Services supports looping intrinsically with two containers called the For Loop and the Foreach Loop. These containers provide a way to repeatedly execute the same workflow in a controlled way. The For Loop uses expressions to determine when the loop should terminate. The Foreach Loop executes the body of the loop once for each item in a collection and terminates after the last element in the collection.

The For Loop

The For Loop is really a pretty simple container. It is useful when you need to execute the same workflow repeatedly for a given number of times. It can also be used to execute what are called "forever loops" to do things like polling for an event or to repeat some action continually when you don't know termination count or time frame. For example, some have used this loop to watch for new files to appear in a folder with a task and then process the file with the rest of the workflow before returning to the start of the loop and waiting for the next file. Whether you need to execute a given control flow a predetermined number of times or until a variable has a certain value, the For Loop is for you.

The For Loop has three expressions that control its execution and termination. Figure 13.1 shows the For Loop designer with a basic setup.

FIGURE 13.1   The For Loop uses three expressions to control execution.

As you can see in Figure 13.1, there are two tabs, the For Loop tab and the Expressions tab. The Expressions tab is generally covered in Chapter 9, "Using Expressions." However, to be clear, that tab is the standard way to add property expressions and is not related to the Init, Eval, and Assign expressions the For Loop provides to control execution.

InitExpression

InitExpression is an abbreviated name for Initialization Expression. The For Loop evaluates the InitExpression exactly once at the start of the For Loop execution. It's useful for initializing values of variables that you use in the other two expressions, but it can also be used to evaluate variable values that are modified with the For Loop control flow.

EvalExpression

EvalExpression is an abbreviated name for Evaluation Expression. The For Loop evaluates the EvalExpression for every iteration of the For Loop. It is evaluated at the top of the loop, which means it is evaluated before the control flow in the For Loop Container is executed but after the InitExpression. So, it's possible to have a valid For Loop that executes successfully without any of its contents executing.

For example, if you set the InitExpression to be

@LOOPINDEX = 1

and the EvalExpression to be

@LOOPINDEX < 1

the For Loop executes successfully, but it does not execute its contents.

TIP

The EvalExpression **must evaluate to a Boolean value. In other words, it must use one of the Boolean operators such as <, >, ==, or TRUE, and so on. In fact, if you want to create a "forever loop," you can set the** EvalExpression **to** TRUE**.**

AssignExpression

AssignExpression is an abbreviated name for Assignment Expression. This expression is evaluated at the bottom of each iteration and you generally use it to increment the index value so that the loop will terminate.

In the sample solution, S13-Loops, the package called ForLoop.dtsx contains the simple For Loop shown in Figure 13.1. Inside the loop is a message box that shows the current value of the variable used to hold the index value called LOOPINDEX. Try changing the expressions and running the package to see the effects your changes have on the For Loop execution.

NOTE

The For **and** Foreach Loops **bear a remarkable resemblance to some programming language intrinsics called** For, Foreach, Do While, **and** While Loops, **and that's no coincidence. These language features have been around as long as structured programming and so have proven their value. The** For **and** Foreach Loops **were modeled on their programming language counterparts.**

A While Loop

In Integration Services, the For Loop **is really the equivalent of a** While Loop. **A common question is: "How do you create a** While Loop **in a package?" Both the** While Loop **and the** For Loop **continue to loop until an expression evaluates to** FALSE. **Perhaps the main difference is that most people think of the** For Loop **as self-terminating—in other words, the loop terminates after so many iterations as defined by the expressions and that the expressions really determine if the loop terminates. On the other hand, many people think of a** While Loop **as being terminated by some change that happens external to the loop, such as an event or a variable value changing.** While Loops **in procedural programming typically have a** break **statement.**

The For Loop supports both models and although it is common to think of the assignment and initialization expressions as ways to initialize and increment an index variable, they are not required and any variable can be used as a pseudo break statement to determine if the For Loop should terminate.

Therefore, to set up a While Loop in the For Loop, simply create an expression that tests a variable that can be modified by some workflow either inside or outside the For Loop. If, like a break statement, you also want to bypass workflow in the For Loop as soon as the variable changes, you can use expressions on precedence constraints that test the same variable you use to terminate the loop.

The Foreach Loop

The Foreach Loop is the answer to the question "How do I process a collection in the control flow?" The Foreach Loop is based on the Foreach construct in C# or VB.NET. If you understand the concept in those languages, the Foreach Loop concept is pretty simple; for each item in a collection of items, do "something." In the Foreach Loop, the "something" is to execute the set of tasks the Foreach Loop contains.

Foreach Enumerators

The Foreach Enumerator is an object the Foreach Loop uses to retrieve elements from collections. Depending on the type of object you need to enumerate, you use a different Foreach Enumerator. The seven stock Foreach Enumerators covered in the following sections provide the ability to enumerate a wide range of collection types.

Types of Foreach Enumerators

Some Foreach Enumerators provide one value per iteration. For example, the Foreach File Enumerator provides an enumeration of the files in a folder. For each iteration of the Foreach File Enumerator, it generates one value, the filename. There are also Foreach Enumerators that enumerate collections of collections or collections of multiple values called Collection Foreach Enumerators. For example, the Foreach Item Enumerator can provide multiple values for each iteration of the Foreach Loop. Figure 13.2 illustrates how the Foreach Loop uses Foreach Enumerators.

Variable Mappings

To make the Foreach Loop useful, you need to have a way for the tasks in the Foreach Loop to use the values found in the collection the loop enumerates over. To do this, the Foreach Loop supports variable mappings, which are a way to associate a variable with an element.

Figure 13.2 shows how the Foreach Loop, variable mappings, and the Foreach Enumerator work for the collections with one value per element.

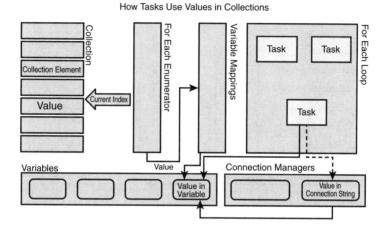

FIGURE 13.2   Foreach Loops use Foreach Enumerators to retrieve elements from collections.

The Foreach Enumerator keeps track of which item in the collection is the current element with an internal index that it increments every time the Foreach Loop requests another element. The variable mappings define which variable should receive the current value. In this way, tasks and connection managers have access to the current enumerated value through the variable. The dashed line represents the fact that sometimes tasks use the enumerated value indirectly by referencing a connection that uses the enumerated value.

Figure 13.3 is a little different than Figure 13.2. It represents a situation in which you are using a Foreach Enumerator that enumerates collections. This is a powerful usage pattern used for a number of dynamic, table- or file-driven scenarios. The difference is that for each iteration, the Foreach Enumerator sets the value of multiple variables and is useful when you need to use the same package workflow pattern just like with a single enumerated value but with multiple values. These are called matrix, multi-valued, or Collection enumerators. The Foreach ADO, Foreach NodeList, and Foreach Item Enumerators are or can be Collection enumerators.

The Foreach Loop Designer
The Foreach Loop designer is a combination of two elements. The base designer with the Collection and Variable Mappings tabs is the dialog box shown in Figure 13.4. The second element is the designer for the Foreach Enumerator. Figure 13.4 shows the Foreach Loop designer with the Collection tab selected and the Foreach Enumerator designer highlighted. Each Foreach Enumerator has its own designer and as you change the enumerator type, the Foreach Enumerator designer also changes.

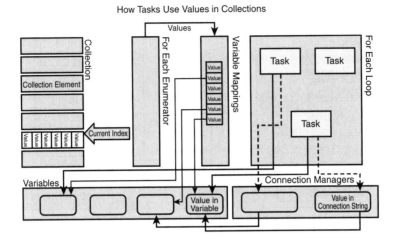

FIGURE 13.3   Tasks use collection element values indirectly through variables.

FIGURE 13.4   The Foreach Loop designer contains the Foreach Enumerator designer.

The Variable Mappings tab shown in Figure 13.5 lets you map the value from the Foreach Enumerator to a variable.

If the Foreach Enumerator only enumerates collections of single elements, the index is always zero. You can add more than one mapping, however. For example, you could have two variables that were both mapped to the same value. This might be useful if one of the variables had an expression that converted the value and one simply provided the value without changing it.

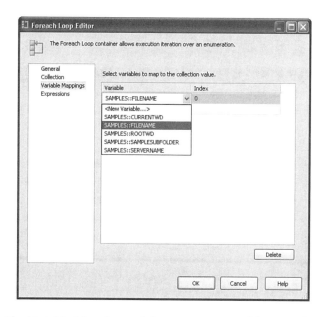

FIGURE 13.5   The Variable Mappings tab lets you map variables to collection elements.

If the Foreach Enumerator is a matrix enumerator, or in other words, each element of the collection is itself a subcollection, the Index field reflects which element of the subcollection you want to map to which variable. For example, if there are three elements in each element collection, you would use an index of 0 (zero) for the first element, 1 for the second, and 2 for the third. Because there is no way for the ForEach Loop designer to know what is contained in each of the elements, there is also no way to specify a more friendly name for a collection element. So, you have to know the order of the elements in the collection.

Stock Foreach Enumerators

Microsoft provides the following stock Foreach Enumerators. Each one has a unique function and provides access to a different type of resource. Although limited in number, this set of enumerators provides access to a broader set of collections than might be immediately obvious.

Foreach File

The Foreach File Enumerator is for enumerating the files in a file system folder. Figure 13.6 shows the designer for this enumerator with the default settings.

The Foreach File Enumerator returns strings that contain the name of a file. The Folder setting is the folder that contains the files you want to enumerate. The Files setting indicates which files to enumerate and supports wildcards. Depending on the settings you specify, the filename can be returned as the fully qualified name (C:\Temp\YourFile.txt), the filename with extension (YourFile.txt), or just the base filename (YourFile). Check the Traverse Subfolders option to enumerate all files that meet the Files specification in the Folders directory and all subdirectories.

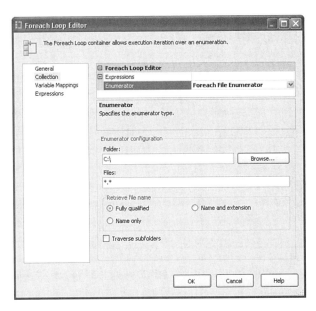

FIGURE 13.6   The Foreach File Enumerator enumerates files in folders.

TIP

The sample package uses a property expression to set the value of the Folder **property to the value of the** WORKINGFOLDER **variable. To see the expression, open the Foreach Loop designer, select the Collection tab, and select the** Expressions **property. The** Directory **property, which is the same as the** Folder **field in the Foreach Loop designer, comes from the** WORKINGFOLDER **variable configured with the** SSISSAMPLESWORKINGFOLDER **environment variable package configuration.**

Foreach Item

The Foreach Item Enumerator is a matrix enumerator that enumerates over a collection of settings you create within the Enumerator designer. It provides a way to create a custom collection and then drive the Foreach Loop with that collection. You specify the columns and column types and then enter data into the columns. The Enumerator designer modifies the entry grid to match the columns you create and checks value types as you enter them.

This Foreach Enumerator is useful when you have a fairly fixed list of nonuniform inputs you want to enumerate repetitively over time. For example, if you need to process the same files, FTP data from the same locations, or perform maintenance tasks on the same servers, you can use the Foreach Item Enumerator to build a custom collection to hold those values. The Foreach Item Enumerator also has the benefit of being independent of connections or outside input, which is useful if you're trying to decrease package dependencies. Figure 13.7 shows the designer for the Foreach Item Enumerator with some data already entered.

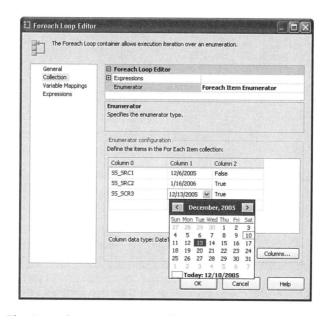

FIGURE 13.7   The Foreach Item Enumerator lets you create custom collections.

The Remove button removes rows. The Columns button allows you to add and remove columns. Depending on the type of the column, you might also get a Type Editor. For example, Column 1 is a DateTime column and so has a Date Type Editor.

The example in Figure 13.7 shows a hypothetical collection you might create if you needed to perform maintenance work on databases every seventh day from the first date in Column1. Column 2 tracks if you want to send email when the loop processes the conditional work.

Because the Foreach Item Enumerator is a matrix enumerator, the Variable Mappings tab looks a little different than nonmatrix enumerators such as the Foreach File Enumerator. Figure 13.8 shows the variable mappings for a sample Foreach Loop with a mapping for each column in the enumerator.

Notice that three variables are defined and that the value from the three columns is mapped to each of them. This one-to-one mapping is typical, but not enforced. You can create multiple mappings per column, which might be useful in rare cases. These variables are used within the loop to control its behavior, and this is what is called a variable-driven loop. For example, the package references the SENDMAIL variable in a precedence constraint to determine if the Send Mail Task should execute. The precedence constraint between the first task and the Conditional Work Task also uses the PROCESSDATE variable to conditionally execute a task on certain dates, but not for all days.

FIGURE 13.8   Matrix enumerators provide more than one variable value per iteration.

TIP

Notice that the variables have been defined at the Foreach Loop scope. It's good practice to define variables at the scope where they are used. If you define the variables at a more global scope, for example at package scope, then tasks outside the loop can modify the variables and alter the behavior of the loop, possibly causing the loop to have timing-related bugs.

Microsoft provided this enumerator as a way to enumerate a collection when there is no default way to generate the collection and to simplify enumerating over custom collections. The Foreach Item Enumerator isn't the right solution for every problem, but it can come in handy when you've got a few manual settings you want to have in a collection and don't want to establish a more formal collection. Try the ForEachItem.dtsx package in the sample solution S13-Loops to better understand the Foreach Item Enumerator. Figure 13.9 shows the workflow of the sample package.

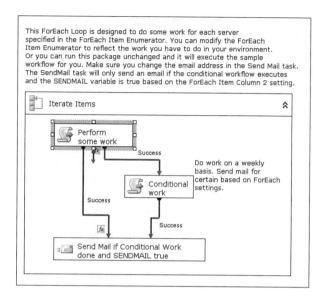

FIGURE 13.9   Matrix enumerators enable complex conditional workflow.

Using matrix enumerators such as the Foreach Item Enumerator, you can drive the behavior of some quite complex Foreach Loops, as you can see in the sample package. The sample package simulates a package that

- Performs some work for every database name in column 0

- Performs conditional work on every seventh day after the date in Column 1 if the previous task was successful

- Sends email conditionally based on the success of the first two tasks and if the value in Column 2 is TRUE

Foreach ADO

The Foreach ADO Enumerator iterates over rows in an ADO recordset or ADO.NET dataset. This is a powerful enumerator for controlling a package with tables. These types of packages are called *table driven* because you can essentially drive a package's execution with the values from rows in a table. Figure 13.10 shows the Foreach ADO Enumerator designer from the sample package.

The sample shows how to enumerate over a set of rows in the first table. It's also possible to iterate over multiple resultsets. The key to setting up this enumerator is creating the resultset. You can do it in a number of ways. The sample package, ForEachADO.dtsx, uses a SQL Task to query the Employee view in the AdventureWorks database for employees with a first name that starts with "C." The SQL Task places the results into a variable of type Object named RESULTSET, which the Foreach ADO Enumerator references. You can also use a Data Flow Task with a Recordset Destination to generate the in-memory results.

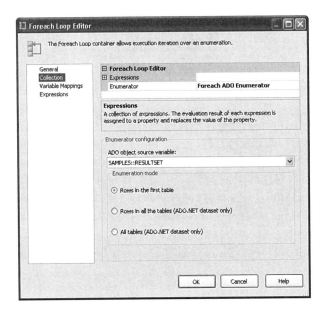

FIGURE 13.10   The Foreach ADO Enumerator supports iterating over an in-memory dataset.

The Foreach ADO Enumerator is also a matrix enumerator. Figure 13.11 shows the Variable Mappings tab from the sample package with the mappings for each of the columns in the query results.

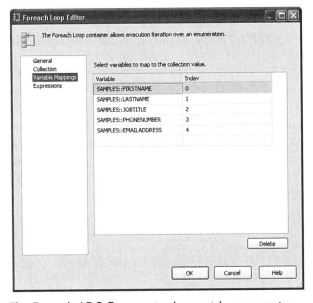

FIGURE 13.11   The Foreach ADO Enumerator is a matrix enumerator.

The Execute SQL Task has the following T-SQL query:

```
USE ADVENTUREWORKS
GO
SELECT      FirstName, LastName, JobTitle, Phone, EmailAddress
FROM            HumanResources.vEmployee
WHERE       FirstName LIKE 'C_____'
```

Notice that five columns are selected which correspond to the five columns in the Variable Mappings tab in Figure 13.11. Figure 13.12 shows the resulting message box with the five values from the five mapped variables.

FIGURE 13.12   The message box shows the results from the SQL Task.

The Foreach ADO Enumerator is a powerful way to drive workflow with data in a table, the results of a query, the results of a data flow, or even a flat file or XML document with the appropriate source adapters in the Data Flow Task. Although the sample is a bit contrived, most users seem to struggle getting the settings on the resultset variable and the mappings correct. So, it's useful as a pattern that you can easily modify to fit your needs.

Foreach ADO.NET Schema Rowset

The ADO.NET Schema Rowset Enumerator provides a way to enumerate the schema for a data source. For example, you can enumerate the tables in a database, catalogs on a server, or columns for a table. For each schema, you can filter the results in a number of ways. Figure 13.13 shows the Foreach ADO.NET Schema Rowset Enumerator Editor with the Catalogs schema selected.

This enumerator is especially useful for maintenance work. For example, you can use this enumerator in combination with the Shrink Database Task to shrink each of your databases within a certain group on an automated regular schedule. Because the enumerator uses a filter to dynamically select the schema instead of a hard-coded set of database names, it would dynamically pick up any new databases and skip any databases that you remove or that happen to be temporarily offline. You can also use it to do auditing of your databases to check security settings, access rights, existence of tables, and so on. Any time you need to perform the same operation on multiple server objects, you can use this enumerator to do it.

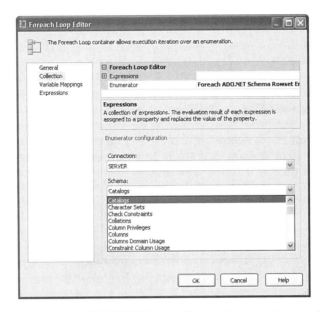

FIGURE 13.13   The Foreach ADO.NET Schema Rowset Enumerator provides a way to enumerate database schema.

Each schema type returns a different set of values, for example, the Catalogs schema contains only one data point, the CATALOG_NAME, and the Column Privileges schema contains TABLE_CATALOG, TABLE_SCHEMA, TABLE_NAME, COLUMN_NAME, GRANTOR, and GRANTEE. You can filter on each of these data points with what are called restrictions. To see the restrictions, click the Set Restrictions button on the Collection tab of the Foreach Loop designer.

Figure 13.14 shows the Tables Schema Restrictions dialog box for the Tables schema.

In this example, the enumerator is referencing the AdventureWorks sample database and enumerating only the tables in the HumanResources schema. Because there are four data elements showing, on the Variable Mappings tab, you can map each of those data elements to variables. The resulting values for tables would be names of tables in the AdventureWorks.HumanResources schema. You can add restrictions for each data point independently as well. For example, in addition to the HumanResources table schema restriction, you could also add a restriction on TABLE_NAME of Employee. This would return one row with the following columns:

- TABLE_CATALOG—AdventureWorks
- TABLE_SCHEMA—HumanResources
- TABLE_NAME—Employee
- TABLE_TYPE—TABLE

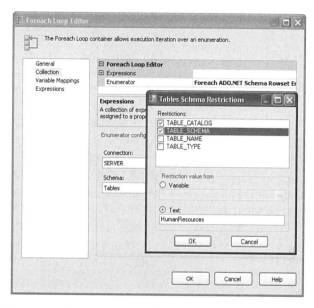

FIGURE 13.14   You can add restrictions to filter the results.

There is no way to specify a wildcard for restrictions.

For those ADO.NET:OLEDB providers that support schema rowsets, the typical collection of supported schema include those in Table 13.1.

TABLE 13.1   Typically Supported Schema

Schema Rowset	Supported Restrictions
DBSCHEMA_CATALOGS	All (CATALOG_NAME)
DBSCHEMA_COLUMN_PRIVILEGES	All (TABLE_CATALOG, TABLE_SCHEMA, TABLE_NAME, COLUMN_NAME, GRANTOR, GRANTEE)
DBSCHEMA_COLUMNS	All (TABLE_CATALOG, TABLE_SCHEMA, TABLE_NAME, COLUMN_NAME)
DBSCHEMA_FOREIGN_KEYS	All (PK_TABLE_CATALOG, PK_TABLE_SCHEMA, PK_TABLE_NAME, FK_TABLE_CATALOG, FK_TABLE_SCHEMA, FK_TABLE_NAME)
DBSCHEMA_INDEXES	1, 2, 3, and 5 (TABLE_CATALOG, TABLE_SCHEMA, INDEX_NAME, TABLE_NAME)

TABLE 13.1 Continued

Schema Rowset	Supported Restrictions
DBSCHEMA_PRIMARY_KEYS	All (TABLE_CATALOG, TABLE_SCHEMA, TABLE_NAME)
DBSCHEMA_PROCEDURE_PARAMETERS	All (PROCEDURE_CATALOG, PROCEDURE_SCHEMA, PROCEDURE_NAME, PARAMETER_NAME)
DBSCHEMA_PROCEDURES	All (PROCEDURE_CATALOG, PROCEDURE_SCHEMA, PROCEDURE_NAME, PROCEDURE_TYPE)
DBSCHEMA_PROVIDER_TYPES	All (DATA_TYPE, BEST_MATCH)
DBSCHEMA_TABLE_PRIVILEGES	All (TABLE_CATALOG, TABLE_SCHEMA, TABLE_NAME, GRANTOR, GRANTEE)
DBSCHEMA_TABLES	All (TABLE_CATALOG, TABLE_SCHEMA, TABLE_NAME, TABLE_TYPE)

To see the Foreach ADO.NET Schema Rowset Enumerator in action, open the sample package ForEachADOSchemaRowset.dtsx in the S13-Loops sample solution. It uses two restrictions to return only the names of the views in the HumanResources schema and shows each of them in a message box. Try changing the restrictions to see how it affects the results.

Foreach From Variable

The Foreach From Variable Enumerator is a little odd because, unlike the other Foreach Enumerators, it doesn't actually represent a domain. In fact, you can create one of the other enumerators in the package with a Script Task, save it to a variable, and use the Foreach From Variable Enumerator to get the Foreach Enumerator you just built. Also, there are certain types of objects in .NET code, such as the String type, that implement the IEnumerator interface. One way the Foreach Loop retrieves elements from collections is through the IEnumerable interface. Because of this, you can enumerate through just about any collection you build in the Script Task with the Foreach Loop. If you build a string with the value "Merry Christmas" and use the Foreach From Variable Enumerator, the Foreach Loop iterates 15 times, each with the next letter in the string starting with 'M' and ending with 's.' This makes the From Variable Enumerator an excellent choice when you want to build collections dynamically.

Figure 13.15 shows the Foreach Loop Editor with the From Variable Enumerator selected.

As you can see, the setup is quite simple. The From Variable Enumerator requires the variable name where the enumerator is stored. The real work is in the package before the ForEach Loop that builds the collection.

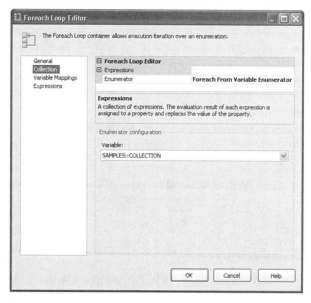

FIGURE 13.15   The Foreach From Variable Enumerator builds enumerators dynamically.

NOTE

The variable must be of type `Object` and the object must support either the managed IEnumerable .NET interface or the IEnumVariant COM interface.

The Sample package `ForEachFromVariable.dtsx` shows how to build a simple array of strings, pass it to a variable, and show it in a message box.

Foreach NodeList

XML documents are basically hierarchical collections of nodes comprised of other nodes, elements, and values. Often, the nodes have a repeating pattern with similar types of information. For example, you might have an XML file that contains a work list. Maybe it's a list of files or tables you need to process. In reality, the types of problems you solve with this enumerator are the same as the other enumerators; the only difference is that the Foreach NodeList Enumerator allows you to drive the `Foreach Loop` with an XML file using the XML concept of the nodelist. The Foreach NodeList Enumerator can function as an array enumerator, providing only one value per iteration, or a matrix enumerator, depending on how you configure it. It can also return different types of values, such as an XML DOM node object, collection, or string. To use this Foreach Enumerator, you'll need a basic understanding of XML and XPath. Printed and web references about these technologies abound, so they aren't explained in detail, but here's a quick review just to get everyone on the same page.

An XML node is a valid, complete structure in an XML document. A node can be very simple, such as this:

```
<simplenode/>
```

or as complex as an entire XML document.

XPath is a way of selecting parts of an XML document. Using simple XPath queries, you can select a set of nodes or values from an XML document. For example, you can write an XPath query to return only one node or one that returns a set of nodes. XPath queries can contain conditional logic or wildcards.

Nodelists are collections of XML nodes and can be returned from an XPath query.

XML navigators are objects that use the cursor model to iterate over nodelists. So, it is possible to write an XPath query that when executed returns a nodelist and then use a navigator to iterate over the nodelist. If you want to find out more, do a search for XPath on MSDN or your favorite search portal.

The sample package, `ForEachNodelist.dtsx` in the sample solution S13-Loops, shows how to configure the Foreach NodeList Enumerator as a matrix enumerator returning two values for each iteration. The XML file that drives the enumerator, `LastProcessed.xml`, is in the `SampleData` subfolder and looks like this:

```
<LastProcessedDate>
 <Info>
  <ID>3</ID>
  <Date>2005-12-13 11:20:00</Date>
 </Info>
 <Info>
  <ID>14</ID>
  <Date>2005-11-12 10:22:00</Date>
 </Info>
</LastProcessedDate>
```

Figure 13.16 shows the Foreach NodeList Enumerator designer with the settings for retrieving the ID number and date as text.

The Document section describes where the enumerator will find the source XML document. The `DocumentSourceType` and `DocumentSource` properties work together to describe to the enumerator where to retrieve the XML source.

The XPath section is where you define the XPath strings the Foreach NodeList Enumerator will use to select nodes from the XML source. The `EnumerationType` property specifies what type the enumerator should return when it finds the selected nodes. The most commonly used setting is likely `NodeText` because it returns a string that other package components can use directly. The `ElementCollection` option is the setting that makes the Foreach NodeList Enumerator a matrix enumerator and enables the properties that are prefixed with "Inner."

FIGURE 13.16   Use the Foreach NodeList Enumerator to retrieve text from XML files.

The "Inner" properties often confuse people, but they are really quite simple. If `EnumerationType` isn't set to `ElementCollection`, you can ignore the "Inner" properties and the Foreach NodeList Enumerator ignores them in that case as well. The enumerator iterates over the nodes returned from the XPath query defined in the `OuterXPathString`. For example, using the source XML shown previously, if the `OuterXPathString` was set to `/LastProcessedDate/Info/ID` and the `EnumerationType` was set to `NodeText`, there would only be one value returned per iteration. The first value returned from the enumerator would be 3, and the last value would be 14. If the `OuterXPathString` was set to `/LastProcessedDate/Info/Date`, the first value returned from the enumerator would be `2005-12-13 11:20:00`, and the last value would be `2005-11-12 10:22:00`.

This is great if all you want to retrieve is one value per iteration. But, what if you need to return multiple nodes per iteration? Well, you could use the XPath query `/LastProcessedDate/Info` to return the node object and use a Script Task to shred the `Date` and `ID` values from the node, or you can specify an inner XPath query.

On the first iteration, the XPath query `/LastProcessedDate/Info` would return the following XML:

```
<ID>3</ID>
<Date>2005-12-13 11:20:00</Date>
```

Now, you need to apply another XPath query to get at the result. The sample uses the simple wildcard character *. However, you can use any valid XPath query to retrieve only the nodes you want. This is how you use the `InnerXPath` properties. The `InnerXPath` properties are a way for you to process the results of the `OuterXPath` properties. The result of the second XPath query on the first iteration is two strings: "3" and "2005-12-13 11:20:00."

<u>CAUTION</u>

To map the results, the index on the Variable Mappings tab corresponds to the order of the nodes in the XML document. For example, the ID node in the sample XML is at index 0 and the Date node is at index 1. If the nodes are not always in the same order, the mappings are confounded and produce incorrect results. You must ensure that the nodes are always in the same order for the entire resultset.

Foreach SMO

The Foreach SMO Enumerator is very similar to the Foreach ADO.NET Schema Rowset Enumerator. It enumerates objects such as tables, databases, servers, views, instances, and logins, but it only supports SQL Server databases and uses a SMO connection. SMO is an abbreviation for SQL Server Management Objects and is the new management API for SQL Server. Figure 13.17 shows the Foreach SMO Enumerator UI.

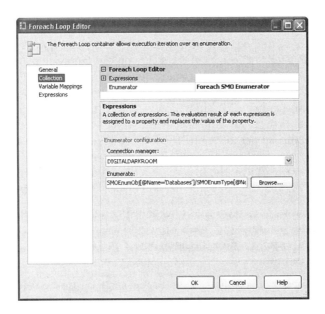

FIGURE 13.17   Use the Foreach SMO Enumerator to iterate over SQL Server objects.

As you can see, the designer is fairly simple because SMO allows you to specify the objects you want to process with a URN. If you know enough about the SMO object model and your servers, you can directly type the URN into the editor in the designer. If you, like the rest of us mortals, need a little help constructing the URN, you can use the URN designer. Click on the Browse button to see the Select SMO Enumeration dialog box, shown in Figure 13.18.

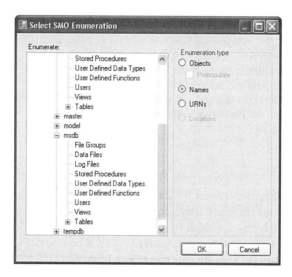

FIGURE 13.18   Build SMO URN strings using the designer.

Simply selecting the item type you want to enumerate builds the URN for you. Later, if you want to further refine the URN to only return a subset of the selected objects, you can do so directly in the Enumerate field by adding qualifiers. For more about this, search Books Online for SQL Management Objects or SMO.

The URN designer also allows you to specify in what form you want the object returned. The Objects option returns the SMO objects the URN returns. SMO has the option of lazy populating objects so that objects don't attempt expensive enumeration or possibly wait for timeouts until absolutely necessary. To disable this feature and populate the objects immediately, select Prepopulate. If you select Names, the enumerator returns strings containing the names of the objects. The URNs option returns a string that contains a URN that uniquely describes the enumerated object. You can use the URN to later retrieve the object using SMO. Finally, some objects such as data files and log files have associated filenames where they are stored. Selecting Locations returns a string with the filename of the object.

This enumerator is very useful for building day-to-day maintenance, validation, and auditing packages that automatically pick up new machines and robustly ignore offline machines. SMO is the same API upon which SQL Server Management Studio is built and is very powerful. The sample package, ForEachSMO.dtsx in the S13-Loops solution, allows you to enumerate various SMO objects. As long as the returned enumerated value is a string, the package functions correctly and shows you the resulting objects. Try changing the package to enumerate different SMO types and select URNs, Locations, and Names.

Summary

These containers have proven useful for a number of applications. For Loops are useful when you need to iterate multiple times and terminate based on a variable that might change by either directly modifying it in an expression or through some component inside or outside the loop. The Foreach Loop provides a way to drive workflow with collections of various types. Foreach Enumerators can enumerate collections of single types or collections of collections. There are Foreach Enumerators for enumerating over files, generic collections, schema rowsets, SMO objects, statically defined collections of strings or ADO rowsets, and datasets.

PART IV

Management Services

IN THIS PART

Configuring and Deploying Solutions

"MOVING BETWEEN DEV, TEST, AND PRODUCTION IS EASIER NOW WITH CONFIGURATIONS."—ERIK VEERMAN

In the typical package development cycle, you build packages on one machine, the development machine. After you get all the settings right and the package is performing to your requirements, you move it to a test machine. After testing is complete, you move the package to the production machine. Although the stages and names might differ, most environments have similar testing and deployment requirements that seem at odds with the very nature of packages. Packages are by necessity tightly bound to the environment in which they run. They reference folders and files on certain drives by name, connect to specific servers by name, and perform other environmentally dependent functions. This is what is called the location-dependent problem. Although it's fairly easy to create a simple package that accomplishes substantial work, it can be a challenge to write the package in such a way that when you deploy it to another machine or when the environment in which the package runs changes, the package will continue to execute without modification or errors. This is one of the most common challenges Integration Services users face and is the primary reason Microsoft created the Integration Services configuration and deployment tools.

Although the tools are helpful in addressing these issues, they're only part of the solution. The other part is the practices you use when building packages. This chapter explains both the tools and the approaches to building packages that address the location dependent package problem so that moving packages from the development environment through your testing processes and onto the production server will be as painless as possible.

Package Configurations

Packages are a collection of objects with properties. The values of some of those properties reflect the environment in which the package runs. For example, tasks need to open files and so need the name of the file to open. Connections need to connect to servers and, therefore, need the connection information for the servers. Each package is different, of course, and not every package has the same type of location dependence. But almost all packages have a reference to some resource such as a file or server that becomes invalid if you move it to another machine.

Another issue that causes long-term package management problems is the reality that the environment in which the package runs will change over time. If the environment never changed, location dependence and resource references wouldn't be a problem. All the environment-specific values could be set once and forgotten. But machines do change, filenames do change, and new servers do replace retired servers. Because the environment changes, your packages need to be edited to adjust property values to reflect the changes so the packages will continue to function correctly.

So, there are really two classes of problems here: those modifications required as a result of moving the package from one machine to another and those caused by environment changes over time. In both cases, you need to modify the package to account for the differences. But, there are also problems associated with editing packages: It can be time consuming, error prone, or against security policies. You need a way to quickly modify packages in a centralized way without physically opening and editing the package directly. This is the purpose of package configurations.

How Package Configurations Work

All package configurations have two essential pieces of information:

- A value for a given property on an object in the package
- The package path to the property of the object

The property values are stored as strings in package configurations. If the property is an integer or other nonstring type, the SSIS runtime converts the value to the correct type before setting the property value. If the SSIS runtime cannot convert the string value to the property's type, you receive a warning when loading the package indicating that the configuration failed.

The path to the property inside the package is stored in what is called a *package path*. Because a package is a hierarchical collection of containers, tasks, and other components, it is possible to uniquely address almost any property on any object in the package using a package path.

Package Paths

Package paths are essentially resource names that point to a property on an object in the package. Here are some examples:

```
\Package.Connections[{E9598474-461E-48F7-B902-52A140B7FE14}].ConnectionString
```

This package path points to the `ConnectionString` property on the `ConnectionManager` using the GUID ID as the index.

```
\Package.Connections[ConnectionName].ConnectionString
```

This package path points to the `ConnectionString` property on the same `ConnectionManager` but uses the `ConnectionManager` name `ConnectionName` as the index instead of the GUID ID.

```
\Package\LoopOverFiles\sql-TruncateLoadTable.SqlStatementSource
```

This package path points to the `SqlStatementSource` property of the Execute SQL Task in the Foreach Loop Container named `LoopOverFiles`.

```
\Package\Foreach Loop Container.ForEachEnumerator.Properties[FileSpec]
```

This package path points to the `FileSpec` property of the Foreach File Enumerator of the `Foreach Loop`.

```
\Package.Variables[FileLocation].Value
```

This package path points to the `Value` property of the `FileLocation` variable.

```
\Package\Data Flow Task.Properties[[DataReader Source].[SqlCommand]]
```

This package path points to the `SqlCommand` property of the `DataReader Source` component in the Data Flow Task.

<u>**CAUTION**</u>

Package configurations physically change packages. When you apply a configuration to a package, it changes the values of variables and properties in the package as though you had opened the package in the designer and typed them in directly. If you save a package after changing properties and variable values with a configuration, it contains the configured property and variable values the next time you load the package.

As you can see from the preceding examples, package paths are composed of the \Package marker, container names, collection element names, and property names.

- All package paths start with the \Package marker.

- The '.' character indicates that a property follows.

- The '\' character indicates that a container or task follows.

- The string between the [and] characters indicates an index into a collection.

<u>**TIP**</u>

When creating configurations, the Package Configuration Wizard by default uses an Objects GUID ID when building the package path. You can also use an object's name in a package path. The ID is safer to use because SSIS never changes IDs. Unless someone manually edits the ID in the package, the ID never changes. If you use the object's name, and someone changes the name during the course of developing the package, the configuration is no longer valid for that object. However, using the name is more portable. For example, a configuration with the previous fourth package path could be applied to all packages that have a variable named FileLocation in the package's variable collection (defined at package scope).

Package Configuration Object

Each entry in the package's Configurations collection has the properties discussed in the following sections.

ConfigurationType   The ConfigurationType property on configuration objects specifies the package configuration type. Although there are only six base types, there are also indirect variants, as described in Table 14.1.

TABLE 14.1   Configuration Type Identifiers

Configuration Type	Identifier	Description
PARENTVARIABLE	0	Parent package variable for setting values of variables in subpackages from parent package variable values
CONFIGFILE	1	XML file configuration
ENVVARIABLE	2	Environment variable configuration; contains one configuration

TABLE 14.1   Continued

Configuration Type	Identifier	Description
REGENTRY	3	Registry entry configuration; contains one configuration
IPARENTVARIABLE	4	Indirect parent package variable
ICONFIGFILE	5	Indirect XML file configuration
IREGENTRY	6	Indirect Registry configuration
SQLSERVER	7	SQLServer table configuration
INIFILE	8	INI file configuration (deprecated)
ISQLSERVER	9	Indirect SQL server table configuration
IINIFILE	10	Indirect INI file configuration (deprecated)

NOTE

There's no need to have an indirect configuration type for an environment variable configuration because they already are, in a sense, indirect configurations.

ConfigurationVariable   This is now a misnomer and is an artifact of an earlier design that supported configuring variables exclusively. It should probably be called ConfigurationPackagePath. It contains the package path for the property to be configured. For configuration types that have more than one configuration, such as SQL table configurations and XML configurations, this value is empty because the package paths are provided in the configuration itself.

TIP

To see the configurations in the XML package, load the package in BIDS, right-click on the package in the Solution Explorer, and select View Code. If you've created a configuration, toward the top of the package XML, you should see some XML that looks similar to the following:

```
<DTS:Configuration>
    <DTS:Property DTS:Name="ConfigurationType">
        2
    </DTS:Property>
    <DTS:Property DTS:Name="ConfigString">
        SSISSAMPLESROOT
    </DTS:Property>
    <DTS:Property DTS:Name="ConfigurationVariable">
        \Package.Variables[SAMPLES::ROOTWD].Properties[Value]
    </DTS:Property>
    <DTS:Property DTS:Name="ObjectName">
        Configure The Root Folder
    </DTS:Property>
```

```
    <DTS:Property DTS:Name="DTSID">
        {90405045-3A91-43C2-B759-6C183C0E81A6}
    </DTS:Property>
    <DTS:Property DTS:Name="Description">
    </DTS:Property>
    <DTS:Property DTS:Name="CreationName">
    </DTS:Property>
  </DTS:Configuration>
```

ConfigString   The ConfigString value contains the information needed to acquire the configuration. For example, for XML configurations, the ConfigString contains the fully qualified path to the XML configuration file, whereas for environment variable configurations, this property contains the name of the environment variable where the configuration is stored.

For indirect configurations, the ConfigString property contains the name of the environment variable that contains the Configuration String for the configuration. For example, for indirect XML configurations, the ConfigString property contains the name of the environment variable that holds the fully qualified path to the XML configuration file.

Indirect Configurations
In the same way that directly specifying the location of a resource is problematic, directly specifying the location of a configuration can be equally problematic. Suppose you create a package with one XML file configuration. In the configurations, you point to the location of the XML file configuration in your D:\Configurations directory. When you move the package to a new machine without a D drive, you're still forced to change the package to account for the differences in available hard drives. These situations make it necessary to have a way to configure the configurations. To do this, Integration Services has what is called indirect configurations.

Indirect configurations use environment variables to store the ConfigString of the configuration and are available for all configuration types except environment variable configurations. When using indirect configurations, the value that you would normally place in the ConfigString property of the configurations goes in the environment variable value and the name of the environment variable goes in the ConfigString property of the configuration.

NOTE

Why are fully qualified directories necessary? Relative paths would make packages more flexible, right? The reason is because relative paths are relative to the package execution location. Because packages can be executed from different utilities and applications, there's no guarantee that the relative path will correctly address a given file. This is one reason IS provides indirect configurations, so that the path can be fully qualified, yet still abstract away environmental differences.

Applying Package Configurations

Packages have a property called *Configurations*, which is a collection of zero to many Package Configuration objects. When you create a package configuration using the Package Configurations Organizer, you are adding an element to the package's Configurations collection. The SSIS runtime stores the configurations information along with the package when you save the package to SQL Server or an XML package file.

When you load the package, the package reads in all the package configurations and applies them in the order in which they were stored in the collection. It's possible to have more than one configuration and more than one type of configuration in the same package. It's also possible to configure the same property with more than one configuration. The last configuration to be applied wins—that is, the configured property retains the value from the most recent configuration.

CAUTION

The load-time behavior of package configurations has confused some users who attempt to change the configuration values and then expect to see the property values change in the package immediately. To see the effects of configurations, you must reload the package.

The Package Configurations Organizer

The designer provides a wizard called the Package Configurations Organizer (Organizer) to help you do just that—organize the packages' configurations. To use the Organizer, right-click on the package design surface and select Package Configurations. Figure 14.1 shows the Organizer with two configurations, a Registry configuration and an XML configuration, already created. You can use the Organizer to create, edit, and delete package configurations.

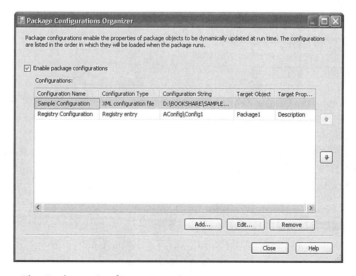

FIGURE 14.1   The Package Configurations Organizer.

Figure 14.1 shows the first dialog box where you create, edit, delete, and order the configurations. The arrows along the right side of the dialog box allow you to modify the order in which the package will apply the configurations. The Configuration Name column is really just for documentation purposes and the package ignores it. The Configuration Type column tells you the type of the configuration. The Configuration String column contains the location of the configuration. The Target Object column tells you which object will be modified by the configuration if it only changes a single property such as Registry configurations. For configuration types that change multiple values such as XML and SQL Server configurations, this value is blank. The Target Property column indicates which property on the target object will be modified. Like the Target Object column, this cell is empty for configurations that change multiple properties.

To turn on configurations, select the Enable Package Configurations check box. If you deselect this check box, configurations for the package are disabled, but the configurations remain so that you can later reenable them.

To create a new configuration, click the Add button. The Package Configuration Wizard opens, as shown in Figure 14.2.

FIGURE 14.2   The Package Configuration Wizard.

You can select the type of configuration you want to create in the Configuration Type drop down. Depending on the type you select, the designer for creating the configuration changes. As each of the configuration types are discussed in the following sections, the settings you should enter into this dialog box are also covered for each type.

Package Configuration Types

Integration Services supports several different types of Package Configuration types. Each type has its strengths and you'll likely find one that is your favorite and perhaps works better given the different requirements in your space. XML configurations are useful when moving packages or when you just prefer working with files and the file system. SQL Package configurations are ideally suited to large production systems with multiple servers and packages that you need to manage centrally in an enterprise environment with elevated security requirements. Environment Variable configurations are useful for describing a machine to packages and simplifying package migration. Parent Package configurations are useful when you need to modify property values on objects in the child package. Registry configurations provide a simple solution similar to environment variables but are more secure. The variety of Package Configurations types provides a lot of flexibility for how to approach the package deployment problems mentioned earlier and discussed in the following sections. Depending on your requirements, you can use one type exclusively or mix them in various ways. The following discussion describes each of the configuration types in detail.

TIP

When using configurations, it can be difficult to know if the configuration failed just by looking at the package. Depending on the type of the property that will be configured, it's a good idea to give the property a well-known default value so that when the configuration fails, it can be detected. Configurations do emit a warning if they fail, but that doesn't help if the configuration is accidentally deleted. So, it's a good practice to give configured properties and variables a value that you will recognize. For example, for string properties, set the value to Default Value. Then, if you see that property anywhere in the package, you'll have a pretty good idea that it was supposed to be configured and wasn't. For numeric property values, use the value 42, because, after all, $6 \times 9 = 42$, which is the ultimate default value, at least according to Douglas Adams.

XML Configuration File

XML configurations are stored in files with the default extension .dtsconfig and can configure more than one property in a package. XML configurations are structured as follows:

```
<?xml version="1.0" ?>
<DTSConfiguration>
  <DTSConfigurationHeading>
    <DTSConfigurationFileInfo GeneratedBy="Kirk Haselden"
    GeneratedFromPackageName="Configurations"
    GeneratedFromPackageID="{ECF155AC-F433-4930-A0A1-BE9B065E004D}"
    GeneratedDate="12/24/2006 12:22:01 PM" />
  </DTSConfigurationHeading>
  <Configuration
    ConfiguredType="Property"
    Path="\Package.Variables[SAMPLES::SERVERNAME].Properties[Value]"
    ValueType="String">
    <ConfiguredValue>ROMEO</ConfiguredValue>
  </Configuration>
</DTSConfiguration>
```

There are two main sections in the XML configuration file shown in bold print in the preceding sample.

- DTSConfigurationHeading—Contains metadata about the file
- Configuration—Contains zero to many configuration entries

When the Integration Services runtime loads an XML configuration, it completely ignores all data in the heading and applies each configuration entry independently in the order found in the file.

NOTE

XML configuration files have the .dtsconfig extension by default, but can have any extension, including .xml or none at all and still be valid.

Package Path

The package path is stored in the Path attribute of the Configuration node. In the preceding example, the package path is
`\Package.Variables[SAMPLES::SERVERNAME].Properties[Value]`, which sets the value of the SERVERNAME variable.

Value

The value is found in the ConfiguredValue node; in the preceding example, the value is the name of the server, ROMEO.

ValueType

The ValueType specifies the type of the value in the Value node. The package uses the ValueType as an aid to convert the value from a string to the correct target type. If it fails to convert the type, you receive a warning similar to the following:

```
Warning loading Package1.dtsx: Failure importing configuration file:
"Package.dtsConfig".
```

The warning is provided to let you know that the configuration failed, but does not affect the outcome of any other configurations the package might have. All configurations that are applied before and after a failed configuration will continue to be valid even if one configuration fails.

ConfiguredType

The ConfiguredType specifies the type of the property to be configured. It is for documentation purposes only.

CAUTION

Although the ConfiguredType is for documentation only, if you remove the attribute from the Configuration node, the configuration is invalid and any package attempting to use the configuration fails to load. The Attribute value can be empty or even contain comments about the configuration if you want, but it must remain intact.

Configurations Editor

Integration Services provides no way to directly edit XML configurations short of opening the configuration in an XML editor or Notepad or opening the Package Configurations Organizer. The problem with using the Package Configurations Organizer is that it depends on the package to generate the configuration and can be cumbersome. Occasionally, it would be nice to open an XML configuration and modify it in a simple way without worrying about corrupting the file or opening the development environment. A simple utility for editing configurations accompanies this book. It currently only supports XML configurations, but could be expanded to support other types as well. You can find it in the samples under the ConfigEdit subfolder. Figure 14.3 shows the editor after loading a configuration.

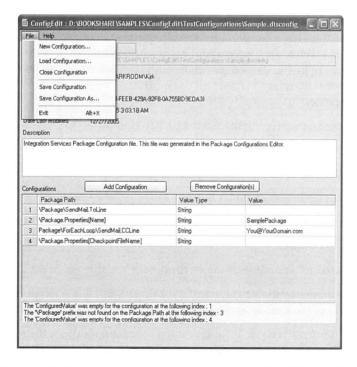

FIGURE 14.3 The Configurations Editor for viewing and editing XML configurations.

You can create a new configuration or edit existing ones. The utility does some lightweight validation on the configuration and alerts you to some common problems with configurations. This utility is perhaps most useful when you need to make small changes or tweaks to existing configurations without loading the designer or if you just want to clearly see what values a configuration changes.

To set up the Configurations Editor utility, go to the Utilities\ConfigEdit subfolder of the Samples folder. Run SetupConfigEdit.exe and it installs the needed components. You can uninstall it from the Add/Remove Programs Control Panel or by running SetupConfgEdit.exe again.

Environment Variable

Environment Variable configurations have two parts: the package path, which is stored in the configuration object's ConfigString property as described previously, and the Value, which the environment variable contains. When the package evaluates the configuration object, it retrieves the ConfigurationType, determines that it is an Environment Variable configuration, and then retrieves the environment variable name from the ConfigString. Then, it retrieves the value from the environment variable. Finally, it retrieves the package path from the ConfigurationVariable property and applies the value to the property.

Setting Up Environment Variables

Environment variables have been around for a long time. Some have commented that they're such an old technology, why would Microsoft build a new feature on them? Well, as it happens, they're just so darned useful. But, on occasion, they can be tricky. So, here's how to set up an environment variable that you can later reference in an Environment Variable configuration.

1. Launch Control Panel by right-clicking on My Computer.

2. Select Properties.

3. Select the Advanced tab.

4. Click the Environment Variables button.

5. The Environment Variables dialog box opens, as shown in Figure 14.4.

6. Click the New button.

7. Type in the name and value of the environment variable you want to create.

8. If the environment variable is for an Environment Variable configuration, set the value to what you want to apply to the property in the package.

9. If the environment variable is for an indirect configuration, set the value to point to the location where the configuration is stored.

FIGURE 14.4   Creating an environment variable.

CAUTION
_____

Environment variables are process specific and inherited from the parent process. Therefore, when you launch the designer, it will have inherited its environment variables from the process that launched it. Even if you change the environment variables in Control Panel or in another command window, the changes are not available to the designer until you shut it down and restart it. If you create an environment variable through Control Panel as described, it is always available on that machine until you remove it through Control Panel. If you create an environment variable programmatically or through the command line, the environment variable is only available to the process that created it.

Setting Up an Environment Variable Configuration

If you already have an environment variable set up as described previously, you can select that type in the drop down and click the Next button to get to the Select Configuration Type dialog box, as shown in Figure 14.5. This is probably the easiest configuration to set up because you need only specify the environment variable. The sample packages that ship with this book use Environment Variable configurations. Figure 14.5 shows the SSIS-SAMPLESERVER environment variable, which the sample packages use in connection strings when accessing the AdventureWorks sample database.

After you've selected the environment variable to use, you need to specify the property that you want to configure and you do that in the Select Target Property dialog box, as shown in Figure 14.6.

FIGURE 14.5   Creating an Environment Variable configuration.

FIGURE 14.6   Specifying the property to configure.

This is where you build the package path. When you select the property to configure, the wizard builds the package path and stores it in the new configuration. This process is essentially the same for all Package Configuration types with one exception. For multi-value configurations such as XML and SQL Server, the wizard allows you to select more than one property to configure.

NOTE

You might notice there is no `ValueType` specified for Environment Variable configurations. The IS runtime successfully converts the value in an Environment Variable configuration to the type of a property (if it can be converted) when configuring properties. It gets tricky when you configure variables. Because variable types change depending on the type of value, when the IS runtime applies the Environment configuration, the variable contains the string "42." However, if you configure an Int32 type property with the same Environment Variable configuration, the IS runtime correctly converts the value to an integer.

The configuration information is stored in the following places:

- **Package path**—Stored in the configuration object

- **New value**—Stored in the value of the environment variable

- **Environment variable name**—Stored in the configuration object

Registry Entry

Registry configurations are fairly straightforward.

The Registry configuration looks for a string value with the name Value in the key that you specify in the configuration. So, for a value stored in the HKEY_CURRENT_USER\AConfig\Config1\Value key, you would specify AConfig\Config1 for the ConfigString. This is also the same string you would type into the Package Configuration Wizard. The HKCU key and the Value string are assumed. You can place these configurations anywhere in the Current User tree and you can create multiple keys under the same tree, as shown in Figure 14.7.

FIGURE 14.7   Registry configurations are stored in the Value string value.

___

NOTE
___

It wasn't Microsoft's intention to make Registry configurations undocumented or difficult to use. They were written very early in the product cycle and seem to have slipped through the documentation cracks unintentionally. Still, after you know the format, it's pretty easy to set them up.

Figure 14.8 shows the Package Configuration Wizard with the correct settings for a Registry configuration stored in the previously mentioned key. The simplest way to set these up is to copy the key in regedit and paste it into the Registry Entry field, deleting the Value and HKCU portions.

FIGURE 14.8   The Registry settings in the Package Configuration Wizard.

For indirect Registry configurations, provide the name of the environment variable that contains the Registry key configuration string, as described previously.

Parent Package Variable

Parent Package Variable configurations provide a way to set a property or variable value in a child package from the value of a variable in the parent package that executes the child. Parent Package Variable configurations use the pull model, which means that you set up the configuration on the child to *pull* the value from the variable in the parent package. This is useful for situations when you want a child package to be controlled or influenced by the executing parent package.

> **NOTE**
>
> Because child packages *inherit* parent package variables, some have questioned the need for Parent Package Variable configurations. The logic being that because the child package can *see* the parent package variables already, the child package can directly reference the parent's variables.
>
> There are a few problems with this assumption. First, during design time, the package does not have access to the parent package variables. Only those tasks that do late variable access by name or GUID ID such as the Script Task can reference parent package variables. Second, child packages that reference parent package variables directly will fail if run independently. If the child package will always be executed by the same parent package, or you're sure that the parent package will always have the correct variable value, you might not need a configuration. However, some tasks require a variable to be available when validating. Because child packages don't have access to the parent

package variables when validating or at design time, these tasks fail to validate. Parent package variables allow you to create your package as a standalone package with a default value stored in a variable or property in the child package, while allowing the variable or property to be configured from the parent package.

PARENT PACKAGE VARIABLE CONFIGURATIONS ARE THE EXCEPTION

Parent Package Variable configurations are the one exception to the rule that configurations are applied to the package at load time. Parent Package Variable configurations are applied when the child package executes. Why the exception? Think about how packages change during execution. If you want to have a child package's execution behavior modified by the parent package, you need to be able to modify the variable before the child uses its value. Put another way, child packages need to see the execution state of the parent package right before the child package executes, not the load time state.

Figure 14.9 shows the Package Configuration Wizard settings for creating a Parent Package Variable configuration.

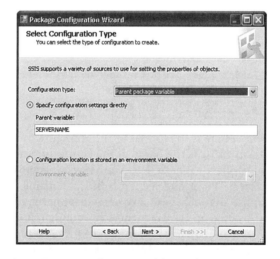

FIGURE 14.9   Creating a Parent Package Variable configuration.

For indirect Parent Package configurations, the environment variable should contain the name of the parent variable.

SQL Server Table

SQL Server Table configurations store the configurations in a SQL Server table and can include multiple configurations per package. The table can reside in any SQL Server database, have any valid SQL Server table name, and must be defined as follows:

```
CREATE TABLE [TABLE NAME]
(
    ConfiguredValue NVARCHAR(255) NULL,
    PackagePath NVARCHAR(255) NOT NULL,
    ConfiguredValueType NVARCHAR(20),
    ConfigurationFilter NVARCHAR(255) NOT NULL
)
```

The ConfiguredValue column specifies the value to apply to the property or variable value. The PackagePath column contains the package path, of course. The ConfiguredValueType specifies the type of the value as a hint to the SSIS runtime for converting to the correct type when applying the configuration. The ConfigurationFilter is how you differentiate between configurations. You might have configurations for all the packages in your solution stored in the table, but only want to apply certain configurations to certain packages. The ConfigurationFilter column allows you to specify a value that the SSIS runtime uses in a SELECT clause. If you view a package with a SQL Server Table Configuration in the Code Editor, you should see something similar to the following abbreviated Configuration node:

```
<DTS:Configuration>
    <DTS:Property DTS:Name="ConfigurationType">
      7
    </DTS:Property>
    <DTS:Property DTS:Name="ConfigString">
      ".\YUKONB3.ISSAMPLES";"[dbo].[SSIS Configurations]";"SAMPLES";
    </DTS:Property>
</DTS:Configuration>
```

The important thing to note here is the format of the configuration string. The first section of the configuration string is the name of the connection manager that the configuration will use to connect to the SQL Server. The connection manager must be defined in the same package. The second section is the table name. Because SQL Server Table configurations can use any table with any name having the correct schema, the configuration requires the name of the table where the configurations are stored. Because of this, it is possible to have more than one configurations table in a server. The last section is the query string or filter. This is the string the SQL Server Table configuration uses in the SELECT clause to filter for the desired configurations. If you need to use a semi-colon in one of the values, use double quotes around the sections, as shown in the preceding example. Figure 14.10 shows the configuration string in the Package Configurations Organizer.

Figure 14.11 shows the same SQL Server Table configuration in the Package Configuration Wizard.

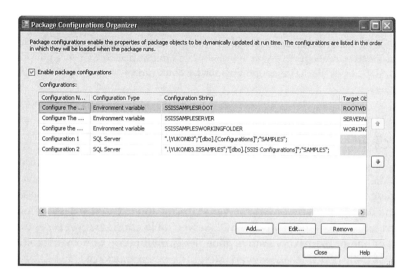

FIGURE 14.10   The configuration string contains the name of the connection manager, the configurations table name, and the configuration Filter string.

FIGURE 14.11   A SQL Server Table configuration in the Package Configuration Wizard.

Notice the Connection, Configuration Table, and Configuration Filter fields correspond to the sections of the configuration string in the package XML in Code View. Finally, the ConfigString has the same format for indirect SQL Server Table configurations. The environment variable would have the format <connection name>;<table name>;<filter>.

TIP

You might notice that SQL Server Package configurations use configurable objects, namely connection managers. If you are clever, you might notice that it is possible to configure SQL Server Package configurations by configuring the connection manager that they use.

Package Configurations Summary

Figure 14.12 shows a diagram of package configurations. The solid lines represent package configurations retrieving settings from the respective sources. The annotations on the solid lines describe what the ConfigString or Indirect Environment Variable configuration contains. The dashed lines represent the values being applied to the destination property or variable value. Notice that XML and SQL Server Table configuration types can configure more than one property or variable value per configuration and that Parent Package configurations pull the value from a variable in the parent package.

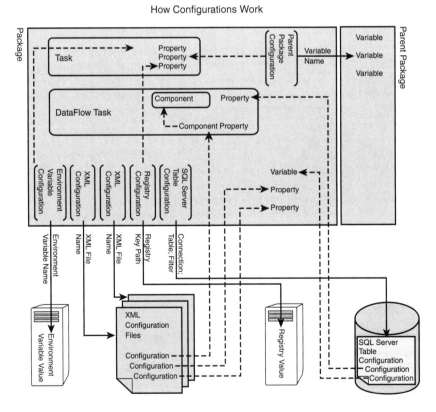

FIGURE 14.12   A diagram of package configurations.

CAUTION

I sometimes receive email or see posts on the SSIS forum from people who are receiving configuration warnings and believe that the warnings are causing their packages to fail loading or executing. Configurations only emit warnings and should never raise an error. Errors cause packages to fail. Often, the packages fail to execute because the configuration fails to configure some critical property that makes the package functional. In any case, the warnings are emitted to alert you to the configuration failure, but they do not fail the package execution and are not fatal.

TIP

Packages have a property called SuppressConfigurationWarnings that filters out all warnings caused by package configuration failures. If you really don't want to see configuration warnings, you can set this property to TRUE and they will all be hidden. Although useful when developing packages, this filter should never be enabled in packages on production machines.

PACKAGE CONFIGURATIONS TIPS

Using one configuration file per server is optimal.

More than one configuration can be applied to the same package.

One configuration can be applied to more than one package.

Each package configuration is applied in the order shown in the Package Configurations Organizer, except Parent Package configurations, which are applied at execution time.

If an entry in a configuration fails, it only emits a warning. Configurations should never raise an error or cause a package load to fail.

The location of a configuration can be explicitly set in the package, or pointed to from an environment variable using indirect configurations.

Deploying Packages

So, you need to move the package? Integration Services provides a utility for moving packages, but for a moment, let's take a step back and think about the deployment problem. What is it you're trying to accomplish? Is there something in the package, some setting or value that can't be moved by simply copying the package to another machine? Not really. However, problems arise when you move a package that references external resources that are available on one machine that aren't available on another. For example, no amount of configuration magic is going to help if you attempt to run a package that references a custom task that isn't installed on the destination machine.

So, the difficult challenge with deployment isn't about moving the package per se. It's really about getting the destination machine to "look" like the machine where the package was built. If the package references a custom task, user account, configuration file, or share on the development machine, the custom task, user account, configuration file, and share must be available on the destination machine. After the destination machine "looks" like the source machine, deployment becomes a simple matter of copying the package. Integration Services provides a way to address some of these issues, notably moving packages and the files they depend upon, in the form of a wizard. This section explains how to use the Deployment Wizard and when it is appropriate and when it is not appropriate to do so.

The Deployment Utility

The designer provides a way to bundle the project packages and miscellaneous files into a folder that you can copy to another machine. The Deployment Utility is a small executable that knows how to install the bundle. When you install the bundle by executing the Deployment Utility the Deployment Utility provides a simple wizard called the Package Installation Wizard to walk you through installing a package. To enable deployment in the designer, right-click on the Integration Services project node in the Solution Explorer and select Properties. Figure 14.13 shows the property pages for the project.

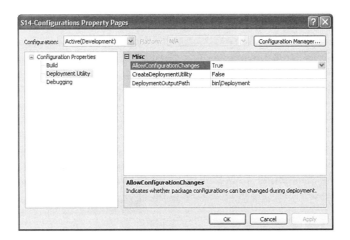

FIGURE 14.13   Use the Property Pages dialog box to set up deployment.

There are three properties that control deployment behavior:

- CreateDeploymentUtility—This is probably a misnomer because it doesn't actually create the Deployment Utility. Rather, it creates the bundle of files that the Deployment Utility installs. Essentially, this tells the designer to copy all the packages and miscellaneous files to a folder and build a deployment manifest, which are described shortly.

- AllowConfigurationChanges—This setting is stored in the deployment manifest and instructs the Deployment Utility to allow the user to make configuration changes.

- DeploymentOutputPath—This setting instructs the designer where to place the deployment manifest, packages, and miscellaneous files.

After enabling deployment, build the SSIS project by right-clicking on the project in the Solution Explorer and selecting Build. The designer copies all the packages, miscellaneous files, and XML configuration files the packages reference to the folder specified in the DeploymentOutputPath setting. Every time you build, it does this. It also creates a file with the SSISDeploymentManifest file extension. The manifest file looks similar to the following:

```
<?xml version="1.0"?>
<DTSDeploymentManifest GeneratedBy="ALPHA\Kirk" GeneratedFromProjectName=
➡"S14-Configurations" GeneratedDate="2006-12-31T00:39:17.
➡6393750-08:00" AllowConfigurationChanges="true">
  <Package>
    ParentPackage.dtsx
  </Package>
  <Package>
    ChildPackage.dtsx
  </Package>
  <Package>
    Configurations.dtsx
  </Package>
</DTSDeploymentManifest>
```

The DTSDeploymentManifest contains some metadata about how and when the manifest was created. The AllowConfigurationChanges specifies that the wizard should show the Configure Packages dialog box after copying all the files. And, of course, the Package nodes specify which packages to copy.

To launch the Deployment Utility, double-click on the manifest file in Windows Explorer. The Package Installation Wizard appears, as shown in Figure 14.14.

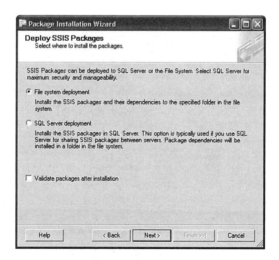

FIGURE 14.14   The Package Installation Wizard.

File System Deployment

As described, if you select the File System Deployment option, the wizard moves all the dependent files, including XML configurations and the files in the miscellaneous node of the project, to a location on the disk. Figure 14.15 shows the next dialog box, Select Installation Folder, in the wizard.

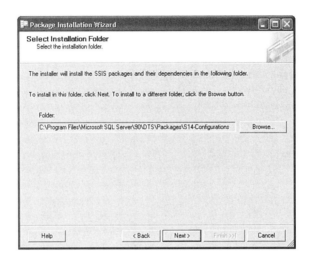

FIGURE 14.15   The default installation folder.

The Deployment Wizard selects the Server Store folder by default. This is the folder where the Integration Services service looks to enumerate packages in the file system. If you look in SQL Server Management Studio under the Stored Packages, File System node, you'll see all the files stored in that folder. Figure 14.16 shows the packages after being deployed.

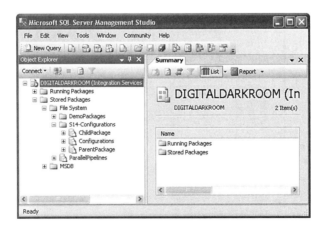

FIGURE 14.16   The packages stored in the File System folder shown in SQL Server Management Studio.

On the IS team, this folder is fondly referred to as the "Magic Folder." You can change the location of this folder in the `MsDtsSrvr.ini.xml` file if you want. Chapter 17, "SQL Server Management Studio" covers this in more detail.

SQL Server Deployment

If you select SQL Server Deployment, the wizard moves the packages to the SQL Server you specify in the dialog box shown in Figure 14.17.

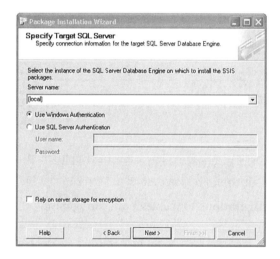

FIGURE 14.17   The packages stored in the file system shown in SQL Server Management Studio.

Because SQL Server package storage only stores packages, the other dependent files must go somewhere, so the wizard places them in the magic folder by default. The next dialog box in the wizard (after the one shown in Figure 14.17) allows you to change the folder where the dependent files are stored.

Because the option to edit the configuration was specified in the Project Properties dialog box, the wizard now provides a way to modify the configuration. After the wizard moves all the packages and dependent files, it shows the Configure Packages dialog box, as shown in Figure 14.18.

If the package references more than one XML configuration, the Configure Packages dialog box allows you to select which configuration to edit using the Configuration File drop down, as shown in Figure 14.18. You can use this dialog box to modify the configuration to have the correct value for a given configuration. For example, in Figure 14.18, no values are specified for `SaveCheckpoints` and `BufferTempStoragePath`, and so on. Using this dialog box, the values can be updated to reflect the destination machine.

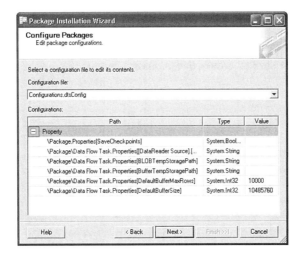

FIGURE 14.18   Use the wizard to update package configurations during deployment.

Deployment Wizard Usage

Let's take another step back now and review what the Deployment Wizard does.

- **Copies packages**—It copies packages to SQL Server or the file system.

- **Copies XML configurations**—It copies XML configuration files the packages reference.

- **Copies dependent files**—It copies the files in the Miscellaneous Files node of the package project.

- **Modify configuration**—It allows you to modify the configurations.

The Deployment Wizard does not do the following:

- **Move custom components**—It doesn't move custom components to the destination machine, such as custom tasks or Data Flow transforms, upon which packages rely.

- **Recognize deltas**—It doesn't recognize when significant changes happen in the package or dependent files or if they are unchanged. Nor does it modify what it deploys based on such information. It simply copies all the files every time you run it.

- **Detect external dependencies**—It doesn't recognize when a package depends on a file that is not included in the Miscellaneous Files node.

So, by now, you might be wondering what the point is. And here it is: Over and over, people misuse the Deployment Utility. The Deployment Utility should only be used in certain circumstances, as follows:

- When you need to create an installation for a new package that has never been installed on a machine before

- When you want to overwrite or otherwise update the dependent files

After you've run the Deployment Wizard on a machine and installed the package, unless you need to update the changes affected by the Deployment Wizard, there is little else to do but copy the package. Is the Deployment Wizard useful for the purpose for which it was designed? Absolutely. Should you use it to repeatedly copy the same package to the same location while developing or updating a package? No. It doesn't gain you anything. In fact, you'll be duplicating efforts and possibly losing or corrupting configurations by overwriting existing configurations or by human error.

So here's a rule of thumb: Only use the Deployment Wizard when something other than the package requires updating. If only the package has changed, simply copy the package or save it to SQL Server.

Moving Packages Around
You can move packages in many ways that are more efficient than the Deployment Wizard, as follows:

- **XCopy/Copy**—You can use the file system commands for moving packages to different file system locations. This is a tried-but-true method.

- **DTUtil**—Use the DTUtil utility to move packages to SQL Server, the file system, or the SSIS server. DTUtil has many useful functions for manipulating packages. See Books Online for more information.

- **Save Copy As**—The Save Copy of <packagename> As menu option in the main File menu of the Business Intelligence Development Studio provides a dialog box for saving packages directly to the file system, SQL Server, or SSIS server. Click on the package Control Flow design surface to ensure this menu option is visible.

- **Import Package**—In SQL Server Management Studio, in the Object Explorer under the Integration Services nodes, you can right-click on the File System or MSDB nodes and select Import Package. This allows you to pull a package into those locations.

- **Export Package**—After you've saved a package to SQL Server or SSIS Server, you can retrieve it again from those locations to a file system folder using the Export Package menu option on the context menu you get by right-clicking on the package nodes in Object Explorer.

<u>TIP</u>

My suggestion is to use the Deployment Wizard whenever you need to move a new package and configurations to a location for the first time and then use one of the preceding methods for moving the package from then on. The only time you might want to use the Deployment Wizard again for the same package and location is if the package or configuration files change significantly. Even then, I would hesitate because you might unintentionally overwrite some settings in a configuration.

Configuration and Deployment Approaches

The following sections provide a few ideas for how to use package configurations and other tools. These ideas are not necessarily original or comprehensive. Undoubtedly, as you and others use Integration Services over time, better and better practices and utilities will emerge. The following sections provide some ideas and approaches to using the tools as a starting point.

Location Dependence and Machine-Resident Configurations

The location dependence problem was touched on earlier but how to work around it wasn't fully described. Now that you've learned about the tools in more detail, you're ready to explore an approach to the problem.

The Problem

Your package references resources such as folders and files in locations that are specific to a given machine.

What's Needed

You need a way to isolate the package from the environment in which it functions, while still providing ways to configure the package so it can reconcile itself and access resources.

The Solution

Create a machine-resident configuration that reflects the machine's environment. Machine-resident configurations stay on one machine and describe the machine environment to the package. Packages reference the configuration through an indirect configuration. The machine-resident configuration configures standard variables that you create in all your packages that specify the locations of files, names, or servers and any other location-dependent settings. The sample packages use this method.

Causes of Location Dependence

The following are some causes of nonportable packages and some suggestions for eliminating those causes:

- **Hard-coded references to files, servers, and other resources**—Eliminate such references as explained previously.

- **Using incorrect package protection level**—For production, use server storage, if possible.

- **Directly referencing configuration files**—Use indirect or SQL Server configurations.

- **Using standard security**—Use integrated security, if possible.

- **References to unavailable subpackages**—Store packages on SQL Server.

- **References to tasks and components not available on a machine**—All components must be installed on the machine where the package that references them is to run.

Database Objects That Move

Some companies are growing very quickly. In fact, they are adding new servers on a regular basis. For them, maintaining packages can be a nightmare because the environment is changing around the packages as they bring new servers online and repurpose older servers.

The Problem

Your packages reference a number of objects that you move regularly and it breaks your packages.

What's Needed

You need a way to specify a reference to a database object, such as a table that will remain valid, even if it moves to a different server. In other words, you need to use a name that is not the four-part specific name.

The Solution

Use synonyms to sever the dependency between physical database object locations and packages. A synonym is a database object that provides an alternative name for another database object. Synonyms provide a layer of abstraction that protects a client application, in this case your packages, from changes made to the name or location of the base object. Using synonyms, you can use a simple naming convention instead of the four-part name form.

```
Server.Database.Schema.ObjectName
```

Using synonyms, even if the location of the object were to change to another server, the package would still remain valid because the synonym will change underneath. The synonym name will remain the same. Use synonyms if you have a fairly dynamic environment where packages reference objects that are moved or changed often.

Overriding Configurations

You want to have a way to temporarily modify the behavior of your packages. For example, you want to change all packages to reference a backup server instead of the production server while you do maintenance.

The Problem

The problem is that you have to physically change configurations. That can be a bit messy and nobody wants to muck around with making quasipermanent changes to functioning systems.

What's Needed

You need a way to temporarily configure packages to reference a different server.

The Solution

The ability to set the same property from multiple configurations is useful when you want to have a default configuration but override it with other package or environment-specific behaviors. For this example, you need to take a server offline for maintenance; you can use this behavior to temporarily switch all packages to reference a backup server.

You do this by creating a secondary or backup configuration in all your packages that is applied after the default configuration. Normally, while running all packages against the default or production server, the backup configuration wouldn't contain any configurations. But, when you need to take the production server offline, you can add a configuration to the backup configuration to point all packages to the backup server. Now, if any of your scheduled packages happen to run during the time the production machine is offline, they will pick up the second backup configuration and point to the backup server. SQL Server Table configurations are especially handy for this because they can be changed in one location, yet referenced across your enterprise. By simply changing the value of one field in one row, you can effectively and temporarily change the behavior of every package in your enterprise. To turn off the secondary configuration, simply remove the secondary configuration value.

> **NOTE**
>
> You can do the same thing with the default configuration. However, this method allows for more flexibility because you can have more than one secondary configuration and segment the packages you redirect by selectively editing configurations.

Configuring Connection Managers

This is really just a more specific location dependence problem, but it has given enough users problems that it is worth mentioning.

The Problem

Your network isn't configured to support Integrated Authentication. You need to automatically configure a password, in this case on connections, noninteractively because you're going to execute the package using SQL Agent.

What's Needed

You need a way to set the password without having to type it in but yet still be secure.

The Solution

Use a SQL Server Table configuration to set the value of a variable, which you later use in a property expression for the connection string, such as the following:

```
"Provider=sqloledb;Data Source=" + @SERVERNAME + ;Initial Catalog=pubs;User
ID=sa;Password=" + @PASSWORD + ";"
```

This expression builds the connection string with the server name and password correctly embedded and looks similar to the following when evaluated:

```
"Provider=sqloledb;Data Source=ROMEO;Initial Catalog=pubs;User ID=sa;Password=foo-
bar;"
```

Summary

Configurations provide a simple, safe, and powerful approach to postdeployment package modification. There are multiple configuration types suitable to different package deployment and management processes. The Deployment Utility is useful for deploying packages the first time, but should be used sparingly thereafter. And, finally, the tools are only part of the solution to configuration and deployment problems. It is also very important to develop solid package management processes and best practices.

Using The Script Task

"THAT'S SO COOL, MAN!"—ASHVINI SHARMA

The Script Task warrants an entire chapter because it is such an important part of the flexibility and extensibility model for Integration Services. Integration Services ships with a rich set of tasks covering a broad range of features, but there always seem to be a few things people want to do in their packages that the stock tasks don't support. The Script Task nicely fills the holes left by the stock tasks and sports its own Visual Studio Designer with a rich set of development bells and whistles, such as object browsing and IntelliSense. If you are only familiar with the DTS ActiveX Task, you are in for a pleasant surprise.

The Script Task gives you access to the full power of .NET coding. It is not scripting, so it has probably been misnamed, but truly compiles the code, giving you a much faster resulting task. You can reference other assemblies, precompile the code, and even work with the Integration Services object model to build other packages. The Integration Services team tried to mitigate the need for coding solutions. By most accounts, they've done a pretty good job, but there are still occasions when you need to break down and write some code. Following are some situations when you might consider using a Script Task:

- No task exists that supports the behavior you need.

- You need to accomplish some simple workflow.

- You will not be using the same code in multiple locations in the package or in multiple packages.

- You need to prototype a custom task.

- You don't care if someone else can see the code.

- You don't have any sensitive information to store in the task.

CAUTION

In DTS, it was common to use an ActiveX Script Task to *self-modify* the package that hosted the task. The Script Task is not capable of modifying its host package and has no access to the package in which it exists.

Generally speaking, if you need to use the logic in more than one location or you have security concerns with the kind of data the task will be manipulating, it is better to build a custom task. Custom tasks are much easier to reuse and are not much harder to build than the Script Task.

The Script Task Environment

The Script Task is a powerful tool for customizing packages. Part of that power comes from the fact that the development environment is so advanced and feature rich. The other part of the power comes from the fact that the Script Task uses Visual Basic .NET and gives you complete access to all the resources of .NET, including WinFX libraries and the ever-burgeoning stock pile of shared source code.

The Script Task Editor

To get started with the Script Task, open the designer and create a new Integration Services project or open one of the sample packages in the S15-ScriptTask sample solution. Figure 15.1 shows the Script Task Editor that opens when you double-click on the task in the Control Flow designer.

Five properties are available in the Script Task Editor dialog box:

- **ScriptLanguage**—The only language available is Microsoft Visual Basic .NET. When the Integration Services team wrote the Script Task, there were plans to support other languages. Those plans did not materialize, so Visual Basic .NET is the only choice.

- **PrecompileScriptIntoBinaryCode**—This setting specifies that the code should be compiled and stored in the package. This property is set to TRUE by default. The compiled code is converted to BASE64 code and stored as part of the package. If you open a package with a Script Task that is precompiled, there is a big block of unintelligible code. If you set it to FALSE, the code is stored in the package, but compiled just in time when the task executes. If it isn't precompiled, there is also a detectable delay when executing the Script Task while the code compiles.

TIP

If you ever get the following error: `The task is configured to precompile the script, but binary code is not found...`, you can resolve the issue by simply loading the package into the designer and opening the offending Script Task designer. In general, it's best to set PreCompile to `TRUE`. For running on 64-bit machines, it must be set to `TRUE` because the Script Task cannot "just in time" compile on 64-bit machines.

This error also sometimes occurs when you attempt to run a package with a Script Task that doesn't successfully compile. The only way to resolve the issue is to fix the code so that it will successfully compile.

- **EntryPoint**—This is the load point for the Script Task. Although you can change this, there is very little reason to do so. If you do decide to change it, you need to change the name of the encompassing main class to match.

- **ReadOnlyVariables**—This setting specifies which variables the script will open for read-only access.

- **ReadWriteVariables**—This setting specifies which variables the script will open for read and write access.

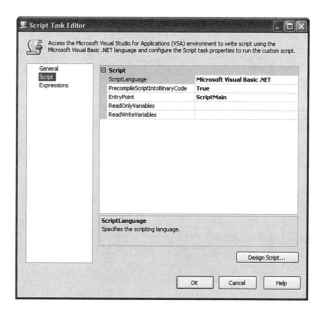

FIGURE 15.1   The Script Task Editor.

The last two properties are a simple way to make variables accessible in the script. To access variables, list them in these fields separated by commas. Or, you can use the VariableDispenser, as follows:

```
Dim vars As Variables
Dim var As Variable
Dts.VariableDispenser.LockForRead("TestVar")
Dts.VariableDispenser.GetVariables(vars)
var = vars.Item(0)
```

CAUTION

When adding variable names to the list of ReadOnly and ReadWrite variables, make sure the names have the correct case and there are no spaces between the names and commas. Also, do not use both methods to access variables. If you reserve a variable for access in the Script Task Editor and then attempt to retrieve a variable using the VariableDispenser, you'll receive an error stating that the variable has already been locked.

The Visual Studio for Applications Design Environment

To open the Visual Studio for Applications designer, click on the Design Script button. The designer appears as shown in Figure 15.2.

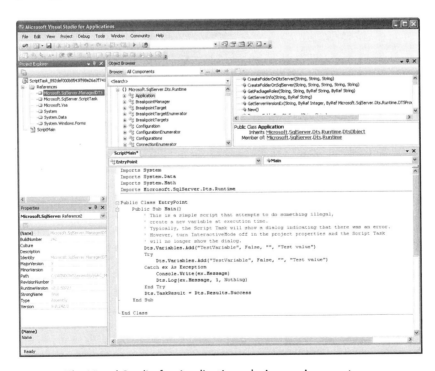

FIGURE 15.2   The Visual Studio for Applications design environment.

The design environment probably looks a little busy, but it doesn't have to be. Figure 15.2 has as many windows open as possible for the screenshot to show you some of the available features, notably the Object Browser, Project Explorer, and Properties windows. Although these windows are not necessary for writing code, they can be helpful if you're trying to find a particular method or when making changes to the project. As you can see, the main code editor has syntax coloring, automatic indenting, and all the other supporting features found in Visual Studio. Because the environment is quite feature rich, every detail is not covered here. But, a few of the more important Script Task–related settings are pointed out next.

Let's take a look at the project first. If you don't have the Project Explorer window open, you can open it from the View menu. In the Project Explorer window, notice the topmost node in the project tree. The name of your project will look similar to the one in Figure 15.2. The Script Task creates a unique name for each Script Task project so that the VSA engine can disambiguate different Script Task code buckets. You shouldn't need to change the name, and the project name doesn't show up in the package. If you're tempted to change the name to make it "prettier" or "consistent," don't do it. It could lead to some odd behavior such as the wrong Script Task opening when a breakpoint is hit, and so forth.

If you right-click on the code node (in Figure 15.2, it is called ScriptMain), there is a menu option for exporting the code to a .vb file. The same option is available on the main File menu for the code currently loaded in the editor. This option allows you to save the code to a file that you can later load into another Script Task. To load a .vb file into the Script Task, right-click on the project and select Add Existing Module. It is useful, although questionable to do this. Arguably, if you're copying code this way, according to the guidelines provided earlier, you should probably be writing a custom task. However, not every case subscribes to the rule, and this feature could be useful for importing a library of useful functions for use in the Script Task. From the project context menu, you can also use the Add menu item to add a new class, and so on.

If you want to add a reference to an assembly, right-click on the References node and select Add Reference. Figure 15.3 shows the Add Reference dialog box that opens.

Select the assemblies you want to reference and click the Add button. After you've added references, you can browse the objects in the assembly in the Object Browser window or create instances of classes in the assembly in your code.

CAUTION

If the assembly you want to reference is not visible in the Add Reference dialog box, you'll need to do a little extra work. Ensure that the assembly is in the global assembly cache and then make a copy of the assembly in the following directory:

```
%WINDIR%\Microsoft.NET\Framework\<latest 2.0 version of .Net>
```

On the sample machine, it's the following directory:

```
C:\WINDOWS\Microsoft.NET\Framework\v2.0.50727
```

Open the Add Reference dialog box again and the assembly should be visible.

This limitation is part of the VSA requirements. The reasons are long and tedious, but basically it's because VSA was built as an application enhancement tool, not a development environment.

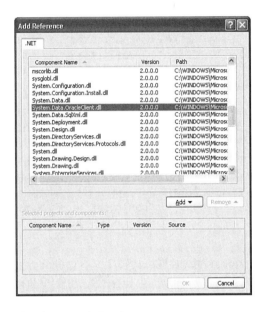

FIGURE 15.3   The Add Reference dialog box.

Script Task Project Properties

If you select Properties from the Script Task project context menu, the dialog box shown in Figure 15.4 opens.

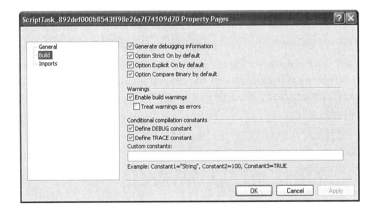

FIGURE 15.4   The Script Task project properties dialog box.

The Build node of this dialog box allows you to toggle some key settings, as follows:

- **Generate Debugging Information**—Generate the debugging information that is normally bound for the .PDB file. If you have set PrecompileScriptIntoBinaryCode to TRUE, the debugging information is also written into the package.

CAUTION

If you are releasing your package to the production environment or concerned about the size of the package, turn this setting off. After you've turned it off, be aware that break-points will no longer function until you turn it back on again.

NOTE

Precompiling a Script Task can increase execution speed because it doesn't need to load every time it executes; this is especially helpful when executing a Script Task in a loop.

- **Option Strict On By Default**—Visual Basic .NET allows implicit conversions of any data type to any other data type. Data loss can occur when the value of one data type is converted to a data type with less precision or smaller capacity. This setting also disallows late binding to an object of type Object. This setting should always remain selected.

- **Option Explicit On By Default**—This option forces explicit declaration of variables using the Dim statement. This setting should always remain selected.

- **Option Compare Binary By Default**—This setting has to do with comparing text. When selected, all text comparisons are case sensitive.

- **Enable Build Warnings**—This setting allows the environment to emit warnings.

- **Treat Warnings as Errors**—This setting elevates any warnings to error status.

- **Define DEBUG Constant**—Turn on the constant DEBUG.

- **Define TRACE Constant**—Turn on the constant TRACE.

- **Custom Constants**—This field allows you to create constant values that will be available in the code.

Interactive Mode

One setting that you won't find in any of the Script Task dialog boxes or anywhere in the environment is the InteractiveMode. Interactive Mode is a package property, but materially affects the Script Task. To see the InteractiveMode property in the designer, open the project properties in the Solution Explorer by right-clicking the project and selecting Properties. The InteractiveMode property is in the Debugging node. By default, the InteractiveMode property on packages is set to FALSE. The package pushes the value of this property to the system variable called System::InteractiveMode. When the designer loads or executes the package, one of the things it does is set the InteractiveMode to TRUE so that error dialog boxes and such will be visible.

> **NOTE**
>
> This variable is available at design time. If you want to see it, look in the Variables window in the designer and make sure the system variables are visible.

Internally, the Script Task references the System::InteractiveMode variable. If InteractiveMode is set to TRUE and there are errors in the Script Task code, the Script Task shows a dialog box containing information about the error. That's why the DTS Script Task: Runtime Error dialog box shown in Figure 15.5 shows up in the designer whenever there's an error.

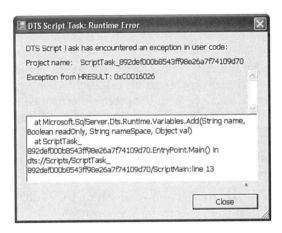

FIGURE 15.5   The DTS Script Task: Runtime Error dialog box is visible if InteractiveMode is set to TRUE.

If you take the same package and run it in DTExec, the Script Task does not, by default, show the error dialog box because DTExec does not set InteractiveMode to TRUE. This is a good thing. You don't exactly want dialog boxes showing up in the middle of the night on a headless production server in a back closet somewhere. All tasks should honor this setting for this very reason.

The sample package called SafeMessageBox.dtsx in the S15-ScriptTask sample solution has a property expression on the package that always sets the InteractiveMode property to TRUE. If you run the package in DTExec, the error dialog box opens just like it does in the designer. Try changing the property expression and see how the behavior changes.

There's a lot to learn about the Script Task environment in general, check the documentation for the designer in Books Online, MSDN, and the Visual Studio documentation.

Setting Breakpoints

The Script Task supports breakpoints, which makes it easier to debug. There are two kinds of breakpoints: those you set in the package Control Flow designer and those you set in the Script Task designer. Like all tasks, you can set breakpoints on the task, but you can also set breakpoints on the code. To set the breakpoint, click on the left margin in the editor; a red dot appears and the designer highlights the adjoining code.

CAUTION

When debugging a Script Task, you might be tempted to make changes in the code before terminating the package. The changes aren't saved unless you edit the code in the Script Task Editor with the package debugging stopped.

Using the Script Task

After you understand the previously described settings, you still need to learn how to write Visual Basic code and how to build Script Tasks. Of course, this chapter isn't a Visual Basic tutorial, so that isn't covered here. This chapter assumes you have a working knowledge of Visual Basic and focuses mainly on working with the Dts object and on practices you should follow when building Script Task code.

The Dts Object

The Dts object or ScriptObjectModel object is the way you access the package object model in the Script Task. The package, application, and other interfaces have been removed to only expose those objects, methods, and interfaces that are legal to use inside of tasks. The Dts object is the base object for accessing all the services available in the SSIS runtime and is how the Script Task interacts with the package.

To see the available collections and methods for this object, find the ScriptObjectModel node in the Object Browser, as shown in Figure 15.6.

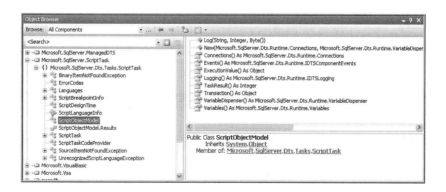

FIGURE 15.6   Viewing the Script Task object model.

The Visual Studio design environment also provides IntelliSense support for the ScriptObjectModel object. Simply type in "Dts." and IntelliSense appears. Because the ScriptObjectModel is how you interact with the package, the following discussion covers each of its methods or objects and how to use them.

The Log Method
This is a shortcut to logging and only takes three parameters:

- **Message text**—The string message

- **DataCode**—The integer identifier for the contents of the DataBytes

- **DataBytes**—The array of bytes storing additional log event–specific information

The New Method
This is the public constructor that has no practical value in the Script Task.

The Connections Collection
This is how the Script Task accesses connection managers. You can use either the connection manager name or ID for the index.

The Events Interface
This is the IDTSComponentEvents interface that supports the following seven events:

- FireBreakpointHit—This event has no practical function. You can use it to fire a breakpoint, but there is no way to enable the breakpoint in the designer because the Script Task does not support registering breakpoints. So, if you fire this event from the Script Task, nothing will be listening on the other side.

- FireCustomEvent—Use this event if you need to fire a custom event.

TIP
This event can also be used as a pseudo custom breakpoint. The Script Task registers custom events, so it is possible to enable a breakpoint on this event and fire it whenever you want to have an event without side effects such as a breakpoint event.

- FireError—Use this event to alert the user to critical errors.

- FireInformation—Use this event to provide information to which the user would not otherwise have access.

- FireWarning—Use this event to provide information about potentially problematic settings or failures that are not critical.

- FireProgress—For long-running tasks, use this event to provide progress information.

- FireQueryCancel—For long-running Script Tasks, use this event to determine if the Script Task should terminate prematurely.

The ExecutionValue

The ExecutionValue is a way to provide more information about the result of the task's execution than just the result provided by the ExecutionResult property. Because it is an object, you have more flexibility in what you return. The SSIS runtime can be set up to place this value in a variable.

The Logging Object

This object provides more information about the logging infrastructure and a more flexible Logging method. The following are the properties and their purpose:

- Enabled—A read-only value that tells you if logging has been enabled for the Script Task.

- GetFilterStatus—A value that returns the filtered event name strings.

- Log—The longer version of the Log method mentioned earlier; it should be avoided because the SSIS runtime overwrites any values you provide for the additional parameters not visible in the abbreviated version.

CAUTION

Although it would appear that, using this method, you can create a new log entry type, the designer does not currently support it. There is no way to register the log event so it cannot be enabled in the designer.

The TaskResult

This is the value you set to establish if the Script Task succeeded or failed. This value must be set intentionally and be accurate because the SSIS runtime keys off this value in determining the evaluation of precedence constraints.

The Transaction Object

This is the transaction created on the Taskhost container and made available to the Script Task to pass to connection managers when calling AcquireConnection so that the connection can enlist in the DTC transaction.

VariableDispenser

This is the mechanism you can use to lock and retrieve variables.

Variables

This is the simplest way to access the Variables collection and contains only those variables that have been reserved by entering them in the Script Task dialog box, as shown previously.

Suggested Practices

After covering the technical details of how to build a Script Task, the following sections cover some suggested practices that will make the Script Tasks in your packages easier to manage and understand. It's easy to get sloppy with the Script Task. After all, it's easy to discover the methods you need to call and the environment goes a long way toward ensuring the viability of the code before you ever run it the first time. But, there are still a lot of "gotchas" and you'll be creating headaches for yourself if you don't follow some basic guidelines, as discussed in the following sections.

Use Exception Handling

This one should go without saying, but is often overlooked or ignored. Using exception handling makes it possible to correctly handle unexpected behavior and, for any substantial code, pays off in the long run, especially if you do some diagnostic output in the Catch block. For example, at a minimum, you should raise an error event in the exception, as follows:

```
' Initialize the task result to success.
Dts.TaskResult = Dts.Results.Success
Try
    ' Try to add a new variable
    Dts.Variables.Add("TestVariable", False, "", "Test value")
Catch ex As Exception
    ' Write out an error, with the exception generating target site
    ' and the exception message
    Dts.Events.FireError(1, ex.TargetSite.ToString(), ex.Message, "", 0)

    ' Always execute this code and return gracefully.
    ' Never return with an exception from script tasks.
    Dts.TaskResult = Dts.Results.Failure
End Try
```

This code attempts to create a new variable during execution. The Integration Services runtime locks all collections at execution time, so this call fails and causes an exception. The Catch block catches the exception and raises an error event. The Integration Services runtime writes a message to the log and DTExec writes the error to the standard output.

Catching exceptions this way is correct. Raising an error this way is good practice. With one simple call, you're able to create an event that can be handled inside the package, write out to the log ensuring that you have some hint why the task failed, and write out the error to the console, making it possible to see the same information, but on the command line. Further, it allows you, the package writer, to handle the failed task in a graceful way because the script actually captures the exception and sets the ExecutionResult to Failure. If you don't correctly handle the exception in this way, the returned ExecutionResult will likely be wrong and the package will proceed as though the task succeeded. The sample package called InteractiveModeTest.dtsx contains this code. When run on the command line with DTExec, you receive the following message:

```
Error: 2006-01-02 19:27:13.01
   Code: 0x00000001
   Source: Test Script for Illustrating InteractiveMode and Handling Exceptions
   Microsoft.SqlServer.Dts.Runtime.Variable Add(System.String, Boolean, System.Str…
   Description: Exception from HRESULT: 0xC0016026
End Error
```

Although not terribly informative, this still provides a hint and a place to start when trying to determine what went wrong with the package, which is much better than the alternative—nothing. The HRESULT is a good place to start, so go to MSDN and find the error. As of this writing, the errors are documented on http://msdn2.microsoft.com/en-us/library/ms345164.aspx. A simple web search for "SSIS Error" or "DTS_E_" takes you to this list.

Scroll down to the error ID for the error and this is what you find.

```
0xC0016026    DTS_E_COLLECTIONLOCKED    This collection cannot be modified during
package validation or execution.
```

Now, because the code adds the TargetSite information, you know that the call causing the error is the Add call. You know the name of the task that caused the error, which is found in the Source. The TargetSite information and the package name combined with the error information makes it clear that the reason the Script Task is failing is because of the Add call.

To summarize, use exception handling to gracefully handle exceptions, log the resulting errors, and correctly set the execution result of the Script Task. If this sounds like too much work, try figuring out what caused your 15-task, 25-transform package to fail with no errors at 2:00 a.m.

Use Meaningful Comments
This is another "yeah, duh" practice, but often falls by the wayside in the rush of hurried projects and tight deadlines. This practice is universally advocated across all coding environments, so there's no need to say much more about it here. Just make it so.

Use FireProgress
If the Script Task is long running, sending progress messages helps the user get a sense that the package is making some progress. At a minimum, progress of 0% and 100% should be fired. The Progress window in the designer shows these events along with the other tasks, making it easy to see the order of package execution. The logs also show these events if they have been enabled in the logging filters.

Avoid Modal Dialog Boxes
Do not use message boxes (or other modal dialog boxes) in production. This probably sounds funny in a book with samples full of message boxes. But, we do a lot of things for illustration purposes that we wouldn't do in production packages. Just understand that placing a message box in a package might cause your package to block until someone

notices after two weeks "Hey, the nightly run isn't finishing" and finds out that the packages are all waiting for someone to click the OK button.

Share Libraries in Assemblies
If you have code that you regularly use in multiple locations, you should place it in a compiled assembly and then reference the code in the Script Task. This is one step closer to a custom task, but allows you to be more flexible in what you place in the library and how you call it. This is ideal for the consultant who wants to combine all the code she's writing at various client sites into one reusable Script Task library assembly.

Use Spacing to Eliminate Code Density
Code is always easier to read if it is phrased. Just like paragraphs of an article or this book, if the script is not separated semantically, it is very hard to understand. The Visual Studio Editor goes a long way toward ensuring that the code subscribes to some modicum of formatting sanity, but it doesn't enforce spacing and good commenting. Pieces of code that are related should be bunched together into groupings with some space between.

Eliminate Junk Code
When asked to review code other developers have written, especially when it's giving them trouble, usually, the first thing to do is delete all the commented code. It's confusing and gets in the way. Often, you think you have some errant code commented out, but don't. Or, you think some code is compiling, but it's commented out. Do yourself a favor and just delete temporary code. At worst, move the code to a temporary file somewhere out of site and mind. It makes the code a lot easier to understand and diagnose.

Use Connection Managers for Accessing Resources
The same rules apply here as for other components. If you hard-code filenames and so on, you'll have to edit the Script Task later for any changes that inevitably happen. Using connection managers for accessing files and servers means the package can be managed and configured more easily.

Use Variables for Parameters
Don't hard-code values that you pass as method parameters. Create variables to contain the parameter values, even if they're just at the scope of the Script Task. Again, variables can be configured or easily modified in the package designer without ever needing to open the Script Task designer.

Don't Write Spaghetti Code
It seems like many Script Tasks have Main functions as long as your arm. Arguably, if the work you're doing is getting that complex, you should break it up into smaller functions, put most of the code into a class library assembly, or write a custom task. A good rule of thumb is if the Main function is much longer than the editor window, you should break it down into subfunctions. This is common coding wisdom, but it is often overlooked when it comes to the Script Task.

Log Well

For very simple Script Tasks, the most you'll likely end up with is an error event in the Catch block, as described previously. However, for complex Script Tasks, you should log significant information.

TaskResult

If you don't correctly set the TaskResult, the parts of the package following the Script Task might be executing under false pretenses. Make sure you check all return paths from the Script Task. If the main section of logic (or, in other words, the thing that you are trying to accomplish with the Script Task) successfully completed, the task is successful. If not, the task failed.

Don't Use the ActiveX Script Task

The ActiveX Script Task is deprecated. Use the Script Task. It's better!

Script Task Samples

The sample solution for this chapter has several packages that illustrate how to build Script Tasks and use them in packages. Each package shows a way to accomplish some useful task. Open the packages and try to figure out how they work. Change something and see how it affects the package. The packages are simple so they'll be easy to understand and primarily focus on one class of problem. You can use these packages as a starting point for your own packages when you're trying to solve a similar problem. The following sections briefly describe each of the sample packages and how they work.

Working Against the SSIS Object Model

The two packages ParentPackage and ChildPackage show how to modify an existing package, save it, and then execute it. The problem these packages solve is how to dynamically change the Transfer Objects Task to move a table. Because the Transfer Objects Task uses a StringCollection to specify the tables to move, property expressions don't work here. So, instead, you can build a StringCollection with the values you want to set, open the package containing it, modify the TablesList property to contain the new StringCollection you just built, and save the package. The StringCollection class is defined in System.Collections.Specialized, so you can also add an Imports statement for it, as follows:

```
Imports System.Collections.Specialized
Public Class ScriptMain
    Public Sub Main()
        Dts.TaskResult = Dts.Results.Success
        Try
            ' Create an Application object to load the package
            Dim application As Microsoft.SqlServer.Dts.Runtime.Application
            Application = New Application()
```

```
          ' Use the File Connection Manager to get the package name
          Dim packagename As Object
          packagename =
Dts.Connections("MoveTablesPackage").AcquireConnection(Nothing)

          ' Load the package
          Dim package As Microsoft.SqlServer.Dts.Runtime.Package
          application.LoadPackage(packagename.ToString(), Nothing)

          ' Get the task host that contains the Transfer Objects Task
          Dim th As TaskHost
          th = package.Executables("TablesToMove")

          ' Build a String Collection with value of the table to move
          ' You can add as many table names as you want here.
          Dim sc As StringCollection = New StringCollection()
          sc.Add(Dts.Variables("TABLETOMOVE").Value.ToString())

          ' Use the properties collection to set the
          ' TableList property to point to our new StringCollection
          th.Properties("TablesList").SetValue(th, sc)
          application.SaveToXml(packagename, package, Nothing)

      ' Catch any exceptions and log them.
      Catch ex As Exception
          Dts.Events.FireError(51, ex.TargetSite().ToString(), ex.Message, "", 0)
          Dts.TaskResult = Dts.Results.Failure
      End Try
   End Sub
End Class
```

The ChildPackage package has only one task in it called TablesToMove. If you run the parent package, it executes the child package and moves the tables you set. You'll need to modify the child package to point to the correct servers. Also, if you run this sample in the designer, it detects that the child package file has changed and asks you if you want to reload. Select Yes so the designer will run the newly saved package. If you run the sample under DTExec, this isn't a problem.

Downloading a File Using HTTP

This sample, DownloadFileViaHTTP.dtsx, shows how to get a connection manager from the Connections collection and call AcquireConnection on it. This also shows how to work with the somewhat peculiar HTTP Connection Manager. The HTTP Connection Manager returns an object that essentially implements all functionality for retrieving files.

This code calls `AcquireConnection` on the HTTP Connection Manager to get the
`HttpClientConnection` and download the file named in the `DOWNLOADEDFILE` variable.

```
Public Class ScriptMain
  Public Sub Main()
    '
    ' Create an HttpClientConnection and use it to download
    ' a file from the location the connection manager specifies
    '
    Dim httpConnection As Microsoft.SqlServer.Dts.Runtime.HttpClientConnection
    Dim temp As Object
    ' Try to get the connection
    Try
      temp = Dts.Connections("FileToDownload").AcquireConnection(Nothing)
      httpConnection = New HttpClientConnection(temp)
      httpConnection.DownloadFile(Dts.Variables("DOWNLOADEDFILE").Value.ToString(),
True)
    Catch ex As Exception
      Dts.Events.FireError(1, ex.TargetSite.ToString(), ex.Message, "", 0)
    End Try
    ' Return that we succeeded
    Dts.TaskResult = Dts.Results.Success
  End Sub
End Class
```

A few things are going on in this package that might not be obvious. The Execute Process
Task has two property expressions that specify the correct working directory and
executable to run. The connection manager is just pointing to the Microsoft.com website,
but doesn't specify a file, so the connection manager picks up the default home page. And
finally, the DOWNLOADEDFILE variable has an expression that builds the fully qualified
filename from the WORKINGFOLDER variable and the name Temp.html.

```
@WORKINGFOLDER + "\\" + @FILENAME
```

Finally, the Execute Process Task launches the default browser showing the Microsoft.com
home page.

This package uses the Script Task and the expressions to pull together stock functionality
in the package to build a fairly complex application with very little code. Hopefully, you
can see that you can take this package as a start and use it anytime you need to access
files on a website.

Loading the Contents of a Text File into a Variable

`LoadingATextFile.dtsx` is a simple package that uses a `Foreach Loop` with a Foreach File
Enumerator to loop over text files in a folder. The Script Task in the `Foreach Loop` opens
each text file and displays the contents in a message box. The sample also shows how to

split up the code to use a subfunction. Make sure there are some .txt files in the working folder before running this package.

The following code reads the name of a file to open from the FileName variable and loads the contents of the file into a string, which it then displays in a message box and also places the contents in the variable named FileContents.

```
Imports System.IO
Public Class ScriptMain
    '
    ' Load a file and show a message box with the contents.
    '
    Public Sub Main()
        Dim errorInfo As String = ""
        Dim Contents As String = ""

        Contents = GetFileContents(Dts.Variables("FileName").Value.ToString(),
errorInfo)
        If errorInfo.Length > 0 Then
            ' Failed to load file
            MsgBox(errorInfo, MsgBoxStyle.Critical, "Error")
            Dts.TaskResult = Dts.Results.Failure
        Else
            ' Do real work here.
            MsgBox(Contents, MsgBoxStyle.OkOnly, "File contents")
            Dts.Variables("FileContents").Value = Contents
            Dts.TaskResult = Dts.Results.Success
        End If
    End Sub
    '
    ' Function for getting the contents of a text file
    '
    ' A subfunction for loading the file.
    Public Function GetFileContents(ByVal filePath As String, _
                                    Optional ByVal ErrorInfo As String = "") As
String
        Dim strContents As String
        Dim objReader As StreamReader
        Try
            objReader = New StreamReader(filePath)
            strContents = objReader.ReadToEnd()
            objReader.Close()
            Return strContents
        Catch Ex As Exception
            ErrorInfo = Ex.Message
```

```
        End Try
    End Function
End Class
```

Simple Custom Logging

The `CustomLogging.dtsx` package is very simple and shows how to use the `Log` method to create a log entry.

```
Public Sub Main()
        '
        ' Add an entry into the logs.
        '
        Dts.TaskResult = Dts.Results.Success
        Try
            Dts.Log("This is a custom log entry from the Script Task", 42, Nothing)
            Dts.Variables.Add("DummyVarName", False, "", Nothing)
        Catch ex As Exception
            Dts.Log(ex.Message, 0, Nothing)
            Dts.TaskResult = Dts.Results.Failure
        End Try
    End Sub
```

Handling Exceptions

The `HandleException` package attempts to do something illegal that causes an exception and handles the exception by firing an error and returning an execution result of failed, exiting gracefully. Notice also that the main class name is `EntryPoint`, not `Main`. Nothing too important, just noting that it doesn't matter so long as the `EntryPoint` property on the Script Task dialog box has the same name.

```
Public Class EntryPoint
    Public Sub Main()
        ' This is a simple script that attempts to do something illegal,
        ' create a new variable at execution time.
        ' Ensure that the error is handled and logged.

        ' Initialize the task result to success.
        Dts.TaskResult = Dts.Results.Success
        Dts.Events.FireProgress("HandleException", 0, 0, 0, "TestExpressions",
True)

        Try
```

```
        ' Try to add a new variable
        Dts.Variables.Add("TestVariable", False, "", "Test value")

    Catch ex As Exception

        ' Write out an error, with the exception generating target site
        ' and the exception message
        Dts.Events.FireError(1, ex.TargetSite.ToString(), ex.Message, "", 0)

        ' Always execute this code and return gracefully.
        ' Never return with an exception from script tasks.
        Dts.TaskResult = Dts.Results.Failure

    End Try
    Dts.Events.FireProgress("HandleException", 100, 0, 0, "TestExpressions",
True)
  End Sub
End Class
```

Safe Message Box

The SafeMessageBox package uses a small function to determine if it is OK to show the message box. Using this function, you can avoid the embarrassing and possibly costly mistake of showing a modal message box in a package on a production machine. Notice the VariableDispenser is used in this code. This makes it so you don't have to remember to put the name of the InteractiveMode variable in the Script Task dialog box.

```
' A function for safely showing message boxes in script tasks
Public Function SafeMessageBox(ByVal prompt As String, ByVal title As String)

    ' Default is off.
    Dim showMessage As Boolean = False
    Try
        ' Get the System InteractiveMode variable to determine if we should show
        Dim vars As Variables
        Dts.VariableDispenser.LockForRead("System::InteractiveMode")
        Dts.VariableDispenser.GetVariables(vars)
        showMessage = vars("System::InteractiveMode").Value
    Catch ex As Exception
        ' Fire an error, we weren't able to get the variable
        Dts.Events.FireError(1, ex.TargetSite.ToString(), ex.Message, "", 0)
    Finally
        If showMessage Then
            ' InteractiveMode is True
```

```
            MsgBox(prompt, MsgBoxStyle.OkOnly, title)
        End If
    End Try
End Function
```

Summary

The Script Task is a powerful tool for performing simple work that is not supported in stock tasks. The Script Task designer is rich with time-saving features and supporting infrastructure. Even though the Script Task is designed to support short, problem-focused scripts, it can be used to tackle more complex problems, such as building or editing packages, parsing files, or downloading files from Internet servers. Also, remember to take a little extra time to comment the code and use exception handling. These and the other best practices mentioned in this chapter will drastically increase the manageability of the script down the road. The samples show how to do some basic work using the Script Task. Although you can perform more complex tasks, this is about the level of work most people perform with the Script Task. If it gets much more complicated than the most complex of these samples, you might want to start thinking about writing a custom task or writing a class library that you reference from the Script Task.

Using Source Control

"BUT THE PLATE DOESN'T HAVE ANY SIDES. IT'S ROUND."—LINDSEY HASELDEN

As anyone who has written code for a living or worked on software development projects of any size will tell you, source control is essential to the success of the project. It is frustrating to develop software without good source control. Your code can be overwritten, lost to accidentally reverted changes, or destroyed when your hard drive goes south. In some cases, not having source control can even be disastrous.

WHEN DISASTER STRIKES

In an article on Embedded.com called "When Disaster Strikes," Jack Ganssle recalls some disasters and what we learn from them while making a good argument for using source control.

"In 1999 a Titan IVb (this is a really big rocket) blasted off the pad, bound for geosynchronous orbit with a military communications satellite aboard. Nine minutes into the flight, the first stage shut down and separated properly. The Centaur second stage ignited and experienced instabilities about the roll axis. That coupled into both yaw and pitch deviations until the vehicle tumbled. Computers compensated by firing the reaction control system thrusters till they ran out of fuel. The Milstar spacecraft wound up in a useless low-elliptical orbit.

"A number of crucial constants specified the launcher's flight behavior. That file wasn't managed by a version control system (VCS) and was lost. An engineer modified a similar file to recreate the data but entered one parameter as -0.1992476 instead of the correct -1.992476. That was it—that one little slipup cost taxpayers a billion dollars.

"We all know to protect important files with a VCS—right? Astonishingly, in 1999 a disgruntled FAA programmer left the Federal Aviation Administration, deleting all of the software needed for on-route control of planes between Chicago O'Hare and the regional airports. He encrypted it on his home computer. The feds busted him, of course, but FBI forensics took six months to decrypt the key."

What Is Source Control?

Source control is first and primarily a way to ensure that your source code remains safe—safe from loss by reversion, deletion, accidental or malicious loss, or theft. There are also a number of services source control software provides for dealing with the realities of software development, such as labeling, branching, merging, and diffing. For the benefit of those who might be unfamiliar with source control, source control software is composed of a source repository and a set of features for managing the source, as discussed in the following sections.

The Source Repository

This is where the source is stored. In large-scale source control systems, this might be built on top of a sophisticated database server such as SQL Server, or for smaller systems, it could be a simple proprietarily formatted file that contains cumulative file deltas. Besides the actual source files, the source repository stores the differences, histories, comments, and other information necessary for safely managing the code.

Syncing

Syncing is what you do to get the source out of the source repository. You sync whenever you want to retrieve the source repository version of the source files. Generally, the result of a sync is that out-of-date files on your local machine get overwritten by files that have changed in the source repository.

Checking Out/Checking In

When you need to make changes to a source file, you check it out. When you're done, you check it in with the changes. The source control system tracks which files get checked out and tracks a history of the differences between the file when it was checked out and checked in. To see the differences in the earlier and later files, you do a diff.

Diffing

Diffing is when you compare two files to determine the differences between the two. This is often part of the merging process but also can be used for code reviewing changes or when viewing change histories. At its heart, source control is about retaining the difference histories of the files in a project throughout the project lifetime so you can reconstruct the product at any stage within the lifetime.

Labeling

Labeling is a source-control feature for creating named code snapshots. A code snapshot is a way to mark code in a project as of a certain date and time so that you can later retrieve the code in that state. Labeling refers to the feature that lets you give the snapshot a name to make it easier to reference the snapshot. Labeling is often used to mark build numbers so that it is easy to reproduce a build from a given date by "syncing" to the code snapshot.

Branching

Branching is a feature used for making copies of all or parts of the code project. In most cases, the intention is to create a sandbox of code that will later be *integrated* back into the mainline. Integration is just another word for a checkin, but implies a larger scale. Because integration is a partial or complete remerge of the files from a branch back into the mainline, integrations usually involve a lot of files with a lot of changes and generally also present a few more challenges. When checking in a file or two, if there are any code changes that collide with changes someone else made, you can usually correctly determine which code should be retained. With integrations, especially for large teams, it can be more complex because of all the changes, files, and potential conflicts involved.

Merging

Merging is how the changes are added to the source. The source system must always merge changes into the source when the checked-out code is checked in. Sometimes, merges result in change collisions. If more than one developer checks out a source file and they make changes to code in the same part of the file, there will be a change collision that will require a merge resolution. The source control system provides a way to view the two changes and select which one is correct. Sometimes, this requires that the person doing the merge manually change the code, especially if both changes are valid.

Source Control in the Designer (BIDS)

One of my first experiences with source control was at a small startup company where our "source control" was a whiteboard. To check out a file, you put a check mark next to the name of the file. Nobody else was allowed to modify the file if it was "checked out." What a mess! Human error reigned supreme and we were always having problems with our code base because of it. Thankfully, the Business Intelligence Development Studio provides integrated support for source control so you don't have to revert to such schemes for controlling your Business Intelligence solutions. Any source control provider that supports the SCCAPI protocol, such as Visual SourceSafe, Clearcase, Visual Studio Team System, PVCS, or QVCS, will integrate with Visual Studio, making it possible to seamlessly add new solutions, projects, and files to your source control repository inside the designer environment. The Solution Explorer gives visual indications as to the source control status of files and even provides views of the pending changes. Essentially, in addition to being a package or cube designer, the Visual Studio environment becomes the source control management interface as well. The Visual Studio source control features are too numerous and rich to fully document here. So, although this chapter can't cover all the details, it does try to cover the most useful, difficult, and problematic elements.

Setting Up

Before you can set up source control in the designer, you need to have a source control provider installed. This chapter demonstrates the provider Visual SourceSafe. After you have the source control provider installed, you can turn on source control in the designer by selecting the main Tools menu and clicking the Options menu option. The Options dialog box opens, as shown in Figure 16.1.

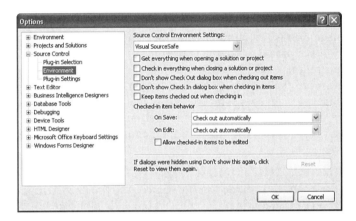

FIGURE 16.1   The Options dialog box with the default source control settings.

The Plug-in Selection tab lets you select which source control provider you want to use. The sample has Visual SourceSafe selected. The Environment tab, shown in Figure 16.1, mainly controls the timing of when projects and files get checked out and checked in. Depending on how you like to work, you can change these settings. The Environment tab shows settings that are universal across source control providers.

CAUTION

Some of these settings are questionable. For example, checking in everything automatically seems dubious. Generally, checkins should be explicit, not implicit. In other words, you should only check in when you intend to check in and then you should be careful and intentional about how you do the checkin. With this setting, and the Don't Show Check In Dialog Box when Checking In Items setting, you could easily forget that files are actually being checked in when closing down a solution and check in code or packages that are broken. It's easy to see how this could become a problem in some environments where central IT departments upgrade machines with the latest virus signature files and reboot the machines automatically. If you ever happen to leave a package partially edited and BIDS shuts down, closing and checking in the solution in this way, you might "break the build" because of your partially edited package or code.

You should also be careful with the Get Everything when Opening a Solution setting. It is generally considered bad form to check out entire projects with all the project files unless you plan to edit each of them simultaneously. This is especially true when working on large teams where you increase the chance of causing a merge resolution or you block them from checking out a file. As a rule, you should only check out files for as long as you need them and no longer. It's similar to the old development wisdom that you should "free all resources as soon as possible, but no sooner."

To see settings that are specific to the source control provider, select the Plug-in Settings tab, and then click the Advanced button; the SourceSafe Options dialog box opens, as shown in Figure 16.2.

FIGURE 16.2   SourceSafe Options.

These settings are covered well in the SourceSafe documentation, so they aren't all explained here. However, you should know where to find these settings in BIDS.

After you've enabled source control, you still need to add solutions to the source control repository. You can add both new and existing solutions. To add an existing solution, right-click on the project or solution node in the Solution Explorer. The context menu shown in Figure 16.3 appears.

If you haven't already logged in to the source control system, a login dialog box opens. After logging in, the Add to SourceSafe Project dialog box opens, as shown in Figure 16.4.

You can create a subfolder here for the solution or add it to an existing folder. Practices for how to structure your source abound, so this chapter doesn't cover that topic. However, it is good to have a dedicated folder for a solution because BIDS manages source control at the solution level.

Figure 16.5 shows the New Project dialog box with the option to add the project to source control.

FIGURE 16.3   Adding solutions to source control.

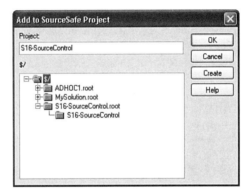

FIGURE 16.4   The Add to SourceSafe Project dialog box.

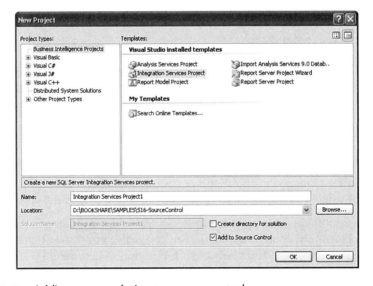

FIGURE 16.5   Adding a new solution to source control.

Using Source Control

After you've set up source control in the Visual Studio environment and then added a solution, a number of changes become available in the designer to enable you to easily work with source control:

- A new Source Control menu appears on the main File menu.

- Small icons appear next to the Solution Explorer nodes.

- A new source control menu section appears on the Solution Explorer context menu.

- The Source Control toolbar is enabled.

Source Control Menu

The Source Control menu has only two menu options when you have no solution loaded. The first is Open from Source Control. This option does a *get* on a solution. You only want to do this if you don't already have a solution on your local machine. After you've sync'ed to the solution in this way, you should open the solution as usual, with the File, Open Solution menu option. The second option is to open the Visual SourceSafe environment. This is usually not necessary unless you need to label, merge, or move files.

The File Source Control menu changes depending on what object you have currently selected. For example, if you have a package open in the designer and you've clicked on the drawing surface, the menu options such as Get, Check Out, and History will act on the selected file. With the solution open, and the YUKONB3.dsv file selected in the Solution Explorer, the Source Control menu looks similar to the one shown in Figure 16.6.

FIGURE 16.6　The Source Control menu allows you to perform the most common operations.

Get the Latest Version　The first menu option is to get the latest version of the file that is currently open in the designer. In this case, it is the YUKONB3 Data Source View. If you

have the file checked out, and you select this option, the Microsoft Visual SourceSafe
dialog box shown in Figure 16.7 opens, giving you several options from which to choose.

FIGURE 16.7   Options for syncing to a file you have checked out.

The Replace option replaces the local file with the one from source safe, overwriting any
changes you may have made. This is useful if you've made changes to the file and want
to back up to the currently checked-in file. This is essentially a big undo. If you regularly
check in your functioning package or other file, you'll always be able to revert to the last
known good state or recover most of your work should you accidentally or catastrophi-
cally lose the file.

Use the Merge option when you want to "pick up" the changes others have made.
However, it is not recommended to use this option when working with packages.

CAUTION

If you choose to use the Merge option, back up the package first. Packages are not like
your average source code that can be compared on a line-by-line basis. There are internal references to other objects within the package. A simple merge can corrupt packages and even make them unusable. Be very careful with this option.

The Leave option simply leaves the local file undisturbed.

Check Out and Check In   These menu options provide a way to check in or check out
the source file. When you check out a file, it also performs a sync. In other words, the
existing local file will be overwritten with the current version of the file found in the
source repository and marked as writable on the local system.

Undo Check Out   This is the "Oops, I really didn't need to check out that file" option.
Or, you might want to use this option when you've made edits that you don't want.
Either way, when you choose this option you lose your edits to the file permanently. Be
careful with this option.

View History   View History lets you view the details of all the checkins for a given file.
When you select this option, the History Options dialog box shown in Figure 16.8 opens.

As you can see, this dialog box allows you to filter the history by date and user. To view
all history items, leave the From, To, and User fields empty. Click the OK button and the
History dialog box shown in Figure 16.9 opens.

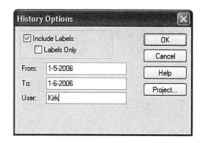

FIGURE 16.8   The History Options dialog box filters the history items to view.

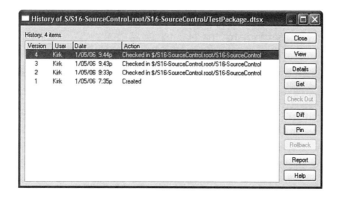

FIGURE 16.9   The History dialog box shows filtered history entries for a file.

From Figure 16.9, you can see that the file has been checked in three times and the dates it was checked in and created. You can also perform other operations such as getting an older file by selecting the version entry in the list and clicking the Get button. If you select two version entries in the list and click Diff, a diff utility graphically shows the differences between the two files. The files do not need to be chronologically adjacent to each other. Figure 16.10 shows the Difference Options dialog box that opens when you click the Diff button.

Various options for the type of diff you want to perform are available, as well as for browsing for different files or creating a report. After you've selected the settings you want, click the OK button and the graphical difference viewer shown in Figure 16.11 opens.

The difference viewer highlights lines that have changed. Some lines might have only a single character difference. Others might be new or deleted. It's a good practice to do a difference on every file before checking it in, right before checking it in.

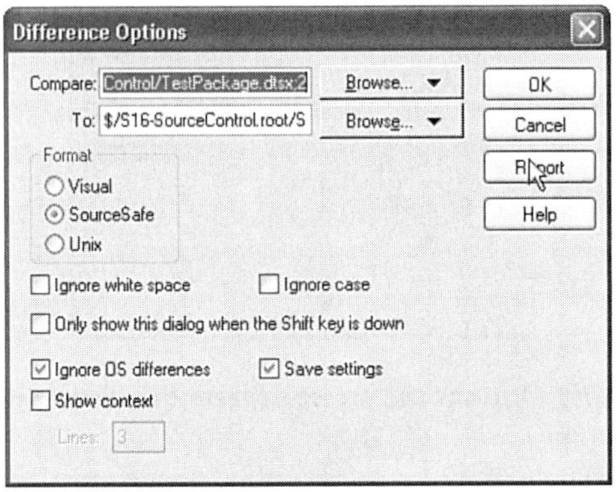

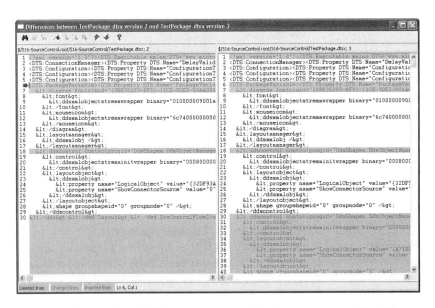

FIGURE 16.10   Select settings for the files to diff.

FIGURE 16.11   The graphical difference viewer makes it easy to spot file differences.

CHECKING IN

On one project, I was just about ready to check in some code. I had performed the code review, done the diff on the files, and was ready to do the checkin. However, I had put off nature for a few hours too long and really needed to see a man about a dog. So, I scuttled off to take care of business and quickly returned, promptly checking in the code. An hour or so later, I received an email that was broadcast to the whole team that said I had broken the build. The error that caused the break was promptly displayed in the email with the embedded string "Kirk is a dork." I was very embarrassed, of course. What happened was, one of my co-workers thought he'd leave me a friendly note in my editor. I did two things wrong, wait, no, three. I didn't lock my machine when I left, I didn't double-check the diffs, and I waited far too long to take care of nature.

Solution Explorer Changes

Figure 16.12 shows the Solution Explorer with source control enabled.

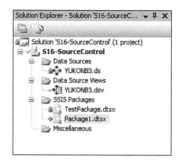

FIGURE 16.12   The Solution Explorer contains visual hints as to file check-in status.

There are primarily three icons that appear:

- **The Lock**—The file is checked in.

- **The Check**—The file is checked out.

- **The Plus**—The file is new and hasn't been added to source control yet.

Source Control Menu Section in the Solution Explorer Context Menu

Most of the same options are found here as on the main File menu. However, the View
Pending Checkins menu option is only found on this menu. Select this option and the
Pending Checkins dockable window opens, as shown in Figure 16.13.

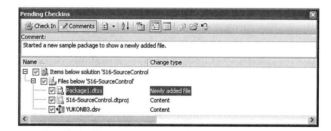

FIGURE 16.13   The Pending Checkins window shows potential solution changes.

The Pending Checkins window makes it easy to see what files are checked out. You can
also directly check files in with comments using this window.

The Source Control Toolbar Is Enabled

Finally, the Source Control toolbar is another way to access the source control features.
All toolbar operations act on the currently selected file in the Solution Explorer.

As you can see, you can interact with the source control system in Visual Studio in many different ways. This seamless integration really makes source control a breeze and enhances the overall development experience.

Practices

Although using source control systems is fairly straightforward, there are a few practices that you should be aware of to help you avoid some of the inevitable source control gotchas. The following are a few suggestions for better source control practices:

- Ensure that the default directory is uniquely defined for each developer on the team. If you specify a shared location for the default directory, you'll have overwrites regularly.

- Ensure that you check in changes to the solution or project as soon as possible because the project and solution files are impacted by all filename changes.

- The default setting for allowing multiple checkouts of the same file is off. Keep it that way, especially if you edit multiple packages simultaneously. As previously mentioned, packages don't merge well.

- Keep files checked out only so long as you must. If you have exclusive checkout turned on, especially on large teams, you might be prohibiting others from editing a file.

- If you need to see who has a file checked out, select the file in the Solution Explorer, choose File, Source Control, and then SourceSafe Properties.

- When opening solutions, use the Get Latest Version option. This updates your current solution files so that you can receive the latest changes from others on your team.

- Before checking in files, always get the latest version of the other files in the solution before testing your changes and checking in. This ensures that your changes will work correctly against the changes others have made in the same project.

- Avoid asymmetrical checkins. Asymetrical checkins are when you check in one file in a change but not another. For example, if you change the name of a file in a project and update the project, you should check in both the project file and the file. Otherwise, when others sync on the project, it will be broken.

- Always do diffs, even on packages. Although it can be difficult to understand what's happening in a package, you can do a sanity diff check. For example, if you do the diff and you see that there is a new executable named "You are a dork," you'll know that there's something amiss in the package. You don't even have to know what that task is. You'll just know that you didn't put it there.

SOURCE CONTROL IN SQL MANAGEMENT STUDIO

SQL Server Management Studio also supports the Project Explorer and source control. Although the types of files that the Management Studio solutions manager contains are constrained to connections, queries, and other miscellaneous files, the same source control features like the Solution Explorer icons, Source Control toolbar, and Pending Checkins window are all there. You enable source control in the same way as in BIDS.

If you have scripts that are related or part of a project you're building in BIDS, consider storing both in the same node in the source repository. This makes it easier to move, back up, restore, and manage the entire solution over time.

Summary

This has been a really quick introduction to using source control for managing your Integration Services solutions. Use source control whether you're a single developer on a small project or on a team of multiple developers. The Visual Studio development environment makes it easy to use source control by providing a rich set of seamlessly integrated source control features. Source control isn't a panacea by any means. Things can still go wrong, but by using source control and exercising a little discipline, you can avoid catastrophic code loss.

SQL Server Management Studio

"IT INCREASES THE NUMBER OF TIMES IT'S NOT GETTING CALLED."— JAMES HOWEY

The chapters so far have mostly covered concepts pertaining to package internals and building packages in the design time environment. As the name implies, SQL Server Management Studio, or just Management Studio, provides the management functions for Integration Services. You'll likely use the design tools for packages as they work their way through your development and testing processes. However, eventually, the packages will land in their final production location in SQL Server or on a server file system. From that point forward, you'll likely store, organize, maintain, and execute those finished packages using Management Studio.

SQL Server Management Studio Overview

One of the biggest theme changes for SQL Server 2005 Business Intelligence applications was the deliberate separation between design time and management features. As you know by now, the Business Intelligence Development Studio (BIDS) now provides the designer features once found in Enterprise Manager. Management Studio is the replacement tool for the management functions SQL Server 2000 Enterprise Manager provided.

Management Studio is based on the Visual Studio platform infrastructure, so it looks similar in many ways to Visual Studio. By using the Visual Studio platform, Management Studio is consistent with the designer in behavior and also shares some of the tools, such as the Object Explorer, Solution Explorer, Source Control, and many others. However, Management Studio is not capable of hosting other tools, such as programming languages, Integration Services, or Reporting Services, the way BIDS can.

This short introduction will be helpful in getting you up to speed on how to move around the Management Studio environment, especially for those of you who are accustomed to working in SQL Server 2000 and have been confused initially by the separation between the designer and Management Studio. Here, a few of the more commonly used features of Management Studio are pointed out just to get you started, and the rest of the chapter covers the topics in more detail.

Figure 17.1 shows a screenshot of Management Studio.

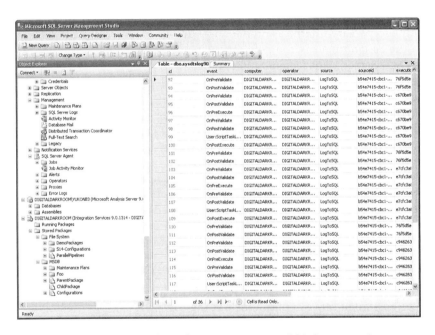

FIGURE 17.1   Management Studio is for managing your SQL Server environment.

Object Explorer

The Object Explorer is where you connect to all the servers, including Integration Services, SQL Server, Analysis Services, and Reporting Services. This window is essentially the home base from which you start almost all operations. In the upper-left portion of the Object Explorer docked window is the Connect button, shown in Figure 17.2.

To create a new query, use the New Query button on the Standard toolbar, located under the main menu by default and shown in Figure 17.3.

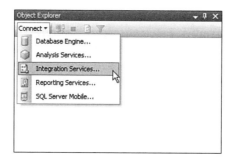

FIGURE 17.2   Use the Connect button to connect to servers.

FIGURE 17.3   Use the Standard toolbar to create new queries and show windows.

The default location of the Standard toolbar is shown in Figure 17.1. However, because the toolbar might have been moved elsewhere or hidden, it might not be visible or in the same location on your screen. To show the Standard toolbar, right-click on the main window header right below the window title bar. The toolbar context menu shown in Figure 17.4 appears.

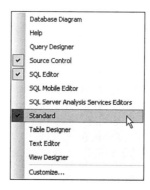

FIGURE 17.4   Use the toolbar context menu to show or hide toolbars.

The Standard toolbar has a number of query buttons for Analysis Services queries to the right of the New Query button. These are useful for quickly loading a new query window. The next few buttons are useful for loading and saving files. Using those buttons, you can open some useful windows, as follows.

Registered Servers
The first button (fifth from the right) opens the Registered Servers window where you can do things like preserve connection information, determine if a registered server is running, view the properties of a server, or connect to the server in the Object Explorer.

To see the properties of a server, right-click on a server node and select Properties. The Edit Server Registration Properties dialog box opens, as shown in Figure 17.5.

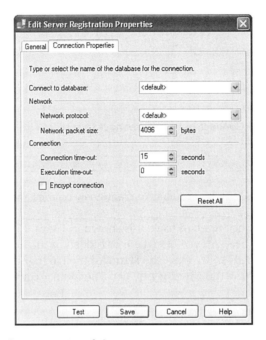

FIGURE 17.5   View the properties of the server.

The Summary Window

The second button (fourth from the right) opens the Summary window. The Summary window presents a polymorphic report on the object currently selected in the Object Explorer. Unfortunately, Integration Services does not fully support the Summary window, so very little information appears for packages. Figure 17.6 shows the Summary window with the column schema for a table in the AdventureWorks database.

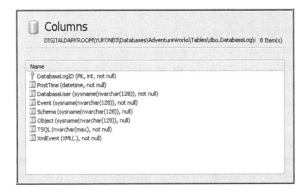

FIGURE 17.6   The Summary window shows information about the selected object.

Template Explorer

The third of the five buttons opens the Object Explorer, and the fourth button (second from the right) on the Standard toolbar opens the Template Explorer. This is a nifty tool that provides what are essentially cookbook T-SQL scripts for accomplishing a wide variety of tasks, such as creating endpoints, creating a login, or attaching a database. Figure 17.7 shows the Template Explorer with a few of the templates showing.

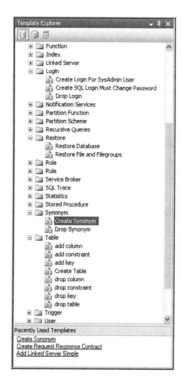

FIGURE 17.7   The Template Explorer contains T-SQL scripts for common tasks.

Viewing the Windows Event Log

One more nifty feature that you should know about is the log viewer. If you right-click on the Integration Services node and select View Logs, the Log File Viewer appears with the Windows Event Log for recently executed packages. This is a helpful feature for getting an overall picture of how well your packages are executing, allowing you to easily and quickly find problem packages.

There's much more to Management Studio than can possibly be covered here. This short introduction should be enough for you to become familiar with the basics. You can find more information in Books Online and MSDN. The remainder of this chapter drills down into the Integration Services–specific features of Management Studio.

Connecting to the Integration Services Server

The Integration Services Server is a Windows NT Service that provides the underlying functionality for the Management Studio Integration Services node. Of course, you can connect to the Integration Services Server only if the service is running. By default, the server is installed and configured to run automatically when you install Integration Services, but you should check just to make sure.

TIP

If you have trouble connecting to the server, you should double-check that the service is running.

Starting the Integration Services Server

To start the server, or to just check if it is running, select the SQL Server Configuration Manager menu option from the Configuration Tools submenu of the SQL Server 2005 Start menu. The SQL Server Configuration Manager appears, as shown in Figure 17.8.

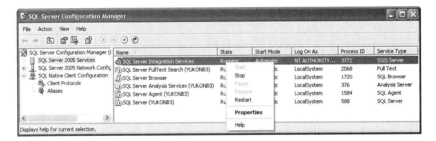

FIGURE 17.8   Use the SQL Server Configuration Manager to check the server status.

NOTE

You can also launch the SQL Server Configuration Manager from any server node in the Registered Servers window by right-clicking on the node and selecting the Configuration Manager menu option. The same configuration features are available from the Computer Management management console in the Services and Applications node under the SQL Server Configuration Manager subnode.

To modify any of the server settings, right-click on the server you want to change, and select Properties. Figure 17.9 shows the SQL Server Integration Services Properties dialog box where you can modify the start mode and change the account to use for logging on. You can also start, stop, and restart the service in this dialog box.

FIGURE 17.9   Use the SQL Server Integration Services Properties dialog box to manage the service.

NOTE

The SSIS Service performs the enumeration of all installed components and caches the information for quicker package and designer startup. The SSIS Service Start Mode should always be set to Automatic so that the designer and executing packages can use the cached enumerations instead of doing the costly enumerations each time the designer is opened or a new package is executed.

Connecting to a Local Server

To connect to the Integration Services Server, perform the following steps.

1. Launch Management Studio.

2. In the Object Explorer window, click the Connect button.

3. Select the Integration Services menu option.

4. The Connect to Server dialog box opens, as shown in Figure 17.10.

5. Select or type in the server name to which you want to connect.

6. Click the Connect button.

FIGURE 17.10   Connecting to the Integration Services Server.

NOTE

For this version, if you open the Server name drop down and select the Browse for More option, the Browse for Servers dialog box only shows you the local servers and doesn't support searching for remote servers. If you click the Options button, the Connection Properties tab is available, but the settings on this tab have no effect on the connection and should be ignored.

Connecting to a Remote SSIS Server

Connecting to the remote server is straightforward. However, because you cannot use the Browse button to discover other IS servers on the network in this version, you need to know the name of the server and type it in directly.

Managing Packages

SQL Server Management Studio allows you to manage packages that are currently executing and those that are stored in SQL Server. The following sections describe how to interact with both types of packages.

Running Packages

After you've established a connection in Management Studio, there will be an Integration Services node in Object Explorer with two subnodes called Running Packages and Stored Packages. The Running Packages folder displays the packages that are currently executing on the node's server and updates regularly as packages start and finish executing. You can also force a package to stop by right-clicking on the package displayed in the Running Packages tree and selecting the Stop menu option. To see this feature, run the sample package WaitUntilTerminated in the sample solution S17-ManagementStudio.

To simulate a long-running package, the WaitUntilTerminated package has two Script Tasks that show message boxes. The second Script Task is constrained with a completion precedence constraint on the first. If you run the package, it shows a message box. You can then refresh the Running Packages node in Management Studio to show the WaitUntilTerminated package. To stop it, right-click on the WaitUntilTerminated package in the Management Studio Running Packages node and select the Stop menu option. Then, wait a second or two and then click the OK button in the message box to dismiss it, and the package will terminate.

NOTE

You need to dismiss the message box because the Stop option does not orphan executing tasks or force packages to stop executing. Rather, it sets the Cancel event in the package object that tells it to cease scheduling new tasks for execution. Therefore, when using the Stop feature, some packages do not immediately stop, especially if tasks aren't checking the Cancel event or calling the FireQueryCancel event regularly.

All packages that are prematurely stopped in this way log that fact in the system log. You can see the message in the Event Viewer in Figure 17.11. This ensures that you have a record of any packages that are canceled.

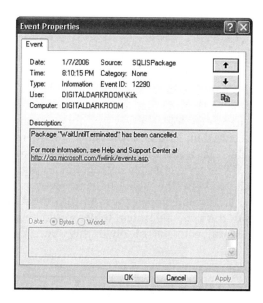

FIGURE 17.11 Packages log a message whenever they are canceled.

Stored Packages

The Stored Packages folder has two subfolders. The File System folder lists the packages that have been stored on the local server. The MSDB folder lists packages stored to the SQL Server instance where the IS Service is configured to enumerate packages.

If you right-click on a package under the Stored Packages node, a context menu appears with one or more of the following menu options:

- **New Folder**—Creates a new subfolder

- **Import Package**—Imports the package from the file system, SQL Server, or SSIS Server storage

- **Export Package**—Exports the package from the location it is stored to the file system, SQL Server, or SSIS Server storage

- **Package Roles**—Launches the Package Roles dialog box for you to select the roles for the package; this feature is not supported for packages stored in the file system

- **Run Package**—Executes the package using the DTExecUI utility

- **Delete**—Deletes the package

- **Rename**—Renames the package

Although these two folders have no subfolders by default, you are free to create, rename, and delete subfolders as you want using the New Folder menu option. When you create a new folder beneath the File System folder, a new directory is created in the file system as well. For folders that are created under the MSDB folder, a new entry is added to the sysdtspackagesfolder90 table that tracks the folder structure. Subfolders make it possible to better organize packages. If you have multiple packages in a solution, you can group them together into one subfolder and give the folder the same name as the solution. This makes it easier to link the production storage location with the solution. In the same way that having all your files in the same file system folder would be a nightmare, it's also easier to manage packages grouped hierarchically in this way.

SQL OR FILE SYSTEM?

Are there any pros/cons for deploying packages into SQL Server versus deploying as a file? The obligatory answer is "It depends." This is not a new question. The options to save packages to SQL Server and to files were available in DTS as well as the option to save to Meta Data Services, which is no longer available in SQL Server 2005. But, it is a good question. It means people are trying to understand the trade-offs. So here are some of them:

Advantages of Saving to Files
- Can use source control to manage
- Ultra secure when using the Encrypt with User Key encryption option
- Not subject to network downtime problems (saved locally)
- May escrow deployment bundles, including miscellaneous files
- Less steps to load into the designer
- Easier direct access for viewing
- May store packages hierarchically in file system
- Projects in Visual Studio are disk based and require the package to be in the file system
- Generally a better experience during development

Advantages of Saving to SQL Server
- Generally easier access by multiple individuals
- Benefits of database security, DTS roles, and Agent interaction
- Packages get backed up with normal DB backup processes
- Able to filter packages via queries
- May store packages hierarchically via new package folders
- Generally a better in-production experience

Managing DTS 2000 Packages

You can also access DTS packages in Management Studio. Whether stored in SQL Server 2005 or SQL Server 2000, the packages are stored in the Legacy tree, as shown in Figure 17.12.

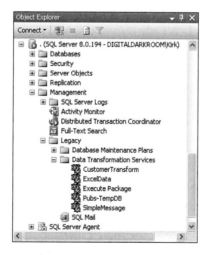

FIGURE 17.12   DTS packages are stored in the legacy node.

If you right-click a package, the context menu has the following options:

- **Open**—Launches the DTS 2000 designer

- **Migrate a Package**—Launches the Migration Wizard to migrate the DTS package to an SSIS package

- **Export**—Exports the package from the msdb database to another SQL Server, the SSIS Server, or the file system

- **Delete**—Deletes the package

- **Rename**—Renames the package

CAUTION

To launch the DTS Package Editor, you must have an existing SQL Server 2000 instance remaining on the machine, or you must download and install the Microsoft SQL Server 2000 DTS Designer Components. To find these components, search MSDN for "DTS Designer Components." See Chapter 2, "Setting Up Integration Services," for more information about setting up the DTS Package Editor.

Server Caching

Besides package execution monitoring and storage management, the server also acts as a systemwide cache for collections of information objects that describe installed Integration Services components. Because there are so many different pluggable components, it's quite expensive to rediscover all the components every time you run a package. In fact, it's prohibitively time consuming. The server shortcuts that by caching information about each of the installed components. After being cached, clients get information about installed components directly from the server. Following is a list of the component collections the server populates and caches:

- ForeachEnumerators

- Tasks

- LogProviders

- Connections

- DBProviders

- Packages

- PipelineComponents

As a package writer, you might never see these collections because the designer and other tools hide them. However, you will see the benefits of having these collections cached. To understand how caching these collections affects the performance of the designer, stop the Integration Services service and load up an Integration Services project. Open a package. There will be a noticeable delay between when you open the package until when the designer is actually ready to edit it. This is because the designer is busy trying to enumerate all the components.

> **NOTE**
>
> If the Integration Services Server is not running when you attempt to open a package in the designer, the server automatically starts. From that time forward, the service is available and will have cached the component collections.

Using SQL Server Agent to Execute Packages

It's common to use SQL Server Agent to schedule and execute packages on the server. With Agent Proxies and Subsystems, it's simple to set up a secure job for executing a package. The following is a quick-start guide to setting up a job:

1. In Management Studio, open the instance of SQL Server in which you want to create the job.

2. In the SQL Server Agent node, right-click on Jobs and select New.

3. On the General tab, provide a name for the job, and select an Owner and Category, as shown in Figure 17.13.

FIGURE 17.13   Create a new job.

4. Make sure the Enabled option is checked so you can schedule the job.

5. Click the Steps tab and then click the New button. The New Job Step dialog box opens, as shown in Figure 17.14.

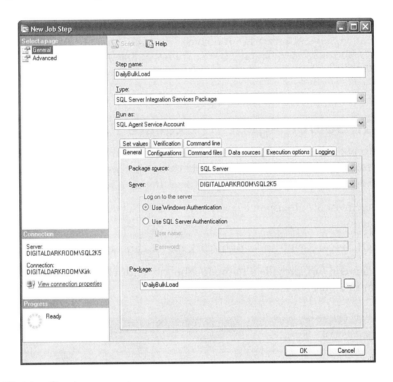

FIGURE 17.14   Create a new step.

6. Give the step a name.

7. In the Type list, select SQL Server Integration Services Package.

8. In the Run As combo box, select the proxy account. This example has the SQL Agent Service account selected. You can create a different proxy account if you create the credential and proxy.

9. On the General tab, select the package source and package to execute.

10. You can set the command line, execution, and other options here as well. This dialog box is the same as for the DTExecUI utility.

11. Click the OK button.

You can set other settings in the dialog boxes, but this is the basic setup and should be enough to get you started. For more information about setting up jobs, credentials, and proxies, search Books Online or MSDN.

CAUTION

Integration Services can be installed on a machine independent of SQL Server. However, the SQL Server Agent service relies on the SQL Server service. If you intend to use SQL Agent to schedule package execution, you need to have SQL Server installed on the machine as well. If you have some policies that don't allow SQL Server on the same box with Integration Services or otherwise govern the installation of SQL Server that prohibits you from running both servers on the same machine, you need to use the Windows Task Scheduler or some other such tool to schedule package execution.

Configuring the Integration Services Server

The Integration Services Server has a number of settings you can configure to customize its behavior. Although the default configuration values work for most users, occasionally you might want to change the settings to make it easier to manage your packages, be consistent with other applications and where they store their data, or just to have naming conventions that make it easier to remember which server is managing which packages. For example, you might want to store all packages on a central file share, making it easier to back up and refresh the packages along with any other important files in your system. The following settings can be used to customize the Integration Services Server in this way.

The configuration settings usually reside in a file called MsDtsSrvr.ini.xml found in the %Program Files%\Microsoft SQL Server\90\DTS\Binn folder. The location and name of the file is stored in the HKLM\SOFTWARE\Microsoft\MSDTS\ServiceConfigFile Registry value. You can change the location and filename by modifying that Registry value to point to a file in a different directory, a file with a different name, or both. By pointing all your machines to the same server configuration file on a common share, you can enforce the same custom package store structure across all the machines in your enterprise.

Restarting the Server

Throughout this discussion, it's important to remember that the server loads these settings when it starts. When you make configuration changes, you need to restart the server. You can do that in a number of ways. Figure 17.15 shows how to restart the Integration Services Server in the Services Control Panel application. Right-click on the SQL Server Integration Services item and select Restart.

You can also restart the server from the SQL Server Configuration Manager, as shown in Figure 17.16. You can launch the SQL Server Configuration Manager from the SQL Server 2005 menu tree.

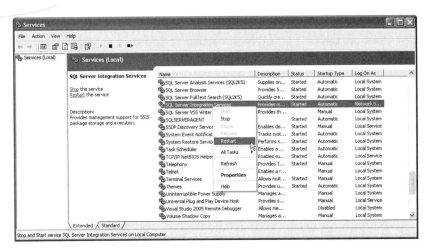

FIGURE 17.15   Restarting the server from the Services Control Panel.

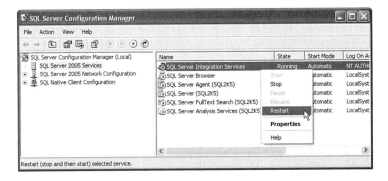

FIGURE 17.16   Restarting the server from SQL Server Configuration Manager.

Server Configurations

So, let's talk a little about how you can configure the server. As mentioned earlier, the default configuration settings work for most people, so you aren't required to make any of these changes. However, if you want to customize the behavior, the following settings make that possible.

The default configuration file looks similar to the following:

```xml
<?xml version="1.0" encoding="utf-8"?>
<DtsServiceConfiguration xmlns:xsd="http://www.w3.org/2001/XMLSchema"
xmlns:xsi="http://www.w3.org/2001/XMLSchema-instance">
  <StopExecutingPackagesOnShutdown>true</StopExecutingPackagesOnShutdown>
  <TopLevelFolders>
```

```
   <Folder xsi:type="SqlServerFolder">
     <Name>MSDB</Name>
     <ServerName>.</ServerName>
   </Folder>
   <Folder xsi:type="FileSystemFolder">
     <Name>File System</Name>
     <StorePath>..\Packages</StorePath>
   </Folder>
 </TopLevelFolders>
</DtsServiceConfiguration>
```

The Header
The header is XML information and should not be changed. In the preceding file, the
header is the first two nodes:

```
<?xml version="1.0" encoding="utf-8"?>
<DtsServiceConfiguration xmlns:xsd="http://www.w3.org/2001/XMLSchema"
xmlns:xsi="http://www.w3.org/2001/XMLSchema-instance">
```

Stop Executing Packages on Shutdown
This Boolean setting tells the server to attempt to shut down executing packages when it
stops. The server uses the same mechanism here as it does when you select the option to
stop a package in Management Studio, the Cancel event. Therefore, packages might not
always terminate immediately.

Folders
There are two types of folders, SqlServerFolders and FileSystemFolders. You can create new
roots for both of these if you want by adding a new node. For example, to create two new
file system folders, you could add the following two nodes within the TopLevelFolders
node:

```
   <Folder xsi:type="FileSystemFolder">
     <Name>File System2</Name>
     <StorePath>..\Packages2</StorePath>
   </Folder>
   <Folder xsi:type="FileSystemFolder">
     <Name>File System3</Name>
     <StorePath>..\Packages3</StorePath>
   </Folder>
```

The resulting folder structure in the Management Studio Integration Services Object
Explorer Stored Packages tree would look similar to the one shown in Figure 17.17.

FIGURE 17.17   The modified file system folder tree.

SQL Server Access

The SqlServerFolder also controls which SQL Server instance the server references when enumerating packages. This is something that will impact you if you're running Integration Services on a machine with multiple instances of SQL Server. The Integration Services Server does not support instances, but is aware of SQL Server instances and can be configured to reference a particular SQL Server instance. For example, on a given machine you may have an instance of SQL Server 2000 as the default instance, and SQL Server 2005 as a secondary instance called SQL2K5. To modify the SSIS Server to find packages in the SQL2K5 instance, you would change the ServerName value to point to the named instance, as follows:

```
<Folder xsi:type="SqlServerFolder">
  <Name>MSDB</Name>
  <ServerName>.\SQL2K5</ServerName>
</Folder>
```

Shared MSDB Store

In many scenarios, it is worthwhile to have all your packages stored on one or more central servers. Again, this makes it easier to secure, back up, and maintain the packages. To do this, you would change the server configuration file on all Integration Services Server machines to point to the same SQL Server machine. In this way, you use the server to indirectly access packages stored on SQL Server instances on other machines. The advantage here is that your automated setup need not change if the central SQL Server ever changes. You need only change the one setting in the server configuration and all your automated processes will continue to access the packages, even though they are stored in a different location. For example, suppose you have a batch file that runs a package using DTExec. The batch file can have the following DTExec command:

```
DTEXEC /Server MyLocalISServer /DTS "\"/MSDB/MyPackage\""
```

Later, if you decide to change the location of the packages, you can change the location in the server configuration file and the batch command remains valid. Also, in this way, end users can run packages without detailed knowledge of where they are stored, while giving control to administrators for where the packages are stored.

Server Diagnostics

There is another server configuration file called msdtssrvr.exe.config in the same folder as the msdtssrvr.ini.xml file. You can use it to turn on and modify server tracing. By default, the file looks like this:

```
<system.diagnostics>
  <switches>
    <add name="TraceClientConnections" value="0" />
    <add name="TraceManagementCalls" value="0" />
    <add name="ServerTraceSwitch" value="0" />
  </switches>
  </system.diagnostics>
```

This is the default setting, which has all the trace switches turned off. If you want to have a view into what the server is doing, you can modify it to send trace output to a file, as follows. The name of the log file can be different, of course.

```
<?xml version="1.0" encoding="utf-8" ?>
<configuration>
  <runtime>
    <gcServer enabled="true"/>
  </runtime>
  <system.diagnostics>
    <switches>
      <add name="TraceClientConnections" value="4" />
      <add name="TraceManagementCalls" value="4" />
      <add name="ServerTraceSwitch" value="4" />
    </switches>
    <trace autoflush="true">
    <listeners>
      <add name="FileLog" type="System.Diagnostics.TextWriterTraceListener"
initializeData="c:\temp\log\Listener.log"/>
    </listeners>
    </trace>
  </system.diagnostics>
</configuration>
```

You can set different values for the three trace categories, as follows:

- **0**—Do not log

- **1**—Log errors only

- 2—Log errors and warnings only

- 3—Log more detailed error information

- 4—Log verbose trace information

When you restart the server and execute a package, the server writes log records similar to the following:

```
Reading configuration file C:\Program Files\Mi…\Binn\MsDtsSrvr.ini.xml
Config processed: 4 root folders
RegisterComObject: Enter
DllGetClassObject: 0x0, System.__ComObject
CoRegisterClassObject: 0
DllGetClassObject: 0x0, System.__ComObject
CoRegisterClassObject: 0
RegisterComObject: Leave
Dropped DtsApplication object
Created DtsApplication object
Opening client's process to get Exited event.
GetRunningPackages
Opening client's process to get Exited event.
Registering package SafeMessageBox (ecf155ac-f433-4930-a0a1-be9b065e004d) for
DIGITALDARKROOM\Kirk, assigned ID 2e570b07-5718-4d7b-b5e1-bfb1a6c0ddbf
Package SafeMessageBox (ecf155ac-f433-4930-a0a1-be9b065e004d)
registered by DIGITALDARKROOM\Kirk, assigned ID 2e570b07-5718-4d7b-b5e1-
bfb1a6c0ddbf
GetRunningPackages
StopPackage 2e570b07-5718-4d7b-b5e1-bfb1a6c0ddbf
Unregister package request: 2e570b07-5718-4d7b-b5e1-bfb1a6c0ddbf
Package unregistered: 2e570b07-5718-4d7b-b5e1-bfb1a6c0ddbf
```

The "4 root folders" entry lets you know how many folders are in the package folders tree. GetRunningPackages is a trace that happens whenever you refresh the packages tree in Management Studio and any other time the service attempts to enumerate running packages. The other bolded entries have to do with packages that execute. In this case, the package named SafeMessageBox was executing. From this log, you can see when a package executes, even if the package execution logs in the event log are somehow erased giving you a history of when packages have been run for a given server. Although not terribly useful for the general day-to-day functions of Integration Services, the trace functions can help you track detailed server activity that doesn't get logged by packages.

CAUTION

Modifying this file is not supported by Microsoft. If you modify it incorrectly, it can cause the server to fail. Be very careful when doing this and always back up the file before modifying it. Also, the format of this file might change over time, from release to release. Modify this file at your own risk.

Summary

SQL Server Management Studio provides the user interface for connecting to the Integration Services Server, managing packages on local or remote servers, managing legacy DTS packages, and scheduling package execution with SQL Server Agent. It also provides a rich environment for building relational databases and managing all aspects of your SQL Server database. Management Studio supports the Integration Services Server in the Object Explorer window and you can configure the locations and folders shown in the Object Explorer by modifying the Integration Services Server configuration file. The Integration Services Server provides component enumeration and caching mechanisms that speed up package execution and load times.

Securing Packages

"EXCUSE ME. I'M IN CHARGE OF SECURITY HERE, MILADY."—ANAKIN SKYWALKER

With all the hackers out there, it's easy to narrowly think of Integration Services security as a set of features that protect against malicious attacks. Although that's certainly part of the security equation, protecting packages is a much broader and more complex problem. You need to prevent the wrong people from changing or executing the package while still allowing the right people that access. You need to provide for access combinations such as allowing some individuals to execute, but not change, a package. Whether by malicious intent or accidental corruption, you need to detect if packages have changed. But you might also need to keep people from viewing certain packages. You might need to protect certain parts of packages that might be more sensitive than others or you might want to send the package via unsecured channels to a partner and need to protect the entire package from being viewed by anyone but the individual to whom you sent it. Finally, you want these features to be easy to use and virtually transparent so that they don't get in the way of day-to-day operations. These are some of the scenarios the Integration Services security feature set supports.

Like other areas of the product, the Integration Services security features have been conceived and developed as a platform of separate but interoperable primitives that you can use exclusively or in combination with other security features to establish a custom security policy that matches the needs of your organization. The security features fall into six functional categories, as follows:

- **Controlling package access**—Controlling who has access to packages

- **Sensitive data marking and identification**—Identifying passwords and other sensitive data so that they are easier to protect

- **Data protection**—Encrypting packages or parts of packages either in the package file or in transit

- **Digital package signing**—Marking a package so it is possible to detect if it has changed

- **Integration with SQL Server Agent**—Securely executing packages in a noninteractive environment

- **Server security**—Securely accessing stored and executing packages enumerated via the Integration Services server

This chapter covers how the SSIS security features address each of these categories and provide some helpful tips on how to diagnose and resolve security-related problems that you might encounter. Finally, the chapter wraps up with some recommended security settings for certain sample environments.

Controlling Package Access

Controlling package access is about providing a way to prohibit certain users from opening or even seeing packages. The way you do this heavily depends on where the package is stored.

Stored in the Integration Services Server

Many, even advanced and corporate SSIS users, prefer to store their packages as files on the file system rather than in SQL Server. The operating system provides the ability to control access to files so file system security is often overlooked as an alternative for controlling package access. However, for those packages and other files that are stored on the file system, including those packages stored in the Integration Services Stored Packages node, it is a viable and worthwhile option.

CAUTION

This chapter assumes that you also take all the precautions necessary to protect your systems. For example, you should prevent physical access, place passwords on the BIOS, turn off BIOS bootup sequences that allow for booting from CD or floppy disks, use a firewall, use least-needed privileges, and so on. How to secure a machine could, of course, constitute an entire book in itself. This chapter only discusses Integration Services–specific security topics. All other security best practices should be followed.

SIMPLE FILE SHARING

Simple File Sharing is always turned on in Windows XP Home Edition–based computers and on by default for Windows XP Professional–based computers that are joined to a workgroup. Windows XP Professional–based computers that are joined to a domain use only the classic file sharing and security user interface. When you use the Simple File Sharing UI, both share and file permissions are automatically configured. Simple File Sharing is intended to be used mostly on home computers. If Simple File Sharing is turned on, you do not have as much flexibility to modify the file permissions and the Security tab for setting file security is not visible.

If you turn off Simple File Sharing, you have more control over the permissions to individual users and groups. However, you should fully understand what you're doing and should have advanced knowledge of NTFS and share permissions to help keep your folders and files more secure.

To turn Simple File Sharing off on Windows XP Professional and higher edition-based computers, open My Computer and select the Tools, Folder Options menu item. Then select the View tab. Scroll down to the bottom of the list and remove the check mark in the Use Simple File Sharing (Recommended) check box, as shown in Figure 18.1.

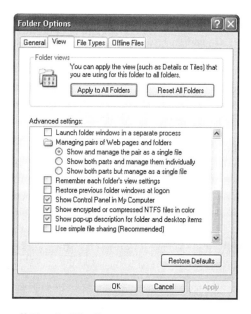

FIGURE 18.1   Turning off Simple File Sharing.

To use Windows XP file system security to protect package access, right-click on the folder or package you want to protect, select the Properties menu item, and select the Security tab. Figure 18.2 shows the Security tab for a folder called Packages2 on a sample machine. Folder access permissions are inherited; so any subfolder or file in the Packages2 folder by default has the same permissions as those specified in this dialog box.

NOTE

The main difference between the Security tab for a folder and a file is that the folder tab has, for obvious reasons, an additional permission option called List Folder Contents.

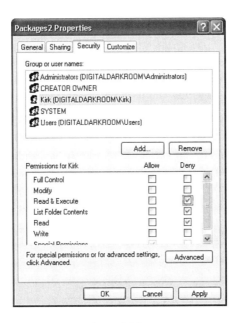

FIGURE 18.2   Setting security options for a folder.

The Security tab allows you to set access rights for individuals or entire Windows System Groups. When setting the Deny rights as shown in Figure 18.2, user Kirk (DIGITALDARK-ROOM\Kirk) is unable to read, execute, or enumerate file contents. If Kirk attempts to access a package within that folder, or even enumerate the packages within it, using SQL Server Management Studio, he receives the error shown in Figure 18.3.

FIGURE 18.3   Attempting to enumerate packages through SQL Server Management Studio in a folder with restricted permissions.

Using this method, you can selectively grant and deny access to different users or groups in your domain by simply modifying the parent folder security permissions. Because the Integration Services server can enumerate multiple folders and display them in the Stored Packages node of SQL Server Management Studio, it's possible to segment the package store into folders with different visibility depending on the user trying to access the folders.

Stored in SQL Server

SSIS uses three standard SQL Server roles to control package access to packages stored in SQL Server.

db_dtsoperator

This is the most limited role. By default, users in this role can only enumerate and execute packages, but cannot create or modify packages in SQL Server.

db_dtsltduser

This role lets users create new packages, modify packages they previously created, and enumerate all other existing packages.

db_dtsadmin

This role lets users create, modify, enumerate, and view all packages. Integration Services stored procedures automatically include sysadmins in the db_dtsadmin role.

A user must be in one of these three roles to enumerate SSIS packages stored in SQL Server because these are the only roles that have access to the following stored procedures. You can find the new SSIS roles in the Management Studio MSDB database node under the Security, Roles, Database Roles node. These roles apply only to MSDB and control access to the sysdtspackages90 table through the stored procedures that Table 18.1 shows. You can find the sysdtspackages90 table and the stored procedures for accessing it in MSDB as well. Because roles rely on the SQL Server roles feature, Integration Services roles are only available for packages stored in SQL Server and do not affect access to packages stored on the Integration Services server or on the file system.

TABLE 18.1   Stored Procedures for Managing Packages in SQL Server

sp_dts_getfolder
sp_dts_addfolder
sp_dts_deletefolder
sp_dts_renamefolder
sp_dts_listfolders
sp_dts_getpackage
sp_dts_putpackage
sp_dts_deletepackage
sp_dts_listpackages
sp_dts_getpackageroles
sp_dts_setpackageroles

To open the Package Roles dialog box, right-click a package in the Packages node and select Package Roles. Figure 18.4 shows the default values the dialog box displays when the Reader and Writer roles are null. When the readrolesid column is null, all users in any IS package role can enumerate and read that package. When the writerolesid column is null, only users in the db_dtsadmin role and the creator of the package can modify or delete the package.

FIGURE 18.4   Default roles for packages stored in SQL Server.

Figure 18.5 shows part of the sysdtspackages90 table in MSDB. There are three columns of particular interest to this discussion. The readrolesid column contains the SID for the user or group that has read access to the package. Readers can enumerate, execute, and export a package from SQL Server. The writerolesid column specifies the SID for the user or role that has write access to the package. Writers can delete, rename, edit, and save a package to SQL Server. By default, these two columns are null.

FIGURE 18.5   Reader and Writer role SIDs in the sysdtspackages90 table.

The third column, ownersid, is not visible in Figure 18.5. It contains the SID of the user who created the package and is stored there to ensure that the user who created the package will always have access to it.

> **NOTE**
>
> A SID is a security identifier and is used within NT/XP. The SID assigned to a user becomes part of an access token, which is then attached to any action attempted or process executed by that user or group. The SID, under normal operation, is unique and identifies an individual object, such as a user, group, or machine.

You can also assign users and roles to the Writer role to let them perform write operations, such as delete and modify, to that package only. To better understand how these roles interact and see which role has what rights, take a look at Table 18.2, which shows the rights assigned to each role and the activities that a user in each role can perform by default.

TABLE 18.2   The Rights Assigned to the Standard Roles

Member of	Read Operations										Write Operations						
	Enumerate Own Packages	Enumerate All Packages	View Own Packages	View All Packages	Execute Own Packages	Execute All Packages	Export Own Packages	Export All Packages	Execute Own Packages in Agent	Execute All Packages in Agent	Import Packages	Delete Own Packages	Delete All Packages	Edit Own Packages	Edit All Packages	Change Own Package Roles	Change All Package Roles
db_dtsadmin	✓	✓	✓	✓	✓	✓	✓	✓	✓	✓	✓	✓	✓	✓	✓	✓	✓
db_dtsltduser	✓	✓	✓		✓		✓		✓		✓	✓		✓		✓	
db_dtsoperator	NA	✓	NA	✓	NA	✓	NA	✓	NA	✓		NA		NA		NA	
Readrole + db_dtsoperator	NA	✓	NA	✓	NA	✓	NA	✓	NA	✓		NA		NA		NA	
Readrole + db_dtsltduser	✓	✓	✓		✓		✓		✓		✓	✓		✓		✓	
Readrole																	
Writerole + db_dtsoperator	✓	✓	✓		✓		✓		✓		NA	✓		✓		✓	
Writerole + db_dtsltduser	✓	✓	✓		✓		✓		✓		✓	✓		✓		✓	
Writerole																	

Identifying Sensitive Data

One of the founding security design principles for Integration Services was that passwords should never be stored in clear text. But it presents a problem. How does the persistence code know what properties are passwords or other sensitive data? For stock components that the SSIS team wrote, this wouldn't be a problem. All the password and sensitive properties could just share a common implementation of some encryption code. But, there needed to be a way to share the encryption code so that third-party custom component writers could also participate in the same encryption mechanism. So, it is necessary to somehow mark properties.

SSIS lets components differentiate between normal package data and sensitive data. To mark a property as sensitive, the component writes a Sensitive=True XML attribute to the property element when saving the component. Generally, when a property is marked as sensitive, it is a password. But the `Sensitive` attribute can protect any information that the custom component writer deems too sensitive to be stored in clear text. SSIS detects that attribute on properties and can give special treatment to a component's sensitive property values depending on the package-protection setting for the package.

For example, the `Sensitive` attribute for a password property on a task in package XML might look similar to the following.

```
<Password Sensitive="1" Encrypted="1">AQAAtAAqEzgw/o80More Data</Password>
```

This is the abbreviated XML for a property in an actual package. The SSIS runtime adds the `Encrypted` attribute so that it can detect that the value is encrypted and decrypt it when loading.

When the SSIS runtime saves a package, it writes all the data out to an in-memory document. It then searches the document for any nodes marked with the `Sensitive` attribute. If the SSIS runtime finds one, it encrypts the value of the node with either a password or user key or simply removes the value altogether, depending on the package-protection option. Then, it saves the entire document to disk.

It's a simple but important concept. This is covered in more detail in Chapter 24, "Building Custom Tasks," but for now it's important to understand how the SSIS runtime identifies sensitive properties.

Protecting Packages and Other Files

SSIS pulls together the concepts of sensitive data identification and encryption by providing six package-protection options. Figure 18.6 shows the dialog box you use to select the appropriate package-protection option whenever you save a package to file or SQL Server, whether you're using the SSIS Import/Export Wizard, DTExecUI, or SQL Server 2005 Management Studio.

The package protection levels are also available in the designer property grid for packages.

TIP
Make sure you click on the package control flow design surface before you look at the property grid.

You should see the option to select the `ProtectionLevel`, as shown in Figure 18.7.

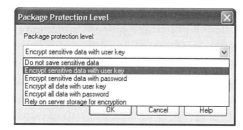

FIGURE 18.6   The Package Protection Level selection dialog box.

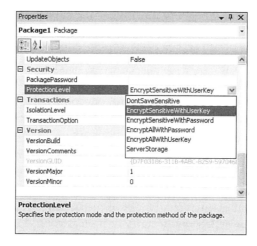

FIGURE 18.7   Selecting the package protection level in the property grid.

The Package Protection Levels

Following is a brief description of each of the package protection levels.

- **Do Not Save Sensitive Data** (DontSaveSensitive)—This option, which eliminates all sensitive data from the package, is useful when you want to purge all passwords from a package. For example, if you write a sample package to share with others or you want to post a package to a support forum to have someone troubleshoot it for you, you can use this option to ensure that you don't share any passwords.

- **Encrypt Sensitive Data with User Key** (EncryptSensitiveWithUserKey)—This option is similar to the *Encrypt All Data with User Key* option, except the user key encrypts only sensitive properties. Users other than the person who saved the package can open packages encrypted at this level, but they'll need to overwrite all sensitive data in the package. This option is the default because it's the easiest way to keep sensitive properties safe while developing packages, but you should use the user-key encryption option only when you want to prevent anyone besides yourself from opening the package. After the package is complete and ready to be deployed, you should consider a different encryption option.

- **Encrypt Sensitive Data with Password** (EncryptSensitiveWithPassword)—This option tells SSIS to encrypt only those properties that are marked as sensitive. This option is useful if you're interested in protecting only the sensitive data in the package and not any of the other data or package logic.

- **Encrypt All Data with Password** (EncryptAllWithPassword)—This option tells SSIS to encrypt the entire package with a password that you provide. The password, which is the encryption key, isn't stored in the package. No user can open the package without the password, and you can't recover a password-encrypted package without the password. This option is useful when you have intellectual property tied up in a package or when you're sending packages across unencrypted channels such as email. The receiving party must know the password, which you can provide in a separate message or other medium. Encrypting an entire package is safer than encrypting only the sensitive data because more data is hidden.

- **Encrypt All Data with User Key** (EncryptAllWithUserKey)—This option is essentially the same as the *Encrypt All Data with Password* option, except that the user key is the encryption key. Only the person who saved the package with this option can open it and only on the same machine. If you create a package with this encryption mode, then attempt to share the package with others, they cannot open it on their machines. For more information about the user key, please see the sidebar "What Is a User Key?" later in this chapter.

- **Rely on Server Storage for Encryption** (ServerStorage)—If you use this option, SSIS doesn't strip out or encrypt any part of the package; you're essentially saying that you want to use SQL Server security to protect your sensitive data. Because SSIS always communicates with SQL Server through an encrypted channel, SSIS doesn't transmit your sensitive data to SQL Server in clear text. This option is available only when you're saving the package to SQL Server.

Table 18.3 gives a little more information about each of the package protection levels. Note that when using server storage, the sensitive data is left in the package. SQL Server 2005 provides an encrypted channel and SSIS uses it to protect the package and all sensitive data en route to the server.

TABLE 18.3   Package Protection Level Notes

Protection Level Setting	Applies to	Encryption	Where Encrypted	Notes
RemoveSensitive	Package file or field in sysdtspackages90	Internal IS methods to strip sensitive data	Client	This option clears all properties on save, which have the sensitive flag set to TRUE.

TABLE 18.3   Continued

Protection Level Setting	Applies to	Encryption	Where Encrypted	Notes
EncryptSensitive WithPassword	Package file or field in sysdtspackages90	Windows Crypto API	Client	
EncryptAllWithPassword	Package file or field in sysdtspackages90	Windows Crypto API	Client	
EncryptAllWithLocalUser Credential	Package file or field in sysdtspackages90	DPAPI	Client	Combination of HW key and current user credentials.
EncryptSensitiveWithLocal UserCredential	Package file or field in sysdtsackages90	DPAPI	Client	Combination of HW key and current user credentials.
ServerStorage	Rows in sysdtspackages 90	SQL certificate	Server	Only allowed when saving to SQL 2005. This option leaves sensitive data in the package data itself, which is then protected in the destination (SQL). Allows the user to execute packages from SQL in a protected and noninteractive way (for example, Agent).

NOTE

If you save with one of the sensitive options—*Encrypt Sensitive Data with Password, Encrypt Sensitive Data with User Key,* or *Do Not Save Sensitive Data*—the package XML will be visible in the designer, so you can recover it if you forget the password or are no longer able to log in as the person who created the package. This tidbit is good to know if you're ever concerned about impending layoffs, disgruntled package developers, or just long-term accessibility of packages and you're not too concerned about losing the intellectual property in your packages. Encrypting the entire package is a safer way of protecting everything in the package, but it also carries more risk than protecting only the sensitive data. If a user-key password is lost or the person who wrote the package leaves and you can't log in with the original credentials, the package is lost for good. No one, including Microsoft, can do anything to recover the package in such a situation. For some packages, such a loss might not be a problem, but it is good to be aware of the risks associated with full encryption.

SSIS lets you use either the user key or a password to encrypt an entire package or just parts of the package. Like your login password, an encryption password can be any password you create. However, Windows generates the user key and you cannot change it. The user key is ideal when you want to protect a package that only you will run. For example, it is a great option when developing packages because you don't need to repeatedly type in a password. The drawback to encrypting packages with a user key is that other users can't open the package unless they log in with the original package creator's credentials. Using a password is more flexible and can add secondary protection to packages, but requires you to type in the password every time you open the package.

WHAT IS A USER KEY?

When a package protection level is `EncryptAllWithUserKey` or `EncryptSensitiveWithUserKey`, the SSIS runtime uses the Windows Data Protection API (DPAPI) to encrypt the package. The DPAPI is a simple symmetric key API and provides two functions for encrypting and decrypting data using the Triple-DES algorithm. The algorithm uses the user credentials as the password for encrypting, which is why packages encrypted with the user key are so bound to the login credentials of the user who creates the package. So, to answer the question "What is a user key?", the simple answer is, it is the user credential. To find out more, search MSDN for "Windows Data Protection."

CAUTION

It is important to understand the implications of using the user key encryption methods. Because the user key is used to generate the decryption key, if by chance, you ever forget your system login password and must have the system administrator perform a password reset, you will be unable to decrypt any packages that were encrypted with the `EncryptAllWithUserKey` protection level. This is really no different than if you forget the password used to encrypt a package with one significant exception: If you forget the password you used to encrypt the package, it's obvious to you and you chalk it up to bad memory. Because the user key encryption methods are somewhat transparent to you as an SSIS user, if you forget your system login password, and you have your password reset, it simply appears that your packages were corrupted somehow. And it only happens when you attempt to open the package after the next time you log in. Figure 18.8 shows the error you receive when attempting to load a package encrypted with the user key after resetting your login password. Use `EncryptAllWithUserKey` carefully.

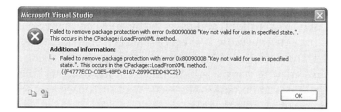

FIGURE 18.8   Attempting to load an encrypted package after resetting the system login password.

Protecting Nonpackage Files

Package encryption only protects the contents of packages and does not protect other files the package generates, such as log files, checkpoint files, or configuration files. Also, child packages do not inherit package protection levels from their parents. Depending on the package and the kind of data you store in variables, you might want to consider encrypting them or storing them in a secured folder.

For example, checkpoint files contain the contents of variables in the package at the last checkpoint saved. If the package is processing Visa numbers or medical records when the package fails, it might be important that you protect the resulting checkpoint file.

For protecting log files and configurations, the easiest way, in many cases, is to use the SQL Server variant. So, for configurations, use SQL Server Configurations and for logging, use SQL Server Logging. But there is no SQL Server variant of checkpoint files, so for checkpoint files you need to secure the folder in which they are stored using file system security, as described previously.

Integrating with SQL Server Agent

To eliminate some of the problematic Agent security practices such as encrypted command lines and so on, Microsoft introduced multiple Agent subsystems, which are dedicated environments for executing particular technologies, such as ActiveX Scripts, Analysis commands or queries, and SSIS packages. By default, only the sysadmin has rights to create jobs. To grant other users the rights to create jobs, the sysadmin creates proxy accounts, which are essentially wrapped credentials with Agent subsystem associations. Proxy accounts let sysadmins grant job creation permissions to other users while finely controlling the kinds of jobs those users can create.

Another problem in SQL Server 2000 DTS shows up when a user deploys a working package to the server but finds that it fails with errors showing that the package didn't have access to certain resources. SQL Server 2005 Agent provides a new *Run As* capability that lets a job step run under the credentials of a user or proxy. This capability means a developer can now create a package under the same credentials under which it runs on the server in Agent.

One more new role in SQL Server 2005 is the SQLAgentUserRole. A user must be in this role to create SQL Server Agent jobs, and users in this role can manage only jobs that they create. This role is important because it affects a common SSIS usage scenario. After they're built, tested, and deployed, a large percentage of packages reside on a SQL Server box in a back room somewhere and a SQL Server Agent job executes them. Because SQL Server Agent integration is important to the security of such packages, the following sections take a closer look at how it works.

Setting Up an Agent Job to Run an SSIS Package

There are several steps to creating an Agent Job to execute a package, as discussed in the following sections.

Create a Login

The SSIS Subsystem job step runs in the context of the SSIS proxy. The owner of the job needs to be given access to the proxy. The proxy has a credential associated with it and runs in the security context of the credential. The following section shows how to do it.

Create a New Login

The first step is to create a login for the user if one does not already exist. In some cases, this might not be a login for any person, but a dedicated login for running packages.

1. Open Microsoft SQL Server Management Studio.

2. Connect to the server where you want to create the user.

3. Open the Security, Logins node under the server.

4. Right-click on the Logins node.

5. Select the New Login menu option.

6. Type in the Login Name and other settings, as shown in Figure 18.9.

7. Select the User Mapping node.

8. Put a check next to msdb.

9. With msdb selected, select the check box next to the database role for this login. This example uses db_dtsltduser.

10. Click the OK button.

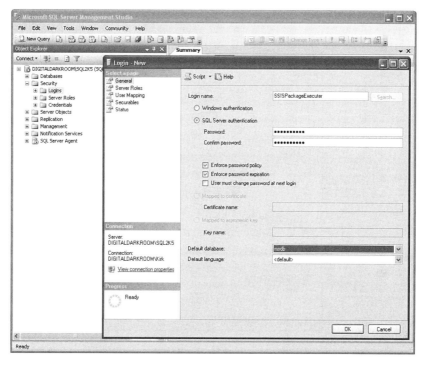

FIGURE 18.9 Creating a new login.

Create a New User

Next, you should create a SQL Server user in one of the SSIS security roles.

1. Open the MSDB database node in the Object Explorer under System Databases.

2. Open the Security, Users node under MSDB.

3. Right-click on the Users node and select the New User menu option.

4. Type in the User Name.

5. Check the SQLAgentUserRole and one of the SSIS roles, for example, db_dtsltduser, as shown in Figure 18.10.

6. Click the "…" button to browse for the login name you just created.

7. Click the Browse button.

8. Select the login name, as shown in Figure 18.11.

9. Click the OK button three times.

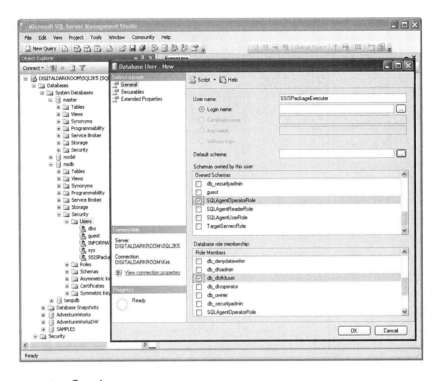

FIGURE 18.10   Creating a new user.

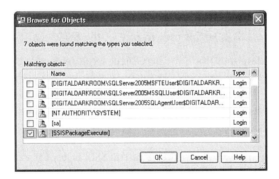

FIGURE 18.11   Selecting the login.

Create a Credential

Next, the credential is a SQL Server object that references a windows account.

1. Right-click on the Credentials node under the server Security node.

2. Select the New Credential menu option.

3. Type in the credential name, windows account name, and password, as shown in Figure 18.12.

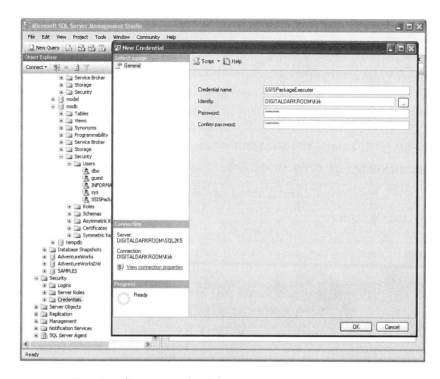

FIGURE 18.12   Creating the new credential.

Create a Proxy and Associate It with the Credential

Next, create a proxy account and associate it with the credential so that the proxy can "run as" under the credential it is assigned.

1. Under the SQL Server Agent node, right-click on the Proxies node.

2. Select the New Proxy menu option.

3. Type in or browse for the credential name.

4. Select the SSIS subsystem, as shown in Figure 18.13.

5. Click the OK button.

Create a New Job

After you've performed the previous steps, you shouldn't need to do them again unless you need to modify the settings in some way. The following steps are necessary whenever you want to create a new job to execute a package.

1. In the SQL Server Agent node, right-click the Jobs node.

2. Select New Job.

3. Type in the name of the job.

4. Click on the Steps tab and click the New button.

5. Give the step a name.

6. Select the SQL Server Integration Services Package type.

7. Select the proxy you just created for Run As.

8. Select the package source and name on the General tab.

9. Add any other settings you want on the tab.

10. Click the OK button.

11. Add any schedules or other Agent settings you want.

12. Click the OK button.

The settings in the dialog box should be as shown in Figure 18.14.

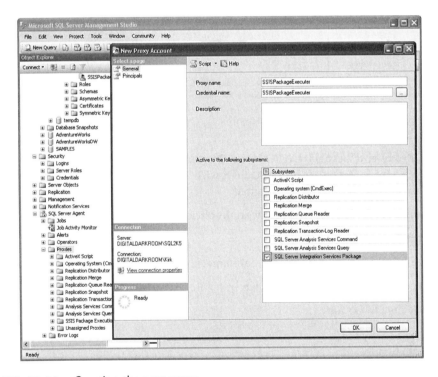

FIGURE 18.13   Creating the new proxy.

With this setup, the job actually runs within the context of the login credential associated with the proxy that runs the package. To put it another way, suppose you used your account when setting up the preceding proxy. When you run the package, it's as if you logged into the server where Agent is running, opened the package, and ran it manually. This design gives you the ability to flexibly control under what security context a package executes.

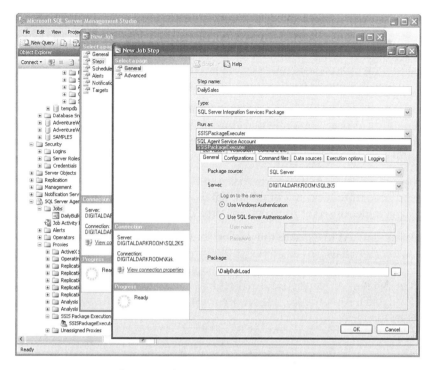

FIGURE 18.14   Creating the new job.

Agent Subsystem Path

The path to each of the Agent subsystems is stored in the msdb.dbo.syssubsystems table. To see the path for the SSIS subsystem, type in the following query:

```
USE msdb
SELECT subsystem, subsystem_dll
FROM msdb.dbo.syssubsystems
WHERE subsystem = 'SSIS'
```

On the sample machine, the query returned the following:

```
SSIS    C:\Program Files\Microsoft SQL Server\MSSQL.1\MSSQL\binn\SQLDTSSS90.DLL
```

You shouldn't need to ever modify this table, but it's good to know that it's there.

Although Agent integration isn't strictly a security-related subject, I've placed this discussion here because it is the only way Microsoft supports securely scheduling package execution in a noninteractive way. Finally, the previous steps are minimal; there are many options and alternative steps that aren't discussed simply to save space. Try different options and test them. For example, use different SSIS roles and logins with different privileges. The possible combinations are virtually limitless.

Permissions Problems When Using Agent

The new Agent Subsystems and Proxy accounts have gone a long way toward eliminating this class of problem; however, calls for help along these lines still find their way to the SSIS forum and my Inbox on regular occasions. So if you're struggling with access to servers or shares, it is not all that uncommon.

The way this problem is typically manifested is something like this: You can run the package fine in your development environment, but then, when you deploy it to the server and attempt to run it through Agent, nothing works. Typically, you'll get errors about insufficient privileges or access denied errors.

As with most diagnostic problems, the first step is to simplify. Create a simple package to run in Agent that reproduces the problem. Often, you'll find that the package is attempting to access a folder or server to which the proxy has no privileges.

If that fails, use Run As to execute the package outside the development environment. Use your own credentials. For example, you can right-click on Command Prompt in the Accessories menu and select the Run As menu option, as shown in Figure 18.15. It is possible that the Run As feature is turned off by security policies. You should check to ensure it is enabled. Also, the Run As service must be started in the Services control panel to use this feature.

FIGURE 18.15   Launching the command prompt with Run As.

A dialog box opens allowing you to select the credentials you want to use for the command prompt. From that point forward, any command you execute inherits the credentials/security context of the command prompt. You can run the package using DTExec or even launch the designer from the command prompt and it loads in that security context. If you can reproduce the problem in the same context that the package is running under on the server, you've found the problem. Likely, you need to modify the privileges of the account under which you are running the package on the server.

Detecting Package Modification

Part of securing a package is recognizing if it has changed. Digital signing is a feature in SSIS that lets you sign a package with a code-signing certificate. With this certificate, you can detect whether a package has been changed in some way. Whether the change was malicious or inadvertent, digital signing lets you ensure that the package you run today is the same package you deployed yesterday. Package signing is not related to package encryption. When a package author *signs* a package, he is simply making it possible for those who open the package to verify that the package came from a trusted source. Anyone, trusted or not, can still open the package.

> **TIP**
>
> As mentioned in Chapter 14, "Configuring and Deploying Solutions," if you configure all transitory settings, such as server names, filenames, and other such values, you'll never need to modify the package, meaning you'll never break the package signing.

Signing Requirements

To sign your package, your certificate must meet the following requirements:

- The root authority must be a trusted publisher.
- The certificate must be in the Current User Personal store.
- The certificate purpose must include "Code Signing."

Signing the Package

Complete the following to sign the package:

1. In Business Intelligence Development Studio, open the Integration Services project that contains the package you want to work with.

2. In the Solution Explorer, double-click the package to open it.

3. In SSIS designer, on the SSIS menu, click Digital Signing.

4. In the Digital Signing dialog box, click Sign.

5. In the Select Certificate dialog box, select a certificate.

6. Click the OK button twice.

7. Save the package.

You can also use DTUtil.exe, the command-line package management utility, to sign packages.

CheckSignatureOnLoad

The CheckSignatureOnLoad package property is a Boolean that indicates if the package should check the digital signature when it loads. If CheckSignatureOnLoad is enabled, all packages are examined for a digital signature when they are loaded. The SSIS runtime validates the signature and if the certificate is valid, loads the package with no messages to the user. If the certificate is not trusted, the SSIS runtime emits a warning and asks you if you want to trust the contents.

To configure the package so that it warns if the signature is trusted, open the Options dialog box by selecting the Tools menu and then selecting Options. In the Business Intelligence Designers node, select Integration Services Designers, General. There are two options:

- **Check Digital Signature when Loading a Package**—Turn this on to check the signature and warn if not trusted.

- **Show Warning if a Package Is Unsigned**—Turn this on to show an error message box giving you the option to cancel opening the package if the signature is invalid.

Security Scenario Settings

The security features in Integration Services have been designed much like the rest of the product. They have been factored to make it possible to support a wide range of customer requirements. Let's look at how to use the SSIS security features in different business scenarios.

Tier-Three Operations

Many large organizations (for example, MSN) encompass multiple operation tiers. Tier-one operators are typically less-technical employees who use step-by-step instructions for every operation. If a problem arises, they pick up the phone and call another tier for help. Tier-two or tier-three employees know systems more intimately and can usually troubleshoot common problems. Tier-three employees are typically quite technical; they might have created the systems, can diagnose difficult problems, and might be on call for troubleshooting serious problems.

Imagine that a tier-one operator, who shouldn't have write access to packages, needs the ability to change the SQL Server Agent schedules and sometimes the jobs that run the packages. The operator also needs to be able to run all the packages. You can give the operator the necessary access by making sure that

- All packages are stored in SQL Server.

- The packages' Reader role is db_dtsoperator.

- The packages' Writer role is NULL, which is the default access for db_dtsadmin.

- The operator is in the SQLAgentUserRole and the db_dtsoperator role.

- The operator is using any OS login credentials, including those in only the user role.

Segmenting Access to Packages Stored in SQL Server

As an observant reader, you will notice that only one role can be specified for the Reader and Writer roles. This is fine for simple access topologies in which all users fit into one of the three standard roles, but what if you want to segment access to classes of packages? For example, suppose you have two groups in your organization, the financial services group and the business intelligence support group, and you want each group to have write access to their own set of packages.

The solution is to create two new user-defined roles called db_finance_package_writers and db_bi_package_writers, one for each class of packages. Each role should be a member of the db_dtsoperator role and then specified as the Reader and Writer role for each package in the given class. So, for all packages that are only to be modified and executed by individuals in the financial services group, they should have as their Reader and Writer role, db_finance_package_writers. Likewise, all business intelligence support group packages should have db_bi_package_writers specified as their Reader and Writer roles.

Using this role topology, sysadmins and users in the db_dtsadmin roles can still read and write all the packages. But only those users in the db_finance_package_writers role can modify, enumerate, or execute the finance class of packages and, likewise, only the users in the db_bi_package_writers role have the same rights on the business intelligence class of packages.

Creating a User-Defined Role   The following steps show how to create a user-defined role.

1. Open SQL Server Management Studio.

2. Click Object Explorer on the View menu.

3. On the Object Explorer toolbar, click Connect, and then click Database Engine Services.

4. In the Connect to Server dialog box, provide a server name and select an authentication mode. You can use a period (.), (local), or localhost to indicate the local server.

5. Click Connect.

6. Expand Databases, System Databases, msdb, Security, and Roles.

7. In the Roles node, right-click Database Roles, and click New Database Role.

8. On the General tab, provide a name and, optionally, specify an owner and owned schemas and add role members.

9. Optionally, click Permissions and configure object permissions.

10. Optionally, click Extended Properties and configure any extended properties.

11. Click the OK button.

Creating Packages Whose Contents Are Invisible to Sysadmins   This typical ISV scenario occurs between users who aren't necessarily in the same company or aren't in the same company as the database administrator. Imagine that some employees are creating packages that contain sensitive data and intellectual property that they don't want to be visible to any other user or administrator. For example, the sysadmin might be a contractor or vendor in your company. Or, you might be saving packages to a SQL Server on your ISP's systems. If your customers are dealing with sensitive data and want to protect their passwords and be assured that nobody outside their group can view their packages, be sure that

- All packages are stored in SQL Server or the file system.

- The packages' Reader role is db_dtsltduser so that no other users can open the packages.

- Users save packages by using one of the password-encryption levels; the password is shared among the users who need it, but administrators don't have package access.

Packages Running on Only One Machine   Suppose you're concerned that sensitive packages might be taken from a given location and opened and plundered offsite. In this scenario, you want to ensure that the package can never be viewed or executed except on a given machine under a certain account. To set these restrictions, be sure that you do the following:

- Save the sensitive packages to SQL Server or the file system. When importing the package into SQL Server, use the *Encrypt Sensitive Data with User Key* option. You must be logged in or running Management Studio with Windows Run As under the same account that the package will be opened or executed under in SQL Server Agent, Development Studio, DTExec.exe, or another such package client.

- Remove all roles from the Reader and Writer roles except the username for the account under which the package will execute or be opened. Although it's not technically necessary because the package is encrypted with the user key and isn't readable even if others attempt to view it, replacing the roles with the name of the account hides the packages from other users.

Summary

The security features in Integration Services have simplified automated execution, protection, scheduling, and editing of packages. Better integration with Agent yields finer control and granularity for configuring Agent package execution schedules. More options for encrypting the package make it possible to custom fit your package security to the requirements of your operation.

PART V

The Data Flow Task

IN THIS PART

Introducing the Data Flow Task

"IT'S ALL JUST BOXES AND LINES."
—BRIAN CHRISTIAN

On its face, the Data Flow Task looks much like workflow in a package. It's all just boxes and lines. You drop components (boxes) onto the surface and then create paths (lines) between them. But that's where the similarity ends. Whereas workflow is a coordinated sequence of atomic units of work possibly executing in parallel, data flow is a set of sequential operations on streaming data necessarily executing in parallel. Workflow executes a task once and moves on (loops excluded), whereas data flow operations process data in parallel until the data stream terminates.

The Data Flow Task is a high-performance data transformation and integration engine. It is the data-processing heart of Integration Services, capable of consuming data from multiple diverse sources, performing multiple transformations in parallel, and outputting to multiple diverse destinations. It supports a pluggable architecture for stock components that ship with Integration Services as well as custom components written by third parties.

With the emergence of the Web and clickstream data, technologies such as Radio Frequency Identification (RFID) and automated scanners, marketplace globalization, increasing regulatory pressures, sophisticated data gathering and analysis techniques, diversity of data formats and sources, and the ever-increasing competitive pressure to make the right decisions at the right time, integrating enterprise data is more important than ever. The Data Flow Task addresses these challenges by providing a rich selection of stock transformations in the box, the ability to process huge volumes of data in very short time frames, and support for structured, semistructured, and nonstructured data sources. Because of these fundamental capabilities, the Data Flow Task is capable of meeting the demanding requirements of traditional Extract, Transform, and Load (ETL) data warehouse scenarios while still providing the flexibility to support emerging data integration needs. This chapter is a gentle introduction to the Data Flow Task and lays the groundwork for the rest of the chapters in this part. If you're already familiar with the Data Flow Task, this chapter probably won't help you much. On the other hand, you should at least skim it because it does present some important basics that you should understand before taking the data flow plunge.

Pipeline Philosophy 101

Throughout the development of the Data Flow Task, there were certain principles that guided its design and implementation. Following are a few of those principles.

Low-Cost Additive Transformations

Before being officially named the "Data Flow Task," it was called the Pipeline Task based on the way data conceptually flows through transformations that modify the data. As the data flows through the Data Flow Task, it visits each transformation, one row at a time. The concept of modifying data row by row has some significant efficiencies over set operations for certain kinds of transformations. There is a one-to-one relationship between all rows and all transformations, or, in other words, all transformations touch all rows exactly once. By combining primitive transformations together, you can build complex additive transformations in limitless ways without undoing incremental per-transformation overhead. Set-based operations lose out when pipelined because there is often no way to eliminate the per-transform cost associated with multiple row visits.

High Performance—No Copying, No Kidding

Copying and moving memory is extremely expensive and over time adds up substantially. The Data Flow Task is built upon the philosophy that unless it is absolutely necessary, after being populated, the memory that holds data should never be moved until it is time to output the data to the destination. Transforms should happen in place, data should only be physically copied when absolutely necessary, and columns that are never transformed or referenced should never be processed. This philosophy or guiding design principle is one of the reasons that the Data Flow Task performs so well. So, although the analogy of a pipeline is useful for instructional purposes, it is only partially correct. Instead of the data flowing through the pipeline, it is actually more accurate to say that the pipeline is moving over the data.

Data Sandboxing

One of the Data Flow Task's strengths is the diversity or data formats it supports. To support both traditional ETL and emerging integration scenarios, it is important that the Data Flow Task be able to access data in multiple formats and to bring that diverse data together in one place where it can be transformed in a common way at the same time. Data sandboxing is a term for describing what happens to data that the Data Flow Task consumes from diversely formatted sources. All the data is retrieved from the source and converted to a columnar data format, making it consistent with the data consumed from other formats. For example, data from an Extensible Markup Language (XML) file can be processed uniformly with data consumed simultaneously from a flat file, a database table, and even a binary file. By supporting multiple diversely typed data sources simultaneously, the Data Flow Task achieves true integration "in the pipe."

Extensibility

Every integration problem is unique and there are times when the components in Integration Services aren't sufficient to build your solution. Therefore, the Data Flow Task is highly extensible in two basic forms: custom components and scripting. If you need a component for accessing some data in a format that isn't currently supported, you can write your own source adapter. Likewise, if you have some business logic for transforming data embedded in custom code, you can write a custom transformation that references that code to do the transformation in the Data Flow Task. Scripting is another way to extend the Data Flow Task by allowing you to write quick and simple data flow logic without having to concern yourself with a fully compiled and installed component. Extensibility makes the Data Flow Task flexible and future-proof because it can be modified to work with data in unforeseen ways.

Data Flow Terms

The following is a list of a few key Data Flow Task–specific terms.

- **Pipeline component**—Pipeline components are all the objects that you drop into the Data Flow Task. These are the boxes. For example, you might say that a Data Flow Task has four pipeline components: a source adapter, two transforms, and a destination adapter.

- **Data flow buffer**—A data flow buffer is a bit of memory that holds data as it "moves through" the transformation pipeline. There is also some metadata associated with the buffer that describes it.

- **Source adapter**—A source adapter is a pipeline component that is responsible for retrieving data from a given source and placing it in the data flow to be processed. Source adapters understand the specific data source. For example, there is a Flat File Source Adapter that knows how to read flat files. There is also an OLEDB Source Adapter that knows how to read data from tables in databases and so forth. Source adapters also know how to place data in the data flow buffers. The source adapters conform data from the format in which it resides to the columnar format of the buffer.

- **Transform**—Transforms are pipeline components that manipulate the data in the buffers in some way. They can change the data, change the order, direct it to following transforms, or simply use it as input for generating new data.

- **Path**—Paths connect pipeline components. Pipeline components expose what are called inputs and outputs. Essentially, these are ports where transforms are able to consume (input) data or generate (output) data. Paths are the lines that connect the outputs to the inputs.

- **Input**—Pipeline components provide inputs as ports where a path can be connected and through which they can consume data from other pipeline components.

- **Output**—Pipeline components provide outputs that can be connected to an input on another pipeline component. Outputs contain metadata that describes the data columns that the pipeline component generates. Outputs can be synchronous or asynchronous. The simple definition for a synchronous output is an output that produces a row for every row on an input on the same transform. Although this isn't completely accurate, it's close enough for now. Later, Chapter 23, "Data Flow Task Internals and Tuning," revisits outputs and provides the technically correct definition. But for now, just think of a synchronous output as being "in sync" with an input. For example, the Data Conversion transform has one input and one output. Every row that enters into the input generates a row on the output. The data is modified in the row as it "passes through" the transform.

- **Asynchronous output**—Asynchronous outputs can generate the same, less, or more rows than those that enter the transform through one or more inputs. The Aggregate transform, for example, generates only one row on its asynchronous output for some operations, no matter how many rows enter on its input. For example, if the Aggregate transform is calculating the average of a column on its input, it only generates one row when it has received all data on its input and the row contains the average.

- **Error output**—You can configure a transform to divert rows with errors to a different output, the "error output." This is useful when you want to better understand what is wrong with the data and even possibly fix the problem in the Data Flow Task and reroute it back into main processing. A typical case is when you have a lookup that fails. You can route the error row to a fuzzy lookup that has algorithms for matching different but similar values. If the fuzzy lookup succeeds, you can reroute the output with the updated key back into the main flow with the other rows.

- **IDs**—Every object in the Data Flow Task has a unique integer ID that aids the user in identifying objects and making the connection between them. The data flow uses IDs whenever it accesses objects, including transforms, adapters, paths, and columns.

- **LineageIDs**—LineageIDs are special IDs on a column that identify the ID of the data's originating source column. Using LineageIDs, it is possible to trace the path of the data in a particular column to its originating source column. Because asynchronous outputs essentially create new data that can only bear a passing resemblance to data on an input, asynchronous outputs sever LineageID paths. The Data Flow Task always creates a new LineageID for every column on an asynchronous output because there is no logical or physical connection between the asynchronous output and the input.

- **Advanced Editor**—The Advanced Editor is the editor you use for pipeline components with no dedicated designer but can be used to modify or scrutinize most pipeline components. The Advanced Editor comes in really handy when you're trying to understand the Data Flow Task diagnostic output because it provides access to the detailed properties on component inputs and outputs, information not available anywhere else in the designer.

- **Truncation**—The Data Flow Task classifies all errors as one of two types: general errors or truncations. General errors can result from a host of operations. Truncations happen as a result of a specific class of operations having to do with types and indicate that data might be lost. For example, attempting to convert a `Double` to an `Integer` or placing a seven-character string value into a five-character column can result in lost data. The Data Flow Task treats these types of errors as special cases because, in some cases, the results might be considered desirable or harmless.

- **Side effects**—Side effects in the Data Flow Task result from operations that affect changes to external data. When `HasSideEffects` is set to `TRUE`, it is an indication to the Data Flow Engine that the component performs some work that the Data Flow Task cannot control or discover. `HasSideEffects` prevents the Data Flow Task from trimming the component on which it is set.

Data Flow Properties

You build a Data Flow Task by adding pipeline components, setting their property values, and creating paths between them. So the behavior of a given data flow is really determined by the collection of subcomponents it contains. But, there are some important properties that the Data Flow Task itself exposes of which you should be aware. You can see them by right-clicking on the Data Flow designer tab and selecting the Properties menu option. The following sections describe each of the important data flow properties. The `Taskhost` properties are covered in other sections of the book, so they aren't revisited here. The following properties are confined to the Misc section in the property grid.

Expressionable Component Properties

Depending on the types of components you have in the data flow, different properties are exposed in the property grid. For example, Figure 19.1 shows the designer with the properties for a Data Flow Task.

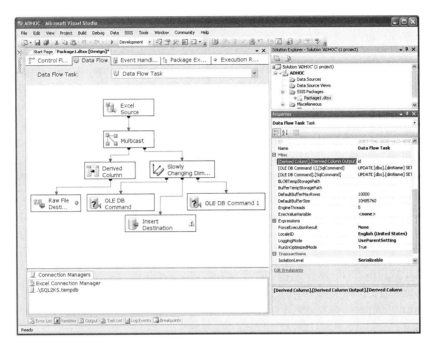

FIGURE 19.1   Data Flow Task properties.

At the top of the Misc properties list, three properties are listed, starting with [Derived Column], [OLE DB Command], and [OLE DB Command 1]. These properties are not really properties of the Data Flow Task, but rather properties of a component in the Data Flow Task that have been advertised as "expressionable" properties. Figure 19.2 shows the Property Expressions Editor for the Data Flow Task in Figure 19.1.

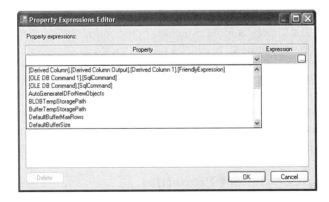

FIGURE 19.2   Data Flow Task properties.

Notice the same properties visible in the drop down. Although the dialog box displays the properties as though they were data flow properties, adding an expression for the property directly affects the property by that name on the component. Figure 19.2 shows how the names are constructed as well. The Derived Column transform is capable of having multiple outputs with properties on each of those outputs. Figure 19.3 shows the Advanced Editor for Derived Column component shown in Figure 19.1.

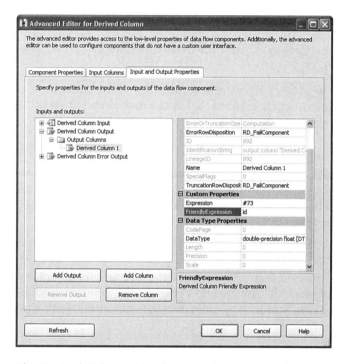

FIGURE 19.3   The Derived Column FriendlyExpression property is expressionable.

So, the property that is exposed on the package,

```
[Derived Column].[Derived Column Output].[Derived Column 1].[FriendlyExpression]
```

is really the path to the FriendlyExpression property on the Derived Column 1 output in the Derived Column Output outputs collection on the Derived Column component.

Because the OLE DB Command components are simpler and the SqlCommand property is a property found directly on the OLE DB Command component, the property is represented as a simple, two-part path. If you remove the OLE DB Command and Derived Column components from the data flow, their properties are also removed from the properties grid.

Storage Paths

Two properties specify temporary storage locations. The BLOBTempStoragePath tells the Data Flow Task what file system folder it should use when storing Binary Large Objects (BLOBs). The BufferTempStoragePath tells the Data Flow Task where to store spooled buffers. The `BLOBTempStoragePath` is always used anytime there are BLOBs in the data. The Data Flow Task only uses the `BufferTempStoragePath` when it runs out of memory and must spool buffers out to disk.

Buffer Size Properties

These are properties that affect the size of the buffer.

- `DefaultMaxBufferRows`—This is the maximum number of rows in a buffer. The default is 10,000.

- `DefaultBufferSize`—This is the maximum size of the buffer in bytes and defaults to 10MB. The minimum is currently 64KB; the maximum is 100MB. Neither the minimum or maximum sizes can be changed in this version.

Engine Threads

This is a hint to the engine for how many worker threads to create. It can be modified to create more threads in the engine thread pool and the number of threads the engine uses is twice the number specified.

RunInOptimizedMode

This is the last of the data flow–specific properties and tells the Data Flow Task to attempt to trim unused components. The data flow engine trims components by simply ignoring them. You might experience some performance gains from this setting because it eliminates components that have no side effects.

Summary

If you don't fully understand all this right now, that's OK. The following chapters should help clarify the concepts for you. It's not necessary to fully understand how the Data Flow Task accomplishes what it does to derive benefits from using it, but if you want to know the technical details, Chapter 22, "Advanced Data Flow Transforms," digs down deep into the Data Flow Task architecture and design. If you want to know how to tune your Data Flow Task so it is more performant, see Chapter 23. Finally, the other three chapters in this section cover the rich set of components that ship with Integration Services.

The Stock Data Flow Components

"I DON'T WANT TO BE SMART!" —ASHVINI SHARMA

This chapter is an introduction to the stock components, the standard Data Flow Task components that ship with Integration Services. Integration Services ships with a wide range of data manipulation transforms and adapters, and so this chapter, like Chapter 8, "The Stock Tasks," provides a general explanation of each component, highlighting their more notable features, their purpose, how to set them up, some tips and tricks, as well as some of the more interesting and/or less-documented component properties. Only the stock components are covered in this chapter. Chapter 21, "Using the Script Component," covers the Script Component and Chapter 22, "Advanced Data Flow Transformations," covers the Slowly Changing Dimension and other advanced transformations.

> **NOTE**
>
> As noted in other sections of this book, Data Flow Adapters and transforms are generally called data flow components, which is also how this chapter refers to them.

Some sample packages are provided to help you understand stock component basics and how to set them up. Each package provides a quick template to draw from when building your own packages. As you read about each of the components in this chapter, it will help your understanding to open the sample package and tinker with it a bit; it's also the quickest way to learn how to set up and use each of the components.

Common Component Conventions

Although each of the stock components is unique, they also share some similarities, especially in the component designers. This section covers the component and designer conventions, which most of the stock components use to some extent.

Custom Component Editors and the Advanced Editor

You can edit data flow components in three ways. Like most objects in the designer, you can modify component properties in the property grid. You can get by with modifying certain properties with only the property grid, but it has limitations.

Another way to edit components in the designer is to use their custom editor. Some, but not all, stock components have a custom editor. Custom component editors only support a given component and provide features for supporting the specific functions and properties of that component.

The final way to modify components is to use the Advanced Editor, which is the default editor for some components with no custom editor and is available to edit most components even if they have custom editors. The Advanced Editor is a generic editor, but it also exposes some component properties that are not visible in any other location; specifically, the input and output properties of components.

You can open the editor or Advanced Editor by either right-clicking on the component and selecting the corresponding menu item for the editor you want to open, or you can click on the Show Editor or Show Advanced Editor links at the bottom of the properties grid. You must have the component selected in the designer for these links to appear. If the links don't appear, right-click on the margin just below the property grid and in the context menu that appears, make sure the Commands menu item is selected. Figure 20.1 shows the editor links.

Error Output

Components might provide a secondary output called, appropriately enough, an *error output*. Error outputs provide a way for a component to redirect rows with one or more columns containing errors. Errors occur when the transform encounters unexpected data. For example, if the transform is expecting a column to contain an integer but it actually contains a date, that would be considered an error. Also, the Data Flow Task treats potential truncations as a different class of errors so that you can handle both with different settings. Although errors are always bad, truncations might be OK or even desirable. Error outputs provide a way for components to divert error and truncation rows to a separate output, providing various options for handling the exceptional data.

Figure 20.2 shows the error row editor for the OLE DB Source Adapter.

FIGURE 20.1   The properties grid for the OLE DB Source Adapter with the editor links.

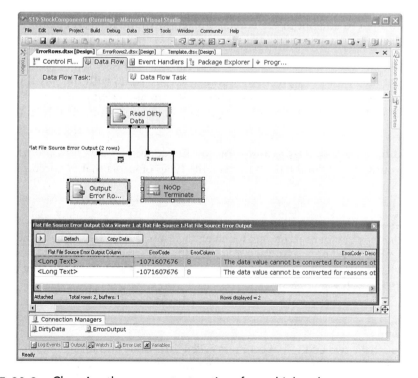

FIGURE 20.2   Changing the error output options for multiple columns.

Using the Error Output Editor, you can specify how the component will handle a row with an error. There are three options:

- **Ignore**—Ignores the error. The row is sent down normal output with the errant data possibly converted to NULL. This is rarely the right choice.

- **Redirect**—Pushes the row to the error output.

- **Fail Component**—Causes the component and, possibly, the data flow to fail.

<u>**CAUTION**</u>

When selecting multiple columns and choosing the error disposition, as shown in Figure 20.2, make sure you click the Apply button so that your change will be applied to all the selected columns.

The option you choose is, of course, dependent on your requirements and how important it is to you that your data be completely clean. Following are some examples of how people process rows with errors.

- **Ignore the rows**—Do this if the column with the error is insignificant and no other transforms in the data flow process the column.

- **Correcting the problem "in situ"**—You can add additional transformations on the error output to attempt to correct the problem with the rows and redirect the corrected rows back into the data flow.

- **Storing the rows**—You can send the error rows to a table or flat file for later analysis. You might find patterns that indicate there are issues with the way the data is being input into the source or processed upstream and attempt to correct the problem either at the source or through additional processing directly in the data flow.

- **Building reports on error rows**—You can run additional data flow processes on the error outputs and build reports to track the types of errors that are occurring.

<u>**NOTE**</u>

Notice that error output settings are found on the Error Output tab. Many of the components support error outputs, but not all of them. Some components have a separate Configure Error Outputs button instead of the tab. Some components have neither if they don't support error outputs.

Error Columns

Error outputs have two additional columns called ErrorCode and ErrorColumn. The ErrorCode column contains the error ID of the error and the ErrorColumn contains the column ID of the column that generated the error. If you create a Data Viewer on the error output, you can see the ErrorCode, ErrorColumn, and ErrorCode Description for each error row. Figure 20.3 shows the ErrorRows sample package in the S20-StockComponents sample solution.

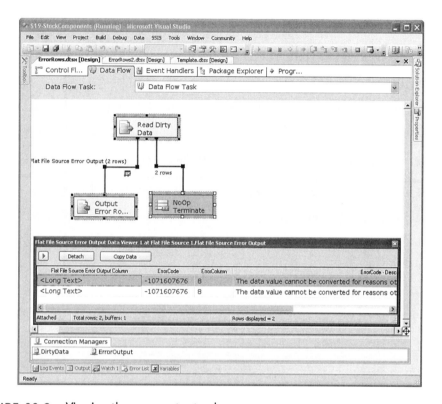

FIGURE 20.3   Viewing the error output columns.

The ErrorCode column gives you an ID that you can look up in the errors list. The ErrorColumn is the ID of the column that caused the error. To use this value, open the Advanced Editor for the component that caused the error and look at the output columns. In this case, the OutputColumn value was 8. Figure 20.4 shows that the column with the ID of 8 was "Column 1" on the Flat File Source Adapter called Read Dirty Data.

Column Mapping

Another thing components have in common is the way they represent columns and column mappings. Figure 20.5 shows the editor for the Flat File Source Adapter. Because it is a source, there are no input columns to which you can map the output columns. You can choose to eliminate columns if you want. In this case, "Column 4" is deselected, making it unavailable to any of the downstream components.

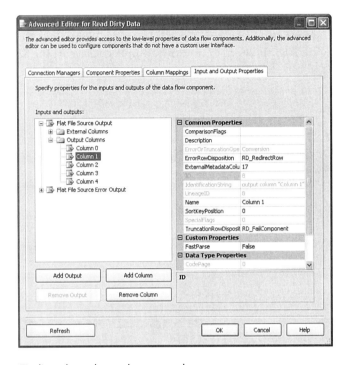

FIGURE 20.4   Finding the column that caused an error.

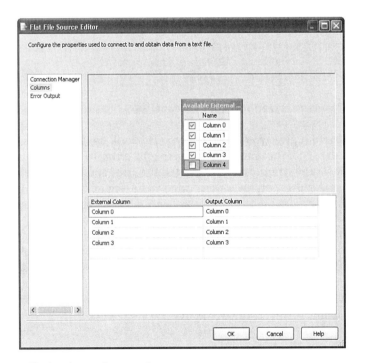

FIGURE 20.5   Eliminating an input column.

Figure 20.6 shows the Flat File Destination Editor with the three columns of the error output from the Flat File Source Adapter called Read Dirty Data in Figure 20.3. To remove one of the mappings, the lines between the columns, you click on it with the mouse and press the Delete key.

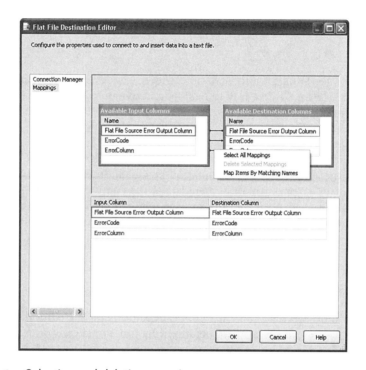

FIGURE 20.6   Selecting and deleting mappings.

You can also right-click in any spot inside the Columns window to access the context menu shown previously. This is a quick way to select and delete all the mappings, which is useful when the metadata on either the input or output changes and you need to remap the columns.

Access Modes

Many components provide different ways to access a given resource. For example, the OLE DB Source Adapter provides four options for where to retrieve rows:

- **Table or View**—Specify the name directly in the designer.

- **Table Name or View Name Variable**—The table or view name is contained in a variable.

- **SQL Command**—Specify the SQL query for retrieving rows directly in the designer.

- **SQL Command from Variable**—The SQL query is stored in a variable; specify the name of the variable.

The XML Source Adapter provides three different ways to access XML data:

- **XML File Location**—Specify the filename.

- **XML File from Variable**—Specify the name of a variable that contains the name of the XML file.

- **XML Data from Variable**—Specify the name of a variable that contains the XML data.

These options for accessing resources are called Access modes and are common throughout components. They provide a way to flexibly and dynamically modify important component settings.

External Metadata

When a component is disconnected from its data source or destination, it has no way to validate against the actual source or destination metadata. Integration Services provides a way to cache the source or destination metadata at the component so that the component can still validate and map columns, even when the component is disconnected. When the component is connected to its data source or destination, it validates its components against the metadata in the source or destination. When disconnected, it validates against the External Metadata cache.

Component Groups

As the thickness of this chapter confirms, there are a lot of data flow components that ship with Integration Services; 45 by my count, depending on the edition you have installed. So, here, the components are organized by functional categories. Source adapters and destination adapters are obvious categories, and the transforms are further organized into three categories:

- Flow Control transforms

- Auditing transforms

- Data Manipulation transforms

Although overlaps exist between the categories, and arguments could be made that a transform doesn't belong in one but should be in another, this categorization is purely for convenience of organization and shouldn't be viewed strictly.

Source Adapters   Source adapters retrieve data from the location and format in which it is stored and convert it to the common data flow buffer format, placing it in a data flow buffer.

Flow Control Transforms   Flow Control transforms direct rows down different paths, create new outputs or columns, merge multiple outputs, or otherwise direct data to different portions of the data flow based on predicates or structure.

Auditing Transforms   Auditing transforms generate metadata about the data flow that is consumed outside of the Data Flow Task. This information can be useful for diagnostic or lineage information.

Data Manipulation Transforms   These are the transforms that perform the heavy data transformation lifting. They vary in data processing extremes from the Character Map transform, which merely performs case conversions on strings, to the Aggregate transform, which consumes all rows on the input while potentially producing only one output row.

Destination Adapters   Destination adapters retrieve data from data flow buffers and insert it into the adapter-specific format and location.

Advanced Components   There are some components that ship with the Developer and Enterprise Editions of SQL Server only or are for specialized purposes, so they are discussed in their own chapter. You can find them in Chapter 22.

- Fuzzy Grouping

- Fuzzy Lookup

- Term Extraction

- Term Lookup

Component Properties   For each component, a table is provided that lists the properties in a condensed format for reference. These aren't properties on the component itself, but rather descriptive properties or classifications to help better characterize the components.

The properties and possible values contained in the tables are as follows:

- **Component Type**—Source, transform, or destination; the component type classification.

- **Has Custom Editor**—Does the component support a Custom Editor? If not, you need to use the Advanced Editor to modify the component.

- **Internal File I/O**—Component works directly with file system files. This is helpful when trying to understand the impact of the file system on the data flow.

- **Output Types**—Synchronous, Asynchronous. Remember the definitions from Chapter 19, "Introducing the Data Flow Task," a synchronous output sends a row out for every row on the component input and asynchronous outputs have a different buffer type than the component's input.

- **Threading**—Single, Multi. Has performance and scale implications.

- **Managed**—Yes/No. Can impact the type of connection manager to use.

- **Number Outputs**—The number of possible outputs. Useful for understanding how data flows through the component.

- **Number Inputs**—The number of possible inputs. Useful for understanding how data flows through the component.

- **Requires Connection Manager**—The component uses a connection manager. Useful for understanding configuration requirements.

- **Supports Error Routing**—The component supports an error output.

- **Constraints**—These are various constraints that could possibly impact the performance of the component. These are not universally applicable and should be viewed purely as performance hints.

Source Adapters

Each of the components in this section are source adapters.

DataReader Source

The DataReader Source Adapter provides a way to retrieve rows from a database table resulting from a SQL query. Table 20.1 provides the standard profile for this component.

TABLE 20.1　The DataReader Source Profile

Property	Value	Description
Component Type	Source	
Has Custom Editor	No	
Internal File I/O	No	
Output Types	Asynchronous	
Threading	Single	
Managed	Yes	
Number Outputs	1	
Number Inputs	0	
Requires Connection Manager	Yes	ADO.NET Connection Manager
Supports Error Routing	Yes	
Constraints	Managed Adapters	Generally, managed adapters slower compared to ODBC or OLEDB
		Query processing

Setting Up the DataReader Source Adapter

To set up the DataReader Source Adapter, you must create a valid ADO.NET Connection Manager, which you select on the Connection Managers tab in the DataReader Source designer. Next, click on the Component Properties tab and type the SQL query you want to use in the `SqlCommand` property. Figure 20.7 shows the Advanced Editor for the DataReader Source Adapter with the query in the generic String Value Editor.

TIP

Only the more masochistic among us enjoy typing complex SQL queries into tiny editors. Because the Advanced Editor is a generic designer and SQL queries are string properties, the default editor is, unfortunately and unavoidably, an edit box. So, to create the query, open SQL Server Management Studio, and build the query there. Or, you can use the query builder that you launch from the SQL Task, and then copy/paste the query into the `SqlQuery` property.

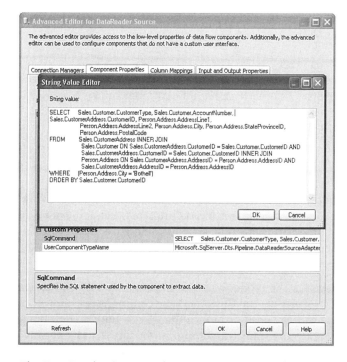

FIGURE 20.7   The DataReader Source Adapter uses a query to fetch rows.

There is little complexity here. The DataReader Source Adapter has one property, `SqlCommand`, which it uses to retrieve rows. The type and number of columns is defined by the query. The columns you select in the query are the columns available for downstream components.

NOTE

Certain terms such as upstream, downstream, and backpressure have come into the vocabulary of Integration Services. Mostly, they are analogic with their physical pipeline counterparts.

The IsSorted **and** SortKeyPosition **Properties**
The DataReader Source Adapter, like other components, has an important property that might easily go unnoticed called IsSorted. Some components, like Merge and MergeJoin, require rows arriving at their inputs to be sorted. This property tells the Data Flow Task that the output from the DataReader Source Adapter is sorted. Obviously, that's not enough information to be useful because it doesn't tell you how they are sorted or on what column. Therefore, there is also a property on columns called SortKeyPosition, where you can specify if the column is sorted, in what column rank (column sorted 1st, 2nd, or 3rd) and in what order (ascending/descending).

> **NOTE**
>
> The output of a component can only be sorted if it is asynchronous. The reason for this is because synchronous transforms can only process rows as they arrive on their outputs. They cannot change the order of rows.

In the sample solution, S20 - StockComponents, there is a package called DataReaderSource.dtsx. That package has a DataReader Source Adapter with a query that is abbreviated as follows:

```
SELECT     Sales.Customer.CustomerType, Sales.CustomerAddress.CustomerID, …
FROM       …
ORDER BY   Sales.Customer.CustomerType ASC, Sales.Customer.CustomerID ASC
```

This is a simple query for building a customer list for all customers living in Bothell, Washington. The ORDER BY clause is important here because it causes the resultset to be sorted on two columns, CustomerType and CustomerID. To represent this sort order in the DataReader Source Adapter (or any other component that generates sorted rows), you set the value of the SortKeyPosition property, as shown in Figure 20.8.

Notice the SortKeyPosition property for the CustomerID column has the value of 2. The SortKeyPosition property on the CustomerType column is not shown, but it has the value of 1. Positive sort key positions mean that the column is sorted in ascending order. A sort key position of zero means the column is not sorted and a negative sort key position means that the column is sorted in descending order. Finally, the numbers for the sort key positions must start with 1 or -1 and increase by 1. The following are valid sequences for defining the sort key positions for columns followed by an explanation. Each number represents the value for the SortKeyPosition for a different column.

- 1 2 3 4 5—The rows are sorted on five columns; all are sorted in ascending order.

- -1 2 -3 4 5—The rows are sorted on five columns; columns with -1 and -3 are sorted in descending order.

- 1—The rows are sorted on one column in ascending order.

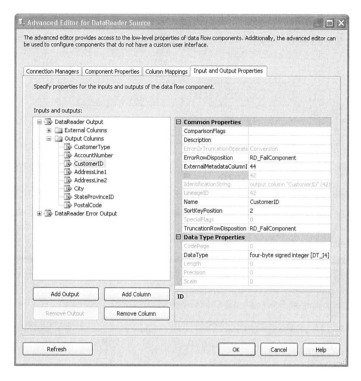

FIGURE 20.8   Use SortKeyPosition to indicate column rank and sort order.

The following sort key positions are invalid:

- **2 3 5**—There is no first sort key column.

- **1 2 3 5**—There is no fourth sort key column set.

- **-1 1 2 3**—There is a duplicate. This says that there are two columns used to sort the rows of the same column rank—one ascending and the other descending. The sort key column numbers must be unique and their absolute values must monotonically at their inputs to be sorted. This property tells the Data Flow increase.

TIP

If you incorrectly specify the sort key columns and attempt to close the component designer, you should receive an error similar to the following: Error at Data Flow Task [DTS.Pipeline]: The IsSorted property of output "DataReader Output" (6) is set to TRUE, but the absolute values of the non-zero output column SortKeyPositions do not form a monotonically increasing sequence, starting at one.

The `IsSorted` and `SortKeyPosition` properties are not specific to the DataReader Source Adapter. Most components that transform or otherwise process data support these properties.

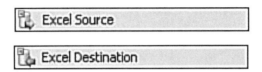

Excel Source and Destination

The Excel Source Adapter is provided to simplify access to Excel data. It is based on and actually uses the same designer as the OLE DB Source. In Chapter 10, "The Stock Connection Managers," there is a discussion about how to set up the Excel Connection Manager or alternatives to using Excel. You might want to quickly review that section. The setup for the Excel Destination Adapter is virtually identical to the Excel Destination Source Adapter. Table 20.2 provides the standard profile for these components.

TABLE 20.2   The Excel Source and Destination Adapter Profiles

Property	Value	Description
Component Type	Source	
Has Custom Editor	Yes	
Internal File I/O	Yes	Accesses Excel file.
Output Types	Asynchronous	
Threading	Single	
Managed	No	
Number Outputs	1	Source Adapter
Number Inputs	1	Destination Adapter
Requires Connection Manager	Yes	Excel Connection Manager
Supports Error Routing	Yes	
Constraints	Uses the Jet provider	File-based access.
	Limited type support	Often necessitates costly
	Network read	type conversions
	performance	
	If reading across network, network traffic can impact read speed.	
	OLEDB provider	Provider implementation performance

There is, at this time, no Jet for Excel or Access provider available for 64 bit. However, you can work around that by using the 32-bit version of DTExec.exe from the Program Files (x86) folder.

Setting Up the Excel Source

One of the first issues you need to contend with when using the Excel Source Adapter is data conversion. The Excel driver supports only six data types and Integration Services maps those types, as shown in Table 20.3.

TABLE 20.3   Excel to Data Flow Type Conversion Table

Excel Type	Data Flow Type	Data Flow Type Identifier
Boolean	Boolean	DT_BOOL
Data/Time	Date	DT_DATE
Currency	Currency	DT_CY
Numeric	Double-precision float	DT_R8
String	Unicode string	
(Max length 255)	DT_WSTR	
Memo	Unicode text string	DT_NTEXT

TIP

When importing data from Excel, you might find it helpful to use the Import/Export Wizard to generate the initial package because the wizard adds a Data Conversion transform to correctly convert the types.

Figure 20.9 shows the Excel Source Editor.

As you can see, the Excel Source Editor is very simple. You define an Excel Connection Manager, select it in the OLE DB Connection Manager, select the table access mode, and then select the name of the Excel sheet.

NOTE

The description for the connection selection drop down reads "OLE DB Connection Manager"; however, that is misnamed because the Excel Source reused the OLE DB Source designer. The designer does not allow you to select an OLE DB Connection Manager. It should read "Excel Connection Manager."

Also, the description for the Excel sheet drop down should read "Name of the Excel sheet or range" because you can also select a named range to load.

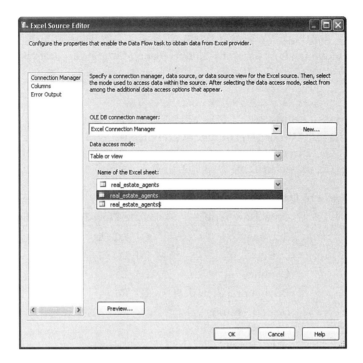

FIGURE 20.9   The Excel Source Editor.

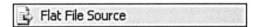

Flat File Source and Destination

The Flat File Source and Destination Adapters provide a high-performance method to work with data from fixed width, delimited, and ragged right flat files. Table 20.4 provides the standard profile for these components.

TABLE 20.4   The Flat File Source and Destination Adapter Profiles

Property	Value	Description
Component Type	Source	
Has Custom Editor	Yes	
Internal File I/O	Yes	
Output Types	Asynchronous	
Threading	Single	
Managed	No	
Number Outputs	1	Source Adapter
Number Inputs	1	Destination Adapter

TABLE 20.4   Continued

Property	Value	Description
Requires Connection Manager	Yes	Flat File Connection Manager
Supports Error Routing	Yes	
Constraints	String conversions	All columns are strings and converting the strings can be expensive. Postpone the conversion or eliminate it completely if possible.

Setting Up the Flat File Source Adapter

To set up the Flat File Source Adapter, you need to first create a Flat File Connection Manager, as described in Chapter 10. The setup for the Flat File Destination Adapter is virtually identical to the Flat File Source Adapter. Figure 20.10 shows the simple Flat File Source Editor.

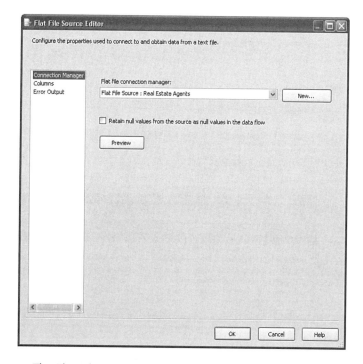

FIGURE 20.10   The Flat File Source Editor.

Most of the work of setting up flat file access is accomplished in the connection manager. However, there are two custom properties worth noting, as described in the following sections.

RetainNulls   You can set the RetainNulls property from two locations. On the custom editor, you enable this property with the Retain Nulls Values check box on the Connection Manager tab. In the Advanced Editor, you can find the property on the Component Properties tab. This setting specifies how the Flat File Source Adapter should handle source NULL values. When this property is set to FALSE, the Flat File Source Adapter replaces NULL values from the source data with appropriate default values for each column, such as zero for numeric columns or empty strings for string columns.

FileNameColumnName   This custom property provides a way to add a column to the output that will contain the name of the file from where the row originates. The property is not available in the Flat File Source Editor and must be set in the Advanced Editor or in the properties grid. The example uses SourceFileName for the column name.

Take a look at Figure 20.11, which shows the column with the name of the file for each row.

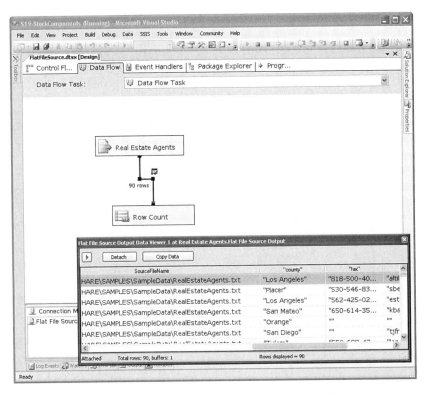

FIGURE 20.11   Viewing the SourceFileName column specified in the FileNameColumnName custom property.

This property is useful for tracking data lineage (where data is coming from) and troubleshooting problem files.

USING THE MULTIFLATFILE CONNECTION MANAGER

There are times when you'd like to process more than one flat file within the same Data Flow Task. If all the flat files have the same format, it would be useful to treat them all as one file. This has several advantages, such as making it possible to perform aggregate operations in one continuous flow without breaking or restarting between files. The Flat File Source Adapter supports this model by doing a little extra work when it reaches the end of the flat file. Instead of simply returning EOR (end of rowset), the Flat File Source Adapter calls the connection manager `AcquireConnection` method. If the connection manager returns NULL, the Flat File Source returns EOF and ends the flow. However, if the connection manager returns the name of another file, the Flat File Source Adapter attempts to open the file and continues reading rows. When using this feature, the `FileNameColumnName` property can help you quickly pinpoint from which of the different source files a row originated.

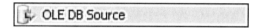

OLE DB Source and Destination

The OLE DB Source Adapter provides a way to retrieve data from sources using OLE DB. Table 20.5 provides the standard profile for these components.

TABLE 20.5   The OLE DB Source and Destination Adapter Profiles

Property	Value	Description
Component Type	Source	
Has Custom Editor	Yes	
Internal File I/O	No	
Output Types	Asynchronous	
Threading	Single	
Managed	No	
Number Outputs	1	Source Adapter
Number Inputs	1	Destination Adapter
Requires Connection Manager	Yes	OLE DB Connection Manager
Supports Error Routing	Yes	
Constraints	Network read performance	
	If reading across network, network traffic can affect read speed.	
	OLE DB Provider	Provider implementation performance

Setting Up the OLE DB Source Adapter

You can configure the OLE DB Source Adapter to consume all columns provided by the connection manager or by using a query. The setup for the OLE DB destination is virtually identical to the source.

There are four access modes:

- **Table or View**—The name is entered directly in the editor.

- **Table Name or View Name Variable**—The name is contained in a variable.

- **SQL Command**—The SQL query is entered directly in the editor.

- **SQL Command from Variable**—The SQL query is contained in a variable.

OLE DB Connection Managers created from a data source can provide additional options such as retrieving rows from a named source.

Figure 20.12 shows the OLE DB Source Editor with the Employee table from AdventureWorks selected.

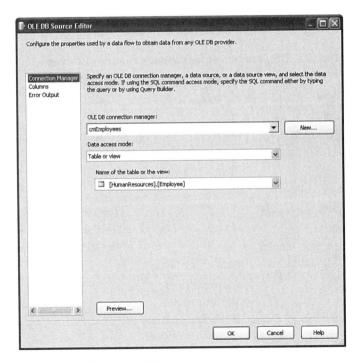

FIGURE 20.12   The OLE DB Source Editor.

```
╔══════════════════════╗
║ ⊞→ Raw File Source    ║
╚══════════════════════╝
```

Raw File Source and Destination

The RawFile Source Adapter provides a way to temporarily stage data to disk. It is an extremely fast storage format because it stores the rows in the same format as the Data Flow Task stores rows in the buffer memory. RawFile adapters do not support Binary Large Object (BLOB) types. The RawFile always loads from files created by the RawFile Destination Adapter and is useful for scenarios in which you need to break up the data flow into smaller units. For example, on underpowered servers, you might experience quicker throughput by breaking large and complex data flows into smaller, less complex data flows connected by raw files. Also, opinions on this vary, but most feel it is important to stage data at key junctures during the Extract, Transform, and Load (ETL) process. The RawFile is ideal for this. The setup for the RawFile destination is virtually identical to the source. Table 20.6 provides the profile for these components.

TABLE 20.6   The Raw File Source and Destination Adapter Profiles

Property	Value	Description
Component Type	Source	
Has Custom Editor	No	
Internal File I/O	Yes	
Output Types	Asynchronous	
Threading	Single	
Managed	No	
Number Outputs	1	Source Adapter
Number Inputs	1	Destination Adapter
Requires Connection Manager	No	
Supports Error Routing	No	

There are two access modes:

- **Filename**—Specify the raw filename directly.
- **Filename from Variable**—Retrieve the raw filename from a variable.

Setting Up the RawFile Source Adapter

Setting up the component is a matter of specifying the filename in the `FileName` property. It is highly recommend that you do not use the filename AccessMode. If you do, whenever you move the package, you might need to modify it to update the raw filename and folder.

```
►_► XML Source
```

XML Source

The XML Source Adapter provides a way to read XML files and convert the contents into tabular form suitable for processing in the Data Flow Task. Table 20.7 provides the profile for this component.

TABLE 20.7   The XML Source Adapter Profile

Property	Value	Description
Component Type	Source	
Has Custom Editor	Yes	
Internal File I/O	Yes	
Output Types	Asynchronous	
Threading	Single	
Managed	Yes	
Number Outputs	1 to n	Depending on the XML schema, it is possible to generate multiple outputs.
Number Inputs	0	
Requires Connection Manager	No	Can access XML files directly via HTTP.
Supports Error Routing	Yes	
Constraints	Default String Length	Default is 255. That might be much too large for some fields.

Setting Up the XML Source Adapter

There are three access modes for the XML Source Adapter, as follows:

- **XML File Location**—Directly specify the location, including an http address.

- **XML File from Variable**—Retrieve the location from a variable.

- **XML Data from Variable**—Retrieve the XML data from a variable.

Figure 20.13 shows the XML Source Editor.

The option for using an inline schema allows you to use an XSD schema that's embedded within the XML file. This is useful if you want to decrease the number of files you work with or if your source system only provides XML files with inline schema.

The XML Source Adapter can have more than one output and more than one error output depending on the shape of the XML. The sample package, XMLSource.dtsx in the sample solution S20-StockComponents, contains a Data Flow Task with an XML Source Adapter having one output on a fairly simplistic XML file. However, files are often structured hierarchically. For example, the sample XML file is a catalog of CDs. A more complex XML file might have a collection of CD catalogs. The XML Source Adapter determines what these hierarchical relationships are and generates outputs based on those relationships.

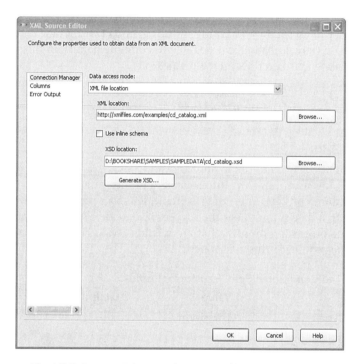

FIGURE 20.13   The XML Source Editor with an XML file specified at an http URL.

<u>**CAUTION**</u>

The schemas can support a single namespace only; they do not support schema collections. The XML Source Adapter also only supports single rooted XML files.

The XML Source Adapter needs a schema to use as metadata for mapping output columns from the source adapter. If a valid schema file (XSD) that describes the XML is available, you can use it. Otherwise, you can click on the GenerateSchema button and generate your own XSD schema file for the selected XML file. After you've supplied a valid schema, make sure you click on the Columns tab to establish the columns that you want to consume.

Finally, the default length for string types is 255 and the default type is Unicode string (DT_WSTR). For columns such as first name or ZIP Code, that's much too much wasted space going through the data flow. You should modify the column types and lengths in the Advanced Editor for those columns to ensure that they are only as large as absolutely necessary, but no larger. This is a good general guideline, but applies especially in this case because the XML Source Adapter defaults to such long strings.

Flow Control Transforms

The following category of transforms pushes data around, but rarely does much with the data directly. They're useful for combining, splitting, and creating new columns, input, and outputs. These transforms make it possible to combine data from different sources and formats, making the data flow incredibly flexible.

Conditional Split

As the name implies, the Conditional Split transform uses expression-based predicates to divide the incoming stream of rows into separate outputs. This is useful when you want to process rows differently based on their content. For example, you might want to remove rows with a date stamp older than a certain date or you might want to perform some special data processing on rows that are missing a value in a given column. Table 20.8 provides the profile for this component.

TABLE 20.8   The Conditional Split Transform Profile

Property	Value	Description
Component Type	Transform	
Has Custom Editor	Yes	
Internal File I/O	No	
Output Types	Synchronous	
Threading	Single	
Managed	No	
Number Outputs	1 to n	Can be split multiple ways depending on the number of expressions entered
Number Inputs	1	
Requires Connection Manager	No	
Supports Error Routing	Yes	

Setting Up the Conditional Split Transform

The Conditional Split transform directs rows to different outputs based on Boolean expressions. If the expression evaluates to TRUE, the row is directed to the associated output. If not, the Conditional Split transform evaluates the next expression, if available, and directs the row based on the results and so on. If none of the expressions evaluate as TRUE, the row is directed to the default output. In many ways, the Conditional Split transform resembles a Switch/Case statement in functional programming languages, such as C, VB, Pascal, or C#. Figure 20.14 shows the Conditional Split Transformation Editor with three conditional outputs.

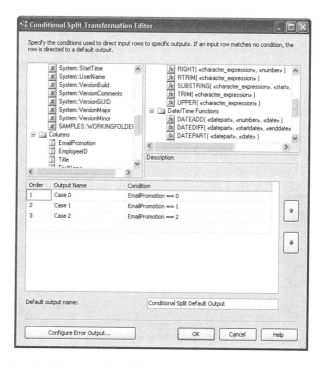

FIGURE 20.14 Redirecting rows based on EmailPromotion.

With the setup displayed in Figure 20.15, there are three conditional outputs and one default output. As you drag the outputs to the next transform or destination, a dialog box opens that gives you the option for which output to use. Figure 20.15 shows the dialog box.

Derived Column

Like the Conditional Split transform, the Derived Column transform uses expressions and has an expression builder as its editor. However, whereas the Conditional Split transform simply directs rows to different outputs, the Derived Column transform actually modifies row metadata and values. The Derived Column transform is used to generate new columns based on expressions that take columns and package variables as inputs. Using the Derived Column transform, it's possible to create a new column or replace an existing one with values *derived* from other columns and variables. Table 20.9 provides the profile for this component.

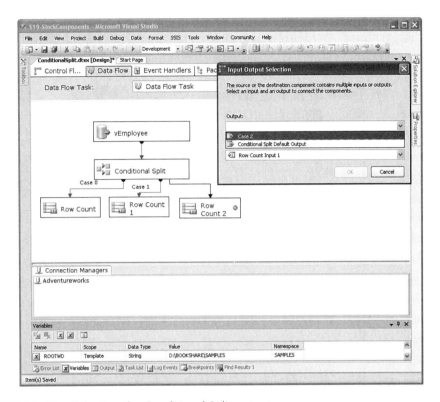

FIGURE 20.15   Selecting the Conditional Split output.

TABLE 20.9   The Derived Column Transform Profile

Property	Value	Description
Component Type	Transform	
Has Custom Editor	Yes	
Internal File I/O	No	
Output Types	Synchronous	
Threading	Single	
Managed	No	
Number Outputs	1	
Number Inputs	1	
Requires Connection Manager	No	
Supports Error Routing	Yes	

Examples of Derived Column Operations

Here are some examples of derived column operations:

- Generate new values by concatenating values from other columns

- Parse out the day of the week from a date column

- Extract fields like city or state from addresses

- Parse multivalue input columns into multiple single value columns

- Convert data formats

Setting Up the Derived Column Transform

Setting up the Derived Column transform is a matter of deciding which columns you want to create and building the expression to generate the output value the new column will contain. The Derived Column transform has synchronous outputs, so every row is processed in order, row by row. The metadata of the resulting output might be virtually identical to the input metadata or drastically different, depending on how many new columns you create and how many columns you overwrite.

Figure 20.16 shows the Derived Column Transformation Editor from the `DerivedColumn.dtsx` package in the StockComponents sample solution.

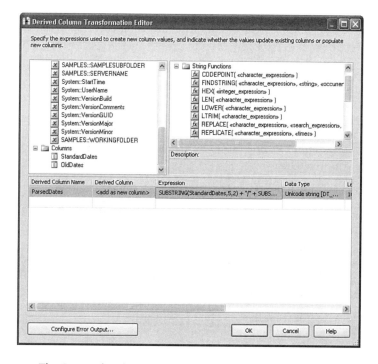

FIGURE 20.16   The Derived Column Transformation Editor.

The upper-left window contains columns and variables. The upper-right window contains functions, operators, and type casts. These two windows are identical to the Expression Editor found in other parts of the product, such as the Stock Task Editors, and use the same expression engine.

The lower window contains the Derived Column Transformation Editor–specific columns, as follows:

- **Derived Column Name**—Specifies the new column name
- **Derived Column**—Specifies if the new column should replace an existing column or create a new one
- **Expression**—Contains the expression
- **Data Type**—Specifies the data type for the new column
- **Length**—Specifies the length for array types
- **Precision**—Indicates the maximum number of digits used by the data type of the column for scalar types, or single value types such as Integer
- **Scale**—Indicates the maximum number of digits to the right of the decimal point

CAUTION

The Derived Column Transformation Editor attempts to discover the data type from the expression. Generally, it is successful and the feature is helpful. However, you must be careful to check the data type any time you modify the expression because it always attempts to modify the type, even when you don't want it to do so.

Building the Expression   To build the expression, you drag and drop variables, columns, and functions from the upper windows down to the Expression field. It is helpful to have all the expression functions in one place, so Appendix B contains an Expression Evaluator cheat sheet for your reference.

To give you an idea how to build expressions, here's a simple example:

```
SUBSTRING(StandardDates,5,2) + "/" + SUBSTRING(StandardDates,7,2) + "/" +
SUBSTRING(StandardDates,1,4)
```

This is the expression from the sample package that takes a string column containing a date in the form YYYYMMDD and converts it to the form MM/DD/YYYY. The SUBSTRING function has the following signature:

```
SUBSTRING( «character_expression», «start», «length» )
```

The first parameter `character_expression` can be a column, a variable, or another expression. All three must be of type `String` (DT_WSTR or DT_STR). In the preceding expression, the `StandardDates` is a column of type DT_WSTR. The second parameter, `start`, is the 1-based index into the string. The third parameter, `length`, specifies the length of the output string and the Expression Evaluator uses it to allocate space for the resulting string value.

The sample package uses the Derived Column transform to parse a date string from an Excel-formatted flat file into two different popular date formats and then converts the date strings into date types using the Data Convert transform. The following four date values represent a row that was generated with the sample package and shows the original or derived values of each of the columns.

```
OldDates   StandardDates     ParsedDates   ConvertedDates
09/24/04   20040924          09/24/2004    9/24/2004 12:00:00 AM
```

This is an example of the kinds of common data manipulation you can do with a simple expression.

TIP

I've seen some very complex expressions used in Derived Column transforms. Sometimes, they can be extremely complex. Although the Expression Evaluator is capable of handling those expressions, one wonders "Why?" A good rule of thumb is if the expression is too complex to edit in the Derived Column Transformation Editor, chances are, you should be using a Script transform. The environment for the Script transform is much more favorable for building complex logic. The Derived Column transform is ideal for simple operations, but is very difficult to maintain when the expressions are more than a few lines long.

Expression and Friendly Expression Properties   In general, people don't remember numbers as well as names. Names have meaning and association. Numbers are mostly symbolic and are difficult to recall. Therefore, the Derived Column and Conditional Split transforms have two properties, the expression and the friendly expression. The expression is the actual string that gets passed to the Expression Evaluator. It contains the ID numbers of any columns that it references. Friendly expressions replace the column ID numbers with the names of the columns. The expression shown previously for parsing a date is the friendly expression. The actual value for the expression property is as follows:

```
[SUBSTRING](#40,5,2) + "/" + [SUBSTRING](#40,7,2) + "/" + [SUBSTRING](#40,1,4)
```

The expression property value is hidden in the custom editors for the Derived Column and Conditional Split transforms. However, you can find these two properties together in the Advanced Editor for either transform. Open the Advanced Editor, select an output, and look in the property grid in the Custom Properties grouping.

Merge

The Merge transform combines exactly two sorted inputs into one sorted output. The Merge transform is useful when you want to retain the sorted order of rows even when the rows must be processed in different execution paths; for example, you might want to process records based on a differentiator key, such as State or County columns. Table 20.10 provides the profile for this component.

TABLE 20.10   The Merge Transform Profile

Property	Value	Description
Component Type	Transform	
Has Custom Editor	Yes	
Internal File I/O	No	
Output Types	Asynchronous	
Threading	Multiple	
Managed	No	
Number Outputs	1	
Number Inputs	2	
Requires Connection Manager	No	
Supports Error Routing	No	
Constraints	Requires sorted inputs	Sorting is an asynchronous and expensive transformation. It is best to sort at the source, if possible.

Depending on the business rules, the rows might have different processing requirements. With the Merge transform, further down the data flow, you can recombine the rows while retaining the sorted order. Figure 20.17 shows the Merge Transformation Editor.

Setting Up the Merge Transform

Setting up the Merge transform is simply a matter of dropping the transform onto the designer and creating paths to it, and then dragging the single output to the next transform. However, if the metadata for a column on the two inputs is not exactly identical, by default, the Merge transform ignores the column and it does not flow through to the output. Also, if you attempt to map two columns of different types or metadata, the Merge transform fails validation. Therefore, it is very important if you want to retain the column that the column metadata matches. Also, the output of the preceding transforms must be sorted. As discussed earlier in this chapter, the IsSorted property of the outputs must be TRUE, at least one column on each output must have its SortKeyPosition property correctly configured, and each sorted column must have the same SortKeyPosition as its mapped column.

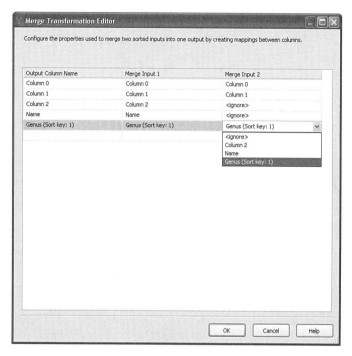

FIGURE 20.17   The Merge Transformation Editor.

NOTE

As Figure 20.17 shows, columns can be mapped to differently named columns. However, because the metadata must match exactly, typically the two inputs are derived from the same output on some upstream transform, so it is uncommon that the names will be different.

Merge Join

The Merge Join transform is similar to the Merge transform in that it requires the inputs to be sorted and combines the rows from the inputs into one output. However, whereas the Merge transform always produces the same amount of rows as the number flowing into both inputs, the Merge Join transform provides the added ability to do joins, which might increase or decrease the total resulting row count. Table 20.11 provides the profile for this component.

TABLE 20.11   The Merge Join Transform Profile

Property	Value	Description
Component Type	Transform	
Has Custom Editor	Yes	
Internal File I/O	No	
Output Types	Asynchronous	
Threading	Multiple	
Managed	No	
Number Outputs	1	
Number Inputs	2	
Requires Connection Manager	No	
Supports Error Routing	No	

Setting Up the Merge Join Transform

The Merge Join transform supports three types of joins:

- **Inner Join**—Only records with matching keys flow to the output.

- **Left Outer Join**—Same as Inner Join, except that all rows from the left input also flow to the output, even if their key does not match a key for a row on the right input.

- **Full Outer Join**—All rows from both inputs flow to the output. Rows without matching keys are still added, but with NULL in the columns from the other input.

You can join on multiple columns, but each of the columns must have identical metadata. Figure 20.18 shows the Merge Join Transformation Editor for the MergeJoin.dtsx package in the sample solution for this chapter.

Try changing the join type and running the package to see the difference in the resultset in the data viewer.

Multicast

The Multicast transform provides a simple way to split a data flow path into multiple identical paths. The Multicast transform essentially duplicates the data from the input for every output. Table 20.12 provides the profile for this component.

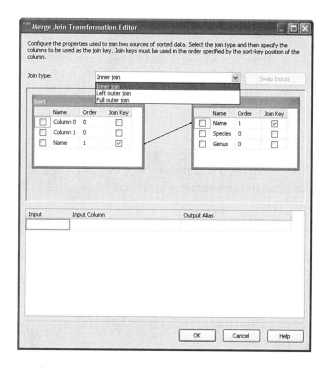

FIGURE 20.18   Use the Merge Join transform to join inputs.

TABLE 20.12   The Multicast Transform Profile

Property	Value	Description
Component Type	Transform	
Has Custom Editor	Yes	
Internal File I/O	No	
Output Types	Synchronous	
Threading	Single	
Managed	No	
Number Outputs	0–Many	
Number Inputs	1	
Requires Connection Manager	No	
Supports Error Routing	No	
Constraints	Synchronous	Because the Multicast is synchronous, it doesn't start any new execution trees. Therefore, it cannot be used to segment package threading.

TIP

The Multicast transform is also useful for easily terminating a data flow path without requiring a variable or connection manager. This comes in really handy when prototyping data flows. Just make sure the `RunInOptimizedMode` property is set to `FALSE` so the Execution Engine won't trim the Multicast's upstream execution tree.

Setting Up the Multicast Transform

Setting up the Multicast transform is quite simple. Just drop it on the designer and start dragging the paths to the various destinations. Paths can be created at any time, and there is no functional limit to the number you can create. Figure 20.19 shows the editor for the Multicast transform.

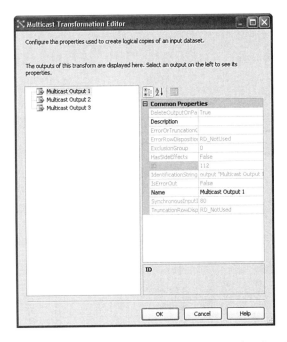

FIGURE 20.19 The Multicast transform is useful for splitting the data flow into identical outputs.

Union All

The Union All transform provides a way to combine multiple data flows into one. It does not have any requirements to be sorted like the Merge transform. The Union All transform is useful for rejoining previously split paths, for example, paths that were split upstream by a Conditional Split or Multicast transform. Table 20.13 provides the profile for this component.

TABLE 20.13   The Union All Profile

Property	Value	Description
Component Type	Transform	
Has Custom Editor	Yes	
Internal File I/O	No	
Output Types	Asynchronous	
Threading	Single	
Managed	No	
Number Outputs	1	
Number Inputs	1–Many	
Requires Connection Manager	No	
Supports Error Routing	No	

Setting Up the Union All Transform

Setting up the Union All transform is simple. Drop it on the surface and drag paths to it. However, you must ensure that the inputs all have the same column metadata or, at least, those columns you want to combine must have the same column metadata.

Figure 20.20 shows the Union All Transformation Editor from the `UnionAll.dtsx` sample package in the S20-StockComponents solution.

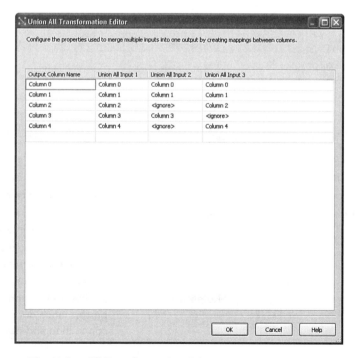

FIGURE 20.20   The Union All Transformation Editor.

There are three inputs on this Union All transform and the mappings as shown were automatically created. Notice that there are some columns in Input 2 and Input 3 that have been marked "<ignore>". This happens whenever there are columns with nonmatching metadata, for example, if the types or length don't match the first input attached to the Union All.

For string types of different lengths, if you correct the mapping, for example, you change column 3 on Input 3 from "<ignore>" to "Column 3," the Union All adjusts the column width to match the length of Column 3 in Input 1. Rows from inputs with columns that are left marked ignore will have NULL values on the output.

Lookup

The Lookup transform provides a way to detect if a given key exists in a reference table. One way the Lookup transform is used is for upserting. Upserting is when you insert a row if it doesn't exist or update it if it does. A classic case of upserting is when checking if a dimension already exists for a given business key when attempting to update or insert a dimension. If you find the key in the reference table, you might want to insert the row if it does not already exist, or update it if it does. Table 20.14 provides the profile for this component.

TABLE 20.14   The Lookup Transform Profile

Property	Value	Description
Component Type	Transform	
Has Custom Editor	Yes	
Internal File I/O	No	
Output Types	Synchronous	
Threading	Single	
Managed	No	
Number Outputs	1	
Number Inputs	1	
Requires Connection Manager	Yes	For the lookup reference table.
Supports Error Routing	Yes	For rows whose key were not found in the reference table.
Constraints	Cache charging	Charging the lookup cache for large reference sets in full cache mode can be time consuming.
	Reference table	Lookup from reference table is performance dependent on the connection and network.

Setting Up the Lookup Transform

To set up the Lookup transform, you need to have a source input and a reference table. The source input must have one or more keys with the same metadata (for example, type and length) as the lookup key(s) in the reference table. The Lookup transform tries to match the incoming keys with the keys in the lookup table or reference set. If it finds the key in the reference set, the Lookup transform pushes the row down the normal output. If it does not find the key, however, it pushes the row out the error output. The Lookup.dtsx package in the sample solution for this chapter shows the basic setup for the Lookup transform. Figure 20.21 shows the first of three tabs in the Lookup Transformation Editor.

FIGURE 20.21   The Lookup Transformation Editor Reference Table tab.

The Reference Table tab allows you to select the data you want to use for the reference set either via a query or by referencing a lookup table. It is generally better to use a query for retrieving the reference set so that you retrieve only what you need, keeping the result size small.

Figure 20.22 shows the Columns tab. You use this tab to specify which column or columns should be used for the lookup. In this case, only one column is selected in the results query. But, it is possible to use more than one column for more complex lookups. To create the lookup, drag and drop an input column onto a lookup column of the exact same metadata. The line between them indicates that if the value in the input column matches the value in the corresponding lookup column, the lookup succeeded. If not, the lookup failed. If the lookup succeeds, you have the option to add a new column with the value of the selected lookup column, or replace an input column as selected in the Lookup Operation in the grid.

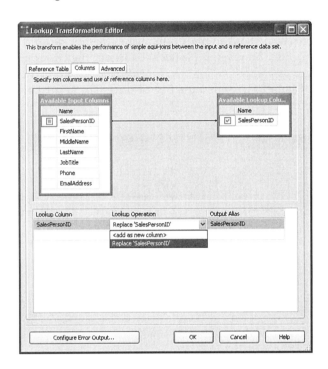

FIGURE 20.22   The Lookup Transformation Editor Columns tab.

Handling Error Rows (Failed Lookups)   If you click on the Configure Error Output button, the Configure Error Output dialog box opens, as shown in Figure 20.23.

As it turns out, this is the same dialog box as for other components. However, the meaning of an error is slightly different. For the Lookup transform, an error can be just like any other error. For example, unexpected types or truncations are still errors. But, failed lookups are also considered errors. So, the option to redirect a row has additional meaning for lookups because failed lookups flow down the error output.

The Advanced Tab, Configuring Reference Caching   Depending on the lookup table or reference set size, you might want to cache the reference set differently. The Advanced tab, shown in Figure 20.24, provides several options from which to choose.

FIGURE 20.23 The Configure Error Output dialog box for the Lookup transform.

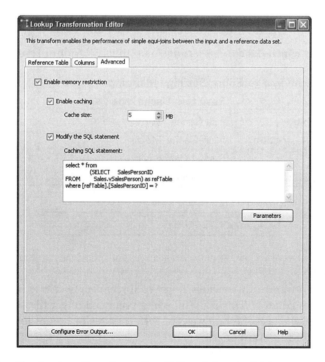

FIGURE 20.24 The Lookup Transformation Editor Advanced tab.

There are three basic options for how the Lookup transform caches the reference set:

- **None**—No rows are cached. Each lookup performs a SELECT statement on the reference table. This is generally not performant, but is useful for very small reference sets.

- **Partial**—Each row is cached the first time the Lookup transform retrieves it. The Lookup transform looks first in the cache; if it doesn't exist there, it retrieves the reference row using the SQL statement. This is useful when the lookup references the same keys repetitively. Also, when using this mode, rows can be removed from the cache when the cache reaches the specified cache size and a new row is fetched into the already full cache.

- **Full**—The entire resultset is precached during the preexecute phase in the Data Flow Task. This is useful when there is a large reference set and any time you're concerned about performance of the lookup operation.

You can set the cache type directly using the CacheType property in the properties grid for the Lookup transform or you can modify the values on the Advanced tab, which indirectly sets those values. Because it's not obvious which settings result in which CacheType, when using the full cache option, the newly added row is not added to the cache because the Lookup transform currently provides no way to update the cache with new rows. However, when using the partial and no cache setting, the new row might possibly be found depending on if the inserted row was committed on insert.

Table 20.15 clarifies which CacheType settings map to which Editor settings.

TABLE 20.15   CacheType to Editor Settings Mapping

Editor Settings	Resulting CacheType
No Settings Enabled	Full Cache Mode
Enable Memory Restriction	Non-Cache Mode
Enable Caching	Partial Cache Mode
Modify the SQL Statement	No Cache Implications

Import Column

The Import Column transform provides a way to insert files from the file system into a column, one file per column. This is useful when you need to get files into a table, for example, when building a real estate website with pictures of homes for sale. Table 20.16 provides a profile for this component.

TABLE 20.16   The Import Column Transform Profile

Property	Value	Description
Has Custom Editor	No	
Component Type	Transform	
Internal File I/O	Yes	
Output Types	Asynchronous	
Threading	Single	
Managed	Yes	
Number Outputs	1	
Number Inputs	1	
Requires Connection Manager	No	
Supports Error Routing	Yes	
Constraints	BLOBs	BLOB processing is expensive and generally slow and should be avoided if possible.
	File I/O Perf	File system and storage subsystems have a drastic impact.
	Memory	Depending on tuning and file sizes, this transform can consume large amounts of memory.

Setting Up the Import Column Transform

You need to have a table or flat file with the names of the files you want to insert, or as shown in the sample package, you can have the source adapter generate rows that contain the filenames. The source adapter reads the filenames from a MultiFile Connection Manager into a column. Then, the Import Column transform reads the filename in each row and loads the file into an output column. The Import Column transformation has two custom properties found on its input columns called ExpectBOM and FileDataColumnID.

- ExpectBOM specifies whether the Import Column transform should expect a BYTE Order Mark (BOM), which is useful for Unicode text types (DT_NTEXT).

- FileDataColumnID specifies the output column ID of the column in which the files should be inserted. If the input column is a simple data column that should flow through unaltered, this property should retain the default value of zero. If the input column contains filenames of files to be inserted into an output column, the FileDataColumnID should contain the ID of the output column where the Import Column transform will insert the files.

To set up the Import Column transform, drag a path from a source adapter or transform with a column that contains rows with filenames. In the sample package, a script component source generates a new name for every file in the samples subdirectory and has two columns on its output, one with the original names of the files and one with the generated output names.

Open the Import Column Transformation Editor and select the Input Columns tab. Check the box to the left of the column with the filenames. Select the Input and Output Properties tab. Open the Import Column Output node, select the Output Columns node, and click the Add Column button. In the sample package, the new output column is called BitmapColumn. Open the Import Column Input node and select the input column you checked earlier. In the `FileDataColumnID` property, type in the ID for the new output column you just created.

Figure 20.25 shows the Advanced Editor with the Input Columns tab selected and the Input Files column checked. This tells the Import Column transform that the Input Files column is the one that contains the names of files to import. For each column you select on this tab, you need to later specify the name of a column on the output that will contain imported files. If you want a column to simply pass through unreferenced, do not put a check in the check box.

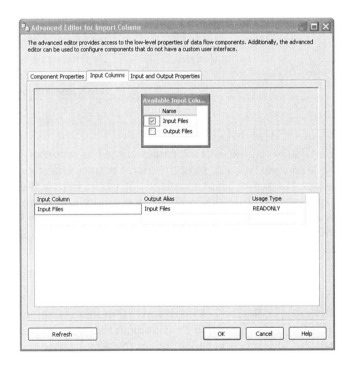

FIGURE 20.25   Selecting the column with filenames.

Figure 20.26 shows the Advanced Editor for the import column with the Input and Output properties showing. A new output column called BitmapColumn was created by selecting the Output Columns node, clicking the Add Column button, and typing in the new name. Note the value of the ID property; in the sample project, it is 699.

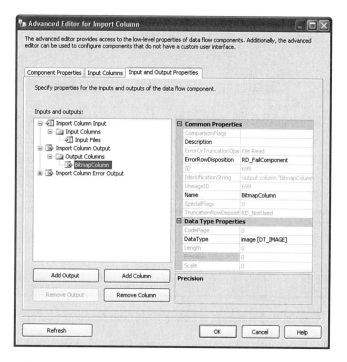

FIGURE 20.26   Adding a new column.

Figure 20.27 shows the correct settings so that the files specified in the Input Files column will be loaded into the output column with the ID of 699 as specified in the `FileDataColumnID`. To see the sample package, open the S20-StockComponents sample solution and open the `ImportExportColumn.dtsx` package.

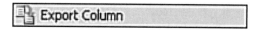

Export Column

The Export Column transform is the converse of the Import Column transform. You use it to export data from a column into files and it requires that there be at least two input columns: one with the data to export into files and the other with the names of the files to create to hold the exported data. Table 20.17 provides a profile for this component.

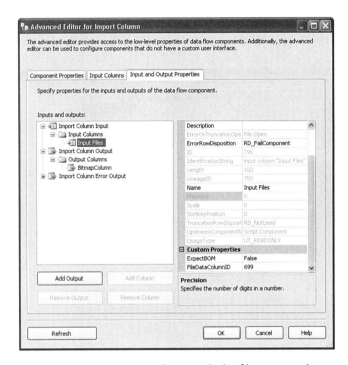

FIGURE 20.27   Connecting the output column with the filenames column.

TABLE 20.17   The Export Column Transform Profile

Property	Value	Description
Component Type	Transform	
Has Custom Editor	Yes	
Internal File I/O	Yes	
Output Types	Asynchronous	
Threading	Single	
Managed	No	
Number Outputs	1	
Number Inputs	1	
Requires Connection Manager	No	
Supports Error Routing	Yes	
Constraints	BLOBs	BLOB processing is expensive and generally slow and should be avoided if possible.
	File I/O Perf	File system and storage subsystems have a drastic impact.
	Memory	Depending on tuning and file sizes, this transform can consume large amounts of memory.

Setting Up the Component

Because the Export Column transform has a custom editor, setting it up is a matter of selecting the column containing the data to export and selecting the File Path Column. Figure 20.28 shows the editor with the correct settings from the sample package.

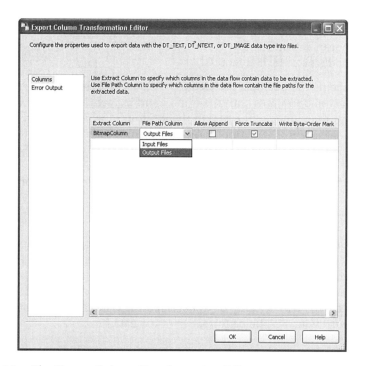

FIGURE 20.28 The Export Column Transformation Editor.

The following are the available settings:

- **Extract Column**—Specifies the column with the data to export into files.

- **File Path Column**—Specifies the column with the names of files to create to hold the extracted data.

- **Allow Append**—Specifies that data should be appended to an existing file.

- **Force Truncate**—Causes any file that might exist with the same name as is specified in the File Path column to be overwritten.

- **Write Byte-Order Mark**—Specifies the ordering of the least significant byte in the Unicode plain text file. If the text in the file is Unicode, you should select this. If the files contain binary data, you should not select this option, as it will corrupt the file.

Some Background on Byte-order Marks Because microprocessors differ in the placement of the least significant byte, it is important to indicate which ordering was used when the

Unicode text file was written. Intel and MIPS processors position the least significant byte first. Motorola processors position it last. At Microsoft, UTF-16/UCS-2 or "little endian" is used.

You should always prefix Unicode plain text files with a *byte-order mark*. Byte-order marks do not control the byte order of the text; they simply inform an application reading the file what its byte ordering is. The Unicode byte-order mark character is not in any code page, so it disappears if Unicode text is converted to ANSI. Also, if a byte-order mark is found in the middle of a file, it is ignored.

The Sample Package   The sample package ImportExportColumn.dtsx in the S20-StockComponents solution uses both the Import and Export Column transforms. It uses a script component to enumerate the files in the location to which the "Files" File Connection Manager points. The Import Column transform imports the files to a column and the following Export Column transform exports the files to a similarly named file in the same folder. The default location for the files is the samples folder, but you can change the property expression on the "Files" Connection Manager to point to any folder.

Auditing Transforms

The following category of transforms provides metadata about the data flow. They're useful for answering *how fast* or *how many* or *from where* type questions. They help you understand what kind of data is flowing through the data flow and how much of it. For example, you can spread these transforms throughout your data flow and log the information they create for later scrutiny or troubleshooting. They are very lightweight transforms and minimally impact the performance of the data flow.

Audit

The Audit transform allows you to create a new column on a given path that will contain system variable information. This is helpful for understanding where data came from and how it was added to a table. Table 20.18 provides a profile for this component.

TABLE 20.18   The Audit Transform Profile

Property	Value	Description
Component Type	Transform	
Has Custom Editor	Yes	
Internal File I/O	No	
Output Types	Synchronous	
Threading	Single	
Managed	No	
Number Outputs	1	

TABLE 20.18   Continued

Property	Value	Description
Number Inputs	1	
Requires Connection Manager	No	
Supports Error Routing	No	

Setting Up the Audit Transform

To set up the Audit transform, simply select the audit type and then input the name of the new column that will contain the audit information. Figure 20.29 shows the Audit Transformation Editor with two new columns created.

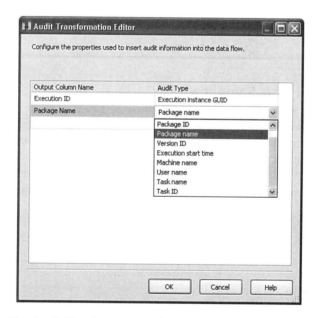

FIGURE 20.29   The Audit Transformation Editor.

Table 20.19 shows the system variables that the Audit transform might use to populate a new column and their description.

TABLE 20.19   System Variables Available to the Audit Transform

System Variable	Index	Description
ExecutionInstanceGUID	0	The GUID that identifies the execution instance of the package
PackageID	1	The unique identifier of the package
PackageName	2	The package name
VersionID	3	The version of the package
ExecutionStartTime	4	The time the package started to run

TABLE 20.19   Continued

System Variable	Index	Description
MachineName	5	The computer name
UserName	6	The login name of the person who started the package
TaskName	7	The name of the Data Flow Task with which the Audit transform is associated
TaskId	8	The unique identifier of the Data Flow Task that contains the Audit transform

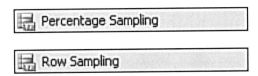

Percentage and Row Sampling

The Percentage and Row Sampling transforms provide a way to select subsets of source data. This is useful in a number of ways. For example, when profiling data, it isn't necessary to process the entire set of data, but rather a statistically significant subset. Using the Percentage Sampling transform, you can reduce the total number of rows that flow through your data profiling process, reducing the total processing time while still ensuring that the row selection is random and relevant. Table 20.20 provides a profile for these components.

TABLE 20.20   The Percentage and Row Sampling Transform Profiles

Property	Value	Description
Component Type	Transform	
Has Custom Editor	Yes	
Internal File I/O	No	
Output Types	Synchronous/Asynchronous	Precentage Sampling/Row Sampling
Threading	Single	
Managed	No	
Number Outputs	2	
Number Inputs	1	
Requires Connection Manager	No	
Supports Error Routing	No	

Setting Up the Row and Percentage Sampling Transforms

Both these transforms are very similar and have very similar editors. The only difference is that the Row Sampling transform allows you to specify the number of rows you want to randomly select and the Percentage Sampling transform allows you to select a specified percentage of rows. Because both are so similar, this section only explains how to set up the Percentage Sampling transform.

The Percentage Sampling transform has two outputs. One contains the dataset sample and the other contains the entire dataset sans the dataset sample. Set the Percentage of Rows settings to what you want to sample. You can name the outputs if you want. Only specify a random seed if you want to return the same rows in subsequent runs, which might be useful for testing purposes. If you leave the Random Seed setting unchecked, the transform picks a different random seed on each subsequent run and returns a different set of data. Figure 20.30 shows the Percentage Sampling Transformation Editor.

FIGURE 20.30   The Percentage Sampling Transformation Editor.

RowCount

The RowCount transform provides a way to track how many rows are flowing through a particular path. You can use this information in logs as diagnostic information or for sending in an email as a notification of the work a package has completed. Table 20.21 provides a profile for this component.

TABLE 20.21   The RowCount Transform Profile

Property	Value	Description
Component Type	Transform	
Has Custom Editor	No	
Internal File I/O	No	
Output Types	Synchronous	
Threading	Single	
Managed	No	
Number Outputs	1	
Number Inputs	1	
Requires Connection Manager	No	
Supports Error Routing	No	

Setting Up the RowCount Transform

The RowCount transform is very simple to set up. Drop it on the design surface, drag an output from another transform, and specify a read/write variable to contain the rowcount. Figure 20.31 shows the Advanced Editor with the rowcount property correctly set.

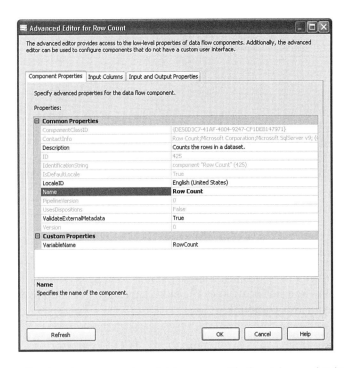

FIGURE 20.31   Setting the rowcount variable name with the Advanced Editor.

Data Manipulation Transforms

These are the transforms you typically think of when you think of transformations. These modify the data, changing it in fundamental ways.

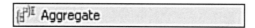

Aggregate

The Aggregate transform provides several different aggregation operations and a Group By feature. It supports multiple simultaneous aggregations on multiple columns as well as multiple aggregations on the same column. You can configure to only have one output or multiple outputs. This transform is useful for Business Intelligence because it supports the aggregation operations needed for things like populating fact tables with fine control over the grain of the aggregations. Table 20.22 provides a profile for this component.

TABLE 20.22   The Aggregate Transform Profile

Property	Value	Description
Component Type	Transform	
Has Custom Editor	Yes	
Internal File I/O	No	
Output Types	Asynchronous	
Threading	Single	
Managed	No	
Number Outputs	1-Many	
Number Inputs	1	
Requires Connection Manager	No	
Supports Error Routing	No	
Constraints	Asynchronous	Blocks. Also creates new execution trees, which help parallelism.

Setting Up the Aggregate Transform

To create a simple aggregation, select the column on which you want to operate in the Available Input Columns window. Figure 20.32 shows the aggregate from the `Aggregate.dtsx` sample package. After you've selected the column, select the operation in the Operation column of the lower grid. Simple aggregations such as sum and average will only output one row. More complex aggregations that use the Group By feature might output multiple rows, based on the data.

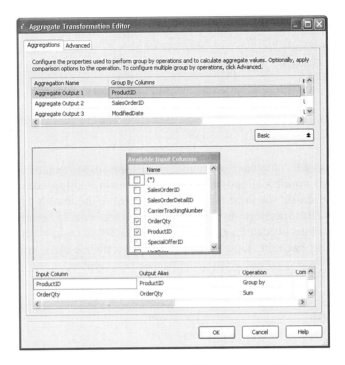

FIGURE 20.32   The Aggregate Transformation Editor Advanced View with two outputs having two aggregation operations.

Table 20.23 shows the operations that are available in the Aggregate transform.

TABLE 20.23   The Aggregation Operations

Operation	Description
Group by	Divides datasets into groups. Columns of any data type can be used for grouping. For more information, see GROUP BY (Transact-SQL).
Sum	Sums the values in a column. Only columns with numeric data types can be summed. For more information, see SUM (Transact-SQL).
Average	Returns the average of the column values in a column. Only columns with numeric data types can be averaged. For more information, see AVG (Transact-SQL).
Count	Returns the number of items in a group. For more information, see COUNT (Transact-SQL).
Count distinct	Returns the number of unique, nonnull values in a group. For more information, see Eliminating Duplicates with DISTINCT.

TABLE 20.23   Continued

Operation	Description
Minimum	Returns the minimum value in a group. For more information, see MIN (Transact-SQL). In contrast to the Transact-SQL MIN function, this operation can be used only with numeric, date, and time data types.
Maximum	Returns the maximum value in a group. For more information, see MAX (Transact-SQL). In contrast to the Transact-SQL MAX function, this operation can be used only with numeric, date, and time data types.

To create multiple outputs, click the Advanced button and select one of the empty rows in the top grid. Type in a name for the output and then select an input column from the Available Input Columns window. You can create any number of outputs this way. The sample package has an aggregate with three outputs, as shown in Figure 20.32. One output tells how many of each product have been sold by doing a sum of the order quantity in the sales order data grouped by the product ID. The second output tells the sum total for all items sold per sales order ID, and the third output tells the sum total dollar amount sold per day based on the change date using Group By.

Character Map

The Character Map transform performs common character conversions typically found in multilanguage environments. Japanese has essentially two alphabets that augment the kanji character set. One, katakana, is used for things like spelling words and names from other languages that cannot be formed with kanji. The other, hiragana, is used for verb conjugations and replacing or simplifying kanji reading. Conversion between hiragana and katakana is direct because there is a hiragana character for every katakana character.

Simplified Chinese is a reduced set of Chinese characters and is a subset of the traditional Chinese character set. Uppercase and lowercase are useful for English as well as other languages and the width operations are useful for character encodings found in Japan and other such countries with more complex character-based writing systems than a simple alphabet. Table 20.24 provides a profile for this component.

TABLE 20.24   The Character Map Transform Profile

Property	Value	Description
Component Type	Transform	
Has Custom Editor	Yes	
Internal File I/O	No	
Output Types	Synchronous	

TABLE 20.24   Continued

Property	Value	Description
Threading	Single	
Managed	No	
Number Outputs	1	
Number Inputs	1	
Requires Connection Manager	No	
Supports Error Routing	Yes	

The operations available in the Character Map transform are noted in Table 20.25.

TABLE 20.25   The Character Map Operations

Operation	Description
Byte reversal	Reverses byte order.
Full width	Maps half-width characters to full-width characters.
Half width	Maps full-width characters to half-width characters.
Hiragana	Maps katakana characters to hiragana characters.
Katakana	Maps hiragana characters to katakana characters.
Linguistic casing	Applies linguistic casing instead of the system rules. Linguistic casing refers to functionality provided by the Win32 API for Unicode simple case mapping of Turkic and other locales.
Lowercase	Converts characters to lowercase.
Simplified Chinese	Maps traditional Chinese characters to simplified Chinese characters.
Traditional Chinese	Maps simplified Chinese characters to traditional Chinese characters.
Uppercase	Converts characters to uppercase.

Setting Up the Character Map Transform

To set up the Character Map transform, select the column you want to use and then the operation to perform on it. There is also an option to either perform the conversion in place, or to create a new column with the modified value. Figure 20.33 shows the Character Map Transformation Editor from the `CharacterMapCopyColumn.dtsx` sample package.

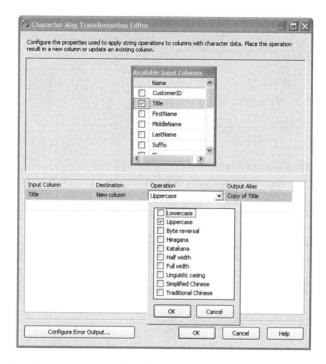

FIGURE 20.33 The Character Map Transformation Editor.

Copy Column

The Copy Column transform is one of the simplest around. It simply creates a clone of a column, copying the value of the source column into the cloned column. This is useful when you need to perform destructive operations on a column, but you want to retain the original column value. For example, you can copy the column and then split it into a different path with an Aggregate transform. This is more efficient than, for example, a multicast because only the columns of interest get copied. Table 20.26 provides a profile for this component.

TABLE 20.26 The Copy Column Transform Profile

Property	Value	Description
Component Type	Transform	
Has Custom Editor	Yes	
Internal File I/O	No	
Output Types	Synchronous	
Threading	Single	
Managed	No	

TABLE 20.26   Continued

Property	Value	Description
Number Outputs	1	
Number Inputs	1	
Requires Connection Manager	No	
Supports Error Routing	No	

Setting Up the Copy Column Transform

To set up the Copy Column transform, simply select the column you want to copy and, if you want, change the name of the output column. Figure 20.34 shows the editor for the Copy Column transform in the CharacterMapCopyColumn.dtsx sample package.

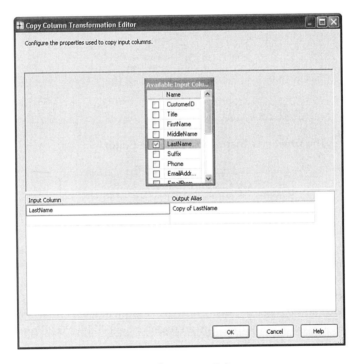

FIGURE 20.34   The Copy Column Transformation Editor.

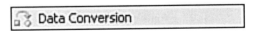

Data Conversion

The Data Conversion transform performs type casting similar to the CAST function in T-SQL. Because the Data Flow Task is very type specific, it is often necessary to convert a column type from the type provided at the source to the type required at the destination. A good example of this is data retrieved from Excel files. If you use the Import/Export Wizard to export data from an Excel file, the Data Flow Task will likely contain a Data Conversion transform because Excel supports so few data types. Table 20.27 provides the profile for this component.

TABLE 20.27   The Data Conversion Transform Profile

Property	Value	Description
Component Type	Transform	
Has Custom Editor	Yes	
Internal File I/O	No	
Output Types	Synchronous	
Threading	Single	
Managed	No	
Number Outputs	1	
Number Inputs	1	
Requires Connection Manager	No	
Supports Error Routing	Yes	
Constraints	Type conversions expensive	You should avoid using this component if possible. If possible, change the column type at the source.

Setting Up the Data Conversion Transform

To set up the Data Conversion transform, select the columns with types you want to convert and in the bottom grid, select the type to which you want to convert the column. You can also change the name of the output column in the Output Alias column of the grid. If you change the output column name to be the same as the corresponding input column name, it overwrites the column. Otherwise, a new column is created with the new name. Figure 20.35 shows the Data Conversion Transformation Editor.

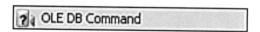

OLE DB Command

The OLE DB Command transform is useful when you want to drive behavior with tables. For example, you could execute a stored procedure for every row in the input set. Table 20.28 provides the profile for this component.

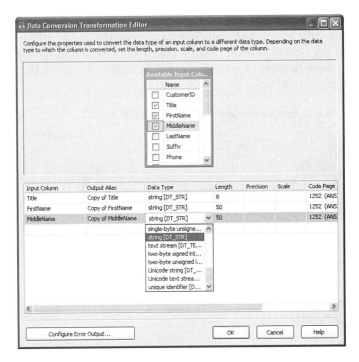

FIGURE 20.35   The Data Conversion Transformation Editor.

TABLE 20.28   The OLE DB Command Transform Profile

Property	Value	Description
Component Type	Transform	
Has Custom Editor	No	
Internal File I/O	No	
Output Types	Synchronous	
Threading	Single	
Managed	No	
Number Outputs	1	
Number Inputs	1	
Requires Connection Manager	Yes	
Supports Error Routing	Yes	
Constraints	Expensive row-based operation	The OLE DB Command transform performs a potentially expensive query for every row. Although useful in some circumstances, it is very expensive and should be avoided where performance is an issue.

Setting Up the Component

The setup for this component can be a little tricky. It doesn't have its own custom editor and it requires an input with columns that you'll likely map as parameters to the OLE DB Command (SQL Query). You must first create a connection to the database that the transform will work against. Select that connection manager in the Connection Manager column.

Next, type in the SqlCommand that you want to execute for every row in the SqlCommand property on the Component Properties tab, as shown in Figure 20.36.

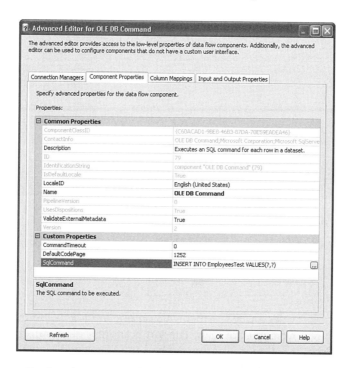

FIGURE 20.36   Setting the SQL query to be executed every row.

Notice that the query has two question mark parameter markers. Go to the Column Mappings tab and click the Refresh button. The Input and Destination columns should be updated to have a destination column for each parameter marker. Drag the input columns to the parameter destination columns, as shown in Figure 20.37.

If there is still an error message in the editor after creating the mappings, click the Refresh button again and it should go away.

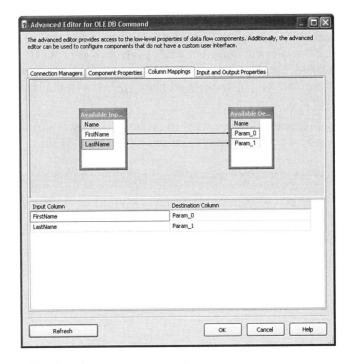

FIGURE 20.37   Creating the parameter mappings.

Sort

The Sort transform provides a way to order rows on one or more columns. It also provides a way to remove duplicate rows. The sort is an important transform because it is used to prepare flows for other transforms, such as the Merge and Merge Join transform. Table 20.29 provides the profile for this component.

TABLE 20.29   The Sort Transform Profile

Property	Value	Description
Component Type	Transform	
Has Custom Editor	Yes	
Internal File I/O	Possibly	When spooling to disk.
Output Types	Asynchronous	
Threading	Multiple	
Managed	No	
Number Outputs	1	
Number Inputs	1	

TABLE 20.29   Continued

Property	Value	Description
Requires Connection Manager	No	
Supports Error Routing	No	
Constraints	Memory	Constrained by memory, the sort will spool to disk if it hits memory limitations. Sorting at the source server is better, if possible.

Setting Up the Sort Transform

The Sort Transformation Editor provides a list of columns that you can sort on as well as those you want to pass through the transform. Figure 20.38 shows the Sort Transformation Editor in the Merge.dtsx sample package.

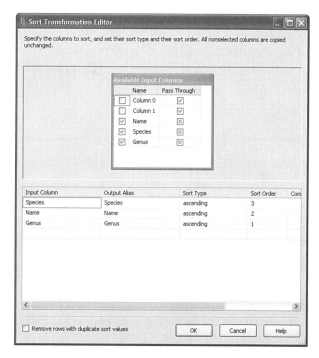

FIGURE 20.38   The Sort Transformation Editor.

In Figure 20.38, the rows are sorted by Genus, Name, and Species columns, all in ascending order. If you want to remove duplicates, select the Remove Rows with Duplicate Sort Values check box at the bottom of the editor. The Sort transform determines duplicates by comparing only the sorted rows. If differences exist in the rows on nonsorted columns, they will still be removed if their sorted column values match.

Destination Adapters

The destination adapters provide the means to write the results of the data flow to an output. The output isn't always a database table or flat file. For example, the DataReader Destination Adapter writes to an in-memory dataset and doesn't even require a connection manager.

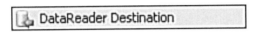

DataReader Destination

The DataReader Destination Adapter is useful for integrating the data flow from a package into external applications that support consuming data from datasets. This destination requires some additional setup on the client that consumes the data. This is useful for getting data into clients that typically only support a specific database server or for doing real-time transformation on data before landing it to the client. Table 20.30 provides the profile for this component.

TABLE 20.30   The DataReader Destination Adapter Profile

Property	Value	Description
Component Type	Destination	
Has Custom Editor	No	
Internal File I/O	No	
Output Types	None	
Threading	Single	
Managed	Yes	
Number Outputs	0	
Number Inputs	1	
Requires Connection Manager	No	
Supports Error Routing	No	

Setting Up the Component

Figure 20.39 shows the Advanced Editor for the DataReader Destination Adapter. The columns selected are included in the dataset.

Recordset Destination

The Recordset Destination Adapter populates an ADO recordset and stores it in a package variable that can be used outside of the data flow. For example, you can generate a recordset that can be used later in the same package workflow in a Foreach Loop or Script Task. Table 20.31 provides the profile for this component.

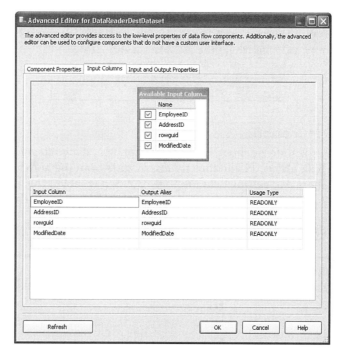

FIGURE 20.39   The DataReader Destination Adapter.

TABLE 20.31   The Recordset Destination Adapter Profile

Property	Value	Description
Component Type	Destination	
Has Custom Editor	No	
Internal File I/O	No	
Output Types	None	
Threading	Single	
Managed	No	
Number Outputs	None	
Number Inputs	1	
Requires Connection Manager	No	
Supports Error Routing	No	
Constraints	Memory Resident	Populates an in-memory recordset and can consume a lot of memory for large datasets.

Setting Up the Recordset Destination Adapter

To set up the Recordset Destination Adapter, simply open the Advanced Editor and specify an object type variable where the recordset will be stored.

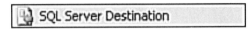

SQL Server Destination

The SQL Server Destination Adapter is a high-performance, shared memory insert mechanism. It uses the bulk insert API and directly inserts rows from the buffer to the SQL Server engine memory. For getting data into new SQL Server tables, this is the fastest method, hands down. Table 20.32 provides the profile for this component.

TABLE 20.32   The SQL Server Destination Adapter Profile

Property	Value	Description
Component Type	Destination	
Has Custom Editor	Yes	
Internal File I/O	No	
Output Types	None	
Threading	Multiple	
Managed	No	
Number Outputs	None	
Number Inputs	1	
Requires Connection Manager	Yes	Only for discovering server and database. Does not use the OLE DB connection.
Supports Error Routing	No	
Constraints	Local Only	Can only be used to access servers running on the same machine as the package.

Setting Up the SQL Server Destination Adapter

To set up the SQL Server Destination Adapter, specify an OLE DB Connection Manager and the table to insert into. Then select the Mapping tab and map the columns. That's about it. Figure 20.40 shows the SQL Server Destination Editor.

Advanced Settings

The SQL Server Destination Adapter also provides some knobs and switches you can tweak to modify the insert. The advanced options are listed in Table 20.33.

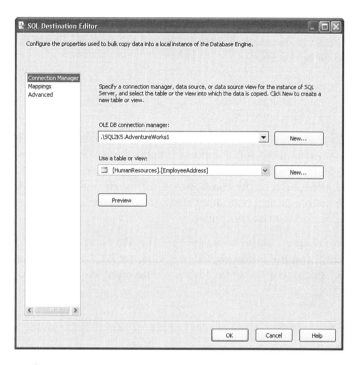

FIGURE 20.40   The SQL Server Destination Editor.

TABLE 20.33   **The SQL Destination Insert Options**

Term	Definition
Check Constraints	Select to check the table and column constraints.
Keep Nulls	Select to replace blank columns from the text file with nulls.
Enable Identity Insert	Select to retain null values during the bulk insert operation, instead of inserting any default values for empty columns.
Table Lock	Select to lock the table during the bulk insert.
Fire Triggers	Select to fire any insert, update, or delete triggers on the table.
First Row	Specify the number of the first row in the input to load during the bulk insert operation.
Last Row	Specify the number of the last row in the input to load during the bulk insert operation.
Max # Errors	Specify the maximum number of errors allowed before the bulk load operation is canceled. Each row that cannot be imported is counted as one error.
Ordered Columns	Specify the sorted columns.

TIP

If possible, for best performance, Table Lock should be enabled and the rest of the options should be turned off.

Summary

This chapter has covered the basics of stock Data Flow Task components. It showed you how to set them up and noted some important applications and typical uses of each. The samples for this chapter provide working packages to see the components in action. There is a sample package for each of the components. Although not mentioned profusely in this chapter, the sample packages are important. Running each of the samples will aid in fully understanding each of the components.

The following two chapters continue where this one leaves off. Chapter 21, "Using the Script Component," and the following chapter, Chapter 22, "Advanced Data Flow Transformations," document the more advanced and complex stock component offerings.

Using the Script Component

CHAPTER 21

"I'VE DONE A DEMO FOR MY TEAM AND THE CONSENSUS WAS THAT SSIS IS 'AWESOME,' 'RIGHTEOUS,' AND 'FUNKADELIC.'"—SCOTT KIM

As you can see from the preceding chapter, a lot of stock transformations and adapters ship in the box. Even so, at times, you'll still need to access some data or perform a transformation that isn't supported with the stock components. The Script Component is provided as an intermediate step between available stock components and writing a custom component.

Introduction to the Script Component

Like the Script Task, the Script Component is a platform within a platform. The environment for the Script Component is very similar to the Script Task. It's the same Visual Studio development environment and provides all the nice bells and whistles, such as IntelliSense and integrated help. If you're unfamiliar with the Visual Studio Integrated Development Environment, a quick review of Chapter 15, "Using the Script Task," might be helpful before moving on.

The Script Component is an easy-to-use mechanism for writing specialized data transformations in Visual Basic .NET. The Script Component provides template functions that allow you to easily add adapter or transformation functionality to your data flow without having to know or understand the details of manipulating metadata and buffers. After you get past the initial and small learning curve of learning the specifics of the Script Component, you need only understand and write code specifically related to your problem domain. Also, the code for the project is stored inside the package so no special steps are needed to register the resulting component as is required for custom components.

The Script Component Is Performant

The Script Component is also quite performant. Traditionally, scripting has been associated with bad performance—with good reason because scripting engines have been late-binding interpreters. Because the Script Component compiles its code into a true .NET binary, it is much faster than JavaScript and VBScript engines. In various tests, the performance of the Script Component measures at or better than roughly 90% of similar components written in native code with the Precompile option enabled.

Building Proofs of Concept

The Script Component is also a valuable way to do proof-of-concept components. The code that you write in a Script Component does, for the most part, transfer nicely to a custom component if you decide to take that step. But, you can do it without having to concern yourself with all the project setup and assembly registration issues. Proving the code in the Script Component lets you get to the heart of the problem without all the fuss. It's also helpful when you want to rapidly build proof-of-concept packages or isolate performance problems in your environment. The Script Component can be used to generate testing data or simply simulate data reads from hardware that might be slowing down your data flow. Using a Script Component, you can eliminate the network bandwidth or hard drive bottlenecks to give you an accurate measurement of the data flow throughput. These varying applications of the Script Component make it a valuable solution implementation.

Accessing Unusual or Unsupported Sources

The Script Component really shines when you need to access data in an unusual or unsupported format or location. For example, a large percentage of corporate information is stored in employee Inboxes. There is currently no source adapter available for reading data from mailboxes. However, using the Script Component, it's very easy to retrieve email, tasks, or any other Microsoft Outlook objects into the data flow. The GetEmail.dtsx package in the S20-ScriptTransform sample solution contains the code that allows you to retrieve email from your Inbox. The following discussion shows how to create a source that reads your Outlook Inbox. You can follow along and create it as you read or just open the package from the Samples folder.

Creating a Source Adapter

When you drop the Script Component onto the Data Flow designer, the first dialog box you'll see is the one shown in Figure 21.1. You can choose the type of component the script will implement from one of three options: Source, Destination, and Transformation.

FIGURE 21.1   The Select Script Component Type dialog box.

Select the Source option and the click the OK button. Double-click on the component and select the Inputs and Outputs node in the left pane. If you open the Output node in the middle pane, you'll notice that there are no defined output columns on Output 0. Also, there are no inputs.

Creating the Component

The source's responsibility is to get data from the medium where the data is stored and place it into the buffer for the downstream transforms to process. The default template for the transform and destination adapters provides a function for processing rows on an input. This is the fundamental difference between sources and other components. Sources have no inputs, only outputs, because they are the components that generate rows and place them in the buffer.

To get to the code, select the Script node in the left pane and click the Design Script button. You should see the default template code, as follows:

```
Public Class ScriptMain
  Inherits UserComponent
    Public Overrides Sub CreateNewOutputRows()
    ' Add code here
    End Sub
End Class
```

You can also override several other methods if you want, as explained in the following section, but this is the one method you must implement in sources and it's where you add rows to the outgoing buffer.

Implementing CreateNewOutputRows

It's important to understand that sources block on the call to `CreateNewOutputRows`, which means that the method is called exactly once on each source adapter for each execution of the package. So, the Data Flow Task knows that the source adapter is done adding rows only when it calls the buffer's `SetEndOfRowset` method and returns from the call. Consequently, for source adapters, you only need to implement this one method.

> **TIP**
>
> As a rule, if you don't call end of rowset, the Data Flow Task does not know if the transform is finished adding rows to the output buffer and, therefore, never finishes. However, in the Script Component there is an exception. The base class sets the end of rowset automatically when you return from the `CreateNewOutputRows` method. So, strictly speaking, you don't need to call `SetEndOfRowset`, but you should as a matter of practice.

Implementing `PreExecute` and `PostExecute`

The `PreExecute` and `PostExecute` methods are not strictly necessary, but if you have any costly startup or shutdown processing that needs to happen, you can do it here. These two methods are useful for any pre- and postprocessing you might want to perform, such as creating member variables, and so on. The idea is that you can initialize and instantiate objects in the `PreExecute` method and release the objects in the `PostExecute` method.

> **TIP**
>
> To see what methods you can override, type in the words "Public Overrides" and then press the spacebar; IntelliSense pops up with a list of available methods.

Implementing `AcquireConnections` and `ReleaseConnections`

As a rule, you should use connection managers to access files or servers and you should implement this method to call `AcquireConnection` on each connection manager you're using. By implementing this method, you ensure that you're calling `AcquireConnections` at the right time because the Data Flow Task calls `AcquireConnections` at the appropriate time. Connections should only be established in the `AcquireConnections` method. `AcquireConnections` is called during both component design and execution. Any connection established during this method should be stored in a member variable and released in the `ReleaseConnections` method.

Creating the Email Source

Microsoft provides an interop assembly for working with Outlook. The assembly allows you to control Outlook and retrieve email, task, schedule, and other Outlook data into your code using the Outlook object model. You'll use it in the Script Component to retrieve email.

CAUTION

If you have Microsoft Office 2003 installed, this should work for you. The Email Source has not been thoroughly tested and you might experience issues with other versions of Office.

Adding the Outputs

When creating the source, you must first add at least one output. When you create an output, the Script Component generates the code for accessing the buffers so that you can add data row by row. The following steps explain how to add an output:

1. Drop the Script Component onto the designer.

2. Select the Source option from the Select Script Component Type dialog box.

3. Open the Script Transformation Editor and select the Inputs and Outputs node.

4. Select the Output node in the middle pane. "Output 0" isn't very descriptive, so change it to "Email" so that it will have a meaningful name.

5. Click the Output Columns node and then click the Add Column button.

6. Name the first column MessageBody and set the type to Unicode Text Stream.

7. Create another column named Sender and set the type to Unicode string.

8. Create another column named Subject and set the type to Unicode string.

9. Create another column named CC and set the type to Unicode string.

10. Create another column named SentOn and set the type to Date.

11. Create another column named Size and set the type to Integer.

The Script Component generates code for each of these columns. As you'll see in a minute, it creates accessor functions as well so that it is very easy to access each column's value. Open the script by selecting the Script node in the left pane and clicking the Design Script button.

Adding a Reference to the Interop Assembly

The first thing you need to do is add a reference to the Outlook interop assembly so that the Script Component can interact with the native Outlook object model library.

1. Double-click on the Script Component.

2. Select the Script node and then click Design Script.

3. In the Project Explorer window, usually in the upper-left of the designer, right-click on the References node and select Add Reference.

4. Select the `Microsoft.Office.Interop.Outlook` assembly. If the interop assembly is not available, you can download it here:
http://support.microsoft.com/default.aspx?scid=kb;en-us;328912

5. Add an imports line, as follows:

```
Imports Microsoft.Office.Interop.Outlook
```

Adding Rows

Now you're ready to implement the `CreateNewOutputRows` method. This method is only called once. When you return from this method, the data flow considers the source complete and begins clearing out buffers. Most of the code in this source is just to get the Outlook objects set up and ready to start reading email. The following code retrieves the Inbox object:

```
' Create an Outlook application object
Dim oApp As Outlook.Application
oApp = New Outlook.Application()

'String used for comparison with mail item.
Dim sClassComp As String = "IPM.Note"

'Get Mapi NameSpace.
Dim oNS As Outlook.NameSpace = oApp.GetNamespace("MAPI")

'Get Messages collection of Inbox.
Dim oInbox As Outlook.MAPIFolder

' Get the default inbox folder
oInbox=oNS.GetDefaultFolder(Outlook.OlDefaultFolders.olFolderInbox)
 ' Get the inbox messages
 Dim oItems As Outlook.Items = oInbox.Items
 Me.Log("Total email items : " + oItems.Count.ToString(), 1001, Nothing)
```

At this point, you have the Inbox and the collection of email objects. You are ready to start creating new rows and reading the contents of the email into the columns, as shown in the following code:

```
'Loop each message.
Dim oMsg As Outlook.MailItem
...
For i = 1 To oItems.Count
   oMsg = oItems.Item(i)
...
```

> **TIP**
>
> This code is simplified to make it easier to read; however, if you were to do this for a production solution, the code to this point should be placed in the `PreExecute` method and cleaned up in the `PostExecute` method. As a general rule, expensive, one-time, and preparation logic should be handled in the `PreExecute` and `PostExecute` methods.

Next, as you loop through the collection of email objects, you'll create a new row for each. The way you create a new row is to call the buffer object `AddRow()` method. The buffer object name is a combination of the output name followed by the word "Buffer." In this case, the output is named "Email," so the buffer object name is "EmailBuffer." As mentioned earlier, the Script Component creates special accessor methods for you to get and set the values of the columns in each row as you add it. The following code adds the Subject line:

```
' Add the subject
EmailBuffer.Subject = oMsg.Subject
```

For each of the columns, you have some code that retrieves the value from the Outlook message object and places it into the buffer object.

> **NOTE**
>
> Note that Binary Large Object (BLOB) columns must be added as an array of bytes. For certain types, you need to convert the data into an array of bytes and then use the column's `AddBlobData` method to insert the array. When retrieving data from BLOB columns, you need to use the `GetBlobData` method.

That's how you create a source. Simple, isn't it?

Creating a Destination Adapter

Destination adapters provide the opposite function than source adapters do, of course. They take data from buffers and write it to their output medium. One valid complaint folks have had about the SQL Server Integration Services (SSIS) component offering is that there is no ADO.NET destination adapter. It's been a real problem for some who have attempted to load into ODBC or ADO.NET adapters for systems that don't support OLE DB. Fortunately, you can use the Script Component to work around the issue by writing a destination adapter. In this section, you create a destination adapter that will take the email inputs from the source just discussed and send them to a table using an ADO.NET Connection Manager.

Get started by dropping a Script Component onto the designer and selecting Destination. Drag a path from the source you just created to the new destination adapter and open the editor. The first thing you'll likely notice is an additional node in the left pane called Input Columns. This is where you tell the component which columns you want to be available in the buffer. If you don't select one of the columns, the Script Component will not create accessors for you. Also, select the Usage Type in the lower-right column. In Figure 21.2, ReadOnly is selected for all the columns because this is a destination and there will be no downstream components that will be impacted by these settings. Figure 21.2 shows the Script Transformation Editor with the input columns selected.

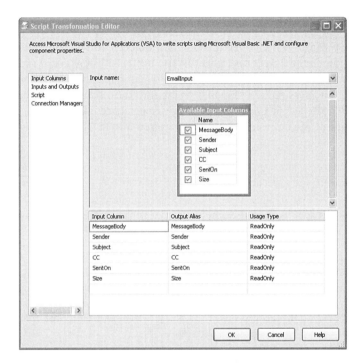

FIGURE 21.2   Selecting the input columns.

Next, click the Inputs and Outputs node in the left pane of the Script Transformation Editor. Here, there are no outputs because destinations are the inverse of sources; they read the data in the buffers on the input and output the data to their respective media. There are no outputs because there are no downstream components to consume them.

NOTE

Strangely enough, you can create a new output on a destination, but then it ceases to be a destination and becomes a transformation.

Figure 21.3 shows the Script Transformation Editor with the selected input columns showing.

FIGURE 21.3   Viewing the selected input columns.

Creating the Component

Select the Script node in the left pane of the Script Transformation Editor to see the properties. This is where you add references to variables if you want to use them in the script. You can also set the PreCompile property and LocaleID, if the defaults don't suit your needs.

> **NOTE**
>
> As a rule, you should turn the PreCompile setting on. It eliminates the compile step that happens at the beginning of package execution and must be set for packages that will run on 64-bit machines. The one drawback is that it can make a package's disk size substantially larger.

Using Connection Managers

If you're creating this package as you read, you'll need to click the Connection Managers node in the left pane and add a new connection manager. In the sample package, an Execute SQL Task creates a table called Email in the TempDB database and executes before the Data Flow Task. The script to create the table is as follows:

```
USE [TEMPDB]
GO

IF OBJECT_ID('dbo.Email') IS NOT NULL
  DROP TABLE dbo.Email
GO

CREATE TABLE [dbo].[Email]
(
    [MessageBody] [ntext]  NULL,
    [Sender] [nvarchar](250)  NULL,
    [Subject] [nvarchar](250)  NULL,
    [CC] [nvarchar](250)  NULL,
    [SentOn] [datetime] NULL,
    [Size] [int] NULL
)
```

NOTE

The table name is hard-coded in the script. That's not a good practice because it means that the package must be changed every time you need to modify the table location, and so forth. Ideally, you should create a property expression on the SQL Task that builds the query with the value of the database passed in from a configurable variable. The sample has the table name hard-coded to simplify the code.

The destination adapter requires an ADO.NET Connection Manager that references the table. You'll need to do the same. Click the Design Script button to open the development environment. The component needs to use an ADO.NET Connection Manager. It's important that you call the AcquireConnections method on connection managers at the appropriate time. The Data Flow Task has a certain order it follows when validating and executing. To ensure that you're playing nicely in the Data Flow Task sandbox, you should override the AcquireConnections method in the Script Component any time you need to use a connection manager and call the connection manager's AcquireConnections method there.

The ADO.NET Connection Manager is named ADONETConnection, so the code looks like this:

```
Public Overrides Sub AcquireConnections(ByVal Transaction As Object)

    connMgr = Me.Connections.ADONETConnection
    sqlConn = CType(connMgr.AcquireConnection(Nothing), SqlConnection)

End Sub
```

NOTE

Notice that the way you access the Connections collection is different than in the Script Task. The Script Component does not have a DTS object, so to access the collections, you simply self-reference. For example, to access the Log method, use Me.Log; for the Connections collection, use Me.Connections; and for variables, use Me.Variables.

You can also access the component's metadata using the ComponentMetadata object. This is useful for things such as firing events, Me.ComponentMetadata.Fire<Event>(), or getting the description of errors, Me.ComponentMetaData.GetErrorDescription().

Adding the Script

Next, you need to add the script for processing the incoming rows. Because destinations actually have inputs, you implement the ProcessInputRow method instead of the CreateNewOutputRows method like you do in source adapters. The code is essentially the opposite of what you have in the source.

Because you're trying to output data to an ADO.NET provider, you need to create a reference to it. Because the ADO.NET provider you'll use is housed in an assembly that's already in the References collection, that is, System.Data, all you need to do is create an Imports entry, as follows:

```
Imports System.Data.SqlClient
```

Next, you need to create an INSERT command and add parameters as follows:

```
sqlCmd = New SqlCommand("INSERT INTO dbo.Email(MessageBody, Sender," & _
    " Subject, CC, SentOn, Size) VALUES(@MessageBody, @Sender, @Subject," & _
    " @CC, @SentOn, @Size)", sqlConn)"
sqlParam = New SqlParameter("@MessageBody", SqlDbType.NText)
sqlCmd.Parameters.Add(sqlParam)
```

For each column, you add a parameter.

NOTE

In the sample package, the INSERT command and parameters are created in the PreExecute method, but it can be done in the ProcessInputRow method as well.

The ProcessInputRow method passes each row in for you to process, so it's easy to get the column value from the row and set the parameter value, as follows:

```
.Parameters("@Subject").Value = Row.Subject
```

After setting up all the parameters, you can execute the insert:

```
.ExecuteNonQuery()
```

Now you have an ADO.NET destination adapter that writes your email out to a table. Hopefully, this gives you a pretty good idea how to create a destination adapter with the Script Component. Open the sample and study it. Try changing it around for different metadata, and so on. The sample package is `Destination.dtsx` and can be found in the S20-ScriptTransform sample solution in the Samples folder.

Creating a Transformation

SSIS doesn't provide a lot of functionality in the box for dealing with BLOBs in the data flow. Yet, I've got some emails that are huge because they're either forum threads or loaded with Hypertext Markup Language (HTML) or from newsgroup posts. What I'd like to do is shorten the email body so that I only get the first few lines, which should be enough to capture the essence of the body. It would be nice to be able to change the length of the body retained based on a value in a variable. It would also be nice to replace any empty column values with a string value from a variable so, for example, instead of being completely empty, the CC field might contain the string "<Empty>. This is much easier to deal with than a NULL. Having the replacement value in a variable makes it easy to change later as well.

> **NOTE**
>
> You can also replace NULL values using a Derived Column transform, but then that wouldn't be as much fun.

Creating the Component

Creating the transform is similar to creating the destination adapter. You have to select the input columns, and so on, but you also need to create outputs like the source. Finally, there are two distinct types of transforms as discussed previously—synchronous and asynchronous. First, you'll create a synchronous transform and then you'll learn how to create an asynchronous transform.

Setting Up the Input Columns

Start by creating the input columns:

1. Drop another Script Component onto the designer and select the Transform option.

2. Delete the path from the source to the destination you just created.

3. Create a new path from the source to the transform.

4. Create a new path from the transform to the destination.

5. Open the Script Transformation Editor.

6. Select the Input Columns node in the left pane.

7. Select the check boxes in all the available input columns.

8. In the grid below, set the usage type for the MessageBody column to ReadWrite. Best practices dictate that you should only set a column to be ReadWrite if you plan to modify it in the transform. Figure 21.4 shows the correct settings.

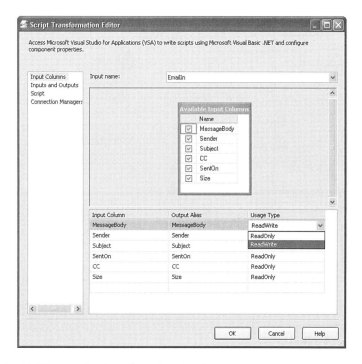

FIGURE 21.4   Setting up the transform input columns.

Setting the Synchronous Input ID

You need to tell the Script Component that it is a synchronous transform. The way you do this is by explicitly linking the output with the input. As mentioned earlier, all objects in the data flow have IDs, including inputs. So, the way you link the output with the input is to specify in the SynchronousInputID property of the output the ID of the associated input. The following steps show you how to do this:

1. Double-click on the Script Component.

2. Select the Inputs and Outputs node.

3. Select the Input node.

4. In the property grid, look at the ID property. In the sample project, the ID is 517.

5. Select the Output node.

6. In the property grid, set the SynchronousInputID to the value you found for the input ID. Figure 21.5 shows the SynchronousInputID settings.

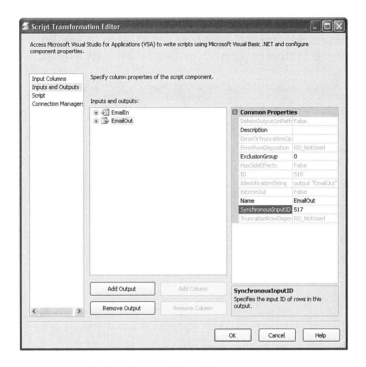

FIGURE 21.5   Setting up the SynchronousInputID.

Setting Up the Variables

Before adding the script, you need to create a couple of variables the Script transform will use as parameters. The first variable is the maximum body length. It's an integer. The second is the default string value you'll use to replace the empty string, which is a string type.

TIP

In the sample, these variables are created at data flow scope because they really have no use elsewhere in the package. Also, if the data flow ever needs to be copied and pasted to another package, the variables will go with the data flow, leaving it valid without the need for creating variables again. It's always a good idea to create variables at the most local scope possible. This helps avoid variable confusion and makes it easier to manage and update packages.

To make the variables accessible within the script, you need to add them to one of the reserve lists. Because you don't need to change their values, you can place their names in the ReadOnlyVariables property.

If you do need to change their values, you should keep two things in mind. You must add the variable name to the `ReadWriteVariables` property and you can only change the value in the `PostExecute` method. Even better, you can use the `VariableDispenser` object to lock the variables directly in the code. This approach is more work, but has the virtue of only locking the variable for as long as it is absolutely needed.

Figure 21.6 shows the Script Transformation Editor with the `ReadOnlyVariables` correctly set.

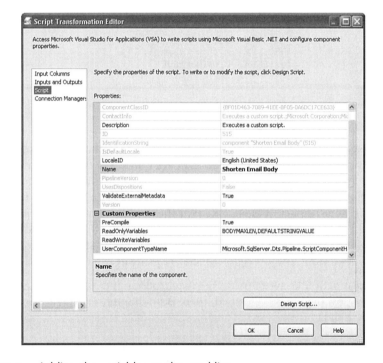

FIGURE 21.6 Adding the variables to the read list.

Adding the Script

Next, you need to set up the script. Because this is a synchronous transform, you only need to modify the rows that are passed to the `ProcessInputRow` method. You don't need to add new rows. Essentially, the Script Component passes each row in succession, allowing the script to modify it in place. Because the Script Component already creates the template `ProcessInputRow` function for you, you need only add the processing code.

The section of code that reads the message body and truncates it is as follows:

```
If Row.MessageBody.Length > Me.Variables.BODYMAXLEN Then
    Dim dBytes As Byte() = Row.MessageBody.GetBlobData(0, Me.Variables.BODYMAXLEN)
    Row.MessageBody.AddBlobData(dBytes)
End If
```

The code tests if the length of the message body is greater than the maximum body length. If it is, it retrieves the message body BLOB, but only the maximum body length bytes. Then, it overwrites the message body BLOB with the shorter value.

The following code, repeated for each string column, checks if the given column is empty. If it is, it replaces it with the string in the DEFAULTSTRINGVALUE variable.

```
If Row.Sender Is Nothing Then
    Row.Sender = Me.Variables.DEFAULTSTRINGVALUE
End If
```

Asynchronous Outputs

To review, asynchronous outputs have a different buffer type than the inputs on the same component. There is a disconnect between the data flowing in on an input and the data flowing out of an asynchronous output. Asynchronous outputs are often called blocking outputs, but that's not entirely accurate. Asynchronous outputs tend to be blocking, but they don't have to be. In fact, it is possible that they produce more data than what the inputs provide. When you think of asynchronous outputs, instead of thinking about whether it blocks or how much data it produces, think "new data" or "new buffer type." Essentially, asynchronous outputs represent newly generated data.

Some make a distinction between partially asynchronous and asynchronous outputs. Where the data flow engine is concerned, there is no difference. The distinction is merely conceptual.

> **NOTE**
>
> Often, people refer to transformations as asynchronous or synchronous. But, that's not an entirely accurate way to classify components. In fact, it's possible to have a transform that has both synchronous and asynchronous outputs. Strictly speaking, there are no synchronous or asynchronous components, only synchronous and asynchronous outputs. However, you'll still hear folks, even SSIS team members, refer to components as synchronous or asynchronous.
>
> But, you know what they really mean.

Making a Script Output Asynchronous

As mentioned earlier, you should check the SynchronousInputID to ensure it had the ID of an input. If you change the SynchronousInputID to zero, you've changed the output to an asynchronous output. It's that simple. When you do this, the Script Component generates a new template function. As you might expect, it is the same template function it generates for the Source, `CreateNewOutputRows`. So, transforms with asynchronous outputs are really like a destination and a source slapped together. The input is like a destination, and the output is like a source, generating new data. Because you've already seen a source and a destination, you already know how to write transforms with asynchronous outputs. In fact, another way to think about it is that sources are components with no inputs and only asynchronous outputs.

Summary

These are some pretty easy examples and show how the Script Component can fill the functional gaps of Integration Services with just a few lines of code. You've seen how to write a source and destination adapter. You've seen how to write a transform with synchronous and asynchronous outputs. Using the Script Component, you can write your own data-processing logic or use existing legacy code. You can even use third-party algorithms or the .NET Framework. The possibilities are nearly infinite.

Advanced Data Flow Transformations

"I KINDA THINK I WAS BEING A BIT VAGUE."—JEFF BERNHARDT

Business Intelligence is a broad and deep field with complex and technical requirements. Take a step back and just think about the Extract, Transform, and Load (ETL) processes for a minute. Think about how many steps it takes to get dirty, duplicate, and out-of-date data from the transactional store, clean it up, transform it into a different schema, aggregate it, deduplicate it, and all the other steps you might have before pushing it into a ROLAP or MOLAP store. Integration Services provides a broad set of features for addressing these steps. To this point, the tasks and transforms covered have been mostly focused around the transformation stage of the ETL and integration processes. This chapter focuses on those components that address some of the more advanced, esoteric, or ETL-specific processes. Some of these components, such as the Slowly Changing Dimension transform and the Fuzzy Lookup transform, are very important tools that require a little more coverage than the average stock component, and so they are covered separately in this chapter.

The components in this chapter fall into three categories.

- Slowly Changing Dimension Wizard and transform

- Data cleansing components

- Text mining and document warehousing components

The Slowly Changing Dimension Wizard provides a simple way to implement a solution to the common problem of how to update dimensions. The data cleansing components represent some cutting-edge algorithms for discovering similarities and groupings. The text mining and document warehousing components provide a way to work with nonformatted or semiformatted data. These are some of the features and components that move Integration Services beyond simple ETL. Also, excepting the Slowly Changing Dimension Transform, these components ship only in the Enterprise Edition of SQL Server.

The Slowly Changing Dimension Wizard and Transform (SCD)

The Slowly Changing Dimension transform makes it easy to quickly generate complex Slowly Changing Dimension transform data flow. Table 22.1 contains the transform profile.

TABLE 22.1   The Slowly Changing Dimension Transform Profile

Property	Value	Description
Component Type	Transform	
Has Custom Designer	Yes	Slowly Changing Dimension Wizard
Internal File I/O	No	
Output Types	Synchronous	
Threading	Single	
Managed	No	
Number Outputs	Up to 6	Depends on change types selected
Number Inputs	1	
Requires Connection Manager	Yes	
Supports Error Routing	No	
Constraints	Nonoptimized	Not optimized, must be tuned to handle larger loads

A full discussion about the nature of dimensions and slowly changing dimensions is beyond the scope of this book, but a brief discussion here will help establish a context for discussing the Slowly Changing Dimension Wizard and transform.

A Typical Slowly Changing Dimension

Generally speaking, Business Intelligence is about capturing, analyzing, and understanding the trends, patterns, and history of a business so that companies can make more informed decisions. Facts record transactions and dimensions contain information about the transactions, such as customer name, time, weather, product, and advertising promotions. Slowly changing dimensions (SCD) result from the fact that over time, the world changes and dimension values must also be updated to reflect those changes. Not every dimension is a slowly changing dimension, and not every slowly changing dimension should be handled in the same way. One example of a dimension might be time. Time doesn't change. October 3, 1963, will always be October 3, 1963. However, marriage status, sales district, last names, and, nowadays, even gender dimension attributes do. Even then, you don't necessarily want to update every change in the same way. You might want to maintain the history of some changes, overwrite others, or simply detect when a change is attempted. For example, if the sales districts for a company are reorganized, to ensure that sales reports and queries remain accurate, you might want to keep a record of the previous sales districts for all salespersons. But, because customer name changes happen so rarely and because names are simply identifiers for the same entity, you might choose to overwrite last name attributes of customer dimensions. This is a fundamental problem with dimensions, and the Slowly Changing Dimension Wizard provides a way to implement the logic to handle these changes.

"Type 1" Slowly Changing Dimensions

Consider a simple example of an existing customer, Tom Brokenjaw, who is moving from Washington to New York on July 21st. If you don't really need to track the fact that, prior to moving to New York, Tom once lived in Washington, you can simply overwrite the state dimension. Table 22.2 shows how the dimension would appear before updating the dimension and Table 22.3 shows the change.

TABLE 22.2   Customer Dim Record Before Type 1 Change

Customer Dimension Key	Customer Business Key	Customer Last Name	Customer State
42	TB2015447815	Brokenjaw	WA

TABLE 22.3   Customer Dim Record After Type 1 Change

Customer Dimension Key	Customer Business Key	Customer Last Name	Customer State
42	TB2015447815	Brokenjaw	NY

In this case, the state value is overwritten. This is known as a Type 1 dimension, and in Integration Services is referred to as a Changing Attribute Change.

"Type 2" Slowly Changing Dimensions

Now, consider a scenario in which it is important to track the fact that Tom lived in Washington before moving to New York on July 21st. To accomplish this, you would create a new record for Tom in the customer dimension table and mark the old record as follows. Table 22.4 shows the record before updating. Table 22.5 shows the additional record.

TABLE 22.4   Customer Dim Record Before Type 2 Change

Customer Dimension Key	Customer Business Key	Customer Last Name	Customer State	Effective Date	Current Record
42	TB2015447815	Brokenjaw	WA	06-01-2000	True

TABLE 22.5   Customer Dim Record After Type 2 Change

Customer Dimension Key	Customer Business Key	Customer Last Name	Customer State	Effective Date	Current Record
42	TB2015447815	Brokenjaw	WA	06-01-2000	False
1001	TB2015447815	Brokenjaw	NY	07-21-2006	True

Notice that there are two more attributes in the dimension for Type 1 records because Type 2 changes preserve history, providing a way to determine when a particular change took effect. Notice also that the old record now has the current record flag set to FALSE and the new record is flagged as the current record indicating that Tom now resides in New York, thus preserving the history of Tom's state of residence. Slowly changing dimensions using this technique are referred to as Type 2 dimensions and are, by far, the most common type of slowly changing dimension. In Integration Services, this type of change is called a Historical Attribute Change.

Additional Slowly Changing Dimension Types

Type 1 or Type 2 are the most common change types, but occasionally you might have late-arriving dimension information or you might want to detect when a dimension attribute changes. Although the SCD does not directly support Type 3 changes, it is possible to detect when a Type 3 change might be appropriate, as described in the following section.

Inferred Member

Traditionally, late-arriving dimensions have been exceptional cases, such as data-entry errors or back-dated, real-world events. For example, occasionally, customers don't alert the company of address changes until months after they occurred or product manufacturing processes or parts change but are not correctly updated.

With the emergence of new technologies and business models, late-arriving dimensions are becoming more common. For example, grocery stores offer membership cards that you can use for discounts on items in the store. The membership card has a unique ID that tracks the buying habits of the card holder even if the card holder hasn't provided any information about herself to the grocery store. The customer might purchase groceries, which represent facts, but might not provide any information about herself at the time she makes her initial purchase with the membership card. Even without the customer information, the grocery store still needs to capture the transaction information as fact records and the fact records need to reference the membership card dimension record. However, the card holder might later provide her personal information, which then needs to be added to the dimension record as the late-arriving dimension.

Another example is furnaces and other home appliances that carry warranties. Large builders sometimes purchase such appliances in bulk to get discounted pricing. When a builder purchases the appliance, they often do not know who the ultimate owner will be or even where the utility will be installed. Only when the owner purchases the house, condo, or other building and registers the appliance will that information become available. When that happens, they will provide new information that needs to be inserted into the existing dimension record for that appliance warranty.

Inferred member changes are dimension records created in anticipation of such late-arriving dimension data.

Fixed Attribute

A Fixed Attribute change type enforces no changes. This change type detects when a record has changed so that it can be recorded and handled in the downstream data flow.

"Type 3" Slowly Changing Dimensions

Type 3 Slowly Changing Dimensions (SCD) are very rare and occur when a business must track the original and current values of only certain specific attributes of a dimension record. Because Type 3 Slowly Changing Dimensions are uncommon and require that the dimension table be modified, the Slowly Changing Dimension Wizard doesn't support them.

TIP

If you want to implement a Type 3 SCD, you can mark the column you want to update with the Fixed Attribute change type and then capture the Fixed Attribute output rows to discover Type 3 attribute candidates.

The Slowly Changing Dimension Wizard

OK, let's put the Slowly Changing Dimension Wizard through its paces. The package you're about to build is the SCD.dtsx package in the book samples in the S21-Advanced solution. The wizard takes you through six dialog boxes and a summary dialog box, as described in the following sections.

The Slowly Changing Dimension Wizard Steps

The following are the general steps the Slowly Changing Dimension Wizard walks you through for defining the additional data flow and the runtime behavior of the Slowly Changing Dimension transform.

1. **Select a Dimension Table and Keys**—This is where you select which dimension table you want to modify and the keys for matching the source records with dimension table records.

2. **Select the Slowly Changing Dimension Columns**—This is where you select the dimension attributes and the change type for each attribute.

3. **Select Fixed and Changing Attribute Options**—This is where you set the SCD transform to fail if a fixed attribute has changed and whether to update all records when a change is detected in a changing attribute.

4. **Select Historical Attribute Options**—This is where you tell the Slowly Changing Dimension Wizard how to detect current and expired records.

5. **Select Inferred Dimension Members**—This is where you turn on inferred member support and how to detect that an incoming record is for a previously inserted inferred dimension record.

6. **Finish the Slowly Changing Dimension Wizard**—This is where you can review the settings before finalizing the wizard.

Running the Slowly Changing Dimension Wizard

The preceding steps show the dialog boxes the wizard walks you through to generate the data flow. Let's run through the wizard and see what it produces. Make sure you have the AdventureWorks and AdventureWorksDW sample databases installed. To run the Slowly Changing Dimension Wizard, open the designer and perform the following steps:

1. Create a new Integration Services project.

2. Click on the package in the new solution.

3. Drop a Data Flow Task onto the workflow.

4. Switch to the Data Flow tab.

5. Drop an OLE DB Source Adapter and double-click on it.

6. Click the New button to create a new OLE DB connection manager.

7. Connect to the AdventureWorks database.

8. Select Table or View for the Data Access mode. (Default)

9. Select [HumanResources].[Employee] for the name of the table.

10. Click on the Columns node.

11. Click the OK button to close the OLE DB Source Adapter dialog box.

12. Drop a Slowly Changing Dimension transform onto the Data Flow designer.

13. Drag the output from the OLE DB Source Adapter to the SCD transform.

CAUTION

The SCD transform doesn't support null business keys. If the source data includes rows in which the Business Key column is null, you should filter those rows from the flow with a conditional split before attempting to process them in the SCD transform.

14. Double-click the Slowly Changing Dimension transform to open the Slowly Changing Dimension Wizard.

15. You should see the Welcome screen shown in Figure 22.1. Click the Next button, if you do.

FIGURE 22.1   The Slowly Changing Dimension Wizard welcome screen.

16. Click the New button to create a connection manager to AdventureWorksDW or select an existing one.

17. From the Table or View drop down, select [dbo].[DimEmployee].

18. In the grid, in the Input Column for EmployeeNationalIDAlternateKey Dimension Column, select NationalIDNumber and set the Key Type to Business Key. The wizard should appear as Figure 22.2 shows. This tells the SCD transform how to match the dimension table record with the source system record and is usually a match between the source table primary key and the dimension table alternate or surrogate key.

19. Click the Next button to take you to the Slowly Changing Dimension Columns dialog box, as shown in Figure 22.3.

20. In the Dimension Columns column of the grid, select BirthDate.

21. Leave it as a Fixed Attribute because someone's birth date should never change. Later in the wizard, you'll tell the wizard what to do if there is a row with a birth date value that has changed.

22. In the Dimension Columns column of the grid, select MaritalStatus.

23. Set this to the Changing Attribute change type to simply overwrite the old value with the new one.

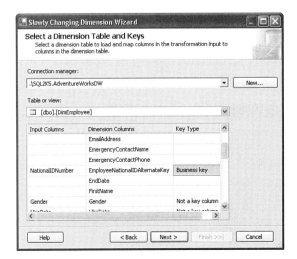

FIGURE 22.2   Matching records from the source to the dimension tables.

24. In the Dimension Columns column of the grid, select SalariedFlag.

25. Set the change type to Historical Attribute, assuming you want to keep a history of when employees become salaried.

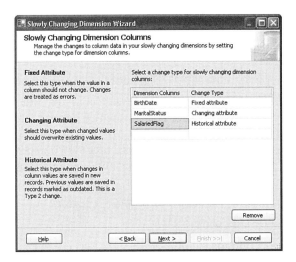

FIGURE 22.3   Setting up the attribute change types.

NOTE

The Slowly Changing Dimension Wizard creates outputs for fixed, changing, and historical change types only if there is at least one dimension with one of those change types. If you do not select a certain change type, for example a fixed change type, for any of the dimension table columns, there will be no Fixed Attribute option.

26. Click the Next button; the Fixed and Changing Attribute Options dialog box opens, as shown in Figure 22.4. If, in the preceding dialog box, you did not create any fixed or changing attributes, these two options will be disabled.

27. Ensure that the changes detected in fixed attributes do not fail the transform by deselecting the top option. This allows the record with the changed fixed attribute to be routed to the error output.

28. Put a check in the Changing Attributes check box to enable Changing Attributes. This ensures that there is only one active dimension record for each employee. As you'll see in a minute, this check box affects the update query by adding an additional condition to the WHERE clause.

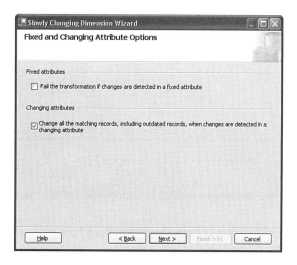

FIGURE 22.4   Setting options for fixed and changing attribute types.

29. Click the Next button, which takes you to the Historical Attribute Options dialog box, shown in Figure 22.5.

30. Select the Use a Single Column to Show Current and Expired Records option because the DimEmployee table has one called CurrentFlag. Alternately, you could use the Use Start and End Dates to Identify Current and Expired Records option.

TIP

If you use the start and end dates option, the Slowly Changing Dimension Wizard populates the start and end date column drop downs with any date-time columns available in the dimension table for you to select. In addition, the Variable to Set Date Values drop down will contain all date-time variables in scope with the Data Flow Task. So, you can create your own and populate it with a date of your choosing, or you can use one of the system date-time variables.

31. In the Column to Indicate Current Record drop down, select CurrentFlag.

32. In the Value when Current drop down, select True.

33. In the Expiration Value drop down, select False.

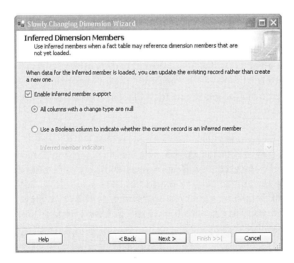

FIGURE 22.5   Setting up the Historical Attribute options.

34. Click the Next button, which takes you to the Inferred Dimension Members dialog box, shown in Figure 22.6.

35. Check the Enable Inferred Member Support check box.

36. Leave the All Columns with a Change Type Are Null option selected. This tells the SCD transform how to detect if a dimension record is an inferred record.

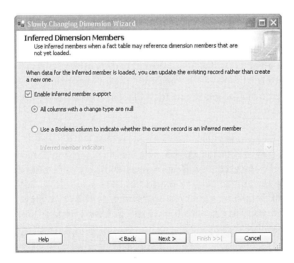

FIGURE 22.6   Enabling inferred dimension members.

37. Click the Next button, which takes you to the summary page.

38. Click the Finish button.

When you finish the wizard, it takes all the settings you've input and creates a data flow. If you've followed along with the preceding steps, the Slowly Changing Dimension Wizard generates a data flow similar to what is shown in Figure 22.7.

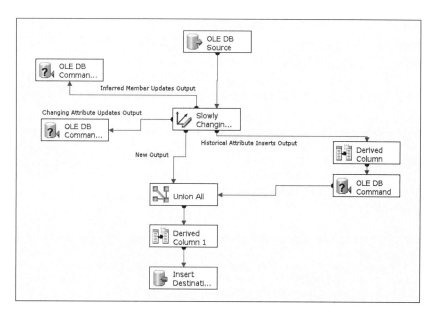

FIGURE 22.7   The data flow resulting from the Slowly Changing Dimension Wizard.

The Generated Data Flow

When you complete the Slowly Changing Dimension Wizard, you end up with a data flow that contains a Slowly Changing Dimension transform, with varying numbers of outputs going to various transforms and destination adapters. At execution time, the Slowly Changing Dimension transform plays the role of row diverter. By applying the rules established in the wizard, the SCD transform decides which output the source rows should flow down, letting the downstream data flow process the rows appropriately. Let's take a look at each of the resulting data flows that result from the settings you entered into the wizard.

The New Output Data Flow

The New Output data flow handles all new dimension rows. Depending upon whether your dimension table supports historical attribute change types, this output might vary. This is basically a straight insert into the dimension table after ensuring that the Current column is set correctly. In the previous example, the DimEmployee table does support the historical attribute change type, so the resulting data flow for the New Output has a Derived Column transformation to set the CurrentFlag column to TRUE.

The Historical Attribute Output Data Flow

The Historical Output data flow is similar to the New Output data flow because it is essentially doing the same thing—inserting a new record. The difference is that the historical attribute must change the last record current column to indicate that it is now expired. So, the additional data flow has an OLE DB Command transform that sets the current record to be expired with the following command:

```
UPDATE [dbo].[DimEmployee] SET [CurrentFlag] = ? WHERE
[EmployeeNationalIDAlternateKey] = ?
```

This sets the current dimension's CurrentFlag to FALSE and the key is the business key.

If you selected the option to set all historical attribute records to be expired in the wizard, the command has the following condition added:

```
UPDATE [dbo].[DimEmployee]
 SET [CurrentFlag] = ?
 WHERE [EmployeeNationalIDAlternateKey] = ?
 AND [CurrentFlag] = '1'
```

This ensures that when the new dimension record is inserted, only the new one will be considered current.

The rest of the data flow for the historical attribute is identical to the New Output and so is merged into the New Output data flow with a Union All.

Changing Attribute Updates Data Flow

The Changing Attribute Updates data flow is quite simple because all it is required to do is update the existing attribute in the given dimension record. Recall that you set the MaritalStatus attribute as the Changing Attribute change type. The resulting data flow is simply an OLE DB Command transform with the following update command:

```
UPDATE [dbo].[DimEmployee] SET [MaritalStatus] = ? WHERE
[EmployeeNationalIDAlternateKey] = ?
```

The MaritalStatus value is the new column value from the source and the key is the current business key.

Inferred Member Updates Data Flow

The records flowing down this output are bound for existing dimension records, so an update is in order. The OLE DB Command transform on this output performs the following UPDATE command:

```
UPDATE [dbo].[DimEmployee]
SET [BirthDate] = ?,
    [CurrentFlag] = ?,
```

```
    [Gender] = ?,
    [HireDate] = ?,
    [LoginID] = ?,
    [MaritalStatus] = ?,
    [SalariedFlag] = ?,
    [SickLeaveHours] = ?,
    [Title] = ?,
    [VacationHours] = ?
WHERE [EmployeeNationalIDAlternateKey] = ?
```

The attribute values are the new values from the source and the key is the current business key.

Fixed Attribute Output Data Flow

The Slowly Changing Dimension Wizard does not automatically generate any data flow for this output, but it might be sent to a destination or other transform to detect possible Type 3 change candidates or as a way to audit columns that should not be changing.

Unchanged Output Data Flow

The Slowly Changing Dimension Wizard does not automatically generate any data flow for this output because the SCD transform doesn't do any work for these rows. You can connect this output and the SCD transform pushes all the rows that were current to the output.

How the SCD Processes Rows

When you first run the Slowly Changing Dimension Wizard, you might be a bit overwhelmed when it generates up to six outputs, each with their own data flow. Previously, you examined the various data flows that the Slowly Changing Dimension Wizard automatically generated. Now let's take a look at how the SCD transform processes each incoming row. Figure 22.8 graphically shows the process the SCD transform uses for diverting rows down its various outputs and the expected processing that should occur for each output.

Performance Considerations

The primary design goals for the Slowly Changing Dimension Wizard and transform were to make the process of building robust SCD handling data flow quick and easy. As you can see, the Slowly Changing Dimension Wizard makes it easy to quickly build data flow for handling slowly changing dimensions and is useful for those wanting to quickly generate such packages. However, after you start dealing with larger dimensional datasets, you'll probably want to modify the automatically generated data flow to improve performance. The following are some optimizations you might consider for optimizing the generated SCD data flow.

FIGURE 22.8   Slowly Changing Dimension transformation processing steps.

Limiting the Dimension Recordset

When processing Type 2 slowly changing dimensions, the SCD transform performs a lookup for every incoming row to determine if there is an existing dimension. You can speed up the lookup by eliminating the number of records in the lookup. In fact, you can have the lookup performed on a different table, perhaps a temporary table with only one indexed column containing the subset of the alternate or surrogate keys that are currently active.

Staging Outputs

The Slowly Changing Dimension Wizard automatically generated data flow makes heavy use of the OLE DB Command transform. Although powerful and useful, this transform performs row-by-row operations, which can be very expensive. To eliminate the OLE DB Command transform, replace it with an OLE DB Destination and stage the data for both update rows and insert rows. Then, later in the workflow, execute separate INSERT and UPDATE commands using the staged data as the source. Because both INSERT and UPDATE statements allow you to join and compare two or more tables, you can conditionally update and insert rows as necessary. Ensure that you run the updates before the inserts. Running them concurrently can create locking issues.

Use a Lookup Transform Before the SCD Transform

Consider using a stock Lookup transform with partial caching turned on right before the SCD to quickly identify rows that don't exist in the dimension table. Those rows that do not exist can be directly inserted. This effectively eliminates the rows flowing through the New Output from the SCD transform and increases the efficiency of the SCD transform lookup step.

New Dimension Tables

When building a new dimension table, the SCD transform has a property named `IncomingRowChangeType` with the default value `Detect`. If the dimension table is empty, you can set this value to `AllNew` the first time you run the package and the SCD redirects all rows to the New Output.

The Slowly Changing Dimension transform provides a way to quickly and easily build complex dimension update data flow logic that is robust and customizable. The SCD transform supports four dimension change types, including changing, historic, fixed, and inferred member. For many applications, the Slowly Changing Dimension Wizard generated data flow is sufficient. However, if needed for increasingly large data loads, the SCD transform also lends itself well to optimizations.

Data Cleansing Components

The Fuzzy Lookup and Fuzzy Grouping components use fuzzy matching algorithms to provide fundamental features or primitives you can use to improve data quality of existing or new data. Together, these two transforms make possible a wide variety of data cleansing operations. The Fuzzy Lookup matches input records with misspellings, unexpected abbreviations, or other irregularities or nonconformant data with clean records in a reference table. The Fuzzy Grouping transform detects similarities between incoming records to find what appear to be duplicate rows. Both transforms use a custom, domain-independent distance algorithm developed by Microsoft Research. The algorithm takes into account the edit distance, token order, number of tokens, and relative frequencies capturing a more detailed structure of the source data. Because the algorithm is token based, it is not limited to a single language. The tokens are basically binary values that can be compared arithmetically. Finally, both transforms have a number of settings for controlling the resulting output and transform performance, so it's possible to tune the transforms to match the requirements of your environment.

Fuzzy Lookup

The Fuzzy Lookup transform makes it possible to look up terms that are close but not exact matches to reference terms. Table 22.6 contains the transform profile.

TABLE 22.6   The Fuzzy Lookup Transform Profile

Property	Value	Description
Component Type	Transform	
Has Custom Designer	Yes	
Internal File I/O	No	
Output Types	Asynchronous	
Threading	Single	
Managed	No	
Number Outputs	1	
Number Inputs	1	
Requires Connection Manager	Yes	OLEDB to reference table.
Supports Error Routing	No	
Constraints	Copies reference table	For large reference tables, the startup time can be substantial.

Figure 22.9 shows a typical use of the Fuzzy Lookup transformation. Because the Lookup transform performs exact match lookups only, if there are slight deviations in the source data from the reference table, the lookup fails. Using the Fuzzy Lookup transform downstream on the Lookup transform error output, you can salvage some of the lookups that failed because the Fuzzy Lookup applies an inexact matching algorithm to determine if a string column is a close approximation of the reference column. To see the package shown in Figure 22.9, open the `FuzzyLookup.dtsx` package in the S21-Advanced sample solution. This sample package uses a sample flat file generated from the contacts table, with some errors introduced into the data, as the source and the contacts table from the AdventureWorks database is the reference data.

NOTE

The Fuzzy Lookup transform only supports input columns of type `DT_WSTR` or `DT_STR` for fuzzy matching, but supports any SSIS data type except `DT_TEXT`, `DT_NTEXT`, and `DT_IMAGE`.

Setting Up the Fuzzy Lookup

Fuzzy Lookup uses what is called the Error-Tolerant Index (ETI) to find matching rows in the reference table. The ETI is an index on a column created to hold a set of tokens that represent the values for each record in the reference table. During runtime, Fuzzy Lookup essentially tokenizes the source rows, compares the tokenized values to the values in the ETI, and derives the similarity and confidence values based on the comparison.

Building the ETI   Depending on the settings you have selected, during the PreExecute phase of the Data Flow Task, the Fuzzy Lookup transform copies the reference table and adds an additional column for storing the tokens for each row and builds the ETI. This can be nontrivial for very large reference tables, so the Fuzzy Lookup transform provides options for storing the ETI on the server and reusing it at a later date.

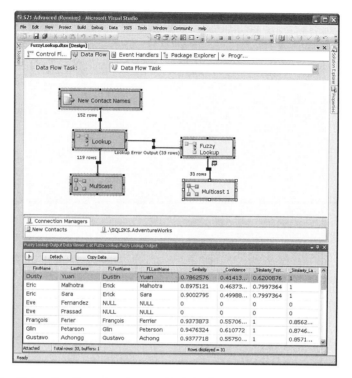

FIGURE 22.9   Using the Fuzzy Lookup to find duplicate names.

The index options shown in Figure 22.10 provide a way to store the index table for later use or update it as changes are made to the reference data. These are the options:

- **Generate New Index**—Use this if your reference data is fairly small. This option copies the table and generates the ETI every time you run the package.

- **Store New Index**—If you plan to use an existing index, you need to run the package with this setting once to generate the index. Then, you can change the setting to one of the following two options to use the generated table and index.

- **Use Existing Index**—This option is for using a reference table you created with the Store New Index option. Select this option when the reference data is fairly static.

- **Maintain Stored Index**—This option is the same as using an existing index, only the Fuzzy Lookup creates a trigger on the reference table to update the index table any time the reference data changes.

When you select one of these options, you receive a warning in the bottom yellow message area, as follows: Connection manager attributes have changed. The mappings of previous columns are no longer valid. **To eliminate the error, go to the Columns tab and remap the columns.**

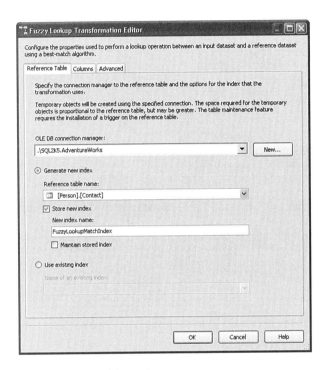

FIGURE 22.10   The Reference Table options.

Setting Up Columns   After you have the reference table set up, you need to set up the columns. The Columns tab allows you to specify which columns you want to fuzzy match and which columns you want to flow to the outputs. As you can see in Figure 22.9, Fuzzy Lookup provides overall similarity and confidence values for each row and similarity values per fuzzy matched columns.

The question often comes up, "What is the difference between similarity and confidence?" Similarity has to do with how close the reference word is to the value. For example, John and Jon are very similar because there is only a one letter difference. John and nohj would be similar as well, because both words have the exact same number of letters and all the letters are the same, but because the algorithm for gauging similarity takes distance, characters, and order into account, Jon would be considered more similar to John than nohj would. Similarity, therefore, is a measure of the differences between the reference word and the value.

Confidence is more related to the uniqueness of the reference word in the reference set. If the name John Smith were to occur several times in the reference set, any exact matches would still have a low confidence score because the algorithm cannot detect which John Smith in the reference table is intended. So, even though the similarity may be 100%, the confidence might still be low.

You can use these results to set minimal bars of acceptance for dirty data and for mapping the dirty data rows back to clean reference data. Figure 22.11 shows the settings from the FuzzyLookup.dtsx sample package. Notice also that the FirstName, LastName columns and their output aliases FLFirstName and FLLastName are the output columns from the Fuzzy Lookup shown in the Data Viewer in Figure 22.9.

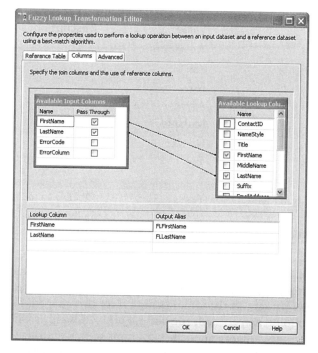

FIGURE 22.11 Creating the column matches and configuring the output.

Tokenizing the Reference Data and the Similarity Threshold The values in the reference data are divided into tokens based on the tokens specified in the Additional Delimiters field on the Advanced tab. For example, if you want to index the string 24^3 instead of 24 and 3, you should remove the ^ character from the list of delimiters.

The similarity threshold is the level of similarity that you're willing to accept as a match. Where to set this value is dependent on your requirements and data. Rows that have similarity values at or above the similarity threshold will pass through with the reference data in the Output column. For example, the FLFirstName and FLLastName from the sample package shown in Figure 22.9 are the results from the Fuzzy Lookup. Those rows that do not meet the similarity threshold have NULLs as the lookup values. Setting the threshold is a trial-and-error iterative process. Run the package against sample data and adjust the threshold based on the results. If there are too many dirty rows accepted, raise the threshold. If there are not enough rows accepted, lower the threshold. Repeat until you're satisfied with the results. You can also allow Fuzzy Lookup to return more than one match per lookup.

The Fuzzy Grouping Transform

The Fuzzy Grouping transform makes it possible to identify possible duplicate terms that are close but not exact matches. Table 22.7 contains the transform profile.

TABLE 22.7   The Fuzzy Grouping Transform Profile

Property	Value	Description
Component Type	Transform	
Has Custom Designer	Yes	
Internal File I/O	No	
Output Types	Asynchronous	
Threading	Multiple	
Managed	No	
Number Outputs	1	
Number Inputs	1	
Requires Connection Manager	Yes	OLEDB to location for temporary tables
Supports Error Routing	No	

Although the Fuzzy Lookup transform is useful for finding correct values for corrupt or dirty data, Fuzzy Grouping is useful for finding duplicated values. Figure 22.12 shows the FuzzyGrouping.dtsx package in the sample solution for this chapter. Notice the output from the Fuzzy Grouping transform in the bottom grid. Those rows with a _score and _similarity value of 1 are cases where the key columns were identical. The rows with _score and _similarity less than 1 are rows where the key columns were only similar.

Whereas naïve approaches such as the following script might work for simple exact match elimination, duplicated data is rarely so clean nor lends itself so well to such elimination techniques. In fact, typically, it is the other way around. Duplicate data is often duplicated when entered into the source system because source entry verification systems frequently use exact match or SOUNDEX checks that are confounded by simple differences in critical columns. Thus, using similar exact matching techniques for deduplication fail for the same reason they fail at the source, making exact matching elimination techniques of limited use.

```
DELETE FROM [dbo].[contact]
WHERE fname=@fname
  AND lname=@lname
  AND address=@address
```

Using the Fuzzy Grouping transform, you can identify both identical and *similar* rows, which you can process in downstream data flow to determine if the rows indeed represent the same business entity and, therefore, should be eliminated.

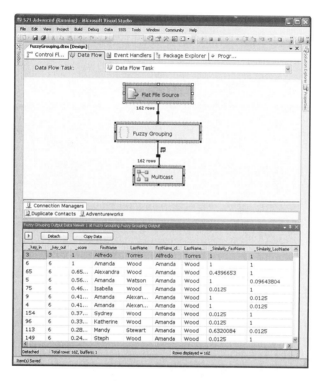

FIGURE 22.12   Grouping like rows together with the Fuzzy Grouping transform.

Setting Up the Fuzzy Grouping Transform

The Fuzzy Grouping transform uses the same underlying technology as the Fuzzy Lookup transform. In fact, under the covers, the Fuzzy Grouping transform builds a Data Flow Task with a Fuzzy Lookup inside to build an ETI table used to determine the similarity values between multiple rows. Consequently, many of the settings for the Fuzzy Grouping transform will look familiar to you after having just read about the Fuzzy Lookup transform.

At runtime, the Fuzzy Grouping transform adds three key fields to the output stream:

- _key_in—The reference key column generated key
- _key_out—The generated key for another reference key from the same input set the fuzzy grouping considers a match according to the similarity threshold setting
- _score—The similarity between the _key_in and _key_out values

The Connection Manager

Figure 22.13 shows the Fuzzy Grouping Transformation Editor Connection Manager tab. This is where you specify where the transform will create the temporary tables the transformation uses.

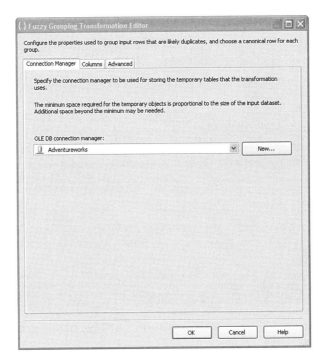

FIGURE 22.13   Selecting the connection manager.

The Key Columns

Figure 22.14 shows the Columns tab where you specify the key columns to use for grouping input rows. The transform does not reference the pass-through rows when grouping the rows, they simply pass through. However, pass-through rows can be useful for distinguishing between rows that are duplicates and those that simply have the same values for the key columns. For example, there might be more than one contact with the name Eve Fernandez. You could use the pass-through columns such as telephone number, birthdate, mother's maiden name, and so on to distinguish between duplicate records of the identical person versus records with identical or similar key values for different people.

FIGURE 22.14   Selecting the input columns.

The Advanced Settings

Figure 22.15 shows the Advanced tab. You can change the name of the columns used to store the keys and similarity score here. You can also change the similarity threshold. The higher the threshold, the more similar the key values must be to be considered duplicates. Finally, the token delimiters are the same as for the Fuzzy Lookup transform. They provide a way to tune how the key values are tokenized.

What to Do with Groups

Great, so you've got groups of rows now. You might be asking yourself, "What do I do with them?" A good example is householding. Simply stated, householding is the process of discovering which of your contacts lives together. This is useful for things like determining if a parent is using a child's name to qualify for more than the per household purchase limit in a limited item sale, target marketing based on family structure, or determining which investors reside at the same address so that a single prospectus or other financial report can be sent to multiple investors at that same address.

Depending on the quality and shape of your data, this might be easy or difficult. For example, if all the addresses in the reference data are up to date and accurate, it should be fairly easy to determine which of your customers live together. Using columns such as age, last moved date, and marital status can help with these kinds of problems as well. For example, people get divorced. If the old address data for one of your contacts implies they were once living with another of your contacts, but the newer data for one contact shows a marital status of divorced with a new address, you could bias the data processing to favor creating a new household for the divorced individual.

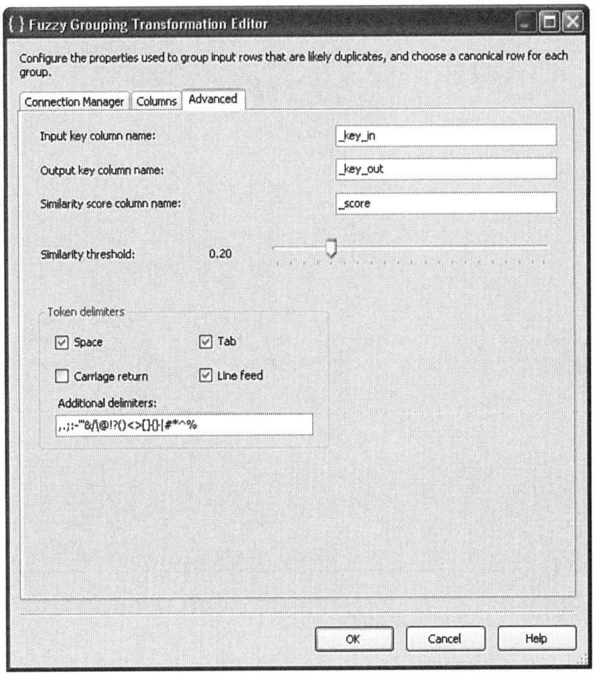

FIGURE 22.15   Selecting the advanced settings.

To find contacts within the same household, you can group by last name. Family members don't always have the same last name, but it's a good start. If you have a Spouse Name column, you can fuzzy match the spouse name with the first name. This might seem a bit odd, but remember, you're not trying to build a clean record of individuals, but rather a single record entity representing a household. Taken together with other fields like address, cross matching helps you find relationships between rows that would otherwise be impossible.

The similarities between all the columns are what constitutes the overall similarity score. After you've configured the column matching, you can set the similarity threshold by iteratively setting, testing, and adjusting it until you arrive at a similarity threshold value that seems to generate the most correct results with the sample data. Then, you can use a Fuzzy Lookup transform on the output of the Fuzzy Grouping transform to look up the house address and other columns as available to arrive at a common address for each of the members of the household. The fuzzy comparison capabilities provide a way to build robust data cleansing solutions using state-of-the-art algorithms for identifying similarities in dirty data. Both transforms support multiple configurable settings for adjusting the parsing, tokenizing, and similarity threshold settings to better adjust the transforms to your business needs. Used separately and together, the Fuzzy Lookup and Fuzzy Grouping transforms can perform a wide range of data cleansing duties.

Text Mining and Document Warehousing Components

Traditional Business Intelligence (BI) processes revolve around managing structured data such as numbers, dates, product and people names, addresses, and other well-structured values that can be aggregated and indexed. Such data is useful for determining what happened, when it happened, and the circumstances and location where it occurred. However, what traditional BI doesn't tell you is why it happened. Document warehousing is concerned with the why behind transactions and trends, and the Term Extraction and Term Lookup transforms provide the primitives for building document warehouses.

The Problem with Text

Text is all around us. The most obvious source is the Internet, but beyond that are other rich and, in some cases, more valuable data, such as whitepapers, patent applications, email, analyst reports, legal briefs, product specifications, financial prospectuses, newspaper articles, and even marketing Fear, Uncertainty, and Doubt (FUD). In many ways, these sources of information are much more helpful than historical data in predicting future trends and supporting decisions. The problem is how to turn the mountains of available nonstructured text into a thematic, accurate, indexable, and relevant archive of searchable summarized data.

The answer, at least in part, is the Term Extraction and Term Lookup transforms, which provide primitives upon which you can build a data warehousing toolbox.

Thematic Categorization

The Term Extraction transform makes it possible to build sets of theme keywords from documents that are representative of a given technology, industry, or other subject area and save them into a reference table. Then, the Term Lookup transform makes it possible to extract the theme keywords from the documents and categorize them according to the frequency of the occurrence of theme keywords.

Creating Indexes

Documents are only useful if you can find them, hence the importance of indexes. The Term Extraction transform uses smart algorithms for extracting significant nouns or noun phrases from text that can be stored in tables and indexed, providing quick access to documents.

Summarizing Text

Summaries are similar to indexes in the way they are built, but instead of each extracted word being stored in a table as an individual record, summaries are collections of extracted words and are meant to be read together with other words, extracted from the same document, to describe the contents of the document.

Relevance

From a human perspective, relevance can be measured intuitively. After reading a sentence or two, it is usually pretty easy to distinguish between a document about Formula 1 *drivers* and a document about video *drivers*. However, for software it's a little more complicated. Term frequency-inverse document frequency (tf-idf) is a way to weight a given term's relevance in a set of documents. *Term frequency* measures the importance of a term within a particular document based on the number of times it occurs relative to the number of all terms in a given document. *Inverse document frequency* is a measure of the importance of a term based upon its occurrence in all documents in a collection. The importance of a term increases with the number of times it appears in a document but is offset by the frequency of the term in all of the documents in the collection. For the previously mentioned set of documents about Formula 1 drivers and video drivers, the word *drivers* is pretty important. However, in those documents that discuss Formula 1 drivers, you would find a very small to negligent incidence of the word *video* and, likewise, for the documents about video drivers, you would find a very small to negligent incidence of the term *Formula 1*. Using the Term Extraction transform and tf-idf weighting, your packages can distinguish between documents about Formula 1 drivers and video drivers.

Term Extraction

The Term Extraction transform makes it possible to extract key terms from nonformatted text. Table 22.8 contains the transform profile.

TABLE 22.8   The Term Extraction Transform Profile

Property	Value	Description
Component Type	Transform	
Has Custom Designer	Yes	
Internal File I/O	No	
Output Types	Asynchronous	
Threading	Single	
Managed	No	
Number Outputs	1	
Number Inputs	1	
Requires Connection Manager	Yes	To exclusion terms
Supports Error Routing	Yes	

The Term Extraction transform currently works only with English text and can be configured to extract nouns, noun phrases, or both nouns and noun phases. A noun is defined as a single noun word. A noun phrase is at least two words, one of which is a noun and the other is a noun or an adjective. The Term Extraction transform ignores articles and pronouns and normalizes words so that the capitalized, noncapitalized, and plural versions of a noun are considered identical.

The Term Extraction Transformation Editor

Figure 22.16 shows the Term Extraction tab of the Term Extraction Transformation Editor. The Term Extraction transform output has only two columns.

- **Term**—Contains the extracted terms

- **Score**—Contains the score for the terms

Because multiple terms can be extracted per input row, there are usually many more output rows than input rows.

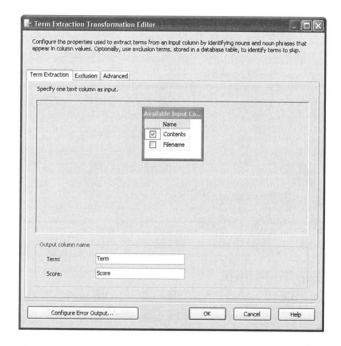

FIGURE 22.16   Setting up the columns.

The Exclusion tab lets you create or select a connection manager to a SQL Server or Access database, table, and column that contains the set of words that the Term Extraction transform should ignore. By adding words to the specified column, you can eliminate them from the term extraction results.

Figure 22.17 shows the Advanced tab where you can tune the term extraction. The Term Type options let you control the types of terms that will be returned in the resultset. The Score Type options allow you to select simple frequency-based score options or the more complex tf-idf scoring algorithm. The Parameters options allow you to control the frequency and length thresholds. For a term to be returned in the resultset, it must occur at least the number of times specified in the Frequency Threshold field. The Maximum Length of Term setting is only enabled when Noun Phrase or Noun and Noun Phrase term types are selected. Finally, check the Use Case-Sensitive Term Extraction check box when you want to retain term and word case.

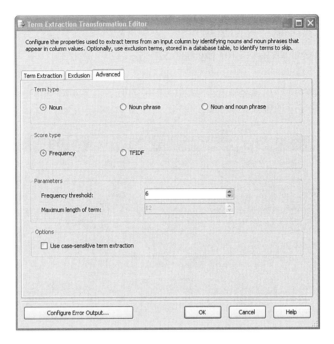

FIGURE 22.17   Use the Advanced tab to tune term extraction.

The Term Lookup Transform

The Term Lookup transform makes it possible to find terms within text and measure the frequency that they occur. Table 22.9 contains the transform profile.

TABLE 22.9   The Term Lookup Transform Profile

Property	Value	Description
Component Type	Transform	
Has Custom Designer	Yes	
Internal File I/O	No	
Output Types	Asynchronous	
Threading	Single	
Managed	No	
Number Outputs	1	
Number Inputs	1	
Requires Connection Manager	Yes	To reference table
Supports Error Routing	Yes	

The Term Lookup transform matches terms in a reference table with terms found in text columns. Using the same method as the Term Extraction transform, the Term Lookup extracts terms from a text column and then attempts to look up the terms in the reference table. The output of the Term Lookup is the columns selected as pass-through columns and the term and frequency. The Term Lookup transform can also be configured to perform case-sensitive matches.

CAUTION

Multiple term and frequency values can be returned from the same row so that for each term and frequency value returned, each pass-through value is duplicated. For large text columns, this can increase the memory usage considerably. Only include pass-through columns if absolutely needed and then be aware of the cost associated with the duplicated values.

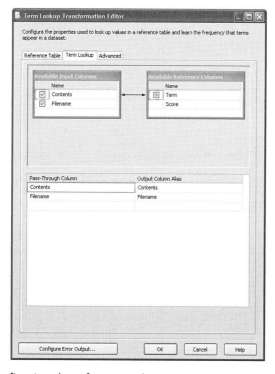

FIGURE 22.18   Configuring the reference columns.

Summary

The components described here are only available in the Enterprise Edition, except the SCD transform, and provide advanced functionality above and beyond typical data transformation. Using these transforms, you can clean and conform data, build a toolbox of packages for categorizing and warehousing documents, and quickly create packages for maintaining slowly changing dimensions.

Data Flow Task Internals and Tuning

"QUICKER THAN A GREASED WEASEL."—EUAN GARDEN

The Data Flow Task is performant by design such that out of the box, without any tuning or optimization, the default settings generally deliver great performance. For less complex data flows, that is data flows with five or six components with small data loads of a gigabyte or less, the default settings are typically sufficient for most applications and do not require any special tuning. However, large and complex data flow loads bring their own challenges and there are often more trade-offs and decisions that need to be made that the Data Flow Task cannot make for the user or over which it has no control.

This chapter starts by describing important Data Flow Task concepts you should understand for the tuning discussion and then proceeds to describe specific ways you can get even more performance using simple settings. These are called turnkey settings because there isn't a lot of measurement or process involved when deciding to use them and the benefits from the settings can usually be seen immediately. The section "An Approach to Data Flow Optimization" discusses a general approach you can use for identifying and resolving performance issues and squeezing every last ounce of performance from the Data Flow Task.

Data Flow Task Under the Hood

Any discussion about tuning the Data Flow Task necessarily starts from the Data Flow Task internals. To truly understand what's happening with data flow performance, you should be familiar with some important data flow concepts.

General Concepts

The Data Flow Task is actually a combination of various subsystems that interact through interfaces. Each subsystem is responsible for managing different aspects of the data flow behavior and is categorized into design time and execution time features. This chapter focuses on the execution time features because they have the most impact upon the performance of the data flow. Figure 23.1 shows a high-level system view of the Data Flow Task.

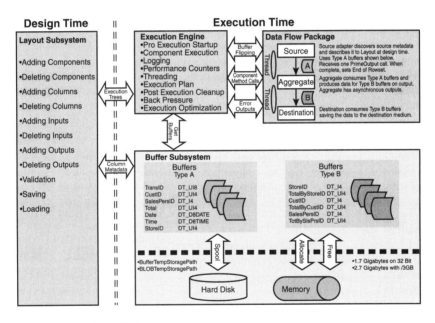

FIGURE 23.1 Data Flow Task system view.

As you can see, there are four major components of interest to this discussion, as follows:

- **Layout Subsystem**—Interacts with the designer and components to provide the design time configuration experience.

- **Buffers**—Contain the data as it flows from the source to the destination.

- **Buffer Subsystem**—Manages memory allocation, buffer creation, and spooling.

- **Execution Engine**—Manages buffer "movement," execution planning, threads, and component calls. In short, this is Data Flow Task execution central, where it all comes together.

Layout Subsystem

The Layout Subsystem is the design time logic for the Data Flow Task. When you create a data flow in the designer, you are using this subsystem. Layout communicates with the Execution Engine and Buffer Subsystem by providing descriptions of the data flow from which the Execution Engine can build execution trees and the Buffer Subsystem can build buffers.

Buffers

Buffers are objects with associated chunks of memory that contain the data to be transformed. As data flows through the Data Flow Task, it lives in a buffer from the time that the source adapter reads it until the time that the destination adapter writes it. Generally speaking, data flow components use buffers for all their major memory needs, including privately created buffers for internal processing. Buffer objects contain pointers to column offsets and methods for accessing their memory chunks. The size and shape of a buffer is determined by several factors:

- Source metadata
- `DefaultBufferMaxRows` property on Data Flow Task
- `DefaultBufferSize` property on Data Flow Task
- `MaxBufferSize/MinBufferSize` internal values
- Buffer width

Source Metadata

If you've worked with the Data Flow Task at all, you're probably aware that it is very metadata dependent. In other words, it generally requires a connection to a server, flat file, or other source before you can start building the data flow. The origin of this metadata dependence is the buffer.

> **NOTE**
>
> One of the reasons the Data Flow Task is so fast is because there is little type ambiguity in the buffer, so very little memory is wasted on unused allocated buffer space and there is little pointer math needed to access a given cell in a buffer. Some users have decried the tight binding between metadata and the data flow because they would like to build more dynamic data flows that adjust to the metadata of the source on the fly. Although there have been long discussions about the legitimacy and value of such a feature, it is clear that the Data Flow Task was designed for optimal loading of big data and dynamically configuring itself to changing metadata was not within the original design goals. Perhaps, in future versions it will be added.

Figure 23.2 shows a simplistic representation of the structure of a buffer in memory.

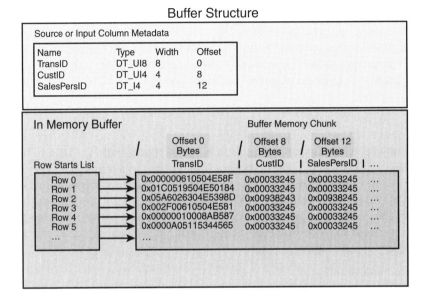

FIGURE 23.2   Data flow buffer system view.

Note the correspondence between the source or output column metadata types and the data column types in the buffer memory. Also note the row starts list. There is more to a buffer than the diagram shows, of course. The point to understand is that, on a simple level, the Data Flow Task is allocating memory to hold data and that components have access to the memory through methods provided on the buffer object.

DefaultBufferMaxRows

This setting controls the maximum allowable number of rows in a buffer and defaults to 10,000.

DefaultBufferSize

This is the default size of the buffer in bytes. The default is 10MB.

MaxBufferSize

This setting is internal and cannot be changed by the user and is the maximum allowable size for a buffer in bytes. In the release version of Integration Services 2005, this value was set to 100MB. The Data Flow Task will refuse to create buffers any larger than this to prevent wasting memory on empty buffers. If you attempt to increase DefaultMaxBufferSize to a value greater than MaxBufferSize, you will get an error similar to the following:

```
Could not set the property value: Error at Data Flow Task [DTS.Pipeline]: The
default buffer size must be between 1048576 and 104857600 bytes. An attempt
was made to set the DefaultBufferSize property to a value that is too small
or too large.
```

`MinBufferSize`

This setting is the minimum allowable size of the buffer. By default, this value is the same as the allocation granularity for memory pages, usually 64K. The reason for this minimum is that memory operations are more efficient when memory is allocated in sizes with granularity the same as the virtual memory page size.

Buffer Width

The buffer width is the total number of bytes required to hold a row plus alignment adjustments. The row width is the sum of the widths of data types for all columns in the row. A row with two 8-byte integers (16), a 25-character Unicode string (50), and a Boolean (2) will be 68 bytes wide. The actual in-memory buffer row width might be wider than the actual data row width if the data row width does not align with the machine word boundary or if the buffer will contain copied columns.

Putting the Buffer Settings Together

The Data Flow Task only takes the `MaxBuffer` property values as suggestions and attempts to match those settings as well as can be done without compromising the performance of the data flow. Also, buffers are rarely exactly the same size as described by the properties because of various memory requirements, such as VirtualAlloc page allocation granularity and the need to align allocated memory structures on machine word boundaries.

Given these settings and their defaults, there are a few things you already know about the size and shape of buffers. First, buffers have a maximum size of 100MB and a minimum size of 64KB. By default, the buffers are 10MB in size and have no more than 10,000 rows per buffer. That much is clear.

What happens if the settings conflict? For example, if the size of a buffer (BufferWidth * DefaultMaxBufferRows) exceeds the `DefaultMaxBufferSize` setting? The Buffer Subsystem decreases the number of rows per buffer. What if the size of a buffer is less than `MinBufferSize`? The Buffer Subsystem increases the number of rows per buffer to meet the `MinBufferSize` setting. If the buffer size is between the minimum and maximum buffer size settings, the Buffer Subsystem attempts to allocate memory so as to match the number of rows requested. Generally speaking, the number of rows setting yields to the buffer size setting and is always rounded to page granularity.

Buffer Subsystem

The Buffer Subsystem manages memory for the Data Flow Task. It communicates with the Layout Subsystem to determine the shape of buffers, allocates memory, generates buffer types, creates and deletes buffers, detects low memory conditions, and responds to low memory conditions by spooling to disk if necessary. It also communicates with the Layout Subsystem to discover metadata and build appropriate buffer types to hold data rows during execution.

Execution Engine

The Execution Engine is at the heart of the data flow execution time behavior. It creates threads, plans executions, calls the various methods on components at the appropriate time and on the appropriate threads, logs output, and handles errors.

To graphically illustrate how the Execution Engine plans the work it will do, Figure 23.3 shows the Aggregate.dtsx package from the S19-StockComponents sample solution with the component, input, and output IDs added to the names.

> **NOTE**
>
> Every object in the data flow is assigned an ID that is unique within the scope of the Data Flow Task. These IDs are how the Data Flow Task internally references all objects, including components, columns, inputs, and outputs.

Adding the input and output IDs in this manner is not something you would typically do, but it helps make the connection between the package data flow and the output the Execution Engine produces.

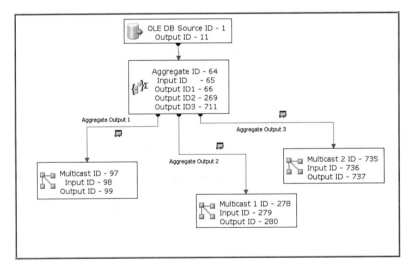

FIGURE 23.3   A data flow annotated with the object IDs.

The data flow itself is very simplistic but ideal because, even though it is quite simple, it produces a fairly interesting and representative execution plan and execution trees and will be instrumental for exploring Execution Engine planning.

Execution Plans

At execution time, one of the first things the Execution Engine does is get the layout information from the Layout Subsystem. This is all the information about inputs, outputs, columns, sources, transforms, and destinations. Then, it builds an execution plan, which is essentially a list of operation codes, or opcodes for short. Each opcode represents a certain operation that the Execution Engine must perform.

Figure 23.4 shows the execution plan for the sample package as viewed in the Log Entry dialog box. To open this dialog box, double-click on any log event in the Log Event window.

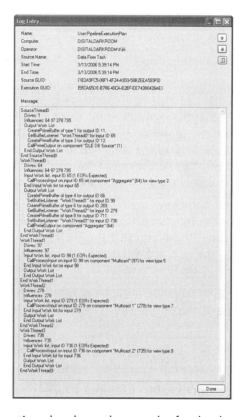

FIGURE 23.4 The execution plan shows the opcodes for the data flow.

There is a lot of information provided in the execution plan and it can be a little confusing at times. However, if you take a little time to understand execution plans, you'll learn a lot about the internals of the Execution Engine. Walk through the plan starting from the top.

The "SourceThread0" Entry   There are three types of threads in the Execution Engine:

- Administrative threads
- Source threads
- Worker threads

Administrative threads are hidden from you. They are the threads that do all the Execution Engine management. Although they are extremely important to the inner workings of the Execution Engine, they are never exposed to the user in the execution plan, and so forth. They are mentioned here simply as a point of interest.

Source threads, as their name implies, are created exclusively for the outputs of sources. When the Execution Engine is ready to have the source adapters start filling buffers with data, it calls the source adapter's `PrimeOutput` method on the source thread. The `PrimeOutput` calls on source adapters blocks. In other words, the call does not return until the source adapter is finished adding rows to the buffer provided in the `PrimeOutput` call.

Worker threads are used for everything else.

The "Drives: 1" Entry   The drives entry lists the components that the given thread drives. In this case, SourceThread0 drives the component with the ID of 1, or the OLE DB Source. What this means is that the methods of the listed components are called from the thread. So, if you look down the execution plan to the other "Drives" entries, and then compare the ID listed with the view of the data flow in Figure 23.3, you can quickly see which components are "driven" by which thread. WorkerThread0 drives the Aggregate with ID 64. WorkerThread1 drives Multicast with the ID 97, and so forth.

The "Influences" Entry   The influences list contains the IDs of those components that are impacted by the work done on the given thread. In this case, all the downstream components are influenced by SourceThread0 because it is such a simple data flow graph. However, this is not always the case and will definitely not be the case for separate data flow graphs within the same Data Flow Task.

Output Work List   The output work list is the set of opcodes that need to be executed on the given thread. For example, the output work list for SourceThread0 contains the following steps:

1. **CreatePrimeBuffer of type 1 for output ID 11**—Create a new buffer for output 11, which is the output for the OLE DB Source Adapter.

2. **SetBufferListener: "WorkThread0" for input ID 65**—Create a new thread to handle the input from the source. Input ID is the Aggregate input.

3. **CreatePrimeBuffer for output ID 12**—This is the error output for the OLE DB Source.

4. **CallPrimeOutput on Component "OLE DB Source"(1)**—This is the method call that kicks off the data flow execution and is the blocking call to the source for retrieving the data into the buffers.

You should be able to read the rest of the execution plan now because the rest of the entries are very similar to the SourceThread0 entry. By matching the execution plan entries and opcodes with the IDs in the package, you can see exactly what work the Execution Engine plans to do on each thread.

Execution Trees

Execution trees are where the output type, buffers, and threads come together to create opportunities for tuning the data flow. To see the execution tree output for a given package, enable the `PipelineExecutionTrees` log event. This log entry is similar to the execution plan log entry but a bit scaled down and only shows the relationship between the outputs and inputs in the data flow. As you'll see later in this chapter, execution trees can greatly impact data flow performance. Figure 23.5 shows the execution trees for the sample data flow in Figure 23.3.

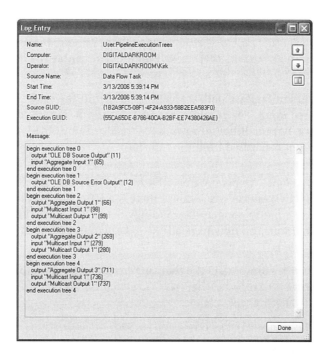

FIGURE 23.5   The execution trees' output shows each thread's inputs and outputs.

The execution trees for the sample package are trivial because it's such a simple package, but execution tree size has no theoretical limits and in practice can contain anywhere from one to tens of output/input pairings.

Although it's fairly easy to look at the execution trees' log output and see where each execution tree is on the data flow, it isn't so easy to understand how the execution trees are defined. A review of output types is in order.

Synchronous Outputs   You will recall that synchronous outputs for a given component use the same buffer type as one of the transforms inputs. Transforms with synchronous outputs generally do not copy memory, but rather modify the data within the buffer where it resides and process each buffer row by row in the order in which they arrive on the input. Synchronous outputs can add additional columns to the input buffers. If they do, the columns will exist on the buffer even before needed. For example, an execution tree containing a Derived Column transform will have additional columns in the buffer for the additional column or columns generated by the Derived Column transform and will only be visible to the Derived Column transform and all that follow it. Another way you can tell if an output is synchronous is it will have a nonzero value for its SynchronousInputID property. Asynchronous outputs have zero for this property value.

Asynchronous Outputs   Also recall that asynchronous outputs copy memory because they populate buffers of a different type than any of the inputs of the same component. There are two factors that cause an output to be asynchronous:

- The output creates data for a new buffer type. For example, the aggregate might release data from its outputs that doesn't remotely resemble the data on any of its inputs.

- The output does not release data at the same rate or in the same order as it appears on its associated input. For example, the Sort transform output buffers have the same metadata, but the inbound rows are all retained until the last one and then the sorted output is released from the transform.

Execution Tree Definitions   Depending on whom you ask, you'll get different definitions of what constitutes an execution tree because there is a lot of confusion about it and an individual must have a pretty good understanding of the Data Flow Task internals to understand the definition. You now have all the information you need to understand what an execution tree is.

An execution tree is a section of data flow starting from an asynchronous output and terminating at inputs on transforms that have no synchronous outputs. Some examples might help to clarify the concept.

Source → Derived Column → Data Conversion → Sort → Destination

Ignoring error outputs, the preceding data flow has two execution trees. Sources are always asynchronous because there is no input for the output. The Derived Column has synchronous outputs as well as the Data Conversion transform. However the Sort has asynchronous outputs and, so, the first execution tree starts at the Source output and ends at the Sort input. The second execution tree starts at the Sort output and ends at the Destination.

Here's another example:

```
Source1->Sort1 \
                 ¦---> Merge ->Aggregate->Destination
Source2->Sort2 /
```

In the preceding data flow, there are exactly six execution trees.

- Source1 Output → Sort1 Input

- Source2 Output → Sort2 Input

- Sort1 Output → Merge Input

- Sort2 Output → Merge Input

- Merge Output → Aggregate Input

- Aggregate Output → Destination

Another way to think about execution trees is what they share in common. With the exception of those including sources, which have their own dedicated thread, transforms on the same execution tree share the same execution thread. They also share the same buffer type. However, as you'll soon discover, all the columns on a buffer are not always visible to all transforms on the same execution tree.

So, why does it matter? Why all this energy to describe execution trees? As it turns out, execution trees are an important concept to understand when tuning data flows. Execution trees are revisited later in this chapter in the "Turnkey Settings for Speedup" section.

Engine Threads   Engine threads are almost synonymous with execution trees. In the data flow shown previously, there are six threads, plus one thread that the runtime provides to the Data Flow Task. Remember that source threads block, so they are exclusively dedicated to the processing of sources. There is generally one thread for every execution tree. The formula for estimating threads needed for a given data flow is as follows:

number of threads = sources + execution trees

Understanding the threading is helpful when tuning data flows to more fully utilize a machine's available resources.

That's a quick primer on the Data Flow Task internals. There is a lot more, of course. This discussion just scratched the surface. You could write a whole book just about the Data Flow Task and someone probably will. However, what is covered here should be sufficient to understand the following discussions about how to tune your data flows.

Turnkey Settings for Speedup

In this section, you'll find a collection of straightforward methods and hints for data flow speedup. The Data Flow Task provides a number of settings and options you can use to eliminate unnecessary work or to diminish the amount of data that must flow through it. Some of these methods involve simple property settings; others are a bit more complex. In addition, you can do a number of things in the environment outside the Data Flow Task to speed up data flow, which are mentioned in this section as well. Although these methods are presented as a series of "do's and don'ts," understand that not every tip applies to every situation and that the items presented here are only guidelines, not hard rules that must always be followed. Knowing when to apply which rules is a matter of experience grown from testing and measuring the results.

Eliminating Unnecessary Work

Often, you might find that the best data flow optimization you can achieve is to simply eliminate work the Data Flow Task must do. Eliminating work is almost always preferable to making the Data Flow Task faster because you get a 100% speedup for every bit of work you eliminate. The following tips describe ways to eliminate work from the Data Flow Task.

Optimize the Sources

Most of the optimizations for eliminating unnecessary work have something to do with eliminating the data coming from the sources. Following are a few ways to eliminate unnecessary data from entering into the data flow.

Remove Unneeded Columns   Unneeded columns are columns that never get referenced in the data flow. The Execution Engine emits warnings for unused columns, so they are easy to identify. This makes the buffer rows narrower. The narrower the row, the more rows that can fit into one buffer and the more efficiently the rows can be processed. Binary Large Objects (BLOBs) are particularly burdensome to the Data Flow Task and should be eliminated if at all possible. Use the queries in the source adapters to eliminate unnecessary columns.

Use a SQL Select Statement to Retrieve Data from a View   Avoid using the *Table or view* access mode in the OLE DB Source Adapter. It is not as performant as using a SELECT statement because the adapter opens a rowset based on the table or view. Then, it calls OpenRowset in the validation phase to retrieve column metadata and later in the execution phase to read out the data.

Testing has shown that using a SELECT statement can be at least an order of magnitude faster because the adapter issues the specified command directly through the provider and fetches the data using sp_prepare without executing the command, avoiding the extra round-trip and a possibly inappropriate cached query plan.

Optimize Source Queries   Using traditional query optimization techniques, optimize the source adapter SQL query. SSIS doesn't optimize the query on your behalf, but passes it on verbatim.

Use Flat File and Other File Sources   Retrieving data from file sources presents its own set of performance challenges because the data is typically in some format that requires conversion. For example, the Jet Provider only supports a limited set of data types when reading Excel files and flat-file data is always of type String until converted. The following sections discuss a few hints for how to eliminate unnecessary data flow work.

Combine Adjacent Unneeded Flat-File Columns   In fixed-width flat files, combine unused columns into one. This eliminates the parsing necessary for the unused columns.

Leave Unneeded Flat-File Columns as Strings   Flat-file columns are all strings when first read from the file. Converting strings to dates, integers, or even Unicode strings is costly. Leave columns as strings unless a conversion is absolutely necessary.

Eliminate Hidden Operations   For the most part, the Data Flow Task is explicit and obvious about what it is doing. For example, in the Derived Column transformation, you must cast column and variable values explicitly. However, there are some components that perform hidden or automatic conversions. For example, the Flat File Source Adapter attempts to convert external column types to their associated output column types. Use the Advanced Editor to explore each column type so that you know where such conversions occur.

Only Parse or Convert Columns When Necessary   Every row with a type conversion costs CPU cycles. Eliminate unnecessary conversions. Reorganize the data flow to eliminate the Type Conversion transform, if possible. Even better, if possible, modify the source column data type to match the type needed in the data flow. Also, if the conversion need not be locale-sensitive, use FastParse.

Use the FastParse Option in Flat File Source Adapter   FastParse is a set of optimized parsing routines that replaces some of the SSIS locale-specific parsing functions. FastParse only supports the more common date format representations and does not use locale when parsing. See Books Online for other FastParse limitations.

To turn on FastParse, follow these steps:

1. Open the Flat File Source Adapter or the Data Conversion transform in the Advanced Editor.

2. Select the Input and Output Properties tab.

3. Open the Flat File Source Output node in the tree on the left.

4. Open the Output Columns.

5. Select one of the columns.

6. Note the FastParse custom property in the property grid.

Eliminate Unneeded Logging

Logging is useful for debugging and troubleshooting. When developing packages, you should pull out the stops. But, when deploying completed packages to production, be mindful and careful about the log entries you leave enabled and the log provider you use. Notably, OnPipelineRowsSent is somewhat verbose. If there is any concern about the write time for logging, you might want to consider turning off logging or at least eliminating the chatty log entries. This is something you need to balance against the need to monitor and troubleshoot packages. Turning off logging might be good for performance, but then you don't get any logs to diagnose when problems arise. You'll have to find the right balance. Logging generally doesn't kill performance. You just need to be aware of the potential performance problems.

Optimizing the Data Flow

The following are some suggestions for tuning the data flow.

Use Indexes

This should probably go without saying, but when accessing data, make sure you use indexes to speed up the process. For example, in certain cases, the Lookup transform can benefit from having an index on the reference table.

Perform Set-based Operations

When possible, perform set-based operations in SQL Server. For example, SQL Server can generally sort faster than the Sort transform, especially if the table being sorted is indexed. Set-based operations, such as joins, unions, and selects with ORDER BY and GROUP BY, tend to be faster on the server.

Be Mindful of Transforms with Internal File IO

In Chapter 20, "The Stock Data Flow Components," some transforms have comments to the effect that they perform internal file Input/Output. For example, the Raw Source and Destination, Import/Export Column transforms, Flat File Source and Destination Adapters, and Excel File Source and Destination Adapters are all directly impacted by the performance of the file system. File IO isn't always a bottleneck, but when combined with low memory conditions, causing spooling, or with other disk-intense operations, it can significantly impact performance. Components that read and write to disk should be scrutinized carefully and, if possible, configured to read and write to dedicated hard drives. Look for ways to optimize the performance of the hard drives using RAID, defragmentation, and/or correct partitioning.

Move to a 64-Bit Platform

As you can see, the Data Flow Task can be very memory intensive. With a few blocking transforms and a large source dataset, it's easily possible to run into the memory limitations of 32-bit systems. The benefit of moving to a 64-bit platform is simple—more memory.

Monitor Memory-Intensive Transforms

If your package is memory bound, look for ways to eliminate the memory-intensive transforms or shift them to another package. Some transforms, such as the Aggregate, Lookup, and Sort transforms, use a lot of memory. The Sort transform, for example, holds all buffers until the last buffer and then releases the sorted rows. If memory runs low, these transforms might spool to disk, causing expensive hard page faults.

Monitor Other Memory-Intensive Applications

When running on the same machine as other memory-intensive applications, the data flow can become memory starved, even if there is plenty of memory on the machine. This is typically true when running packages on the same machine with SQL Server. SQL Server is aggressive about using memory. You can use the sp_configure system stored procedure to instruct SQL Server to limit its memory usage.

Eliminate Unnecessary Operations

If you don't need to process a column, keep the column in the original format in which you find it. For example, don't convert strings to dates if you never do any date-related transformations.

Pare Down the Lookup Reference Data

The default lookup query for the Lookup transform is

```
'SELECT * FROM …'
```

Select the option to use the results of a query for the reference data. Generally, the reference data should only contain the key and the desired lookup column. So, for a dimension table lookup, that would be the natural key and the surrogate key.

Use Lookup Partial or Full Cache Mode

Depending on the requirements and the data, you should choose one of these two modes to speed up the Lookup transform. Partial cache mode is useful when the incoming data is repetitive and only references a small percentage of the total reference table. Full cache mode is useful when the reference table is relatively small and the incoming data references the full spectrum of reference table rows.

Consider Transforms with Asynchronous Outputs

As the mantra goes, "Asynchronous transforms aren't good because they copy memory." In practice, however, it's not always so conclusive. Recall the earlier discussion about asynchronous outputs being the start of a new execution tree. Because introducing a new execution tree provides another worker thread to do work, in some cases, introducing a transform with an asynchronous output can actually benefit data flow performance. For example, introducing an asynchronous output into a data flow running on a machine with only one CPU will likely slow down the data flow because of the memory copying. However, introduce asynchronous outputs into a data flow with only two execution trees running on a machine with eight CPUs, and you'll likely see a performance gain because more CPUs can be enlisted in processing the data flow. There's no magic pill here. This is one of those cases where you have to set, test, and measure.

Eliminate Lookup, Aggregate, and Sort Transforms

Although performant for what they do, and important when absolutely necessary, these transforms invariably degrade data flow performance. If possible, eliminate them from your data flows. Sort and aggregate data at the source, and use the Merge Join transform instead of the Lookup transform, if possible.

Set `BufferTempStoragePath` and `BlobTempStoragePath` to Fast Drives

If the data flow does need to spool to disk, these two locations point to where the Execution Engine stores the memory. In truth, if you're swapping out to these locations, you should try to decrease the memory load and eliminate the swapping. However, that's not always possible, so both properties should point to fast drives that are in low demand. Ideally, `BufferTempStoragePath` and `BlobTempStoragePath` should be on separate spindles.

Increase `DefaultBufferMaxSize` **and** `DefaultBufferMaxRows`
Increasing the values for these two properties can boost performance by decreasing the number of buffers moving through the data flow. However, you should avoid increasing the values too much to the point where the Execution Engine starts swapping out buffers to disk. That would defeat the purpose.

Use Match Indexes for Repeat Data-Cleansing Sessions

On subsequent runs, the Fuzzy Lookup transform can either use an existing match index or create a new index. If the reference table is static, the package can avoid the potentially expensive process of rebuilding the index for repeat package runs. If you choose to use an existing index, the index is created the first time that the package runs. If multiple Fuzzy Lookup transformations use the same reference table, they can all use the same index. To reuse the index, the lookup operations must be identical; the lookup must use the same columns. You can name the index and select the connection to the SQL Server database that saves the index. Doing this can save substantial startup time that would be wasted rebuilding the index.

Implement Parallel Execution

Both the Execution Engine for the Data Flow Task and the Execution Engine for the Control Flow are multithreaded. The following settings can be used to take full advantage of Execution Engine threading.

Use the `EngineThreads` **Property**   There is a property on the Data Flow Task called `EngineThreads`, which controls the number of worker threads the Execution Engine uses. The default for this property is 5, which means that five worker threads and five source threads will be used. However, as you now know, by simply adding a few components, data flow thread requirements will quickly exceed the default. If the `EngineThreads` value is less than the number of worker threads, or execution trees, the Data Flow Task uses one thread for multiple execution trees. This isn't always a bad thing. You might notice very little difference in performance with different `EngineThreads` settings depending on the package and the environment. On the other hand, boosting the number of threads can drastically improve performance for some data flows—especially on high-end, multi-processor machines. The important point here is to be aware of how many threads the data flow naturally needs and try to keep the `EngineThreads` value reasonably close to it.

Set `MaxConcurrentExecutables`   Recall the description of this property from Chapter 7, "Grouping Control Flow with Containers." It is the number of threads the control flow or runtime execution engine will use. The default is 4 and the maximum is 128. If you set the value to -1, the number of threads used will be the number of processors on the machine plus 2. For hyperthreaded enabled CPUs, the number of processors used is the logical processor count. If there are multiple Data Flow Tasks in the Control Flow, for example 10, and `MaxConcurrentExecutables` is set to 4, only four of the Data Flow Tasks will execute simultaneously. Set, test, and measure various value combinations of this property and the `EngineThreads` property to determine the optimal setting for your packages.

Handle Errors

Instead of handling errors in the data flow, you can choose to ignore them and then use the Conditional Split transform to filter through them, moving the error rows to a different output where you can later analyze and process them in a separate process. Handling errors in the data flow can be expensive. If the number of errors is typically low, then there's little worry. However, if you have a lot of errors, for example, when using the Lookup transform, using the Conditional Split transform is the way to go.

Scrutinize Components with Row-Intensive Operations

All the components perform operations on a row-by-row basis, but there are some that perform expensive operations such as the OLE DB Command transform, which executes a query for every row in the buffer. Although useful and even indispensable at times, it should be avoided if at all possible. Other transforms with row-intensive operations are as follows:

- Fuzzy Lookup

- Data Conversion

- Export/Import Column

- Term Lookup

Insert Performance

Often the greatest data flow performance inhibitor is the sustained write speed of the destination hard drives. But other elements impact destinations as well. Depending on where you are inserting data, you can speed up the inserts in the following ways.

Use the SQL Server Destination Adapter

If running on the same machine as SQL Server, use the SQL Server Destination Adapter instead of OLE DB Destination Adapter. Tests show a marked performance gain with the SQL Server Destination Adapter over the OLE DB Destination Adapter, especially when loading into empty nonindexed tables. This is almost always a slam-dunk performance improvement.

Set the Commit Size

The Commit Size option allows you to set a larger buffer commit size for loading into SQL Server. This setting is only available in the OLE DB Destination Adapter when using the SQL Server OLEDB driver. A setting of zero indicates that the adapter should attempt to commit all rows in a single batch.

Turn on Table Lock

This option is available in the OLE DB Destination Editor. Selecting Table Lock also enables a fast load, which tells the adapter to use the `IRowsetFastload` bulk insert interface for loading.

NOTE

Fastload delivers much better performance; however, it does not provide as much information if there is an error. Generally, for development, you should turn it off and then turn it on when deploying to production.

Disable Constraints

This option is also available in the OLE DB Destination Editor by deselecting the Check Constraints option.

Use Minimal Logging

Using the Simple or Bulk-Logged Recovery model, bulk import operations are minimally logged, which can significantly decrease insert times. To learn more about minimal logging, search MSDN or Books Online for "minimally logged operations."

Disable Indexes

Depending on the amount of time you save on the load, it might benefit you to disable indexes. The choice depends on how much you gain versus how much you lose. If disabling the index saves you 20 minutes of load time and rebuilding the index takes 10, you've saved yourself 10 minutes. However, in practice, the index rebuild time often takes longer than the amount of time you save by disabling it.

An Approach to Data Flow Optimization

The preceding section presents a pretty long list of methods to improve the performance of your data flows and addresses a large percentage of the data flow performance problems you'll run into. However, if after applying all those suggestions, you still need to squeeze some performance from your data flow, you might need to step back and take a more holistic approach to analyzing your packages. This section presents a disciplined and somewhat theoretical approach you can use to evaluate and incrementally optimize your data flows.

The Theory of Constraints

One of the more impressive books I read in college was *The Goal* by Eliyahu M. Goldratt. For me, it was an epiphany. In *The Goal*, Dr. Goldratt deftly articulates the kinds of problems businesses face when continually improving their processes and trying to get the most from their resources. Although the book was about how to improve the throughput of a manufacturing plant, the underlying concept is about optimizing processes, identifying resources and constraints, and consistently and significantly increasing the overall performance of systems. Sounds an awful lot like a process we could use for optimizing data flows, doesn't it?

NOTE

For more information regarding the Theory of Constraints and its Thinking Processes, or The Goldratt Institute's products and services, visit www.goldratt.com.

The Five Steps of the Theory of Constraints

Dr. Goldratt has codified his process of improvement into five steps, as follows:

- *Identify* the constraint.

- Decide how to *exploit* the constraint.

- *Subordinate and synchronize* everything else to the preceding decisions.

- *Elevate* the performance of the constraint.

- If in any of the previous steps, the constraint has shifted, *go back to Step 1*.

Let's apply the Theory of Constraints to optimizing data flow.

Identifying and Prioritizing Resource Constraints

The first step is to identify the constraints, which are elements of a system that limit the overall system's performance. In this step, you should focus on educating yourself about your computing environment. What are your resources and in what ways are those resources constrained? For a simple example, evaluate your machine memory. How much is installed? Open Windows Task Manager and look at the Performance tab. How much total physical memory is available? A common mistake people make is to forget how much memory other processes on a machine consume. They might have 2GB of RAM, but only have 500MB available because they are running SQL Server and a plethora of other processes on the machine. If a package running on the machine must sort 1GB of data, even though they have 2GB of memory, the data flow will likely spool (swap buffers) to disk and the performance will suffer because only 500MB is available to SSIS. Try to understand your system's resources and how they are or potentially can be constrained.

The second part of this step is to prioritize the constraints in order of importance. Prioritizing constraints is important because, although a given constraint might exist on all your machines, it might not be significant enough to factor into your optimization for a given package. For example, recently a customer asked how to optimize a package's startup time. Their system was not concerned with throughput, or even data flow processing speed, as the loads were very small. Rather, they were interested in how to speed up the startup time of packages because they were running them on demand as part of a reporting system and the load time for the package constituted a large percentage of the overall report load time. Although memory might be a high-priority constraint for packages processing very large datasets, for these particular packages, memory was a low-priority constraint. However, task types, hard drive speed, configuration type, and package size were high-priority constraints. Understand the priorities of the constraints.

Some Common Constraints

The following is a partial list of constraints of which you should be aware. There are more, no doubt, but this list is a good start.

- **Amount of memory installed**—This is perhaps the most important factor for processing complex data.

- **Disk IO speed**—Using slow IDE or optimized RAID drives? This is important for big data throughput that involves hard drives.

- **Available memory**—Changes based on other processes should be monitored and understood. For example, how much memory SQL Server is using.

- **CPU cache**—This can increase processing for certain transforms that do repetitive, same-memory access, such as the Lookup transform.

- **Query performance**—Queries should be optimized for speed.

- **Package size**—Larger packages take longer to load.

- **CPU speed**—The raw processing power is important for processing throughput.

- **Amount of data to process**—Generally speaking, the more data, the longer the processing time.

- **Complexity of data flow**—More complex data flow can take longer and more memory, especially if it involves multiple blocking transforms.

- **Number of CPUs**—More CPUs widen the processing pipe.

- **Server availability**—Server availability impacts connection times and query performance.

- **Logging**—Although quite efficient, logging can impact performance when verbose.

- **Other software running on the same machine**—Other software reduces available memory, reads and writes to disk, and occupies the bus.

- **Order of data**—Sorted data might process faster for data flows with certain transforms, such as Merge and Merge Join.

- **Event handlers**—Event handlers are useful, but can be expensive if overused.

- **Indexes**—Table access is improved; joins and searching speed improves.

- **Designer environment**—The Business Intelligence Development Studio is a full-featured development platform, but does not function well as a package execution platform for production or performance testing purposes.

- **Bus speed**—Bus speed impacts memory and disk access speeds.

- **Network Speed**—Impacts cross network loads, extracts, and queries.

Most Common High-Priority Constraints

Having listed all these constraints, it's important to stress that a handful will be the most common high-priority constraints, in no particular order:

- Memory

- CPU speed

- Number of CPUs

- Hard drive speed

- Network speed

How to Identify and Prioritize Constraints

To identify constraints, you need to witness the effect of the constraints. The priorities naturally fall out of the identification process. The most drastic decreases in performance are caused by the highest-priority constraints. To witness the effect of constraints, you need a baseline against which you can measure decreases in performance.

Get a Baseline   To understand where a given package spends its processing time, it's necessary to decompose the package into its processing time constituent parts. To do that, you must decompose the package and get a baseline measurement of its core processing time, then measure each incremental processing time increase as more components and other package parts are added to the core package. It is very important to isolate what you are measuring so that when you measure deltas, you know what causes them. Start by decomposing the package and eliminating unmeasured constraints.

Eliminate Unmeasured Constraints   To ensure that you have the most control over the system, try to get total control over everything happening on the machine. Eliminate as much outside influence as you can.

- **Shut down other applications that might consume memory or impact other resources**—Applications can do unexpected things, such as read from disk at unexpected times or launch a reminder message box.

- **Make sure you have enough memory for package execution**—If you swap to disk, it ruins your measurement.

- **Disconnect from networks, if possible**—If you're accessing flat files across the network, copy them locally to eliminate the network element. Later, you can add it back to measure it.

- **Shut down SQL Server, if possible**—If the package connects to SQL Server, replace the destination or source with a rowcount, trash, or Data Generation transform.

TIP

One of the biggest unmeasured constraints that is too often ignored is the Business Intelligence Development Studio. Don't use the designer for measuring performance. If you do, you're measuring the designer performance, not the package performance. Execute packages in DTExec.exe. It is ideal for measuring package performance because it is very lightweight and generally resembles how packages will be executed in production.

Build a Baseline   The following are some typical baseline measurements. You should pick one with which you are comfortable. If you want to measure source performance, you should choose the first one. If you're more interested in the destination performance, choose the second one, and so forth.

- Source→Multicast
- Source→Destination
- Source→Transforms→Multicast

NOTE

For measuring an existing package, try to deconstruct it into simple parts that you can measure using this approach.

TIP

Because the Multicast does almost nothing, if there are no outputs, using it as a replacement for destinations is a great way to measure the performance impact of destinations or transforms. However, be sure that RunInOptimized mode is turned off. Otherwise, the Execution Engine trims the execution trees.

Note the differences in performance between the different baselines. After you've done that, you'll have a good idea where some of your bottlenecks are. For example, when you replace the Multicast with a real destination, the execution time might increase, even drastically. But, when you add in transforms, you might see very little performance degradation. This is what is meant by witnessing or measuring the impact of changes.

NOTE

What's the difference between a constraint and a bottleneck? Constraints always exist, but they might not be a factor in the performance of the system because they are hidden by bottlenecks or they are low-priority constraints. Bottlenecks are constraints that are actually limiting the overall system's performance in some way. Remove a bottleneck, and you'll expose another one—turning a previously hidden constraint into a bottleneck.

Add Elements Back to the Package and Measure Performance Impact   After you've established these baseline measurements, you can start incrementally adding previously removed elements to measure the impact each has on the overall system. Make sure you only add them back and measure them one by one, otherwise you won't know which element is causing the impact you measure. Continue this "Set, Test, and Measure" process until you have reconstructed the package and the environment. Also, don't do this in a straight line. Try adding components in a different order and in different combinations.

Measure with Performance Counters   Performance counters are useful for 'measuring internal or otherwise hidden processes. Integration Services provides the following useful performance counters:

- Buffers in Use

- Flat Buffers in Use

- Private Buffers in Use

- Rows Read

- Rows Written

- Buffers Spooled

The most useful of these for performance measurements is *Buffers Spooled*. Values greater than zero indicate that the Execution Engine has swapped buffers to disk. You should always try to avoid swapping out buffers to disk, which is usually an indication that you don't have enough memory or that you need to rearrange your data flow.

Rows Read and *Rows Written* help gauge the overall progress of the data flow and can be useful as sanity checks. For example, as you increase the number of rows a data flow processes, you would expect a commensurate increase in processing time. These measurements help' you quickly determine if the increased processing times are warranted.

Deciding How to *Exploit* the Constraint

This step is about making sure the bottleneck is never overutilized. Applying this to data flow, always try to match the data load at a transform's input with its throughput capacity. The Data Flow Task already attempts to do this using back pressure, but that only temporarily masks the problem. It doesn't improve throughput, it just slows down the data flow. This is a tough one to get right because throughput and processing loads at an input aren't constant, so you have to rely on the Data Flow Task for the most part.

Subordinating and Synchronizing Everything Else to the Preceding Decisions

After you've identified the bottleneck, and you've fully exploited it as described in the preceding step, you should apply all the other nonconstrained resources to breaking the bottleneck. If you've got resources that are not fully utilized in your environment and that are waiting around because of a bottleneck in your package, you're wasting resources. Try to get those underutilized resources to take on more of the work that the bottleneck is performing. You can decrease the data loads flowing into the bottleneck or ease the bottleneck processing burden using the following techniques:

- Filtering the data before it flows into the bottleneck transform, for example, prebuilding a Lookup transform dimension reference table from the new facts so that only those dimensions that are required end up in the reference table.

- Ignoring errors and using a conditional split to filter them, for example, when doing upserts, testing shows that it is generally faster to ignore errors from the Lookup transform and conditionally split the not-found rows into an insert than to try and handle the not-found rows with an error output.

- Preprocessing the data the constrained transform will process, for example, placing a Lookup transform before the Slowly Changing Dimension transform to filter out nonexistent rows.

- Postprocessing the data in lieu of a transformation, for example, the OLEDB Command transform performs row-by-row expensive operations, which you can optimize by eliminating the transform and flowing the data to a table. Later, use SQL Server to perform the set-based operations instead.

- Cloning and parallelizing the data flow around the bottleneck. For example, if the bottleneck is a transform, segment the rows with a Conditional Split transform into clones of the bottleneck, then union all the rows back into the next transform.

In other words, off-load work from your overutilized bottleneck resources and load it onto the laggard, underutilized resources. Optimizing nonbottleneck resources doesn't help much if they're all constrained by the bottleneck.

Elevating the Bottlenecks

As you continue to increase the performance of the bottleneck by off-loading work from it and placing more of the load on other less-utilized resources, the system becomes more balanced and the bottleneck is eventually broken.

If in any of the Previous Steps the Constraint Has Shifted, *Go Back to Step 1*

When you take these steps, what you'll find is that you're in an iterative improvement loop. After you eliminate one bottleneck, you'll find others. So, you start the process again until you reach your performance goal.

Summary

The Data Flow Task is pretty fast by default, but as the data flow grows more complex and the size of data loads increase, the opportunities for tuning the data flow also increase. The guidelines and methods for tuning the data flow described here address a large percentage of the performance issues you'll run into. However, if you still want to get the last drop of performance out of the Data Flow Task, use the Theory of Constraints as your guide to find and eliminate bottlenecks.

PART VI

Programming Integration Services

IN THIS PART

Building Custom Tasks

"SOMEBODY MUST HAVE BEEN REALLY HUNGRY IN THIS HALL."— MATT DAVID

If you were to decompose Integration Services and remove all the components, you'd be left with very little value because packages wouldn't do anything. They would just sit there, wishing you'd build a task or other component to plug into them so they would have something to do. The tasks, transforms, Foreach Enumerators, connection managers, data flow adapters, and log providers are what provide the power of SSIS. Without them, you'd be left with two snoozing engines and a designer. What's interesting is that, as a third-party developer, you can write components that are exactly like the stock components that ship with Integration Services. The SSIS team used the same infrastructure to write components as you can use to build custom components. This chapter generically describes how to start a project for building all the custom components and then covers in detail how to write custom tasks just like the stock tasks that ship with the product. The next chapter, Chapter 25, "Building Custom Data Flow Components," covers how to build adapters and transforms.

Custom Runtime Components

Integration Services supports five different custom component types; however, this book only covers how to write custom tasks and data flow components in detail because those are the most commonly required. The other custom components you can write are as follows:

- Foreach Enumerators
- Connection managers
- Log providers

By now, you know that Foreach Enumerators are the components that plug into the ForEach Loop. They iterate over collections of objects and provide an element or collection of elements on each Foreach Loop iteration. Because the stock Foreach Enumerators are very flexible and provide a way to iterate over SQL Server Management Objects (SMO) objects, static text, ADO recordsets, schema rowsets, files, nodelists, or even generic .NET collections, there doesn't seem to be a lot of demand for custom Foreach Enumerators. However, if you want to write one, you can.

The stock connection managers give pretty good coverage for database connections, but if you need to access an unsupported protocol, server, or other resource, for example, Lightweight Directory Access Protocol (LDAP), Simple Object Access Protocol (SOAP), or build an enhanced File Transfer Protocol (FTP) Connection Manager, you can write a custom connection manager.

Log providers are extensible as well and provide a layer between the package logging infrastructure and the destination logging medium. Here again, the stock log providers provide pretty good coverage, including SQL Server, text, XML, SQL Profiler, and Windows event logging.

Only a brief introduction to these custom component types is provided here because they share common setup with custom tasks and data flow components. Books Online provides excellent resources if you want to further pursue writing one of these component types.

Requirements for Building Custom Components

Before digging into the nuts and bolts of developing the components, let's talk a little about the requirements. You should be familiar with the following tools and have them installed. If you have Visual Studio installed, they should already be available. Also, if you have never used these tools, you should become familiar with them and understand the basics of how they function.

Development Platform

Visual Studio is the preferred platform, but any environment that supports .NET will do, for example Borland Delphi or #develop will also work. It is important that the tools are compatible with .NET Framework 2.0.

Debugging Environment

Whatever platform you choose, it should have a development environment. For this chapter, the Visual Studio development and debugging environment is assumed. If you're using a different environment, you'll need to extrapolate the instructions to match the environment.

Strong Name Utility and GACUtil

All Integration Services custom components must be placed in the Global Assembly Cache (GAC) and so need to be strongly named. It is best if the Strong Name Utility (sn.exe) is on the path so that it can be executed from any directory. The same goes for GACUtil.exe. You'll use this utility for adding and possibly removing assemblies to the GAC.

Programming Languages Supported

You can use any .NET language to write custom components for Integration Services, including VB.NET, COBOL.NET or Delphi.NET. You can even write custom components in C++, although Microsoft does not support it. However, the examples in this chapter are in C# because that is the language used to write the managed stock components. For VB.NET developers, search Books Online for "custom task" to find a wealth of sample code you can reference.

Computer Needed

As in previous chapters, you'll not fully understand the code presented here until you actually work through the samples on your machine, step through it in the debugger, and so on. There are numerous aspects to developing components and only a few can be documented here. Working through the samples is the best way to understand this chapter.

The Sample Tasks

There are four sample tasks in the samples folder. Each is in various stages of development so you can see what is possible. This chapter includes parts of those tasks when needing to explain certain concepts. Studying the code for these sample tasks in detail is a great way to quickly get up to speed on writing your own. The tasks are as follows:

- StarterTask—This is a sample task with a fully functional task user interface (task UI) you can use as a starting point for writing your own custom tasks. The task UI uses the same task UI infrastructure as the stock tasks. The task has two properties of type integer and string. The properties serve no purpose but to illustrate how to add properties and support them in the UI.

- HTTPTask—This is a stripped-down custom task for downloading HTML pages. It has no user interface and is very rudimentary. The HTTPTask is the kind of task someone might write for internal use only to eliminate the continual copying and pasting of Script Tasks or to make task configuration easier. It shows how easy it is to create a functional custom task without a lot of effort.

- ExpressionTask—This is a simple task that supports assigning values to variables through expressions using the SSIS Expression Evaluator. This task is useful in situations in which you need to modify the value of a variable and don't want to use a

Script Task. For example, you can use this task as a way to prematurely break out of a For Loop based on workflow.

- CryptoTask—This is a fully functional task and task UI similar to the stock tasks. It provides the ability to encrypt and decrypt text files with a password. It also has the kind of validation, with warnings and errors, that you would expect from a fully functional task.

Deciding to "Roll Your Own"

Any discussion about writing custom components wouldn't be complete without some mention of the criteria for deciding when you should do so. For example, how do you decide if it is better to invest time in a Script Task or write a custom task instead? The following list offers a few guidelines to follow when deciding to write a custom component:

- **Resurrecting legacy code**—You might have legacy business rules or other code that you want to reuse. Rewriting might not be an option, but the code has well-understood interfaces or call points. Calling these methods from a Script Task might be cumbersome and repetitive. Wrapping up the calls in a component abstracts away the details of the legacy code.

- **Simplifying code reuse**—If you plan to use the logic for the component in multiple packages and don't want to copy and paste to multiple locations, writing a custom component is the right answer.

- **Hiding intellectual property**—There is no way to hide code in the Script Task or script component. If the algorithm you are writing is sensitive or you simply want to hide the details of the implementation from those who might innocently break the code, you should write a custom component.

- **Selling components**—If you want to write components to sell, you, of course, need to write the component.

- **Dealing with complex problems**—If the logic and code you need to implement is even slightly complex, you are likely better off writing a custom component so that you can break up the code into more manageable units.

- **Getting better performance**—Although the Script Task and components are pretty performant, there is no good way to profile or optimize them.

- **Supporting an unsupported protocol**—If you want support for an existing or new unsupported protocol, you need to write a custom connection manager and possibly other components as well. The Script Task or component cannot be used to create any of the other three component types.

It's also important to understand when you shouldn't roll your own. The following list enumerates a few reasons why you wouldn't write a custom component:

- **Similar component exists**—This is likely obvious, but true nonetheless. When a similar component already exists that will do what you need, why write a new one? What isn't so obvious is what components are already available. To find out more about available components, go to the Community menu in Visual Studio and select the Partner Products Catalog menu option, which takes you to the Visual Studio Industry Partners Product Catalog website.

- **Function achievable by combining existing components**—Integration Services is designed with the toolbox approach. Components provide slices of well-defined behavior that you combine together to build functionality. Sometimes, it is easy to overlook the power of this approach and think that a particular task simply cannot be performed with the existing toolset. Before starting a custom component, give some consideration to how you can accomplish the given function with a clever combination of existing tools.

- **Function only needed for the short term or in few packages**—If the feature or function you need will only be useful for a short time, is just a proof of concept, or will only be used in a few packages, your efforts would probably be better spent writing the function in a Script Task or component.

- **Function available in an executable**—If you can spawn a command-line executable to do the same thing as your required function, consider doing that instead.

There are a lot of considerations and trade-offs to make when deciding to write a custom component. The listed guidelines are just a start and should be considered along with the myriad of other considerations that aren't listed, such as scheduling and budgetary constraints, long-term maintenance, area expertise, and future project viability expectations that are specific to a given project. Hopefully, these guidelines will get you started with your decision.

Starting an SSIS Custom Component Project

Although each of the component types performs very different functions, the way you build each custom component type is very similar. To set up each of the component types, start with the following general steps:

1. Create the solution.

2. Add a strong name and key file.

3. Reference SSIS and other assemblies.

4. Define the class.

5. Compile and install.

Creating the Solution

In this step, you'll create a new solution for the component to live in. This step is identical for all component types, but for this discussion you'll be building a task.

1. Open Microsoft Visual Studio.

2. Select File, New, Project. The New Project dialog box opens, as shown in Figure 24.1.

3. Select the Visual C# project type and the Class Library template.

4. Type in the name and location of the solution.

5. Click the OK button.

6. Right-click on the `.cs` source file in the Solution Explorer, and select the Rename menu option.

7. Change the name of the source file to something meaningful. The sample source file is `SampleTask.cs`.

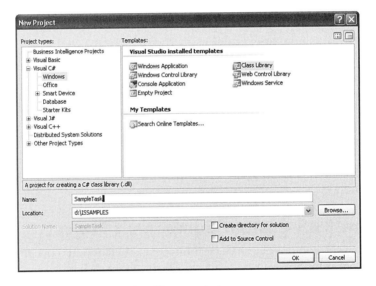

FIGURE 24.1   Setting up a new class library solution.

Adding a Strong Name and Key File

.NET requires that the component have a strong name. To do this, you must create a key file and link the key file to the component. This step is identical for all component types. Fortunately, Visual Studio makes this very easy, as follows:

1. Right-click on the project in the Solution Explorer, and select Properties.

2. Select the Signing tab in the Project Properties dialog box. Figure 24.2 shows the Signing tab with the settings input.

3. Put a check in the Sign the Assembly check box.

4. Click the drop down to choose a strong name key file.

5. Select New to create a new key file.

6. The Create Strong Name Key dialog box opens. Type in a new key file name. The sample key file name is SampleKeyfile.snk.

7. Click the OK button.

8. Uncheck the option to protect the key file with a password for this sample.

9. Click the OK button.

10. Save the project ([Ctrl+S]) and close the Project Properties dialog box.

FIGURE 24.2   Signing the assembly.

Referencing SSIS and Other Assemblies

All component types need this step, but depending on the type of component, the assemblies you reference will be different. For Foreach Enumerators, connection managers, log providers, and tasks, you need to reference the Microsoft.SqlServer.Dts.Runtime assembly.

CAUTION

In rare circumstances, you might need to reference the Microsoft.SqlServer.Dts.Runtime.Wrapper assembly as well. However, doing so can cause some confusion as there are many similarly named objects in both assemblies. As a rule, when building runtime components, you should not need to reference the wrapper assembly and should avoid doing so unless absolutely required.

For data flow components, you need to use the following namespaces and reference the associated assemblies:

- `Microsoft.SqlServer.Dts.Runtime` found in the `Microsoft.SqlServer.ManagedDTS` assembly

- `Microsoft.SqlServer.Dts.Runtime.Wrapper` found in the `Microsoft.SqlServer.DTSRuntimeWrap` assembly

- `Microsoft.SqlServer.Dts.Pipeline` found in the `Microsoft.SqlServer.PipelineHost` assembly

- `Microsoft.SqlServer.Dts.Pipeline.Wrapper` found in the `Microsoft.SqlServer.DtsPipelineWrap` assembly

To reference each of the assemblies in your project, follow these steps:

1. Right-click on the References node in the Solution Explorer and select Add Reference. The Add Reference dialog box opens, as shown in Figure 24.3.

2. Select the `Microsoft.SqlServer.ManagedDTS` assembly.

3. At the top of the source file, for example `SampleTask.cs`, type in the `USING` statement. For `Microsoft.SqlServer.Dts.Runtime`, type in the following case-sensitive code:

   ```
   using Microsoft.SqlServer.Dts.Runtime;
   ```

4. Repeat these steps for each assembly you want to reference.

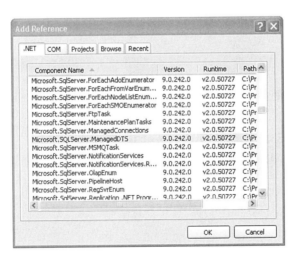

FIGURE 24.3   Adding a reference to the `ManagedDTS` assembly.

Defining the Class

There are two parts to this step. One is to derive from the base component so that you get the default behavior of the base class. The other is adding attributes. The attributes provide information that the runtime examines when enumerating the components. This step is different for each component type.

Deriving from the Base Class

Integration Services provides an abstract base class for each of the component types. Following is a list of the base class names:

- Task
- LogProviderBase
- ConnectionManagerBase
- ForEachEnumerator
- PipelineComponent

By deriving from one of these base classes, you can create the corresponding SSIS class. For this sample, derive the `SampleTask` from the `Task` base. When you have done so, the `SampleTask.cs` file should contain the following code:

```
using System;
using System.Collections.Generic;
using System.Text;
using Microsoft.SqlServer.Dts.Runtime;


namespace SampleTask
{
    public class SampleTask : Task
    {
    }
}
```

Adding Attributes

The second part of this step is to identify the new class to Integration Services. Integration Services enumerates components based on two criteria: location and attributes.

Location   Integration Services components are installed in the DTS subfolder of the SQL Server installation location. The default location is in the Program Files directory.

```
C:\Program Files\Microsoft SQL Server\90\DTS
```

Under this folder, there are five folders of interest to this discussion, as follows:

- `Connections`
- `ForEachEnumerators`
- `LogProviders`
- `PipelineComponents`
- `Tasks`

This is where Integration Services looks when enumerating components and does not detect managed components in any other location. In the Compile and Install step described later, you'll see how to set up the project to directly compile the component into the correct folder.

Attributes   Integration Services opens each of the assemblies in those folders and reflects on the attributes of the contained classes. This is how the `TaskInfos`, `PipelineComponentInfos`, and other info objects on the `Application` object are enumerated.

Table 23.1 shows the attributes and their purpose.

TABLE 23.1   SSIS Custom Component Attributes

Attributes Where Found	Parameters	Description
All Attributes		
(`DtsTask`, `DtsPipelineComponent`, `DtsForEachEnumerator`, `DtsConnection`,		
`DtsLogProvider`)	Description	Contains the description for the task that is displayed in various designer locations
All Attributes	DisplayName	Specifies the name used to build the component name in the designer; for example, FTPTask, FTPTask 1, FTPTask 2, and so forth and shown in ToolTips
All Attributes	IconResource	Points to the icon for the task
All Attributes	LocalizationType	Provides the class type that provides values for the DtsLocalizableAttribute.
All Attributes	UITypeName	Specifies the qualified name of the User Interface assembly and class for the component
DtsPipelineComponent	NoEditor	Indicates if the component supports the Advanced Editor

TABLE 23.1   Continued

Attributes Where Found	Parameters	Description
DtsPipelineComponent, DtsTask	RequiredProductLevel	Indicates the edition of SQL Server that must be installed for this component to be available
DtsTask	TaskType	Specifies what version of SSIS the task was created; typically "DTS90"
DtsPipelineComponent	ComponentType	Specifies the type of component: Transform, Destination, or Source
DtsLogProvider	LogProviderType	Specifies what version of SSIS the task was created; typically "DTS90"
DtsConnection	ConnectionType	Specifies the type of connection manager, for example FILE, FTP, or SMOServer
DtsPipelineComponent	CurrentVersion	Specifies the version of the component and is used when automatically upgrading components
DtsTask	TaskContact	Specifies contact information
DtsLogProvider	LogProviderContact	Specifies contact information
DtsForEachEnumerator	ForEachEnumeratorContact	Specifies contact information
DtsConnection	ConnectionContact	Specifies contact information

For the sample task, in the line above the class declaration, add the following attribute and parameters:

```
[
DtsTask(
    DisplayName="SampleTask",
    Description="A sample task",
    TaskContact="SampleTask, Copyright © Your Name")
]
```

With the attribute added, everything necessary for the designer to identify and load the component is in place. The next step is to compile and install the component.

Compiling and Installing

To make a component visible to Integration Services, you need to compile it, place it in the GAC, and move the component assembly to one of the enumeration folders under the DTS folder mentioned previously. For the sample task, that is the DTS\Tasks folder.

Setting the Output Path

To automatically move the component to the correct folder when you build it, set the output path on the Project Properties Build page.

> **NOTE**
>
> It's important to remember that, when correctly installed, there is a copy of the component in two locations. The following location, on the file system under the SQL Server folder, is for enumeration only. In fact, if you never do any design work on a machine, but only run packages, there is no need for the components in the special folders.
>
> When loading packages, SSIS only references the copies of the components in the GAC.

The following steps show how to set up the output path for the compiled component:

1. Right-click on the project in the Solution Explorer.

2. Select the Properties menu option to open the Project Properties dialog box.

3. Select the Build tab.

4. In the Output Path field, type in the folder where the tasks are stored. Typically, it is C:\Program Files\Microsoft SQL Server\90\DTS\Tasks.

Figure 24.4 shows the correct settings in the Project Properties dialog box.

Installing into the GAC

The next step is to install the component into the GAC:

1. Select the Build Events tab in the Project Properties dialog box.

2. In the Post-Build Event Command Line field, enter the following command:

   ```
   gacutil /if "C:\program Files\microsoft sql Server\90\DTS\Tasks\
   $(TargetFileName)"
   ```

3. Ensure that the Run the Post-Build Event option is set to On Successful Build.

4. Close the Project Properties dialog box.

5. Save the project ([Ctrl+S]).

> **CAUTION**
>
> Make sure that the gacutil.exe utility is on the path so that this command will succeed.

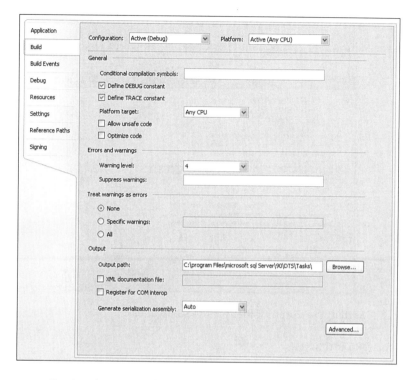

FIGURE 24.4   Setting the output folder for the sample task.

Building the Component

Now you need to build the component. If you've got everything right in the sample, the assembly compiles directly to the folder location where it can be enumerated by the designer and another copy gets placed into the GAC. Then, you can open the Business Intelligence Development Studio (BIDS) and add the task in the Toolbox.

1. From the Build menu, select Build Solution.

2. Right-click on the Solution node in the Solution Explorer.

3. Select Add, New Project to open the Add New Project dialog box.

4. In the Name field, type in `SampleTaskTest`.

5. Click the OK button.

6. The Add New Project dialog box closes and a new SSIS project is created with the package open.

7. If the Toolbox isn't visible, select View, Toolbox ([Ctrl+Alt+X]).

8. Right-click anywhere on the Toolbox and select Choose Items to open the Choose Toolbox Items dialog box. It might take a few seconds to open because it has to enumerate all the components.

9. Choose the SSIS Control Flow Items tab to see the available tasks.

10. Check the SampleTask component check box, as shown in Figure 24.5.

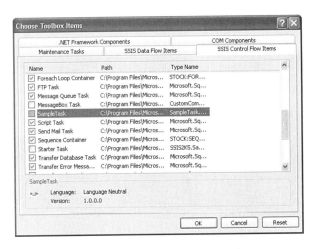

FIGURE 24.5   Setting the output folder for the sample task.

11. Click the OK button.

12. Notice that the SampleTask is now available in the Toolbox.

13. Drag the task over to the designer.

14. Double-click the task and get the message shown in Figure 24.6.

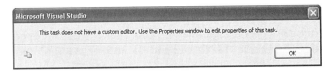

FIGURE 24.6   The SampleTask has no task UI.

The message box is telling you that there is no TaskUI for the task. That's because you haven't built a TaskUI for the sample task yet. However, if you run the package, the task will still successfully execute because the base class provides the default `Execute` methods. Also, even though there is no task UI, you can still modify properties through the property grid.

How the Runtime Finds Your Installed Tasks

To understand how the runtime finds your custom task and other components, take a look at the Registry by opening regedit.

1. Click the Start menu.

2. Select Run.

3. Type **regedit** in the Open text box.

4. Click the OK button.

5. Find `HKEY_LOCAL_MACHINE\Software\Microsoft\MSDTS\Setup`.

A number of subkeys are in the Setup key. Click on the DTSPath key and look at the Default value. For most installs, this is `C:\Program Files\Microsoft SQL Server\90\DTS\` and is the fully qualified path to the base directory where tasks are stored. If this key isn't there, the application object searches: `HKLM\Software\Microsoft\MSSQLServer\Setup` for the fully qualified base directory. If neither of these values is found, the enumeration fails.

After retrieving the base directory, the runtime appends "\tasks" to the base path to create the final directory where tasks assemblies are stored to generate the folder path. The runtime reflects on all assemblies in this folder and tries to find classes with the `DtsTask` attribute. If you look in that folder, you'll notice that the stock task assemblies are also stored there. Again, Microsoft has no special location or process for including stock components. The same rules apply to stock and custom components, so all components are enumerated and included in the designer in the same way.

This sample task is an example of the most rudimentary component you can write. It shows how simple it is to start, code, install, add to the designer, and execute with very little effort. However, it is only a simple component with no real purpose other than to serve as a sample. The following discussion describes how to expand on the basic sample and make it a full-featured SSIS citizen.

Developing and Debugging the Task

The preceding discussion applies to all the component types and shows how to start any one of the component type projects. From this point forward, this chapter covers how to write a task in detail. Before starting to build tasks, it's helpful to understand the general relationships between the various high-level elements in the SSIS runtime, so a review of Chapter 7, "Grouping Control Flow with Containers," is worthwhile, especially the discussion about `Taskhosts`. Also, because the `CryptoTask` is complete and implements all the task features, the remaining discussion focuses on the `CryptoTask` sample in the `SAMPLES\SRC\SampleComponents\CryptoTask` folder.

Giving the Task an Identity

As you've seen, without the `DtsTask` attribute, the SSIS runtime considers your task assembly as just another class library. The attribute is what identifies the class library as a task and provides information about the task that the designer can use to describe it. `CryptoTask` has the following `DtsTask` attribute in `CryptoTask.cs`.

```
[
DtsTask(
  TaskType = "DTS90",
```

```
        DisplayName="CryptoTask",
        IconResource="SSIS2K5.Samples.Tasks.CryptoTask.TaskIcon.ico",
        Description="A task for encrypting text files",
        UITypeName = "SSIS2K5.Samples.Tasks.CryptoTask.CryptoTaskUI,
            SSIS2K5.Samples.CryptoTaskUI, Version=1.0.0.1, Culture=Neutral,
            PublicKeyToken=844aba2619516093",
        TaskContact = "CryptoTask; Microsoft SQL Server Integration Services 2005,
            By Kirk Haselden; For Version 9.0 of Integration Services;
            (c) 2006 Kirk Haselden;http://www.CustomTask.com/CryptoTask")
    ]
```

The TaskType parameter is not required, but is useful for identifying the target SSIS version for the task. The DisplayName parameter is required. The DisplayName is the name shown in the Toolbox and to name the task. If you don't provide a DisplayName parameter, the designer attempts to use the Description parameter value. If you don't provide either parameter, the designer cannot create the task. The IconResource parameter points to the icon to be used in the Toolbox. It is not required. If not provided, the designer uses a default icon. However, if you do provide this, the name of the resource must be "TaskIcon" and you must provide the fully qualified name. The UITypeName parameter is required if you want to provide a TaskUI for the task and contains the fully qualified type name of your Task UI class. The following is the format of the UITypeName attribute:

UITypeName = "*NamespaceTypeName*, *AssemblyName*, Version=*AssemblyVersion*, Culture=Neutral, PublicKeyToken= *PublicKeyToken*".

The UITypeName parameter seems to be the most problematic for custom task writers to get right, so this is covered in detail in the "Building the Task User Interface" section.

Provide the TaskContact parameter in case the SSIS runtime is unable to load the task. The SSIS runtime saves the TaskContact information with the task and displays it in the designer with an error when the task fails to load. This parameter is not required, but is suggested as a way to inform users how to correct the load problem. Chapter 7 describes this feature in detail.

Adding Feature-Specific Properties and Functions

You need to perform two types of coding when creating a task. One type is implementing the functionality that allows the task to function in the SSIS environment as a good SSIS citizen. The other type is the actual functionality that the task will provide to the packages that use it. For the CryptoTask, the task-specific behavior is provided by the encryption and decryption helper functions found in Rijndael.cs. All the task code is found in the CryptoTask.cs file.

NOTE
_____

A quick search on the Web yields a robust and highly reusable code library for encryption that Obviex wrote and freely distributes. This library is entirely contained with the

`Rijndael.cs` file in the `CryptoTask` sample solution. To find out more about the folks at Obviex, go to their website at http://www.obviex.com.

Thanks to Alex Bandukov and the folks at Obviex for permission to use this code.

Adding the Feature Properties

Although these properties are specific to the `CryptoTask`, they are also fairly representative of the kinds of properties most tasks will need, and so this is a good set to discuss. The `CryptoTask` has five feature-related properties, as follows:

- `Password`
- `SourceFileConnectionManager`
- `DestinationFileConnectionManager`
- `EncryptionOperation`
- `OverwriteDestination`

Passwords and Other Sensitive Properties   Passwords are interesting properties because of their sensitive nature. A number of conventions are used to avoid displaying the password.

Write Only   Passwords should always be write-only to prevent accidental exposure of the password. The code for the `Password` property is simple:

```
public string Password
{
   set
   {
      m_password = value;
   }
}
```

Note that there is only a SET method and no GET method. The code gets interesting when it is saved.

CAUTION

It is very important that password encryption and other protection measures discussed in this section be considered only as password obfuscation and do not protect passwords 100% from those with unfettered package access. In other words, if you have a package that is encrypted, and you give the package and password for the package to another person, having a write-only password property on a task or marking the password as sensitive only makes it difficult to get the password, not impossible. To fully protect passwords in packages, you must use one of the encryption package protection options and not share the password. As soon as someone has access to the unencrypted package, all data within the package should be considered compromised.

Marked as Sensitive   To allow the SSIS runtime to detect properties that should be encrypted, properties must be marked as sensitive in the SaveToXML method.

SaveToXML

```
// Save the password
private const string PERSIST_CONST_SENSITIVE    = "Sensitive";
private const string PERSIST_CONST_PASSWORD     = "Password";


// Create the password element
XmlElement pswdElement = doc.CreateElement("", PERSIST_CONST_PASSWORD, "");
rootElement.AppendChild(pswdElement);


// Set the password element as sensitive so that the runtime will encrypt it.
pswdElement.InnerText = m_password;
XmlAttribute attr = doc.CreateAttribute(PERSIST_CONST_SENSITIVE);
attr.Value = "1";
pswdElement.Attributes.Append(attr)
```

This code creates a new element for the password value and adds an attribute called Sensitive, setting the value equal to 1 or TRUE. The SSIS runtime, when saving the task, looks for all properties with the Sensitive attribute and encrypts the value for the property in memory before saving to the destination. In this way, the value is never written out to disk.

Masked in the UI   Passwords should always be masked in the UI. This is covered later in the "Building the Task User Interface" section.

Connection Managers
The SourceFileConnectionManager and DestinationFileConnectionManager properties are of type string and store the names of the connection managers the CryptoTask uses. Here again, the properties are simple accessor methods, but with a twist.

```
    // SourceConnection manager
    public string SourceFileConnectionManager
    {
        get
        {
            return GetConnectionName(m_connections, m_source);
        }
        set
        {
            m_source = GetConnectionID(m_connections, value);
        }
    }
```

Using names to reference connection managers makes sense from a human perspective. Humans don't remember numbers, especially globally unique identifiers (GUIDs) as well as they do names. However, connection manager names change. Their IDs, which are GUIDs, don't. So, the connection manager properties actually store the GUID ID of the connection manager instead of the name. That way, if the user changes the connection manager name, the connection manager reference is still valid. The `GetConnectionName` and `GetConnectionID` functions are conveniently provided on the base task class. All you need to do is store a reference to the connections and pass it in. The methods do the work of getting the name from the ID and the ID from the name. The task should only store the ID because it is guaranteed not to change, unless you edit the package XML directly, of course.

> **NOTE**
>
> Hard-core .NET developers will perhaps cringe at the member variable names using the "m_" prefix. FxCop might emit a warning about this not being Pascal cased. Ignore it. Resist the flood of conventionalism!

`EncryptionOperation`   The `EncryptionOperation` property illustrates how custom types can be used in tasks to clearly describe optional task behavior. *EncryptionOp* is an enum defined within the task and represents the two operations the task can perform. A Boolean property could have worked here, but the values `Encrypt` and `Decrypt` are much more direct and clearly indicate what the operation will be. Later, if you decide to modify the task to perform more operations, adding another enum value is easy.

```
public EncryptOp EncryptionOperation
{
   get
   {
      return m_operation;
   }
   set
   {
      m_operation = value;
   }
}
```

Again, the `EncryptionOperation` is a simple accessor property. This is how properties on tasks should be. There should rarely be any complicated logic in task properties. Also, the functionality of the task is generally something that can and should be developed and tested separately. For example, in the `CryptoTask` example, the code that interacts with the SSIS runtime is contained in the `CryptoTask.cs` file and the code that implements the actual features, the functionality of the task, is contained in the `Rijndael.cs` file. This makes it easy to isolate, test, and debug the code.

Adding SSIS-Specific Properties and Functions

As you have seen, you build customassembly. The base class implements three methods that you should override when creating a custom task:

- InitializeTask—Do initialization functions, such as creating log events, custom events, and breakpoints
- Validate—Validate if the task will run successfully when Execute is called
- Execute—Do the work the task is configured to do

There are also some execution-related properties that the custom task can provide:

- ExecutionValue—Provides a task-defined value with information resulting from the task execution.
- WaitForMe—Indicates if the task is an event-driven task. If the task has no bounded execution lifetime, this property should be set to FALSE. The default is TRUE.

In addition, there are some properties and a method related to task upgrade:

- CanUpdate—Indicates if the task supports upgrading other tasks
- Version—Indicates the version of the task
- Update—Tells the task to update another task

Finally, there are two utility methods for handling connection manager names and IDs just mentioned:

- GetConnectionName
- GetConnectionID

Only the Execute method must be implemented. The Validate method is extremely important as well. However, the rest of the methods need to be implemented only if you want your task to have the functionality that they provide.

The InitializeTask Method

The InitializeTask method is called when the task is first created. In the designer, that happens when you drag the task from the Toolbox and drop it onto the Control Flow surface or when loading a package. Following is the method signature:

```
public virtual void
InitializeTask(
   Connections connections,               //The package connections reference
   VariableDispenser variableDispenser,   //The package variables reference
   IDTSInfoEvents events,                 //The collection you use to raise events
   IDTSLogging log,                       //The package logging reference
   EventInfos eventInfos,                 //The collection used to describe events
```

```
   LogEntryInfos logEntryInfos,       //The collection used to describe log
entries
   ObjectReferenceTracker refTracker   //This parameter should be ignored.
)
```

You can perform any initialization that is needed here; however, this method is provided as a way for the task to communicate to the SSIS runtime what events the task will raise and what log entries it will log. You might notice that the events parameter is different than the one passed into `Validate` and `Execute`. This is because the runtime is only prepared to receive `Error`, `Warning`, and `Information` events at the time it calls `InitializeTask`.

Creating Custom Events   Tasks use the `EventInfos` parameter to describe custom events they raise. The SSIS runtime exposes the events to the designer where users can create event handlers for the custom events. The code to add a custom event with two parameters is as follows:

```
string[] parameterNames = new string[2] {"Parameter1", "Parameter2"};
TypeCode[] parameterTypes = new TypeCode[2] {TypeCode.String, TypeCode.Int32};
string[] parameterDescriptions = new string[2] {"Parameter desc1.",
➥"Parameter desc2" };
Boolean allowEventHandlers = true;
eventInfos.Add(
   "CustomEventName",
   "A custom event to show how they are created",
   allowEventHandlers,
   parameterNames,
   parameterTypes,
   parameterDescriptions
);
```

The first parameter is a `string` containing the name of the event. The second parameter is a `string` containing the description. The third parameter is a Boolean and specifies if event handlers should be created for the event. The last three parameters are for describing the event parameters. The SSIS runtime uses these parameters to build system variables on the event handler that will contain the event parameters.

Adding a custom event has the following effects:

- A new `Log` event is added for the event. If the `Log` event is enabled in the Configure SSIS Logs dialog box, whenever the task fires the event, the SSIS runtime also logs the event.

- A new event handler type becomes available in the EventHandlers collection. Figure 24.7 shows the event handler for the custom event added with the sample code.

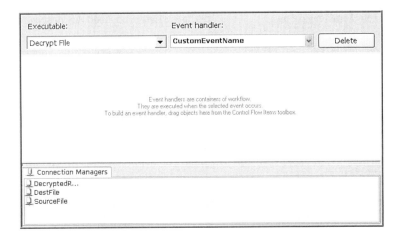

FIGURE 24.7   The sample custom event handler in the designer.

- A new system variable becomes available within the event handler for each event parameter. Figure 24.8 shows the two system variables, `Parameter1` and `Parameter2`, that will contain the values for the custom event parameters created in the sample code.

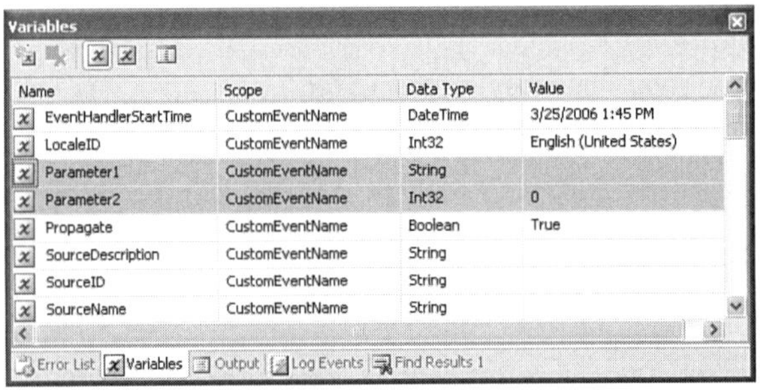

Name	Scope	Data Type	Value
EventHandlerStartTime	CustomEventName	DateTime	3/25/2006 1:45 PM
LocaleID	CustomEventName	Int32	English (United States)
Parameter1	CustomEventName	String	
Parameter2	CustomEventName	Int32	0
Propagate	CustomEventName	Boolean	True
SourceDescription	CustomEventName	String	
SourceID	CustomEventName	String	
SourceName	CustomEventName	String	

FIGURE 24.8   The system variables that will contain the values for the custom event parameters.

Creating Custom Log Events   The task must add a `LogEntryInfo` for custom log events. This informs the SSIS runtime about the log entry so that it can filter the log entry and provides an entry in the designer's Configure SSIS Logs dialog box. Figure 24.9 shows the custom log entry for the `CryptoTask` called `CryptoFileLogEntry`. Also, notice the custom log entry for the custom event called `CustomEventName` created with the sample code.

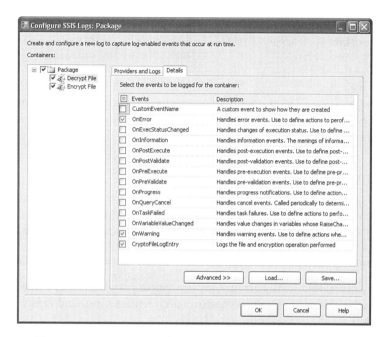

FIGURE 24.9   The CryptoTask custom log entry and custom event log entry.

The code to add this custom log entry is as follows:

```
// Adds a log entry info so users can filter the log entries of this type in the
designer.
// Creates an entry in the logging dialog box under details to filter the log
entry.
logEntryInfos.Add(
    "CryptoFileLogEntry",
    "Logs the file and encryption operation performed",
    DTSLogEntryFrequency.Occasional
);
```

The first parameter is a string that contains the name of the log entry. The second para-meter is a string that contains the description of the log entry. The third parameter is the LogEntryFrequency parameter and indicates how often the task logs the custom log entry. The SSIS runtime currently ignores this parameter.

The Validate Method

Validate is called whenever the runtime wants to ensure that the task is valid. It is guar-anteed to be called at least once immediately before the Execute method is called. It can be called multiple times before and after execution.

```
public virtual DTSExecResult
Validate(
    Connections connections,          //Used to access connection managers
```

```
    VariableDispenser variableDispenser, //Used to access variables
    IDTSComponentEvents componentEvents, //Used to raise events
    IDTSLogging log                      //Used to make log entries
)
```

Validation is what a component does to detect if there are any issues that would cause it to fail during execution. The following are some guidelines for what your component should do during validation:

- When a component validates, it should always validate that given its current property settings, it will succeed during execution.

- Components should not return when they find the first error or warning. They should continue to validate until finding all errors and warnings. This provides more information and helps the user better understand all the problems with the component up front because an entire error stack for the component is visible instead of just one error or warning.

- Components should emit warnings for less severe errors. But that can be a difficult call to make. Where do you draw the line between warnings and errors?

To Warn or To Err   You should think of warnings as errors that won't cause the component to fail. For example, the Send Mail Task emits a warning when there is no subject specified, but it emits an error when there is no connection manager specified. Clearly, the former isn't critical, whereas the latter causes the task to fail.

Another example is the validation code for the `CryptoTask`. If no password is specified, this is bad. The document gets encrypted, but without a password. Anyone can decrypt the document by simply running the task without a password. So, it is important to ensure that there is a password and emit an error if there isn't one.

```
// Validate that the password exists
if (m_password.Length == 0)
{
    events.FireError(15, "",
    "There is no password specified.", "", 0);
}
```

You can also validate that the password conforms to a password complexity policy. For the sake of simplicity, the code checks if the password is empty. You definitely want to emit an error in this case because the task will be silently behaving in an unexpected way.

On the other hand, there are cases when the task is expecting that something will be configured in a certain way or that a given file exists but doesn't. Packages are sometimes built to prepare files for processing by other parts of the same package. For example, to error if a file doesn't exist would essentially eliminate this pattern and create an inflexible component. When it comes to elements of the system that can be altered by previous package control flow or data flow, it is wise to only emit a warning. The

ValidateConnectionManager function in CryptoTask.cs emits a warning for this case, as follows:

```
// Does the file even exist?
// If not and it's the source Connection Manager, let the user know.
if (!fiSource.Exists)
{
    if( !bDest) // Don't warn if it's the destination cuz we'll be creating the dest
file.
    {
        // Only fire a warning because the file may become available later in the
package.
        StringBuilder sb = new StringBuilder("The specified connection manager : " +
            sCMName + " points to the following file which does not exist : " +
sFile);
        events.FireWarning(3, "", sb.ToString(), "", 0);
    }
}
```

If the source file to encrypt doesn't exist, the CryptoTask emits the following warning:

```
Warning   1 Validation warning. Encrypt File : The specified connection manager :
SourceFile points to the following file which does not exist :
D:\SAMPLES\SAMPLE.TXT
```

Seriously consider what constitutes a validation warning or error. Although the runtime design encourages static package designs, a certain amount of flexibility is necessary. Think about how the task will be used in different situations. Issues that cannot be resolved at execution time should always be considered errors. The following are some examples of issues that should always be considered errors:

- **Missing connection manager**—Connection managers can only be created at design time. The package cannot correct the problem during execution time.

- **Silent unexpected behavior**—Task would behave in a way that is undesirable because, for example, a property value is out of bounds.

- **Missing variables**—Opinions differ, but it is safest to emit an error.

- **Internal errors**—Always catch exceptions and correct the problem internally or emit an error with a detailed explanation. This is the one case in which validation should return Failure.

Errors Are Not Failures   There has been some confusion about how errors affect the success or failure of validation or execution. Errors do not constitute failure. It is the MaximumErrorCount property on containers that defines how many errors constitute failure. The Validate and Execute methods should never return Failure because of errors or warnings except when the errors are a result of an exception that cannot be corrected in code. Typical cases are when there is an exception or fatal error such as when the `AcquireConnection` call fails to return a valid connection.

The `Execute` Method

The `Execute` method is where the task performs its work. `Execute` cannot be called at all if the package flow doesn't reach the task or if the task is disabled. Otherwise, it is called at least once during the execution of a package and can be called more than once if the task is in a loop. The parameters are the same as for validation with the addition of the transaction object.

```
public virtual DTSExecResult
Execute(
    Connections connections,
    VariableDispenser variableDispenser,
    IDTSComponentEvents componentEvents,
    IDTSLogging log,
    object transaction
)
```

The `Connections` Parameter   At design time, a user creates a new connection manager and sets its properties. During execution, tasks retrieve the desired connection manager in the collection and call `AcquireConnection` on the connection manager, which yields a number of values depending on the connection manager type. For example, the Flat File Connection Manager returns a string containing the fully qualified filename of the flat file, the OLE DB Connection Manager returns a pointer to an IDBSession OLEDB interface, and an ADO.NET Connection Manager returns an `IdbConnection` object.

How Tasks Use Connections   Tasks use connections by creating a task property where the name or ID of the connection can be specified. At design time, the user places the name or ID of the connection to use by setting this property. In the `CryptoTask`, these properties are called `DestinationFileConnectionManager` and `SourceFileConnectionManager`. During execution, the task uses the name or ID to retrieve the specified connection manager and call `AcquireConnection`. Here is the code from the `CryptoTask`.

```
// Get the source filename string
ConnectionManager cm = connections[m_source];
if (cm != null)
{
    // Get the filename
    sourceFileName = (string)cm.AcquireConnection(null);
}
```

The m_source member variable is a string that contains the ID of the source connection manager. The `AcquireConnection` call takes one parameter, which is a transaction object. In this case, the File Connection Manager does not support transactions, so simply passes in null. Later, the code uses the returned string, `sourceFileName`, to open the file to encrypt it with this code.

```
// Read the file into a string
TextReader trSource = System.IO.File.OpenText(sourceFileName);
string sSource = trSource.ReadToEnd();

// Release the file
trSource.Close();
```

The `VariableDispenser` **Parameter**   The second parameter is the `VariableDispenser` object. Users create variables and populate them by directly entering values, configuring them with package configurations, or by adding an expression to the variable. Variable values can also change during the execution of the package. The `VariableDispenser` provides accessor methods for retrieving variables.

How Tasks Use the Variable Dispenser   Generally, a task exposes a property with a name that indicates it is used to store a variable name or ID. A name like `ConnectionStringVariable` is appropriate. Similar to the way connections are used, the task uses the name as an index into the Variables collection to retrieve the specified variable during execution. Because SSIS packages do work in parallel, variables can have multiple simultaneous readers and writers. Therefore, it is necessary to serialize access to variables. The runtime does this using what is called the Variable Dispenser. To gain access to a variable, the task must first reserve the variable. This essentially locks variables so that other tasks or components cannot access them simultaneously. The following code is an example of how to access variables:

```
// Lock the variable with the initialization vector string
variableDispenser.LockForRead(m_InitVectorVariable);

// Get the locked variables collection
// In this case the collection has only the one variable, InitVector.
variableDispenser.GetVariables(ref variables);

// Use the variable value
string sVector = variables[m_InitVectorVariable].Value;
```

The `IDTSComponentEvents` **Parameter**   The third parameter passed is the Component Events interface. The `ComponentEvents` interface provides a way for the task to raise events. Events that a task raises can be handled within the package in event handler workflow or simply flow up through the container hierarchy until it reaches the package. After the event arrives at the package, it is sent to the client events interface passed into the `Execute` method on the package. Figure 24.10 illustrates how a typical event is generated and propagated through the package. The solid lines represent method calls and the dotted lines represent the method returning. The client represents the designer, `DTExec.exe`, or any other object model client. The client passes in an `IDTSEvents` interface so that it can "listen" for all events that are raised within the package as it executes. Likewise, each container also implements the `IDTSEvents` interface. Events bubble up through the container hierarchy, giving each container an opportunity to handle the event before passing it on. Figure 24.10 illustrates the life cycle of an event starting with the client application calling the package's Execute method and finishing with the event call returning to the task and the task continuing execution. Events are synchronous, meaning that when the task raises an event by calling one of the "fire" methods on the IDTSComponentEvents interface, the method does not return until the event has completed the entire event handling cycle from the event handlers all the way up to the client application.

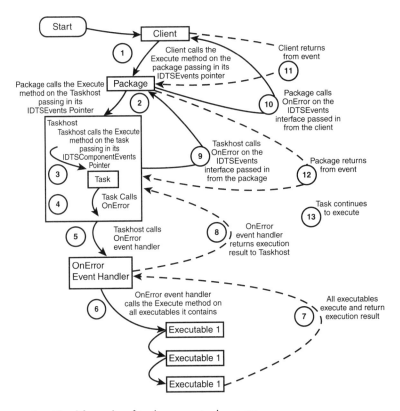

FIGURE 24.10   The life cycle of task-generated events.

Notice that each container passes its own IDTSEvents interface into the Execute method of its child executable and that the Taskhost has the OnError event handler defined in its EventHandlers collection. Notice also, that the OnError method is called on each container in the hierarchy, providing an opportunity for each container to handle the event. This design makes it possible to localize event handlers to the section of the package that raises the event. It also makes it possible to generalize event handling, that is, create global event handlers that handle all events from the entire package. If an event handler was defined for OnError at package scope, that event handler would be called for each OnError event in the package. The event bubbles up to the client where events can be reflected in the UI or trigger some logic in the client. For example, the designer uses the ExecutionStatusChanged event to determine whether to color the tasks red or green when they complete execution.

The following events are available on the Component Events interface:

- FireBreakpointHit—This event is fired when an active breakpoint is hit. For more about implementing breakpoints, see the "Developing and Debugging the Task" section later in this chapter.

- FireCustomEvent—This event is for custom, task-specific information. See "Firing Custom Events" in the next section.

- FireError—This event is for reporting critical errors.

- FireInformation—There are many situations when the task needs to provide information about internal events that are not appropriately surfaced as warnings or errors. For example, some tasks can feature the ability to execute in a smart way. Maybe they optimize some aspects of their configuration or change the way they execute based on some heuristic. The custom task should alert the user to this behavior by raising a FireInfo event. For another example, consider a custom task that uses the wildcard feature on the file connection manager to process multiple files that are unknown at package design time. By raising a FireInfo event for each file used, there is a record of which files were processed and in what order. You should raise the FireInfo event whenever there is nonerror information available that will help the user understand what is happening inside the task.

- FireProgress—This event is for reporting progress. Tasks should raise this event to inform clients about the status of the task's execution. Even for short-running tasks, when the progress goes from 0% to 100% instantly, this event should be called.

- FireQueryCancel—At various intervals in the execution of the task, the task should call this event. This is especially true if the task has the potential to be long running. Long-running tasks are those that take much more time than the other tasks in the package or longer than 15 or 20 seconds. This allows the runtime to gracefully terminate execution. The task raises this event to determine whether the package wants the task to cease executing. Because the package gives control to the task to execute and will not terminate it randomly, there needs to be a juncture at which the package can inform the task that it is attempting to shut down. OnQueryCancel provides that juncture.

- FireWarning—This event is for reporting noncritical errors.

Firing Custom Events   The discussion so far has focused on how to raise events with the "Fire" events methods. Custom events are the extensible mechanism for raising task-defined events. Tasks can advertise the custom event by populating a special collection of event information objects that the runtime reads. This makes it possible to create DTS event handlers in the package workflow that will handle the events. Although the available set of stock events is rich and useful, there are many circumstances when the stock events don't provide the needed functionality. For example, a task might need to raise a custom event when a hard drive is full. The task could raise a custom DTS event with information about which drive is full and workflow can be created in the DTS event handler to clean up the hard drive.

Custom events are added during design time. As the package writer modifies properties and operations, the task is free to add and remove custom events. If you've defined a custom event, you'll need to use the FireCustomEvent method, as follows:

```
// Check whether the client wants to continue receiving events.
Boolean fireAgain = true;

// Set up the event parameters
object[] objArgs = new object[2] {"Parameter1 Value", 42};

// Fire the custom event
events.FireCustomEvent(
   "CustomEventName",
   "Custom event fired",
   ref objArgs, "", ref fireAgain
);
```

The SSIS runtime places the passed parameter values into the system variables it created to hold the values. Notice that the parameter values passed in are "Parameter1 Value" for the string parameter and "42" for the integer parameter. Figure 24.11 shows the custom event parameter system variables in the Watch window.

FIGURE 24.11   Viewing the value of custom event parameter system variables.

The IDTSLogging **Parameter**   The IDTSLogging parameter is a pointer to the logging interface the task can use to create log entries. IDTSLogging has one property and two methods.

- Enabled—Specifies if logging is enabled for the task
- GetFilterStatus—Specifies if an event is filtered
- Log—Adds log entries when called

In practice, the GetFilterStatus method is rarely used. If you do use it, call it once in the Execute method to determine if a given log entry has been filtered. If so, you can eliminate the log.

The `Enabled` property is useful to determine if logging is enabled for the task. If not, you can short circuit the log calls and save some time.

The `Log` method has the following signature:

```
void Log (
    string eventName,
    string computerName,
    string operatorName,
    string sourceName,
    string sourceGuid,
    string executionGuid,
    string messageText,
    DateTime startTime,
    DateTime endTime,
    int dataCode,
    ref byte[] dataBytes
)
```

The SSIS runtime overwrites the `computerName`, `operatorName`, `sourceName`, `sourceGuid`, and `executionGuid`. Even if you provide values for these parameters, they will not be logged. For most tasks, it is easier to have a helper function for logging, such as the following:

```
// A simplified method for logging.
// Does not require the additional overwritten parameters.
private void WriteLog(IDTSLogging log, string logEventName, string message)
{
    // Only log if we have a valid log object and logging is enabled
    if (log != null && log.Enabled)
    {
        byte[] nothing = null;
        log.Log(
            logEventName, null, null, null, null, null,
            message, DateTime.Now, DateTime.Now, 0, ref nothing );
    }
}
```

The `Transaction` **Object**

The last parameter passed into the `Execute` method is the transaction. Transactions in SSIS are thin wrappers around an `ITransaction Distributed Transaction` pointer. The `Transaction` object has two properties, one is the `ITransaction` pointer and the other is a Boolean flag called `isActive`. The `isActive` flag is used internally to evaluate the transaction requirements imposed on the containers and is not of particular interest to the task author nor should it be modified in the task code.

Package writers configure transactions on the Taskhost or other parent container in the tasks hierarchy and at execution time, the container creates the distributed transaction and passes the transaction pointer to its children when it calls their Execute method. If your task uses a connection to a server that supports transactions and you want your task to participate in transactions, using the Transaction object is simple. When the SSIS runtime calls the task's Execute method, it passes in the Transaction object. The responsibility of the task is to pass the Transaction object into the connection when calling AcquireConnection. If your task uses a connection that doesn't support transactions, the Transaction object is of no interest to your task and the task should pass null to the AcquireConnection call.

The scope and lifetime of the transaction is determined by the owning container, which is the container that creates the transaction. The transaction is active as long as its owning container is executing. Depending on how the transaction is configured and the execution result of the owning container, the owning container commits or rolls back the transaction when the container completes execution.

```
public override DTSExecResult
Execute( Connections connections,
                VariableDispenser variableDispenser,
                IDTSComponentEvents events,
                IDTSLogging log,
                object transaction)
{
    // Get the connection manager.
    AcquireConnection(connections, transaction);

    //Other execution code that uses the connection…

    return DTSExecResult.Success;
}
```

Task Breakpoints

To expose breakpoints, a task must implement the IDTSBreakpointSite interface which is derived from IDTSSuspend. When a task is first created, the runtime calls IDTSBreakpointSite.AcceptBreakpointManager on the task, passing in a breakpoint manager that the task can use to inform the runtime of the breakpoints it wants to expose and to check whether those breakpoints have been enabled by the client. The task retains a reference to the breakpoint manager and creates breakpoints during the AcceptBreakpointManager call. The task then calls IsBreakpointEnabled while executing. Each breakpoint is identified by a task-defined and task-scoped ID. The following code shows how to create a custom breakpoint:

```
AcceptBreakpointManager( BreakpointManager breakPointManager)
{
   m_pManager = breakPointManager;
   m_pManager.CreateBreakpoint(1, "Break when the task is about to do X");
}
```

Then, in the `Execute` method, the following code is called when the breakpoint is hit:

```
Execute(...)
{
   // Other code...

   // At the point in the code where you wish to fire the breakpoint
   if( m_pManager.IsBreakpointTargetEnabled( 1 ) == true )
   {
      events.OnBreakpointHit( m_pManager.GetBreakpointTarget( 1 ) );
   }

   // Other code...
}
```

The `IsBreakpointEnabled` function must be called each time the task encounters a breakpoint in its code. This can become expensive if called too much. As a result, `IDTSBreakpointSite` contains a flag, `DebugMode`, which is set to `TRUE` when the executable is to be debugged. When this flag is set to `FALSE`, the task can avoid the breakpoint logic altogether and save some performance. Figure 24.12 illustrates the order of processing that occurs when execution reaches a task breakpoint.

ExecutionValue

`ExecutionValue` is a read-only variant property. This property is a task-defined value that provides an opportunity for the task writer to expose more information about the execution of the task than merely if the execution succeeded or failed. For example, the Execute Process Task returns the exit code from the last process executed in this property. As a task author, you are free to use this property for whatever purposes you deem appropriate. However, the property should hold a value that relates to the execution of the task and should add information about the reasons for the success or failure of the task.

WaitForMe

The `WaitForMe` property is a special read-only Boolean property the task can expose to indicate that the package should not wait on the task to complete and set the `Cancel` event. Remember that the `Cancel` event is the windows event that the SSIS runtime flags to indicate that it is attempting to shut down, and tasks access the event through the `CancelEvent` system variable. The `WaitForMe` property is implemented in the task base class and is `TRUE` by default. This property should only be implemented in custom tasks that implement eventing. Eventing class tasks are tasks that have no defined execution life cycle. For example, the stock WMI Event Watcher Task is of this class. This type of tasks waits for events and when an event happens, they can return from their Execute method or continue waiting for more events for an indeterminant length of time.

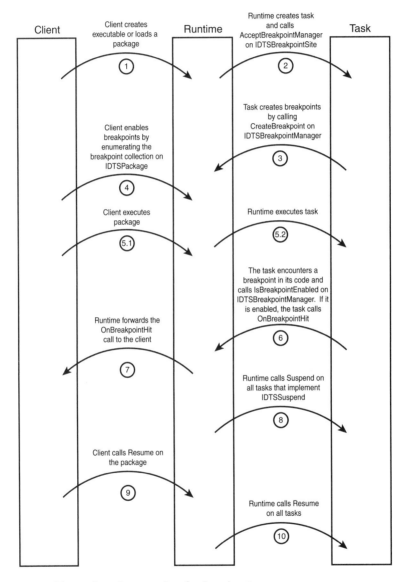

FIGURE 24.12   The order of processing for breakpoints.

The SSIS runtime knows it is time to return from executing when every task in the package has completed. However, if there is an eventing task still waiting, the package would never complete. So packages wait until all tasks with the WaitForMe property set to TRUE have completed. Then they signal the Cancel event, through the CancelEvent system variable. Eventing class tasks should wait on this event and when it is signaled, cancel execution, and return, allowing the package to complete.

Update Properties and Method

Integration Services provides a way for later version tasks to update earlier version tasks. For example, if you ship a task and then, a year later, update the task, you'd want the newer task to update the older task. This is what the Update methods are for. CanUpdate has the following signature:

```
public virtual bool CanUpdate(string CreationName)
{
    return false; //default implementation
}
```

The string parameter contains the CLSID or fully qualified name of a task. Return TRUE from CanUpdate if the task can update the task with the given CreationName.

Version is the version of the task. The default is 0 and should be incremented whenever you update a task.

```
public virtual int Version
{
    get{return 0;}     //default implementation
}
```

The Update method is called by the SSIS runtime to perform the update of the older task. The persisted state of the older version of the task is passed, giving the newer version task a chance to read in the property values for the older task and replace the XML with its own persisted state. In this way, the property values for the older task are retained while simultaneously upgrading to a newer version.

```
public virtual void Update(ref string ObjectXml)
{
}
```

Saving and Loading Tasks

DTS packages are persisted in XML. Tasks can participate in persistence by deriving the task from IDTSTaskPersist, which has two methods called SaveToXML and LoadFromXML that must be implemented. The following code illustrates in a basic way how this can be done. Error handling and other code is omitted in the interest of clarity. For more sample code, see the CryptoTask sample task.

```
using System;
using System.Xml;
using Microsoft.SqlServer.Dts.Runtime;

class MyTask : Task, IDTSTaskPersist
{
```

```
    // Other code…
    // IDTSTaskPersist interface methods
    public void SaveToXML(XmlDocument doc)
    {
        // Create element for the task info w/ prefix, name, namespace
        XmlNode dataNode = doc.CreateElement( null, "MyData", mytask.uri");

        // Append the node to the package document
        doc.AppendChild(dataNode);

        // Add text to the element, the value of MyTask's member data
        XmlNode textNode = doc.CreateTextNode( m_value.ToString() );

        // Add the node under our main node.
        dataNode.AppendChild(textNode);
    }
    public void LoadFromXML(XmlElement element)
    {
        m_value = System.Convert.ToInt32(element.FirstChild.Value);
    }
    private int m_value = 123;
}
```

There are a few things worth mentioning about the previous snippet of code. First, notice that SaveToXML takes one parameter that is an XmlDocument while LoadFromXML takes an XmlElement as the parameter. When loading, the runtime creates an instance of the task and passes in the task's node. Everything below the task node, including content and format, is opaque to the package. So tasks have total control over what is stored inside their node. The one exception is that nodes marked as sensitive are handled in a special way as previously mentioned in the discussion "Passwords and Other Sensitive Properties." Also, if a task is simple with no special persistence requirements, you can simply not implement IDTSTaskPersist and the SSIS runtime will save and load your task for you.

Building the Task User Interface

This section describes how to create a user interface for your task. The task UI is developed in a separate project and compiled to a separate assembly from the task to simplify localization and maintenance. Other than the DTSTask attribute, the task has no connection to its TaskUI. This section starts by describing how to build a rudimentary custom task UI for the sample task and then moves on to describe how to use the foundation class Microsoft used for building rich task UI.

Building the Sample Task UI (Simple)

To start the TaskUI project, step through the same steps used to start any of the custom components. Because they were covered in detail earlier, only the high-level steps are given here.

1. Create a Class Library project. Call the project TaskUI.

2. Rename the generated source file to `SampleTaskUI.cs`.

3. Add a strong name and key file. You can use the key file already generated for the sample task.

4. Reference SSIS and other assemblies. You need to reference the `Microsoft.SqlServer.Dts.Runtime` namespace in the `Microsoft.SqlServer.ManagedRuntime` assembly as before, but you must also reference the `Microsoft.SqlServer.Dts.Runtime.Design` namespace in the `Microsoft.SqlServer.Dts.Design.dll` assembly.

5. Define the class. Change the namespace in `SampleTaskUI.cs` to be the same as the sample task, namely SampleTask.

6. Compile and install. You need only place this assembly in the GAC. You do not need to copy it to the `DTS\Tasks` directory.

Adding the Form

At this point, you have a compiling component, but it contains no form and it has no relationship to the sample task. To add the TaskUI form, complete the following steps:

1. Right-click on the TaskUI project in the Solution Explorer, and select Add, New Item.

2. Select Windows Form and name the new file `SampleTaskUIWnd.cs`, as shown in Figure 24.13.

3. Right-click on the `SampleUIWnd.cs` file in the Solution Explorer, and select View Designer.

4. Drag two Label controls over to the form, and change the text to *Name* for one and *Description* for the other.

5. Drag two text boxes to the form.

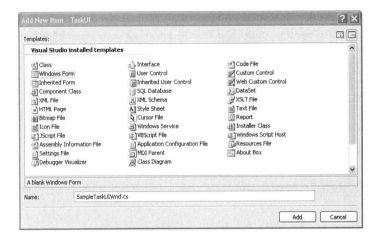

FIGURE 24.13   Adding a form to the TaskUI project.

6. Drag a button to the form and change the text to "OK" in the property grid.

7. Change the `DialogResult` property to "OK."

8. The form should look similar to the one shown in Figure 24.14.

FIGURE 24.14   The TaskUI form.

9. Double-click on the text box below the Name label and enter the following event handler code. Make sure the text box name matches the event name. In the sample, the text box name is textBox1.

```
private string name;
private void textBox1_TextChanged(object sender, EventArgs e)
{
    name = textBox1.Text;
}
```

10. Go back to the designer and do the same for the other text box below the Description label.

```
private string description;
private void textBox2_TextChanged(object sender, EventArgs e)
{
    description = textBox2.Text;
}
```

11. Modify the constructor code as follows to store the Taskhost reference and to initialize the name and description text boxes.

```
private TaskHost m_taskHost;
public SampleTaskUIWnd(TaskHost taskHost)
{
    m_taskHost = taskHost;
    InitializeComponent();
    textBox1.Text = m_taskHost.Name;
    textBox2.Text = m_taskHost.Description;
}
```

12. Go back to the designer one more time, double-click the OK button, and enter the following code to set the name and description on the task.

TIP

In the TaskUI, it's best to wait until the end before committing task property value changes. With this code, changes are only committed when the user clicks the OK button. If you directly change the values on the Taskhost, you would have to change them back if the user cancels the edit.

```
private void button1_Click(object sender, EventArgs e)
{
    m_taskHost.Name = name;
    m_taskHost.Description = description;
}
```

13. The final step is to derive the SampleTaskUI class from the IdtsTaskUI interface defined in the Microsoft.SqlServer.Dts.Design namespace. Open the SampleTaskUI.cs source file and modify the code to look like the following:

```
using System;
using System.Collections.Generic;
using System.Text;
using System.Windows.Forms;
using Microsoft.SqlServer.Dts.Runtime.Design;
using Microsoft.SqlServer.Dts.Design;
```

```
namespace SampleTask
{
   public partial class SampleTaskUI : IDtsTaskUI
   {
      private Microsoft.SqlServer.Dts.Runtime.TaskHost m_taskHost;

      public void
      Initialize(Microsoft.SqlServer.Dts.Runtime.TaskHost taskHost,
               System.IServiceProvider serviceProvider)
      {  // Save the taskhost reference
         m_taskHost = taskHost;
      }

      public ContainerControl GetView()
      {  // Show the TaskUI
         return new SampleTaskUIWnd(m_taskHost);
      }

      public void Delete(System.Windows.Forms.IWin32Window form)
      {
      }

      public void New(System.Windows.Forms.IWin32Window form)
      {
      }
   }
}
```

As you can see, the interface for task UIs is called IDTSTaskUI. This interface has four methods:

- Initialize—This method is called by the client (that is, the designer application) to associate a task UI with the task. Note that the Taskhost is passed in as the first parameter. The logic of the task UI can use this pointer to access the variables collection on the Taskhost, get the task pointer by calling GetInnerUnknown on the Taskhost, or view the errors collection, and so forth. The ServiceProvider provides a way to access services such as the connection service for accessing or creating connection managers. This Initialize method should be implemented at a minimum so that you can save the Taskhost reference.

- GetView—This method is called by the client whenever the task UI should show itself. This method must be implemented.

- New—This method is called when a new task is added to the package. This method is rarely implemented.

- Delete—This method is called when a task is about to be deleted. This method is rarely implemented.

This code saves the Taskhost reference and then passes it into the form when the GetView method is called. The form sets properties on the Taskhost and on the task as well if you add properties to the task. There is one more thing to do now and that is to connect the task with the task UI. You do this with the DTSTask attribute UITypeName parameter. You will remember that the format for the UITypeName is as follows:

UITypeName = "*NamespaceTypeName, AssemblyName*, Version=*AssemblyVersion*, Culture=Neutral, PublicKeyToken= *PublicKeyToken*".

- NamespaceTypeName—This is the fully qualified name of the TaskUI. In the SampleTaskUI case, it is SampleTask.SampleTaskUI.

- AssemblyName—This is the filename of the TaskUI assembly sans the .dll extension. For the SampleTaskUI assembly, this is SampleTaskUI.

- Version—This is the version of the task UI assembly specified in the AssemblyInfo.cs file.

- Culture—This is the culture of the TaskUI assembly and can be discovered by looking at the properties of the assembly, as shown in Figure 24.15.

- PublicKeyToken—You find this value by examining the properties of the TaskUI assembly in the GAC. Go to C:\Windows\Assembly and find the TaskUI assembly. Right-click on the assembly name and select Properties. Figure 24.15 shows the properties dialog box for the SampleTaskUI assembly. Notice the public key token that is highlighted.

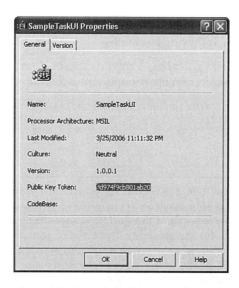

FIGURE 24.15   Finding the public key token for the TaskUI assembly.

After you get the `UITypeName` right, you're ready to build and install the task and task UI assemblies. Make sure the task assembly is installed in the GAC and the DTS subfolder. Also, make sure the task UI assembly is installed in the GAC. Create a new SSIS project, add the SampleTask to the Toolbox if you haven't already, and drop it onto the package surface. Double-click on the task to open the task UI.

> **TIP**
>
> After you have opened the task UI inside the designer, the designer caches a reference to the assembly. If you make subsequent changes to the task UI, they are not reflected in the designer until you close down all instances of the designer that have previously opened the task UI. If you make changes to the task UI, close down the designer containing the package you use to test the task UI, rebuild the entire task and task UI project, and reload the test package. That is the only way to consistently ensure that the designer picks up the updated task UI.

If you get lost or just want to go straight to the code, you can look at the SampleTask solution in the samples under `SAMPLES\SRC\SampleComponents\SampleTask`.

Building a Sophisticated TaskUI (Complex)

Although simple taskUIs might be sufficient for some tasks, if you want your tasks to have the same look and feel as the stock tasks, you need to create a more sophisticated taskUI. Integration Services provides a standard framework for taskUIs. It is the same framework Microsoft used for building all the stock taskUIs and supports the Property Expression page and Expression Builder by default. The taskUI foundation classes and definitions are found in the following assemblies:

- `Microsoft.SQLServer.Dts.Design`—Contains `IDtsConnectionService` for creating new connection managers and other important definitions.

- `Microsoft.DataTransformationServices.Controls`—Contains `DtsBaseTaskUI` and other important classes.

> **CAUTION**
>
> When you right-click on the References node for your taskUI project and select Add References, the `Microsoft.DataTransformationService.Controls` assembly does not show up in the .NET assemblies tab of the Add Reference dialog box. You need to select the Browse tab and search for the assembly. This makes a copy of the assembly while you are designing the UI. You do not need to install this assembly, however, because it is in the GAC. You only need a copy of the assembly while developing the task UI. On machines where SSIS has been installed, you'll find this assembly in the `C:\Windows\Assemblies` folder or its equivalent.

There are two sample tasks that use the framework. `StarterTaskUI` in the `StarterTask` sample solution is a rudimentary taskUI you can use for starting your own tasks and taskUIs. CryptoTask is a complete task and taskUI and uses some of the more interesting features of the framework such as custom UITypeEditors. The samples shown here are from the CryptoTask sample code. Only the more interesting aspects of the code are covered here because the taskUI code is somewhat lengthy. You can find both projects in the SAMPLES\SRC\SampleComponents folder.

Figure 24.16 shows the CryptoTask taskUI settings node. This taskUI has four custom properties that are typical of the kinds of properties that you might want to support on your taskUIs. The four property types are as follows:

- Connection Managers, Source and Destination
- Password
- Custom Enum type selector
- Boolean

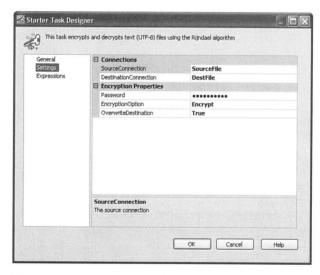

FIGURE 24.16   The CryptoTask Settings node.

By now, the taskUI design should be familiar to you. On the left side of the taskUI is the tree view that contains nodes that when selected present you with different property grids or *views* on the right side of the taskUI. The upper-left of the taskUI shows an icon and description. Each of these sections of the taskUI is customizable.

Starting the Project
To get started with the taskUI, you can use the same steps as described for the simple taskUI by creating a class library project, deriving the class from IDtsTaskUI, and implementing the Initialize and GetView methods or you can use the StarterTask project and modify it as needed. The following is the code for the CryptoTask IDtsTaskUI interface methods:

```
namespace SSIS2K5.Samples.Tasks.CryptoTask
{
    public class CryptoTaskUI : IDtsTaskUI
    {
        // TaskUI receives a TaskHost and we cache it here.
        private TaskHost taskHost = null;

        // Get the connection service for creating connections if needed.
        private IDtsConnectionService connectionService = null;

        // Called by the designer to initialize the taskHost UI
        public void Initialize(TaskHost taskHost, System.IServiceProvider
➥serviceProvider)
        {
            this.taskHost = taskHost;
            this.connectionService = serviceProvider.GetService(typeof
➥(IDtsConnectionService)) as IDtsConnectionService;
        }

        // Called by the designer to show the window
        public ContainerControl GetView()
        {
            return new CryptoTaskUIMainWnd(taskHost, connectionService);
        }

        /// <summary>
        ///  Called when a new Task is added to the package.
        /// </summary>
        public void New(IWin32Window parentWindow)
        {
            // do nothing
        }

        /// <summary>
        /// Called when an existing taskHost is about to be deleted from the package
        /// </summary>
        public void Delete(IWin32Window parentWindow)
        {
            // do nothing
        }
    }
}
```

If you worked through the simple task sample, this code should look familiar to you. It's almost exactly the same and is how the designer communicates with the taskUI. Notice that the Initialize method stores a reference to the serviceProvider parameter and that in the GetView method a new form called CryptoTaskUIMainWnd is created. The serviceProvider parameter is later used for creating connection managers. When the designer calls GetView on CryptoTaskUI, it simply creates an instance of the CryptoTaskUIMainWnd. The CryptoTaskUIMainWnd is derived from the taskUI framework DTSBaseTaskUI base class.

The taskUI code has five source files:

- CryptoTaskUI.cs—Contains the portion of the taskUI that interacts with the Business Intelligence Development Studio.

- CryptoTaskUIMainWnd.cs—Contains the partial class definition of the CryptoTaskUIMainWnd main form you see when you open the taskUI. There is little code in this file, but it is important code nonetheless.

- CryptoTaskUIMainWnd.Designer.cs—Contains the forms editor generated code for the CryptoTaskUIMainWnd form.

- GeneralView.cs—Contains the code that implements the General view in the taskUI and is derived from IDtsTaskUIView.

- SettingsView.cs—Contains the code that implements the Settings view in the taskUI and is derived from IDtsTaskUiView.

TaskUI Foundation Classes, Interfaces, and Terms
The following list of terms are used throughout the TaskUI Foundation Classes. Understanding these terms will help you better understand the taskUI code.

- **Tree-panel**—This is the name used to describe the layout of the taskUI with the tree on the left and the panel or views on the right.

- **Hosted view**—The hosted view is the property grid control hosted inside the panel on the right side of the tree-panel dialog box.

- **Tree**—The tree is the selection of nodes on the left side of the taskUI.

- **IDTSTaskUIView**—This interface is implemented by the hosted views, which change depending on the node selected in the tree.

- **DTSBaseTaskUI**—This is the abstract base class from which you derive the taskUI form.

- **IDTSTaskUIHost**—This interface is used by the hosted views to communicate with the tree, and is also used by the tree to communicate with the views. This interface is implemented in the base class so you do not implement it.

- **IDtsTaskUI**—This is the interface with which the designer interacts.

The IDTSTaskUIHost **Interface**   The IDTSTaskUIHost interface is used for communicating back and forth between the tree and the views. You do not need to implement this interface because it is already implemented in the base DTSBseTaskUI. The IDTSTaskUIHost interface has the following methods and properties:

```
// Add an IDTSTaskUIView derived view to the right side panel
void AddView(
    string viewName,
    IDTSTaskUIView view,
    TreeNode parentNode
);

// Add an IDTSTaskUIView derived view to the right side panel with an image.
// Provide an index into the image list for displaying in the tree
void AddView(
    string viewName,
    int imageIndex,
    IDTSTaskUIView view,
    TreeNode parentNode
);

// Return the TreeNode associated with a view
TreeNode GetViewNode(IDTSTaskUIView view);

// Return the view associated with a TreeNode
IDTSTaskUIView GetView(TreeNode treeNode);

// Add an imagelist for displaying in the tree.
void SetImageList(ImageList imageList);

// Remove a view from tree
void RemoveView(IDTSTaskUIView view);

// Remove a view from tree
void RemoveView(TreeNode viewNode);

// display a specific view
void SelectView(IDTSTaskUIView view);

// display a specific view
void SelectView(TreeNode viewNode);

// Display the error message in the error area of the form
void DisplayError(string errorMessage);

// By default set to true. If set to false the views will be initialized
bool FastLoad{ get; set; }
```

```
// If true the dialog can be closed with the OK button.
// true by default if all the views return true from OnValidate method
bool CanCommit{ get; set; }
```

The IDTSTaskUIView Interface   This interface must be implemented by hosted views and allows the tree view to communicate various changes to the hosted view. The following code shows the IDTSTaskUIView methods and how they are used.

```
public interface IDTSTaskUIView
{
   // If FastLoad from IDTSTaskUIHost is set to true,
   // this method is called when the view is added to the tree.
   // Otherwise it will be called when the view is about to
   // be displayed for the first time
   void OnInitialize(
    IDTSTaskUIHost treeHost,                 // IDTSTaskUIHost that hosts the view.
    System.Windows.Forms.TreeNode viewNode, // The task that is being edited.
    object taskHost,                         // The tree node associated with
➥this view.
    object connections                       // The connection managers in
➥the package.
   );

   // Called whenever the view is about to be displayed
   void OnSelection();

   // Called whenever the view is about to be exited.
   // You can use this method to refuse to leave the view.
   void OnLoseSelection(
      ref bool bCanLeaveView, // True if the view can be left.
      ref string reason       // Error message if bCanLeaveView returned false.
   );

   // Called when the OK button is clicked to validate the input.
   void OnValidate(
      ref bool bViewIsValid, // Result of the validation, true if validated
➥successfully.
      ref string reason       // Error message if bViewIsValid returned false.
   );

   // Called when OK button is clicked, but only if all OnValidate
➥calls succeeded.
   void OnCommit(
      object taskHost   // The TaskHost for the task to modify.
   );
}
```

TaskUI Provided Attributes

The TaskUI foundation classes also provide a set of attributes you can use to modify the hosted views. These attributes control the behavior of the property grid cells and provide a way to easily support properties of different types.

`EnableExpandable`   Use the `EnableExpandableAttribute` to specify whether a user-defined type is to be expandable or nonexpandable in the property grid based on a Boolean property defined by the user-defined type.

> **CAUTION**
>
> The type must have a copy constructor defined and expandable types must have the `RefreshProperties(RefreshProperties.All)` **attribute.**

The following code sample is an example of an expandable type and how to set one up in a view:

```
EnableExpandable("DTSExpandable")]
public class ExpandableType
{
   private bool bExpandable = false;
   private bool bExpanded = true;

   // Constructor
   public ExpandableType()
   {
   }

   // Copy constructor
   public ExpandableType(ExpandableType xt)
   {
      this.DTSExpandable = xt.DTSExpandable;
      this.bExpanded = xt.Expanded;
   }

   // Don't show in the designer
   [Browsable(false)]
   public bool DTSExpandable
   {
      get{ return bExpandable; }
      set{ bExpandable = value; }
   }

   public bool Expanded
   {
      get { return bExpanded; }
```

```
      set { bExpanded = false; }
   }
}
```

In the hosted view class, you would have the following code to add the type to the property grid:

```
Public class Class1
{
   …
   Public ExpandableType xpand = new ExpandableType();

   [RefreshProperties(RefreshProperties.All)]
   public ExpandableType ExpandableProperty
   {
      get{ return m_xtVal; }
      set{ m_xtVal = value;}
   }
}
```

The ExpandableProperty is a property on the hosted view, but stores the value in a member variable. Later, when the user closes the taskUI with the OK button and commits the changes, the hosted view can set the task's property value to the value in the member variable.

EnableDisable   Use the EnableDisable attribute to disable a property in the property grid based on an array of values of another property. One of the two properties needs to have the RefreshProperties attribute, as shown for the EnableExpandable attribute.

SortProperties   Use this attribute to dictate the order of properties in the property grid. This attribute receives an array of strings containing one of the following:

- All of the properties of the type in the order you want to sort them.
- Some of the properties' names. Those passed in are sorted according to the order found in the array. The rest are sorted alphabetically.
- The array is NULL. The properties are sorted in alphabetical order, which is the same as if you didn't add the attribute at all.

LocalizablePropertyDescription   The LocalizablePropertyDescription attribute provides a way to retrieve a localizable description for the property that will appear in the description section at the bottom of the property grid.

LocalizablePropertyName   The LocalizablePropertyName provides a way to retrieve a localizable name for the property.

LocalizablePropertyCategory   The LocalizablePropertyCategory provides a way to retrieve a localizable category name that shows in between the properties and categorizes them into groups.

Using the TaskUI Foundation Classes

Take a look at the sample code to see some of these pieces working together. In CryptoTaskUIMainWnd.cs, you'll find the constructor for the CryptoTaskUIMainWnd class where the hosted views are created and added to the main form.

```
public partial class CryptoTaskUIMainWnd : DTSBaseTaskUI
{
   #region members
   private const string Title = "Crypto Task Editor";
   private const string Description = "This task encrypts and decrypts text.";
   public static Icon taskIcon = new
Icon(typeof(SSIS2K5.Samples.Tasks.CryptoTask.CryptoTask),"TaskIcon.ico");
   #endregion

   // Construct and pass base class to the
   // title, taskicon, desc., taskhost, & connections.
   public CryptoTaskUIMainWnd(TaskHost taskHost, object connections) :
     base(Title, taskIcon, Description, taskHost, connections)
   {
     // Proactively assert that the taskHost is valid
     Debug.Assert(taskHost != null);

     // Create a new general hosted view
     GeneralView generalView = new GeneralView();
     // Add the view to the main form
     this.DTSTaskUIHost.AddView("General", generalView, null);

     // Create a new settings view
     SettingsView settingsView = new SettingsView();
     // Add the view to the main form
     this.DTSTaskUIHost.AddView("Settings", settingsView, null);

     InitializeComponent();
   }
}
```

The description is what shows up on the top of the taskUI with the icon. The constructor also calls into the base class constructor to ensure that the icon, description, and other elements are correctly displayed. Then, the code adds the two hosted views. The hosted views are where the really interesting things happen.

Getting the Connections   The following code shows how to retrieve only the connections of a given type in the internal class `FileConnections`, which is a `TypeConverter`:

```
/// <summary>
/// Method to get the file connections created or available in the package
/// </summary>
/// <param name="retrievalObject"></param>
/// <returns>list of FILE connections</returns>
private ArrayList getFileConnections(object retrievalObject)
{
    SettingsNode node = (SettingsNode)retrievalObject;

    Connections runTimeCons = ((IDtsConnectionService)node.Connections).
➥GetConnections();
    ArrayList list = new ArrayList();

    list.Add(NEW_CONN);
    foreach (ConnectionManager conn in runTimeCons)
    {
        if (conn.CreationName.CompareTo("FILE") == 0 ¦¦ conn.CreationName.
➥CompareTo("FLATFILE") == 0)
        {
            list.Add(conn.Name);
        }
    }

    if (list.Count > 0))
        list.Sort();

    return list;
}
```

The `FileConnections` TypeConverter is used to provide the names of file connection managers in the taskUI by passing it as a parameter to the `TypeConverter` attribute on the `SourceConnection` and `DestinationConnection` properties, as follows:

```
[
Category("Connections"),
Description("The destination connection"),
TypeConverter(typeof(FileConnections))
]
public string DestinationConnection
{
    get { return _destConnection; }
    set { _destConnection = value; }
}
```

Notice also that the `Category` attribute creates a grouping of properties based on the string passed as a parameter, in this case "Connections."

Handling Connection Manager Events   The special handling needed for the Connection Manager combo box is done in the `PropertyValueChanged` event handler in the `SettingsView.cs` source code, as follows:

```
private const string NEW_CONN = "<New Connection...>";

private void propertyGridSettings_PropertyValueChanged(object s,
System.Windows.Forms.PropertyValueChangedEventArgs e)
{
    #region New File Connection for Source path
    if (e.ChangedItem.PropertyDescriptor.Name.CompareTo("SourceConnection") == 0)
    {
        if (e.ChangedItem.Value.Equals(NEW_CONN))
        {
            ArrayList list = null;

            this.Cursor = Cursors.WaitCursor;
            if (!((settingsNode.SourceCMName == null) || (settingsNode.SourceCMName
➥ == "")))
                    settingsNode.SourceCMName = null;

            list = ((IDtsConnectionService)settingsNode.Connections).
➥CreateConnection("FILE");
            this.Cursor = Cursors.Default;
            if ((list != null) && (list.Count > 0))
            {
                ConnectionManager cMgr = (ConnectionManager)list[0];

                settingsNode.SourceCMName = cMgr.Name;
            }
            else
            {
                if (e.OldValue == null)
                {
                    settingsNode.SourceCMName = null;
                }
                else
                {
                    settingsNode.SourceCMName = (string)e.OldValue;
                }
            }
        }
    }
}
```

In the preceding code, the event handler checks to see whether the <New Connection> option was chosen from the Connection Manager combo box. If it was, the code uses the IDtsConnectionService to create a new connection manager of type FILE. This is how the taskUI launches the correct Connection Manager creation dialog box.

The taskUI is perhaps the most complex part of building a custom task; however, with the taskUI foundation class library, you can quickly build a professional looking and functional taskUI that looks identical to the stock taskUIs and automatically take advantage of the built-in property expression hosted view. This introduction didn't cover every aspect of writing taskUIs, but should get you started. You can study the sample code to get a better understanding of how to roll your own taskUIs. Also, you can copy the starter task and taskUI project into a new folder and quickly start building your custom tasks and taskUIs beginning with what is already in those projects.

Debugging the Task

Because of the way the designer (BIDS) executes packages, you must take two different approaches to debugging your custom task based on whether you are executing the package. The designer has a special debugging host called DTSDebugHost that it launches. The host prevents problems with orphaned packages or rogue tasks and helps the designer be more robust, but it also makes it a little tricky to debug components.

Debugging Tasks During Design Time   When debugging tasks and taskUIs in the designer, it is easiest to create a testing package in another instance of the designer and then attach to the second instance of the designer from the task project designer. Following are the steps to set up for debugging a task.

1. Create a new Integration Services project.

2. In the Visual Studio Development Studio (DevEnv) where you have your task project, set a breakpoint in either the task or taskUI code that you want to debug.

3. From the Debug menu, select Attach to Process. The Attach to Process dialog box opens.

4. Select the devenv.exe process with the title that appears the same as the title of the DevEnv containing your test solution, as shown in Figure 24.17.

5. Ensure that the code type is correct by clicking the Select button.

6. Click the Attach button.

7. Switch back to the DevEnv containing your test solution and open the taskUI or do something else such as change a property so that your breakpoint gets hit.

8. In the sample case, the breakpoint is on the constructor for the CryptoTaskUIMainWnd class, as shown in Figure 24.18. When opening the taskUI for the CryptoTask, the breakpoint is hit and the development environment takes control. You can now step through the taskUI code.

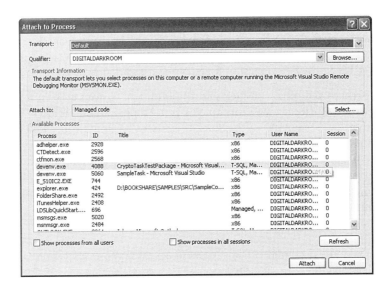

FIGURE 24.17   Attaching to the Development Studio process.

```
namespace SSIS2K5.Samples.Tasks.CryptoTask
{
    public partial class CryptoTaskUIMainWnd : DTSBaseTaskUI
    {
        #region members
        private const string Title = "Crypto Task Editor";
        private const string Description = "This task encrypts and decrypts text (UTF-8) files using the Rijndael algorithm";

        public static Icon taskIcon = new Icon(typeof(SSIS2K5.Samples.Tasks.CryptoTask.CryptoTask),"TaskIcon.ico");

        #endregion

        public CryptoTaskUIMainWnd(TaskHost taskHost, object connections) :
            base(Title, taskIcon, Description, taskHost, connections)
        {
            Debug.Assert(taskHost != null);

            GeneralView generalView = new GeneralView();
            // Add the view to the main form
            this.DTSTaskUIHost.AddView("General", generalView, null);

            SettingsView settingsView = new SettingsView();
            // Add the view to the main form
            this.DTSTaskUIHost.AddView("Settings", settingsView, null);

            InitializeComponent();
        }
    }
}
```

FIGURE 24.18   Hitting the breakpoint in the development environment.

This also works for the task code. However, because only certain task code paths are executed during design time, you have to judiciously decide where to put the breakpoint. For example, you can place a breakpoint in a property GET method and then modify the method through the property grid in BIDS.

Debugging Tasks During Execution Time   During execution, it's a little trickier, but not much. Instead of attaching to a running instance of BIDS, you attach to `DTSDebugHost`. Also, you need to set a breakpoint in the package so the package doesn't complete execution before you have a chance to attach to it. Finally, if you want to debug the `InitializeTask` or `Validate` methods, you need to use the design time debugging method. The designer calls those methods before loading the package into the debug host and executing it. The following steps show one way to debug a task's `Execute` method:

1. Create a new Integration Services project.

2. In the package, drag a task onto the Control Flow surface and configure it as you like.

3. Set a breakpoint on the package `OnPreExecute` event.

4. Run the package and let it hit the breakpoint.

5. In the DevEnv where you have your task project, set a breakpoint on the `Execute` method of the task you want to debug.

6. From the Debug menu, select Attach to Process. Look for the `DtsDebugHost.exe` process. There are usually two processes, but only one is correct. Select the one that has managed code available for debugging. Experiences differ on whether it is the first or second entry. Whatever order in which you find the processes listed, it seems to remain consistent.

7. Click the Attach button.

8. Go back to the Integration Services project where the package is waiting on a breakpoint and let the package run.

9. When the package executes your task, the breakpoint should get hit and the development environment should take over.

10. You can now step through the task's Execution method code.

Custom Task Best Practices

To this point, the discussion has centered on programming details. However, you should also take a number of design considerations into account while developing a custom task. They are hard-learned lessons codified here as best practices after experiences with developing a number of custom tasks as well as designing most of the stock tasks that ship in the SQL Server box. The practices are organized in no particular order.

Conventions and Constraints

Although building a no-op custom task is trivial, you should follow a few guidelines when writing a fully functional custom task so that the task supports the features and facilities found in the SSIS runtime. Following these guidelines ensures that a custom task will play nice in the SSIS sandbox.

Do Not Retain Internal State

Don't retain state in your task after returning from the Execute method. What does that mean? You have properties right, and that's state? It is possible for Execute to be called multiple times per one instance of a task. If this happens and internal state is retained between executions, the task might behave differently even if all its properties have the same values. This is nondeterministic behavior and is undesirable.

It's important that a task's behavior is *solely* determined by its internal logic based on exposed read/write properties. In other words, if you have a property value that represents state and that should be retained across instances or executions, it should be a writable property that can only be changed externally.

Do Not Internally Change Writable Property Values

The second rule is a corollary to the first. Don't internally change writable property values. If the property is writable, it is an indication that it is to be set by the user. Changing it could cause unexpected, even damaging behavior. If you have state that you want to expose to the user and the state is volatile due to internal functions of the task, make it a read-only property. This indicates to the user that the property is for information only and does not control or affect execution of the task.

Do Use Logging

This is very important. If the custom task doesn't log progress, errors, warnings, information, or other events, the user will have little in the way of troubleshooting the task when things go sideways with the task. Logging makes it possible to clearly indicate what the task is doing at any time. If you are concerned about performance, understand that logging is turned off by default and you can also check to see if logging is enabled before even attempting to log.

Always Exit Gracefully

Tasks should always exit their methods from the same location, ensuring that they have cleaned up resources and returned the correct execution result. For managed tasks, that means using try/catch blocks around any potentially failing code, especially the Validate and Execute methods. If code in the task generates an exception during validation or execution, it should log the error and/or raise an OnError or OnWarning event with descriptions of the errors. Tasks that are unable to recover due to a failure should indicate that the failure occurred by returning DTSER_FAILED for their execution result. Tasks that raise exceptions are considered an exceptional case and cause the package to shut down.

Honor the InteractiveMode System Variable

If your custom task shows any sort of UI during execution time, it should check the InteractiveMode system variable. If the package is executing, and the InteractiveMode system variable is set to FALSE, the task should not show the UI. Most tasks don't show UI at all unless their taskUI is launched, so this is rare.

Do Not Choose Taskhost Conflicting Names

Care should be taken to avoid property names that conflict with names found on the Taskhost. For example, if the name "Description" is used for a property on a task, it conflicts with the `Description` property found on task hosts and is hidden in the designer. To avoid confusion, the following names should not be used for properties on tasks:

- Name
- Description
- CreationName
- ID

Task UI

A task writer is not required to create a task UI to accompany his task. However, it is highly recommended. It is practically mandatory if you plan to sell the task. Tasks that do not provide a task UI are only editable using the property grid in the designer. For very simple tasks, this might be acceptable, especially for internal-only tasks. For tasks with several properties or having even mildly complex settings, a task UI is essential.

List Resources
When listing resources in list boxes or combo boxes, the taskUI should only show valid options. Two examples are list boxes that show Variables or Connection Managers.

Filter Variables   Filter out read-only variables when showing variables that the package will write to and only display variables that are in scope.

Filter Connection Managers   Connection managers should be filtered by type required. For example, if the task requires a file connection manager, the taskUI should only show the available file connection managers in the package.

Correctly Name Log Events   Log event names should be named by combining the task's type name with the log event. For example, if the task is a SQL Task and the log event was SQL Statement Processed, the log event name should be `SQLTaskSQLStatementProcessed`.

Log event names should use proper case and no spaces. Log events should not use abbreviated words nor should they be prefixed. It is common to prefix log entries with common prefixes such as On, Log, Event, or LogEvent. These are usually redundant and add to the log entry name length without adding uniqueness.

Use Custom Breakpoints Wisely
Breakpoints should only be implemented if there is a good reason, for example, if a task performs multiple, repeated operations or executes for a long period of time doing variable operations with external side effects. The user might be interested in understanding how the task settings impact the side effects. Breakpoints are useful for stalling the task execution long enough to watch the impact unfold. This is unusual, however, and should only be done if the stock breakpoints do not provide an adequate debugging facility.

General Guidelines

These guidelines are miscellaneous suggestions that make the task easier to use.

Use Connection Managers for Accessing Resources

Tasks should use connection managers for accessing any external resources such as files or connections. The benefits are numerous, including packages that are easier to understand and maintain. The taskUI should be written so that it is easy to create a new connection manager within the taskUI.

The TaskUI Should Be in a Separate Assembly   This is primarily for economy. For example, it is possible to eliminate all the taskUIs on server machines, making the packages safer and saving some drive space. However, there are also memory benefits. If the taskUI is in the same assembly, the taskUI can consume memory unnecessarily.

Summary

Writing a custom task isn't always the best solution and this chapter has provided some guidelines for you to consider before undertaking a custom task effort. However, if you do decide to write custom tasks, the provided sample tasks and descriptions make it possible to write fully featured and professional tasks with the same look and feel as stock tasks.

Building Custom Data Flow Components

"HE MAKES ME LOOK LIKE LAURA FROM *LITTLE HOUSE ON THE PRAIRIE.*"—MIKE BLASZCZAK

In this chapter, you'll learn how to write custom components for the Data Flow Task. Starting with a concepts discussion to help you understand the general design of components, the chapter then digs down into code. The two types of components, adapters and transforms, are covered and four sample components are provided in the sample source that will serve as the baseline for the discussion.

Custom Component Concepts

If you've just finished reading the preceding chapter about writing custom tasks, you might think there are similarities between how you write a custom task and how you write a custom data flow component, and there are. As noted in Chapter 24, "Building Custom Tasks," the setup for all the components is virtually identical with the exception of a few minor differences such as the attributes and names you use. However, after you get past the initial setup, you'll want to do a reset and clear the brain slate a bit. Implementing custom data flow components is very different from implementing custom tasks. Writing a custom task is like writing a windows application. For example, applications have "main" functions, which are the primary entry and exit points for the application. Tasks have the `Execute` method as the primary entry and exit point and it is called only once for the entire execution life cycle of the task.

Because of the nature of data flow, data flow components have a little different life cycle and function call order than you might expect. There are two time frames when methods get called. The first is design time and the other is runtime. Some methods get called exclusively during design time, others might get called during design time and runtime, while others might get called exclusively during runtime. Still other methods might be called multiple times during execution, and sometimes which method is called depends on the component type. If this is a bit confusing, don't worry. We'll sort it out in a minute. The point is that you can't approach component development in the same way that you approach writing custom tasks or any other application for that matter. You need to keep an open mind. Understanding a little more about the architecture of the Data Flow Task, specifically those parts relating to data flow components, is useful as well. The remainder of this section provides a few insights into how the Data Flow Task interacts with components that should be helpful when writing your custom components.

Design Time

Recall the discussion in Chapter 23, "Data Flow Task Internals and Tuning," that briefly touched on the Layout Subsystem and mentioned that it provides the design time behavior for components, notably adding, deleting, validating, loading, and saving components and their inputs, outputs, and columns. See Figure 23.1. The Layout Subsystem also provides the column metadata to the Buffer Subsystem and execution tree information to the Execution Engine. Therefore, when components interact with the Data Flow Task, they are interacting with the Layout Subsystem and providing information that flows throughout the Layout Subsystem to the Buffer Subsystem for creating buffers that the component will use at runtime.

The `ComponentMetaData` **Object**

For the component writer, the first and foremost interactions with the Layout Subsystem (Layout) are usually through the `ComponentMetaData` object. When you drop a component onto the designer, Layout creates a new `ComponentMetaData` object for the component to house all the information about the component. Components store and retrieve information into and from the `ComponentMetadata` object. They also use the `ComponentMetaData` object to interact with the designer or other programmatic client through events and logging.

Think metaphorically for a moment about when you get up in the morning and start your day. One of the first things you do is get dressed. The hat you wear determines the role you play at work. You might wear multiple hats. The uniform you wear represents the kind of work you do. You store information in your clothes such as your wallet or purse that identify who you are, where you live, and where you shop. The `ComponentMetaData` object is similar. Like the hat, components declare what role they play, whether they are source, destination, or transform through `ComponentMetaData`. Like the uniform, the component populates the `ComponentMetaData` object with columns and other metadata that represent how the component will function. Finally, like the wallet or purse, the component communicates its own ID and stores information such as connections needed and columns used in the ComponentMetaData object. Like most analogies, if you stretch it too far, it doesn't make much sense and underwear has no parallel. But hopefully, you get the point, which is that the component describes itself to the ComponentMetaData object and then the ComponentMetaData object works with the other data flow subsystems to build the buffers, execution trees, threads, and other internal structures to properly interact with the component.

Data Flow Component Design Lifetime

Before plunging into the code, it's helpful to have a high-level view of what it is you are going to write. Figure 25.1 shows the design lifetime of a typical data flow component. Although not completely accurate for every operation sequence, it should give you an idea of how the user, layout, designer, and component interact.

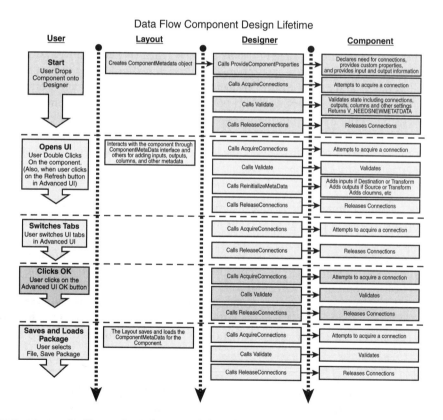

FIGURE 25.1   An illustration of a typical data flow component design lifetime.

Ceaseless Validation   Figure 25.1 illustrates a few interesting and helpful points. One thing to notice is that Validate gets called a lot. So do the AcquireConnections and ReleaseConnections calls. Just about every time you do something with the component in the designer, you get the validation sandwich. `AcquireConnections` and `ReleaseConnections` are the bread and the `Validate` call is the meat, or cheese if you are a vegetarian, or lettuce if you're vegan. This makes sense when you think about it because just about everything that happens in the data flow is related in some way to external data.

Providing Component Properties   Also, notice that `ProvideComponentProperties` is where you declare the need for connections and publish custom component properties. `ProvideComponentProperties` is only called once when the component is first dropped onto the designer. From the package writer perspective, this isn't all that interesting. However, from your perspective as a component writer, you should keep this in mind—especially if you ever add a new custom property or connection to your component. For example, if there are existing packages with your custom component in them, and you add a new custom property, the components in the old packages will not show you the new custom properties because `ProvideComponentProperties` is only called once for the entire lifetime of the component within a package. You'll have to delete the old component and add a new one anytime you change anything affected by the code in `ProvideComponentProperties`.

Work Done for the Component   Notice also that the designer is doing a lot of work for the component. This is important to keep in mind when you write code that builds packages. Your custom code must do everything that the designer does when setting up a package. Notice that the layout persists the component, instead of the component handling the task. This simplifies the component somewhat and eliminates some of the coding the custom component writers must do. It also makes it possible for the layout to do some validation on the component XML. Finally, when an adapter is added to a data flow, `ReinitializeMetaData` must be called after `ProvideComponentProperties` to ensure that the metadata for the source and destinations is correctly established.

Runtime

As mentioned previously, during runtime or package execution, the Data Flow Task manages the data in buffers and "moves" the buffers around or, more accurately, does some pointer magic to make buffers always look fresh to the components. At some point, the Execution Engine needs to present the buffers to the components so that the components can read the data and process it according to their functionality. For example, sources need to receive a buffer that they can fill with data. Destinations need to receive a buffer that they can read and send to the destination medium. Transforms need to read and write to buffers. The way the Execution Engine provides access to the buffers is through two methods, `PrimeOutput` and `ProcessInput`. There are more than just these two methods on the runtime interface, which are covered in a bit, but these two methods are extremely important because it is inside them where the real data-processing work happens in the Data Flow Task.

The `PrimeOutput` Method

`PrimeOutput` is the method the Execution Engine uses for providing a buffer to sources and transforms and is only called on components with asynchronous outputs. Synchronous outputs don't need a `PrimeOutput` call because they don't generate new buffers. They only fill buffers that are provided to them on their `ProcessInput` calls. Destinations don't receive `PrimeOutput` calls because they don't have outputs and they don't send data to buffers; they send it to their respective media. `PrimeOutput` is only called once on asynchronous outputs at the beginning of the Data Flow Task execution. The component then holds onto a reference to the buffer and stuffs it with data until it runs out. After the component runs out of data, it sets the buffer's end-of-file flag to tell the Execution Engine that the component has completed processing. Again, for synchronous outputs, the end-of-rowset flag isn't necessary because the Execution Engine already knows how many buffers are arriving at the synchronous input of the output.

Figure 25.2 illustrates two views of buffers. One is how the component views the buffer it is passed in `PrimeOutput`. The component never gets another call to `PrimeOutput` so it holds onto the buffer reference and continues adding rows to the buffer until it is done. To the component, it would seem that the buffer is huge. In fact, even if the component processes billions of rows, it only receives one buffer. However, the Execution Engine has a different view, which is the second part of Figure 25.2. When the component attempts to insert a row of data into the buffer and if the buffer is full, the Execution Engine "flips" the buffer with a fresh (empty) buffer. The former buffer is then available for processing by another component; however, it is rarely moved. When the downstream component is ready to process a new buffer, the Execution Engine calls the component's `ProcessInput` method and passes the pointer to the next available processed buffer.

The `ProcessInput` Method

`ProcessInput` is the method the Execution Engine uses for providing buffers to transform and destination inputs. `ProcessInput` is called for every buffer on an input and is called until the buffers on the input run out or the data flow terminates because of errors or exceptions. It can be a bit confusing as to which types of components get which calls and on what locations, so the various possibilities are captured in Table 25.1.

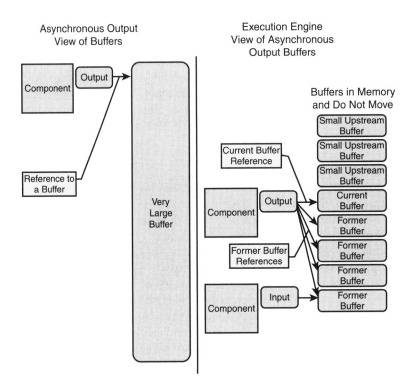

Asynchronous Output
View of Buffers

Execution Engine
View of Asynchronous
Output Buffers

FIGURE 25.2   Components only see one buffer.

TABLE 25.1   `ProcessInput` and `PrimeOutput` **Call Sites**

Component Type	Process Input Called	Prime Output Called	Description
Source	No	Yes	Sources have no inputs. Sources have pure asynchronous outputs.
Transform with Asynchronous Outputs	Yes	Yes	Prime Output called only on components with asynchronous outputs. It is possible, though rare, to have multiple output types on one transform.
Transform with Synchronous Outputs	Yes	No	Synchronous outputs simply pass along the buffer from the input after modifying its contents.
Destination	Yes	No	Destinations have no outputs but may have an error output

This has been a short overview of how components interact with the Data Flow Task environment. Hopefully, this gives you some perspective going into the development process. Now, take a look at the sample components that have been provided.

The Sample Components

There are three sample components provided, as discussed in the following sections.

JPG File EXIF Reader Source Adapter

JPEG or JPG files are a common image file format developed by the Joint Photographic Experts Group (JPEG). EXIF data can be embedded in JPG files to provide information about how, when, and where the image was captured. EXIF stands for Exchangeable Image File Format and can be very useful for keeping track of your image library. Currently, there are an ever-increasing number of tools being generated for reading the EXIF information from image files. For example, Windows XP, given certain settings, shows you some of the EXIF information by simply hovering over an image in an Explorer window. Figure 25.3 shows an example.

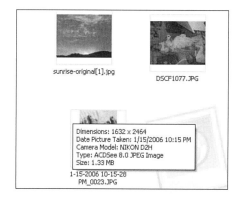

FIGURE 25.3   Viewing JPG image EXIF information in Windows XP.

The JPG File EXIF Reader Source or just Image File Source for short is a Data Source Adapter for reading the EXIF data. There are a number of fields that can be extracted, over 100. However, the Image File Source only extracts a few of the most interesting fields. It uses a MultiFile Connection Manager to point to where the image files are stored and produces one row with the EXIF data for every image file. Figure 25.4 shows a screenshot of the adapter at work.

The source is interesting because it shows just how flexible Integration Services can be. By marrying the Execution Engines with your custom components, you can build an entire custom solution stack. The source is also interesting because it is a working sample that you can debug, add to, and otherwise study. The sample source is available in the SAMPLES\SRC\CustomComponents\ImageFileSrc folder.

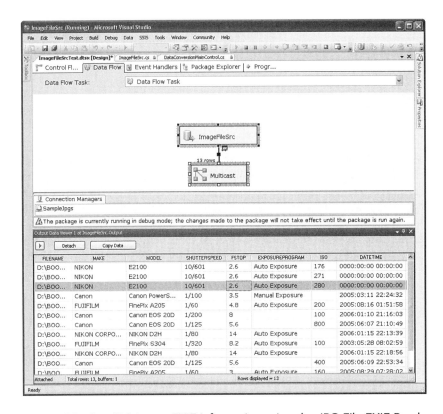

FIGURE 25.4   Viewing JPG image EXIF information using the JPG File EXIF Reader Source Adapter.

Data Profiler Transform

At the beginning of any Data Quality, Integration, Warehouse, or other Business Intelligence project, one of the most important and most overlooked steps is to profile the existing data. Profiling tells you how much work there will be to clean and conform your data. It gives you a better idea what kinds of data you have and what sorts of problems there will be with implementing the project. It helps you to understand things like how much space you'll need for storing the processed data or if you need to dedup source data.

The Data Profiler transform does rudimentary profiling, including string length, nulls, maximum, and minimum values. It is a simple sample, but could easily be expanded to do much more and different profiling operations. The Data Profiler is an asynchronous transform and consumes all data on the input to produce one row for every profile type on every column profiled. For example, if you select two columns on the input to be profiled, and there are two profile types available for the selected column's type, the Data Profiler transform produces four rows.

The SQL Client and ODBC Destination Adapters

Although these are two distinct components, they are really just two sides of the same coin and should help you understand how to modify a sample to meet your specific requirements. The SQL Client Destination uses the Microsoft SQL Client ADO.NET Destination Adapter. It also uses the batching capability to help speed performance. It has a custom property called BatchSize you can set to tune the performance. The ODBC.NET Destination Adapter is a slightly modified version of the SQL Client Adapter to reflect the differences in the two providers. Either one of these two adapters could easily be modified to create other destination adapters.

Sample Transform UI

There is no sample transform user interface (UI) provided because, unlike the control flow that provides no standard UI for tasks, the data flow provides a standard component UI in the Advanced Editor. Although it is possible to write a custom component UI, few seem interested because the Advanced Editor covers most of the custom component UI requirements.

> **TIP**
>
> The Advanced UI is not capable of editing components with multiple inputs. If you write such a component, you need to also provide a custom component UI. The one exception to this is if the custom component has only component-level properties, in which case the Advanced UI will suffice.

Also, you can associate custom TypeEditors with custom properties that the Advanced Editor will use for editing properties. Finally, there is some especially well-done documentation on writing custom components found in Books Online. Perform a search for "Developing Custom Data Flow Components" for the index into the content.

> **NOTE**
>
> Chapter 24 covers in detail how to start the custom component projects. The differences between component types are also noted there. If you need to start from scratch, please review that chapter.

The Design Time Methods

The design time interface is for establishing and managing the component's metadata. The sample components are derived from the base class Microsoft.SqlServer.Dts. PipelineComponent in the Microsoft.SqlServer.PipelineHost assembly and provide the default behavior for most of the methods while hiding much of the complexity involved in writing native code custom components. Although the base class supports many methods, fortunately it also handles the implementation of most of the methods. You only need override a few of the important methods, as discussed in the following sections.

ProvideComponentProperties

This is the method you use to set up your component and is called the first time you drop the component onto the design surface. Typically, the kinds of things you do in this method are as follows:

- Add inputs and outputs

- Define connection requirements

- Define custom properties such as `BatchSize` or `Timeout`

ReinitializeMetaData

You use this method to provide the column-level information for the component. It is called when the `Validate` method returns `VS_NEEDSNEWMETADATA` or when the user clicks the Refresh button in the Advanced UI. When initially called, this method adds all the columns and column information. Upon subsequent calls, this method is where column metadata can be fixed if corrupted.

Validate

You use this method to verify the correctness of the column metadata and other component settings such as connection availability. It is called repeatedly during package design, and once right before the `PrimeOutput/ProcessInput` calls. You should never modify the column or other component metadata during this call. During validation, you should verify the following:

- Component custom properties exist and are valid values.

- A runtime connection is specified and a connection manager exists.

- The connection manager is of the correct type.

- The component has the correct number of inputs.

- The component has the correct number of outputs.

If validation succeeds, the component should return `DTSValidationStatus.VS_ISVALID`. If validation fails, the component should raise appropriate errors and warnings to alert the user to the problems and then return one of the following `DTSValidationStatus` values.

- `VS_ISBROKEN`—Indicates that the component is not configured correctly but could be fixed by the user.

- `VS_NEEDSNEWMETADATA`—Indicates that the validation errors could be fixed by a call to `ReinitializeMetaData`.

- `VS_ISCORRUPT`—Indicates that the `ComponentMetaData` is corrupt and cannot be repaired by a call to the `ReinitializeMetaData` method or by edits to the component.

NOTE

If the DelayValidation property of the Data Flow Task is set to TRUE, the designer will not call Validate on the component. Validate is only called during package execution.

AcquireConnections **and** ReleaseConnections

These methods are called for every major component operation and establish and release connections. If the component uses connection managers, these methods must be implemented. If not, they are not needed and can be ignored.

RegisterEvents

If your component fires any custom events, you should register them with this method. It performs the same function as the EventInfos do for custom tasks. In fact, when you register events using the RegisterEvents method, the Data Flow Task creates a corresponding EventInfos entry for the event at the task level.

RegisterLogEntries

If your component logs custom log entries, you should register them with this method. It performs the same function as the LogEntryInfos does for custom tasks. Like the preceding RegisterEvents method, this method generates a new LogEntryInfo at the Data Flow Task level.

PerformUpgrade

This method is only useful when you release a new version of the component. It allows a newer version of a component to update an older version of the same component. If you release a component, and then subsequently want to add a property or output or any other change for that matter, you'll need to implement this method on the component so that it can replace previous versions seamlessly.

The Runtime Methods

The runtime methods are, of course, the methods called during the execution of the package and are responsible for either processing the data in buffers or for preparing the component to do so. The PrimeOutput and ProcessInput methods have already been described.

Now, let's put them in context with the other runtime methods in the order that they are called.

PrepareForExecute

This method is almost identical to the PreExecute method and has no common uses. In rare cases, you might need to have all components do timing-based initialization simultaneously, such that certain settings get initialized for all components of a given type before some other processing or initialization occurs in PreExecute. This type of thing is very rare, however, and so PrepareForExecute and its mirror method, Cleanup, are rarely necessary.

PrepareForExecute happens before PreExecute and is provided for doing work before execution that does not require a lot of resources. If a component needs to acquire and hold onto a resource needed during execution, it should do so in PreExecute because it happens closer to execution time. Also, the AcquireConnections method is called on components after PrepareForExecute and before PreExecute; therefore, any work requiring connections should happen in PreExecute. Finally, the buffer manager is not available to components in PrepareForExecute but is available in PreExecute.

PreExecute

PreExecute is called once per Data Flow Task execution and is called right before the PrimeOutput/ProcessInput methods. This method is provided as a way to do any potentially expensive or time-consuming operations, such as allocating memory or preparing data column-to-buffer column mappings. For example, you can use this method to discover which output columns the user has selected for output.

PrimeOutput

PrimeOutput is the method called on components with an asynchronous output to pass the buffer. This method is only called once per Data Flow Task execution and has the following parameters:

- outputs—An integer value containing the count of the outputs
- outputIDs—An array of integer IDs for the output columns
- buffers—An array of PipelineBuffer objects containing the buffers for each of the outputs

Each output on the component gets its own buffer. For example, a component that supports error outputs would receive two buffers, one for the main output and one for the error output. A component with four outputs and one error output receives five buffers.

ProcessInput

This method is called for every buffer on an input and passes the following parameters:

- inputID—An integer value containing the ID of the input Indicates from which input the buffer originates
- buffer—A PipelineBuffer object containing the buffer to be processed

PostExecute

This is the mirror method for the PreExecute and can be used to do any cleanup necessary. Usually, if there are resources you've acquired during PreExecute you'll want to release them here.

Cleanup

This is the mirror method for the `PrepareForExecute` method and is rarely used.

To better understand how to write custom data flow components, the following samples have been provided. These samples are a little more complex than what you normally see in a book like this, and because the source is quite functional, to better represent a real custom component, it is also fairly verbose. Only the more difficult and interesting sections are covered here. For a full understanding of the code, load it up in Visual Studio and step through it in the debugger.

Writing a Source Adapter

This section describes how to build a source adapter and walks through the implementation of the Image File Source Adapter example. Open the `ImageFileSrc` sample solution in the `SAMPLES\SRC\SampleComponents\ImageFileSrc` folder to follow along. The Image File Source Adapter is a bit unusual in that it does not rely on external metadata. The columns to retrieve are relatively static having been defined in the EXIF standard. The component could conceivably open one of the source files, retrieve the supported EXIF fields for that file, and then configure the columns based on the supported fields; however, the next file might support a different set of fields. To keep things simple, only the most commonly supported and interesting fields are supported for this source.

Setup and the Design Time Methods

The setup for the component is very similar to custom tasks, but this section covers some of the differences as well as how to implement some of the design time methods.

The `DtsPipelineComponent` Attribute

The `DtsPipelineComponent` attribute identifies the component to Integration Services and provides a number of important pieces of information.

```
[ DtsPipelineComponent(
ComponentType = ComponentType.SourceAdapter,
IconResource = "SSIS2K5.Samples.Transforms.ImageFileSrc.component.ico",
DisplayName="ImageFile Source",
Description="Retrieves EXIF information from JPG files",
CurrentVersion = 1) ]
```

There are a few important points to notice about the attribute. `ComponentType` is required. Without it, Integration Services will not recognize the component. `IconResource` must be the fully qualified name of the icon. The `DisplayName` and `Description` are important and you must include one or the other. The `CurrentVersion` attribute is not required, but comes in handy when you ship the next version of the component. Attribute parameters not used are `NoEditor`, `LocalizationType`, `RequiredProductLevel`, `ShapeProgID`, and `UITypeName`, which are described in Chapter 24.

`ProvideComponentProperties`

This method cleans up any other possible settings and then sets up the connection, output, and `ComponentInformation`. It might not seem necessary to do the cleanup because the designer calls this method only when the component is first created. However, there are other clients besides the designer, for example, custom written code for generating packages. Those clients might call the component methods in a different order and even multiple times. It's important to guard against such clients and always implement these methods as though they were getting called in the wrong way at the wrong time by cleaning up, checking assumptions, and building from scratch.

```
public override void ProvideComponentProperties()
{
    // start out clean, remove anything put on by the base class
    RemoveAllInputsOutputsAndCustomProperties();
```

Setting Up the Runtime Connection   This section of code reserves a reference to a runtime connection. This confuses some, so an explanation is in order. The Data Flow Task has a special collection called the `RuntimeConnectionCollection`. This is not a collection of connection managers. It is a collection of objects specific to the Data Flow Task and indicates components needed for a connection manager. By creating a `RuntimeConnection` as shown next, the component is saying to the Data Flow Task that it needs to use a connection. The name can be any string and is used for later retrieving the `RuntimeConnection` object, which will contain a reference to a connection manager. Why? This design makes it possible to better validate at the Data Flow Task level and hides connection manager name changes from components.

```
    // Get the runtime connection collection.
    IDTSRuntimeConnectionCollection90 pIDTSRuntimeConnectionCollection =
ComponentMetaData.RuntimeConnectionCollection;
    // See if there is already a runtime connection
    IDTSRuntimeConnection90 pIDTSRuntimeConnection;
    try
    {
        pIDTSRuntimeConnection = pIDTSRuntimeConnectionCollection[CONNECTION_NAME];
    }
    catch (Exception)
    {
        // Must not be there, make one
        pIDTSRuntimeConnection = pIDTSRuntimeConnectionCollection.New();
        pIDTSRuntimeConnection.Name = CONNECTION_NAME;
        pIDTSRuntimeConnection.Description = CONNECTION_DESC;
    }
```

Setting Up Component Outputs   This section of code sets up an output and declares that the component wants to use external metadata columns. External metadata columns have a number of benefits, including the ability to validate even when there is no connection available. In this case, the metadata is static, but the external metadata columns are still useful because the Advanced UI uses the external metadata columns to display the links in the mapping columns. Users indicate that they don't want a particular column by deleting the mapping, which also eliminates the output column.

```
// Add an output
IDTSOutput90 output = ComponentMetaData.OutputCollection.New();
```

The output.Name is the name that shows up in the Input and Output Properties tab in the Advanced UI.

```
// Name the output
output.Name = "Image Source Output";

// Set external metadata used.
ComponentMetaData.OutputCollection[0].ExternalMetadataColumnCollection.IsUsed =
true;

// We don't have connected metadata, just external metadata.
// Don't provide connected validation.
ComponentMetaData.ValidateExternalMetadata = false;
```

The component supports error dispositions. As a rule, components should support error dispositions. They make it easier to troubleshoot problems with the data. Setting UsesDispositions generally indicates that the component provides error input. However, it doesn't have to do this and might simply provide better error handling. Without error dispositions, the component will fail the first time data fails to correctly insert into the buffer.

```
ComponentMetaData.UsesDispositions = true;
```

The ContactInfo information is useful when a package that references the component is loaded, but the component isn't installed. In that event, this information is displayed to the user in an error message when loading the package.

```
// Get the assembly version and set that as our current version.
SetComponentVersion();

// Name the component and add component information
ComponentMetaData.Name = "ImageFileSrc";
ComponentMetaData.Description = "Sample Image File Source Adapter";
ComponentMetaData.ContactInfo = ComponentMetaData.Description +
    ";Microsoft SQL Server Integration Services 2005, By Kirk Haselden;" +
    " (c) 2006 Kirk Haselden" +
ComponentMetaData.Version.ToString();
```

ReinitializeMetadata
ReinitializeMetadata is called when the Refresh button in the Advanced UI is clicked or
when the Validate method returns VS_NEEDSNEWMETADATA.

```
public override void ReinitializeMetaData()
{
   // Baseclass may have some work to do here
   base.ReinitializeMetaData();

   // Get the output
   IDTSOutput90 output = ComponentMetaData.OutputCollection[0];

   // Start from a clean slate
   output.OutputColumnCollection.RemoveAll();
   output.ExternalMetadataColumnCollection.RemoveAll();
```

This is where the column information is added. The ExternalMetadataColumn is added to
the ExternalMetadataColumnCollection on the output it describes. Note that the column
data is statically defined. This is not typical. Most sources reference an external source
such as a table, flat file, or spreadsheet to determine the metadata for the columns. In this
case, the data we want to expose is known beforehand and is statically defined in the
ColumnInfos array. As a general rule, you should avoid removing columns in source
adapters unless absolutely necessary because this causes downstream data flow to break
when the lineage IDs change.

```
m_columnInfos = new ColumnInfo[12]
{
   new ColumnInfo("FILENAME", DataType.DT_STR, 1028),
   new ColumnInfo("MAKE", DataType.DT_STR, 30),
   new ColumnInfo("MODEL", DataType.DT_STR, 30),
   new ColumnInfo("SHUTTERSPEED", DataType.DT_STR, 10),
   new ColumnInfo("FSTOP", DataType.DT_STR, 10),
   new ColumnInfo("EXPOSUREPROGRAM", DataType.DT_STR, 20),
   new ColumnInfo("ISO", DataType.DT_STR, 10),
   new ColumnInfo("DATETIME", DataType.DT_STR, 40),
   new ColumnInfo("IMAGEWIDTH", DataType.DT_STR, 10),
   new ColumnInfo("IMAGELENGTH", DataType.DT_STR, 10),
   new ColumnInfo("BITSPERSAMPLE", DataType.DT_STR, 10),
   new ColumnInfo("COMPRESSION", DataType.DT_STR, 20),
};
```

The ReinitializeMetadata method uses the array of ColumnInfos to populate the output
columns.

```
   // Add the EXIF column information
   for (int i = 0; i < m_columnInfos.Length;i++ )
   {
```

```
// Create a new output column
IDTSOutputColumn90 column = output.OutputColumnCollection.NewAt(i);
IDTSExternalMetadataColumn90 externalColumn =
    output.ExternalMetadataColumnCollection.NewAt(i);
```

Set the properties of each column. In this sample, all the columns are of type `string` so only the length and code page parameters are needed. The `SetDataTypeProperties` method sets the data type, length, precision, scale, and code page for the column simultaneously.

```
// Set the column properties
column.SetDataTypeProperties(m_columnInfos[i].type,
    m_columnInfos[i].length, 0, 0, 1252);
column.Name = m_columnInfos[i].name;
```

Set the properties of each external metadata column. These should be the same as their corresponding columns.

```
// Set the external column properties
externalColumn.DataType = m_columnInfos[i].type;
externalColumn.Length = m_columnInfos[i].length;
externalColumn.Name = m_columnInfos[i].name;

// Assign the output column to the external metadata
column.ExternalMetadataColumnID = externalColumn.ID;
```

This component has only one output so this setting is redundant. However, if a component has more than one output that are in sync with the same input, the `ExclusionGroup` property should be set to a nonzero value and the `DirectRow` method should be used to tell the Execution Engine to which output the row should be sent. If the `DirectRow` method is not called to indicate the output to which the row should be sent, the row is not sent to an output. Outputs in sync with the same input and with exclusion group 0 are automatically forwarded to all outputs.

```
// Exclusion group
output.ExclusionGroup = 0;
```

This setting is also redundant because it is zero by default. But setting it makes it explicitly understood that the output is an asynchronous output. You will recall that an asynchronous output is the start of a new execution tree and consequently a new buffer type. Therefore, asynchronous outputs have no synchronous input ID value.

```
    // Synchronous input
    output.SynchronousInputID = 0;
    }
}
```

The `Validate` Method

The `Validate` method is where the component has the opportunity to sanity check some of its own settings. When validating, it's important to remember that not all settings come directly through a well-developed UI that checks for bounds violations or other invalid values. It's possible that someone modified the package XML directly or that the component was created by a different client application than the designer. Validation should be a little pessimistic and check all the assumptions. The sample `Validate` method for the Image File Source shows a few examples of the kind of checks validation should make.

```
public override DTSValidationStatus Validate()
{
   // Make sure base call is successful
   DTSValidationStatus status = base.Validate();
   if (status == DTSValidationStatus.VS_ISCORRUPT)
   {
      return status;
   }
}
```

If there are no external metadata columns, `ReinitializeMetadata` probably hasn't been called yet. This is probably the first time `Validate` is called and the component was probably just created. Short circuit the call here so that the Data Flow Task calls `ReinitializeMetadata`. Later, `Validate` will be called again and make it past this check.

```
   // If there are no external metadata columns, then return that we need some
   // Short circuit the validation since there is no metadata to validate at this
point.
   if (ComponentMetaData.OutputCollection[0].ExternalMetadataColumnCollection.Count
== 0)
   return DTSValidationStatus.VS_NEEDSNEWMETADATA;
```

This is a source; there should be no inputs and only one output because the component doesn't support an error output.

```
   // should have no inputs
   if (ComponentMetaData.InputCollection.Count != 0)
      return DTSValidationStatus.VS_ISCORRUPT;

   // should have two outputs
   if (ComponentMetaData.OutputCollection.Count != 1)
      return DTSValidationStatus.VS_ISCORRUPT;
```

The following code is an example of pessimistic validation. The component sets `UsesDispositions` to `TRUE`, but this code still checks it to ensure that the value hasn't been altered in some way.

```
    // See if the UsesDispositions is set.
    if (!ComponentMetaData.UsesDispositions)
    {
        bool bCancel;
        ComponentMetaData.FireError( 99, "ImageFile Source",
          "Uses dispositions setting is incorrect", "", 0, out bCancel);
        return DTSValidationStatus.VS_ISCORRUPT;
    }
    return status;
}
```

AcquireConnections **and** ReleaseConnections

Acquire and Release Connections methods are called the most because they bracket any of the other calls, including Validate, ReinitializeMetadata, ProcessInput/PrimeOutput, and PreExecute/PostExecute. They do not bracket PrepareForExecute and Cleanup calls.

AcquireConnections   Because getting a connection is such a commonly required thing to do in the component, the AcquireConnection method has been provided. You could get away with not implementing this method by simply doing the same code in all the methods that require connections, but then you'd have duplicated code in all of them and the Data Flow Task wouldn't be able to do some of its own validation on the connection managers. Implementing the AcquireConnections and ReleaseConnections methods correctly ensures that the component will always have a valid and up-to-date connection available before the other methods are called. The up-to-date part is important because, if the component simply calls AcquireConnection on a connection manager and stores the returned connection object as a member variable, numerous problems could result. For example, the connection might time out or it might be changed by a property expression or a Foreach Loop. It is important to implement AcquireConnections correctly and to release the connection object in the ReleaseConnections method to minimize the chance that those bad things happen.

```
// Called multiple times during design and once during execution
public override void AcquireConnections(object transaction)
{
```

Get the RuntimeConnection that was created in ProvideComponentProperties.

```
    IDTSRuntimeConnection90 conn;
    try
    {
        // get the runtime connection
        conn = ComponentMetaData.
                    RuntimeConnectionCollection[CONNECTION_NAME];
    }
    catch (Exception ex)
    {
```

```
    bool bCancel;
    ComponentMetaData.FireError(1, "ImageFileSrc",
                "Could not find the runtime connection.",
                "", 0, out bCancel );
    throw ex;
}


// Get the connection manager host from the connection
ConnectionManagerHost cmh =
(ConnectionManagerHost)conn.ConnectionManager;

if (cmh == null)
{
    bool bCancel;
    ComponentMetaData.FireError(2, "ImageFileSrc",
                "Could get the runtime Connection Manager.",
                "", 0, out bCancel );
}
```

The Image File Source only supports the Multifile type of connection manager. The component simply cannot function without one, so alert the user with an error if it isn't the correct type.

```
// Make sure it is a multifile connection manager
else if ( cmh.CreationName != "MULTIFILE")
{
    bool bCancel;
    ComponentMetaData.FireError(2, "ImageFileSrc",
                "Connection manager must be of type MULTIFILE",
                "", 0, out bCancel);
}
```

The connection manager was the correct type, so store it in a member variable. Note that it is stored there, but updated every time `AcquireConnections` is called. This is different than getting a reference to the connection manager once and holding onto it for the life of the component.

```
else
{
    try
    {
        // Store the connection manager for validation and execution
        m_cm = conn.ConnectionManager;
    }
    catch (Exception ex)
    {
```

```
            bool bCancel;
            ComponentMetaData.FireError(10, "ImageFileSrc",
                    "Could not get the runtime connection.",
                    "", 0, out bCancel);
            throw ex;
        }
    }
}
```

ReleaseConnections   Normally, the ReleaseConnections is where you would release the connection object you retrieved from the connection manager. Because MultiFile Connection Managers only return strings containing a filename, there is nothing to release here.

```
// Release if you have one, multifile only returns strings
public override void ReleaseConnections()
{
    // Nothing to do here because we're using file connection managers
    base.ReleaseConnections();
}
```

General Runtime Approach
The general approach for this component is as follows:

- **Get columns**—Establish the set of columns that will be populated with EXIF field information.

- **Store column ID**—Set the column ID in the array of structures containing the column information based on the field metadata.

- **Loop through files**—Retrieve the filename for each file returned from the MultiFile Connection Manager.

  •Call **AcquireConnection**—Retrieve the name of the file.

    - **Read EXIF data**—Create an ExifFileReader object to open the file and read the EXIF information.

    - **Call AddRow**—Add a new row to contain the EXIF information.

    - **Insert data**—Copy the EXIF information to the buffer.

    - **Handle dispositions**—If the column insert fails, determine the reason and warn the user.

- **Set EndOfRowset**—When the MultiFile Connection Manager returns null, indicating that there are no more files to open, set EndOfRowset on the buffer.

Take a look at the code now and see how each of the steps is implemented.

Get Columns

```
// Called once right before executing.
public override void PreExecute()
{
   base.PreExecute();

   // Find out which output columns exist
   IDTSOutput90 output = ComponentMetaData.OutputCollection[0];
   int countColumns = output.OutputColumnCollection.Count;
```

Check whether output columns exist. This is how the component knows if the user deleted a path between the ExternalMetadata column and the output column.

```
   // Iterate through the columns
   for( int iColumn = 0; iColumn < countColumns; iColumn++ )
   {
      // Set the exists flag for the column info.
      m_columnInfos[iColumn].outputExists =
               (output.OutputColumnCollection[iColumn] == null ? false : true);
```

Store Column ID   The ColumnInfos array stores the output ID of the given column. Later, the component uses the ID to access the column on the buffer.

```
      m_columnInfos[iColumn].outputID = iColumn;
   }
}
```

The processing of the output buffers happens in the PrimeOutput method. Note that this method is only called once. It's a blocking call and the component does not return from the call until it has added all the rows to the buffer. Also note that the component only processes one buffer. To the component, it appears as though there is one endless buffer available for filling.

```
// Called to provide a buffer to fill. Only called once per execution.
public override void PrimeOutput(int outputs, int[] outputIDs,
➡PipelineBuffer[] buffers)
{
```

Get the buffer. In this case, there is only one because there is only one output.

```
   // Only have one output, so
   PipelineBuffer buffer = buffers[0];

   // The name of the jpg file
   string fileName;
```

Loop Through Files   While the MultiFile Connection returns a valid filename, the component needs to do the following steps.

```
// For each jpg file, get the EXIF data
// MultiFile connection managers return null from
// AcquireConnection when the file list is exausted.
object conn;
```

Call AcquireConnection

```
while (null != (conn = m_cm.AcquireConnection(null)))
```

Read EXIF Data   The MultiFile Connection Manager returns the filename as an object. Convert to a string.

```
// Get the name of the file
fileName = conn.ToString();
```

Create a new ExifReader object to open the file and read the EXIF information. The ExifReader is found in the EXIFReader.cs file in the sample project.

```
// Open each file and read the EXIF information
ExifReader reader = new ExifReader(fileName);
```

Call AddRow   This method adds a row to the buffer. If the buffer is full, the Execution Engine performs the buffer flip and then adds a row to the new buffer.

```
// Add a new row to the buffer
buffer.AddRow();
```

Insert Data   Insert data into the buffer using the SetString method. This code makes a big assumption to simplify the code. Most of the time, sources have columns of varying types. In these cases, the component needs to use the various type-specific insert methods, such as SetBoolean, SetByte, SetInt16, or SetDateTime.

```
// Insert each column into the buffer.
foreach (ColumnInfo ci in m_columnInfos)
{
  try
  {
    // Only output to columns the user has chosen
    if (ci.outputExists)
    {
      // We only have string types
      // For other types, switch/case works.
      buffer.SetString(ci.outputID, reader.GetProperty(ci.name));
    }
  }
```

Handle Dispositions   In the `ProvideComponentProperties` method, the component sets the `UsesDispositions` flag to `TRUE`. If the component supports an error output, it directs the row to the error output. Otherwise, the component might simply handle the error rows in the exception handler.

```
catch (Exception ex)
{
    if (ex is DoesNotFitBufferException)
    {
        DTSRowDisposition rd =
            ComponentMetaData.OutputCollection[0].TruncationRowDisposition;
        if (rd == DTSRowDisposition.RD_IgnoreFailure)
        {
            // Ignore the error and continue.
            ComponentMetaData.FireWarning(100, "ImageFleSrc",
                "The file property " + ci.name + " for file " +
                    reader.FileName + " was too long. Ignoring truncation.", "", 0);
        }
        else
        {
            bool bCancel = false;
            ComponentMetaData.FireError(100, "ImageFleSrc",
                "The file property " + ci.name + " for file " + reader.FileName +
                " was too long.", "", 0, out bCancel);
            throw ex;
        }
```

Set `EndOfRowset`   The `EndOfRowset` method tells the Execution Engine that the output is done generating rows. If this method is not called, the Data Flow Task never terminates and continues waiting for more rows. However, for source adapters, the Execution Engine considers the source complete when the `PrimeOutput` call returns. If the `EndOfRowset` is not set by the source before returning from `PrimeOutput`, the Execution Engine fires an error before terminating.

```
        // Tell the buffer that we're done now.
        buffer.SetEndOfRowset();
```

Source adapters are examples of pure asynchronous outputs. Although the metadata for asynchronous outputs on a transform might sometimes reflect the metadata on the transforms inputs, sources have no inputs and all the data comes from some source outside of the pipeline. The primary responsibilities of a source adapter, therefore, are as follows:

- Describe the source data to the Data Flow Task

- Retrieve data from some source medium

- Convert the source data into buffer format

- Insert the source data into the buffer
- Tell the Execution Engine when the source data is exhausted

Writing a Destination Adapter

In many ways, destination adapters are the corollary opposites of source adapters. They do everything that source adapters do, only in reverse. They convert buffer types to destination types and they extract data from the buffer and insert it into the destination medium. Many of the functions are almost identical with the exception that the direction of the operations and data movement is reversed. Therefore, the methods that are virtually identical are not covered here. With a brief look at the code, you should be able to make the short conceptual leap between writing sources and destinations. However, there are a few differences worth noting and the destination component implements error outputs. This section covers those differences. Also, this section focuses on the SQLClientDest sample solution because it contains a few more interesting elements. The differences between the SQLClientDest and the ODBCDest are minor.

The Destination Adapter General Approach

Although the Image File Source has hard-coded component metadata, the sample destination is a little more complex and discovers the destination metadata from the destination table. This section focuses on how that is done. The ADO.NET SQL Client Destination (SQLClientDest) uses the ADO.NET SqlClient Data provider for inserting data into SQL Server data tables. Internally, the component uses two DataTable objects: one for holding the metadata for the destination table (m_metadataTable) and the other for inserting the rows from the buffer into the destination table (m_batchTable). The component first retrieves the metadata from the destination SQL Server table and then builds the batch table to match. The component also builds an INSERT statement to use for inserting the data from the buffer into the batch table.

During execution, the component extracts the column data from the buffer and inserts it into the batch table. The component calls the Update method and the ADO.NET provider takes over, inserting the data from the batch table into the destination SQL Server table. The batch size, or number of rows sent at a time, is determined by the BatchSize custom property.

Adding Custom Properties

The sample component adds a custom property for the batch size and the destination table. Figure 25.5 shows the properties in the Advanced Editor for the SQLClientDest component.

This code adds the TableName and BatchSize custom properties.

```
// Add the TableName property and set it as expressionable
IDTSCustomProperty90 propTableName =
ComponentMetaData.CustomPropertyCollection.New();
```

```
propTableName.Name = TABLE_NAME;
propTableName.Description = "The name of the table to insert into";
propTableName.ExpressionType = DTSCustomPropertyExpressionType.CPET_NOTIFY;

// Add the batch size property and make it expressionable.
IDTSCustomProperty90 propBatchSize =
ComponentMetaData.CustomPropertyCollection.New();
propBatchSize.Name = BATCH_SIZE;
propBatchSize.Description = "The number of rows to insert per batch.";
propBatchSize.ExpressionType = DTSCustomPropertyExpressionType.CPET_NOTIFY;
propBatchSize.Value = 1000;
```

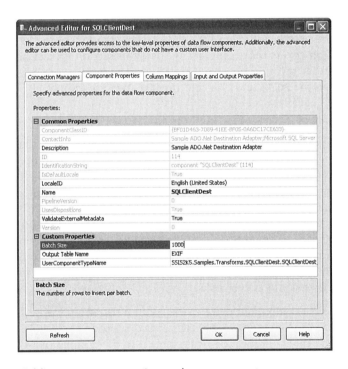

FIGURE 25.5   Adding custom properties to the component.

Notice also that the ExpressionType is specified. By default, the type is CPET_NONE. By setting the property ExpressionType to CPET_NOTIFY, the component has made the properties "expressionable." Figure 25.6 shows the Property Expressions Editor for a Data Flow Task containing the SQL Client Destination. Notice that the BatchSize and OutputTable properties are available.

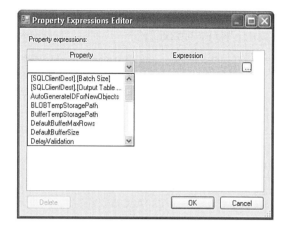

FIGURE 25.6   Custom properties can be made expressionable.

The `ReinitializeMetaData` Method

Most of what you see in the `ReinitializeMetaData` method is similar to the Image File Source, so it isn't reviewed here. The code relating to discovering the destination table metadata, however, is interesting and generally the kind of thing that destination adapters need to do.

Discovering the Destination Table Metadata

For source and destination adapters, part of the challenge is to create a mapping between the columns found on the buffer and the source or destination table. To create the mapping, one of the first things the destination must accomplish is to discover the metadata on the destination table.

The SQL Client Destination uses the `GetSchema` method to retrieve a set of rows containing the metadata for the destination table. Each row in the rowset returned contains the information about one column in the destination table. The columns for the returned rowset have 17 columns. Table 25.2 contains the schema and indexes for the rows.

TABLE 25.2   Connection Managers Required Per Operation

Numeric Index	String Name Index	Description
1	TABLE_CATALOG	Database (AdventureWorks)
2	TABLE_SCHEMA	Table Schema (dbo)
3	TABLE_NAME	Name of the table (Authors)
4	COLUMN_NAME	Name of the column (Age)
5	ORDINAL_POSITION	Position of the column in the table
6	COLUMN_DEFAULT	Default value
7	IS_NULLABLE	NULLs allowed for values

TABLE 25.2   Continued

Numeric Index	String Name Index	Description
8	DATA_TYPE	The type of the column
9	CHARACTER_MAXIMUM_LENGTH	Length of varchar and other character type columns
10	CHARACTER_OCTET_LENGTH	Length without terminator
11	NUMERIC_PRECISION	Precision
12	NUMERIC_PRECISION_RADIX	Radix
13	NUMERIC_SCALE	Scale
14	DATETIME_PRECISION	Date-time precision
15	CHARACTER_SET_CATALOG	Catalog name
16	CHARACTER_SET_SCHEMA	Unqualified schema name
17	CHARACTER_SET_NAME	Unqualified schema name

The GetSchema method discovers the catalog name from the connection manager and then builds the restrictions array to only retrieve the schema for the destination table columns.

```
private void CreateSchemaTable(string strTableName)
{
   try
   {
      // Create the table to hold the table metadata
      m_metaDataTable = new DataTable();

      // Get the InitialCatalog
      string initialCatalog = "";
      IDTSConnectionManager90 cm = GetConnectionManager();
```

Get the catalog name from the connection manager host properties. The ConnectionManagerHost is a host similar to the Taskhost and all connection managers have one with a properties provider containing all the property values of the connection manager.

```
      // What you really have here is a ConnectionManagerHost which implements
      // IDTSPropertiesProvider90 from which you can get the extended properties.
      if (cm is IDTSPropertiesProvider90)
      {
         IDTSPropertiesProvider90 pp = (IDTSPropertiesProvider90)cm;
         initialCatalog = pp.Properties["InitialCatalog"].GetValue(cm).ToString();
      }
```

Next, you specify the catalog, table name, and that you only want column schema information.

```
    // Build the restrictions. We just want to get column information for the
table.
    string[] restrictions = new string[4] { initialCatalog, null, strTableName,
null };

    // Get the schema.
    m_metaDataTable = m_conn.GetSchema("Columns", restrictions);
  }
}
```

Creating the External Metadata Columns

Now that the component has built the metadata table, it can start to create the
ExternalMetaData Columns. ExternalMetaData Columns are useful for validating the
component when there is no connection available, but they also are used to represent the
source or destination table when creating mappings. For each row in the metadata table,
there should be a new column created, as follows. The following code has been abbreviated from the source to save space. This code shows the crucial logic for converting the
metadata rows to ExternalMetaData Columns.

```
// Every row of the table describes one column
// Now set up the ExternalMetadata Columns
m_countMetaDataColumns = m_metaDataTable.Rows.Count;
for (int iColumn = 0;
           iColumn < m_countMetaDataColumns;
           iColumn++)
{
   // Create a new column
   IDTSExternalMetadataColumn90 inputcolNewMain =
inputMain.ExternalMetadataColumnCollection.NewAt(iColumn);
   // Point to the row describing this column
   DataRow rowCurr = m_metaDataTable.Rows[iColumn];

   // Get the name
   inputcolNewMain.Name = rowCurr["COLUMN_NAME"].ToString();

   int CodePage = 0;
```

TranslateSqlTypeToDts is a special method to convert the SQL Client data types to
Integration Services buffer types.

```
   // Convert the type to a pipeline type
   DataType dtstype = DataType.DT_EMPTY;
   TranslateSqlTypeToDts(rowCurr["DATA_TYPE"].ToString(), ref dtstype);
```

Set the length and other type-related properties:

```
// Set the length where the type does not determine the length
int Length = 0;
// Create input columns with the ideal type for conversion
inputcolNewMain.CodePage = CodePage;
inputcolNewMain.DataType = dtstype;
inputcolNewMain.Length = Length;
inputcolNewMain.Precision = Precision;
inputcolNewMain.Scale = Scale;
}
```

The PreExecute Method

The PreExecute method is where the batch table and INSERT statement are created and
the columns are mapped.

Creating the Batch Table

The batch table is the location where rows are inserted and temporarily held until the
SQL Adapter sends off a batch of rows to the destination. The logic for creating the batch
table is found in the CreateBatchTable method, as follows:

```
// Get a table to hold the rows temporarily until it contains BatchSize rows
// Then we'll update the destination in bigger batches.
private void CreateBatchTable(string strTableName)
{
    // Get the Schema into m_metaDataTable;
    CreateSchemaTable(strTableName);

    // Create new data table
    m_batchTable = new DataTable();

    // Build the table MetaData.
    int countColumns = m_metaDataTable.Rows.Count;
```

In this step, you precreate the number of columns you need so that you can place the
columns in the correct order. If each column is added in the order found in the metadata
table, the columns will not be in the correct order when inserting the data with the
query.

```
    // Preload with columns
    DataColumn[] columns = new DataColumn[countColumns];

    for (int iColumn = 0; iColumn < countColumns; iColumn++)
    {
        // Point to the row describing this column
        DataRow rowCurr = m_metaDataTable.Rows[iColumn];
```

The ORDINAL_POSITION string is a string index into the ordinal position of the column in the source table. It is a 1-based index but the columns collection is 0-based, so the code subtracts one to correct the off-by-one index.

```
        // Build the columns array in the order found in the table.
        // Makes it easier on the user and the programmer.
        columns[Convert.ToInt16(rowCurr["ORDINAL_POSITION"])-1] = new DataColumn(
                rowCurr["COLUMN_NAME"].ToString(),
                GetSqlDbTypeFromName(rowCurr["DATA_TYPE"].ToString()).GetType());
    }
```

Now, all the columns have been added in the correct order; the code adds them to the batch table.

```
    m_batchTable.Columns.AddRange(columns);
}
```

Generating the INSERT Statement

To insert data into the batch table, the code dynamically creates an INSERT statement from the columns in the metadata table by adding parameters for each column.

```
for (int i = 0; i < m_countMetaDataColumns; i++)
{
    sb.Append("@p" + i.ToString() + ", ");

    // Point to the row describing this column
    DataRow rowCurr = m_metaDataTable.Rows[i];

    // Get the length for character types
    string strLen = rowCurr["CHARACTER_MAXIMUM_LENGTH"].ToString();
    int len = strLen.Length == 0 ? 0 : Convert.ToInt32( strLen );


    // Set the parameter with name, type and length.
    cmd.Parameters.Add("@p" + i.ToString(),
        GetSqlDbTypeFromName(rowCurr["DATA_TYPE"].ToString()),
        len,
        m_batchTable.Columns[i].ColumnName);

}
// Add the closing parenthesis
// Remove the last comma
sb.Remove(sb.Length - 2, 2);
sb.Append(" )");
```

The completed INSERT statement looks similar to the following:

```
INSERT INTO TableName VALUES( @p0, @p1, @p3 )
```

Mapping the Columns

The code that maps the ExternalMetaData columns to the buffer columns is perhaps the most complex in the SQL Client Destination and requires some explanation.

Discovering Which Input Columns Map to External Columns   It's important to remember all through this discussion that input columns represent buffer columns and external columns represent destination table columns. When a user edits the component in the Advanced Editor, the two sets of columns visible in the editor represent those to column collections. When creating or deleting a mapping between two columns in the Advanced Editor, the user is selecting which input columns should flow to each table column. Another way of thinking about it is the user is specifying which buffer column should flow to which ExternalMetaData Column.

ExternalMetaData Columns unfortunately do not have the name or ID of the buffer column. In fact, they don't even contain the ID of the input column. To discover which buffer (input) column should flow to a given table (ExternalMetaData) column, it is necessary to work backward from the input ID of the input column to the ExternalMetaData Column ID to the ExternalMetaData Column name to the Destination Table column name. When it is all done, the component will have established which column on the destination table maps to which column on the input buffer. Take a look at the following code to see how this is done:

```
// Get the input and the external column collection
IDTSInput90 input = ComponentMetaData.InputCollection[0];
IDTSExternalMetadataColumnCollection90 externalcols =
➥ input.ExternalMetadataColumnCollection;
```

This hash table makes it possible to retrieve the ID for an ExternalMetaData Column by name to get its ID. Later the code uses this hash to match the column name on the batch table to the ExternalMetaData Column name and then get the ExternalMetaData Column ID to match with the input column that references the ExternalMetaData Column and then get the LineageID from the input column. The LineageID can then be used to retrieve the buffer column index.

```
// Make a hash table for the names of the external columns and contains the ID
int cExternalCol = externalcols.Count;
System.Collections.Hashtable hashExternalNameToID = new
➥ System.Collections.Hashtable(cExternalCol);
// Build a mapping between the external column name and its ID
for (int iExternalCol = 0; iExternalCol < cExternalCol; iExternalCol++)
{
   IDTSExternalMetadataColumn90 externalcol = externalcols[iExternalCol];
   hashExternalNameToID.Add(externalcol.Name, externalcol.ID);
}

// Get the input columns collection and make a hash table to map the external
// ID that it references to the lineage ID of the column
```

```
IDTSInputColumnCollection90 inputcols = input.InputColumnCollection;
int cInputCol = inputcols.Count;
System.Collections.Hashtable hashReferenceIDToLineageID = new
➥  System.Collections.Hashtable(cInputCol);
// Build a mapping between external columns and input buffer columns IDs
for (int iInputCol = 0; iInputCol < cInputCol; iInputCol++)
{
   IDTSInputColumn90 inputcol = inputcols[iInputCol];
   if (inputcol.ExternalMetadataColumnID > 0)
   hashReferenceIDToLineageID.Add(inputcol.ExternalMetadataColumnID,
➥inputcol.LineageID);
}
```

Now that you have a way to discover which LineageID is connected to which ExternalMetaData Column name, you can get the buffer index from the column name on the batch table.

```
// Loop over all columns in the batchTable
for (int iRSCol = 0; iRSCol < cBTCol; iRSCol++)
{
   // Get the name for the column at the current index
   string strRSColName = m_batchTable.Columns[iRSCol].ColumnName;

   // Find the ID of the external column from the name
   // ExternalMetaData is driven from the destination table.
   // This should not fail unless ExternalMetadata is corrupt.
   int idExternal = (int)hashExternalNameToID[strRSColName];

   // Find the ExternalMetadata column that points to this ID
   try
   {
      int linid = (int)hashReferenceIDToLineageID[idExternal];
      // Get the index in the buffer of this column
      int idx = (int)BufferManager.FindColumnByLineageID(input.Buffer, linid);
```

This is the mapping array. The array is in order of the columns found in the batch table and the values are the indexes into the buffer for those columns. In the ProcessInput method, the component can now simply loop through this collection for each batch table column and find the index into the buffer for transferring the buffer data into the columns of the batch table using the INSERT statement shown earlier.

```
      m_idxColumn[iRSCol] = idx;
   }
}
```

The ProcessInput Method

The PreExecute method built the mapping array that maps the column to the buffer index. The ProcessInput method has a pretty simple job. Get each of the rows from the buffers passed into the method and pass the column values from the buffer row into the parameters for the INSERT statement.

Getting Data from the Input Buffer

```
for (; iCol < cCols; iCol++)
{
    // Which buffer column is this ?
    int idxCol = m_idxColumn[iCol];

    // Set the parameter value for the insert.
    m_sqlAdapter.InsertCommand.Parameters[iCol].Value = buffer[idxCol];
}
```

There is some more code in the sample project for handling blobs and so forth, but this is the essential code that extracts data out of the buffer using the buffer index array built in the PreExecute method.

Inserting the Data

The following statement performs the insert. The Update method gives ADO.NET an opportunity to send the batch of rows.

```
m_sqlAdapter.InsertCommand.ExecuteNonQuery();
m_sqlAdapter.Update(m_batchTable);
```

Handling Error Rows

If a row fails to correctly insert, there will be an exception. Depending on the Error Disposition settings the user has selected, you might want to either ignore the error, redirect the error row, or fail the component.

```
catch (Exception e)
{
    if (m_rowdisp == DTSRowDisposition.RD_FailComponent)
    throw e;

    if (m_rowdisp == DTSRowDisposition.RD_IgnoreFailure)
        continue;

    if (m_rowdisp == DTSRowDisposition.RD_RedirectRow)
    {
        buffer.DirectErrorRow(errorOutputID, 100, iCol);
    }
}
```

Incrementing Pipeline Performance Counters

A commonly missed detail of custom components is updating the performance counters. The following code shows how easy it is to add support for the performance counters with methods provided on the `ComponentMetaData` interface.

```
finally
{
   // Update the number of rows we inserted
   ComponentMetaData.IncrementPipelinePerfCounter(DTS_PIPELINE_
➡ CTR_ROWSWRITTEN, uiRowsWritten);

   // Update the number of blob bytes we wrote
ComponentMetaData.IncrementPipelinePerfCounter(DTS_PIPELINE
➡ _CTR_BLOBBYTESWRITTEN, uiBlobBytesWritten);
}
```

The SQL Client Destination code has more code than you see here. This discussion has focused on those sections of code that might be difficult to understand or that cover new ground. As always, stepping through the code in the debugger is the best way to understand it completely. Writing a destination is not difficult, even one that dynamically discovers and maps columns as this one does. You can convert the sample destinations into your own. Adapting the code to the specific ADO.NET provider and the ADO.NET ODBC SQL Client shows how to use this same SQL Client Destination code for a different provider with little effort.

Writing a Transform

Transforms are last because in many ways they are no more than source and destination components bound together into one component. This is especially true of transforms with asynchronous outputs. Think of the input of a transform as a destination adapter and the output as a source adapter and you'll understand. So, what is left to talk about? Although sources and destinations only convert data to and from various media, they don't actually transform it. What transforms do that sources and destinations don't is actually modify the data. That's what this section focuses on. How transforms perform the actual work they do. The Data Profiler sample is an excellent example because it is simple, easy to understand, and built to be extended. There are currently only a few profiling options, but by simply adding a new profile type class, you can add new profiling operations to the transform.

Types of Transforms

You will remember that there are two general types of transforms: those with synchronous outputs and those with asynchronous outputs. Transforms with synchronous outputs do not handle the `PrimeOutput` method and it will never get called even if they do. Sync outputs with nonzero exclusion groups get their rows as directed by the `DirectRow` method called by the transform. Synchronous outputs with exclusion group of zero automatically receive all rows from their synchronous input. Implementing

`ProcessInput` for transforms with synchronous outputs is quite simple and virtually identical between the two types of transforms. Because transforms with synchronous outputs do not have any behavior or interesting challenges beyond those found in transforms with asynchronous outputs, this section only describes transforms with asynchronous outputs and specifically focuses on the DataProfiler transform.

Setting Up the Transform

The process for setting up a transform is identical to any of the other components with the exceptions previously noted.

Setting Up the Attributes   The following are the attributes for the DataProfiler transform. Notice that the `ComponentType` parameter is set to `ComponentType.Transform`:

```
[DtsPipelineComponent(
    DisplayName = "Data Profiler",
    Description = "Computes profile metrics for input data",
    IconResource = "SSIS2K5.Samples.Transforms.DataProfiler.Component.ico",
    ComponentType = ComponentType.Transform )]
```

The `ProvideComponentProperties` Method   Because the set of output columns for the DataProfiler is fixed, the `ProvideComponentProperties` method statically defines the output columns and there is little need for the `ReinitializeMetaData` method. No matter what the shape of the input columns, the output columns and their types will always be fixed. The following code is repeated for each output column and adds the Column, Type, ProfileType, and ProfileValue columns to the output.

```
IDTSOutputColumn90 outputColumn = outputColumnCollection.New();
outputColumn.Name = "Column";
outputColumn.SetDataTypeProperties(DataType.DT_WSTR, 50, 0, 0, 0);
```

The `PreExecute` Method   In the `PreExecute` method, the component examines each of the columns, creates column profilers for each column, and determines which of the column profilers can profile the column. Note that it is easy to add a new profile type by simply creating a new profile class.

```
foreach(IDTSInputColumn90 inputColumn in inputColumnCollection)
{
    // For each column profiler...
    for (int j = 0; j < columnProfilerCount; j++)
    {
        ColumnProfilerBase columnProfiler = null;

        // Create column profiler object of the desired type
        switch(j)
        {
            case 0:
```

```csharp
            columnProfiler = new ColumnProfilerMin();
         break;

      case 1:
            columnProfiler = new ColumnProfilerMax();
         break;

      case 2:
            columnProfiler = new ColumnProfilerAvgStrLen();
         break;

      case 3:
            columnProfiler = new ColumnProfilerPercentageNulls();
         break;
   }

   // Give column profiler the information about the input column
   columnProfiler.ColumnIndex = BufferManager.FindColumnByLineageID(
      input.Buffer,
      inputColumn.LineageID);

   columnProfiler.ColumnName = inputColumn.Name;

   // And tell the details of that column (type, length, etc)
   BufferManager.GetColumnInfo(
      input.Buffer,
      columnProfiler.ColumnIndex,
      ref columnProfiler.ColumnInfo);

   // The column profiler might not be able to profile this column,
   // so ask beforehand.
   if (!columnProfiler.CanProfile())
   {
      // If we can't profile this column, null out the column profiler
      // object and our ProcessInput method will ignore this element.
      columnProfiler = null;
   }
   else
   {
      columnProfiler.Prepare();
   }

   // Save the new object in the array of column profilers
   columnProfilers.Add(columnProfiler);
   }
}
```

The PrimeOutput **Method**   The PrimeOutput method is about as simple as it gets. It stores the output buffer reference for use in the ProcessInput method. The Data Flow Task guarantees that PrimeOutput will be called before ProcessInput.

<u>TIP</u>

Remember also, that this is different from synchronous outputs on source adapters that do not return from the PrimeOutput method until the source has completed.

```
public override void PrimeOutput(int outputs, int[] outputIDs, PipelineBuffer[]
buffers)
{
   outputBuffer = buffers[0];
}
```

The ProcessInput **Method**   The ProcessInput method loops through each of the rows performing the profile operation. When the EndOfRowset is reached, each of the profiling classes is asked for their final profile values and the output buffer receives a number of rows based on the number of columns multiplied times the number of profile types. At last, the code calls SetEndOfRowset to indicate that the transform is done.

```
public override void ProcessInput(int inputID, PipelineBuffer buffer)
{
   // Check if this is all the data
   if (!buffer.EndOfRowset)
   {
      // While there are rows, profile columns.
      while (buffer.NextRow())
      {
         // Iterate through the profilers and apply the profiles
         for (int i = 0; i < columnProfilers.Count; i++)
         {
            ColumnProfilerBase columnProfiler =
            (ColumnProfilerBase)columnProfilers[i];

            if (columnProfiler != null)
            {
               columnProfiler.Profile(buffer);
            }
         }
      }
   }
   else
   {
```

```
      // When we reach end of rowset, output final profile values.
      for (int i = 0; i < columnProfilers.Count; i++)
      {
         ColumnProfilerBase columnProfiler =
         (ColumnProfilerBase) columnProfilers[i];

         if (columnProfiler != null)
         {
            outputBuffer.AddRow();
            outputBuffer[columnIndex] = columnProfiler.ColumnName;
            outputBuffer[typeIndex] =
columnProfiler.ColumnInfo.DataType.ToString();
            outputBuffer[profileTypeIndex] = columnProfiler.GetProfileType();
            outputBuffer[profileValueIndex] = columnProfiler.GetProfileValue();
         }
      }
      outputBuffer.SetEndOfRowset();
      outputBuffer = null;
   }
}
```

Performing the Transformation

The actual work of transforming the data is done by each of the profiler classes. The
following code is the definition for the average string length profile.

```
namespace SSIS2K5.Samples.Transforms.DataProfiler
{
   class ColumnProfilerAvgStrLen : SSIS2K5.Samples.Transforms.DataProfiler.
➥ ColumnProfilerBase
   {
       private double rows = 0;
       private double length = 0;
       public override string GetProfileType() { return "AVGSTRLEN"; }
```

Only profile string type columns.

```
      public override bool CanProfile()
      {
          return ColumnInfo.DataType == DataType.DT_WSTR
                 || ColumnInfo.DataType == DataType.DT_STR;
      }
```

The profile method is called for every row and simply stores the number of rows and the
length.

```
public override void Profile(PipelineBuffer buffer)
{
    rows++;
    object o = buffer[ColumnIndex];
    if (o != null) length += ((string) o).Length;
}
```

When the last row is processed, the resulting average row length is the length of all rows divided by the number of rows.

```
    public override string GetProfileValue() { return Math.Ceiling(length/rows)
➥.ToString(); }
    };
}
```

Summary

This chapter showed you how to write custom data flow components by starting with a conceptual overview of the component design and execution life cycles and then it covered the design time and runtime interfaces. Details of how to implement the various required functions were covered and sample code is available in the SampleComponents folder for you to study. Although Integration Services does provide a broad and deep set of components, there will still be times when it is necessary to roll your own. This chapter should get you off to a good start.

Error, Warning, and Information Events

Error Code	Symbolic Name	Description
0x8002F347	DTS_E_STOREDPROCSTASK_OVERWRITINGSPATDESTINATION	Overwriting Stored Procedure "__" at destination.
0xC0000032	DTS_E_NOTINITIALIZED	An internal object or variable was not initialized. This is an internal product error. This error is returned when a variable should have a valid value but does not.
0xC0000033	DTS_E_EXPIRED	Data Transformation Services evaluation period has expired.
0xC0000034	DTS_E_NEGATIVEVALUESNOTALLOWED	This property cannot be assigned a negative value. This error occurs when a negative value is assigned to a property that can only contain positive values, such as the COUNT property.
0xC0000035	DTS_E_NEGATIVEINDEXNOTALLOWED	Indexes cannot be negative. This error occurs when a negative value is used as an index to a collection.
0xC00060AB	DTS_E_INVALIDSSISSERVERNAME	Invalid server name "__". SSIS service does not support multi-instance; use just server name instead of "server name\instance".
0xC0010001	DTS_E_VARIABLENOTFOUND	The variable cannot be found. This occurs when an attempt is made to retrieve a variable from the Variables collection on a container during execution of the package, and the variable is not there. The variable name may have changed or the variable is not being created.
0xC0010003	DTS_E_VARIABLEREADONLY	Error trying to write to a read-only variable, "__".
0xC0010004	DTS_E_MANAGEDCOMPONENTSTORENOTFOUND	Unable to find the directories containing Tasks and Data Flow Task components. Check the integrity of your installation.
0xC0010006	DTS_E_PACKAGENAMETOOLONG	Package name is too long. The limit is 128 characters. Shorten the package name.
0xC0010007	DTS_E_PACKAGEDESCRIPTIONTOOLONG	Package description is too long. The limit is 1024 characters. Shorten the package description.
0xC0010008	DTS_E_VERCOMMENTSTOOLONG	VersionComments property is too long. The limit is 1024 characters. Try shortening the VersionComments.
0xC0010009	DTS_E_ELEMENTNOTFOUND	The element cannot be found in a collection. This error happens when you try to retrieve an element from a collection on a container during execution of the package and the element is not there.
0xC001000A	DTS_E_PACKAGENOTFOUND	The specified package could not be loaded from the SQL Server database.
0xC001000C	DTS_E_INVALIDVARIABLEVALUE	The variable value assignment is not valid. This error happens when the client or a task assigns a runtime object to a variable value.

Error Code	Symbolic Name	Description
0xC001000D	DTS_E_RESERVEDNAMESPACE	Error assigning namespace to the variable. The namespace "System" is reserved for system use. This error happens when a component or task attempts to create a variable with a namespace of "System".
0xC001000E	DTS_E_CONNECTIONNOTFOUND	The connection "__" is not found. This error is thrown by Connections collection when the specific connection element is not found.
0xC001000F	DTS_E_64BITVARIABLERECAST	The variable "__" is a 64-bit integer variable, which is not supported on this operating system. The variable has been recast to 32-bit integer. Variables of type VT_I8 and VT_UI8 are not supported on Microsoft Windows 2000.
0xC0010010	DTS_E_CANTCHANGEREADONLYATRUNTIME	An attempt change to a read-only attribute on variable "__" occurred. This error happens when a read-only attribute for a variable is being changed at runtime. Read-only attributes can be changed only at design time.
0xC0010011	DTS_E_VARIABLEINVALIDCONTAINERREF	Invalid attempt to set a variable to a container reference. Variables are not allowed to reference containers.
0xC0010013	DTS_E_INVALIDVARVALUE	Assigning invalid value or object to variable "__". This error happens when a value is not appropriate for variables.
0xC0010014	DTS_E_GENERICERROR	One or more errors occurred. There should be more specific errors preceding this one that explain the details of the errors. This message is used as a return value from functions that encounter errors.
0xC0010016	DTS_E_INVALIDARRAYVALUE	Error getting or setting an array value. The type "__" is not allowed. This occurs when loading an array into a variable.
0xC0010017	DTS_E_UNSUPPORTEDARRAYTYPE	Unsupported type in array. This happens when saving an array of unsupported types into a variable.
0xC0010018	DTS_E_PERSISTENCEERROR	Error loading value "__" from node "__".
0xC0010019	DTS_E_INVALIDNODE	Node "__" is not a valid node. This happens when saving fails.
0xC0010020	DTS_E_ERRORLOADINGTASK	Error loading a task. The contact information for the task is "__". This happens when loading a task fails.
0xC0010021	DTS_E_ERRORELEMENTNOTINCOLL	Element "__" does not exist in collection "__".
0xC0010022	DTS_E_MISSINGOBJECTDATA	The ObjectData element is missing in the XML block of a hosted object. This occurs when the XML parser attempts to locate the data element for an object and it cannot be found.

Error Code	Symbolic Name	Description
0xC0010023	DTS_E_VARIABLENOTFOUNDINCOLL	The variable "___" cannot be found. This error occurs when an attempt to retrieve a variable from a variables collection on a container during execution of the package occurs, and the variable is not there. A variable name may have changed or the variable is not being created.
0xC0010025	DTS_E_HASEMPTYTASKHOSTS	The package cannot execute because it contains tasks that failed to load.
0xC0010026	DTS_E_TASKISEMPTY	The task has failed to load. The contact information for this task is "___".
0xC0010027	DTS_E_ERRORLOADINGTASKNOCONTACT	Error loading task "___".
0xC0010028	DTS_E_ERRORATLOADTASK	Error loading task. This happens when loading a task from XML fails.
0xC0011001	DTS_E_CANTLOADFROMNODE	The runtime object cannot be loaded from the specified XML node. This happens when trying to load a package or other object from an XML node that is not of the correct type, such as a non-SSIS XML node.
0xC0011002	DTS_E_OPENPACKAGEFILE	Failed to open package file "___" due to error 0x___ "___". This happens when loading a package and the file cannot be opened or loaded correctly into the XML document. This can be the result of either providing an incorrect file name was specified when calling LoadPackage or the XML file was specified and has an incorrect format.
0xC0011003	DTS_E_LOADPACKAGEXML	Failed to load XML due to error 0x___ "___". This happens when loading a package and the file cannot be opened or loaded correctly into XML document. This can be the result of either providing an incorrect file name to the LoadPackage method or the XML file specified having an incorrect format.
0xC0011004	DTS_E_LOADPACKAGEXMLFILE	Failed to load XML from package file "___" due to error 0x___ "___". This happens when loading a package and the file cannot be opened or loaded correctly into an XML document. This can be the result of either providing an incorrect file name to the LoadPackage method or the XML file specified having an incorrect format.
0xC0011005	DTS_E_OPENFILE	Failed to open package file. This happens when loading a package and the file cannot be opened or loaded correctly into an XML document. This can be the result of either providing an incorrect file name to the LoadPackage method or the XML file specified having an incorrect format.
0xC0011006	DTS_E_UNABLETODECODEBINARYFORMAT	Unable to decode a binary format in the package.
0xC0011007	DTS_E_FUNDAMENTALLOADINGERROR	Unable to load the package as XML because the package does not have a valid XML format. A specific XML parser error will be posted.

Error Code	Symbolic Name	Description
0xC0011008	DTS_E_LOADFROMXML	Error loading from XML. No further detailed error information can be specified for this problem because no Events object was passed where detailed error information can be stored.
0xC0011009	DTS_E_XMLDOMERROR	Cannot create an instance of the XML Document Object Model. MSXML may not be registered.
0xC001100D	DTS_E_CANNOTLOADOLDPACKAGES	The package cannot be loaded. This occurs when attempting to load an older version package, or the package file refers to an invalid structured object.
0xC001100E	DTS_E_SAVEFILE	Failed to save package file.
0xC001100F	DTS_E_SAVEPACKAGEFILE	Failed to save package file "___" with error 0x___ "___".
0xC001200D	DTS_E_IDTSNAMENOTSUPPORTED	The object must inherit from IDTSName90 and does not.
0xC0012018	DTS_E_CONFIGFORMATINVALID_PACKAGEDELIMITER	The configuration entry, "___", has an incorrect format because it does not begin with package delimiter. There was no "\package" delimiter.
0xC0012019	DTS_E_CONFIGFORMATINVALID	The configuration entry "___" had an incorrect format. This can occur because of a missing delimiter or formatting errors, like an invalid array delimiter.
0xC001201B	DTS_E_CONFIGFILEFAILEDEXPORT	Failure exporting configuration file.
0xC0012021	DTS_E_PROPERTIESCOLLECTIONREADONLY	Properties collection cannot be modified.
0xC0012022	DTS_E_DTRXMLSAVEFAILURE	Unable to save configuration file. The file may be read only.
0xC0012023	DTS_E_FAILPACKAGEONFAILURENA	FailPackageOnFailure property is not applicable to the package container.
0xC0012024	DTS_E_TASKPRODUCTLEVEL	The task "___" cannot run on this edition of Integration Services. It requires a higher level edition.
0xC0012029	DTS_E_UNABLETOSAVETOFILE	Unable to save xml to "___". The file may be read only.
0xC0012037	DTS_E_CONFIGTYPECONVERSIONFAILED	Failed to convert a type in the configuration "___" for the package path "___". This happens when a configuration value cannot be converted from a string to the appropriate destination type. Check the configuration value to ensure it can be converted to the type of the destination property or variable.
0xC0012049	DTS_E_CONFIGFAILED	Configuration failure. This is a generic warning for all configuration types. Other warnings should precede this with more information.
0xC0012050	DTS_E_REMOTEPACKAGEVALIDATION	Package failed validation from the ExecutePackage task. The package cannot run.
0xC0014003	DTS_E_INVALIDTASKPOINTER	The wrapper's task pointer is not valid. The wrapper has an invalid pointer to a task.

Error Code	Symbolic Name	Description
0xC0014004	DTS_E_ALREADYADDED	The executable has been added to the Executables collection of another container. This occurs when a client tries to add an executable to more than one Executables collection. You need to remove the executable from the current Executables collection before attempting to add it.
0xC0014005	DTS_E_UNKNOWNCONNECTIONMANAGERTYPE	The connection type "__" specified for connection manager "__" is not recognized as a valid connection manager type. This error is returned when an attempt is made to create a connection manager for an unknown connection type. Check the spelling in the connection type name.
0xC0014006	DTS_E_COLLECTIONCOULDNTADD	An object was created but the attempt to add it to a collection failed. This can occur due to an out-of-memory condition.
0xC0014007	DTS_E_ODBCERRORENV	There was an error creating an Open Database Connectivity (ODBC) environment.
0xC0014008	DTS_E_ODBCERRORDBC	There was an error creating an Open Database Connectivity (ODBC) database connection.
0xC0014009	DTS_E_ODBCERRORCONNECT	There was an error trying to establish an Open Database Connectivity (ODBC) connection with the database server.
0xC001400A	DTS_E_CONNECTIONMANAGERQUALIFIERALREADYSET	The qualifier is already set on this instance of the connection manager. The qualifier may be set once per instance.
0xC001400B	DTS_E_CONNECTIONMANAGERQUALIFIERNOTSET	The qualifier has not been set on this instance of the connection manager. Setting the qualifier is required to complete initialization.
0xC001400C	DTS_E_CONNECTIONMANAGERQUALIFIERNOTSUPPORTED	This connection manager does not support specification of qualifiers.
0xC001400D	DTS_E_CANNOTCLONECONNECTIONMANAGER	Connection manager "0x__" cannot be cloned for out-of-process execution.
0xC001400E	DTS_E_NOSQLPROFILERDLL	The log provider for SQL Profiler was unable to load pfclnt90.dll. Please check that the SQL Profiler is installed.
0xC001400F	DTS_E_LOGFAILED	The SSIS logging infrastructure failed with error code 0x__. This error indicates that this logging error is not attributable to a specific log provider.
0xC0014010	DTS_E_LOGPROVIDERFAILED	The SSIS logging provider "__" failed with error code 0x__ (__). This indicates a logging error attributable to the specified log provider.
0xC0014011	DTS_E_SAVETOSQLSERVER_OLEDB	The SaveToSQLServer method has encountered OLE DB error code 0x__ (__). The SQL statement that was issued has failed.

Error Code	Symbolic Name	Description
0xC0014012	DTS_E_LOADFROMSQLSERVER_OLEDB	The LoadFromSQLServer method has encountered OLE DB error code 0x__ (__). The SQL statement that was issued has failed.
0xC0014013	DTS_E_REMOVEFROMSQLSERVER_OLEDB	The RemoveFromSQLServer method encountered OLE DB error code 0x__ (__). The SQL statement that was issued has failed.
0xC0014014	DTS_E_EXISTSONSQLSERVER_OLEDB	The ExistsOnSQLServer method has encountered OLE DB error code 0x__ (__). The SQL statement issued has failed.
0xC0014015	DTS_E_CONNECTIONSTRING	OLE DB has failed making a database connection when using the supplied connection string.
0xC0014016	DTS_E_FROMEXECISNOTCHILD	When adding a precedence constraint, a From executable was specified that is not a child of this container.
0xC0014017	DTS_E_TOEXECISNOTCHILD	When adding a precedence constraint, the To executable specified is not a child of this container.
0xC0014018	DTS_E_ODBCTRANSACTIONENLIST	There was an error trying to enlist an ODBC connection in a transaction. The SQLSetConnectAttr failed to set the SQL_ATTR_ENLIST_IN_DTC attribute.
0xC0014019	DTS_E_CONNECTIONOFFLINE	The connection manager "__" will not acquire a connection because the package OfflineMode property is TRUE. When the OfflineMode is TRUE, connections cannot be acquired.
0xC001401A	DTS_E_BEGINTRANSACTION	The SSIS Runtime has failed to start the distributed transaction due to error 0x__ "__". The DTC transaction failed to start. This could occur because the MSDTC Service is not running.
0xC001401B	DTS_E_SETQUALIFIERDESIGNTIMEONLY	The SetQualifier method cannot be called on a connection manager during package execution. This method is used at design-time only.
0xC001401C	DTS_E_SQLPERSISTENCEVERSION	Storing packages in SQL Server requires database server version 9.0 or higher. Storing packages in SQL Server is not supported on earlier versions of servers.
0xC001401D	DTS_E_CONNECTIONVALIDATIONFAILED	Connection "__" failed validation.
0xC001401E	DTS_E_INVALIDFILENAMEINCONNECTION	The file name "__" specified in the connection was not valid.
0xC001401F	DTS_E_MULTIPLEFILESONRETAINEDCONNECTION	Multiple file names cannot be specified on a connection when the Retain property is TRUE. Vertical bars were found on the connection string, meaning multiple file names are being specified and, in addition, the Retain property is TRUE.
0xC0014020	DTS_E_ODBCERROR	An ODBC error __ has occurred.
0xC0014021	DTS_E_PRECEDENCECONSTRAINT	There was an error in the precedence constraint between "__" and "__".

Error Code	Symbolic Name	Description
0xC0014022	DTS_E_FAILEDPOPNATIVEFEE	Failed to populate the ForEachEnumeratorInfos collection with native ForEachEnumerators with the following error code: ___.
0xC0014023	DTS_E_GETENUMERATOR	The GetEnumerator method of the ForEach Enumerator has failed with error 0x___ " ___ ". This occurs when the ForEach Enumerator cannot enumerate.
0xC0014024	DTS_E_CANTGETCERTDATA	The raw certificate data cannot be obtained from the supplied certificate object (error: ___). This occurs when CPackage::put_CertificateObject cannot instantiate the ManagedHelper object, when the ManagedHelper object fails, or when the ManagedHelper object returns a malformed array.
0xC0014025	DTS_E_CANTCREATECERTCONTEXT	Failed to create certificate context (error: ___). This occurs in CPackage::put_CertificateObject or CPackage::LoadFromXML when the corresponding CryptoAPI function fails.
0xC0014026	DTS_E_CANTOPENCERTSTORE	Opening MY certificate store failed with error " ___ ".This occurs in CPackage::LoadUserCertificateByName and CPackage::LoadUserCertificateByHash.
0xC0014027	DTS_E_CANTFINDCERTBYNAME	The certificate specified by name in MY store cannot be found (error: ___). This occurs in CPackage::LoadUserCertificateByName.
0xC0014028	DTS_E_CANTFINDCERTBYHASH	Unable to find the specified certificate by hash in "MY" store (error: ___). Occurs in CPackage::LoadUserCertificateByHash.
0xC0014029	DTS_E_INVALIDCERTHASHFORMAT	The hash value is not a one-dimensional array of bytes (error: ___). This occurs in CPackage::LoadUserCertificateByHash.
0xC001402A	DTS_E_CANTACCESSARRAYDATA	The data in the array cannot be accessed (error: ___). This error can occur whenever GetDataFromSafeArray is called.
0xC001402B	DTS_E_CREATEMANAGEDHELPERFAILED	The SSIS managed helper object failed during creation with error 0x___ " ___ ". This occurs whenever CoCreateInstance CLSID_DTSManagedHelper fails.
0xC001402C	DTS_E_OLEDBTRANSACTIONENLIST	The SSIS Runtime has failed to enlist the OLE DB connection in a distributed transaction with error 0x___ " ___ ".
0xC001402D	DTS_E_SIGNPACKAGEFAILED	Package signing failed with error 0x___ " ___ ". This occurs when the ManagedHelper.SignDocument method fails.
0xC001402E	DTS_E_CHECKENVELOPEFAILED	Failed to check for XML signature envelope in package XML with error 0x___ " ___ ".This occurs in CPackage::LoadFromXML.
0xC001402F	DTS_E_GETXMLSOURCEFAILED	Failed to obtain XML source from XML DOM object with error 0x___ " ___ ". This occurs when IXMLDOMDocument::get_xml fails.

Error Code	Symbolic Name	Description
0xC0014030	DTS_E_PACKAGEVERIFICATIONFAILED	The cryptographic signature of the package failed verification due to error 0x___ "___". This occurs when the signature verification operation fails.
0xC0014031	DTS_E_GETKEYFROMCERTFAILED	Failed to obtain cryptographic key pair associated with the specified certificate with error 0x___ "___". Verify that you have the key pair for which the certificate was issued. This error usually occurs when trying to sign a document using a certificate for which the person does not have the private key.
0xC0014032	DTS_E_INVALIDSIGNATURE	The digital signature is not valid. The contents of the package have been modified.
0xC0014033	DTS_E_UNTRUSTEDSIGNATURE	The digital signature is valid; however the signer is not trusted and, therefore, authenticity cannot be guaranteed.
0xC0014034	DTS_E_TRANSACTIONENLISTNOTSUPPORTED	The connection does not support enlisting in distributed transaction.
0xC0014035	DTS_E_PACKAGEPROTECT	Failed to apply package protection with error 0x___ "___". This error occurs when saving to Xml.
0xC0014036	DTS_E_PACKAGEUNPROTECT	Failed to remove package protection with error 0x___ "___". This occurs in the CPackage::LoadFromXML method.
0xC0014037	DTS_E_PACKAGEPASSWORD	The package is encrypted with a password. The password was not specified, or is not correct.
0xC0014038	DTS_E_DUPLICATECONSTRAINT	A precedence constraint already exists between the specified executables. More than one precedence constraint is not allowed.
0xC0014039	DTS_E_PACKAGELOADFAILED	The package failed to load due to error 0x___ "___". This occurs when CPackage::LoadFromXML fails.
0xC001403A	DTS_E_PACKAGEOBJECTNOTENVELOPED	Failed to find package object in signed XML envelope with error 0x___ "___". This occurs when signed XML does not contain a SSIS package, as expected.
0xC001403B	DTS_E_JAGGEDEVENTINFO	The lengths of parameter names, types, and description arrays are not equal. The lengths must be equal. This occurs when the lengths of the arrays are mismatched. There should be one entry per parameter in each array.
0xC001403C	DTS_E_GETPACKAGEINFOS	An OLE DB error 0x___ (___) occurred while enumerating packages. A SQL statement was issued and failed.
0xC001403D	DTS_E_UNKNOWNLOGPROVIDERTYPE	The log provider type "___" specified for log provider "___" is not recognized as a valid log provider type. This error occurs when an attempt is made to create a log provider for unknown log provider type. Verify the spelling in the log provider type name.

Error Code	Symbolic Name	Description
0xC001403E	DTS_E_UNKNOWNLOGPROVIDERTYPENOSUBS	The log provider type is not recognized as a valid log provider type. This error occurs when an attempt is made to create a log provider for unknown log provider type. Verify the spelling in the log provider type name.
0xC001403F	DTS_E_UNKNOWNCONNECTIONMANAGERTYPENOSUBS	The connection type specified for connection manager is not a valid connection manager type. This error occurs when an attempt is made to create a connection manager for unknown connection type. Verify the spelling of the connection type name.
0xC0014040	DTS_E_PACKAGEREMOVEFAILED	An error was encountered when trying to remove the package "__" from SQL Server.
0xC0014042	DTS_E_FOLDERADDFAILED	An error was encountered when trying to create a folder on SQL Server named "__" in folder "__".
0xC0014043	DTS_E_CREATEFOLDERONSQLSERVER_OLEDB	The CreateFolderOnSQLServer method has encountered OLE DB error code 0x__ (__). The SQL statement issued has failed.
0xC0014044	DTS_E_FOLDERRENAMEFAILED	An error occurred when renaming folder "%1__" to "%1__" on SQL Server.
0xC0014045	DTS_E_RENAMEFOLDERONSQLSERVER_OLEDB	The RenameFolderOnSQLServer method encountered OLE DB error code 0x__ (__). The SQL statement issued has failed.
0xC0014046	DTS_E_FOLDERDELETEFAILED	Error deleting SQL Server folder "__".
0xC0014047	DTS_E_REMOVEFOLDERFROMSQLSERVER_OLEDB	The RemoveFolderOnSQLServer method encountered OLE DB error code 0x__ (__). The SQL statement issued has failed.
0xC0014048	DTS_E_INVALIDPATHTOPACKAGE	The specified package path does not contain a package name. This occurs when the path does not contain at least one backslash or one forward slash.
0xC0014049	DTS_E_FOLDERNOTFOUND	Cannot find folder "__".
0xC001404A	DTS_E_FINDFOLDERONSQLSERVER_OLEDB	While trying to find a folder on SQL an OLE DB error was encountered with error code 0x__ (__).
0xC001404B	DTS_E_OPENLOGFAILED	The SSIS logging provider has failed to open the log. Error code: 0x__.
0xC001404C	DTS_E_GETCONNECTIONINFOS	Failed to get ConnectionInfos collection with error 0x__ "__". This error occurs when the call to IDTSApplication90::get_ConnectionInfos fails.
0xC001404D	DTS_E_VARIABLEDEADLOCK	Deadlock detected while trying to lock variables. The locks cannot be acquired after 16 attempts. The locks timed out.
0xC001404E	DTS_E_NOTDISPENSED	The Variables collection has not been returned from the VariableDispenser. An operation was attempted that is only allowed on dispensed collections.

Error Code	Symbolic Name	Description
0xC001404F	DTS_E_VARIABLESALREADYUNLOCKED	This Variables collection has already been unlocked. The Unlock method is called only once on a dispensed Variables collection.
0xC0014050	DTS_E_VARIABLEUNLOCKFAILED	One or more variables failed to unlock.
0xC0014051	DTS_E_DISPENSEDREADONLY	The Variables collection was returned from the VariableDispenser and cannot be modified. Items cannot be added to or removed from dispensed collections.
0xC0014052	DTS_E_VARIABLEALREADYONREADLIST	The variable "__" is already on the read list. A variable may only be added once to either the read lock list or the write lock list.
0xC0014053	DTS_E_VARIABLEALREADYONWRITELIST	The variable "__" is already on the write list. A variable may only be added once to either the read lock list or the write lock list.
0xC0014054	DTS_E_LOCKVARIABLEFORREAD	Failed to lock variable "__" for read access with error 0x__"__".
0xC0014055	DTS_E_LOCKVARIABLEFORWRITE	Failed to lock variable "__" for read/write access with error 0x__"__".
0xC0014056	DTS_E_CUSTOMEVENTCONFLICT	The custom event "__" is already declared with a different parameter list. A task is trying to declare a custom event, which another task has already declared with a different parameter list.
0xC0014057	DTS_E_EVENTHANDLERNOTALLOWED	The task providing the custom event "__" does not allow this event to be handled in the package. The custom event was declared with AllowEventHandlers = FALSE.
0xC0014059	DTS_E_UNSAFEVARIABLESALREADYSET	The VariableDispenser received an unsafe Variables collection. This operation cannot be repeated.
0xC001405A	DTS_E_INVALIDPARENTPACKAGEPATH	GetPackagePath was called on the ForEachEnumerator but there was no ForEachLoop package path specified.
0xC001405B	DTS_E_VARIABLEDEADLOCK_READ	A deadlock was detected while trying to lock variable "__" for read access. A lock could not be acquired after 16 attempts and timed out.
0xC001405C	DTS_E_VARIABLEDEADLOCK_READWRITE	A deadlock was detected while trying to lock variables "__" for read/write access. A lock cannot be acquired after 16 attempts. The locks timed out.
0xC001405D	DTS_E_VARIABLEDEADLOCK_BOTH	A deadlock was detected while trying to lock variables "__" for read access and variables "__" for read/write access. A lock cannot be acquired after 16 attempts. The locks timed out.
0xC001405E	DTS_E_PACKAGEPASSWORDEMPTY	The protection level of the package requires a password, but PackagePassword property is empty.

Error Code	Symbolic Name	Description
0xC001405F	DTS_E_DECRYPTXML_PASSWORD	Failed to decrypt an encrypted XML node because the password was not specified or not correct. Package load will attempt to continue without the encrypted information.
0xC0014060	DTS_E_DECRYPTPACKAGE_USERKEY	Failed to decrypt a package that is encrypted with a user key. You may not be the user who encrypted this package, or you are not using the same machine that was used to save the package.
0xC0014061	DTS_E_SERVERSTORAGEDISALLOWED	The protection level, ServerStorage, cannot be used when saving to this destination. The system could not verify that the destination supports secure storage capability.
0xC0014062	DTS_E_LOADFROMSQLSERVER	LoadFromSQLServer method has failed.
0xC0014100	DTS_E_NAMEALREADYADDED	The object cannot be added because another object with the same name already exists in the collection. Use a different name to resolve this error.
0xC0014101	DTS_E_NAMEALREADYEXISTS	The object name cannot be changed from "___" to "___" because another object in the collection already uses that name. Use a different name to resolve this error.
0xC0014103	DTS_E_FAILEDDEPENDENCIES	There was an error enumerating the package dependencies. Check other messages for more information.
0xC0015001	DTS_E_BPDUPLICATE	The specified breakpoint ID already exists. This error occurs when a task calls CreateBreakpoint with the same ID multiple times. It is possible to create a breakpoint with the same ID multiple times if the task calls RemoveBreakpoint on the first creation before creating the second one.
0xC0015002	DTS_E_BPUNKNOWNID	The specified breakpoint ID does not exist. This error occurs when a task references a breakpoint that does not exist.
0xC0015004	DTS_E_CANTWRITETOFILE	The file, "___", could not be opened for writing. The file could be read-only, or you do not have the correct permissions.
0xC0015005	DTS_E_NOROWSETRETURNED	No result rowset is associated with the execution of this query. The result is not correctly specified.
0xC0016001	DTS_E_INVALIDURL	The URL specified is not valid. This can happen when the server or proxy URL is null, or in an incorrect format. A valid URL format is in the form of http://ServerName:Port/ResourcePath or https://ServerName:Port/ResourcePath.

Error Code	Symbolic Name	Description
0xC0016002	DTS_E_INVALIDSCHEME	The URL __ is not valid. This can happen when a scheme other than http or https is specified, or the URL is in an incorrect format. A valid URL format is in the form of http://ServerName:Port/ResourcePath or https://ServerName:Port/ResourcePath.
0xC0016003	DTS_E_WINHTTPCANNOTCONNECT	Connection to server __ cannot be established. This error can occur when the server does not exist, or the proxy settings are incorrect.
0xC0016004	DTS_E_CONNECTIONTERMINATED	The connection with the server has been reset or terminated. Try again later.
0xC0016005	DTS_E_LOGINFAILURE	The login attempt failed for "__". This error occurs when the login credentials provided are incorrect. Verify the login credentials.
0xC0016006	DTS_E_INVALIDSERVERNAME	The server name specified in the URL__ cannot be resolved.
0xC0016007	DTS_E_PROXYAUTH	Proxy authentication failed. This error occurs when login credentials are not provided, or the credentials are incorrect.
0xC0016008	DTS_E_SECUREFAILURE	SSL certificate response obtained from the server was not valid. Cannot process the request.
0xC0016009	DTS_E_TIMEOUT	The request has timed out. This error can occur when the timeout specified was too short, or a connection to the server or proxy cannot be established. Ensure that the server and proxy URL are correct.
0xC001600A	DTS_E_CLIENTAUTH	Client certificate is missing. This error occurs when the server is expecting an SSL client certificate and the user has provided an invalid certificate, or has not provided a certificate. A client certificate must be configured for this connection.
0xC001600B	DTS_E_REDIRECTFAILURE	The specified server, URL__, has a redirect and the redirect request failed.
0xC001600C	DTS_E_SERVERAUTH	Server authentication failed. This error occurs when login credentials are not provided, or the credentials are incorrect.
0xC001600D	DTS_E_WINHTTPUNKNOWNERROR	Request cannot be processed. Try again later.
0xC001600E	DTS_E_UNKNOWNSTATUSCODE	Server returned status code - __ : __. This error occurs when the server is experiencing problems.
0xC001600F	DTS_E_WINHTTPNOTSUPPORTED	This platform is not supported by WinHttp services.
0xC0016010	DTS_E_INVALIDTIMEOUT	Timeout value is not valid. Timeout should be in the range of __ to __ (in seconds).

Error Code	Symbolic Name	Description
0xC0016011	DTS_E_INVALIDCHUNKSIZE	The chunk size is not valid. The ChunkSize property should be in the range of __ to __ (in KB).
0xC0016012	DTS_E_CERTERROR	Error processing client certificate. This error can occur when the client certificate provided was not found in the Personal Certificate Store. Verify that the client certificate is valid.
0xC0016013	DTS_E_FORBIDDEN	Server returned error code "403 - Forbidden". This error can occur when the specified resource needs "https" access, but the certificate validity period has expired, the certificate is not valid for the use requested, or the certificate has been revoked or revocation cannot be checked.
0xC0016014	DTS_E_WINHTTPOPEN	Error initializing HTTP session with proxy " __ ". This error can occur when an invalid proxy was specified. HTTP connection manager only supports CERN-type proxies.
0xC0016015	DTS_E_OPENCERTSTORE	Error opening certificate store.
0xC0016016	DTS_E_UNPROTECTXMLFAILED	Failed to decrypt protected XML node " __ " with error 0x__ " __ ". You may not be authorized to access this information. This error occurs when there is a cryptographic error. Verify that the correct key is available.
0xC0016017	DTS_E_UNPROTECTCONNECTIONSTRINGFAILED	Failed to decrypt protected connection string for server " __ " with error 0x__ " __ ". You may not be authorized to access this information. This error occurs when there is a cryptographic error. Verify that the correct key is available.
0xC0016018	DTS_E_NEGATIVEVERSION	The version number cannot be negative. This error occurs when the VersionMajor, VersionMinor, or VersionBuild property of the package is set to a negative value.
0xC0016019	DTS_E_PACKAGEMIGRATED	The package has been migrated to a later version during loading. It must be reloaded to complete the process. This is an internal error code.
0xC0016020	DTS_E_PACKAGEMIGRATIONFAILED	Package migration from version __ to version __ failed with error 0x__ " __ ".
0xC0016021	DTS_E_PACKAGEMIGRATIONMODULELOAD	Package migration module has failed to load.
0xC0016022	DTS_E_PACKAGEMIGRATIONMODULE	Package migration module has failed.
0xC0016023	DTS_E_CANTDETERMINEWHICHPROPTOPERSIST	Unable to persist object using default persistence. This error occurs when the default persistence is unable to determine which objects are on the hosted object.

Error Code	Symbolic Name	Description
0xC0016024	DTS_E_CANTADDREMOVEWHENEXECUTING	Cannot add or remove an element from a package in runtime mode. This error occurs when an attempt is made to add or remove an object from a collection while the package is executing.
0xC0016025	DTS_E_NODENOTFOUND	Node cannot be found in custom default persistence. This error occurs if the default saved XML of an extensible object was changed in a way that a saved object is no longer found, or if the extensible object itself changed.
0xC0016026	DTS_E_COLLECTIONLOCKED	This collection cannot be modified during package validation or execution.
0xC0016027	DTS_E_COLLOCKED	The "__" collection cannot be modified during package validation or execution. "__" cannot be added to the collection.
0xC0016029	DTS_E_FTPNOTCONNECTED	Connection with the FTP server has not been established.
0xC001602A	DTS_E_FTPERROR	An error occurred in the requested FTP operation. Detailed error description: __.
0xC001602B	DTS_E_FTPINVALIDRETRIES	The number of retries is not valid. The number of retries should be between __ and __.
0xC001602C	DTS_E_LOADWININET	The FTP connection manager needs the following DLL to function: __.
0xC001602D	DTS_E_FTPINVALIDCONNECTIONSTRING	The port specified in the connection string is not valid. The ConnectionString format is ServerName:Port. Port should be an integer value between __ and __.
0xC001602E	DTS_E_FTPCREATEFOLDER	Creating folder "__" ... __.
0xC001602F	DTS_E_FTPDELETEFOLDER	Deleting folder "__" ... __.
0xC0016030	DTS_E_FTPCHANGEFOLDER	Changing current directory to "__".
0xC0016031	DTS_E_FTPFILESEMPTY	No files to transfer. This error can occur when performing a Send or Receive operation and no files are specified for the transfer.
0xC0016032	DTS_E_FTPINVALIDLOCALPATH	Specified local path is not valid. Specify a valid local path. This can occur when the specified local path is null.
0xC0016033	DTS_E_FTPNOFILESTODELETE	No files specified to delete.
0xC0016034	DTS_E_WINHTTPCERTDECODE	Internal error occurred while loading the certificate. This error could occur when the certificate data is invalid.
0xC0016035	DTS_E_WINHTTPCERTENCODE	Internal error occurred while saving the certificate data.
0xC0016049	DTS_E_CHECKPOINTMISMATCH	Checkpoint file "__" does not match this package. The ID of the package and the ID in the checkpoint file do not match.

Error Code	Symbolic Name	Description
0xC001604A	DTS_E_CHECKPOINTFILEALREADYEXISTS	An existing checkpoint file is found with contents that do not appear to be for this package, so the file cannot be overwritten to start saving new checkpoints. Remove the existing checkpoint file and try again. This error occurs when a checkpoint file exists, the package is set to not use a checkpoint file, but to save checkpoints. The existing checkpoint file will not be overwritten.
0xC001604B	DTS_E_CHECKPOINTFILELOCKED	The checkpoint file "__" is locked by another process. This may occur if another instance of this package is currently executing.
0xC001604C	DTS_E_OPENCHECKPOINTFILE	Checkpoint file "__" failed to open due to error 0x__"__".
0xC001604D	DTS_E_CREATECHECKPOINTFILE	Checkpoint file "__" failed during creation due to error 0x__"__".
0xC0016050	DTS_E_FTPINVALIDPORT	The FTP Port contains an invalid value. The FTP Port value should be an integer between __ and __.
0xC00160AA	DTS_E_CONNECTTOSERVERFAILED	Connect to SSIS Service on machine "__" failed: __.
0xC0017002	DTS_E_PROPERTYEXPRESSIONSDISABLEDONVARIABLES	The Expression property is not supported on Variable objects. Use the EvaluateAsExpression property instead.
0xC0017003	DTS_E_PROPERTYEXPRESSIONEVAL	The expression "__" on property "__" cannot be evaluated. Modify the expression to be valid.
0xC0017004	DTS_E_PROPERTYEXPRESSIONSET	The result of the expression "__" on property "__" cannot be written to the property. The expression was evaluated, but cannot be set on the property.
0xC0017005	DTS_E_FORLOOPEVALEXPRESSIONINVALID	The evaluation expression for the loop is not valid. The expression needs to be modified. There should be additional error messages.
0xC0017006	DTS_E_EXPRESSIONNOTBOOLEAN	The expression "__" must evaluate to True or False. Change the expression to evaluate to a Boolean value.
0xC0017007	DTS_E_FORLOOPHASNOEXPRESSION	There is no expression for the loop to evaluate. This error occurs when the expression on the For Loop is empty. Add an expression.
0xC0017008	DTS_E_FORLOOPPASSIGNEXPRESSIONINVALID	The assignment expression for the loop is not valid and needs to be modified. There should be additional error messages.
0xC0017009	DTS_E_FORLOOPINITEXPRESSIONINVALID	The initialization expression for the loop is not valid and needs to be modified. There should be additional error messages.
0xC001700A	DTS_E_INVALIDVERSIONNUMBER	The version number in the package is not valid. The version number cannot be greater than current version number.
0xC001700C	DTS_E_INVALIDVERNUMCANTBENEGATIVE	The version number in the package is not valid. The version number is negative.

Error Code	Symbolic Name	Description
0xC001700D	DTS_E_PACKAGEUPDATEDISABLED	The package has an older format version, but automatic package format upgrading is disabled.
0xC001700E	DTS_E_EXPREVALTRUNCATIONASERROR	A truncation occurred during evaluation of the expression.
0xC0019001	DTS_E_FAILEDSETEXECVALVARIABLE	The wrapper was unable to set the value of the variable specified in the ExecutionValueVariable property.
0xC0019004	DTS_E_VARIABLEEXPRESSIONERROR	The expression for variable "__" failed evaluation. There was an error in the expression.
0xC001A003	DTS_E_TXNSPECINVALID	Transaction cannot be specified when a retained connection is used. This error occurs when Retain is set to TRUE on the connection manager, but AcquireConnection was called with a non-null transaction parameter.
0xC001A004	DTS_E_INCOMPATIBLETRANSACTIONCONTEXT	Incompatible transaction context was specified for a retained connection. This connection has been established under a different transaction context. Retained connections can be used under exactly one transaction context.
0xC001B001	DTS_E_NOTSUSPENDED	Resume call failed because the package is not suspended. This occurs when the client calls resume, but the package is not suspended.
0xC001B002	DTS_E_ALREADYEXECUTING	Execute call failed because the executable is already executing. This error occurs when the client calls Execute on a container that is still executing from the last Execute call.
0xC001B003	DTS_E_NOTEXECUTING	Suspend or Resume call failed because the executable is not executing, or is not the top-level executable. This occurs when the client calls Suspend or Resume on an executable that is not currently processing an Execute call.
0xC001C002	DTS_E_INVALIDFILE	The file specified in the For Each File enumerator is not valid. Check that the file specified in the For Each File enumerator exists.
0xC001C010	DTS_E_VALUEINDEXNOTINTEGER	The value index is not an integer. Mapping a For Each Variable number __ to the variable "__".
0xC001C011	DTS_E_VALUEINDEXNEGATIVE	The value index is negative. The ForEach Variable Mapping number __ to variable "__".
0xC001C012	DTS_E_FOREACHVARIABLEMAPPING	ForEach Variable Mapping number __ to variable "__" cannot be applied.
0xC001C013	DTS_E_OBJECTNOTINFOREACHLOOP	Failure when adding an object to a ForEachPropertyMapping that is not a direct child of the ForEachLoop container.

Error Code	Symbolic Name	Description
0xC001F001	DTS_E_FAILEDSYSTEMVARIABLEREMOVE	Failed to remove a system variable. This error occurs when removing a variable that is a required variable. Required variables are variables that are created by the runtime for communicating between tasks and the runtime.
0xC001F002	DTS_E_CHANGESYSTEMVARIABLEREADONLYFAILED	Changing the property of a variable failed because it is a system variable. System variables are read-only.
0xC001F003	DTS_E_CHANGESYSTEMVARIABLENAMEFAILED	Changing the name of a variable failed because it is a system variable. System variables are read-only.
0xC001F004	DTS_E_CHANGESYSTEMVARIABLENAMESPACEFAILED	Changing the namespace of a variable failed because it is a system variable. System variables are read-only.
0xC001F006	DTS_E_EVENTHANDLERNAMEREADONLY	Changing the event handler name failed. Event handler names are read-only.
0xC001F008	DTS_E_PATHUNKNOWN	Cannot retrieve path to object. This is a system error.
0xC001F009	DTS_E_RUNTIMEVARIABLETYPECHANGE	The type of the value being assigned to variable "__" differs from the current variable type. Variables may not change type during execution. Variable types are strict, except for variables of type Object.
0xC001F010	DTS_E_INVALIDSTRING	Invalid characters in string: "__". This occurs when a string supplied for a property value contains unprintable characters.
0xC001F011	DTS_E_INVALIDOBJECTNAME	SSIS object name is invalid. More specific errors would have been raised explaining the exact naming problem.
0xC001F021	DTS_E_PROPERTYREADONLY	The property "__" is read only. This occurs when a change to a read-only property is attempted.
0xC001F022	DTS_E_FAILEDGETTYPEINFO	The object does not support type information. This occurs when the runtime attempts to get the type information from an object to populate the Properties collection. The object must support type information.
0xC001F023	DTS_E_FAILEDPROPERTYGET	An error occurred while retrieving the value of property "__". The error code is 0x__.
0xC001F024	DTS_E_FAILEDPROPERTYGET_ERRORINFO	An error occurred while retrieving the value of property "__". The error code is 0x__.
0xC001F025	DTS_E_FAILEDPROPERTYSET	An error occurred while setting the value of property "__". The error returned is 0x__.
0xC001F026	DTS_E_FAILEDPROPERTYSET_ERRORINFO	An error occurred while setting the value of property "__". The error returned is 0x__.

Error Code	Symbolic Name	Description
0xC001F027	DTS_E_PROPERTYWRITEONLY	The property " __ " is write-only. This error occurs when trying to retrieve the value of a property through a property object, but the property is write-only.
0xC001F028	DTS_E_NODISPATCH	The object does not implement IDispatch. This error occurs when a property object or properties collection attempts to access an IDispatch interface on an object.
0xC001F029	DTS_E_NOCONTAININGTYPELIB	Unable to retrieve the type library of the object. This error occurs when the Properties collection attempts to retrieve the type library for an object through its IDispatch interface.
0xC001F02A	DTS_E_INVALIDTASKMONIKER	Cannot create a task with the name " __ ". Verify that the name is correct.
0xC001F02C	DTS_E_FAILEDCREATEXMLDOCUMENT	Failed to create an XML document " __ ".
0xC001F02D	DTS_E_PMVARPROPTYPESDIFFERENT	An error occurred because there is a property mapping from a variable to a property with a different type. The property type must match the variable type.
0xC001F02E	DTS_E_PMINVALIDPROPMAPTARGET	Attempted to set property mapping to target unsupported object type. This error occurs when passing an unsupported object type to a property mapping.
0xC001F02F	DTS_E_COULDNOTRESOLVEPACKAGEPATH	Cannot resolve a package path to an object in the package " __ ". Verify that the package path is valid.
0xC001F030	DTS_E_PMNODESTPROPERTY	The destination property for the property map is empty. Set the destination property name.
0xC001F031	DTS_E_INVALIDPROPERTYMAPPINGSFOUND	The package failed to restore at least one property mapping.
0xC001F032	DTS_E_AMBIGUOUSVARIABLENAME	The variable name is ambiguous because multiple variables with this name exist in different namespaces. Specify namespace-qualified name to prevent ambiguity.
0xC001F033	DTS_E_DESTINATIONOBJECTPARENTLESS	The destination object in a property mapping has no parent. The destination object is not a child of any sequence container. It may have been removed from the package.
0xC001F036	DTS_E_INVALIDPROPERTYMAPPING	The property mapping is not valid. The mapping is ignored.
0xC001F038	DTS_E_PMFAILALERTREMOVE	Failure when alerting property mappings that a target is being removed.
0xC001F03A	DTS_E_INVALIDFOREACHPROPERTYMAPPING	An invalid property mapping is found on the For Each Loop. This occurs when the ForEach property mapping fails to restore.
0xC001F040	DTS_E_PMPROPERTYINVALID	A destination property was specified on a property mapping that is invalid. This occurs when a property is specified on a destination object that in not found on that object.

Error Code	Symbolic Name	Description
0xC001F041	DTS_E_INVALIDTASKMONIKERNOPARAM	Cannot create a task from XML. This occurs when the runtime is unable to resolve the name to create a task. Verify that the name is correct.
0xC001F080	DTS_E_COULDNOTREPLACECHECKPOINTFILE	Cannot replace the existing checkpoint file with the updated checkpoint file. The checkpoint was successfully created in a temporary file, but overwriting the existing file with the new file failed.
0xC001F081	DTS_E_CHECKPOINTFILENOTSPECIFIED	The package is configured to always restart from a checkpoint, but checkpoint file is not specified.
0xC001F082	DTS_E_CHECKPOINTLOADXML	The attempt to load the XML checkpoint file "___" failed with error 0x___ "___". Check that the file name specified is correct, and that the file exists.
0xC001F083	DTS_E_LOADCHECKPOINT	The package failed during execution because the checkpoint file cannot be loaded. Further execution of the package requires a checkpoint file. This error usually occurs when the CheckpointUsage property is set to ALWAYS, which specifies that the package always restarts.
0xC001F185	DTS_E_NOEVALEXPRESSION	The evaluation condition expression on the For Loop "___" is empty. There must be a Boolean evaluation expression in the For Loop.
0xC001F186	DTS_E_EXPREVALASSIGNMENTTYPEMISMATCH	The result of the assignment expression "___" cannot be converted to a type that is compatible with the variable that it was assigned to.
0xC001F187	DTS_E_EXPREVALASSIGNMENTTOREADONLYVARIABLE	Error using a read-only variable "___" in an assignment expression. The expression result cannot be assigned to the variable because the variable is read only. Choose a variable that can be written to, or remove the expression from this variable.
0xC001F188	DTS_E_EXPREVALASSIGNMENTVARIABLELOCKFORWRITEFAILED	Cannot evaluate expression "___" because the variable "___" does not exist or cannot be accessed for writing. The expression result cannot be assigned to the variable because the variable was not found, or could not be locked for write access.
0xC001F189	DTS_E_EXPREVALRESULTTYPENOTSUPPORTED	The expression "___" has a result type of "___", which cannot be converted to a supported type.
0xC001F18A	DTS_E_EXPREVALRESULTTYPECONVERSIONFAILED	The conversion of the result of the expression "___" from type "___" to a supported type failed with error code 0x___. An unexpected error occurred when trying to convert the expression result to a type supported by the runtime engine, even though the type conversion is supported.

Error Code	Symbolic Name	Description
0xC001F200	DTS_E_DTSNAME_NOTNULL	The object name is not valid. The name cannot be set to NULL.
0xC001F201	DTS_E_DTSNAME_NOTEMPTY	The object name is not valid. The name cannot be empty.
0xC001F202	DTS_E_DTSNAME_LEGAL	The object name "___" is not valid. The name cannot contain any of the following characters: / \ : [ ] . = .
0xC001F203	DTS_E_DTSNAME_PRINTABLE	Object name "___" is not valid. The name cannot contain control characters that render it unprintable.
0xC001F204	DTS_E_DTSNAME_NOLEADWHITESP	Object name "___" is not valid. Name cannot begin with a whitespace.
0xC001F205	DTS_E_DTSNAME_NOTRAILWHITESP	Object name "___" is not valid. Name cannot end with a whitespace.
0xC001F206	DTS_E_DTSNAME_BEGINSWITHALPHA	Object name "___" is not valid. Name must begin with an alphabetical character.
0xC001F207	DTS_E_DTSNAME_BEGINSWITHALPHAUNDERBAR	Object name "___" is not valid. Name must begin with an alphabetical character or underscore "_".
0xC001F208	DTS_E_DTSNAME_ALPHADIGITUNDERBAR	Object name "___" is not valid. Name must contain only alphanumeric characters or underscores "_".
0xC001F209	DTS_E_DTSNAME_VALIDFILENAME	Object name "___" is not valid. The name cannot contain any of the following characters: / \ : ? " < > |.
0xC00220DE	DTS_E_TKEXECPACKAGE_UNABLETOLOADFILE	Error 0x___ while loading package file "___.___".
0xC00220DF	DTS_E_TKEXECPACKAGE_UNSPECIFIEDPACKAGE	The package is not specified.
0xC00220E0	DTS_E_TKEXECPACKAGE_UNSPECIFIEDCONNECTION	The connection is not specified.
0xC00220E2	DTS_E_TKEXECPACKAGE_INCORRECTCONNECTIONMANAGERTYPE	The connection manager "___" has an unsupported type "___". Only "FILE" and "OLEDB" connection managers are supported.
0xC00220E3	DTS_E_TKEXECPACKAGE_UNABLETOLOADXML	Error 0x___ while loading package file "___" into an XML document.___
0xC00220E4	DTS_E_TKEXECPACKAGE_UNABLETOLOAD	Error 0x___ while preparing to load the package. ___.
0xC0024102	DTS_E_TASKVALIDATIONFAILED	The Validate method on the task failed, and returned error code 0x___ (___). The Validate method must succeed and indicate the result using an "out" parameter.
0xC0024104	DTS_E_TASKEXECUTEFAILED	The Execute method on the task returned error code 0x___ (___). The Execute method must succeed, and indicate the result using an "out" parameter.
0xC0024105	DTS_E_RETRIEVINGDEPENDENCIES	A failure occurred on task "___": 0x___ while retrieving dependencies. The runtime was retrieving dependencies from the task's dependencies collection when the error occurred. The task may have incorrectly implemented one of the dependency interfaces.

Error Code	Symbolic Name	Description
0xC0024107	DTS_E_TASKVALIDATIONERROR	There were errors during task validation.
0xC0024108	DTS_E_CONNECTIONSTRINGFORMAT	The connection string format is not valid. It must consist of one or more components of the form X=Y, separated by semicolons. This error occurs when a connection string with zero components is set on database connection manager.
0xC0024109	DTS_E_UNQUOTEDSEMICOLON	The connection string components cannot contain unquoted semicolons. If the value must contain a semicolon, enclose the entire value in quotes. This error occurs when values in the connection string contain unquoted semicolons, such as the InitialCatalog property.
0xC002410A	DTS_E_LOGPROVIDERVALIDATIONFAILED	Validation of one or more log providers failed. The package cannot execute. The package does not execute when a log provider fails validation.
0xC002410B	DTS_E_INVALIDVALUEINARRAY	Invalid value in array.
0xC002410C	DTS_E_ENUMERATIONELEMENTNOTENUMERABLE	An element of the enumerator returned by the ForEach Enumerator does not implement IEnumerator, contradicting the CollectionEnumerator property of the ForEach Enumerator.
0xC0029100	DTS_E_AXTASK_MISSING_ENTRY_METHOD_NAME	Function not found.
0xC0029101	DTS_E_AXTASK_EMPTY_SCRIPT	Function not found.
0xC0029102	DTS_E_AXTASK_INITIALIZATION_WITH_WRONG_XML_ELEMENT	ActiveX Script Task was initiated with a wrong XML element.
0xC0029105	DTS_E_AXTASK_HANDLER_NOT_FOUND	Handler not found.
0xC0029106	DTS_E_AXTASKUTIL_ENUMERATE_LANGUAGES_FAILED	An error occurred while attempting to retrieve the scripting languages installed on the system.
0xC0029107	DTS_E_AXTASKUTIL_SCRIPTHOST_CREATE_FAILED	An error occurred while creating the ActiveX script host. Verify that you have the script host installed properly.
0xC0029108	DTS_E_AXTASKUTIL_SCRIPTHOSTINIT_FAILED	An error occurred while trying to instantiate the script host for the chosen language. Verify that the script language you have chosen is installed on your system.
0xC0029109	DTS_E_AXTASKUTIL_ADDVARIABLES_FAILED	An error occurred while adding the SSIS variables to the script host namespace. This might prevent the task from using SSIS variables in the script.
0xC002910A	DTS_E_AXTASKUTIL_SCRIPT_PARSING_FAILED	A fatal error occurred while trying to parse the script text. Verify that the script engine for the chosen language is installed properly.

Error Code	Symbolic Name	Description
0xC002910B	DTS_E_AXTASKUTIL_MSG_BAD_FUNCTION	The function name entered is not valid. Verify that a valid function name has been specified.
0xC002910C	DTS_E_AXTASKUTIL_EXECUTION_FAILED	An error occurred while executing the script. Verify that the script engine for the selected language is installed properly.
0xC002910D	DTS_E_AXTASKUTIL_ADDTYPELIB_FAILED	An error occurred while adding the managed type library to the script host. Verify that the DTS 2000 runtime is installed.
0xC002910E	DTS_E_BITASK_INITIALIZATION_WITH_WRONG_XML_ELEMENT	Bulk Insert Task was initiated with a wrong XML element.
0xC002910F	DTS_E_BITASK_DATA_FILE_NOT_SPECIFIED	Data file name not specified.
0xC0029110	DTS_E_BITASK_HANDLER_NOT_FOUND	Handler not found.
0xC0029111	DTS_E_BITASK_CANNOT_ACQUIRE_CONNECTION	Failed to acquire the specified connection: "___".
0xC0029112	DTS_E_BITASK_NO_CONNECTION_MANAGER_SPECIFIED	Attempt to obtain the Connection Manager failed.
0xC0029113	DTS_E_BITASK_INVALID_CONNECTION	The connection is not valid.
0xC0029114	DTS_E_BITASK_NULL_CONNECTION	The connection is null.
0xC0029115	DTS_E_BITASK_EXECUTE_FAILED	Execution failed.
0xC0029116	DTS_E_BITASK_CANNOT_RETRIEVE_TABLES	An error occurred while retrieving the tables from the database.
0xC0029117	DTS_E_BITASK_CANNOT_RETRIEVE_COLUMN_INFO	An error occurred while retrieving the columns of the table.
0xC0029118	DTS_E_BITASK_ERROR_IN_DB_OPERATION	An error occurred in the database operation.
0xC0029119	DTS_E_BITASK_INVALIDSOURCECONNECTIONNAME	The specified connection "___" is either not valid, or points to an invalid object. To continue, specify a valid connection.
0xC002911A	DTS_E_BITASK_INVALIDDESTCONNECTIONNAME	The destination connection specified is not valid. Supply a valid connection to continue.
0xC002911B	DTS_E_BITASK_DESTINATION_TABLE_NOT_SPECIFIED	You must specify a table name to continue.
0xC002911C	DTS_E_BITASK_ERROR_IN_LOAD_FROM_XML	Error occurred in LoadFromXML at the tag "___".
0xC002911D	DTS_E_BITASK_ERROR_IN_SAVE_TO_XML	Error occurred in SaveToXML at the tag "___".
0xC002911E	DTS_E_BITASKUNMANCONNECTION_INVALID_CONNECTION	The connection is not valid.
0xC002911F	DTS_E_BITASKUNMANCONNECTION_EXECUTE_FAILED	Execution failed.

Error Code	Symbolic Name	Description
0xC0029120	DTS_E_BITASKUNMANCONNECTION_CANNOT_RETRIEVE_TABLES	Error occurred while retrieving the tables from the database.
0xC0029121	DTS_E_BITASKUNMANCONNECTION_CANNOT_RETRIEVE_COLUMN_INFO	Error occurred while retrieving the columns of the table.
0xC0029122	DTS_E_BITASKUNMANCONNECTION_CANNOT_OPEN_FILE	Error occurred while trying to open the data file.
0xC0029123	DTS_E_BITASKUNMANCONNECTION_OEM_CONVERSION_FAILED	Cannot convert the input OEM file to the specified format.
0xC0029124	DTS_E_BITASKUNMANCONNECTION_ERROR_IN_DB_OPERATION	Error in database operation.
0xC0029125	DTS_E_DTSPROCTASK_NOCONNECTIONSPECIFIED	No connection manager specified.
0xC0029126	DTS_E_DTSPROCTASK_CONNECTIONMANAGERNOTOLAP	Connection " __ " is not an Analysis Services connection.
0xC0029127	DTS_E_DTSPROCTASK_UNABLETOLOCATECONNECTIONMANAGER	Unable to locate connection " __ ".
0xC0029128	DTS_E_DTSPROCTASK_INVALIDTASKDATANODEEXE	Analysis Services Execute DDL task received an invalid task data node.
0xC0029129	DTS_E_DTSPROCTASK_INVALIDTASKDATANODEPROC	Analysis Services Processing task received an invalid task data node.
0xC002912A	DTS_E_DTSPROCTASK_INVALIDDDL	The DDL is not valid.
0xC002912B	DTS_E_DTSPROCTASK_INVALIDDDLPROCESSINGCOMMANDS	The DDL found in ProcessingCommands is not valid.
0xC002912C	DTS_E_DTSPROCTASK_CANNOTWRITEINAREADONLYVARIABLE	The Execution result cannot be saved in a read-only variable.
0xC002912D	DTS_E_DTSPROCTASK_INVALIDVARIABLE	Variable " __ " is not defined.
0xC002912E	DTS_E_DTSPROCTASK_CONNECTIONNOTFOUND	Connection Manager " __ " is not defined.
0xC002912F	DTS_E_DTSPROCTASK_INVALIDCONNECTION	Connection Manager " __ " is not a FILE Connection Manager.
0xC0029130	DTS_E_DTSPROCTASK_NONEXISTENTATTRIBUTE	" __ " was not found during deserialization.
0xC0029131	DTS_E_DTSPROCTASK_TRACEHASBEENSTOPPED	The trace has been stopped due to an exception.
0xC0029132	DTS_E_DTSPROCTASK_DDLEXECUTIONFAILED	Execution of DDL failed.

Error Code	Symbolic Name	Description
0xC0029133	DTS_E_DTSPROCTASK_FILEDOESNOTEXIST	There is no file associated with connection "__".
0xC0029134	DTS_E_DTSPROCTASK_VARIABLENOTDEFINED	Variable "__" is not defined.
0xC0029135	DTS_E_DTSPROCTASK_FILECONNECTIONNOTDEFINED	File connection "__" is not defined.
0xC0029136	DTS_E_EXEC2000PKGTASK_INITIALIZATION_WITH_WRONG_XML_ELEMENT	Execute DTS 2000 Package task is initiated with a wrong XML element.
0xC0029137	DTS_E_EXEC2000PKGTASK_HANDLER_NOT_FOUND	Handler not found.
0xC0029138	DTS_E_EXEC2000PKGTASK_PACKAGE_NAME_NOT_SPECIFIED	Package name is not specified.
0xC0029139	DTS_E_EXEC2000PKGTASK_PACKAGE_ID_NOT_SPECIFIED	Package ID is not specified.
0xC002913A	DTS_E_EXEC2000PKGTASK_PACKAGE_VERSIONGUID_NOT_SPECIFIED	Package version GUID is not specified.
0xC002913B	DTS_E_EXEC2000PKGTASK_SQLSERVER_NOT_SPECIFIED	SQL Server is not specified.
0xC002913C	DTS_E_EXEC2000PKGTASK_SQL_USERNAME_NOT_SPECIFIED	SQL Server user name not specified.
0xC002913D	DTS_E_EXEC2000PKGTASK_FILE_NAME_NOT_SPECIFIED	Storage file name not specified.
0xC002913E	DTS_E_EXEC2000PKGTASK_DTS2000CANTBEEMPTY	The DTS 2000 package property is empty.
0xC002913F	DTS_E_EXEC2000PKGTASK_ERROR_IN_PACKAGE_EXECUTE	An error occurred while executing the DTS 2000 package.
0xC0029140	DTS_E_EXEC2000PKGTASK_SQLSERVER_NOT_AVAILABLE_NETWORK	Cannot load the available SQL Servers from the network. Check the network connection.
0xC0029141	DTS_E_EXEC2000PKGTASK_DATATYPE_NULL	The data type cannot be null. Please specify the correct data type to use for validating the value.
0xC0029142	DTS_E_EXEC2000PKGTASK_NULL_VALUE	Cannot validate a null against any data type.
0xC0029143	DTS_E_EXEC2000PKGTASK_NULL_VALUE_ARGUMENT	A required argument is null.

Error Code	Symbolic Name	Description
0xC0029144	DTS_E_EXEC2000PKGTASK_CLS_NOT_REGISTRED_EXCEPTION	To execute the DTS 2000 Package task, start SQL Server Setup and use the Advanced button from the Components to Install dialog to select Data Transformation Services 2000 Runtime.
0xC0029145	DTS_E_EXEC2000PKGTASK_NOT_PRIMITIVE_TYPE	" __ " is not a value type.
0xC0029146	DTS_E_EXEC2000PKGTASK_CONVERT_FAILED	Could not convert " __ " to " __ ".
0xC0029147	DTS_E_EXEC2000PKGTASK_ERROR_IN_VALIDATE	Could not validate " __ " against " __ ".
0xC0029148	DTS_E_EXEC2000PKGTASK_ERROR_IN_LOAD_FROM_XML	Error occurred in LoadFromXML at the tag " __ ".
0xC0029149	DTS_E_EXEC2000PKGTASK_ERROR_IN_SAVE_TO_XML	Error occurred in SaveToXML at the tag " __ ".
0xC002914A	DTS_E_EXECPROCTASK_INVALIDTIMEOUT	The time-out value provided is not valid. Specify the number of seconds that the task allows the process to run. The minimum time-out is 0, which indicates that no time-out value is used and the process runs to completion or until an error occurs. The maximum time-out is 2147483 (((2^31) − 1)/1000).
0xC002914B	DTS_E_EXECPROCTASK_CANTREDIRECTIO	Cannot redirect streams if the process can continue executing beyond the lifetime of the task.
0xC002914C	DTS_E_EXECPROCTASK_PROCESSHASTIMEDOUT	The process timed out.
0xC002914D	DTS_E_EXECPROCTASK_EXECUTABLENOTSPECIFIED	The executable is not specified.
0xC002914E	DTS_E_EXECPROCTASK_STDOUTVARREADONLY	The standard out variable is read-only.
0xC002914F	DTS_E_EXECPROCTASK_STDERRVARREADONLY	The standard error variable is read-only.
0xC0029150	DTS_E_EXECPROCTASK_RECEIVEDINVALIDTASKDATANODE	The Execute Process task received a task data node that is not valid.
0xC0029151	DTS_E_EXECPROCTASK_PROCESSEXITCODEEXCEEDS	In Executing " __ " " __ " at " __ ", the process exit code was " __ " while the expected was " __ ".
0xC0029152	DTS_E_EXECPROCTASK_WORKINGDIRDOESNOTEXIST	The directory " __ " does not exist.
0xC0029153	DTS_E_EXECPROCTASK_FILEDOESNOTEXIST	File/Process " __ " does not exist in directory " __ ".
0xC0029154	DTS_E_EXECPROCTASK_FILENOTINPATH	File/Process " __ " is not in path.
0xC0029156	DTS_E_EXECPROCTASK_WORKINGDIRECTORYDOESNOTEXIST	Working Directory " __ " does not exist.
0xC0029157	DTS_E_EXECPROCTASK_ERROREXECUTIONVALUE	The process exited with return code " __ ". However, " __ " was expected.
0xC0029158	DTS_E_FSTASK_SYNCFAILED	Synchronization object failed.
0xC0029159	DTS_E_FSTASK_INVALIDDATA	The File System task received an invalid task data node.

Error Code	Symbolic Name	Description
0xC002915A	DTS_E_FSTASK_DIRECTORYEXISTS	The Directory already exists.
0xC002915B	DTS_E_FSTASK_PATHNOTVALID	"__" is not valid on operation type "__".
0xC002915C	DTS_E_FSTASK_DESTINATIONNOTSET	Destination property of operation "__" not set.
0xC002915D	DTS_E_FSTASK_SOURCENOTSET	Source property of operation "__" not set.
0xC002915E	DTS_E_FSTASK_CONNECTIONTYPENOTFILE	Type of Connection "__" is not a file.
0xC002915F	DTS_E_FSTASK_VARIABLEDOESNTEXIST	Variable "__" does not exist.
0xC0029160	DTS_E_FSTASK_VARIABLENOTASTRING	Variable "__" is not a string.
0xC0029163	DTS_E_FSTASK_FILEDOESNOTEXIST	File or directory "__" represented by connection "__" does not exist.
0xC0029165	DTS_E_FSTASK_DESTCONNNUSAGETYPEINVALID	The destination file connection manager "__" has an invalid usage type: "__".
0xC0029166	DTS_E_FSTASK_SRCCONNNUSAGETYPEINVALID	The source file connection manager "__" has an invalid usage type "__".
0xC0029167	DTS_E_FSTASK_LOGENTRYGETTINGFILEOPERATION	FileSystemOperation
0xC0029168	DTS_E_FSTASK_LOGENTRYGETTINGFILEOPERATIONDESC	Provides information regarding File System operations.
0xC0029169	DTS_E_FSTASK_TASKDISPLAYNAME	File System Task
0xC002916A	DTS_E_FSTASK_TASKDESCRIPTION	Perform file system operations, such as copying and deleting files.
0xC002916B	DTS_E_FTPTASK_SYNCOBJFAILED	Synchronization object failed.
0xC002916C	DTS_E_FTPTASK_UNABLETOOBTAINFILELIST	Unable to obtain the file list.
0xC002916D	DTS_E_FTPTASK_LOCALPATHEMPTY	The local path is empty.
0xC002916E	DTS_E_FTPTASK_REMOTEPATHEMPTY	The remote path is empty.
0xC002916F	DTS_E_FTPTASK_LOCALVARIBALEEMPTY	The local variable is empty.
0xC0029170	DTS_E_FTPTASK_REMOTEVARIBALEEMPTY	The remote variable is empty.
0xC0029171	DTS_E_FTPTASK_FTPRCVDINVLDDATANODE	The FTP task received an invalid task data node.
0xC0029172	DTS_E_FTPTASK_CONNECTION_NAME_NULL	The connection is empty. Verify that a valid FTP connection is provided.
0xC0029173	DTS_E_FTPTASK_CONNECTION_NOT_FTP	The connection specified is not an FTP connection. Verify that a valid FTP connection is provided.
0xC0029175	DTS_E_FTPTASK_INITIALIZATION_WITH_NULL_XML_ELEMENT	Cannot initialize the task with a null XML element.
0xC0029176	DTS_E_FTPTASK_SAVE_TO_NULL_XML_ELEMENT	Cannot save the task to a null XML document.

Error Code	Symbolic Name	Description
0xC0029177	DTS_E_FTPTASK_ERROR_IN_LOAD_FROM_XML	Error occurred in LoadFromXML at the tag "__".
0xC0029178	DTS_E_FTPTASK_NOFILESATLOCATION	There are no files at "__".
0xC0029179	DTS_E_FTPTASK_LOCALVARIABLEISEMPTY	The variable "__" is empty.
0xC002917A	DTS_E_FTPTASK_REMOTEVARIABLEISEMPTY	The variable "__" is empty.
0xC002917B	DTS_E_FTPTASK_NOFILESINCONNMGR	The File "__" doesn't contain file path(s).
0xC002917C	DTS_E_FTPTASK_NOFILEPATHSINLOCALVAR	The variable "__" doesn't contain file path(s).
0xC002917D	DTS_E_FTPTASK_VARIABLENOTASTRING	Variable "__" is not a string.
0xC002917E	DTS_E_FTPTASK_VARIABLENOTFOUND	Variable "__" does not exist.
0xC002917F	DTS_E_FTPTASK_INVALIDPATHONOPERATION	Invalid path on operation "__".
0xC0029180	DTS_E_FTPTASK_DIRECTORYEXISTS	"__" already exists.
0xC0029182	DTS_E_FTPTASK_CONNECTIONTYPENOTFILE	Type of Connection "__" is Not a file.
0xC0029183	DTS_E_FTPTASK_FILEDOESNOTEXIST	File represented by "__" does not exist.
0xC0029184	DTS_E_FTPTASK_INVALIDDIRECTORY	Directory is not specified in the variable "__".
0xC0029185	DTS_E_FTPTASK_NOFILESFOUND	No files found in "__".
0xC0029186	DTS_E_FTPTASK_NODIRECTORYPATHINCONMGR	Directory is not specified in the file connection manager "__".
0xC0029187	DTS_E_FTPTASK_UNABLETODELETELOCALEFILE	Unable to delete local file "__".
0xC0029188	DTS_E_FTPTASK_UNABLETOREMOVELOCALDIRECTORY	Unable to remove local directory "__".
0xC0029189	DTS_E_FTPTASK_UNABLETOCREATELOCALDIRECTORY	Unable to create local directory "__".
0xC002918A	DTS_E_FTPTASK_UNABLETORECEIVEFILES	Unable to receive files using "__".
0xC002918B	DTS_E_FTPTASK_UNABLETOSENDFILES	Unable to send files using "__".
0xC002918C	DTS_E_FTPTASK_UNABLETOMAKEDIRREMOTE	Unable to create remote directory using "__".
0xC002918D	DTS_E_FTPTASK_UNABLETOREMOVEDIRREMOTE	Unable to remove remote directory using "__".
0xC002918E	DTS_E_FTPTASK_UNABLETODELETEREMOTEFILES	Unable to delete remote files using "__".
0xC002918F	DTS_E_FTPTASK_UNABLETOCONNECTTOSERVER	Unable to connect to FTP server using "__".
0xC0029190	DTS_E_FTPTASK_INVALIDVARIABLEVALUE	Variable "__" doesn't start with "/".
0xC0029191	DTS_E_FTPTASK_INVALIDREMOTEPATH	Remote path "__" doesn't start with "/".

Error Code	Symbolic Name	Description
0xC0029192	DTS_E_DTS_E_FTPTASK_CANNOT_ACQUIRE_CONNECTION	There was an error acquiring the FTP connection. Please check if you have specified a valid connection type "__".
0xC0029193	DTS_E_MSGQTASKUTIL_CERT_OPEN_STORE_FAILED	Opening the certificate store failed.
0xC0029194	DTS_E_MSGQTASKUTIL_CERT_FAILED_GETTING_DISPLAY_NAME	An error occurred while retrieving the display name of the certificate.
0xC0029195	DTS_E_MSGQTASKUTIL_CERT_FAILED_GETTING_ISSUER_NAME	An error occurred while retrieving the issuer name of the certificate.
0xC0029196	DTS_E_MSGQTASKUTIL_CERT_FAILED_GETTING_FRIENDLY_NAME	An error occurred while retrieving the friendly name of the certificate.
0xC0029197	DTS_E_MSMQTASK_NO_CONNECTION	The MSMQ connection name is not set.
0xC0029198	DTS_E_MSMQTASK_INITIALIZATION_WITH_WRONG_XML_ELEMENT	Task was initialized with the wrong XML element.
0xC0029199	DTS_E_MSMQTASK_DATA_FILE_NAME_EMPTY	Data file name is empty.
0xC002919A	DTS_E_MSMQTASK_DATA_FILE_SAVE_NAME_EMPTY	The name specified for the data file to save is empty.
0xC002919B	DTS_E_MSMQTASK_DATA_FILE_SIZE_ERROR	File size should be less than 4 MB.
0xC002919C	DTS_E_MSMQTASK_DATA_FILE_SAVE_FAILED	Saving the data file failed.
0xC002919D	DTS_E_MSMQTASK_STRING_COMPARE_VALUE_MISSING	String filter value is empty.
0xC002919E	DTS_E_MSMQTASK_INVALID_QUEUE_PATH	Queue path is not valid.
0xC002919F	DTS_E_MSMQTASK_QUEUE_NOT_TRANSACTIONAL	Message is part of a transaction, but the queue is not transactional.
0xC00291A0	DTS_E_MSMQTASK_INVALID_MESSAGE_TYPE	The message type is not valid.
0xC00291A1	DTS_E_MSMQTASK_TASK_TIMEOUT	The message queue timed out. No message has been received.
0xC00291A2	DTS_E_MSMQTASK_INVALID_PROPERTY_VALUE	The property specified is not valid. Verify that the argument type is correct.
0xC00291A3	DTS_E_MSMQTASK_MESSAGE_NON_AUTHENTICATED	Message is not authenticated.
0xC00291A4	DTS_E_MSMQTASK_INVALID_ENCRYPTION_ALGO_WRAPPER	You are trying to set the value of Encryption Algorithm with an invalid object.
0xC00291A5	DTS_E_MSMQTASK_VARIABLE_TO_RECEIVE_STRING_MSG_EMPTY	The variable to receive string message is empty.

Error Code	Symbolic Name	Description
0xC00291A6	DTS_E_MSMQTASK_RECEIVE_VARIABLE_EMPTY	Variable to receive variable message is empty.
0xC00291A7	DTS_E_MSMQTASK_CONNECTIONTYPENOTMSMQ	Connection " __ " is not of type MSMQ.
0xC00291A8	DTS_E_MSMQTASK_DATAFILE_ALREADY_EXISTS	The data file " __ " already exists at the specified location. Cannot overwrite the file as the Overwrite option is set to false.
0xC00291A9	DTS_E_MSMQTASK_STRING_MSG_TO_VARIABLE_NOT_FOUND	The specified variable " __ " to receive string message is not found in the package variable collection.
0xC00291AA	DTS_E_MSMQTASK_CONNMNGRNULL	The connection manager " __ " is empty.
0xC00291AB	DTS_E_MSMQTASK_CONNMNGRDOESNOTEXIST	The connection manager " __ " does not exist.
0xC00291AC	DTS_E_SCRIPTTASK_COMPILEERRORMSG	Error " __ ": " __ " \r\nLine " __ " Column " __ " through " __ ".
0xC00291AD	DTS_E_SCRIPTTASK_COMPILEERRORMSG2	There was an error compiling the script: " __ ".
0xC00291AE	DTS_E_SCRIPTTASK_COMPILEERRORMSG3	Error " __ ": " __ " \r\nLine " __ " Columns " __ "-" __ " \r\nLine Text: " __ ".
0xC00291AF	DTS_E_SCRIPTTASK_SCRIPTREPORTEDFAILURE	User script returned a failure result.
0xC00291B0	DTS_E_SCRIPTTASK_SCRIPTFILESFAILEDTOLOAD	User script files failed to load.
0xC00291B1	DTS_E_SCRIPTTASK_SCRIPTTHREWEXCEPTION	User script threw an exception: " __ ".
0xC00291B2	DTS_E_SCRIPTTASK_COULDNOTCREATEENTRYPOINTCLASS	Could not create an instance of entrypoint class " __ ".
0xC00291B3	DTS_E_SCRIPTTASK_LOADFROMXMLEXCEPTION	There was an exception while loading Script Task from XML: " __ ".
0xC00291B4	DTS_E_SCRIPTTASK_SOURCEITEMNOTFOUNDEXCEPTION	Source item " __ " was not found in the package.
0xC00291B5	DTS_E_SCRIPTTASK_BINARYITEMNOTFOUNDEXCEPTION	Binary item " __ " was not found in the package.
0xC00291B6	DTS_E_SCRIPTTASK_UNRECOGNIZEDSCRIPTLANGUAGEEXCEPTION	" __ " was not recognized as a valid script language.
0xC00291B7	DTS_E_SCRIPTTASK_ILLEGALSCRIPTNAME	The script name is not valid. It cannot contain spaces, slashes, special characters, or begin with a number.
0xC00291B8	DTS_E_SCRIPTTASK_INVALIDSCRIPTLANGUAGE	The script language specified is not valid.
0xC00291B9	DTS_E_SCRIPTTASK_CANTINITNULLTASK	Cannot initialize to a null task.
0xC00291BA	DTS_E_SCRIPTTASK_MUSTINITWITHRIGHTTASK	The Script Task user interface must initialize to a Script Task.
0xC00291BB	DTS_E_SCRIPTTASK_WASNOTINITED	The Script Task user interface is not initialized.
0xC00291BC	DTS_E_SCRIPTTASK_HOST_NAME_CANT_EMPTY	Name cannot be empty.

Error Code	Symbolic Name	Description
0xC00291BD	DTS_E_SCRIPTTASK_INVALID_SCRIPT_NAME	The project name is not valid. It cannot contain spaces, slashes, special characters, or begin with a number.
0xC00291BE	DTS_E_SCRIPTTASK_INVALID_SCRIPT_LANGUAGE	The script language specified is not valid.
0xC00291BF	DTS_E_SCRIPTTASK_INVALID_ENTRY_POINT	Entry point not found.
0xC00291C0	DTS_E_SCRIPTTASK_LANGUAGE_EMPTY	The script language is not specified. Verify that a valid script language is specified.
0xC00291C1	DTS_E_SCRIPTTASK_INITIALIZATION_WITH_NULL_TASK	User interface initialization: The task is null.
0xC00291C2	DTS_E_SCRIPTTASK_UI_INITIALIZATION_WITH_WRONG_TASK	The Script Task user interface is initialized with an incorrect task.
0xC00291C3	DTS_E_SENDMAILTASK_RECIPIENT_EMPTY	No recipient is specified.
0xC00291C4	DTS_E_SENDMAILTASK_SMTP_SERVER_NOT_SPECIFIED	The Simple Mail Transfer Protocol (SMTP) server is not specified. Provide a valid name or IP address of the SMTP server.
0xC00291C5	DTS_E_SENDMAILTASK_TASK_INITIALIZATION_WITH_WRONG_XML_ELEMENT	Send Mail task is initiated with an incorrect XML element.
0xC00291CB	DTS_E_SENDMAILTASK_INVALIDATTACHMENT	Either the file "__" does not exist or you do not have permissions to access the file.
0xC00291CD	DTS_E_SENDMAILTASK_CHECK_VALID_SMTP_SERVER	Verify that the Simple Mail Transfer Protocol (SMTP) server specified is valid.
0xC00291CE	DTS_E_SENDMAILTASK_CONNECTIONTYPENOTFILE	Connection "__" is not of type File.
0xC00291CF	DTS_E_SENDMAILTASK_FILEDOESNOTEXIST	On operation "__", file "__" does not exist.
0xC00291D0	DTS_E_SENDMAILTASK_VARIABLETYPEISNOTSTRING	Variable "__" is not of type string.
0xC00291D1	DTS_E_SENDMAILTASK_CONNECTIONTYPENOTSMTP	Connection "__" is not of type SMTP.
0xC00291D2	DTS_E_SENDMAILTASK_CONNMNGRNULL	Connection "__" is empty.
0xC00291D3	DTS_E_SENDMAILTASK_NOCONNMNGR	The specified connection "__" does not exist.
0xC00291D4	DTS_E_SQLTASK_NOSTATEMENTSPECIFIED	No Transact-SQL statement specified.
0xC00291D5	DTS_E_SQLTASK_NOXMLSUPPORT	The connection does not support XML result sets.
0xC00291D6	DTS_E_SQLTASK_NOHANDLERFORCONNECTION	Cannot locate a handler for the specified connection type.

Error Code	Symbolic Name	Description
0xC00291D7	DTS_E_SQLTASK_NOCONNECTIONMANAGER	No connection manager is specified.
0xC00291D8	DTS_E_SQLTASK_CANNOTACQUIRECONNMANAGER	Cannot acquire a connection from the connection manager.
0xC00291D9	DTS_E_SQLTASK_NULLPARAMETERNAME	Cannot have a null parameter name.
0xC00291DA	DTS_E_SQLTASK_INVALIDPARAMETERNAME	The parameter name is not valid.
0xC00291DB	DTS_E_SQLTASK_VALIDPARAMETERTYPES	Valid parameter names are of type Int or String.
0xC00291DC	DTS_E_SQLTASK_READONLYVARIABLE	Variable "__" cannot be used in a result binding because it is read-only.
0xC00291DD	DTS_E_SQLTASK_INDESNOTINCOLLECTION	The index is not assigned in this collection.
0xC00291DE	DTS_E_SQLTASK_ROVARINOUTPARAMETER	The variable "__" cannot be used as an "out" parameter or return value in a parameter binding because it is read-only.
0xC00291DF	DTS_E_SQLTASK_OBJECTNOTINCOLLECTION	The object does not exist in this collection.
0xC00291E0	DTS_E_SQLTASK_UNABLETOACQUIREMANAGEDCONN	Cannot acquire a managed connection.
0xC00291E1	DTS_E_UNABLETOPOPRESULT	Cannot populate the result columns for a single row result type. The query returned an empty result set.
0xC00291E2	DTS_E_SQLTASK_INVALIDNUMOFRESULTBINDINGS	There is an invalid number of result bindings returned for the ResultSetType: "__".
0xC00291E3	DTS_E_SQLTASK_RESULTBINDTYPEFORROWSETXML	The result binding name must be set to zero for full result set and XML results.
0xC00291E4	DTS_E_SQLTASK_INVALIDEPARAMDIRECTIONFALG	The parameter directions flag is not valid.
0xC00291E5	DTS_E_SQLTASK_NOSQLTASKDATAINXMLFRAGMENT	The XML fragment does not contain SQL Task data.
0xC00291E6	DTS_E_SQLTASK_MULTIPLERETURNVALUEPARAM	A parameter with type return value is not the first parameter, or there are more than one parameter of type return value.
0xC00291E7	DTS_E_SQLTASK_CONNECTIONTYPENOTFILE	Connection "__" is not a file connection manager.
0xC00291E8	DTS_E_SQLTASK_FILEDOESNOTEXIST	File represented by "__" does not exist.
0xC00291E9	DTS_E_SQLTASK_VARIABLETYPEISNOTSTRING	Type of variable "__" is not string.
0xC00291EA	DTS_E_SQLTASK_VARIABLENOTFOUND	Variable "__" does not exist or could not be locked.
0xC00291EB	DTS_E_SQLTASK_CANNOTLOCATECONNMANAGER	Connection manager "__" does not exist.
0xC00291EC	DTS_E_SQLTASK_FAILEDTOACQUIRECONNECTION	Failed to acquire connection "__". Connection may not be configured correctly or you may not have the right permissions on this connection.

Error Code	Symbolic Name	Description
0xC00291ED	DTS_E_SQLTASK_RESULTBYNAMENOTSUPPORTED	Result binding by name " __ " is not supported for this connection type.
0xC00291EE	DTS_E_SQLTASKCONN_ERR_NO_ROWS	A result set type of single row is specified, but no rows were returned.
0xC00291EF	DTS_E_SQLTASKCONN_ERR_NO_DISCONNECTED_RS	No disconnected record set is available for the Transact-SQL statement.
0xC00291F0	DTS_E_SQLTASKCONN_ERR_UNSUPPORTED_TYPE	Unsupported type.
0xC00291F1	DTS_E_SQLTASKCONN_ERR_UNKNOWN_TYPE	Unknown type.
0xC00291F2	DTS_E_SQLTASKCONN_ERR_PARAM_DATA_TYPE	Unsupported data type on parameter binding \"%s\".
0xC00291F3	DTS_E_SQLTASKCONN_ERR_PARAM_NAME_MIX	Parameter names cannot be a mix of ordinal and named types.
0xC00291F4	DTS_E_SQLTASKCONN_ERR_PARAM_DIR	The parameter direction on parameter binding \"%s\" is not valid.
0xC00291F5	DTS_E_SQLTASKCONN_ERR_RESULT_DATA_TYPE	The data type on result set binding \"%s\" is not supported.
0xC00291F6	DTS_E_SQLTASKCONN_ERR_RESULT_COL_INDEX	The result column index __ is not valid.
0xC00291F7	DTS_E_SQLTASKCONN_ERR_UNKNOWN_RESULT_COL	Cannot find column \"%s\" in the result set.
0xC00291F9	DTS_E_SQLTASKCONN_ERR_NOROWSET	No result rowset is associated with the execution of this query.
0xC00291FA	DTS_E_SQLTASKCONN_ERR_ODBC_DISCONNECTED	Disconnected recordsets are not available from ODBC connections.
0xC00291FB	DTS_E_SQLTASKCONN_ERR_RESULT_SET_DATA_TYPE	The data type in the result set, column __, is not supported.
0xC00291FC	DTS_E_SQLTASKCONN_ERR_CANT_LOAD_XML	Cannot load XML with query result.
0xC00291FD	DTS_E_TTGENTASK_NOCONNORVARIABLE	A connection name or variable name for the package must be specified.
0xC00291FE	DTS_E_TTGENTASK_FAILEDCREATE	Failed to create the package.
0xC00291FF	DTS_E_TTGENTASK_BADTABLEMETADATA	The TableMetaDataNode is not an XMLNode.
0xC0029200	DTS_E_TTGENTASK_FAILEDCREATEPIPELINE	Failed to create the pipeline.
0xC0029201	DTS_E_TTGENTASK_BADVARIABLETYPE	The variable is not the correct type.
0xC0029202	DTS_E_TTGENTASK_NOTFILECONNECTION	The connection manager specified is not a FILE connection manager.
0xC0029203	DTS_E_TTGENTASK_BADFILENAME	Invalid file name specified on the connection manager " __ ".
0xC0029204	DTS_E_WEBSERVICETASK_CONNECTION_NAME_NULL	The connection is empty. Verify that a valid HTTP connection is specified.
0xC0029205	DTS_E_WEBSERVICETASK_CONNECTION_NOT_FOUND	The connection does not exist. Verify that a valid, existing HTTP connection is specified.

Error Code	Symbolic Name	Description
0xC0029206	DTS_E_WEBSERVICETASK_CONNECTION_NOT_HTTP	The connection specified is not an HTTP connection. Verify that a valid HTTP connection is specified.
0xC0029207	DTS_E_WEBSERVICETASK_SERVICE_NULL	The Web Service name is empty. Verify that a valid web service name is specified.
0xC0029208	DTS_E_WEBSERVICETASK_METHODNAME_NULL	The web method name is empty. Verify that a valid web method is specified.
0xC0029209	DTS_E_WEBSERVICETASK_WEBMETHODINFO_NULL	The web method is empty or may not exist. Verify that there is an existing web method to specify.
0xC002920A	DTS_E_WEBSERVICETASK_OUTPUTLOC_NULL	The output location is empty. Verify that an existing file connection or variable is specified.
0xC002920B	DTS_E_WEBSERVICETASK_VARIABLE_NOT_FOUND	The variable cannot be found. Verify that the variable exists in the package.
0xC002920C	DTS_E_WEBSERVICETASK_VARIABLE_READONLY	Cannot save the result. Verify that the variable is not read-only.
0xC002920D	DTS_E_WEBSERVICETASK_ERROR_IN_LOAD_FROM_XML	Error occurred in LoadFromXML at the tag " __ ".
0xC002920E	DTS_E_WEBSERVICETASK_ERROR_IN_SAVE_TO_XML	Error occurred in SaveToXML at the tag " __ ".
0xC002920F	DTS_E_WEBSERVICETASK_SAVE_TO_NULL_XML_ELEMENT	Cannot save the task to a null XML document.
0xC0029210	DTS_E_WEBSERVICETASK_TASK_INITIALIZATION_WITH_NULL_XML_ELEMENT	Cannot initialize the task with a null XML element.
0xC0029211	DTS_E_WEBSERVICETASK_TASK_INITIALIZATION_WITH_WRONG_XML_ELEMENT	The Web Service Task is initiated with an incorrect XML element.
0xC0029212	DTS_E_WEBSERVICETASK_UNEXPECTED_XML_ELEMENT	Unexpected XML element found.
0xC0029213	DTS_E_WEBSERVICETASK_CANNOT_ACQUIRE_CONNECTION	There was an error acquiring the HTTP connection. Verify that a valid connection type is specified.
0xC0029214	DTS_E_WEBSERVICETASK_FILE_CONN_NOT_FOUND	Cannot save the result. Verify that there is an existing file connection.
0xC0029215	DTS_E_WEBSERVICETASK_FILE_NOT_FOUND	Cannot save the result. Verify that the file exists.
0xC0029216	DTS_E_WEBSERVICETASK_FILE_NULL	Cannot save the result. The file name is empty or the file is in use by another process.

Error Code	Symbolic Name	Description
0xC0029217	DTS_E_WEBSERVICETASK_CANNOT_ACQUIRE_FILE_CONNECTION	There was an error in acquiring the file connection. Verify that a valid file connection is specified.
0xC0029218	DTS_E_WEBSERVICETASK_DATATYPE_NOT_SUPPORTED	Only Complex Types with Primitive values, Primitive Arrays, and Enumerations are supported.
0xC0029219	DTS_E_WEBSERVICETASK_PARAMTYPE_NOT_SUPPORTED	Only Primitive, Enum, Complex, PrimitiveArray, and ComplexArray types are supported.
0xC002921A	DTS_E_WEBSERVICETASK_WSDL_VERSION_NOT_SUPPORTED	This version of WSDL is not supported.
0xC002921B	DTS_E_WEBSERVICETASK_WRONG_XML_ELEMENT	Initialized with an incorrect XML element.
0xC002921C	DTS_E_WEBSERVICETASK_XML_ATTRIBUTE_NOT_FOUND	A mandatory attribute is not found.
0xC002921D	DTS_E_WEBSERVICETASK_ENUM_NO_VALUES	The enum "___" does not have any values. The WSDL is corrupted.
0xC002921E	DTS_E_WEBSERVICETASK_CONNECTIONNOTFOUND	The connection cannot be found.
0xC002921F	DTS_E_WEBSERVICETASK_CONNECTION_ALREADY_EXISTS	Connection by this name already exists.
0xC0029220	DTS_E_WEBSERVICETASK_NULL_CONNECTION	Connection cannot be null or empty.
0xC0029221	DTS_E_WEBSERVICETASK_NOT_HTTP_CONNECTION	The connection specified is not an HTTP connection. Verify that a valid HTTP connection is specified.
0xC0029222	DTS_E_WEBSERVICETASK_WSDL_NOT_FOUND	The specified Uniform Resource Identifier (URI) does not contain a valid WSDL.
0xC0029223	DTS_E_WEBSERVICETASK_ERROR_IN_DOWNLOAD	Could not read the WSDL file. The input WSDL file is not valid. The reader threw the following error: "___".
0xC0029224	DTS_E_WEBSERVICETASK_SERVICE_DESC_NULL	Service Description cannot be null.
0xC0029225	DTS_E_WEBSERVICETASK_SERVICENULL	Service name cannot be null.
0xC0029226	DTS_E_WEBSERVICETASK_WSDL_NULL	URL cannot be null.
0xC0029227	DTS_E_WEBSERVICETASK_SERVICE_NOT_FOUND	The service is not currently available.
0xC0029228	DTS_E_WEBSERVICETASK_SOAPPORT_NOT_FOUND	The service is not available on the SOAP port.
0xC0029229	DTS_E_WEBSERVICETASK_SOAPBINDING_NOT_FOUND	Failed to parse the Web Services Description Language (WSDL). Cannot find the Binding that corresponds to the SOAP port.
0xC002922A	DTS_E_WEBSERVICETASK_SOAPPORTTYPE_NOT_FOUND	Failed to parse the Web Services Description Language (WSDL). Cannot find a PortType that corresponds to the SOAP port.

Error Code	Symbolic Name	Description
0xC002922B	DTS_E_WEBSERVICETASK_MSG_NOT_FOUND	Cannot find the message that corresponds to the method specified.
0xC002922C	DTS_E_WEBSERVICETASK_CANNOT_GEN_PROXY	Could not generate the proxy for the given web service. The following errors were encountered while generating the proxy " __ ".
0xC002922D	DTS_E_WEBSERVICETASK_CANNOT_LOAD_PROXY	Could not load the proxy for the given web service. The exact error is as follows: " __ ".
0xC002922E	DTS_E_WEBSERVICETASK_INVALID_SERVICE	Could not find the specified service. The exact error is as follows: " __ ".
0xC002922F	DTS_E_WEBSERVICETASK_WEBMETHOD_INVOKE_FAILED	The Web Service threw the following error during method execution: " __ ".
0xC0029230	DTS_E_WEBSERVICETASK_INVOKE_ERR	Could not execute the web method. The exact error is as follows: " __ ".
0xC0029231	DTS_E_WEBSERVICETASK_METHODINFO_NULL	MethodInfo cannot be null.
0xC0029232	DTS_E_WEBSERVICETASK_VALUE_NOT_PRIMITIVE	The specified WebMethodInfo is not correct. The ParamValue supplied does not match the ParamType. The DTSParamValue is not of type PrimitiveValue.
0xC0029233	DTS_E_WEBSERVICETASK_VALUE_NOT_ENUM	The WebMethodInfo specified is not correct. The ParamValue supplied does not match the ParamType. The DTSParamValue found is not of type EnumValue.
0xC0029234	DTS_E_VALUE_WEBSERVICETASK_NOT_COMPLEX	The WebMethodInfo specified is not correct. The ParamValue supplied does not match the ParamType. The DTSParamValue found is not of type ComplexValue.
0xC0029235	DTS_E_WEBSERVICETASK_VALUE_NOT_ARRAY	The WebMethodInfo specified is not correct. The ParamValue supplied does not match the ParamType. The DTSParamValue found is not of type ArrayValue.
0xC0029236	DTS_E_WEBSERVICETASK_TYPE_NOT_PRIMITIVE	The WebMethodInfo you have specified is wrong. " __ " is not Primitive Type.
0xC0029237	DTS_E_WEBSERVICETASK_ARRAY_VALUE_INVALID	The format of the ArrayValue is not valid. There should be at least one element in the array.
0xC0029238	DTS_E_WEBSERVICETASK_SELECTED_VALUE_NULL	The value of the enumeration cannot be null. Select a default value for the enumeration.
0xC0029239	DTS_E_WEBSERVICETASK_NULL_VALUE	Cannot validate a null against any datatype.
0xC002923A	DTS_E_WEBSERVICETASK_ENUM_VALUE_NOT_FOUND	The enumeration Value is not correct.
0xC002923B	DTS_E_WEBSERVICETASK_PROP_NOT_EXISTS	The class specified does not contain a public property by the name " __ ".
0xC002923C	DTS_E_WEBSERVICETASK_CONVERT_FAILED	Could not convert " __ " to " __ ".
0xC002923D	DTS_E_WEBSERVICETASK_CLEANUP_FAILED	Cleanup failed. The proxy that was created for the web service may not have been deleted.

Error Code	Symbolic Name	Description
0xC002923E	DTS_E_WEBSERVICETASK_CREATE_INSTANCE_FAILED	Could not create an object of type " __ ". Please check whether the default constructor exists.
0xC002923F	DTS_E_WEBSERVICETASK_NOT_PRIMITIVE_TYPE	" __ " is not a value type.
0xC0029240	DTS_E_WEBSERVICETASK_ERROR_IN_VALIDATE	Could not validate " __ " against " __ ".
0xC0029241	DTS_E_WEBSERVICETASK_DATATYPE_NULL	The data type cannot be null. Specify the value of the data type to validate.
0xC0029242	DTS_E_WEBSERVICETASK_INDEX_OUT_OF_BOUNDS	The ParamValue cannot be inserted at this position. The index specified might be less than zero or greater than the length.
0xC0029243	DTS_E_WEBSERVICETASK_WRONG_WSDL	The input WSDL file is not valid.
0xC0029244	DTS_E_WMIDRTASK_SYNCOBJECTFAILED	Synchronization object failed.
0xC0029245	DTS_E_WMIDRTASK_MISSINGWQLQUERY	The WQL query is missing.
0xC0029246	DTS_E_WMIDRTASK_DESTINATIONMUSTBESET	The destination must be set.
0xC0029247	DTS_E_WMIDRTASK_MISSINGCONNECTION	No WMI connection is set.
0xC0029248	DTS_E_WMIDRTASK_INVALIDDATANODE	WMI Data Reader Task received an invalid task data node.
0xC0029249	DTS_E_WMIDRTASK_FAILEDVALIDATION	The task failed validation.
0xC002924A	DTS_E_WMIDRTASK_FILEDOESNOTEXIST	File " __ " does not exist.
0xC002924B	DTS_E_WMIDRTASK_CONNECTIONMNGRDOESNTEXIST	Connection manager " __ " does not exist.
0xC002924C	DTS_E_WMIDRTASK_VARIABLETYPEISNOTSTRINGOROBJECT	Variable " __ " is not of type string or object.
0xC002924D	DTS_E_WMIDRTASK_CONNECTIONTYPENOTFILE	Connection " __ " is not of type "FILE".
0xC002924E	DTS_E_WMIDRTASK_CONNECTIONTYPENOTWMI	Connection " __ " is not of type "WMI".
0xC002924F	DTS_E_WMIDRTASK_FILEALREADYEXISTS	File " __ " already exists.
0xC0029250	DTS_E_WMIDRTASK_CONNECTIONMANAGEREMPTY	Connection manager " __ " is empty.
0xC0029251	DTS_E_WMIDRTASK_VARNOTOBJECT	Variable " __ " should be of type object to be assigned a data table.
0xC0029252	DTS_E_WMIDRTASK_TASKFAILURE	Task failed due to invalid WMI query: " __ ".
0xC0029253	DTS_E_WMIDRTASK_CANTWRITETOVAR	Unable to write to variable " __ " since it is set to keep its original value.
0xC0029254	DTS_E_WMIEWTASK_SYNCOBJECTFAILED	Synchronization object failed.
0xC0029255	DTS_E_WMIEWTASK_MISSINGWQLQUERY	The WQL query is missing.
0xC0029256	DTS_E_WMIEWTASK_MISSINGCONNECTION	The WMI connection is missing.

Error Code	Symbolic Name	Description
0xC0029257	DTS_E_WMIEWTASK_QUERYFAILURE	The task failed to execute the WMI query.
0xC0029258	DTS_E_WMIEWTASK_INVALIDDATANODE	The WMI Event Watcher Task received a task data node that is not valid.
0xC0029259	DTS_E_WMIEWTASK_CONNECTIONMNGRDOESNTEXIST	Connection manager "__" does not exist.
0xC002925A	DTS_E_WMIEWTASK_FILEDOESNOTEXIST	File "__" does not exist.
0xC002925B	DTS_E_WMIEWTASK_VARIABLETYPEISNOTSTRING	Variable "__" is not of type string.
0xC002925C	DTS_E_WMIEWTASK_CONNECTIONTYPENOTFILE	Connection "__" is not of type "FILE".
0xC002925D	DTS_E_WMIEWTASK_CONNECTIONTYPENOTWMI	Connection "__" is not of type "WMI".
0xC002925E	DTS_E_WMIEWTASK_FILEALREADYEXISTS	File "__" already exists.
0xC002925F	DTS_E_WMIEWTASK_CONNECTIONMANAGEREMPTY	Connection manager "__" is empty.
0xC0029260	DTS_E_WMIEWTASK_TIMEOUTOCCURRED	Timeout of "__" second(s) occurred before event represented by "__".
0xC0029261	DTS_E_WMIEWTASK_ERRMESSAGE	Watching for the Wql query caused the following system exception: "__". Check the query for errors or WMI connection for access rights/permissions.
0xC0029262	DTS_E_XMLTASK_NODEFAULTOPERTION	The Operations specified is not defined.
0xC0029263	DTS_E_XMLTASK_CONNECTIONTYPENOTFILE	The connection type is not File.
0xC0029264	DTS_E_XMLTASK_CANTGETREADERFROMSOURCE	Cannot get an XmlReader from the source XML document.
0xC0029265	DTS_E_XMLTASK_CANTGETREADERFROMDEST	Cannot get an XmlReader from the changed XML document.
0xC0029266	DTS_E_XMLTASK_CANTGETREADERFROMDIFFGRAM	Cannot get the XDL diffgram reader from the XDL diffgram XML.
0xC0029268	DTS_E_XMLTASK_EMPTYNODELIST	The node list is empty.
0xC0029269	DTS_E_XMLTASK_NOELEMENTFOUND	The element was not found.
0xC002926A	DTS_E_XMLTASK_UNDEFINEDOPERATION	The Operations specified is not defined.
0xC002926B	DTS_E_XMLTASK_XPATHNAVERROR	Unexpected content item in XPathNavigator.
0xC002926C	DTS_E_XMLTASK_NOSCHEMAFOUND	No schema found to enforce validation.
0xC002926D	DTS_E_XMLTASK_VALIDATIONERROR	A validation error occurred when validating the instance document.
0xC002926E	DTS_E_XMLTASK_SYNCOBJECTFAILED	Synchronization object failed.
0xC002926F	DTS_E_XMLTASK_ROOTNOODESNOTMATCHED	The root nodes do not match.
0xC0029270	DTS_E_XMLTASK_INVALIDEDITSCRIPT	The Edit Script Operation type in the final Edit Script is not valid.

Error Code	Symbolic Name	Description
0xC0029271	DTS_E_XMLTASK_CDATANODESISSUE	CDATA nodes should be added with DiffgramAddSubtrees class.
0xC0029272	DTS_E_XMLTASK_COMMENTSNODEISSUE	Comment nodes should be added with DiffgramAddSubtrees class.
0xC0029273	DTS_E_XMLTASK_TEXTNODEISSUES	Text nodes should be added with DiffgramAddSubtrees class.
0xC0029274	DTS_E_XMLTASK_WHITESPACEISSUE	Significant white space nodes should be added with DiffgramAddSubtrees class.
0xC0029275	DTS_E_XMLTASK_DIFFENUMISSUE	Correct the OperationCost array so that it reflects the XmlDiffOperation enumeration.
0xC0029276	DTS_E_XMLTASK_TASKISEMPTY	There are no operations in the task.
0xC0029277	DTS_E_XMLTASK_DOCUMENTHASDATA	The document already contains data and should not be used again.
0xC0029278	DTS_E_XMLTASK_INVALIDENODETYPE	The node type is not valid.
0xC0029279	DTS_E_XMLTASK_INVALIDDATANODE	The XML Task received a task data node that is not valid.
0xC002927B	DTS_E_XMLTASK_VARIABLETYPEISNOTSTRING	Variable data type is not a String.
0xC002927C	DTS_E_XMLTASK_COULDNOTGETENCODINGFROMDOCUMENT	Cannot get encoding from XML.
0xC002927D	DTS_E_XMLTASK_MISSINGSOURCE	Source is not specified.
0xC002927E	DTS_E_XMLTASK_MISSINGSECONDOPERAND	Second operand is not specified.
0xC002927F	DTS_E_XMLTASK_INVALIDPATHDESCRIPTOR	Invalid XDL diffgram. " __ " is an invalid path descriptor.
0xC0029280	DTS_E_XMLTASK_NOMATCHINGNODE	Invalid XDL diffgram. No node matches the path descriptor " __ ".
0xC0029281	DTS_E_XMLTASK_EXPECTINGDIFFGRAMELEMENT	Invalid XDL diffgram. Expecting xd:xmldiff as a root element with namespace URI " __ ".
0xC0029282	DTS_E_XMLTASK_MISSINGSRCDOCATTRIBUTE	The XDL diffgram is not valid. The srcDocHash attribute on the xd:xmldiff element is missing.
0xC0029283	DTS_E_XMLTASK_MISSINGOPTIONSATTRIBUTE	The XDL diffgram is not valid. The options attribute on the xd:xmldiff element is missing.
0xC0029284	DTS_E_XMLTASK_INVALIDSRCDOCATTRIBUTE	The XDL diffgram is not valid. The srcDocHash attribute has an invalid value.
0xC0029285	DTS_E_XMLTASK_INVALIDOPTIONSATTRIBUTE	The XDL diffgram is not valid. The options attribute has an invalid value.
0xC0029286	DTS_E_XMLTASK_SRCDOCMISMATCH	The XDL diffgram is not applicable to this XML document. The rcDocHash value does not match.
0xC0029287	DTS_E_XMLTASK_MORETHANONENODEMATCHED	Invalid XDL diffgram; more than one node matches the " __ " path descriptor on the xd:node or xd:change element.

Error Code	Symbolic Name	Description
0xC0029288	DTS_E_XMLTASK_XMLDECLMISMATCH	The XDL diffgram is not applicable to this XML document. A new XML declaration cannot be added.
0xC0029289	DTS_E_XMLTASK_INTERNALERRORMORETHANONENODEINLIST	Internal Error. XmlDiffPathSingleNodeList can contain only one node.
0xC002928A	DTS_E_XMLTASK_INTERNALERRORMORETHANONENODELEFT	Internal Error. "__" nodes left after patch, expecting 1.
0xC002928B	DTS_E_XMLTASK_XSLTRESULTFILEISNOTXML	The File/Text Produced by the XSLT is not a valid XmlDocument, thus cannot be set as result of operation: "__".
0xC002928E	DTS_E_XMLTASK_FILEDOESNOTEXIST	There is no file associated with connection "__".
0xC002928F	DTS_E_XMLTASK_XMLTEXTEMPTY	Property "__" has no source Xml text; Xml Text is either invalid, null, or empty string.
0xC0029290	DTS_E_XMLTASK_FILEALREADYEXISTS	File "__" already exists.
0xC0029293	DTS_E_TRANSFERTASKS_SRCCONNECTIONREQUIRED	A source connection must be specified.
0xC0029294	DTS_E_TRANSFERTASKS_DESTCONNECTIONREQUIRED	A destination connection must be specified.
0xC0029295	DTS_E_TRANSFERTASKS_CONNECTIONNOTFOUND	The connection "__" could not be found in the package.
0xC0029296	DTS_E_TRANSFERTASKS_SERVERVERSIONNOTALLOWED	The connection "__" specifies a SQL server with a version that is not supported for transfer. Only version 7, 2000, and 2005 are supported.
0xC0029297	DTS_E_TRANSFERTASKS_SRCSERVERLESSEQUALDESTSERVER	The source connection "__" must specify a SQL server with a version less than or equal to the destination connection "__".
0xC0029298	DTS_E_TRANSFERTASKS_SRCDBREQUIRED	A source database must be specified.
0xC0029299	DTS_E_TRANSFERTASKS_SRCDBMUSTEXIST	The source database "__" must exist on the source server.
0xC002929A	DTS_E_TRANSFERTASKS_DESTDBREQUIRED	A destination database must be specified.
0xC002929B	DTS_E_TRANSFERTASKS_SRCDBANDDESTDBTHESAME	The source database and the destination database cannot be the same.
0xC002929C	DTS_E_TRANSFERDBTASK_FILENAMEREQUIRED	The transfer file information __ is missing the filename.
0xC002929D	DTS_E_TRANSFERDBTASK_FOLDERREQUIRED	The transfer file information __ is missing the folder part.
0xC002929E	DTS_E_TRANSFERTASKS_NETSHAREREQUIRED	The transfer file information __ is missing the network share part.
0xC002929F	DTS_E_TRANSFERTASKS_FILELISTSCOUNTMISMATCH	The number of source transfer files and the number of destination transfer files must be the same.

Error Code	Symbolic Name	Description
0xC00292A0	DTS_E_DOESNOTSUPPORTTRANSACTIONS	Enlisting in transactions is not supported.
0xC00292A1	DTS_E_TRANSFERDBTASK_OFFLINEERROR	The following exception occurred during an offline database transfer: ___.
0xC00292A2	DTS_E_TRANSFERDBTASK_NETSHAREDOESNOTEXIST	The network share "___" could not be found.
0xC00292A3	DTS_E_TRANSFERDBTASK_NETSHARENOACCESS	The network share "___" could not be accessed. The error is: ___.
0xC00292A4	DTS_E_TRANSFERDBTASK_USERMUSTBEDBOORSYSADMIN	The user "___" must be a DBO or a sysadmin for "___" in order to perform an online database transfer.
0xC00292A5	DTS_E_TRANSFERDBTASK_USERMUSTBESYSADMIN	The user "___" must be a sysadmin on "___" to perform an offline database transfer.
0xC00292A6	DTS_E_TRANSFERDBTASK_FTCATALOGSOFFLINEYUKONONLY	Full text catalogs can only be included when performing an offline database transfer between 2 SQL Server 2005 servers.
0xC00292A7	DTS_E_TRANSFERDBTASK_NOOVERWRITEDB	The database "___" already exists on the destination server "___".
0xC00292A8	DTS_E_TRANSFERDBTASK_MUSTHAVESOURCEFILES	At least one source file must be specified.
0xC00292A9	DTS_E_TRANSFERDBTASKS_SRCFILENOTFOUND	Could not find the file "___" in the source database "___".
0xC00292B3	DTS_E_MSMQTASK_FIPS1402COMPLIANCE	The operation requested is not allowed in systems compliant with U.S. FIPS 140-2.
0xC002F210	DTS_E_SQLTASK_ERROREXECUTINGTHEQUERY	Executing the query "___" failed with the following error: "___". Possible failure reasons: Problems with the query, "ResultSet" property not set correctly, parameters not set correctly, or connection not established correctly.
0xC002F300	DTS_E_TRANSFERSPTASK_ERRORREADINGSPNAMES	Error reading stored procedure names from the xml file.
0xC002F301	DTS_E_TRANSFERSPTASK_INVALIDDATANODE	Invalid data node for the Transfer Stored Procedure task.
0xC002F302	DTS_E_TRANSFERTASKS_CONNECTIONTYPEISNOTSMOSERVER	Connection "___" is not of type "SMOServer".
0xC002F303	DTS_E_TRANSFERSPTASK_EXECUTIONFAILED	Execution failed with the following error "___".
0xC002F304	DTS_E_ERROROCCURREDWITHFOLLOWINGMESSAGE	An error occurred with the following error message: "___".
0xC002F305	DTS_E_BITASK_EXECUTION_FAILED	Bulk insert execution failed.
0xC002F306	DTS_E_FSTASK_INVALIDDESTPATH	Invalid destination path.
0xC002F307	DTS_E_FSTASK_CANTCREATEDIR	Cannot create directory. User chose to fail the task if directory exists.
0xC002F308	DTS_E_SQLTASK_ODBCNOSUPPORTTRANSACTION	The task has a transaction option of "Required" and connection "___" is of type "ODBC". ODBC connections don't support transactions.

Error Code	Symbolic Name	Description
0xC002F309	DTS_E_SQLTASK_ERRORASSIGINGVALUETOVAR	An error occurred while assigning a value to variable " __ "; " __ ".
0xC002F30A	DTS_E_FSTASK_SOURCEISEMPTY	The source is empty.
0xC002F30B	DTS_E_FSTASK_DESTINATIONISEMPTY	The destination is empty.
0xC002F30C	DTS_E_FSTASK_FILEDIRNOTFOUND	File or directory " __ " does not exist.
0xC002F30D	DTS_E_FSTASK_VARSRCRDESTISEMPTY	Variable " __ " is used as a source or destination and is empty.
0xC002F30E	DTS_E_FSTASK_FILEDELETED	File or directory " __ " was deleted.
0xC002F30F	DTS_E_FSTASK_DIRECTORYDELETED	Directory " __ " was deleted.
0xC002F310	DTS_E_WMIDRTASK_VARIABLETYPEISNOTOBJECT	The variable " __ " should be of type object to be assigned a data table.
0xC002F311	DTS_E_WMIDRTASK_VARIABLETYPEISNOTSTRING	The variable " __ " does not have a string data type.
0xC002F312	DTS_E_FTPTASK_CANNOTACQUIRECONNECTION	There was an error acquiring the FTP connection. Verify that a valid connection type is specified in " __ ".
0xC002F313	DTS_E_FTPTASK_CONNECTIONNOTFOUND	Connection manager " __ " cannot be found.
0xC002F314	DTS_E_FTPTASK_FILEUSAGETYPEERROR	File usage type of connection " __ " should be " __ " for operation " __ ".
0xC002F315	DTS_E_TRANSFERTASKS_SOURCECANTBESAMEASDESTINATION	The source server cannot be the same as the destination server.
0xC002F316	DTS_E_ERRMSGTASK_EMPTYSOURCELIST	There are no Error Messages to transfer.
0xC002F317	DTS_E_ERRMSGTASK_DIFFERENTMESSAGEANDLANGUAGESIZES	The lists of error messages and their corresponding languages are of different sizes.
0xC002F318	DTS_E_ERRMSGTASK_ERRORMESSAGEOUTOFRANGE	The error message id " __ " is out of the allowed range of user defined error messages. User defined error message ids are between 50000 and 2147483647.
0xC002F319	DTS_E_TRANSFERTASKS_NOTRANSACTIONSUPPORT	This task cannot participate in a transaction.
0xC002F320	DTS_E_ERRMSGTASK_FAILEDTOTRANSFERERRORMESSAGES	Failed to transfer some or all of the Error Messages.
0xC002F321	DTS_E_ERRMSGTASK_ERRORMESSAGEALREADYEXISTS	The error message " __ " already exists at destination server.
0xC002F324	DTS_E_ERRMSGTASK_ERRORMESSAGECANTBEFOUND	The error message " __ " cannot be found at source server.
0xC002F325	DTS_E_TRANSFERTASKS_EXECUTIONFAILED	Execution failed with the following error: " __ ".

Error Code	Symbolic Name	Description
0xC002F327	DTS_E_JOBSTASK_FAILEDTOTRANSFERJOBS	Failed to transfer the Job(s).
0xC002F330	DTS_E_JOBSTASK_EMPTYSOURCELIST	There are no Jobs to transfer.
0xC002F331	DTS_E_JOBSTASK_JOBEXISTSATDEST	The job "__" already exists at destination server.
0xC002F334	DTS_E_JOBSTASK_JOBCANTBEFOUND	The job "__" cannot be found at source server.
0xC002F337	DTS_E_LOGINSTASK_EMPTYLIST	The list of "Logins" to transfer is empty.
0xC002F338	DTS_E_LOGINSTASK_CANTGETLOGINSNAMELIST	Cannot get the list of "Logins" from source server.
0xC002F340	DTS_E_LOGINSTASK_ERRORLOGINEXISTS	Login "__" already exists at destination server.
0xC002F342	DTS_E_LOGINSTASK_LOGINNOTFOUND	Login "__" does not exist at source.
0xC002F344	DTS_E_LOGINSTASK_FAILEDTOTRANSFERLOGINS	Failed to transfer some or all of the logins.
0xC002F345	DTS_E_STOREDPROCSTASK_FAILEDTOTRANSFERSPS	Failed to transfer the stored procedure(s). More informative error should have been raised.
0xC002F346	DTS_E_STOREDPROCSTASK_STOREDPROCNOTFOUND	Stored Procedure "__" is not found at the source.
0xC002F349	DTS_E_STOREDPROCSTASK_ERRORSTOREDPROCEDUREEXISTS	Stored procedure "__" already exists at destination server.
0xC002F350	DTS_E_STOREDPROCSTASK_EMPTYSOURCELIST	There are no stored procedures to transfer.
0xC002F353	DTS_E_TRANSOBJECTSTASK_FAILEDTOTRANSFEROBJECTS	Failed to transfer the object(s).
0xC002F354	DTS_E_TRANSOBJECTSTASK_EMPTYLIST	The list of "Objects" to transfer is empty.
0xC002F355	DTS_E_TRANSOBJECTSTASK_NOSPATSOURCE	Stored procedure "__" does not exist at the source.
0xC002F356	DTS_E_TRANSOBJECTSTASK_SPALREADYATDEST	Stored procedure "__" already exists at destination.
0xC002F357	DTS_E_TRANSOBJECTSTASK_ERRORHANDLINGSPS	An error occurred while trying to get set the Stored Procedures list to transfer: "__".
0xC002F359	DTS_E_TRANSOBJECTSTASK_NORULEATSOURCE	Rule "__" does not exist at the source.
0xC002F360	DTS_E_TRANSOBJECTSTASK_RULEALREADYATDEST	Rule "__" already exists at destination.
0xC002F361	DTS_E_TRANSOBJECTSTASK_ERRORHANDLINGRULES	An error occurred while trying to get set the Rules list to transfer: "__".
0xC002F363	DTS_E_TRANSOBJECTSTASK_NOTABLEATSOURCE	Table "__" does not exist at the source.
0xC002F364	DTS_E_TRANSOBJECTSTASK_TABLEALREADYATDEST	Table "__" already exists at destination.

Error Code	Symbolic Name	Description
0xC002F365	DTS_E_TRANSOBJECTSTASK_ ERRORHANDLINGTABLES	An error occurred while trying to get set the Tables list to transfer: "___".
0xC002F367	DTS_E_TRANSOBJECTSTASK_NOVIEWATSOURCE	View "___" does not exist at the source.
0xC002F368	DTS_E_TRANSOBJECTSTASK_ VIEWALREADYATDEST	View "___" already exists at destination.
0xC002F369	DTS_E_TRANSOBJECTSTASK_ ERRORHANDLINGVIEWS	An error occurred while trying to get set the Views list to transfer: "___".
0xC002F371	DTS_E_TRANSOBJECTSTASK_NOUDFATSOURCE	User Defined Function "___" does not exist at the source.
0xC002F372	DTS_E_TRANSOBJECTSTASK_UDFALREADYATDEST	User Defined Function "___" already exists at destination.
0xC002F373	DTS_E_TRANSOBJECTSTASK_ ERRORHANDLINGUDFS	An error occurred while trying to get set the User Defined Functions list to transfer: "___".
0xC002F375	DTS_E_TRANSOBJECTSTASK_ NODEFAULTATSOURCE	Default "___" does not exist at the source.
0xC002F376	DTS_E_TRANSOBJECTSTASK_ DEFAULTALREADYATDEST	Default "___" already exists at destination.
0xC002F377	DTS_E_TRANSOBJECTSTASK_ ERRORHANDLINGDEFAULTS	An error occurred while trying to get set the Defaults list to transfer: "___".
0xC002F379	DTS_E_TRANSOBJECTSTASK_NOUDDTATSOURCE	User Defined Data Type "___" does not exist at the source.
0xC002F380	DTS_E_TRANSOBJECTSTASK_ UDDTALREADYATDEST	User Defined Data Type "___" already exists at destination.
0xC002F381	DTS_E_TRANSOBJECTSTASK_ ERRORHANDLINGUDDTS	An error occurred while trying to get set the User Defined Data Types list to transfer: "___".
0xC002F383	DTS_E_TRANSOBJECTSTASK_NOPFATSOURCE	Partition Function "___" does not exist at the source.
0xC002F384	DTS_E_TRANSOBJECTSTASK_PFALREADYATDEST	Partition Function "___" already exists at destination.
0xC002F385	DTS_E_TRANSOBJECTSTASK_ERRORHANDLINGPFS	An error occurred while trying to get set the Partition Functions list to transfer: "___".
0xC002F387	DTS_E_TRANSOBJECTSTASK_NOPSATSOURCE	Partition Scheme "___" does not exist at the source.
0xC002F388	DTS_E_TRANSOBJECTSTASK_PSALREADYATDEST	Partition Scheme "___" already exists at destination.
0xC002F389	DTS_E_TRANSOBJECTSTASK_ERRORHANDLINGPSS	An error occurred while trying to get set the Partition Schemes list to transfer: "___".

Error Code	Symbolic Name	Description
0xC002F391	DTS_E_TRANSOBJECTSTASK_NOSCHEMAATSOURCE	Schema "___" does not exist at the source.
0xC002F392	DTS_E_TRANSOBJECTSTASK_SCHEMAALREADYATDEST	Schema "___" already exists at destination.
0xC002F393	DTS_E_TRANSOBJECTSTASK_ERRORHANDLINGSCHEMAS	An error occurred while trying to get set the Schemas list to transfer: "___".
0xC002F395	DTS_E_TRANSOBJECTSTASK_NOSQLASSEMBLYATSOURCE	SqlAssembly "___" does not exist at the source.
0xC002F396	DTS_E_TRANSOBJECTSTASK_SQLASSEMBLYALREADYATDEST	SqlAssembly "___" already exists at destination.
0xC002F397	DTS_E_TRANSOBJECTSTASK_ERRORHANDLINGSQLASSEMBLIES	An error occurred while trying to get set the SqlAssemblys list to transfer: "___".
0xC002F399	DTS_E_TRANSOBJECTSTASK_NOAGGREGATEATSOURCE	User Defined Aggregate "___" does not exist at the source.
0xC002F400	DTS_E_TRANSOBJECTSTASK_AGGREGATEALREADYATDEST	User Defined Aggregate "___" already exists at destination.
0xC002F401	DTS_E_TRANSOBJECTSTASK_ERRORHANDLINGAGGREGATES	An error occurred while trying to get set the User Defined Aggregates list to transfer: "___".
0xC002F403	DTS_E_TRANSOBJECTSTASK_NOTYPEATSOURCE	User Defined Type "___" does not exist at the source.
0xC002F404	DTS_E_TRANSOBJECTSTASK_TYPEALREADYATDEST	User Defined Type "___" already exists at destination.
0xC002F405	DTS_E_TRANSOBJECTSTASK_ERRORHANDLINGTYPES	An error occurred while trying to get set the User Defined Types list to transfer: "___".
0xC002F407	DTS_E_TRANSOBJECTSTASK_NOXMLSCHEMACOLLECTIONATSOURCE	XmlSchemaCollection "___" does not exist at the source.
0xC002F408	DTS_E_TRANSOBJECTSTASK_XMLSCHEMACOLLECTIONALREADYATDEST	XmlSchemaCollection "___" already exists at destination.
0xC002F409	DTS_E_TRANSOBJECTSTASK_ERRORHANDLINGXMLSCHEMACOLLECTIONS	An error occurred while trying to get set the XmlSchemaCollections list to transfer: "___".
0xC002F411	DTS_E_TRANSOBJECTSTASK_SUPPORTEDONYUKONONLY	Objects of type "___" are only supported between SQL Server 2005 servers.
0xC002F413	DTS_E_LOGINSTASK_EMPTYDATABASELIST	The databases list is empty.

Error Code	Symbolic Name	Description
0xC002F414	DTS_E_TRANSOBJECTSTASK_NOLOGINATSOURCE	Login " __ " does not exist at the source.
0xC002F416	DTS_E_TRANSOBJECTSTASK_LOGINALREADYATDEST	Login " __ " already exists at destination.
0xC002F417	DTS_E_TRANSOBJECTSTASK_ERRORHANDLINGLOGINS	An error occurred while trying to get set the Logins list to transfer: " __ ".
0xC002F419	DTS_E_TRANSOBJECTSTASK_NOUSERATSOURCE	User " __ " does not exist at the source.
0xC002F41B	DTS_E_TRANSOBJECTSTASK_USERALREADYATDEST	User " __ " already exists at destination.
0xC002F41C	DTS_E_TRANSOBJECTSTASK_ERRORHANDLINGUSERS	An error occurred while trying to get set the Users list to transfer: " __ ".
0xC002F41F	DTS_E_BITASK_CANNOTRETAINCONNINTRANSACTION	The task cannot have a retained connection manager in a transaction.
0xC0047000	DTS_E_CYCLEINEXECUTIONTREE	An execution tree contains a cycle.
0xC0047001	DTS_E_DISCONNECTEDOBJECT	The __ object " __ " (__) is disconnected from the layout.
0xC0047002	DTS_E_INVALIDOBJECTID	The ID for the layout object is not valid.
0xC0047003	DTS_E_INPUTWITHOUTPATHS	A required input object is not connected to a path object.
0xC0047005	DTS_E_INVALIDSYNCHRONOUSINPUT	__ has an invalid synchronous input ID __.
0xC0047006	DTS_E_INVALIDOUTPUTLINEAGEID	__ has lineage ID __, but should have had __.
0xC0047008	DTS_E_DUPLICATENAMESINCOLLECTION	The package contains two objects with the duplicate name of " __ " and " __ ".
0xC0047009	DTS_E_INVALIDEXCLUSIONGROUP	The " __ " and the " __ " are in the same exclusion group, but they do not have the same synchronous input.
0xC004700A	DTS_E_DUPLICATELINEAGEIDSINCOLLECTION	Two objects in the same collection have a duplicate lineage ID of __. The objects are __ and __.
0xC004700B	DTS_E_VALIDATIONFAILEDONLAYOUT	The layout failed validation.
0xC004700C	DTS_E_VALIDATIONFAILEDONCOMPONENTS	One or more components failed validation.
0xC004700D	DTS_E_VALIDATIONFAILED	The layout and one or more components failed validation.
0xC004700E	DTS_E_THREADSTARTUPFAILED	The Data Flow task engine failed at startup because it cannot create one or more required threads.
0xC004700F	DTS_E_CANTGETMUTEX	A thread failed to create a mutex at initialization.

Error Code	Symbolic Name	Description
0xC0047010	DTS_E_CANTGETSEMAPHORE	A thread failed to create a semaphore at initialization.
0xC0047011	DTS_E_BUFFERFAILUREDETAILS	The system reports __ percent memory load. There are __ bytes of physical memory with __ bytes free. There are __ bytes of virtual memory with __ bytes free. The paging file has __ bytes with __ bytes free.
0xC0047012	DTS_E_BUFFERALLOCFAILED	A buffer failed while allocating __ bytes.
0xC0047013	DTS_E_CANTCREATEBUFFERMANAGER	The Buffer Manager could not be created.
0xC0047015	DTS_E_BUFFERBADSIZE	Buffer Type __ had a size of __ bytes.
0xC0047016	DTS_E_DANGLINGWITHPATH	__ is marked as dangling, but has a path attached to it.
0xC0047017	DTS_E_INDIVIDUALVALIDATIONFAILED	__ failed validation and returned error code 0x__.
0xC0047018	DTS_E_INDIVIDUALPOSTEXECUTEFAILED	__ failed the post-execute phase and returned error code 0x__.
0xC0047019	DTS_E_INDIVIDUALPREPAREFAILED	__ failed the prepare phase and returned error code 0x__.
0xC004701A	DTS_E_INDIVIDUALPREEXECUTEFAILED	__ failed the pre-execute phase and returned error code 0x__.
0xC004701B	DTS_E_INDIVIDUALCLEANUPFAILED	__ failed the cleanup phase and returned error code 0x__.
0xC004701C	DTS_E_INVALIDINPUTLINEAGEID	__ has lineage ID __ that was not previously used in the Data Flow task.
0xC004701E	DTS_E_EXECUTIONTREECYCLE	Cannot connect __ to __ because a cycle would be created.
0xC004701F	DTS_E_CANTCOMPARE	The data type " __ " cannot be compared. Comparison of that data type is not supported, so it cannot be sorted or used as a key.
0xC0047020	DTS_E_REFUSEDFORSHUTDOWN	This thread has shut down and is not accepting buffers for input.
0xC0047021	DTS_E_THREADFAILED	Thread " __ " has exited with error code 0x__.
0xC0047022	DTS_E_PROCESSINPUTFAILED	The ProcessInput method on component " __ " (__) failed with error code 0x__. The identified component returned an error from the ProcessInput method. The error is specific to the component, but the error is fatal and will cause the Data Flow task to stop running.
0xC0047023	DTS_E_CANTREALIZEVIRTUALBUFFERS	A set of virtual buffers cannot be realized.
0xC0047024	DTS_E_PIPELINETOOCOMPLEX	The number of threads required for this pipeline is __, which is more than the system limit of __. The pipeline requires too many threads as configured. There are either too many asynchronous outputs, or EngineThreads property is set too high. Split the pipeline into multiple packages, or reduce the value of the EngineThreads property.
0xC0047028	DTS_E_SCHEDULERCOULDNOTCOUNTSOURCES	The Data Flow engine scheduler cannot obtain a count of the sources in the layout.

Error Code	Symbolic Name	Description
0xC0047029	DTS_E_SCHEDULERCOULDNOTCOUNTDESTINATIONS	The Data Flow engine scheduler cannot obtain a count of the destinations in the layout.
0xC004702A	DTS_E_COMPONENTVIEWISUNAVAILABLE	The component view is unavailable. Make sure the component view has been created.
0xC004702B	DTS_E_INCORRECTCOMPONENTVIEWID	The component view ID is incorrect. The component view may be out of synchronization. Try releasing the component view and recreating it.
0xC004702C	DTS_E_BUFFERNOTLOCKED	This buffer is not locked and cannot be manipulated.
0xC004702D	DTS_E_CANTBUILDBUFFERTYPE	The Data Flow task cannot allocate memory to build a buffer definition. The buffer definition had __ columns.
0xC004702E	DTS_E_CANTREGISTERBUFFERTYPE	The Data Flow task cannot register a buffer type. The type had __ columns and was for execution tree __.
0xC004702F	DTS_E_INVALIDUSESDISPOSITIONSVALUE	The UsesDispositions property cannot be changed from its initial value. This occurs when the XML is edited and the UsesDispositions value is modified. This value is set by the component when it is added to the package and is not allowed to change.
0xC0047030	DTS_E_THREADFAILEDINITIALIZE	The Data Flow task failed to initialize a required thread and cannot begin execution. The thread previously reported a specific error.
0xC0047031	DTS_E_THREADFAILEDCREATE	The Data Flow task failed to create a required thread and cannot begin running. This usually occurs when there is an out-of-memory state.
0xC0047032	DTS_E_EXECUTIONTREECYCLEADDINGSYNCHRONOUSINPUT	The synchronous input of " __ " cannot be set to " __ " because a cycle would be created.
0xC0047033	DTS_E_INVALIDCUSTOMPROPERTYNAME	A custom property named " __ " is invalid because there is a stock property with that name. A custom property cannot have the same name as a stock property on the same object.
0xC0047035	DTS_E_BUFFERLOCKUNDERFLOW	The buffer was already unlocked.
0xC0047036	DTS_E_INDIVIDUALCACHEINTERFACESFAILED	__ failed initialization and returned error code 0x__.
0xC0047037	DTS_E_INDIVIDUALRELEASEINTERFACESFAILED	__ failed during shut down and returned error code 0x__. A component failed to release its interfaces.

Error Code	Symbolic Name	Description
0xC0047038	DTS_E_PRIMEOUTPUTFAILED	The PrimeOutput method on __ returned error code 0x__. The component returned a failure code when the pipeline engine called PrimeOutput(). The meaning of the failure code is defined by the component, but the error is fatal and the pipeline stopped executing.
0xC0047039	DTS_E_THREADCANCELLED	Thread " __ " received a shutdown signal and is terminating. The user requested a shutdown, or an error in another thread is causing the pipeline to shutdown.
0xC004703A	DTS_E_DISTRIBUTORCANTSETPROPERTY	Distributor for thread " __ " failed to initialize property " __ " on component " __ " because of error 0x__8X. The distributor could not initialize the component's property and cannot continue running.
0xC004703B	DTS_E_CANTREGISTERVIEWBUFFERTYPE	The Data Flow task cannot register a view buffer type. The type had __ columns and was for input ID __.
0xC004703F	DTS_E_CANTCREATEEXECUTIONTREE	There is not enough memory to create an execution tree.
0xC0047040	DTS_E_CANTINSERTINTOHASHTABLE	There is not enough memory to insert an object into the hash table.
0xC0047041	DTS_E_OBJECTNOTINHASHTABLE	The object is not in the hash table.
0xC0047043	DTS_E_CANTCREATECOMPONENTVIEW	Cannot create a component view because another one already exists. Only one component view can exist at a time.
0xC0047046	DTS_E_LAYOUTCANTSETUSAGETYPE	At input " __ " (__), the virtual input column collection does not contain a virtual input column with lineage ID __.
0xC0047047	DTS_E_WRONGOBJECTTYPE	The requested object has the incorrect object type.
0xC0047048	DTS_E_CANTCREATESPOOLFILE	The buffer manager cannot create a temporary storage file on any path in the BufferTempStoragePath property. There is an incorrect file name or no permission.
0xC0047049	DTS_E_SEEKFAILED	The buffer manager could not seek to offset __ in file " __ ". The file is damaged.
0xC004704A	DTS_E_EXTENDFAILED	The buffer manager cannot extend the file " __ " to length __. There was insufficient disk space.
0xC004704B	DTS_E_FILEWRITEFAILED	The buffer manager cannot write __ bytes to file " __ ". There was insufficient disk space or quota.
0xC004704C	DTS_E_FILEREADFAILED	The buffer manager cannot read __ bytes from file " __ ". The file is damaged.
0xC004704D	DTS_E_VIRTUALNOTSEQUENTIAL	Buffer ID __ supports other virtual buffers and cannot be placed into sequential mode. IDTSBuffer90.SetSequentialMode was called on a buffer that supports virtual buffers.

Error Code	Symbolic Name	Description
0xC004704E	DTS_E_BUFFERISREADONLY	This operation could not be performed because buffer is in read-only mode. A read-only buffer cannot be modified.
0xC004704F	DTS_E_EXECUTIONTREECYCLESETTINGID	ID __ cannot be set to __ because a cycle would be created.
0xC0047050	DTS_E_NOMOREBUFFERTYPES	The buffer manager ran out of memory while trying to extend the table of buffer types. This is caused by an out-of-memory condition.
0xC0047051	DTS_E_CANTCREATENEWTYPE	The buffer manager failed to create a new buffer type.
0xC0047053	DTS_E_SCHEDULERBADTREE	The Data Flow engine scheduler failed to retrieve the execution tree with index __ from the layout. The scheduler received a count containing more execution trees than actually exist.
0xC0047056	DTS_E_CANTCREATEPRIMEOUTPUTBUFFER	The Data Flow task failed to create a buffer to call PrimeOutput for output " __ " (__) on component " __ " (__). This error usually occurs due to an out-of-memory condition.
0xC0047057	DTS_E_SCHEDULERTHREADMEMORY	The Data Flow engine scheduler failed to create a thread object because not enough memory is available. This is caused by an out-of-memory condition.
0xC004705A	DTS_E_SCHEDULEROBJECT	The Data Flow engine scheduler cannot retrieve object with ID __ from the layout. The Data Flow engine scheduler previously located an object that is now no longer available.
0xC004705B	DTS_E_PREPARETREENODEFAILED	The Data Flow task failed to prepare buffers for the execution tree node beginning at output " __ " (__).
0xC004705C	DTS_E_CANTCREATEVIRTUALBUFFER	The Data Flow task cannot create a virtual buffer to prepare for execution.
0xC004705E	DTS_E_NOMOREIDS	The maximum ID has been reached. There are no more IDs available to assign to objects.
0xC004705F	DTS_E_ALREADYATTACHED	The __ is already attached and cannot be attached again. Detach it and try again.
0xC0047060	DTS_E_OUTPUTCOLUMNNAMECONFLICT	Column name " __ " on output " __ " cannot be used because it conflicts with a column of the same name on synchronous input " __ ".
0xC0047061	DTS_E_EOFANNOUNCEMENTFAILED	The Data Flow task cannot create a buffer to mark the end of the rowset.
0xC0047062	DTS_E_USERCOMPONENTEXCEPTION	A managed user component has thrown exception " __ ".
0xC0047063	DTS_E_SCHEDULERMEMORY	The Data Flow engine scheduler cannot allocate enough memory for the execution structures. The system was low on memory before execution started.

Error Code	Symbolic Name	Description
0xC0047064	DTS_E_BUFFERNOOBJECTMEMORY	An out-of-memory condition prevented the creation of the buffer object.
0xC0047065	DTS_E_BUFFERNOMAPMEMORY	An out-of-memory condition prevents the mapping of a buffer's lineage IDs to DTP_HCOL indexes.
0xC0047066	DTS_E_INDIVIDUALPUTVARIABLESFAILED	
0xC0047067	DTS_E_INDIVIDUALPUTCOMPONENTMETADATAFAILED	The "__" failed to cache the component metadata object and returned error code 0x__.
0xC0047068	DTS_E_SORTEDOUTPUTHASINVALIDSORTKEYPOSITION	"__" has a non-zero SortKeyPosition, but its value (__) is too large. It must be less than or equal to the number of columns.
0xC004706A	DTS_E_SORTEDOUTPUTHASINVALIDSORTKEYPOSITIONS	The IsSorted property of __ is set to TRUE, but the absolute values of the non-zero output column SortKeyPositions do not form a monotonically increasing sequence, starting at one.
0xC004706B	DTS_E_INDIVIDUALVALIDATIONSTATUSFAILED	"__" failed validation and returned validation status "__".
0xC004706C	DTS_E_CANTCREATECOMPONENT	Component "__" could not be created and returned error code 0x__. Make sure that the component is registered correctly.
0xC004706D	DTS_E_COMPONENTNOTREGISTERED	The module containing "__" is not registered or installed correctly.
0xC004706E	DTS_E_COMPONENTNOTFOUND	The module containing "__" cannot be located, even though it is registered.
0xC004706F	DTS_E_BINARYCODENOTFOUND	The script component is configured to pre-compile the script, but binary code is not found. Please visit the IDE in Script Component Editor by clicking Design Script button to cause binary code to be generated.
0xC0047070	DTS_E_CANTCREATEBLOBFILE	The buffer manager cannot create a file to spool a long object on the directories named in the BLOBTempStoragePath property. Either an incorrect file name was provided, or there are no permissions.
0xC0047071	DTS_E_SYNCHRONOUSIDMISMATCH	The SynchronousInputID property on "__" was __, and __ was expected.
0xC0047072	DTS_E_OBJECTIDNOTFOUND	No object exists with the ID __.
0xC0047073	DTS_E_OBJECTIDLOOKUPFAILED	Unable to locate an object with ID __ because of the error code 0x__.
0xC0047074	DTS_E_INVALIDCODEPAGE	The code page __ specified on output column "__" (__) is not valid. Select a different code page for output column "__".
0xC0047075	DTS_E_INDIVIDUALPUTEVENTINFOSFAILED	The EventInfos collection could not be cached by "__" and returned error code 0x__.
0xC0047077	DTS_E_DUPLICATEOUTPUTCOLUMNNAMES	The name for "__" is a duplicate. All names must be unique.
0xC0047078	DTS_E_NOOUTPUTCOLUMNFORINPUTCOLUMN	There is no output column associated with input column "__" (__).

Error Code	Symbolic Name	Description
0xC0047079	DTS_E_EXCLGRPNOSYNCINP	" __ " has a virtual buffer extending from a root source. There is an exclusion group that is not zero with a synchronous input that is zero.
0xC004707A	DTS_E_ERROROUTCANTBEONSYNCNONEXCLUSIVEOUTPUT	" __ " cannot be an error output because error outputs cannot be placed on synchronous, non-exclusive outputs.
0xC004707B	DTS_E_EXPREVALDIVBYZERO	A divide-by-zero error occurred. The right side operand evaluates to zero in the expression " __ ".
0xC004707C	DTS_E_EXPREVALLITERALOVERFLOW	The literal " __ " is too large to fit into type __. The magnitude of the literal overflows the type.
0xC004707D	DTS_E_EXPREVALBINARYOPNUMERICOVERFLOW	The result of the binary operation " __ " on data types __ and __ exceeds the maximum size for numeric types. The operand types could not be implicitly cast into a numeric (DT_NUMERIC) result without loss of precision or scale. To perform this operation, one or both operands need to be explicitly cast with a cast operator.
0xC004707E	DTS_E_EXPREVALBINARYOPOVERFLOW	The result of the binary operation " __ " exceeds the maximum size for result data type " __ ". The magnitude of the result of the operation overflows the type of the result.
0xC004707F	DTS_E_EXPREVALFUNCTIONOVERFLOW	The result of the function call " __ " is too large to fit in type " __ ". The magnitude of the result of the function call overflows the type of the operand. An explicit cast to a larger type may be required.
0xC0047080	DTS_E_EXPREVALBINARYTYPEMISMATCH	The data types " __ and " __ " are incompatible for binary operator " __ ". The operand types could not be implicitly cast into compatible types for the operation. To perform this operation, one or both operands need to be explicitly cast with a cast operator.
0xC0047081	DTS_E_EXPREVALUNSUPPORTEDBINARYTYPE	The data type " __ " cannot be used with binary operator " __ ". The type of one or both of the operands is not supported for the operation. To perform this operation, one or both operands need to be explicitly cast with a cast operator.
0xC0047082	DTS_E_EXPREVALBINARYSIGNMISMATCH	There is a sign mismatch for the bitwise binary operator " __ " in operation " __ ". Both operands for this operator must be positive or negative.
0xC0047083	DTS_E_EXPREVALBINARYOPERATIONFAILED	The binary operation " __ " failed with error code 0x__. An internal error occurred, or an out-of-memory condition exists.

Error Code	Symbolic Name	Description
0xC0047084	DTS_E_ EXPREVALBINARYOPERATIONSETTYPEFAILED	Attempt to set the result type of binary operation " __ " failed with error code 0x__.
0xC0047085	DTS_E_EXPREVALSTRINGCOMPARISONFAILED	Comparing " __ " to string " __ " failed.
0xC0047086	DTS_E_EXPREVALUNSUPPORTEDUNNARYTYPE	The data type " __ " cannot be used with unary operator " __ ". This operand type is not supported for the operation. To perform this operation, the operand needs to be explicitly cast with a cast operator.
0xC0047087	DTS_E_EXPREVALUNARYOPERATIONFAILED	The unary operation " __ " failed with error code 0x__. An internal error occurred, or there is an out-of-memory condition.
0xC0047088	DTS_E_ EXPREVALUNARYOPERATIONSETTYPEFAILED	Attempt to set the result type of unary operation " __ " failed with error code 0x__.
0xC0047089	DTS_E_EXPREVALPARAMTYPEMISMATCH	The function " __ " does not support the data type " __ " for parameter number __. The type of the parameter could not be implicitly cast into a compatible type for the function. To perform this operation, the operand needs to be explicitly cast with a cast operator.
0xC004708A	DTS_E_EXPREVALINVALIDFUNCTION	The function " __ " was not recognized. Either the function name is incorrect or does not exist.
0xC004708B	DTS_E_EXPREVALFNSUBSTRINGINVALIDLENGTH	The length __ is not valid for function " __ ". The length parameter cannot be negative. Change the length parameter to zero or a positive value.
0xC004708C	DTS_E_ EXPREVALFNSUBSTRINGINVALIDSTARTINDEX	The start index __ is not valid for function " __ ". The start index value must be an integer greater than 0. Start index is one-based, not zero-based.
0xC004708E	DTS_E_EXPREVALCHARMAPPINGFAILED	The function " __ " cannot perform the character mapping on string " __ ".
0xC004708F	DTS_E_EXPREVALINVALIDDATEPART	" __ " is not a valid date part for function " __ ".
0xC0047090	DTS_E_EXPREVALINVALIDNULLPARAM	Parameter number __ of the function NULL with data type " __ " is not valid. The parameters of NULL() must be static, and cannot contain dynamic elements such as input columns.
0xC0047091	DTS_E_EXPREVALINVALIDNULLPARAMTYPE	Parameter number __ of the function NULL with data type " __ " is not an integer. A parameter of NULL() must be an integer or a type that can be converted to an integer.
0xC0047092	DTS_E_EXPREVALFUNCTIONPARAMNOTSTATIC	Parameter number __ of the function " __ " is not static. This parameter must be static, and cannot contain dynamic elements such as input columns.

Error Code	Symbolic Name	Description
0xC0047093	DTS_E_EXPREVALINVALIDCASTPARAM	Parameter number __ of the cast to data type " __ " is not valid. The parameters of cast operators must be static, and cannot contain dynamic elements such as input columns.
0xC0047094	DTS_E_EXPREVALINVALIDCASTPARAMTYPE	Parameter number __ of the cast to data type " __ " is not an integer. A parameter of a cast operator must be an integer or a type that can be converted to an integer.
0xC0047095	DTS_E_EXPREVALINVALIDCAST	Cannot cast expression " __ " from data type " __ " to data type " __ ". The requested cast is not supported.
0xC0047096	DTS_E_EXPREVALINVALIDTOKEN	Attempt to parse the expression " __ " failed. The token " __ " at line number " __ ", character number " __ " was not recognized. The expression cannot be parsed because it contains invalid elements at the location specified.
0xC0047097	DTS_E_EXPREVALUNEXPECTEDPARSEERROR	An error occurred when parsing the expression " __ ". The expression failed to parse for an unknown reason.
0xC0047098	DTS_E_EXPREVALFAILEDTOPARSEEXPRESSIONWITHHR	Attempt to parse the expression " __ " failed and returned error code 0x__. The expression cannot be parsed. It might contain invalid elements or it might not be well-formed. There may also be an out-of-memory error.
0xC0047099	DTS_E_EXPREVALFAILEDTOPARSEEXPRESSION	The expression " __ " is not valid and cannot be parsed. The expression may contain invalid elements or it may not be well-formed.
0xC004709A	DTS_E_EXPREVALEXPRESSIONEMPTY	There was no expression to compute. An attempt was made to compute or get the string of an empty expression.
0xC004709B	DTS_E_EXPREVALCOMPUTEFAILED	Attempt to compute the expression " __ " failed with error code 0x__.
0xC004709C	DTS_E_EXPREVALBUILDSTRINGFAILED	Attempt to generate a string representation of the expression failed with error code 0x__. Failed when attempting to generate a displayable string that represents the expression.
0xC004709D	DTS_E_EXPREVALCANNOTCONVERTRESULT	Cannot convert the expression result data type " __ " to the column data type " __ ". The result of the expression should be written to an input/output column, but the data type of the expression cannot be converted to the data type of the column.
0xC004709E	DTS_E_EXPREVALCONDITIONALOPINVALIDCONDITIONTYPE	The conditional expression " __ " of the conditional operator has an invalid data type of " __ ". The conditional expression of the conditional operator must return a Boolean, which is type DT_BOOL.

Error Code	Symbolic Name	Description
0xC004709F	DTS_E_EXPREVALCONDITIONALOPTYPEMISMATCH	The data types "___" and "___" are incompatible for the conditional operator. The operand types cannot be implicitly cast into compatible types for the conditional operation. To perform this operation, one or both operands need to be explicitly cast with a cast operator.
0xC00470A0	DTS_E_EXPREVALCONDITIONALOPSETTYPEFAILED	Attempt to set the result type of conditional operation "___" failed with error code 0x___.
0xC00470A1	DTS_E_BUFFERORPHANED	This buffer has been orphaned. The buffer manager has shut down, leaving an outstanding buffer and no cleanup will occur for the buffer. There is a potential for memory leaks and other problems.
0xC00470A2	DTS_E_EXPREVALINPUTCOLUMNNAMENOTFOUND	Attempt to find the input column named "___" failed with error code 0x___. The input column specified was not found in the input column collection.
0xC00470A3	DTS_E_EXPREVALINPUTCOLUMNIDNOTFOUND	Attempt to find the input column with lineage ID ___ failed with error code 0x___. The input column was not found in the input column collection.
0xC00470A4	DTS_E_EXPREVALNOINPUTCOLUMNCOLLECTIONFORCOLUMNNAME	The expression contains unrecognized token "___". If "___" is a variable, it should be expressed as "@___". The specified token is not valid. If the token is intended to be a variable name, it should be prefixed with the @ symbol.
0xC00470A5	DTS_E_EXPREVALNOINPUTCOLUMNCOLLECTIONFORCOLUMNID	The expression contains unrecognized token "#___".
0xC00470A6	DTS_E_EXPREVALVARIABLENOTFOUND	The variable "___" was not found in the Variables collection. The variable might not exist in the correct scope.
0xC00470A7	DTS_E_EXPREVALINVALIDTOKENSTATE	Attempt to parse the expression "___" failed. The expression might contain an invalid token, an incomplete token, or an invalid element. It might not be well-formed, or might be missing part of a required element such as a parenthesis.
0xC00470A8	DTS_E_BLANKOUTPUTCOLUMNNAME	The name for "___" is blank, and names cannot be blank.
0xC00470A9	DTS_E_HASSIDEEFFECTSWITHSYNCINP	The "___" has the HasSideEffects property set to TRUE, but "___" is synchronous and cannot have side effects. Set the HasSideEffects property to FALSE.

Error Code	Symbolic Name	Description
0xC00470AA	DTS_E_EXPREVALINVALIDCASTCODEPAGE	The value, ___, specified for the code page parameter of the cast to data type "___", is not valid. The code page is not installed on the machine.
0xC00470AB	DTS_E_EXPREVALINVALIDCASTPRECISION	The value ___ specified for the precision parameter of the cast to data type "___" is not valid. Precision must be in the range ___ to ___ and the precision value is out of range for the type cast.
0xC00470AC	DTS_E_EXPREVALINVALIDCASTSCALE	The value ___ specified for the scale parameter of the cast to data type "___" is not valid. The scale must be in the range ___ to ___ and the scale value is out of range for the type cast. Scale must not exceed precision and must be positive.
0xC00470AD	DTS_E_NONSORTEDOUTPUTHASSORTKEYPOSITIONS	The IsSorted property for "___" is false, but ___ of its output columns' SortKeyPositions are non-zero.
0xC00470AF	DTS_E_EXPREVALCONDITIONALOPCODEPAGEMISMATCH	The code pages must match for operands of conditional operation "___" for type ___. The code page of the left operand does not match the code page of the right operand. For the conditional operator on the specified type, the code pages must be the same.
0xC00470B1	DTS_E_REFERENCEDMETADATABADCOUNT	Input "___" (___) references input "___" (___), but they do not have the same number of columns. Input ___ has ___ columns, while input ___ has ___ columns.
0xC00470B2	DTS_E_OBJECTLINEAGEIDNOTFOUND	No object exists with a lineage ID of ___.
0xC00470B3	DTS_E_FILENAMEOUTPUTCOLUMNNOTFOUND	The output column for the file name cannot be found.
0xC00470B4	DTS_E_FILENAMEOUTPUTCOLUMNINVALIDDATATYPE	The output column for the file name is not a null-terminated Unicode character string, which is data type DT_WSTR.
0xC00470B5	DTS_E_DISTRIBUTORADDFAILED	A distributor failed to give a buffer to thread "___" because of error 0x___. The target thread is probably shutting down.
0xC00470B6	DTS_E_LOCALENOTINSTALLED	The LocaleID ___ is not installed on this system.
0xC00470B7	DTS_E_EXPREVALILLEGALHEXESCAPEINSTRINGLITERAL	The string literal "___" contains an illegal hexadecimal escape sequence of "\x___". The escape sequence is not supported in string literals in the expression evaluator. The hexadecimal escape sequences must be of the form \xhhhh where h is a valid hexadecimal digit.
0xC00470B8	DTS_E_EXPREVALILLEGALESCAPEINSTRINGLITERAL	The string literal "___" contains an illegal escape sequence of "___". The escape sequence is not supported in string literals in the expression evaluator. If a backslash is needed in the string, use a double backslash, "\\".
0xC00470B9	DTS_E_NOOUTPUTCOLUMNS	"___" contains no output columns. An asynchronous output must contain output columns.

Error Code	Symbolic Name	Description
0xC00470BA	DTS_E_LOBDATATYPENOTSUPPORTED	The " __ " has a long object data type of DT_TEXT, DT_NTEXT, or DT_IMAGE, which is not supported.
0xC00470BB	DTS_E_OUTPUTWITHMULTIPLEERRORS	Output ID __ was given multiple error output configurations. First __ and __, then __ and __.
0xC00470BC	DTS_E_	The OLE DB provider failed during the data type conversion verification for " __ ".
		FAILEDDURINGOLEDBDATATYPECONVERSIONCHECK
0xC00470BD	DTS_E_BUFFERISEOR	This buffer represents the end of the rowset and its row count cannot be altered. An attempt was made to call AddRow or RemoveRow on a buffer that has the end of rowset flag.
0xC00470BE	DTS_E_EXPREVALUNSUPPORTEDTYPE	The data type " __ " is not supported in an expression. The specified type is not supported or is not valid.
0xC00470BF	DTS_E_PRIMEOUTPUTNOEOR	The PrimeOutput method on " __ " returned success, but did not report an end of the rowset. There is an error in the component. It should have reported an end-of-row. The pipeline will shut down execution to avoid unpredictable results.
0xC00470C0	DTS_E_EXPREVALDATACONVERSIONOVERFLOW	An overflow occurred while converting from data type " __ " to data type " __ ". The source type is too large for the destination type.
0xC00470C1	DTS_E_EXPREVALDATACONVERSIONNOTSUPPORTED	Conversion from data type " __ " to data type " __ " is unsupported. The source type cannot be converted to the destination type.
0xC00470C2	DTS_E_EXPREVALDATACONVERSIONFAILED	Error code 0x__ occurred attempting to convert from data type __ to data type __.
0xC00470C3	DTS_E_EXPREVALCONDITIONALOPERATIONFAILED	The conditional operation " __ " failed with error code 0x__. There was an internal error or an out-of-memory error.
0xC00470C4	DTS_E_EXPREVALCASTFAILED	Casting expression " __ " from data type " __ " to data type " __ " failed with error code 0x__.
0xC00470C5	DTS_E_EXPREVALFUNCTIONCOMPUTEFAILED	Evaluating function " __ " failed with error code 0x__.
0xC00470C6	DTS_E_EXPREVALFUNCTIONCONVERTPARAMTOMEMBERFAILED	Parameter number __ of the function " __ " cannot be converted to a static value.

Error Code	Symbolic Name	Description
0xC00470C7	DTS_E_REDIRECTROWUNAVAILABLEWITH FASTLOADANDZEROMAXINSERTCOMMITSIZE	The error row disposition on "___" cannot be set to redirect the row when the fast load option is turned on, and the maximum insert commit size is set to zero.
0xC00470CE	DTS_E_ EXPREVALBINARYOPERATORCODEPAGEMISMATCH	The code pages for operands of binary operator "___" for type "___" must match. Currently, the code page of the left operand does not match the code page of the right operand. For the specified binary operator on the specified type, the code pages must be the same.
0xC00470CF	DTS_E_EXPREVALVARIABLECOMPUTEFAILED	Retrieving the value of Variable "___" failed with error code 0x___.
0xC00470D0	DTS_E_EXPREVALVARIABLETYPENOTSUPPORTED	The data type of variable "___" is not supported in an expression.
0xC00470D1	DTS_E_EXPREVALCASTCODEPAGEMISMATCH	Unable to cast expression "___" from data type "___" to data type "___" because the code page of the value being cast (___) does not match the requested result code page (___). The code page of the source must match the code page requested for the destination.
0xC00470D2	DTS_E_BUFFERSIZEOUTOFRANGE	The default buffer size must be between ___ and ___ bytes. An attempt was made to set the DefaultBufferSize property to a value that is too small or too large.
0xC00470D3	DTS_E_BUFFERMAXROWSIZEOUTOFRANGE	The default buffer maximum rows must be larger than ___ rows. An attempt was made to set the DefaultBufferMaxRows property to a value that is too small.
0xC00470D4	DTS_E_EXTERNALCOLUMNMETADATACODEPAGE MISMATCH	The code page on ___ is ___ and is required to be ___.
0xC00470D5	DTS_E_THREADCOUNTOUTOFRANGE	The EngineThreads property of the Data Flow task must be between ___ and ___. An attempt was made to set the property to a value that is too small.
0xC00470D6	DTS_E_EXPREVALINVALIDTOKENSINGLEQUOTE	Parsing the expression "___" failed. The single quotation mark at line number "___", character number "___", was not expected.
0xC00470D7	DTS_E_EXPREVALINVALIDTOKENSINGLEEQUAL	Parsing the expression "___" failed. The equal sign (=) at line number "___", character number "___", was not expected. A double equals sign (==) may be required at the location specified.
0xC00470DA	DTS_E_INDIVIDUALPUTREFTRACKERFAILED	Component "___" failed to cache the runtime object reference tracker collection and returned error code 0x___.
0xC00470DB	DTS_E_EXPREVALAMBIGUOUSINPUTCOLUMNNAME	There are multiple input columns with the name "___". The desired input column must be specified uniquely as [Component Name].[%2] or referenced by lineage ID. Currently, the input column specified exists on more than one component.

Error Code	Symbolic Name	Description
0xC00470DC	DTS_E_EXPREVALDOTTEDINPUTCOLUMNNAME NOTFOUND	Locating the input column named "[%1].[%2]" failed with error code 0x__. The input column was not found in the input column collection.
0xC00470DD	DTS_E_EXPREVALAMBIGUOUSVARIABLENNAME	There are multiple variables with the name " __ ". The desired variable must be specified uniquely as @[Namespace::%2]. The variable exists in more than one namespace.
0xC00470DE	DTS_E_REDUCTIONFAILED	The Data Flow engine scheduler failed to reduce the execution plan for the pipeline. Set the OptimizedMode property to false.
0xC00470DF	DTS_E_EXPREVALSQRTINVALIDPARAM	The function SQRT cannot operate on negative values, and a negative value was passed to the SQRT function.
0xC00470E0	DTS_E_EXPREVALLNINVALIDPARAM	The function LN cannot operate on zero or negative values, and a zero or negative value was passed to the LN function.
0xC00470E1	DTS_E_EXPREVALLOGINVALIDPARAM	The function LOG cannot operate on zero or negative values, and a zero or negative value was passed to the LOG function.
0xC00470E2	DTS_E_EXPREVALPOWERINVALIDPARAM	The parameters passed to the function POWER cannot be evaluated and yield an indeterminate result.
0xC00470E3	DTS_E_NOCANCELEVENT	The runtime cannot provide a cancel event because of error 0x__.
0xC00470E4	DTS_E_CANCELRECEIVED	The pipeline received a request to cancel and is shutting down.
0xC00470E5	DTS_E_EXPREVALUNARYOPOVERFLOW	The result of the unary minus (negation) operation " __ " exceeds the maximum size for result data type " __ ". The magnitude of the result of the operation overflows the type of the result.
0xC00470E6	DTS_E_EXPREVALPLACEHOLDERINEXPRESSION	The placeholder " __ " was found in an expression. This must be replaced with an actual parameter or operand.
0xC00470E7	DTS_E_EXPREVALFNRIGHTINVALIDLENGTH	The length __ specified for function " __ " is negative, and is not valid. The length parameter must be positive.
0xC00470E8	DTS_E_ EXPREVALFNREPLICATEINVALIDREPEATCOUNT	The repeat count __ is negative and is not valid for function " __ ". The repeat count parameter cannot be negative.
0xC00470EA	DTS_E_EXPREVALVARIABLECOULDNOTBEREAD	Reading the variable " __ " failed with error code 0x__.
0xC00470EC	DTS_E_EXPREVALBINARYOPDTSTRNOTSUPPORTED	For operands of a binary operation, the data type DT_STR is supported only for input columns and cast operations. The expression " __ " has a DT_STR operand that is not an input column or the result of a cast, and cannot be used in a binary operation. To perform this operation, the operand needs to be explicitly cast with a cast operator.

Error Code	Symbolic Name	Description
0xC00470ED	DTS_E_EXPREVALCONDITIONALOPDTSTRNOTSUPPORTED	For operands of the conditional operator, the data type DT_STR is supported only for input columns and cast operations. The expression "__" has a DT_STR operand that is not an input column or the result of a cast, and cannot be used with the conditional operation. To perform this operation, the operand needs to be explicitly cast with a cast operator.
0xC00470EE	DTS_E_EXPREVALFNFINDSTRINGINVALIDOCCURRENCECOUNT	The occurrence count __ is not valid for function "__". This parameter must be greater than zero.
0xC00470EF	DTS_E_INDIVIDUALPUTLOGENTRYINFOS	"__" failed to cache the LogEntryInfos collection and returned error code 0x__.
0xC00470F0	DTS_E_EXPREVALINVALIDDATEPARTNODE	The date part parameter specified for function "__" is not valid. It must be a static string. The date part parameter cannot contain dynamic elements, such as input columns, and must be of type DT_WSTR.
0xC00470F1	DTS_E_EXPREVALINVALIDCASTLENGTH	The value __ specified for the length parameter of the cast to data type __ is negative and not valid. The length must be positive.
0xC00470F2	DTS_E_EXPREVALINVALIDNULLCODEPAGE	The value __ specified for the code page parameter of the NULL function with data type "__" is not valid. The code page is not installed on the computer.
0xC00470F3	DTS_E_EXPREVALINVALIDNULLPRECISION	The value __ specified for the precision parameter of the NULL function with data type "__" is out of range. Precision must be in the range __ to __.
0xC00470F4	DTS_E_EXPREVALINVALIDNULLSCALE	The value __ specified for the scale parameter of the NULL function with data type __ is out of range. Scale must be in the range __ to __. Scale must not exceed precision and must not be negative.
0xC00470F5	DTS_E_EXPREVALINVALIDNULLLENGTH	The value __ specified for the length parameter of the "NULL" function with data type __ is negative and not valid. The length must be positive.
0xC00470F6	DTS_E_NEGATIVESNOTALLOWED	The __ can't be assigned a negative value.
0xC00470F7	DTS_E_FASTPARSENOTALLOWED	The "__" custom property for "__" cannot be set to true. The column data type must be one of the following: DT_I1, DT_I2, DT_I4, DT_I8, DT_UI1, DT_UI2, DT_UI4, DT_UI8, DT_R4, DT_R8, DT_DBTIMESTAMP, DT_DBDATE, DT_DBTIME, or DT_FILETIME.
0xC00470F8	DTS_E_CANNOTREATTACHPATH	The "__" cannot be reattached. Delete the path, add a new one, and attach it.
0xC00470F9	DTS_E_EXPREVALINVALIDNUMBEROFPARAMSPLURALSINGULAR	The function "__" requires __ parameters, not __ parameter. The function name was recognized, but the number of parameters is not valid.
0xC00470FA	DTS_E_EXPREVALINVALIDNUMBEROFPARAMSSINGULARPLURAL	The function "__" requires __ parameter, not __ parameters. The function name was recognized, but number of parameters is not valid.

Error Code	Symbolic Name	Description
0xC00470FB	DTS_E_EXPREVALINVALIDNUMBEROFPARAMS PLURALPLURAL	The function " __ " requires __ parameters, not __ parameters. The function name was recognized, but the number of parameters is not valid.
0xC00470FC	DTS_E_EXPREVALFAILEDTOPARSEEXPRESSION OUTOFMEMORY	Attempt to parse the expression " __ " failed because there was an out-of-memory error.
0xC00470FD	DTS_E_INDIVIDUALCHECKPRODUCTLEVELFAILED	The __ failed to be able to perform its required product level check and returned error code 0x__.
0xC00470FE	DTS_E_PRODUCTLEVELTOLOW	The product level is insufficient for __.
0xC00470FF	DTS_E_EXPREVALSTRINGLITERALTOOLONG	A string literal in the expression exceeds the maximum allowed length of __ characters.
0xC0047100	DTS_E_EXPREVALSTRINGVARIABLETOOLONG	The variable __ contains a string that exceeds the maximum allowed length of __ characters.
0xC0048000	DTS_E_CANNOTOPENREGISTRYKEY	The registry key " __ " cannot be opened.
0xC0048001	DTS_E_INVALIDCOMPONENTFILENAME	Cannot get the file name for the component with a CLSID of " __ ". Verify that the component is registered properly or that the CLSID provided is correct.
0xC0048002	DTS_E_UNKNOWNCOMPONENTHASINVALIDCLSID	The CLSID for one of the components is not valid. Verify that all the components in the pipeline have valid CLSIDs.
0xC0048003	DTS_E_COMPONENTHASINVALIDCLSID	The CLSID for one of the components with ID __ is not valid.
0xC0048004	DTS_E_INVALIDINDEX	The index is not valid.
0xC0048005	DTS_E_CANNOTACCESSDTSAPPLICATIONOBJECT	The Application object cannot be accessed. Verify that SSIS is correctly installed.
0xC0048006	DTS_E_ ERROROCCURREDWHILERETRIEVINGFILENAME	Retrieving the file name for a component failed with error code 0x__.
0xC0048007	DTS_E_ CANNOTRETRIEVEPROPERTYFORCOMPONENT	Cannot retrieve property " __ " from component with ID __.
0xC0048008	DTS_E_DUPLICATEIDFOUND	Attempting to use ID __ more than once in the Data Flow Task.
0xC0048009	DTS_E_CANNOTRETRIEVEBYLINEAGE	Cannot retrieve an item by lineage ID from a collection that does not contain columns.
0xC004800B	DTS_E_ CANNOTMAPRUNTIMECONNECTIONMANAGER	Cannot find the connection manager with ID " __ " in the connection manager collection due to error code 0x__. That connection manager is needed by " __ " in the connection manager collection of " __ ". Verify that a connection manager in the connection manager collection, Connections, has been created with that ID.

Error Code	Symbolic Name	Description
0xC004800E	DTS_E_INPUTNOTKNOWN	Thread " __ " received a buffer for input __, but this thread is not responsible for that input. An error occurred, causing the Data Flow engine scheduler to build a bad execution plan.
0xC004800F	DTS_E_GETRTINTERFACEFAILED	The component " __ " (__) cannot provide an IDTSRuntimeComponent90 interface.
0xC0048011	DTS_E_CANTGIVEAWAYBUFFER	The Data Flow task engine attempted to copy a buffer to assign another thread, but failed.
0xC0048012	DTS_E_CANTCREATEVIEWBUFFER	[Message not provided.]
0xC0048013	DTS_E_UNUSABLETEMPORARYPATH	The buffer manager could not create a temporary file on the path " __ ". The path will not be considered for temporary storage again.
0xC0048014	DTS_E_DIRECTTONONERROROUTPUT	The buffer manager attempted to push an error row to an output that was not registered as an error output. There was a call to DirectErrorRow on an output that does not have the IsErrorOut property set to TRUE.
0xC0048015	DTS_E_BUFFERISPRIVATE	A call was made to a buffer method on a private buffer and private buffers do not support this operation.
0xC0048016	DTS_E_BUFFERISFLAT	Private mode buffers do not support this operation.
0xC0048017	DTS_E_BUFFERISPRIMEOUTPUT	This operation cannot be called on a buffer passed to PrimeOutput. A call was made to a buffer method during PrimeOutput, but that call is not allowed during PrimeOutput.
0xC0048018	DTS_E_BUFFERISPROCESSINPUT	This operation cannot be called on a buffer passed to ProcessInput. A call was made to a buffer method during ProcessInput, but that call is not allowed during ProcessInput.
0xC0048019	DTS_E_BUFFERGETTEMPFILENAME	The buffer manager could not get a temporary file name. The call to GetTempFileName failed.
0xC004801A	DTS_E_REFERENCECOLUMNTOOWIDE	The code encountered a column that was too wide.
0xC004801B	DTS_E_CANNOTGETRUNTIMECONNECTIONMANAGERID	Cannot get the ID of the runtime connection manager specified by " __ " in the connection manager collection, Connections, of " __ " due to error code 0x__. Verify that the ConnectionManager.ID property of the runtime connection object has been set for the component.
0xC004801C	DTS_E_EMPTYRUNTIMECONNECTIONMANAGERID	The " __ " in the connection manager collection, Connections, of " __ " does not have a value for the ID property. Verify that the ConnectionManagerID property of the runtime connection object has been set for the component.

Error Code	Symbolic Name	Description
0xC004801D	DTS_E_METADATAREADONLY	Metadata cannot be changed during execution.
0xC004801F	DTS_E_UPGRADEFAILED	The component metadata for "___" could not be upgraded to the newer version of the component. The PerformUpgrade method failed.
0xC0048020	DTS_E_COMPONENTVERSIONMISMATCH	The version of ___ is not compatible with this version of the DataFlow.
0xC0048021	DTS_E_ERRORCOMPONENT	The component is missing, not registered, not upgradeable, or missing required interfaces. The contact information for this component is "___".
0xC0048022	DTS_E_BUFFERISNOTPRIMEOUTPUT	The method was called on the wrong buffer. Buffers that are not used for component output do not support this operation.
0xC0049014	DTS_E_EXPREVALSTATIC_COMPUTATIONFAILED	An error occurred during computation of the expression.
0xC0049030	DTS_E_EXPREVALSTATIC_DIVBYZERO	Division by zero occurred in the expression.
0xC0049031	DTS_E_EXPREVALSTATIC_LITERALOVERFLOW	The magnitude of the literal value was too big to fit in the type requested.
0xC0049032	DTS_E_EXPREVALSTATIC_BINARYOPNUMERICOVERFLOW	The result of a binary operation was too big for the maximum size for numeric types. The operand types could not be implicitly cast into a numeric (DT_NUMERIC) result without loss of precision or scale. To perform this operation, one or both operands need to be explicitly cast with a cast operator.
0xC0049033	DTS_E_EXPREVALSTATIC_BINARYOPOVERFLOW	The magnitude of the result of a binary operation overflows the maximum size for result data type.
0xC0049034	DTS_E_EXPREVALSTATIC_FUNCTIONOVERFLOW	The magnitude of the result of a function call was too big to fit in the result type, and overflowed the type of the operand. An explicit cast to a larger type may be required.
0xC0049035	DTS_E_EXPREVALSTATIC_BINARYTYPEMISMATCH	Incompatible data types were used with a binary operator. The operand types could not be implicitly cast into compatible types for the operation. To perform this operation, one or both operands need to be explicitly cast with a cast operator.
0xC0049036	DTS_E_EXPREVALSTATIC_UNSUPPORTEDBINARYTYPE	An unsupported data type was used with a binary operator. The type of one, or both, of the operands is not supported for the operation. To perform this operation, one or both operands need to be explicitly cast with a cast operator.
0xC0049037	DTS_E_EXPREVALSTATIC_BINARYSIGNMISMATCH	There is a sign mismatch for the bitwise binary operator. The operands for this operator must be both positive or both negative.
0xC0049038	DTS_E_EXPREVALSTATIC_BINARYOPERATIONFAILED	A binary operation failed. There was an out-of-memory condition, or an internal error occurred.

Error Code	Symbolic Name	Description
0xC0049039	DTS_E_EXPREVALSTATIC_BINARYOPERATIONSETTYPEFAILED	Setting the result type of a binary operation failed.
0xC004903A	DTS_E_EXPREVALSTATIC_STRINGCOMPARISONFAILED	Cannot compare two strings.
0xC004903B	DTS_E_EXPREVALSTATIC_UNSUPPORTEDUNNARYTYPE	An unsupported data type is used with a unary operator. The operand type is not supported for the operation. To perform this operation, the operand needs to be explicitly cast with a cast operator.
0xC004903C	DTS_E_EXPREVALSTATIC_UNARYOPERATIONFAILED	A unary operation failed. An out-of-memory condition occurred, or there was an internal error.
0xC004903D	DTS_E_EXPREVALSTATIC_UNARYOPERATIONSETTYPEFAILED	Setting the result type of a unary operation failed.
0xC004903E	DTS_E_EXPREVALSTATIC_PARAMTYPEMISMATCH	A function has a parameter with an unsupported data type. The type of the parameter cannot be implicitly cast into a compatible type for the function. To perform this operation, the operand needs to be explicitly cast with a cast operator.
0xC004903F	DTS_E_EXPREVALSTATIC_INVALIDFUNCTION	An invalid function name appeared in the expression. Verify that the function name is correct and does exist.
0xC0049040	DTS_E_EXPREVALSTATIC_FNSUBSTRINGINVALIDLENGTH	The length parameter was not valid for function SUBSTRING. The length parameter cannot be negative.
0xC0049041	DTS_E_EXPREVALSTATIC_FNSUBSTRINGINVALIDSTARTINDEX	The start index was not valid for function SUBSTRING. The start index value must be an integer greater than zero. The start index is 1-based, not 0-based.
0xC0049042	DTS_E_EXPREVALSTATIC_INVALIDNUMBEROFPARAMS	An incorrect number of parameters was given to a function. The function name was recognized, but the number of parameters was not correct.
0xC0049043	DTS_E_EXPREVALSTATIC_CHARMAPPINGFAILED	A character mapping function failed.
0xC0049044	DTS_E_EXPREVALSTATIC_INVALIDDATEPART	An unrecognized date part parameter was specified for a date function.
0xC0049045	DTS_E_EXPREVALSTATIC_INVALIDNULLPARAM	An invalid parameter was given for function NULL. The parameters of NULL must be static, and cannot contain dynamic elements such as input columns.
0xC0049046	DTS_E_EXPREVALSTATIC_INVALIDNULLPARAMTYPE	An invalid parameter was given for function NULL. A parameter of NULL must be an integer, or a type that can be converted to an integer.
0xC0049047	DTS_E_EXPREVALSTATIC_FUNCTIONPARAMNOTSTATIC	An invalid parameter was given for a function. This parameter must be static and cannot contain dynamic elements such as input columns.

Error Code	Symbolic Name	Description
0xC0049048	DTS_E_EXPREVALSTATIC_INVALIDCASTPARAM	An invalid parameter was given for a cast operation. Parameters of cast operators must be static, and cannot contain dynamic elements such as input columns.
0xC0049049	DTS_E_EXPREVALSTATIC_INVALIDCASTPARAMTYPE	An invalid parameter was given for a cast operation. A parameter of a cast operator must be an integer, or a type that can be converted to an integer.
0xC004904A	DTS_E_EXPREVALSTATIC_INVALIDCAST	The expression contained an unsupported type cast.
0xC004904B	DTS_E_EXPREVALSTATIC_INVALIDTOKEN	The expression contained a token that was not recognized. The expression could not be parsed because it contains invalid elements.
0xC004904C	DTS_E_EXPREVALSTATIC_FAILEDTOPARSEEXPRESSION	The expression is not valid and could not be parsed. It might contain invalid elements, or it might not be well-formed.
0xC004904D	DTS_E_EXPREVALSTATIC_UNARYOPOVERFLOW	The result of a unary minus (negation) operation overflowed the maximum size for result data type. The magnitude of the result of the operation overflows the type of the result.
0xC004904E	DTS_E_EXPREVALSTATIC_COMPUTEFAILED	Attempt to compute the expression failed.
0xC004904F	DTS_E_EXPREVALSTATIC_BUILDSTRINGFAILED	Attempt to generate a string representation of the expression failed.
0xC0049050	DTS_E_EXPREVALSTATIC_CANNOTCONVERTRESULT	Cannot convert the expression result data type to the column data type. The result of the expression should be written to an input/output column, but the data type of the expression cannot be converted to the data type of the column.
0xC0049051	DTS_E_EXPREVALSTATIC_CONDITIONALOPINVALIDCONDITIONTYPE	The conditional expression of the conditional operator has invalid data type. The conditional expression must be of type DT_BOOL.
0xC0049052	DTS_E_EXPREVALSTATIC_CONDITIONALOPTYPEMISMATCH	The data types of the operands of the conditional operator were incompatible. The operand types could not be implicitly cast into compatible types for the conditional operation. To perform this operation, one or both operands need to be explicitly cast with a cast operator.
0xC0049053	DTS_E_EXPREVALSTATIC_CONDITIONALOPSETTYPEFAILED	Setting the result type of a conditional operation failed.
0xC0049054	DTS_E_EXPREVALSTATIC_INPUTCOLUMNNAMENOTFOUND	The input column specified was not found in the input column collection.
0xC0049055	DTS_E_EXPREVALSTATIC_INPUTCOLUMNIDNOTFOUND	Attempt to find an input column by lineage ID failed. The input column was not found in the input column collection.

Error Code	Symbolic Name	Description
0xC0049056	DTS_E_EXPREVALSTATIC_ NOINPUTCOLUMNCOLLECTION	The expression contains an unrecognized token that appears to be an input column reference, but the input column collection is not available to process input columns. The input column collection has not been provided to the expression evaluator, but an input column was included in the expression.
0xC0049057	DTS_E_EXPREVALSTATIC_VARIABLENOTFOUND	A variable specified was not found in the collection. It might not exist in the correct scope. Verify that the variable exists and that the scope is correct.
0xC0049058	DTS_E_EXPREVALSTATIC_INVALIDTOKENSTATE	Attempt to parse the expression failed. The expression contains an invalid or incomplete token. It may contain invalid elements, be missing part of a required element such as closing parentheses, or may not be well formed.
0xC0049059	DTS_E_EXPREVALSTATIC_INVALIDCASTCODEPAGE	The value specified for the code page parameter of the cast to data type DT_STR or DT_TEXT is not valid. The specified code page is not installed on the computer.
0xC004905A	DTS_E_EXPREVALSTATIC_INVALIDCASTPRECISION	The value specified for the precision parameter of a cast operation is out of range for the type cast.
0xC004905B	DTS_E_EXPREVALSTATIC_INVALIDCASTSCALE	The value specified for the scale parameter of a cast operation is out of range for the type cast. Scale must not exceed precision and must not be negative.
0xC004905C	DTS_E_EXPREVALSTATIC_ CONDITIONALOPCODEPAGEMISMATCH	The code pages do not match in a conditional operation. The code page of the left operand does not match the code page of the right operand. For the conditional operator of that type, the code pages must be the same.
0xC004905D	DTS_E_EXPREVALSTATIC_ ILLEGALHEXESCAPEINSTRINGLITERAL	A string literal contains an illegal hexadecimal escape sequence. The escape sequence is not supported in string literals in the expression evaluator. Hexadecimal escape sequences must be of the form \xhhhh where h is a valid hexadecimal digit.
0xC004905E	DTS_E_EXPREVALSTATIC_ ILLEGALESCAPEINSTRINGLITERAL	The string literal contains an illegal escape sequence. The escape sequence is not supported in string literals in the expression evaluator. If a backslash is needed in the string, format it as a double backslash, "\\".
0xC004905F	DTS_E_EXPREVALSTATIC_UNSUPPORTEDTYPE	An unsupported or unrecognized data type was used in the expression.
0xC0049060	DTS_E_EXPREVALSTATIC_ DATACONVERSIONOVERFLOW	An overflow occurred while converting between data types. The source type is too large to fit in the destination type.
0xC0049061	DTS_E_EXPREVALSTATIC_ DATACONVERSIONNOTSUPPORTED	The expression contains an unsupported data type conversion. The source type cannot be converted to the destination type.

Error Code	Symbolic Name	Description
0xC0049062	DTS_E_EXPREVALSTATIC_DATACONVERSIONFAILED	An error occurred while attempting to perform data conversion. The source type could not be converted to the destination type.
0xC0049063	DTS_E_EXPREVALSTATIC_CONDITIONALOPERATIONFAILED	The conditional operation failed.
0xC0049064	DTS_E_EXPREVALSTATIC_CASTFAILED	An error occurred while attempting to perform a type cast.
0xC0049065	DTS_E_EXPREVALFAILEDTOCONVERTSTRCOLUMNTOWSTR	Converting " __ " from type DT_STR to type DT_WSTR failed with error code 0x__. An error occurred while performing the implicit conversion on the input column.
0xC0049066	DTS_E_EXPREVALSTATIC_FAILEDTOCONVERTSTRCOLUMNTOWSTR	Converting an input column from type DT_STR to type DT_WSTR failed. An error occurred while performing the implicit conversion on the input column.
0xC0049067	DTS_E_EXPREVALSTATIC_FUNCTIONCOMPUTEFAILED	An error occurred while evaluating the function.
0xC0049068	DTS_E_EXPREVALSTATIC_FUNCTIONCONVERTPARAMTOMEMBERFAILED	A function parameter cannot be converted to a static value. The parameter must be static and cannot contain dynamic elements such as input columns.
0xC0049088	DTS_E_EXPREVALSTATIC_FNRIGHTINVALIDLENGTH	The length parameter is not valid for function RIGHT. The length parameter cannot be negative.
0xC0049089	DTS_E_EXPREVALSTATIC_FNREPLICATEINVALIDREPEATCOUNT	The repeat count parameter is not valid for function REPLICATE. This parameter cannot be negative.
0xC0049096	DTS_E_EXPREVALSTATIC_BINARYOPERATORCODEPAGEMISMATCH	The code pages do not match in a binary operation. The code page of the left operand does not match the code page of the right operand. For this binary operation, the code pages must be the same.
0xC0049097	DTS_E_EXPREVALSTATIC_VARIABLECOMPUTEFAILED	Retrieving the value for a variable failed.
0xC0049098	DTS_E_EXPREVALSTATIC_VARIABLETYPENOTSUPPORTED	The expression contains a variable with an unsupported data type.
0xC004909B	DTS_E_EXPREVALSTATIC_CASTCODEPAGEMISMATCH	Unable to cast the expression because the code page of the value being cast does not match the requested result code page. The code page of the source must match the code page requested for the destination.
0xC004909C	DTS_E_EXPREVALSTATIC_INVALIDTOKENSINGLEQUOTE	The expression contains an unexpected single quotation mark. A double quotation mark may be required.
0xC004909D	DTS_E_EXPREVALSTATIC_INVALIDTOKENSINGLEEQUAL	The expression contains an unexpected equal sign (=). This error usually occurs when a double equals sign (==) is needed.

Error Code	Symbolic Name	Description
0xC00490AA	DTS_E_EXPREVALSTATIC_AMBIGUOUSINPUTCOLUMNNAME	An ambiguous input column name was specified. The column must be qualified as [Component Name].[Column Name] or referenced by lineage ID. This error occurs when the input column exists on more than one component, and must be differentiated by the addition of component name or by using the lineage ID.
0xC00490AB	DTS_E_EXPREVALSTATIC_PLACEHOLDERINEXPRESSION	A placeholder function parameter or operand was found in an expression. This should be replaced with an actual parameter or operand.
0xC00490AC	DTS_E_EXPREVALSTATIC_AMBIGUOUSVARIABLENNAME	An ambiguous variable name was specified. The desired variable must be qualified as @[Namespace::Variable]. This error occurs when the variable exists in more than one namespace.
0xC00490D3	DTS_E_EXPREVALSTATIC_BINARYOPDTSTRNOTSUPPORTED	For operands of binary operation, the data type DT_STR is only supported for input columns and cast operations. A DT_STR operand that is not an input column or the result of a cast cannot be used with a binary operation. To perform this operation, the operand needs to be explicitly cast with a cast operator.
0xC00490D4	DTS_E_EXPREVALSTATIC_CONDITIONALOPDTSTRNOTSUPPORTED	For operands of the conditional operator, the data type DT_STR is only supported for input columns and cast operations. A DT_STR operand that is not an input column or the result of a cast cannot be used with the conditional operation. To perform this operation, the operand needs to be explicitly cast with a cast operator.
0xC00490D5	DTS_E_EXPREVALSTATIC_FNFINDSTRINGINVALIDOCCURRENCECOUNT	The occurrence count parameter is not valid for function FINDSTRING. This parameter must be greater than zero.
0xC00490DD	DTS_E_EXPREVALSTATIC_INVALIDDATEPARTNODE	The "date part" parameter specified for a date function is not valid. "Date part" parameters must be static strings, and cannot contain dynamic elements such as input columns. They must be of type DT_WSTR.
0xC00490DE	DTS_E_EXPREVALSTATIC_INVALIDCASTLENGTH	The value specified for the length parameter of a cast operation is not valid. The length must be positive. The length specified for the type cast is negative. Change to a positive value.
0xC00490DF	DTS_E_EXPREVALSTATIC_INVALIDNULLLENGTH	The value specified for the length parameter of a NULL function is not valid. The length must be positive. The length specified for the NULL function is negative. Change to a positive value.

Error Code	Symbolic Name	Description
0xC00490E0	DTS_E_EXPREVALSTATIC_INVALIDNULLCODEPAGE	The value specified for the code page parameter of the NULL function with data type DT_STR or DT_TEXT is not valid. The code page specified is not installed on the computer. Either change the code page that is specified, or install the code page on the computer.
0xC00490E1	DTS_E_EXPREVALSTATIC_INVALIDNULLPRECISION	The value specified for the precision parameter of a NULL function is not valid. The precision that was specified is out of range for the NULL function.
0xC00490E2	DTS_E_EXPREVALSTATIC_INVALIDNULLSCALE	The value specified for the scale parameter of a NULL function is not valid. The scale that was specified is out of range for the NULL function. Scale must not exceed precision and must be positive.
0xC00490F5	DTS_E_TXLOOKUP_CANCEL_REQUESTED	Lookup transform has received a cancel request from the user.
0xC0202001	DTS_E_MISSINGSQLCOMMAND	The SQL command has not been set correctly. Check SQLCommand property.
0xC0202002	DTS_E_COMERROR	COM error object information is available. Source: "___" error code: 0x___ Description: "___".
0xC0202003	DTS_E_ACQUIREDCONNECTIONUNAVAILABLE	Unable to access the acquired connections.
0xC0202004	DTS_E_INCORRECTCOLUMNCOUNT	The number of columns is incorrect.
0xC0202005	DTS_E_COLUMNNOTFOUND	Column "___" cannot be found at the datasource.
0xC0202007	DTS_E_OLEDBRECORD	An OLE DB record is available. Source: "___" Hresult: 0x___ Description: "___".
0xC0202009	DTS_E_OLEDBERROR	An OLE DB error has occurred. Error code: 0x___.
0xC020200A	DTS_E_ALREADYCONNECTED	Component is already connected. The component needs to be disconnected before attempting to connect it.
0xC020200B	DTS_E_INCORRECTSTOCKPROPERTYVALUE	The value of the property "___" is incorrect.
0xC020200E	DTS_E_CANNOTOPENDATAFILE	Cannot open the datafile "___".
0xC0202010	DTS_E_DESTINATIONFLATFILEREQUIRED	No destination flat file name was provided. Make sure the flat file connection manager is configured with a connection string. If the flat file connection manager is used by multiple components, ensure that the connection string contains enough file names.
0xC0202011	DTS_E_TEXTQUALIFIERNOTFOUND	The text qualifier for column "___" cannot be found.
0xC0202014	DTS_E_CANNOTCONVERTTYPES	Conversion from "___" to "___" is not supported.
0xC0202015	DTS_E_PROBLEMDETECTINGTYPECOMPATIBILITY	The error code 0x___ was returned when validating type conversion from ___ to ___.

Error Code	Symbolic Name	Description
0xC0202016	DTS_E_CANNOTMAPINPUTCOLUMNTOOUTPUTCOLUMN	Cannot find input column with lineage ID " __ " which is needed by " __ ". Check SourceInputColumnLineageID custom property of the output column.
0xC0202017	DTS_E_INCORRECTMINIMUMNUMBEROFOUTPUTS	The number of outputs is incorrect. There must be at least __ outputs.
0xC0202018	DTS_E_INCORRECTEXACTNUMBEROFOUTPUTS	The number of outputs is incorrect. There must be exactly __ output(s).
0xC0202019	DTS_E_STRINGCONVERSIONTOOLONG	A string was too long to be converted.
0xC020201A	DTS_E_INCORRECTEXACTNUMBEROFINPUTS	The number of inputs is incorrect. There must be exactly __ inputs.
0xC020201B	DTS_E_CANNOTHAVEZEROINPUTCOLUMNS	The number of input columns for __ cannot be zero.
0xC020201C	DTS_E_CANNOTHAVEINPUTS	This component has __ inputs. No input is allowed on this component.
0xC020201D	DTS_E_PROCESSINPUTCALLEDWITHINVALIDINPUTID	ProcessInput was called with an invalid input ID of __.
0xC020201F	DTS_E_INCORRECTCUSTOMPROPERTYTYPE	The custom property " __ " needs to be of type __.
0xC0202020	DTS_E_INVALIDBUFFERTYPE	The buffer type is not valid. Make sure the Pipeline layout and all components pass validation.
0xC0202021	DTS_E_INCORRECTCUSTOMPROPERTYVALUE	The value for custom property " __ " is incorrect.
0xC0202022	DTS_E_CONNECTIONREQUIREDFORMETADATA	An error occurred due to no connection. A connection is required when requesting metadata.
0xC0202023	DTS_E_CANTCREATECUSTOMPROPERTY	The custom property " __ " cannot be created.
0xC0202024	DTS_E_CANTGETCUSTOMPROPERTYCOLLECTION	The custom property collection cannot be retrieved for initialization.
0xC0202025	DTS_E_CANNOTCREATEACCESSOR	Cannot create an OLE DB accessor. Verify that the column metadata is valid.
0xC0202026	DTS_E_PRIMEOUTPUTCALLEDWITHINVALIDOUTPUTID	PrimeOutput was called with an invalid output ID of __.
0xC0202027	DTS_E_INCORRECTSTOCKPROPERTY	The value for property " __ " on " __ " is not valid.
0xC0202028	DTS_E_CONNECTIONREQUIREDFORREAD	A connection is required to read data.
0xC020202C	DTS_E_ERRORWHILEREADINGHEADERROWS	An error occurred while reading header rows.
0xC020202D	DTS_E_DUPLICATECOLUMNNAME	Duplicate column name " __ ".
0xC0202030	DTS_E_CANNOTGETCOLUMNNAME	Cannot get the name of the column with ID __.
0xC0202031	DTS_E_CANTDIRECTROW	Direct row to output " __ " (__) failed.
0xC020203A	DTS_E_CANNOTCREATEBULKINSERTHREAD	Cannot create the bulk insert thread due to error " __ ".
0xC020203B	DTS_E_BULKINSERTHREADINITIALIZATIONFAILED	The thread for the SSIS Bulk Insert task failed initialization.

Error Code	Symbolic Name	Description
0xC020203E	DTS_E_BULKINSERTTHREADALREADYRUNNING	The thread for the SSIS Bulk Insert task is already running.
0xC020203F	DTS_E_BULKINSERTTHREADABNORMALCOMPLETION	The thread for the SSIS Bulk Insert task terminated with errors or warnings.
0xC0202040	DTS_E_CANNOTGETIROWSETFASTLOAD	Failed to open a fastload rowset for " __ ". Check that the object exists in the database.
0xC0202041	DTS_E_CONNECTREQUIREDFORMETADATAVALIDATION	Error due to no connection. A connection is required before metadata validation can proceed.
0xC0202042	DTS_E_DESTINATIONTABLENAMENOTPROVIDED	A destination table name has not been provided.
0xC0202043	DTS_E_ICONVERTTYPEUNAVAILABLE	The OLE DB provider used by the OLE DB adapter does not support IConvertType. Set the adapter's ValidateColumnMetaData property to FALSE.
0xC0202044	DTS_E_OLEDBPROVIDERDATATYPECONVERSION UNSUPPORTED	The OLE DB provider used by the OLE DB adapter cannot convert between types " __ " and " __ " for " __ ".
0xC0202045	DTS_E_VALIDATECOLUMNMETADATAFAILED	Column metadata validation failed.
0xC0202047	DTS_E_ATTEMPTINGTOINSERTINTOAROWIDCOLUMN	" __ " is a row ID column and cannot be included in a data insertion operation.
0xC0202048	DTS_E_ATTEMPTINGTOINSERTINTOAROWVERCOLUMN	Attempting insertion into the row version column " __ ". Cannot insert into a row version column.
0xC0202049	DTS_E_ATTEMPTINGTOINSERTINTOAREADONLYCOLUMN	Failure inserting into the read-only column " __ ".
0xC020204A	DTS_E_UNABLETORETRIEVECOLUMNINFO	Unable to retrieve column information from the data source. Make sure your target table in the database is available.
0xC020204B	DTS_E_CANTLOCKBUFFER	A buffer could not be locked. The system is out of memory or the buffer manager has reached its quota.
0xC020204C	DTS_E_INVALIDCOMPARISONFLAGS	The __ has a ComparisonFlags property that includes extra flags with the value __ .
0xC020204D	DTS_E_COLUMNMETADATAUNAVAILABLEFORVALIDATION	The column metadata was unavailable for validation.
0xC0202053	DTS_E_CANNOTWRITETODATAFILE	Cannot write to the data file.
0xC0202055	DTS_E_COLUMNDELIMITERNOTFOUND	The column delimiter for column " __ " was not found.
0xC0202058	DTS_E_COLUMNPARSEFAILED	Failed to parse the column " __ " in the data file.

Error Code	Symbolic Name	Description
0xC020205A	DTS_E_RAWFILENAMEREQUIRED	The file name is not properly specified. Supply the path and name to the raw file either directly in the FileName property or by specifying a variable in the FileNameVariable property.
0xC020205B	DTS_E_RAWFILECANTOPEN	File " __ " cannot be opened for writing. Error may occur when there are no file privileges or the disk is full.
0xC020205C	DTS_E_RAWFILECANTBUFFER	An I/O buffer cannot be created for the output file. Error may occur when there are no file privileges or the disk is full.
0xC020205D	DTS_E_RAWCANTWRITE	Cannot write __ bytes to file " __ ". See previous error messages for details.
0xC020205E	DTS_E_RAWBADHEADER	Encountered bad metadata in file header. The file is damaged or not a SSIS-produced raw data file.
0xC020205F	DTS_E_RAWEXISTSCREATEONCE	Error occurred because the output file already exists and the WriteOption is set to Create Once. Set the WriteOption property to Create Always, or delete the file.
0xC0202060	DTS_E_RAWCANTAPPENDTRUNCATE	Error caused by conflicting property settings. Both the AllowAppend property and the ForceTruncate property are set to TRUE. Both properties cannot be set to TRUE. Set one of the two properties to FALSE.
0xC0202061	DTS_E_RAWBADVERSION	The file had bad version and flags information. The file is damaged or not a SSIS-produced raw data file.
0xC0202062	DTS_E_RAWVERSIONINCOMPATIBLEAPPEND	The output file was written by an incompatible version and cannot be appended. The file may be an older file format that is no longer useable.
0xC0202064	DTS_E_RAWMETADATAMISMATCH	Cannot append output file because no column in the existing file matches column " __ " from the input. Old file does not match in metadata.
0xC0202065	DTS_E_RAWMETADATACOUNTMISMATCH	Cannot append output file because the number of columns in the output file does not match the number of columns in this destination. The old file does not match in metadata.
0xC0202067	DTS_E_ERRORRETRIEVINGCOLUMNCODEPAGE	There was an error retrieving column code page information.
0xC0202068	DTS_E_RAWCANTREAD	Cannot read __ bytes from file " __ ". The cause of the failure should have been previously reported.
0xC0202069	DTS_E_RAWUNEXPECTEDEOF	Unexpected end-of-file encountered while reading __ bytes from file " __ ". The file ended prematurely because of an invalid file format.
0xC020206A	DTS_E_RAWNOLONGTYPES	The raw adapters do not support image, text, or ntext data.

Error Code	Symbolic Name	Description
0xC020206B	DTS_E_RAWUNEXPECTEDTYPE	The adapter encountered an unrecognized data type of __. This could be caused by a damaged input file (source) or by an invalid buffer type (destination).
0xC020206C	DTS_E_RAWSTRINGTOOLONG	String too long. The adapter read a string that was __ bytes long, and expected a string no longer than __ bytes, at offset __. This could indicate a damaged input file. The file shows a string length that is too large for the buffer column.
0xC020206E	DTS_E_RAWSKIPFAILED	The raw adapter attempted to skip __ bytes in the input file for unreferenced column "__" with lineage ID __, but there was an error. The error returned from the operating system should have been previously reported.
0xC020206F	DTS_E_RAWREADFAILED	The raw adapter attempted to read __ bytes in the input file for column "__" with lineage ID __, but there was an error. The error returned from the operating system should have been previously reported.
0xC0202070	DTS_E_RAWFILENAMEINVALID	The file name property is not valid. The file name is a device or contains invalid characters.
0xC0202071	DTS_E_BULKINSERTAPIPREPARATIONFAILED	Unable to prepare the SSIS bulk insert for data insertion.
0xC0202072	DTS_E_INVALIDDATABASEOBJECTNAME	Database object name "__" is not valid.
0xC0202073	DTS_E_INVALIDORDERCLAUSE	Order clause is not valid.
0xC0202074	DTS_E_RAWFILECANTOPENREAD	File "__" cannot be opened for reading. Error may occur when there are no privileges or the file is not found. Exact cause is reported in previous error message.
0xC0202075	DTS_E_TIMEGENCANTCREATE	Unable to create the Microsoft.AnalysisServices.TimeDimGenerator.TimeDimGenerator.
0xC0202076	DTS_E_TIMEGENCANTCONFIGURE	Unable to configure the Microsoft.AnalysisServices.TimeDimGenerator.
0xC0202077	DTS_E_TIMEGENCANTCONVERT	Unsupported datatype for column __.
0xC0202079	DTS_E_TIMEGENCANTREAD	The attempt to read from the Microsoft.AnalysisServices.TimeDimGenerator failed with error code 0x__.
0xC020207A	DTS_E_TIMEGENCANTREADCOLUMN	The attempt to read column "__" data from the Microsoft.AnalysisServices.TimeDimGenerator failed with error code 0x__.
0xC020207B	DTS_E_RSTDESTBADVARIABLENAME	The VariableName property is not set to the name of a valid variable. Need a runtime variable name to write to.
0xC020207C	DTS_E_RSTDESTRSTCONFIGPROBLEM	Unable to create or configure the ADODB.Recordset object.
0xC020207D	DTS_E_RSTDESTRSTWRITEPROBLEM	Error writing to the ADODB.Recordset object.

Error Code	Symbolic Name	Description
0xC020207E	DTS_E_FILENAMEINVALID	The file name is not valid. The file name is a device or contains invalid characters.
0xC020207F	DTS_E_FILENAMEINVALIDWITHPARAM	The file name " __ " is not valid. The file name is a device or contains invalid characters.
0xC0202080	DTS_E_CMDDESTNOPARAMS	Unable to retrieve destination column descriptions from the parameters of the SQL command.
0xC0202081	DTS_E_CMDDESTNOTBOUND	Parameters are not bound. All parameters in the SQL command must be bound to input columns.
0xC0202082	DTS_E_TXPIVOTBADUSAGE	The PivotUsage value for the input column " __ " (__) is not valid.
0xC0202083	DTS_E_TXPIVOTTOOMANYPIVOTKEYS	Too many Pivot Keys found. Only one input column can be used as the Pivot Key.
0xC0202084	DTS_E_TXPIVOTNOPIVOTKEY	No Pivot Key found. One input column must be used as the Pivot Key.
0xC0202085	DTS_E_TXPIVOTINPUTALREADYMAPPED	More than one output column (such as " __ " (__)) is mapped to input column " __ " (__).
0xC0202086	DTS_E_TXPIVOTCANTMAPPIVOTKEY	Output column " __ " (__) cannot be mapped to PivotKey input column.
0xC0202087	DTS_E_TXPIVOTCANTMAPPINGNOTFOUND	Output column " __ " (__) has a SourceColumn __ that is not a valid input column lineage ID.
0xC0202088	DTS_E_TXPIVOTEMPTYPIVOTKEYVALUE	Output column " __ " (__) is mapped to a Pivoted Value input column, but its PivotKeyValue property value is missing.
0xC0202089	DTS_E_TXPIVOTDUPLICATEPIVOTKEYVALUE	Output column " __ " (__) is mapped to a Pivoted Value input column with a non-unique PivotKeyValue property value.
0xC020208A	DTS_E_TXPIVOTOUTPUTNOTMAPPED	Input column " __ " (__) is not mapped to any output column.
0xC020208B	DTS_E_TXPIVOTCANTCOMPARESETKEYS	Failure occurred while comparing values for the set keys.
0xC020208D	DTS_E_TXPIVOTNOBLOB	The Input column " __ " (__) cannot be used as a Set Key, Pivot Key, or Pivot Value because it contains long data.
0xC020208E	DTS_E_TXPIVOTBADOUTPUTTYPE	Incorrect output type. The output column " __ " (__) must have the same data type and metadata as the input column to which it is mapped.
0xC020208F	DTS_E_TXPIVOTPROCESSERROR	Failure when trying to pivot the source records.
0xC0202090	DTS_E_TXPIVOTBADPIVOTKEYVALUE	The pivot key value " __ " is not valid.
0xC0202091	DTS_E_ERRORWHILESKIPPINGDATAROWS	An error occurred while skipping data rows.
0xC0202092	DTS_E_ERRORWHILEREADINGDATAROWS	An error occurred while processing file " __ " on data row __.

Error Code	Symbolic Name	Description
0xC0202093	DTS_E_FAILEDTOINITIALIZEFLATFILEPARSER	An error occurred while initializing the flat file parser.
0xC0202094	DTS_E_UNABLETORETRIEVECOLUMNINFOFROM FLATFILECONNECTIONMANAGER	Unable to retrieve column information from the flat file connection manager.
0xC0202095	DTS_E_FAILEDTOWRITEOUTCOLUMNNAME	Failed to write out column name for column "___".
0xC0202096	DTS_E_INVALIDFLATFILECOLUMNTYPE	The column type for column "___" is incorrect. It is type "___". It can only be either "___" or "___".
0xC0202097	DTS_E_DISKIOBUFFEROVERFLOW	The attempt to write data of __ bytes into the disk I/O failed. The disk I/O buffer has __ free bytes.
0xC0202098	DTS_E_FAILEDTOWRITEOUTHEADER	An error occurred while writing out the file header.
0xC0202099	DTS_E_FAILEDTOGETFILESIZE	An error occurred while getting the file size for file "___".
0xC020209A	DTS_E_FAILEDTOSETFILEPOINTER	An error occurred while setting the file pointer for file "___".
0xC020209B	DTS_E_UNABLETOSETUPDISKIOBUFFER	An error occurred while setting up the disk I/O buffer.
0xC020209C	DTS_E_COLUMNDATAOVERFLOWDISKIOBUFFER	The column data for column "___" overflowed the disk I/O buffer.
0xC020209D	DTS_E_DISKIOFAILED	An unexpected disk I/O error occurred while reading the file.
0xC020209E	DTS_E_DISKIOTIMEDOUT	An disk I/O time out occurred while reading the file.
0xC020209F	DTS_E_INPUTSNOTREADONLY	The Usage Type specified for the input columns to this transform cannot be read/write. Change the Usage Type to be read-only.
0xC02020A0	DTS_E_CANNOTCOPYORCONVERTFLATFILEDATA	Cannot copy or convert flat file data for column "___".
0xC02020A1	DTS_E_FAILEDCOLUMNDATACONVERSIONSTATUS	Data conversion failed. The data conversion for column "___" returned status value __ and status text "___".
0xC02020A2	DTS_E_VARIABLESCOLLECTIONUNAVAILABLE	The Variables collection is not available.
0xC02020A3	DTS_E_TXUNPIVOTDUPLICATEPIVOTKEYVALUE	Duplicate PivotKeyValue. Input column "___" (__) is mapped to a Pivoted Value output column and has a non-unique PivotKeyValue.
0xC02020A4	DTS_E_TXUNPIVOTNOUNPIVOTDESTINATION	No unpivot destination found. At least one input column must be mapped with a PivotKeyValue to an DestinationColumn in the output.
0xC02020A5	DTS_E_TXUNPIVOTBADKEYLIST	PivotKeyValue is not valid. In an UnPivot transform with more than one unpivoted DestinationColumn, the set of PivotKeyValues per destination must match exactly.
0xC02020A6	DTS_E_TXUNPIVOTBADUNPIVOTMETADATA	Incorrect UnPivot metadata. In an UnPivot transform, all input columns with a PivotKeyValue that is set, and are pointing to the same DestinationColumn, must have metadata that exactly matches the DestinationColumn.

Error Code	Symbolic Name	Description
0xC02020A7	DTS_E_TXPIVOTBADPIVOTKEYCONVERT	Cannot convert the pivot key value " __ " to the data type of the pivot key column.
0xC02020A8	DTS_E_TXUNPIVOTTOOMANYPIVOTKEYS	Too many Pivot Keys specified. Only one output column can be used as the Pivot Key.
0xC02020A9	DTS_E_TXUNPIVOTUNMAPPEDOUTPUT	Output column " __ " (__) is not mapped by any input column's DestinationColumn property.
0xC02020AA	DTS_E_TXUNPIVOTNOPIVOT	No output column is marked as the PivotKey.
0xC02020AB	DTS_E_TXUNPIVOTNOTINPUTMAP	Input column " __ " (__) has a DestinationColumn property value that does not refer to a valid output column LineageID.
0xC02020AC	DTS_E_TXUNPIVOTDUPLICATEDESTINATION	Duplicate destination error. More than one non-pivoted input column is mapped to the same destination output column.
0xC02020AD	DTS_E_TOTALINPUTCOLSCANNOTBEZERO	No input columns found. At least one input column must be mapped to an output column.
0xC02020AE	DTS_E_TXMERGEJOINMUSTHAVESAMENUMBEROFINPUTANDOUTPUTCOLS	The number of input and output columns are not equal. The total number of input columns on all inputs must be the same as the total number of output columns.
0xC02020AF	DTS_E_INPUTMUSTBESORTED	The input is not sorted. The " __ " must be sorted.
0xC02020B0	DTS_E_TXMERGEJOININVALIDJOINTYPE	The JoinType custom property for the __ contains a value of __, which is not valid. Valid values are 0 (full), 1 (left), or 2 (inner).
0xC02020B1	DTS_E_TXMERGEJOININVALIDNUMKEYCOLS	The NumKeyColumns value is not valid. In the __, the value for the NumKeyColumns custom property must be between 1 and __.
0xC02020B2	DTS_E_NOKEYCOLS	No key columns are found. The __ must have at least one column with a SortKeyPosition that is non-zero.
0xC02020B3	DTS_E_TXMERGEJOINNOTENOUGHKEYCOLS	Not enough key columns. The __ must have at least __ columns with non-zero SortKeyPosition values.
0xC02020B4	DTS_E_TXMERGEJOINDATATYPEMISMATCH	Datatype mismatch occurred. The datatypes for the columns with SortKeyPosition value __ do not match.
0xC02020B5	DTS_E_TXMERGEJOININVALIDSORTKEYPOS	The column with the SortKeyPosition value of __ is not valid. It should be __.
0xC02020B6	DTS_E_TXMERGEJOINSORTDIRECTIONMISMATCH	Sort direction mismatch. The sort directions for the columns with SortKeyPosition value __ do not match.

Error Code	Symbolic Name	Description
0xC02020B7	DTS_E_TXMERGEJOINOUTPUTCOLMUSTHAVE ASSOCIATEDINPUTCOL	Missing column. The __ must have an associated input column.
0xC02020B8	DTS_E_TXMERGEJOINREADONLYINPUTCOLSWITH NOOUTPUTCOL	Input columns must have output columns. There are input columns with a usage type of read-only that do not have associated output columns.
0xC02020B9	DTS_E_TXMERGEJOINNONSTRINGCOMPARISON FLAGSNOTZERO	The comparison flags are not zero. The comparison flags for non-string columns must be zero.
0xC02020BA	DTS_E_ TXMERGEJOINCOMPARISONFLAGSMISMATCH	The comparison flags for the columns with SortKeyPosition value __ do not match.
0xC02020BB	DTS_E_TXPIVOTBADPIVOTKEYVALUENOSTRING	Unrecognized pivot key value.
0xC02020BC	DTS_E_TXLINEAGEINVALIDLINEAGEITEM	Lineage item value __ is not valid. The valid range is between __ and __.
0xC02020BD	DTS_E_CANNOTHAVEANYINPUTCOLUMNS	Input columns not allowed. The number of input columns must be zero.
0xC02020BE	DTS_E_TXLINEAGEDATATYPEMISMATCH	The datatype for " __ " is not valid for the specified lineage item.
0xC02020BF	DTS_E_TXLINEAGEINVALIDLENGTH	The length for " __ " is not valid for the specified lineage item.
0xC02020C1	DTS_E_ METADATAMISMATCHWITHOUTPUTCOLUMN	The metadata for " __ " does not match the metadata for the associated output column.
0xC02020C3	DTS_E_TXMERGESORTKEYPOSMISMATCH	There are output columns that have SortKeyPosition values that don't match the associated input columns' SortKeyPosition.
0xC02020C4	DTS_E_ADDROWTOBUFFERFAILED	The attempt to add a row to the Data Flow task buffer failed with error code 0x__.
0xC02020C5	DTS_E_DATACONVERSIONFAILED	Data conversion failed while converting column " __ " (__) to column " __ " (__). The conversion returned status value __ and status text " __ ".
0xC02020C6	DTS_E_FAILEDTOALLOCATEROWHANDLEBUFFER	The attempt to allocate a row handle buffer failed with error code 0x__.
0xC02020C7	DTS_E_FAILEDTOSENDROWTOSQLSERVER	The attempt to send a row to SQL Server failed with error code 0x__.
0xC02020C8	DTS_E_FAILEDTOPREPAREBUFFERSTATUS	The attempt to prepare the buffer status failed with error code 0x__.
0xC02020C9	DTS_E_FAILEDTOBUFFERROWSTARTS	The attempt to retrieve the start of the buffer row failed with error code 0x__.
0xC02020CA	DTS_E_BULKINSERTTHREADTERMINATED	The thread for the SSIS Bulk Insert is no longer running. No more rows can be inserted. Try increasing the bulk insert thread timeout.
0xC02020CB	DTS_E_RAWTOOMANYCOLUMNS	The source file is not valid. The source file is returning a count of more than 131,072 columns. This usually occurs when the source file is not produced by the raw file destination.

Error Code	Symbolic Name	Description
0xC02020CC	DTS_E_TXUNIONALL_EXTRADANGLINGINPUT	The __ is an extra unattached input and will be removed.
0xC02020CD	DTS_E_TXUNIONALL_NONDANGLINGUNATTACHEDINPUT	The __ is not attached but is not marked as dangling. It will be marked as dangling.
0xC02020CF	DTS_E_TXPIVOTRUNTIMEDUPLICATEPIVOTKEYVALUE	Duplicate pivot key value "__".
0xC02020D0	DTS_E_TXPIVOTRUNTIMEDUPLICATEPIVOTKEYVALUENOSTRING	Duplicate pivot key value.
0xC02020D1	DTS_E_FAILEDTOGETCOMPONENTLOCALEID	Failure retrieving component locale ID. Error code 0x__.
0xC02020D2	DTS_E_MISMATCHCOMPONENTCONNECTIONMANAGERLOCALEID	Mismatched locale IDs. The component locale ID (__) does not match the connection manager locale ID (__).
0xC02020D3	DTS_E_LOCALEIDNOTSET	The component locale ID has not been set. Flat file adapters need to have the locale ID on the flat file connection manager set.
0xC02020D4	DTS_E_RAWBYTESTOOLONG	The binary field is too large. The adapter attempted to read a binary field that was __ bytes long, but expected a field no longer than __ bytes at offset __. This usually occurs when the input file is not valid. The file contains a string length that is too large for the buffer column.
0xC02020D5	DTS_E_TXSAMPLINGINVALIDPCT	The percentage, __, is not valid for the "__" property. It must be between 0 and 100.
0xC02020D6	DTS_E_TXSAMPLINGINVALIDROWS	The number of rows, __, is not valid for the "__" property. It must be greater than 0.
0xC02020D7	DTS_E_RAWSTRINGINPUTTOOLONG	The adapter was asked to write a string that was __ bytes long, but all data must be less than 4294967295 bytes in length.
0xC02020D9	DTS_E_ATLEASTONEINPUTMUSTBEMAPPEDTOOUTPUT	No inputs were mapped to an output. The "__" must have at least one input column mapped to an output column.
0xC02020DB	DTS_E_CANNOTCONVERTDATATYPESWITHDIFFERENTCODEPAGES	Conversion from "__" with code page __ to "__" with code page __ is not supported.
0xC02020DC	DTS_E_COLUMNNOTMAPPEDTOEXTERNALMETADATACOLUMN	The external metadata column mapping for __ is not valid. The external metadata column ID cannot be zero.
0xC02020DD	DTS_E_COLUMNMAPPEDTONONEXISTENTEXTERNALMETADATACOLUMN	The __ is mapped to an external metadata column that does not exist.

Error Code	Symbolic Name	Description
0xC02020E5	DTS_E_UNABLETOWRITELOBDATATOBUFFER	Writing long object data of type DT_TEXT, DT_NTEXT, or DT_IMAGE to Data Flow task buffer failed for column "__".
0xC02020E8	DTS_E_CANNOTGETIROWSET	Opening a rowset for "__" failed. Check that the object exists in the database.
0xC02020E9	DTS_E_VARIABLEACCESSFAILED	Accessing variable "__" failed with error code 0x__.
0xC02020EA	DTS_E_CONNECTIONMANAGERNOTFOUND	The connection manager "__" is not found. A component failed to find the connection manager in the Connections collection.
0xC02020EB	DTS_E_VERSIONUPGRADEFAILED	The upgrade from version "__" to version __ failed.
0xC02020EC	DTS_E_RSTDESTBIGBLOB	A value in an input column is too large to be stored in the ADODB.Recordset object.
0xC02020ED	DTS_E_CANNOTCONVERTBETWEENUNICODE ANDNONUNICODESTRINGCOLUMNS	Columns "__" and "__" cannot convert between Unicode and non-Unicode string data types.
0xC02020EE	DTS_E_ROWCOUNTBADVARIABLENAME	The variable "__" specified by VariableName property is not a valid variable. Need a valid variable name to write to.
0xC02020EF	DTS_E_ROWCOUNTBADVARIABLETYPE	The variable "__" specified by VariableName property is not an integer. Change the variable to be of type VT_I4, VT_UI4, VT_I8, or VT_UI8.
0xC02020F0	DTS_E_NOCOLUMNADVANCETHROUGHFILE	No column was specified to allow the component to advance through the file.
0xC02020F1	DTS_E_MERGEJOINSORTEDOUTPUTHASNOSORT KEYPOSITIONS	The "__" has IsSorted set to TRUE, but the SortKeyPosition on all output columns are zero. Either change the IsSorted to FALSE, or select at least one output column to contain a non-zero SortKeyPosition.
0xC02020F2	DTS_E_METADATAMISMATCHWITHINPUTCOLUMN	The "__" metadata does not match the metadata of the input column.
0xC02020F3	DTS_E_RSTDESTBADVARIABLE	The value of the specified variable cannot be located, locked, or set.
0xC02020F4	DTS_E_CANTPROCESSCOLUMNTYPECODEPAGE	The column "__" cannot be processed because more than one code page (__ and __) are specified for it.
0xC02020F5	DTS_E_CANTINSERTCOLUMNTYPE	The column "__" can't be inserted because the conversion between types __ and __ is not supported.
0xC02020F6	DTS_E_CANNOTCONVERTBETWEENUNICODE ANDNONUNICODESTRINGCOLUMN	Column "__" cannot convert between Unicode and non-Unicode string data types.
0xC02020F8	DTS_E_COULDNOTFINDINPUTBUFFERCOLUMN BYLINEAGE	The __ cannot find the column with LineageID __ in its input buffer.
0xC02020F9	DTS_E_ COULDNOTGETCOLUMNINFOFORINPUTBUFFER	The __ cannot get the column information for column __ from its input buffer.

Error Code	Symbolic Name	Description
0xC02020FA	DTS_E_COULDNOTGETCOLUMNINFOFORCOPYBUFFER	The __ cannot get the column information for column " __ " from its copy buffer.
0xC02020FB	DTS_E_COULDNOTREGISTERCOPYBUFFER	The __ cannot register a buffer type for its copy buffer.
0xC02020FC	DTS_E_COULDNOTCREATECOPYBUFFER	The __ cannot create a buffer to copy its data into for sorting.
0xC02020FD	DTS_E_DATAREADERDESTREADFAILED	DataReader client has failed to call Read or has closed the DataReader.
0xC0204000	DTS_E_PROPERTYNOTSUPPORTED	The property " __ " cannot be set on " __ ". The property being set is not supported on the specified object. Check the property name, case, and spelling.
0xC0204002	DTS_E_CANTCHANGEPROPERTYTYPE	The property type cannot be changed from the type that was set by the component.
0xC0204003	DTS_E_CANTADDOUTPUTID	Output ID __ failed during insert. The new output was not created.
0xC0204004	DTS_E_CANTDELETEOUTPUTID	Cannot delete output ID __ from the output collection. The ID may not be valid, or the ID may have been the default or error output.
0xC0204006	DTS_E_FAILEDTOSETPROPERTY	Failed to set property " __ " on " __ ".
0xC0204007	DTS_E_FAILEDTOSETOUTPUTCOLUMNTYPE	Failed to set the type of __ to type: " __ ", length: __ precision: __ scale: __ codepage: __.
0xC0204008	DTS_E_MORETHANONEERROROUTPUTFOUND	More than one error output was found on the component, and there can be only one.
0xC020400A	DTS_E_CANTSETOUTPUTCOLUMNPROPERTY	The property on an output column cannot be set.
0xC020400B	DTS_E_CANTMODIFYERROROUTPUTCOLUMNDATATYPE	The data type for " __ " cannot be modified in the error " __ ".
0xC020400E	DTS_E_CANONLYSETISSORTEDONSOURCE	The " __ " cannot have its IsSorted property set to TRUE because it is not a source output. A source output has a SynchronousInputID value of zero.
0xC020400F	DTS_E_CANONLYSETSORTKEYONSOURCE	The " __ " cannot have a SortKeyPosition property set to non-zero because " __ " is not a source output. The output column "colname" (ID) cannot have its SortKeyPosition property set to non-zero because its output "outputname" (ID) is not a source output.
0xC0204010	DTS_E_CANONLYSETCOMPFLAGSONSOURCE	The ComparisonFlags property cannot be set to a non-zero value for " __ " because the __ " is not a source output. The output column "colname" (ID) cannot have a ComparisonFlags property set to non-zero because its output "outputname" (ID) is not a source output.

Error Code	Symbolic Name	Description
0xC0204011	DTS_E_NONSTRINGCOMPARISONFLAGSNOTZERO	The comparison flags for " __ " must be zero because its type is not a string type. ComparisonFlags can only be non-zero for string type columns.
0xC0204012	DTS_E_COMPFLAGSONLYONSORTCOL	The " __ " cannot have a ComparisonFlags property set to non-zero because its SortKeyPosition is set to zero. An output column's ComparisonFlags can only be non-zero if its SortKeyPosition is also non-zero.
0xC0204013	DTS_E_READONLYSTOCKPROPERTY	The property is read-only.
0xC0204014	DTS_E_INVALIDDATATYPE	The __ had an invalid datatype value (__) set.
0xC0204015	DTS_E_CODEPAGEREQUIRED	The " __ " requires a code page to be set but the value passed was zero.
0xC0204016	DTS_E_INVALIDSTRINGLENGTH	The " __ " has a length that is not valid. The length must be between __ and __.
0xC0204017	DTS_E_INVALIDSCALE	The " __ " has a scale that is not valid. The scale must be between __ and __.
0xC0204018	DTS_E_INVALIDPRECISION	The " __ " has a precision that is not valid. The precision must be between __ and __.
0xC0204019	DTS_E_PROPVALUEIGNORED	The " __ " has a value set for length, precision, scale, or code page that is a value other than zero, but the data type requires the value to be zero.
0xC020401A	DTS_E_CANTSETOUTPUTCOLUMNDATATYPEPROPERTIES	The __ does not allow setting output column datatype properties.
0xC020401B	DTS_E_INVALIDDATATYPEFORERRORCOLUMNS	The " __ " contains an invalid data type. " __ " is a special error column, and the only valid data type is DT_I4.
0xC020401C	DTS_E_NOERRORDESCFORCOMPONENT	The component does not supply error code descriptions.
0xC020401D	DTS_E_UNRECOGNIZEDERRORCODE	The specified error code is not associated with this component.
0xC020401F	DTS_E_TRUNCATIONTRIGGEREDREDIRECTION	A truncation caused a row to be redirected, based on the truncation disposition settings.
0xC0204020	DTS_E_CANTSETUSAGETYPETOREADWRITE	The " __ " is unable to make the column with lineage ID __ read/write because that usage type is not allowed on this column. An attempt was made to change the usage type of an input column to a type, UT_READWRITE, that is not supported on this component.
0xC0204023	DTS_E_CANTSETUSAGETYPE	The __ has forbidden the requested use of the input column with lineage ID __.
0xC0204024	DTS_E_FAILEDTOSETUSAGETYPE	The " __ " was unable to make the requested change to the input column with lineage ID __. The request failed with error code 0x__. The specified error occurred while attempting to set the usage type of an input column.

Error Code	Symbolic Name	Description
0xC0204025	DTS_E_FAILEDTOSETOUTPUTCOLUMNDATA TYPEPROPERTIES	Attempt to set the data type properties on " ___ " failed with error code 0x___. The error occurred while attempting to set one or more of the data type properties of the output column.
0xC0204026	DTS_E_UNABLETORETRIEVEMETADATA	The metadata for " ___ " cannot be retrieved. Make sure the object name is correct and the object exists.
0xC0204027	DTS_E_CANNOTMAPOUTPUTCOLUMN	The output column cannot be mapped to an external metadata column.
0xC0204028	DTS_E_UNSUPPORTEDVARIABLETYPE	The variable ___ is required to be of type " ___ ".
0xC020402A	DTS_E_CANTSETEXTERNALMETADATACOLUMN DATATYPEPROPERTIES	The ___ does not allow setting external metadata column datatype properties.
0xC020402B	DTS_E_IDNOTINPUTNOROUTPUT	The ID, ___, is neither an input ID nor an output ID. The specified ID must be the input ID or the output ID that the external metadata collection is associated with.
0xC020402C	DTS_E_METADATACOLLECTIONNOTUSED	The external metadata collection on " ___ " is marked as not used, so no operations can be performed on it.
0xC020402D	DTS_E_NOBUFFERTYPEONSYNCOUTPUT	The ___ is a synchronous output and the buffer type cannot be retrieved for a synchronous output.
0xC0207000	DTS_E_INPUTCOLUMNUSAGETYPENOTREADONLY	The input column " ___ " must be read-only. The input column has a usage type other than read-only, which is not allowed.
0xC0207001	DTS_E_MISSINGCUSTOMPROPERTY	The " ___ " is missing the required property " ___ ". The object is required to have the specified custom property.
0xC0207002	DTS_E_ILLEGALCUSTOMOUTPUTPROPERTY	The output ___ cannot have property " ___ ", but currently has that property assigned.
0xC0207003	DTS_E_INVALIDOUTPUTEXCLUSIONGROUP	The ___ must be in exclusion group ___. All outputs must be in the specified exclusion group.
0xC0207004	DTS_E_PROPERTYISEMPTY	The property " ___ " is empty. The property cannot be empty.
0xC0207005	DTS_E_CREATEEXPRESSIONOBJECTFAILED	Memory cannot be allocated for the expression " ___ ". There was an out-of-memory error while creating an internal object to hold the expression.
0xC0207006	DTS_E_EXPRESSIONPARSEFAILED	Cannot parse the expression " ___ ". The expression was not valid, or there is an out-of-memory error.

Error Code	Symbolic Name	Description
0xC0207007	DTS_E_EXPRESSIONCOMPUTEFAILED	Computing the expression " __ " failed with error code 0x__. The expression may have errors, such as divide by zero, that cannot be detected at parse time, or there may be an out-of-memory error.
0xC0207008	DTS_E_FAILEDTOCREATEEXPRESSIONARRAY	Memory cannot be allocated for the Expression objects. An out-of-memory error occurred while creating the array of Expression object pointers.
0xC020700A	DTS_E_FAILEDTOCREATEEXPRESSIONMANANGER	The __ failed with error code 0x__ while creating the Expression Manager.
0xC020700B	DTS_E_SPLITEXPRESSIONNOTBOOLEAN	The expression " __ " is not Boolean. The result type of the expression must be Boolean.
0xC020700C	DTS_E_EXPRESSIONVALIDATIONFAILED	The expression " __ " on " __ " is not valid.
0xC020700E	DTS_E_COLUMNNOTMATCHED	The column " __ " (__) cannot be matched to any input file column. The output column name or input column name cannot be found in the file.
0xC020700F	DTS_E_SETRESULTCOLUMNFAILED	Attempting to set the result column for the expression " __ " on __ failed with error code 0x__. The input or output column that was to receive the result of the expression cannot be determined, or the expression result cannot be cast to the column type.
0xC0207011	DTS_E_FAILEDTOGETLOCALEIDFROMPACKAGE	The __ failed to get the locale ID from the package.
0xC0207012	DTS_E_INCORRECTPARAMETERMAPPINGFORMAT	The parameter mapping string is not in the correct format.
0xC0207013	DTS_E_NOTENOUGHPARAMETERSPROVIDED	The SQL command requires __ parameters, but the parameter mapping only has __ parameters.
0xC0207014	DTS_E_PARAMETERNOTFOUNDINMAPPING	The SQL command requires a parameter named " __ ", which is not found in the parameter mapping.
0xC0207015	DTS_E_DUPLICATEDATASOURCECOLUMNNAME	There is more than one data source column with the name " __ ". The data source column names must be unique.
0xC0207016	DTS_E_DATASOURCECOLUMNWITHNONAMEFOUND	There is a data source column with no name. All data source columns must have a name.
0xC0208001	DTS_E_DISCONNECTEDCOMPONENT	A component is disconnected from the layout.
0xC0208002	DTS_E_INVALIDCOMPONENTID	The ID for a layout component is not valid.
0xC0208003	DTS_E_INVALIDINPUTCOUNT	A component has an invalid number of inputs.
0xC0208004	DTS_E_INVALIDOUTPUTCOUNT	A component has an invalid number of outputs.
0xC0208005	DTS_E_NOINPUTSOROUTPUTS	A component does not have any inputs or outputs.

Error Code	Symbolic Name	Description
0xC0208007	DTS_E_CANTALLOCATECOLUMNINFO	Not enough memory was available to allocate a list of the columns that are being manipulated by this component.
0xC0208008	DTS_E_OUTPUTCOLUMNNOTININPUT	Output column "__" (__) references input column with lineage ID __, but no input could be found with that lineage ID.
0xC0208009	DTS_E_SORTNEEDSONEKEY	At least one input column must be marked as a sort key, but no keys were found.
0xC020800A	DTS_E_SORTDUPLICATEKEYWEIGHT	Both column "__" (__) and column "__" (__) were marked with sort key weight __.
0xC020800D	DTS_E_CANTMODIFYINVALID	The component cannot perform the requested metadata change until the validation problem is fixed.
0xC020800E	DTS_E_CANTADDINPUT	An input cannot be added to the inputs collection.
0xC020800F	DTS_E_CANTADDOUTPUT	An output cannot be added to the outputs collection.
0xC0208010	DTS_E_CANTDELETEINPUT	An input cannot be deleted from the inputs collection.
0xC0208011	DTS_E_CANTDELETEOUTPUT	An output cannot be removed from the outputs collection.
0xC0208014	DTS_E_CANTCHANGEUSAGETYPE	The usage type of the column cannot be changed.
0xC0208016	DTS_E_INVALIDUSAGETYPEFORCUSTOMPROPERTY	The __ must be read/write to have custom property "__". The input or output column has the specified custom property, but is not read/write. Remove the property, or make the column read/write.
0xC0208017	DTS_E_READWRITECOLUMNMISSINGREQUIREDCUSTOMPROPERTY	The __ is read/write and is required to have custom property "__". Add the property, or remove the read/write attribute from the column.
0xC0208018	DTS_E_CANTDELETECOLUMN	The column cannot be deleted. The component does not allow columns to be deleted from this input or output.
0xC0208019	DTS_E_CANTADDCOLUMN	The component does not allow adding columns to this input or output.
0xC020801A	DTS_E_CANNOTTFINDRUNTIMECONNECTIONOBJECT	The connection "__" cannot be found. Verify that the connection manager has a connection with that name.
0xC020801B	DTS_E_CANNOTFINDRUNTIMECONNECTIONMANAGER	The runtime connection manager with the ID "__" cannot be found. Verify that the connection manager collection has a connection manager with that ID.
0xC020801C	DTS_E_CANNOTACQUIRECONNECTIONFROMCONNECTIONMANAGER	The AcquireConnection method call to the connection manager __ "failed with error code 0x__.
0xC020801D	DTS_E_ACQUIREDCONNECTIONISINVALID	The connection acquired from the connection manager "__" is not valid.
0xC020801E	DTS_E_INCORRECTCONNECTIONMANAGERTYPE	The connection manager __ "is an incorrect type. The type required is "__". The type available to the component is "__".

Error Code	Symbolic Name	Description
0xC020801F	DTS_E_CANNOTACQUIREMANAGEDCONNECTION FROMCONNECTIONMANAGER	Cannot acquire a managed connection from the run-time connection manager.
0xC0208020	DTS_E_CANTINITINPUT	An input cannot be created to initialize the inputs collection.
0xC0208021	DTS_E_CANTINITOUTPUT	An output cannot be created to initialize the outputs collection.
0xC0208023	DTS_E_EXTRACTORCANTWRITE	Writing to the file "__" failed with error code 0x__.
0xC0208024	DTS_E_INCORRECTCONNECTIONOBJECTTYPE	The connection manager "__" returned an object of an incorrect type from the AcquireConnection method.
0xC0208025	DTS_E_INPUTCOLPROPERTYNOTFOUND	The "__" property is required on input column "__" (__), but is not found. The missing property should be added.
0xC0208026	DTS_E_EXTRACTORUNREFERENCED	The "__" is marked read-only, but is not referenced by any other column. Unreferenced columns are not allowed.
0xC0208027	DTS_E_EXTRACTORREFERENCEDCOLUMNNOTFOUND	The "__" references column ID __, and that column is not found on the input. A reference points to a non-existent column.
0xC0208028	DTS_E_EXTRACTORDATACOLUMNNOTBLOB	The "__" references "__", and that column is not of a BLOB type.
0xC0208029	DTS_E_INSERTERREFERENCEDCOLUMNNOTFOUND	The "__" references output column ID __, and that column is not found on the output.
0xC020802A	DTS_E_INSERTERCANTREAD	Reading from the file "__" failed with error code 0x__.
0xC020802B	DTS_E_TXSCD_NOTYPEDCOLUMNSATINPUT	There must be at least one column of Fixed, Changing, or Historical type on the input of a Slowly Changing Dimension transform. Verify that at least one column is a FixedAttribute, ChangingAttribute, or HistoricalAttribute.
0xC020802C	DTS_E_TXSCD_INVALIDINPUTCOLUMNTYPE	The ColumnType property of "__" is not valid. The current value is outside the range of acceptable values.
0xC020802D	DTS_E_TXSCD_CANNOTMAPDIFFERENTTYPES	The input column "__" cannot be mapped to external column "__" because they have different data types. The Slowly Changing Dimension transform does not allow mapping between columns of different types except for DT_STR and DT_WSTR.
0xC020802E	DTS_E_NTEXTDATATYPENOTSUPPORTEDWITHANSIFILES	The data type for "__" is DT_NTEXT, which is not supported with ANSI files. Use DT_TEXT instead and convert the data to DT_NTEXT using the data conversion component.
0xC020802F	DTS_E_TEXTDATATYPENOTSUPPORTEDWITH UNICODEFILES	The data type for "__" is DT_TEXT, which is not supported with Unicode files. Use DT_NTEXT instead and convert the data to DT_TEXT using the data conversion component.

Error Code	Symbolic Name	Description
0xC0208030	DTS_E_IMAGEDATATYPENOTSUPPORTED	The data type for "___" is DT_IMAGE, which is not supported. Use DT_TEXT or DT_NTEXT instead and convert the data from, or to, DT_IMAGE using the data conversion component.
0xC0208031	DTS_E_FLATFILEFORMATNOTSUPPORTED	Format "___" is not supported by Flat File Connection Manager. Supported formats are Delimited, FixedWidth, RaggedRight, and Mixed.
0xC0208032	DTS_E_EXTRACTORFILENAMECOLUMNNOTSTRING	The "___" should contain a file name, but it is not of a String type.
0xC0208033	DTS_E_EXTRACTORCANTAPPENDTRUNCATE	Error caused by conflicting property settings. The "___" has both the AllowAppend property and the ForceTruncate property set to TRUE. Both properties cannot be set to TRUE. Set one of the two properties to FALSE.
0xC0208034	DTS_E_EXTRACTORCOLUMNALREADYREFERENCED	The ___ references column ID ___ but that column is already referenced by ___. Remove one of the two reference to the column.
0xC0208035	DTS_E_CONNECTIONMANANGERNOTASSIGNED	A connection manager has not been assigned to the ___.
0xC0208036	DTS_E_INSERTERCOLUMNALREADYREFERENCED	The ___ references the output column with ID ___, but that column is already referenced by ___.
0xC0208037	DTS_E_INSERTERCOLUMNNOTREFERENCED	The "___" is not referenced by any input column. Each output column must be referenced by exactly one input column.
0xC0208038	DTS_E_INSERTERDATACOLUMNNOTBLOB	The "___" references "___", and that column is not the correct type. It must be DT_TEXT, DT_NTEXT, or DT_IMAGE. A reference points to a column that must be a BLOB.
0xC0208039	DTS_E_INSERTERFILENAMECOLUMNNOTSTRING	The "___" should contain a file name, but it is not a String type.
0xC020803A	DTS_E_INSERTEREXPECTBOMINVALIDTYPE	The "___" has the ExpectBOM property set to TRUE for ___, but the column is not NT_NTEXT. The ExpectBOM specifies that the Import Column transformation expects a byte-order mark (BOM). Either set the ExpectBOM property to false or change the output column data type to DT_NTEXT.
0xC020803B	DTS_E_INSERTERINVALIDDATACOLUMNSETTYPE	Data output columns must be DT_TEXT, DT_NTEXT, or DT_IMAGE. The data output column may only be set to a BLOB type.
0xC020803C	DTS_E_TXSCD_FIXEDATTRIBUTECHANGE	If the FailOnFixedAttributeChange property is set to TRUE, the transformation will fail when a fixed attribute change is detected. To send rows to the Fixed Attribute output, set the FailOnFixedAttributeChange property to FALSE.
0xC020803D	DTS_E_TXSCD_LOOKUPFAILURE	The Lookup transformation failed to retrieve any rows. The transform fails when the FailOnLookupFailure is set to TRUE and no rows are retrieved.

Error Code	Symbolic Name	Description
0xC020803E	DTS_E_TXSCD_INVALIDNUMBERSOFPARAMETERS	There must be at least one column type of Key on the input of a Slowly Changing Dimension transformation. Set at least one column type to Key.
0xC020803F	DTS_E_TXSCD_CANNOTFINDEXTERNALCOLUMN	Cannot find external column with name " __ ".
0xC0208040	DTS_E_TXSCD_INFFEREDINDICATORNOTBOOL	Inferred indicator column " __ " must be of type DT_BOOL.
0xC0208107	DTS_E_ERRORROWDISPMUSTBENOTUSED	The __ must have its error row disposition value set to RD_NotUsed.
0xC0208108	DTS_E_TRUNCROWDISPMUSTBENOTUSED	The __ must have its truncation row disposition value set to RD_NotUsed.
0xC0208201	DTS_E_TXAGG_INPUTNOTFOUNDFOROUTPUT	Cannot find input column with lineage ID __ needed by output column with ID __.
0xC0208202	DTS_E_TXAGG_INVALIDOUTPUTDATATYPEFORAGGREGATE	Invalid output data type for aggregate type specified at output column ID __.
0xC0208203	DTS_E_TXAGG_INVALIDINPUTDATATYPEFORAGGREGATE	Invalid input data type for __ used for the specified aggregate at __.
0xC0208204	DTS_E_TXAGG_INPUTOUTPUTDATATYPEMISMATCH	Data types of input column lineage ID __ and output column ID __ do not match.
0xC0208205	DTS_E_UNABLETOGETINPUTBUFFERHANDLE	Cannot get input buffer handle for input ID __.
0xC0208206	DTS_E_UNABLETOGETOUTPUTBUFFERHANDLE	Cannot get output buffer handle for output ID __.
0xC0208207	DTS_E_UNABLETOFINDCOLUMNHANDLEINOUTPUTBUFFER	Cannot find column with lineage ID __ in output buffer.
0xC0208208	DTS_E_UNABLETOFINDCOLUMNHANDLEININPUTBUFFER	Cannot find column with lineage ID __ in input buffer.
0xC0208209	DTS_E_CANNOTHAVEZEROOUTPUTCOLUMNS	The number of output columns for __ cannot be zero.
0xC020820A	DTS_E_CONNECTIONMANAGERCOLUMNCOUNTMISMATCH	The number of columns in the flat file connection manager must be the same as the number of columns in the flat file adapter. The number of columns for the flat file connection manager is __, while the number of columns for the flat file adapter is __.
0xC020820B	DTS_E_MISMATCHCONNECTIONMANAGERCOLUMN	The column " __ " at index __ in the flat file connection manager was not found at index __ in the column collection of the flat file adapter.
0xC020820D	DTS_E_EXTERNALMETADATACOLUMNISALREADYMAPPED	The external metadata column with ID __ has already been mapped to __.
0xC020820E	DTS_E_TXAGG_STRING_TOO_LONG	The transform encountered a key column that was larger than __ characters.

Error Code	Symbolic Name	Description
0xC020820F	DTS_E_DERIVEDRESULT_TOO_LONG	The transform encountered a result value that was longer than __ bytes.
0xC0208210	DTS_E_TXAGG_MEMALLOCERROUTPUT DESCRIPTORS	Unable to allocate memory.
0xC0208211	DTS_E_TXAGG_MEMALLOCERRWORKSPACE DESCRIPTORS	Unable to allocate memory.
0xC0208212	DTS_E_TXAGG_MEMALLOCERRSORTORDER DESCRIPTORS	Unable to allocate memory.
0xC0208213	DTS_E_TXAGG_MEMALLOCERRNUMERIC DESCRIPTORS	Unable to allocate memory.
0xC0208214	DTS_E_TXAGG_MEMALLOCERRCOUNTDISTINCT DESCRIPTOR	Unable to allocate memory.
0xC0208215	DTS_E_TXAGG_MEMALLOCERRWORKSPACESORT ORDERDESCRIPTORS	Unable to allocate memory.
0xC0208216	DTS_E_TXAGG_MEMALLOCERRWORKSPACE NUMERICDESCRIPTORS	Unable to allocate memory.
0xC0208217	DTS_E_TXAGG_MEMALLOCERRWORKSPACE BUFFCOLS	Unable to allocate memory.
0xC0208218	DTS_E_UNREFERENCEDINPUTCOLUMN	The input column "__" is not referenced.
0xC0208219	DTS_E_CANTBUILDTHREADPOOL	The Sort transformation could not create a thread pool with __ threads. Not enough memory is available.
0xC020821A	DTS_E_QUEUEWORKITEMFAILED	The Sort transformation cannot queue a work item to its thread pool. There is not enough memory available.
0xC020821B	DTS_E_SORTTHREADSTOPPED	A worker thread in the Sort transformation stopped with error code 0x__. A catastrophic error was encountered while sorting a buffer.
0xC020821E	DTS_E_SORTBADTHREADCOUNT	MaxThreads was __, and should be between 1 and __, inclusive or -1 to default to the number of CPUs.
0xC020821F	DTS_E_DTPXMLLOADFAILURE	Unable to load from XML.
0xC0208220	DTS_E_DTPXMLSAVEFAILURE	Unable to save to XML.
0xC0208221	DTS_E_DTPXMLINT32CONVERTERR	Unable to convert the value "__" to an integer.
0xC0208222	DTS_E_DTPXMLBOOLCONVERTERR	Unable to convert the value "__" to a Boolean.

Error Code	Symbolic Name	Description
0xC0208223	DTS_E_DTPXMLPARSEERRORNEARID	Load error encountered near object with ID __.
0xC0208226	DTS_E_DTPXMLPROPERTYTYPEERR	The value " __ " is not valid for the attribute " __ ".
0xC0208228	DTS_E_DTPXMLSETUSAGETYPEERR	The value " __ " is not valid for the attribute " __ ".
0xC0208229	DTS_E_DTPXMLDATATYPEERR	The value " __ " is not valid for the attribute " __ ".
0xC020822A	DTS_E_UNMAPPEDINPUTCOLUMN	The __ is not mapped to an output column.
0xC020822B	DTS_E_INPUTCOLUMNBADMAP	The __ has a mapping that is not valid. An output column with an ID of __ does not exist on this component.
0xC020822D	DTS_E_MULTIPLYMAPPEDOUTCOL	The __ is mapped to an output column that already has a mapping on this input.
0xC020822E	DTS_E_TXAGG_STRINGPROMOTIONFAILED	Could not convert input column with Lineage ID __ to DT_WSTR due to error 0x__.
0xC0208230	DTS_E_DTPXMLIDLOOKUPERR	Referenced object with ID __ not found in package.
0xC0208231	DTS_E_DTPXMLINVALIDXMLPERSISTPROPERTY	Cannot read a persistence property required for the pipelinexml module. The property was not provided by the pipeline.
0xC0208232	DTS_E_DTPXMLPROPERTYSTATEERR	The value " __ " is not valid for the attribute " __ ".
0xC0208233	DTS_E_CANTGETCUSTOMPROPERTY	Cannot retrieve custom property " __ ".
0xC0208234	DTS_E_UNABLETOLOCATEINPUTCOLUMNID	An input column with the lineage ID __, referenced in the ParameterMap custom property with the parameter on position number __, cannot be found in the input columns collection.
0xC0208235	DTS_E_TXLOOKUP_UNABLETOLOCATEREFCOLUMN	Unable to locate reference column " __ ".
0xC0208236	DTS_E_TXLOOKUP_INCOMPATIBLEDATATYPES	__ and reference column named " __ " have incompatible data types.
0xC0208237	DTS_E_TXLOOKUP_PARAMMETADATAMISMATCH	The parameterized SQL statement yields metadata which does not match the main SQL statement.
0xC0208238	DTS_E_TXLOOKUP_INCORRECTNUMOFPARAMETERS	The parameterized SQL statement contains an incorrect number of parameters. Expected __, but found __.
0xC0208239	DTS_E_TXLOOKUP_INVALIDJOINTYPE	__ has a datatype which cannot be joined on.
0xC020823A	DTS_E_TXLOOKUP_INVALIDCOPYTYPE	__ has a datatype which cannot be copied.
0xC020823B	DTS_E_INSERTERINVALIDCOLUMNDATATYPE	The __ has an unsupported datatype. It must be DT_STR or DT_WSTR.
0xC020823C	DTS_E_EXTRACTORINVALIDCOLUMNDATATYPE	The __ has an unsupported datatype. It must be DT_STR, DT_WSTR, DT_TEXT, DT_NTEXT, or DT_IMAGE.

Error Code	Symbolic Name	Description
0xC020823D	DTS_E_TXCHARMAPINVALIDCOLUMNDATATYPE	The __ has an unsupported datatype. It must be DT_STR, DT_WSTR, DT_TEXT, or DT_NTEXT.
0xC020823E	DTS_E_SORTCANTCREATEEVENT	The Sort transformation cannot create an event to communicate with its worker threads. Not enough system handles are available to the Sort transformation.
0xC020823F	DTS_E_SORTCANTCREATETHREAD	The Sort transformation cannot create a worker thread. Not enough memory is available to Sort transformation.
0xC0208240	DTS_E_SORTCANTCOMPARE	The Sort transformation failed to compare row __ in buffer ID __ to row __ in buffer ID __.
0xC0208242	DTS_E_TXLOOKUP_TOOFEWREFERENCECOLUMNS	The Lookup transformation reference metadata contains too few columns. Check the SQLCommand property. The SELECT statement must return at least one column.
0xC0208243	DTS_E_TXLOOKUP_MALLOCERR_REFERENCECOLUMNINFO	Unable to allocate memory for an array of ColumnInfo structures.
0xC0208244	DTS_E_TXLOOKUP_MALLOCERR_REFERENCECOLUMNPAIR	Could not allocate memory for an array of ColumnPair structures.
0xC0208245	DTS_E_TXLOOKUP_MALLOCERR_BUFFCOL	Unable to allocate memory for an array of BUFFCOL structures for the creation of a main workspace.
0xC0208246	DTS_E_TXLOOKUP_MAINWORKSPACE_CREATEERR	Unable to create a main workspace buffer.
0xC0208247	DTS_E_TXLOOKUP_HASHTABLE_MALLOCERR	Unable to allocate memory for hash table.
0xC0208248	DTS_E_TXLOOKUP_HASHNODEHEAP_CREATEERR	Unable to allocate memory to create a heap for hash nodes.
0xC0208249	DTS_E_TXLOOKUP_HASHNODEHEAP_MALLOCERR	Unable to allocate memory for a hash node heap.
0xC020824A	DTS_E_TXLOOKUP_LRUNODEHEAP_CREATEERR	Unable to create a heap for LRU nodes. An out-of-memory condition occurred.
0xC020824B	DTS_E_TXLOOKUP_LRUNODEHEAP_MALLOCERR	Unable to allocate memory for the LRU node heap. An out-of-memory condition occurred.
0xC020824C	DTS_E_TXLOOKUP_OLEDBERR_LOADCOLUMNMETADATA	OLE DB error occurred while loading column metadata. Check SQLCommand and SqlCommandParam properties.
0xC020824D	DTS_E_TXLOOKUP_OLEDBERR_GETIROWSET	OLE DB error occurred while fetching rowset. Check SQLCommand and SqlCommandParam properties.
0xC020824E	DTS_E_TXLOOKUP_OLEDBERR_FILLBUFFER	OLE DB error occurred while populating internal cache. Check SQLCommand and SqlCommandParam properties.

Error Code	Symbolic Name	Description
0xC020824F	DTS_E_TXLOOKUP_OLEDBERR_BINDPARAMETERS	OLE DB error occurred while binding parameters. Check SQLCommand and SqlCommandParam properties.
0xC0208250	DTS_E_TXLOOKUP_OLEDBERR_CREATEBINDING	OLE DB error occurred while creating bindings. Check SQLCommand and SqlCommandParam properties.
0xC0208251	DTS_E_TXLOOKUP_INVALID_CASE	An invalid case was encountered in a switch statement during runtime.
0xC0208252	DTS_E_TXLOOKUP_MAINWORKSPACE_MALLOCERR	Unable to allocate memory for a new row for the main workspace buffer. An out-of-memory condition occurred.
0xC0208253	DTS_E_TXLOOKUP_OLEDBERR_GETPARAMIROWSET	OLE DB error occurred while fetching parameterized rowset. Check SQLCommand and SqlCommandParam properties.
0xC0208254	DTS_E_TXLOOKUP_OLEDBERR_GETPARAMSINGLEROW	OLE DB error occurred while fetching parameterized row. Check SQLCommand and SqlCommandParam properties.
0xC0208255	DTS_E_TXAGG_MAINWORKSPACE_MALLOCERR	Unable to allocate memory for a new row for the main workspace buffer. An out-of-memory condition occurred.
0xC0208256	DTS_E_TXAGG_MAINWORKSPACE_CREATEERR	Unable to create a main workspace buffer.
0xC0208257	DTS_E_TXAGG_HASHTABLE_MALLOCERR	Unable to allocate memory for the hash table.
0xC0208258	DTS_E_TXAGG_HASHNODEHEAP_CREATEERR	Unable to allocate memory to create a heap for the hash nodes.
0xC0208259	DTS_E_TXAGG_HASHNODEHEAP_MALLOCERR	Unable to allocate memory for the hash node heap.
0xC020825A	DTS_E_TXAGG_CDNODEHEAP_CREATEERR	Unable to allocate memory to create a heap for CountDistinct nodes.
0xC020825B	DTS_E_TXAGG_CDNODEHEAP_MALLOCERR	Unable to allocate memory for CountDistinct node heap.
0xC020825C	DTS_E_TXAGG_CDCHAINHEAP_CREATEERR	Unable to allocate memory to create a heap for CountDistinct chains.
0xC020825D	DTS_E_TXAGG_CDHASHTABLE_CREATEERR	Unable to allocate memory for CountDistinct hash table.
0xC020825E	DTS_E_TXAGG_CDWORKSPACE_MALLOCERR	Unable to allocate memory for a new row for the CountDistinct workspace buffer.
0xC020825F	DTS_E_TXAGG_CDWORKSPACE_CREATEERR	Unable to create a CountDistinct workspace buffer.
0xC0208260	DTS_E_TXAGG_CDCOLLASSEARRAY_MALLOCERR	Unable to allocate memory for CountDistinct Collapse array.
0xC0208261	DTS_E_TXAGG_CDCHAINHEAP_MALLOCERR	Unable to allocate memory for CountDistinct chains.
0xC0208262	DTS_E_TXCOPYMAP_MISMATCHED_COLUMN_METADATA	Columns with lineage IDs __ and __ have mismatched metadata. The input column that is mapped to an output column for copymap does not have the same metadata (datatype, precision, scale, length, or codepage).

Error Code	Symbolic Name	Description
0xC0208263	DTS_E_TXCOPYMAP_INCORRECT_OUTPUT_COLUMN_MAPPING	The output column with lineage ID "___" is incorrectly mapped to an input column. The CopyColumnId property of the output column is not correct.
0xC0208265	DTS_E_CANTGETBLOBDATA	Failed to retrieve long data for column "___".
0xC0208266	DTS_E_CANTADDBLOBDATA	Long data was retrieved for a column but cannot be added to the Data Flow task buffer.
0xC0208267	DTS_E_MCASTOUTPUTCOLUMNS	Output "___" (___) has output columns, but multicast outputs do not declare columns. The package is damaged.
0xC0208273	DTS_E_UNABLETOGETLOCALIZEDRESOURCE	Unable to load a localized resource ID ___. Verify that the RLL file is present.
0xC0208274	DTS_E_DTPXMLEVENTSCACHEERR	Cannot acquire Events Interface. An invalid Events interface was passed to the data flow module for persisting to XML.
0xC0208275	DTS_E_DTPXMLPATHLOADERR	An error occurred while setting a path object during XML load.
0xC0208276	DTS_E_DTPXMLINPUTLOADERR	Error setting input object during XML load.
0xC0208277	DTS_E_DTPXMLOUTPUTLOADERR	Error setting output object during XML load.
0xC0208278	DTS_E_DTPXMLINPUTCOLUMNLOADERR	Error setting input column object during XML load.
0xC0208279	DTS_E_DTPXMLOUTPUTCOLUMNLOADERR	Error setting output column object during XML load.
0xC0208280	DTS_E_DTPXMLPROPERTYLOADERR	Error setting property object during XML load.
0xC0208281	DTS_E_DTPXMLCONNECTIONLOADERR	Error setting connection object during XML load.
0xC0208282	DTS_E_FG_MISSING_OUTPUT_COLUMNS	Special transformation-specific columns are either missing or have incorrect types.
0xC0208283	DTS_E_FG_PREPARE_TABLES_AND_ACCESSORS	Fuzzy Grouping transformation failed to create required tables and accessors.
0xC0208284	DTS_E_FG_COPY_INPUT	Fuzzy Grouping transformation failed to copy input.
0xC0208285	DTS_E_FG_GENERATE_GROUPS	Fuzzy Grouping transformation failed to generate groups.
0xC0208286	DTS_E_FG_LEADING_TRAILING	An unexpected error occurred in Fuzzy Grouping when applying the settings of property "%1'.
0xC0208287	DTS_E_FG_PICK_CANONICAL	The Fuzzy Grouping transformation failed to pick a canonical row of data to use in standardizing the data.
0xC0208288	DTS_E_FG_NOBLOBS	Fuzzy Grouping does not support input columns of type IMAGE, TEXT, or NTEXT.
0xC0208289	DTS_E_FG_FUZZY_MATCH_ON_NONSTRING	A fuzzy match is specified on column "___" (___) that is not a data type of DT_STR or DT_WSTR.

Error Code	Symbolic Name	Description
0xC020828A	DTS_E_FUZZYGROUPINGINTERNALPIPELINEERROR	A Fuzzy Grouping transformation pipeline error occurred and returned error code 0x__: "__".
0xC020828B	DTS_E_CODE_PAGE_NOT_SUPPORTED	The code page __ specified on column "__" (__) is not supported. You must first convert this column to DT_WSTR which can be done by inserting a Data Conversion Transform before this one.
0xC0208294	DTS_E_SETEODFAILED	Failure encountered while setting end of data flag for the buffer driving output "__" (__).
0xC0208296	DTS_E_CANTCLONE	The input buffer could not be cloned. An out-of-memory condition occurred or there was an internal error.
0xC02082F9	DTS_E_TXCHARMAP_CANTKATAKANAHIRAGANA	Column "__" requests that Katakana and Hiragana characters be produced at the same time.
0xC02082FA	DTS_E_TXCHARMAP_CANTSIMPLECOMPLEX	Column "__" requests that Simple Chinese and Traditional Chinese characters be produced at the same time.
0xC02082FB	DTS_E_TXCHARMAP_CANTFULLHALF	Column "__" requests operations to generate both full width and half width characters.
0xC02082FC	DTS_E_TXCHARMAP_CANTCHINAJAPAN	Column "__" combines operations on Japanese characters with operations for Chinese characters.
0xC02082FD	DTS_E_TXCHARMAP_CANTCASECHINESE	Column "__" combines operations on Chinese characters with uppercase and lowercase operations.
0xC02082FE	DTS_E_TXCHARMAP_CANTCASEJAPANESE	Column "__" combines operations on Japanese characters with uppercase and lowercase operations.
0xC02082FF	DTS_E_TXCHARMAP_CANTBOTHCASE	Column "__" maps the column to both uppercase and lowercase.
0xC0208300	DTS_E_TXCHARMAP_CANTLINGUISTIC	Column "__" combines flags other than uppercase and lowercase with the linguistic casing operation.
0xC0208301	DTS_E_TXCHARMAP_INVALIDMAPFLAGANDDATATYPE	The data type of column "__" cannot be mapped as specified.
0xC0208302	DTS_E_TXFUZZYLOOKUP_UNSUPPORTED_MATCH_INDEX_VERSION	The version (__) of the pre-existing match index "__" is not supported. The version expected is "__". This error occurs if the version persisted in the index metadata does not match the version which the current code was built for. Fix the error by rebuilding the index with the current version of the code.
0xC0208303	DTS_E_TXFUZZYLOOKUP_INVALID_MATCH_INDEX	The table "__" does not appear to be a valid pre-built match index. This error occurs the metadata record cannot be loaded from the specified pre-built index.

Error Code	Symbolic Name	Description
0xC0208304	DTS_E_TXFUZZYLOOKUP_UNABLE_TO_READ_MATCH_INDEX	Unable to read specified pre-built match index " __ ". OLEDB Error code: 0x __.
0xC0208305	DTS_E_TXFUZZYLOOKUP_NO_JOIN_COLUMNS	There were no input columns with a valid join to a reference table column. Make sure that there is at least one join defined using the input column properties JoinToReferenceColumn and JoinType.
0xC0208306	DTS_E_TXFUZZYLOOKUP_INDEX_DOES_NOT_CONTAIN_COLUMN	The specified pre-existing match index " __ " was not originally built with fuzzy match information for column " __ ". It must be rebuilt to include this informa-tion. This error occurs when the index was built with the column not being a fuzzy join column.
0xC0208307	DTS_E_TXFUZZYLOOKUP_IDENTIFIER_PROPERTY	The name " __ " given for property " __ " is not a valid SQL identifier name. This error occurs if the name for the property does not conform to the specifications for a valid SQL identifier name.
0xC0208309	DTS_E_TXFUZZYLOOKUP_MINSIMILARITY_INVALID	The MinSimilarity threshold property on the Fuzzy Lookup transformation must be a value greater than or equal to 0.0 but less than 1.0.
0xC020830A	DTS_E_TXFUZZYLOOKUP_INVALID_PROPERTY_VALUE	The value " __ " for property " __ " is not valid.
0xC020830B	DTS_E_TXFUZZYLOOKUP_INCOMPATIBLE_FUZZY_JOIN_DATATYPES	The fuzzy lookup specified between input column " __ " and reference column " __ " is not valid because fuzzy joins are only supported between string columns, types DT_STR and DT_WSTR.
0xC020830C	DTS_E_TXFUZZYLOOKUP_INCOMPATIBLE_EXACT_JOIN_DATATYPES	The exact lookup columns, " __ " and " __ ", do not have equal data types or are not comparable string types. Exact joins are supported between columns with equal data types or a DT_STR and DT_WSTR combination.
0xC020830D	DTS_E_TXFUZZYLOOKUP_INCOMPATIBLE_COPYCOLUMN_DATATYPES	The copy columns, " __ " and " __ ", do not have equal data types or are not trivially convertible string types. This occurs because copying from reference to output between columns with equal data types, or a DT_STR and DT_WSTR combination, is supported, but other types are not.
0xC020830E	DTS_E_TXFUZZYLOOKUP_INCOMPATIBLE_PASSTHRUCOLUMN_DATATYPES	The passthrough columns, " __ " and " __ ", do not have equal data types. Only columns with equal data types are supported as passthrough columns from input to output.
0xC020830F	DTS_E_TXFUZZYLOOKUP_UNABLETOLOCATEREFCOLUMN	Cannot locate reference column " __ ".

Error Code	Symbolic Name	Description
0xC0208311	DTS_E_TXFUZZYLOOKUP_OUTPUT_COLUMN_MUST_BE_PASSTHRU_COLUMN_OR_A_COPY_COLUMN	An output column must have exactly one CopyColumn or PassThruColumn property specified. This error occurs when neither the CopyColumn or the PassThruColumn properties, or both the CopyColumn and PassThruColumn properties, are set to non-empty values.
0xC0208312	DTS_E_TXFUZZYLOOKUP_PASSTHRU_COLUMN_NOT_FOUND	The source lineage id '%1ldl' specified for property '%2' on output column '%3' was not found in the input column collection. This occurs when the input column id specified on an output column as a passthrough column is not found in the set of inputs.
0xC0208313	DTS_E_TXFUZZYLOOKUP_INDEXED_COLUMN_NOT_FOUND_IN_REF_TABLE	The column "___" in the pre-built index "___" was not found in the reference table/query. This happens if the schema/query of the reference table has changed since the pre-existing match index was built.
0xC0208314	DTS_E_TXFUZZYLOOKUP_TOKEN_TOO_LONG	The component encountered a token that was larger than 2147483647 characters.
0xC0208315	DTS_E_RAWMETADATAMISMATCHTYPE	The output file cannot be appended. Column "___" matches by name, but the column in the file has type ___ and the input column has type ___. The metadata for the column does not match on data type.
0xC0208316	DTS_E_RAWMETADATAMISMATCHSIZE	The output file cannot be appended. Column "___" matches by name, but the column in the file has maximum length ___ and the input column has type ___. The metadata for the column does not match in length.
0xC0208317	DTS_E_RAWMETADATAMISMATCHCODEPAGE	The output file cannot be appended. Column "___" matches by name, but the column in the file has code page ___ and the input column has code page ___. The metadata for the named column does not match on code page.
0xC0208318	DTS_E_RAWMETADATAMISMATCHPRECISION	The output file cannot be appended. Column "___" matches by name, but the column in the file has precision ___ and the input column has precision ___. The metadata for the named column does not match on precision.
0xC0208319	DTS_E_RAWMETADATAMISMATCHSCALE	The output file cannot be appended. Column "___" matches by name, but the column in the file has scale ___ and the input column has scale ___. The metadata for the named column does not match on scale.
0xC020831A	DTS_E_COULD_NOT_DETERMINE_DATASOURCE_DBMSNAME	Unable to determine the DBMS name and version on "___". This occurs if the IDBProperties on the connection did not return information needed to verify the DBMS name and version.

Error Code	Symbolic Name	Description
0xC020831B	DTS_E_INCORRECT_SQL_SERVER_VERSION	The DBMS type or version of "__" is not supported. A connection to Microsoft SQL Server version 8.0 or later is required. This occurs if IDBProperties on the connection did not return a the correct version.
0xC020831D	DTS_E_CANTDELETEERRORCOLUMNS	The __ is a special error output column and cannot be deleted.
0xC020831E	DTS_E_UNEXPECTEDCOLUMNDATATYPE	The data type specified for column "__" is not the expected type "__".
0xC020831F	DTS_E_INPUTCOLUMNNOTFOUND	The input column lineage ID "__" referenced by property "__" on output column "__" could not be located in the input column collection.
0xC0208320	DTS_E_TXGROUPDUPS_ INPUTCOLUMNNOTJOINED	The input column "__" referenced by the "__" property on output column "__" must have property ToBeCleaned=True and have a valid ExactFuzzy property value.
0xC0208322	DTS_E_TXFUZZYLOOKUP_REF_TABLE_MISSING_ IDENTITY_INDEX	The reference table '%1' does not have a clustered index on an integer identity column, which is required if the property 'CopyRefTable' is set to FALSE. If CopyRefTable is false, the reference table must have a clustered index on an integer identity column.
0xC0208323	DTS_E_TXFUZZYLOOKUP_REF_CONTAINS_NON_ INTEGER_IDENT_COLUMN	The reference table '%1' contains a non-integer type identity column which is not supported. Use a view of the table without the column '%2'. This error occurs because when a copy is made of the reference table, an integer identity column is added, and only one identity column is allowed per table.
0xC0208324	DTS_E_TXFUZZY_MATCHCONTRIBUTION_AND_ HIERARCHY_SPECIFIED	Both MatchContribution and hierarchy information cannot be specified at the same time. This is not allowed because these properties are both weighing factors for scoring.
0xC0208325	DTS_E_TXFUZZY_HIERARCHY_INCORRECT	Levels in hierarchy should be unique numbers. Valid level in hierarchy values are integers greater than or equal to 1. The smaller the number is, the lower the column is in the hierarchy. The default value is 0, indicating that the column is not part of a hierarchy. Overlaps and gaps are not allowed.
0xC0208326	DTS_E_TXFUZZYGROUPING_INSUFFICIENT_ FUZZY_JOIN_COLUMNS	No columns to fuzzy group on were defined. There must be at least one input column with column properties ToBeCleaned=true and ExactFuzzy=2.
0xC0208329	DTS_E_TXFUZZYLOOKUP_COLUMNINVALID	The column with ID '%1!d!' was not valid for an undetermined reason.
0xC020832A	DTS_E_TXFUZZYLOOKUP_UNSUPPORTEDDATATYPE	The data type of column '%1' is not supported.
0xC020832C	DTS_E_TXFUZZYLOOKUP_ OUTPUTLENGTHMISMATCH	The length of output column '%1' is less than that of its source column '%2'.

Error Code	Symbolic Name	Description
0xC020832F	DTS_E_TERMEXTRACTION_ INCORRECTEXACTNUMBEROFINPUTCOLUMNS	There should be only one input column.
0xC0208330	DTS_E_TERMEXTRACTION_ INCORRECTEXACTNUMBEROFOUTPUTCOLUMNS	There should be exactly two output columns.
0xC0208331	DTS_E_TERMEXTRACTION_ INCORRECTDATATYPEOFINPUTCOLUMN	The input column can only have DT_WSTR or DT_NTEXT as its data type.
0xC0208332	DTS_E_TERMEXTRACTION_ INCORRECTDATATYPEOFOUTPUTCOLUMN	The output column [%1!d!] can only have '%2' as its data type.
0xC0208333	DTS_E_TERMEXTRACTION_ INCORRECTDATATYPEOFREFERENCECOLUMN	The reference column can only have DT_STR or DT_WSTR as its data type.
0xC0208334	DTS_E_TERMEXTRACTION_ UNABLETOLOCATEREFCOLUMN	An error occurred while locating the reference column '%1'.
0xC0208335	DTS_E_TERMEXTRACTION_INCORRECTTERMTYPE	The Term Type of the transformation can only be WordOnly, PhraseOnly, or WordPhrase.
0xC0208336	DTS_E_TERMEXTRACTION_ INCORRECTFREQUENCYTHRESHOLD	The value of Frequency Threshold should not be lower than '%1!d!'.
0xC0208337	DTS_E_TERMEXTRACTION_ INCORRECTMAXLENOFTERM	The value of Max Length of Term should not be lower than '%1!d!'.
0xC0208338	DTS_E_TERMEXTRACTION_ TOOFEWREFERENCECOLUMNS	Term Extraction reference metadata contains too few columns.
0xC0208339	DTS_E_TERMEXTRACTION_MALLOCERR_ REFERENCECOLUMNINFO	An error occurred while allocating memory.
0xC020833A	DTS_E_TERMEXTRACTION_MAINWORKSPACE_ CREATEERR	An error occurred while creating a workspace buffer.
0xC020833B	DTS_E_TERMEXTRACTION_OLEDBERR_ CREATEBINDING	An OLEDB error occurred while creating bindings.
0xC020833C	DTS_E_TERMEXTRACTION_OLEDBERR_ GETIROWSET	An OLEDB error occurred while fetching rowsets.
0xC020833D	DTS_E_TERMEXTRACTION_OLEDBERR_FILLBUFFER	An OLEDB error occurred while populating internal cache.
0xC020833E	DTS_E_TERMEXTRACTION_PROCESSERR	An error occurred while extracting terms on row __, column __. The error code returned was 0x__. Please remove it from the input as a work-around.

Error Code	Symbolic Name	Description
0xC020833F	DTS_E_TERMEXTRACTIONORLOOKUP_PROCESSERR_DEPOSITFULL	The number of the term candidates exceeds its limit, 4G.
0xC0208340	DTS_E_TERMEXTRACTION_INVALIDOUTTERMTABLEORCOLUMN	The reference table, view, or column that is used for Exclusion Terms is not valid.
0xC0208341	DTS_E_TXFUZZYLOOKUP_STRINGCOLUMNTOOLONG	The length of string column '%1' exceeds 4000 characters. A conversion from DT_STR to DT_WSTR is necessary, so a truncation would occur. Either reduce the column width or use only DT_WSTR column types.
0xC0208342	DTS_E_TERMEXTRACTION_OUTTERMTABLEANDCOLUMNNOTSET	The reference table, view, or column to be used for an Exclusion Terms has not been set.
0xC0208343	DTS_E_TERMLOOKUP_TOOFEWOUTPUTCOLUMNS	Term Lookup contains too few output columns.
0xC0208344	DTS_E_TERMLOOKUP_INCORRECTDATATYPEOFREFERENCECOLUMN	The reference column can only have DT_STR or DT_WSTR as its data type.
0xC0208345	DTS_E_TERMLOOKUP_UNABLETOLOCATEREFCOLUMN	An error occurred while locating the reference column '%1'.
0xC0208346	DTS_E_TERMLOOKUP_TOOFEWREFERENCECOLUMNS	Term Lookup reference metadata contains too few columns.
0xC0208347	DTS_E_TERMEXTRACTIONORLOOKUP_TESTOFFSETERROR	An error occurred while normalizing words.
0xC0208348	DTS_E_TERMLOOKUP_MAINWORKSPACE_CREATEERR	An error occurred while creating a workspace buffer.
0xC0208349	DTS_E_TERMLOOKUP_OLEDBERR_CREATEBINDING	An OLEDB error occurred while creating bindings.
0xC020834A	DTS_E_TERMLOOKUP_OLEDBERR_GETIROWSET	An OLEDB error occurred while fetching rowsets.
0xC020834B	DTS_E_TERMLOOKUP_OLEDBERR_FILLBUFFER	An OLEDB error occurred while populating internal cache.
0xC020834C	DTS_E_TERMLOOKUP_PROCESSERR	An error occurred while looking up terms on row ___, column ___. The error code returned was 0x___. Please remove it from the input as a work-around.
0xC020834D	DTS_E_TERMLOOKUP_TEXTIDINPUTCOLUMNNOTMAPPEDWITHOUTPUTCOLUMN	At least one Passthrough column is not mapped to an output column.
0xC020834E	DTS_E_TERMLOOKUP_INCORRECTEXACTNUMBEROFTEXTCOLUMNS	There should be exactly one input column mapped to one reference column.
0xC020834F	DTS_E_TERMLOOKUP_TEXTINPUTCOLUMNHAVEINCORRECTDATATYPE	The input column mapped to a reference column can only have DT_NTXT or DT_WSTR as its data type.

Error Code	Symbolic Name	Description
0xC0208354	DTS_E_TXFUZZYLOOKUP_INVALID_MATCH_INDEX_NAME	The reference table name " __ " is not a valid SQL identifier. This error occurs when the table name cannot be parsed from the input string. There may be unquoted spaces in the name. Verify that the name is correctly quoted.
0xC0208355	DTS_E_TERMEXTRACTION_TERMFILTERSTARTITERATIONERROR	An error occurred while the Term Filter was starting its iteration.
0xC0208356	DTS_E_TERMEXTRACTION_EMPTYTERMRESULTERROR	An error occurred while reclaiming the buffer used for caching terms. The error code returned was 0x__.
0xC0208357	DTS_E_TERMEXTRACTION_STDLENGTHERROR	An std::length_error occurred from the STL containers.
0xC0208358	DTS_E_TERMLOOKUP_SAVEWORDWITHPUNCTERROR	An error occurred while saving words with punctuation characters. The error code returned was 0x__.
0xC0208359	DTS_E_TERMLOOKUP_ADDREFERENCETERM	An error occurred while processing the __ reference term. The error code returned was 0x__. Please remove the reference term from your reference table as a work-around.
0xC020835A	DTS_E_TERMLOOKUP_SORREFERENCETERM	An error occurred while sorting reference terms. The error code returned was 0x__.
0xC020835B	DTS_E_TERMLOOKUP_COUNTTERM	An error occurred while counting term candidates. The error code returned was 0x__.
0xC020835C	DTS_E_FUZZYLOOKUP_REFERENCECACHEFULL	Fuzzy Lookup was unable to load the entire reference table into main memory as is required when the Exhaustive property is enabled. Either we ran out of system memory or a limit was specified for MaxMemoryUsage which was not sufficient to load the reference table. Either set MaxMemoryUsage to 0 or increase it significantly. Alternatively, disable Exhaustive.
0xC020835D	DTS_E_TERMLOOKUP_INITIALIZE	An error occurred while initializing the engine of Term Lookup. The error code returned was 0x__.
0xC020835E	DTS_E_TERMLOOKUP_PROCESSSENTENCE	An error occurred while processing sentences. The error code returned was 0x__.
0xC020835F	DTS_E_TEXTMININGBASE_APPENDTOTEMPBUFFER	An error occurred while adding strings to an internal buffer. The error code returned was 0x__.
0xC0208360	DTS_E_TERMEXTRACTION_SAVEPOSTAG	An error occurred while saving part-of-speech tags from an internal buffer. The error code returned was 0x__.
0xC0208361	DTS_E_TERMEXTRACTION_COUNTTERM	An error occurred while counting term candidates. The error code returned was 0x__.

Error Code	Symbolic Name	Description
0xC0208362	DTS_E_TERMEXTRACTION_INITPOSPROCESSOR	An error occurred while initializing the part-of-speech processor. The error code returned was 0x__.
0xC0208363	DTS_E_TERMEXTRACTION_INITFSA	An error occurred while loading the finite state automata. The error code returned was 0x__.
0xC0208364	DTS_E_TERMEXTRACTION_INITIALIZE	An error occurred while initializing the engine of Term Extraction. The error code returned was 0x__.
0xC0208365	DTS_E_TERMEXTRACTION_PROCESSSENTENCE	An error occurred while processing within a sentence. The error code returned was 0x__.
0xC0208366	DTS_E_TERMEXTRACTION_INITPOSTAGVECTOR	An error occurred while initializing the part-of-speech processor. The error code returned was 0x__.
0xC0208367	DTS_E_TERMEXTRACTION_SAVEPTRSTRING	An error occurred while adding strings to an internal buffer. The error code returned was 0x__.
0xC0208368	DTS_E_TERMEXTRACTION_ADDWORDTODECODER	An error occurred while adding words to a statistical decoder. The error code returned was 0x__.
0xC0208369	DTS_E_TERMEXTRACTION_DECODE	An error occurred while decoding for a sentence. The error code returned was 0x__.
0xC020836A	DTS_E_TERMEXTRACTION_SETEXCLUDEDTERM	An error occurred while setting exclusion terms. The error code returned was 0x__.
0xC020836B	DTS_E_TERMEXTRACTION_PROCESSDOCUMENT	An error occurred while processing a document in the input. The error code returned was 0x__.
0xC020836C	DTS_E_TEXTMININGBASE_TESTPERIOD	An error occurred while testing whether a dot is a part of an acronym. The error code returned was 0x__.
0xC020836D	DTS_E_TERMLOOKUP_ENGINEADDREFERENCETERM	An error occurred while setting reference terms. The error code returned was 0x__.
0xC020836E	DTS_E_TERMLOOKUP_PROCESSDOCUMENT	An error occurred while processing a document in the input. The error code returned was 0x__.
0xC020836F	DTS_E_INVALIDBULKINSERTPROPERTYVALUE	The value for the property __ is __, which is not allowed. The value must be greater than or equal to __.
0xC0208370	DTS_E_INVALIDBULKINSERTFIRSTROWLASTROWVALUES	The value for the property __ is __, which must be less than or equal to the value of __ for property __.

Error Code	Symbolic Name	Description
0xC0208371	DTS_E_FUZZYLOOKUPUNABLETODELETEEXISTING MATCHINDEX	An error was encountered when trying to delete the existing fuzzy match index named "___". It is possible that this table was not created by Fuzzy Lookup (or this version of Fuzzy Lookup), it has been damaged, or there is another problem. Try manually deleting the table named "___" or specify a different name for the MatchIndexName property.
0xC0208372	DTS_E_TERMEXTRACTION_INCORRECTSCORETYPE	The Score Type of the transformation can only be Frequency or TFIDF.
0xC0208373	DTS_E_FUZZYLOOKUPREFTABLETOOBIG	The reference table specified has too many rows. Fuzzy Lookup only works with reference tables having less than 1 billion rows. Consider using a smaller view of your reference table.
0xC0208374	DTS_E_FUZZYLOOKUPUNABLETODETERMINE REFERENCETABLESIZE	Unable to determine the size of the reference table '%1'. It is possible that this object is a view and not a table. Fuzzy Lookup does not support views when CopyReferentaceTable=false. Make sure that the table exists and that CopyReferenceTable=true.
0xC0208377	DTS_E_XMLSRCOUTPUTCOLUMNDATATYPENOT SUPPORTED	The SSIS Data Flow Task data type "___" on the ___ is not supported for the ___.
0xC0208378	DTS_E_XMLSRCCANNOTFINDCOLUMNTOSETDATATYPE	Unable to set data type properties for the output column with ID ___ on the output with ID ___. The output or column could not be found.
0xC0208379	DTS_E_CUSTOMPROPERTYISREADONLY	The value of custom property "___" on the ___ cannot be changed.
0xC020837A	DTS_E_OUTPUTCOLUMNHASNOERRORCOLUMN	The ___ on the non-error output has no corresponding output column on the error output.
0xC020837B	DTS_E_ERRORCOLUMNHASNOOUTPUTCOLUMN	The ___ on the error output has no corresponding output column on the non-error output.
0xC020837C	DTS_E_ERRORCOLUMNHASINCORRECTPROPERTIES	The ___ on the error output has properties that do not match the properties of its corresponding data source column.
0xC020837D	DTS_E_ADOSRCOUTPUTCOLUMNDATATYPE CANNOTBECHANGED	The data type of output columns on the ___ cannot be changed.
0xC020837E	DTS_E_ADOSRCDATATYPENOTSUPPORTED	The data type "___" found on column "___" is not supported for the ___.
0xC020837F	DTS_E_ADOSRCDATATYPEMISMATCH	The data type of "___" does not match the data type "___" of the source column "___".
0xC0208380	DTS_E_ADOSRCCOLUMNNOTINSCHEMAROWSET	The ___ does not have a matching source column in the DataReader schema.

Error Code	Symbolic Name	Description
0xC0208381	DTS_E_TERMLOOKUP_INVALIDREFERENCETERM TABLEORCOLUMN	The reference table/view or column used for the reference terms is invalid.
0xC0208382	DTS_E_TERMLOOKUP_REFERENCETERMTABLE ANDCOLUMNNOTSET	The reference table/view or column used for the reference terms has not been set.
0xC0208383	DTS_E_COLUMNMAPPEDTOALREADYMAPPED EXTERNALMETADATACOLUMN	The __ is mapped to the external metadata column with ID __, which is already mapped to another column.
0xC0208384	DTS_E_TXFUZZYLOOKUP_TOOMANYPREFIXES	The SQL object name "%1" specified for property "%2" contains more than the maximum number of prefixes. The maximum is 2.
0xC0208385	DTS_E_MGDSRCSTATIC_OVERFLOW	The value was too large to fit in the column.
0xC0208386	DTS_E_DATAREADERDESTREADERISCLOSED	The SSIS IDataReader is closed.
0xC0208387	DTS_E_DATAREADERDESTREADERISATEND	The SSIS IDataReader is past the end of the result set.
0xC0208388	DTS_E_ DATAREADERDESTINVALIDCOLUMNORDINAL	The ordinal position of the column is not valid.
0xC0208389	DTS_E_DATAREADERDESTCANNOTCONVERT	Cannot convert the __ from data type " __ " to data type " __ ".
0xC020838A	DTS_E_DATAREADERDESTINVALIDCODEPAGE	The __ has unsupported code page __.
0xC020838B	DTS_E_XMLSRCEXTERNALMETADATACOLUMN NOTINSCHEMA	The __ has no mapping to the XML schema.
0xC020838C	DTS_E_XMLSRCSCHEMACOLUMNNOTIN EXTERNALMETADATA	The column __ in table __ in the XML schema does not have a mapping in the external metadata column collection.
0xC020838D	DTS_E_TXTERMLOOKUP_MISMATCHED_COLUMN_ METADATA	Columns with lineage IDs __ and __ have mismatched metadata. The input column that is mapped to an output column does not have the same metadata (datatype, precision, scale, length, or codepage).
0xC020838E	DTS_E_DATAREADERDESTREADERTIMEOUT	The SSIS IDataReader is closed. The read timeout has expired.
0xC020838F	DTS_E_ADOSRCINVALIDSQLCOMMAND	An error occurred executing the provided SQL command.
0xC0208390	DTS_E_JOINTYPEDOESNTMATCHETI	The JoinType property specified for input column "%1" differs from the JoinType specified for the corresponding reference table column when the Match Index was initially created. Either rebuild the Match Index with the given JoinType or change the JoinType to match the type used when the Match Index was created.
0xC0209001	DTS_E_FAILEDTOFINDCOLUMNINBUFFER	Failed to find column " __ " with lineage ID __ in the buffer. The buffer manager returned error code 0x__.

Error Code	Symbolic Name	Description
0xC0209002	DTS_E_FAILEDTOGETCOLUMNINFOFROMBUFFER	Failed to get information for column "__" (__) from the buffer. The error code returned was 0x__.
0xC0209011	DTS_E_TXAGG_ARITHMETICOVERFLOW	Arithmetic overflow encountered while aggregating "__".
0xC0209012	DTS_E_FAILEDTOGETCOLINFO	Failed to get information for row __, column __ from the buffer. The error code returned was 0x__.
0xC0209013	DTS_E_FAILEDTOSETCOLINFO	Failed to set information for row __, column __ into the buffer. The error code returned was 0x__.
0xC0209015	DTS_E_REQUIREDBUFFERISNOTAVAILBLE	A required buffer is not available.
0xC0209016	DTS_E_FAILEDTOGETBUFFERBOUNDARYINFO	The attempt to get buffer boundary information failed with error code 0x__.
0xC0209017	DTS_E_FAILEDTOSETBUFFERENDOFROWSET	Setting the end of rowset for the buffer failed with error code 0x__.
0xC0209018	DTS_E_FAILEDTOGETDATAFORERRORROUTPUTBUFFER	Failed to get data for the error output buffer.
0xC0209019	DTS_E_FAILEDTOREMOVEROWFROMBUFFER	Removing a row from the buffer failed with error code 0x__.
0xC020901B	DTS_E_FAILEDTOSETBUFFERERRORINFO	The attempt to set buffer error information failed with error code 0x__.
0xC020901C	DTS_E_COLUMNSTATUSERROR	There was an error with __ on __. The column status returned was: "__".
0xC020901D	DTS_E_TXLOOKUP_METADATAXMLCACHEERR	Unable to cache reference metadata.
0xC020901E	DTS_E_TXLOOKUP_ROWLOOKUPERROR	Row yielded no match during lookup.
0xC020901F	DTS_E_INVALIDERRORDISPOSITION	The __ has an invalid error or truncation row disposition.
0xC0209022	DTS_E_FAILEDTODIRECTERRORROW	Directing the row to the error output failed with error code 0x__.
0xC0209023	DTS_E_FAILEDTOPREPARECOLUMNSTATUSESFORINSERT	Preparing column statuses for insert failed with error code 0x__.
0xC0209024	DTS_E_FAILEDTOFINDCOLUMNBYLINEAGEID	An attempt to find __ with lineage ID __ in the Data Flow Task buffer failed with error code 0x__.
0xC0209025	DTS_E_FAILEDTOFINDNONSPECIALERRORCOLUMN	Failed to find any non-special error column in __.
0xC0209029	DTS_E_INDUCEDTRANSFORMFAILUREONERROR	The "__" failed because error code 0x__ occurred, and the error row disposition on "__" specifies failure on error. An error occurred on the specified object of the specified component.
0xC020902A	DTS_E_INDUCEDTRANSFORMFAILUREONTRUNCATION	The "__" failed because truncation occurred, and the truncation row disposition on "__" specifies failure on truncation. A truncation error occurred on the specified object of the specified component.

Error Code	Symbolic Name	Description
0xC020902B	DTS_E_TXSPLITEXPRESSIONEVALUATEDTONULL	The expression "__" on "__" evaluated to NULL, but the "__" requires a Boolean result. Modify the error row disposition on the output to treat this result as False (Ignore Failure) or to redirect this row to the error output (Redirect Row). The expression results must be Boolean for a Conditional Split. A NULL expression result is an error.
0xC020902C	DTS_E_TXSPLITSTATIC_EXPRESSIONEVALUATEDTONULL	The expression evaluated to NULL, but a Boolean result is required. Modify the error row disposition on the output to treat this result as False (Ignore Failure) or to redirect this row to the error output (Redirect Row). The expression results must be Boolean for a Conditional Split. A NULL expression result is an error.
0xC020902D	DTS_E_UTF16BIGENDIANFORMATNOTSUPPORTED	The file format of UTF-16 big endian is not supported. Only UTF-16 little endian format is supported.
0xC020902E	DTS_E_UTF8FORMATNOTSUPPORTEDASUNICODE	The file format of UTF-8 is not supported as Unicode.
0xC020902F	DTS_E_DTPXMLCANTREADIDATTR	Cannot read ID attribute.
0xC0209069	DTS_E_COMMANDDESTINATIONADAPTERSTATIC_CANTCONVERTVALUE	The data value cannot be converted for reasons other than sign mismatch or data overflow.
0xC020906A	DTS_E_COMMANDDESTINATIONADAPTERSTATIC_SCHEMAVIOLATION	The data value violated the schema constraint.
0xC020906B	DTS_E_COMMANDDESTINATIONADAPTERSTATIC_TRUNCATED	The data was truncated.
0xC020906C	DTS_E_COMMANDDESTINATIONADAPTERSTATIC_SIGNMISMATCH	Conversion failed because the data value was signed and the type used by the provider was unsigned.
0xC020906D	DTS_E_COMMANDDESTINATIONADAPTERSTATIC_DATAOVERFLOW	Conversion failed because the data value overflowed the type used by the provider.
0xC020906E	DTS_E_COMMANDDESTINATIONADAPTERSTATIC_UNAVAILABLE	No status is available.
0xC020906F	DTS_E_COMMANDDESTINATIONADAPTERSTATIC_PERMISSIONDENIED	The user did not have the correct permissions to write to the column.
0xC0209070	DTS_E_COMMANDDESTINATIONADAPTERSTATIC_INTEGRITYVIOLATION	The data value violated the integrity constraints for the column.
0xC0209071	DTS_E_OLEDBSOURCEADAPTERSTATIC_UNAVAILABLE	No status is available.

Error Code	Symbolic Name	Description
0xC0209072	DTS_E_OLEDBSOURCEADAPTERSTATIC_CANTCONVERTVALUE	The data value cannot be converted for reasons other than sign mismatch or data overflow.
0xC0209073	DTS_E_OLEDBSOURCEADAPTERSTATIC_TRUNCATED	The data was truncated.
0xC0209074	DTS_E_OLEDBSOURCEADAPTERSTATIC_SIGNMISMATCH	Conversion failed because the data value was signed and the type used by the provider was unsigned.
0xC0209075	DTS_E_OLEDBSOURCEADAPTERSTATIC_DATAOVERFLOW	Conversion failed because the data value overflowed the type used by the provider.
0xC0209076	DTS_E_OLEDBDESTINATIONADAPTERSTATIC_SCHEMAVIOLATION	The data value violated the schema constraint.
0xC0209077	DTS_E_OLEDBDESTINATIONADAPTERSTATIC_CANTCONVERTVALUE	The data value cannot be converted for reasons other than sign mismatch or data overflow.
0xC0209078	DTS_E_OLEDBDESTINATIONADAPTERSTATIC_TRUNCATED	The data was truncated.
0xC0209079	DTS_E_OLEDBDESTINATIONADAPTERSTATIC_SIGNMISMATCH	Conversion failed because the data value was signed and the type used by the provider was unsigned.
0xC020907A	DTS_E_OLEDBDESTINATIONADAPTERSTATIC_DATAOVERFLOW	Conversion failed because the data value overflowed the type used by the provider.
0xC020907B	DTS_E_OLEDBDESTINATIONADAPTERSTATIC_UNAVAILABLE	No status is available.
0xC020907C	DTS_E_OLEDBDESTINATIONADAPTERSTATIC_PERMISSIONDENIED	The user did not have the correct permissions to write to the column.
0xC020907D	DTS_E_OLEDBDESTINATIONADAPTERSTATIC_INTEGRITYVIOLATION	The data value violates integrity constraints.
0xC020907F	DTS_E_TXDATACONVERTSTATIC_CANTCONVERTVALUE	The data value cannot be converted for reasons other than sign mismatch or data overflow.
0xC0209080	DTS_E_TXDATACONVERTSTATIC_TRUNCATED	The data was truncated.
0xC0209081	DTS_E_TXDATACONVERTSTATIC_SIGNMISMATCH	Conversion failed because the data value was signed and the type used by the provider was unsigned.
0xC0209082	DTS_E_TXDATACONVERTSTATIC_DATAOVERFLOW	Conversion failed because the data value overflowed the type used by the data conversion transform.

Error Code	Symbolic Name	Description
0xC0209083	DTS_E_FLATFILESOURCEADAPTERSTATIC_ UNAVAILABLE	No status is available.
0xC0209084	DTS_E_FLATFILESOURCEADAPTERSTATIC_ CANTCONVERTVALUE	The data value cannot be converted for reasons other than sign mismatch or data overflow.
0xC0209085	DTS_E_FLATFILESOURCEADAPTERSTATIC_ TRUNCATED	The data was truncated.
0xC0209086	DTS_E_FLATFILESOURCEADAPTERSTATIC_ SIGNMISMATCH	Conversion failed because the data value was signed and the type used by the flat file source adapter was unsigned.
0xC0209087	DTS_E_FLATFILESOURCEADAPTERSTATIC_ DATAOVERFLOW	Conversion failed because the data value overflowed the type used by the flat file source adapter.
0xC020908E	DTS_E_TXDATACONVERTSTATIC_UNAVAILABLE	No status is available.
0xC0209090	DTS_E_FILEOPENERR_FORREAD	Opening the file " __ " for reading failed with error code 0x__.
0xC0209091	DTS_E_TXFILEINSERTERSTATIC_FILEOPENERR_ FORREAD	Failed to open file for reading.
0xC0209092	DTS_E_FILEOPENERR_FORWRITE	Opening the file " __ " for writing failed with error code 0x__.
0xC0209093	DTS_E_TXFILEEXTRACTORSTATIC_FILEOPENERR_ FORWRITE	Failed to open file for writing.
0xC0209094	DTS_E_TXFILEINSERTERSTATIC_ INSERTERCANTREAD	Failed to read from file.
0xC0209095	DTS_E_TXFILEEXTRACTORSTATIC_ EXTRACTORCANTWRITE	Failed to write to file.
0xC0209099	DTS_E_DTPXMLINVALIDPROPERTYARRAYTOO MANYVALUES	Too many array elements were found when parsing a property of type array. The elementCount is less than the number of array elements found.
0xC020909A	DTS_E_DTPXMLINVALIDPROPERTYARRAYNOT ENOUGHVALUES	Too few array elements were found when parsing a property of type array. The elementCount is more than the number of array elements found.
0xC020909E	DTS_E_FILEOPENERR_FORWRITE_FILENOTFOUND	Opening the file " __ " for writing failed. The file cannot be found.
0xC020909F	DTS_E_TXFILEEXTRACTORSTATIC_FILEOPENERR_ FORWRITE_FILENOTFOUND	Opening the file for writing failed. The file cannot be found.
0xC02090A0	DTS_E_FILEOPENERR_FORWRITE_PATHNOTFOUND	Opening the file " __ " for writing failed. The path cannot be found.
0xC02090A1	DTS_E_TXFILEEXTRACTORSTATIC_FILEOPENERR_ FORWRITE_PATHNOTFOUND	Opening the file for writing failed. The path cannot be found.

Error Code	Symbolic Name	Description
0xC02090A2	DTS_E_FILEOPENERR_FORWRITE_TOOMANYOPENFILES	Opening the file "__" for writing failed. There are too many files open.
0xC02090A3	DTS_E_TXFILEEXTRACTORSTATIC_FILEOPENERR_FORWRITE_TOOMANYOPENFILES	Opening the file for writing failed. There are too many files open.
0xC02090A4	DTS_E_FILEOPENERR_FORWRITE_ACCESSDENIED	Opening the file "__" for writing failed. You do not have the correct permissions.
0xC02090A5	DTS_E_TXFILEEXTRACTORSTATIC_FILEOPENERR_FORWRITE_ACCESSDENIED	Opening the file for writing failed. You do not have the correct permissions.
0xC02090A6	DTS_E_FILEOPENERR_FORWRITE_FILEEXISTS	Opening the file "__" for writing failed. The file exists and cannot be overwritten. If the AllowAppend property is FALSE and the ForceTruncate property is set to FALSE, the existence of the file will cause this failure.
0xC02090A7	DTS_E_TXFILEEXTRACTORSTATIC_FILEOPENERR_FORWRITE_FILEEXISTS	Opening a file for writing failed. The file already exists and cannot be overwritten. If both the AllowAppend property and the ForceTruncate property are set to FALSE, the existence of the file will cause this failure.
0xC02090A8	DTS_E_INCORRECTCUSTOMPROPERTYVALUEFOROBJECT	The value for custom property "__" on __ is incorrect.
0xC02090A9	DTS_E_COLUMNSHAVEINCOMPATIBLEMETADATA	Columns "__" and "__" have incompatible metadata.
0xC02090AD	DTS_E_FILEWRITEERR_DISKFULL	Opening the file "__" for writing failed because the disk is full. There is not sufficient disk space to save this file.
0xC02090AE	DTS_E_TXFILEEXTRACTORSTATIC_FILEWRITEERR_DISKFULL	Attempting to open the file for writing failed because the disk is full.
0xC02090B9	DTS_E_TXAGG_SORTKEYGENFAILED	Generating a sort key failed with error 0x__. The ComparisonFlags are enabled, and generating a sortkey with LCMapString failed.
0xC02090BA	DTS_E_TXCHARMAPLCMAPFAILED	Transform failed to map string and returned error 0x__. The LCMapString failed.
0xC02090BB	DTS_E_FILEOPENERR_FORREAD_FILENOTFOUND	Opening the file "__" for reading failed. The file was not found.
0xC02090BC	DTS_E_TXFILEINSERTERSTATIC_FILEOPENERR_FORREAD_FILENOTFOUND	Opening a file for reading failed. The file was not found.
0xC02090BD	DTS_E_FILEOPENERR_FORREAD_PATHNOTFOUND	Opening the file "__" for reading failed. The path cannot be found.
0xC02090BE	DTS_E_TXFILEINSERTERSTATIC_FILEOPENERR_FORREAD_PATHNOTFOUND	Opening a file for reading failed. The path was not found.

Error Code	Symbolic Name	Description
0xC02090BF	DTS_E_FILEOPENERR_FORREAD_TOOMANYOPENFILES	Opening the file " __ " for reading failed. There are too many files open.
0xC02090C0	DTS_E_TXFILEINSERTERSTATIC_FILEOPENERR_FORREAD_TOOMANYOPENFILES	Opening the file for reading failed. There are too many files open.
0xC02090C1	DTS_E_FILEOPENERR_FORREAD_ACCESSDENIED	Attempting to open the file " __ " for reading failed. Access is denied.
0xC02090C2	DTS_E_TXFILEINSERTERSTATIC_FILEOPENERR_FORREAD_ACCESSDENIED	Opening the file for reading failed. You do not have the correct permissions.
0xC02090C3	DTS_E_INSERTERINVALIDBOM	The byte order mark (BOM) value for the file " __ " is 0x__4XI, but the expected value is 0x__4XI. The ExpectBOM property was set for this file, but the BOM value in the file is missing or not valid.
0xC02090C4	DTS_E_TXFILEINSERTERSTATIC_INSERTERINVALIDBOM	The byte order mark (BOM) value for the file is not valid. The ExpectBOM property was set for this file, but the BOM value in the file is missing or not valid.
0xC02090C5	DTS_E_NOCOMPONENTATTACHED	The __ is not attached to a component. It is required that a component be attached.
0xC02090C9	DTS_E_TXLOOKUP_INVALIDMAXMEMORYPROP	The value for custom property __ is incorrect. It should be a number between __ and __.
0xC02090CA	DTS_E_TXAGG_COMPFLAGS_BADAGGREGATIONTYPE	The custom property " __ " cannot be specified for the aggregation type selected for this column. The comparison flags custom property can only be specified for group by and count distinct aggregation types.
0xC02090CB	DTS_E_TXAGG_COMPFLAGS_BADDATATYPE	The comparison flags custom property " __ " can only be specified for columns with datatype DT_STR or DT_WSTR.
0xC02090CD	DTS_E_TXAGG_AGGREGATION_FAILURE	Aggregation on __ failed with error code 0x__.
0xC02090CF	DTS_E_MAPPINGSETUPERROR	There was an error setting up the mapping. %1
0xC02090D0	DTS_E_XMLSRCUNABLETOREADXMLDATA	The __ was unable to read the XML data.
0xC02090D1	DTS_E_XMLSRCUNABLETOGETXMLDATAVARIABLE	The __ was unable to get the variable specified by the " __ " property.
0xC02090D2	DTS_E_NODATATABLEMATCHROWID	The __ contains a RowsetID with a value of __ that does not reference a data table in the schema.
0xC02090D6	DTS_E_TXAGG_BADKEYSVALUE	The property __ must either be empty, or a number between __ and __. The Keys or CountDistinctKeys property has an invalid value. The property should be a number between 0 and ULONG_MAX, inclusive, or not be set.

Error Code	Symbolic Name	Description
0xC02090D7	DTS_E_TXAGG_TOOMANYKEYS	The aggregate component encountered too many distinct key combinations. It cannot accommodate more than __ distinct key values. There is more than ULONG_MAX distinct key values in the main workspace.
0xC02090D8	DTS_E_TXAGG_TOOMANYCOUNTDISTINCTVALUES	The aggregate component encountered too many distinct values while calculating the count distinct aggregate. It cannot accommodate more than __ distinct values. There were more than ULONG_MAX distinct values while calculating the count distinct aggregation.
0xC02090D9	DTS_E_FAILEDTOWRITETOTHEFILENAMECOLUMN	The attempt to write to the filename column failed with error code 0x__.
0xC02090DC	DTS_E_FAILEDTOFINDERRORCOLUMN	An error occurred, but the column that caused the error cannot be determined.
0xC02090E3	DTS_E_TXLOOKUP_FAILEDUPGRADE_BAD_VERSION	Unable to upgrade lookup metadata from version __ to __. The Lookup transform was unable to upgrade metadata from the existing version number in a call to PerformUpgrade().
0xC02090E5	DTS_E_TERMEXTRACTIONORLOOKUP_NTEXTSPLITED	Failed to locate the ending boundary of a sentence.
0xC02090E6	DTS_E_TERMEXTRACTION_EXCEED_MAXWORDNUM	The Term Extraction transformation is unable to process the input text because a sentence from the input text is too long. The sentence is segmented into several sentences.
0xC02090E7	DTS_E_XMLSRCFAILEDTOCREATEREADER	The __ was unable to read the XML data. %2
0xC02090F0	DTS_E_TXLOOKUP_REINITMETADATAFAILED	The call to Lookup transform method, ReinitializeMetadata, failed.
0xC02090F1	DTS_E_TXLOOKUP_NOJOINS	The lookup transform must contain at least one input column joined to a reference column, and none were specified. You must specify at least one join column.
0xC02090F2	DTS_E_MANAGEDERR_BADFORMATSPECIFICATION	The message string being posted by the managed error infrastructure contains a bad format specification. This is an internal error.
0xC02090F3	DTS_E_MANAGEDERR_UNSUPPORTEDTYPE	While formatting a message string using the managed error infrastructure, there was a variant type that does not have formatting support. This is an internal error.
0xC02090F5	DTS_E_DATAREADERSRCUNABLETOPROCESSDATA	The __ was unable to process the data.
0xC02090F6	DTS_E_XMLSRCEMPTYPROPERTY	The property " __ " on the __ was empty.
0xC02090F7	DTS_E_XMLSRCINVALIDOUTPUTNAME	Attempting to create an output with the name " __ " for the XML table with the path " __ " failed because the name is invalid.

Error Code	Symbolic Name	Description
0xC02090F8	DTS_E_MGDSRC_OVERFLOW	The value was too large to fit in the ___.
0xC02090F9	DTS_E_DATAREADERDESTUNABLETOPROCESSDATA	The ___ was unable to process the data.
0xC0209291	DTS_E_SQLCEDESTSTATIC_FAILEDTOSETVALUES	The SQLCE destination could not set the column values for the row.
0xC0209292	DTS_E_SQLCEDESTSTATIC_FAILEDTOINSERT	The SQLCE destination could not insert the row.
0xC0209293	DTS_E_TXFUZZYLOOKUP_OLEDBERR_LOADCOLUMNMETADATA	Encountered OLEDB error while loading column metadata.
0xC0209294	DTS_E_TXFUZZYLOOKUP_TOOFEWREFERENCECOLUMNS	Lookup reference metadata contains too few columns.
0xC0209295	DTS_E_TXSCD_OLEDBERR_LOADCOLUMNMETADATA	Encountered OLEDB error while loading column metadata.
0xC0209296	DTS_E_TXSCD_TOOFEWREFERENCECOLUMNS	Lookup reference metadata contains too few columns.
0xC0209297	DTS_E_TXSCD_MALLOCERR_REFERENCECOLUMNINFO	Unable to allocate memory.
0xC0209298	DTS_E_TXSCD_MALLOCERR_BUFFCOL	Unable to allocate memory.
0xC0209299	DTS_E_TXSCD_MAINWORKSPACE_CREATEERR	Unable to create workspace buffer.
0xC020929A	DTS_E_DTPXMLDOMCREATEERROR	Unable to instantiate XML DOM document, please verify that MSXML binaries are properly installed and registered.
0xC020929B	DTS_E_DTPXMLDOMLOADERROR	Unable to load XML data into a local DOM for processing.
0xC020929C	DTS_E_RSTDESTBADVARIABLETYPE	The type of the runtime variable "___" is incorrect. The runtime variable type must be Object.
0xC020929E	DTS_E_XMLDATAREADERMULTIPLEINLINEXMLSCHEMASNOTSUPPORTED	The XML Source Adapter was unable to process the XML data. Multiple inline schemas are not supported.
0xC020929F	DTS_E_XMLDATAREADERANYTYPENOTSUPPORTED	The XML Source Adapter was unable to process the XML data. The content of an element cannot be declared as anyType.
0xC02092A0	DTS_E_XMLDATAREADERGROUPREFNOTSUPPORTED	The XML Source Adapter was unable to process the XML data. The content of an element cannot contain a reference (ref) to a group.
0xC02092A1	DTS_E_XMLDATAREADERMIXEDCONTENTFORCOMPLEXTYPESNOTSUPPORTED	The XML Source Adapter does not support mixed content model on Complex Types.
0xC02092A2	DTS_E_XMLDATAREADERINLINESCHEMAFOUNDINSOURCEXML	The XML Source Adapter was unable to process the XML data. An inline schema must be the first child node in the source Xml.

Error Code	Symbolic Name	Description
0xC02092A3	DTS_E_XMLDATAREADERNOINLINESCHEMAFOUND	The XML Source Adapter was unable to process the XML data. No inline schema was found in the source XML, but the "UseInlineSchema" property was set to true.
0xC02092A4	DTS_E_CONNECTIONMANAGERTRANSACTED ANDRETAINEDINBULKINSERT	The component cannot use a connection manager that retains its connection in a transaction with fastload or bulk insert.
0xC02092A5	DTS_E_OUTPUTREDIRECTINTRANSACTIONNOT ALLOWED	The ___ cannot be set to redirect on error using a connection in a transaction.
0xC02092A6	DTS_E_FOUNDORPHANEDEXTERNALMETADATA COLUMN	The ___ does not have a corresponding input or output column.
0xC02092A9	DTS_E_RAWDESTNOINPUTCOLUMNS	There is no selected column to be written to the file.
0xC02092AA	DTS_E_RAWDESTBLOBDATATYPE	The ___ has an invalid data type. Columns with data types DT_IMAGE, DT_TEXT, and DT_NTEXT cannot be written to raw files.
0xC02092AB	DTS_E_RAWDESTWRONGEXTERNALMETADATA USAGE	The external metadata collection is improperly used by this component. The component should use external metadata when appending or truncating an existing file. Otherwise, the external metadata is not needed.
0xC02092AC	DTS_E_RAWDESTMAPPEDINPUTCOLUMN	The ___ is mapped to an external metadata column with the id ___. Input columns should not be mapped to external metadata columns when selected Write Option value is Create Always.
0xC02092AD	DTS_E_RAWFILECANTOPENFORMETADATA	The file cannot be opened for reading the metadata. If the file does not exist, and the component has already defined external metadata, you can set the "ValidateExternalMetadata" property to "false" and the file will be created at the runtime.
0xC02092AE	DTS_E_FAILEDTOACCESSLOBCOLUMN	Failed to access LOB data from the data flow buffer for data source column "___" with error code 0x___.
0xC02092AF	DTS_E_XMLSRCUNABLETOPROCESSXMLDATA	The ___ was unable to process the XML data. %2
0xC02092B0	DTS_E_XMLSRCSTATIC_ UNABLETOPROCESSXMLDATA	The XML Source Adapter was unable to process the XML data.
0xC02092B1	DTS_E_RAWINVALIDACCESSMODE	The value ___ is not recognized as a valid access mode.
0xC02092B2	DTS_E_INCOMPLETEDATASOURCECOLUMNFOUND	Complete metadata information for the data source column "___" is not available. Make sure the column is correctly defined in the data source.
0xC02092B3	DTS_E_TXAUDIT_ ONLYUSERNAMELENGTHCHANGEALLOWED	Only a username audit column's length can be changed. All other audit column datatype information is read only.
0xC02092B4	DTS_E_ROWSETUNAVAILABLE	A rowset based on the SQL command was not returned by the OLE DB provider.

The symbolic names of Integration Services warning messages begin with DTS_W_.

Error Code	Symbolic Name	Description
0x80000036	DTS_W_COUNTDOWN	There are __ days left in the evaluation. When it expires, packages will not be able to be executed.
0x80010015	DTS_W_GENERICWARNING	Warning(s) raised. There should be more specific warnings preceding this one that explain the specifics of the warning(s).
0x80012010	DTS_W_FAILEDXMLDOCCREATION	Cannot create an XML document object instance. Verify that MSXML is installed and registered correctly.
0x80012011	DTS_W_FAILEDCONFIGLOAD	Cannot load the XML configuration file. The XML configuration file may be malformed or not valid.
0x80012012	DTS_W_CONFIGFILENAMEINVALID	The configuration file name " __ " is not valid. Check the configuration file name.
0x80012013	DTS_W_CONFIGFILEINVALID	The configuration file loaded, but is not valid. The file is not formatted correctly, may be missing an element, or may be damaged.
0x80012014	DTS_W_CONFIGFILENOTFOUND	The configuration file " __ " cannot be found. Check the directory and file name.
0x80012015	DTS_W_CONFIGKEYNOTFOUND	Configuration registry key " __ " was not found. A configuration entry specifies a registry key that is not available. Check the registry to ensure that the key is there.
0x80012016	DTS_W_CONFIGTYPEINVALID	The configuration type in one of the configuration entries was not valid. Valid types are listed in the DTSConfigurationType enumeration.
0x80012017	DTS_W_CANNOTFINDOBJECT	The package path referenced an object that cannot be found: " __ ". This occurs when an attempt is made to resolve a package path to an object that cannot be found.
0x80012018	DTS_W_CONFIGFORMATINVALID_PACKAGEDELIMITER	The configuration entry, " __ ", has an incorrect format because it does not begin with the package delimiter. Prepend "\package" to the package path.
0x80012019	DTS_W_CONFIGFORMATINVALID	The configuration entry " __ " had an incorrect format. This can occur because of a missing delimiter or formatting errors, like an invalid array delimiter.
0x8001201A	DTS_W_NOPARENTVARIABLES	Configuration from a parent variable " __ " did not occur because there was no parent variable collection.
0x8001201B	DTS_W_CONFIGFILEFAILEDIMPORT	Failure importing configuration file: " __ ".
0x8001201C	DTS_W_PARENTVARIABLENOTFOUND	Configuration from a parent variable " __ " did not occur because there was no parent variable. Error code: 0x__.

Error Code	Symbolic Name	Description
0x8001201D	DTS_W_CONFIGFILEEMPTY	The configuration file was empty and contained no configuration entries.
0x80012023	DTS_W_INVALIDCONFIGURATIONTYPE	The configuration type for configuration " __ " is not valid. This may occur when an attempt is made to set the type property of a configuration object to an invalid configuration type.
0x80012025	DTS_W_REGISTRYCONFIGURATIONTYPENOTFOUND	The configuration type for the registry configuration was not found in key " __ ". Add a value called ConfigType to the registry key and give it a string value of "Variable", "Property", "ConnectionManager", "LoggingProvider", or "ForEachEnumerator".
0x80012026	DTS_W_REGISTRYCONFIGURATIONVALUENOTFOUND	The configuration value for the registry configuration was not found in key " __ ". Add a value called Value to the registry key of type DWORD or String.
0x80012028	DTS_W_PROCESSCONFIGURATIONFAILEDSET	Process configuration failed to set the destination at the package path of " __ ". This occurs when attempting to set the destination property or variable fails. Check the destination property or variable.
0x80012032	DTS_W_CONFIGUREDVALUESECTIONEMPTY	Failed to retrieve value from the .ini file. The ConfiguredValue section is either empty, or does not exist: " __ ".
0x80012033	DTS_W_CONFIGUREDTYPESECTIONEMPTY	Failed to retrieve value from the .ini file. The ConfiguredType section is either empty, or does not exist: " __ ".
0x80012034	DTS_W_PACKAGEPATHSECTIONEMPTY	Failed to retrieve value from the .ini file. The PackagePath section is either empty, or does not exist: " __ ".
0x80012035	DTS_W_CONFIGUREDVALUETYPE	Failed to retrieve value from the .ini file. The ConfiguredValueType section is either empty, or does not exist: " __ ".
0x80012051	DTS_W_SQLSERVERFAILEDIMPORT	Configuration from SQL Server was not successfully imported: " __ ".
0x80012052	DTS_W_INICONFIGURATIONPROBLEM	The .ini configuration file is not valid due to empty or missing fields.
0x80012054	DTS_W_NORECORDSFOUNDINTABLE	Table " __ " does not have any records for configuration. This occurs when configuring from a SQL Server table that has no records for the configuration.
0x80012055	DTS_W_DUPLICATECUSTOMEVENT	Error using same name for different custom events. The custom event " __ " was defined differently by different children of this container. There may be an error when executing the event handler.
0x80012057	DTS_W_CONFIGREADONLYVARIABLE	The configuration attempted to change a read-only variable. The variable is at the package path " __ ".

Error Code	Symbolic Name	Description
0x80012058	DTS_W_CONFIGPROCESSCONFIGURATIONFAILED	Calling ProcessConfiguration on the package failed. The configuration attempted to change the property at the package path "___".
0x80012059	DTS_W_ONEORMORECONFIGLOADFAILED	Failed to load at least one of the configuration entries for the package. Check configuration entries and previous warnings to see descriptions of which configuration failed.
0x8001205A	DTS_W_CONFIGNODEINVALID	The configuration entry "___" in the configuration file was not valid, or failed to configure the variable. The name indicates which entry failed. In some cases, the name will not be available.
0x80014058	DTS_W_FAILURENOTRESTARTABLE	This task or container has failed, but because FailPackageOnFailure property is FALSE, the package will continue. This warning is posted when the SaveCheckpoints property of the package is set to TRUE and the task or container fails.
0x80017101	DTS_W_EMPTYPATH	The path is empty.
0x80019002	DTS_W_MAXIMUMERRORCOUNTREACHED	The Execution method succeeded, but the number of errors raised (___) reached the maximum allowed (___); resulting in failure. This occurs when the number of errors reaches the number specified in MaximumErrorCount. Change the MaximumErrorCount or fix the errors.
0x80019003	DTS_W_CONFIGENVVARNOTFOUND	The configuration environment variable was not found. The environment variable was: "___". This occurs when a package specifies an environment variable for a configuration setting but it cannot be found. Check the configurations collection in the package and verify that the specified environment variable is available and valid.
0x8001C004	DTS_W_FILENUMEMPTY	The For Each File enumerator is empty. The For Each File enumerator did not find any files that matched the file pattern, or the specified directory was empty.
0x8001F02F	DTS_W_COULDNOTRESOLVEPACKAGEPATH	Cannot resolve a package path to an object in the package "___". Verify that the package path is valid.
0x8001F203	DTS_W_ITERATIONEXPRESSIONISBOOLEAN	The iteration expression is Boolean. The expressions found in this position are not usually Boolean: "___". This error usually occurs when the expression in the assignment expression on the ForLoop is Boolean.
0x8001F204	DTS_W_INITIALIZATIONEXPRESSIONISBOOLEAN	Initialization expression is Boolean. The expressions found in this position are not usually Boolean: "___". This error usually occurs when the expression in the iterate expressions on the ForLoop is Boolean.

Error Code	Symbolic Name	Description
0x80020918	DTS_W_FTPTASK_OPERATIONFAILURE	Operation "__" failed.
0x80029164	DTS_W_FSTASK_OPERATIONFAILURE	Task failed to execute operation "__".
0x80029185	DTS_W_EXECPROCTASK_FILENOTINPATH	File/Process "__" is not in path.
0x800291C6	DTS_W_SENDMAILTASK_SUBJECT_MISSING	The subject is empty.
0x800291C7	DTS_W_SENDMAILTASK_ERROR_IN_TO_LINE	The address in the "To" line is malformed. It is either missing the "@" symbol or is not valid.
0x800291C8	DTS_W_SENDMAILTASK_AT_MISSING_IN_FROM	The address in the "From" line is malformed. It is either missing the "@" symbol or is not valid.
0x8002927A	DTS_W_XMLTASK_DIFFFAILURE	The two XML documents are different.
0x8002928C	DTS_W_XMLTASK_DTDVALIDATIONWARNING	DTD Validation will use the DTD file defined in the DOCTYPE line in the XML document. It will not use what is assigned to the property "__".
0x8002928D	DTS_W_XMLTASK_VALIDATIONFAILURE	Task failed to validate "__".
0x80029291	DTS_W_TRANSFERDBTASK_ACTIONSETTOCOPY	The transfer action value was invalid. It is being set to copy.
0x80029292	DTS_W_TRANSFERDBTASK_METHODSETTOONLINE	The transfer method value was invalid. It is being set to an online transfer.
0x8002F304	DTS_W_PROBLEMOCCURREDWITHFOLLOWINGMESSSAGE	A problem occurred with the following messages: "__".
0x8002F322	DTS_W_ERRMSGTASK_ERRORMESSAGEALREADYEXISTS	The error message "__" already exists at destination server.
0x8002F331	DTS_W_JOBSTASK_JOBEXISTSATDEST	The job "__" already exists at destination server.
0x8002F332	DTS_W_JOBSTASK_SKIPPINGJOBEXISTSATDEST	Skipping the transfer of job "__" since it already exists at destination.
0x8002F333	DTS_W_JOBSTASK_OVERWRITINGJOB	Overwriting the job "__" at destination server.
0x8002F339	DTS_W_LOGINSTASK_ENUMVALUEINCORRECT	Persisted enumeration value of property "FailIfExists" was changed and rendered invalid. Resetting to default.
0x8002F343	DTS_W_LOGINSTASK_OVERWRITINGLOGINATDEST	Overwriting Login "__" at destination.
0x8002F356	DTS_W_TRANSOBJECTSTASK_SPALREADYATDEST	Stored procedure "{0}" already exists at destination.
0x8002F360	DTS_W_TRANSOBJECTSTASK_RULEALREADYATDEST	Rule "__" already exists at destination.
0x8002F364	DTS_W_TRANSOBJECTSTASK_TABLEALREADYATDEST	Table "__" already exists at destination.

Error Code	Symbolic Name	Description
0x8002F368	DTS_W_TRANSOBJECTSTASK_VIEWALREADYATDEST	View "__" already exists at destination.
0x8002F372	DTS_W_TRANSOBJECTSTASK_UDFALREADYATDEST	User Defined Function "__" already exists at destination.
0x8002F376	DTS_W_TRANSOBJECTSTASK_DEFAULTALREADYATDEST	Default "__" already exists at destination.
0x8002F380	DTS_W_TRANSOBJECTSTASK_UDDTALREADYATDEST	User Defined Data Type "__" already exists at destination.
0x8002F384	DTS_W_TRANSOBJECTSTASK_PFALREADYATDEST	Partition Function "__" already exists at destination.
0x8002F388	DTS_W_TRANSOBJECTSTASK_PSALREADYATDEST	Partition Scheme "__" already exists at destination.
0x8002F391	DTS_W_TRANSOBJECTSTASK_SCHEMAALREADYATDEST	Schema "__" already exists at destination.
0x8002F396	DTS_W_TRANSOBJECTSTASK_SQLASSEMBLYALREADYATDEST	SqlAssembly "__" already exists at destination.
0x8002F400	DTS_W_TRANSOBJECTSTASK_AGGREGATEALREADYATDEST	User Defined Aggregate "__" already exists at destination.
0x8002F404	DTS_W_TRANSOBJECTSTASK_TYPEALREADYATDEST	User Defined Type "__" already exists at destination.
0x8002F408	DTS_W_TRANSOBJECTSTASK_XMLSCHEMACOLLECTIONALREADYATDEST	XmlSchemaCollection "__" already exists at destination.
0x8002F412	DTS_W_TRANSOBJECTSTASK_NOELEMENTSPECIFIEDTOTRANSFER	There are no elements specified to transfer.
0x8002F415	DTS_W_TRANSOBJECTSTASK_LOGINALREADYATDEST	Login "__" already exists at destination.
0x8002F41A	DTS_W_TRANSOBJECTSTASK_USERALREADYATDEST	User "__" already exists at destination.
0x80047007	DTS_W_NOLINEAGEVALIDATION	The lineage IDs of the input columns cannot be validated because the execution trees contain cycles.
0x80047034	DTS_W_EMPTYDATAFLOW	The DataFlow task has no components. Add components or remove the task.
0x80047069	DTS_W_SORTEDOUTPUTHASNOSORTKEYPOSITIONS	The IsSorted property of __ is set to TRUE, but all of its output columns' SortKeyPositions are set to zero.

Error Code	Symbolic Name	Description
0x8004706F	DTS_W_SOURCEREMOVED	Source " _ " (_) will not be read because none of its data ever becomes visible outside the Data Flow Task.
0x80047076	DTS_W_UNUSEDOUTPUTDATA	The output column " _ " (_) on output " _ " (_) and component " _ " (_) is not subsequently used in the Data Flow task. Removing this unused output column can increase Data Flow task performance.
0x800470AE	DTS_W_COMPONENTREMOVED	Component " _ " (_) has been removed from the Data Flow task because its output is not used and its inputs have no side effects. If the component is required, then the HasSideEffects property on at least one of its inputs should be set to true, or its output should be connected to something.
0x800470B0	DTS_W_NOWORKTODO	Rows were given to a thread, but that thread has no work to do. The layout has a disconnected output. Running the pipeline with the RunInOptimizedMode property set to TRUE will be faster, and prevents this warning.
0x800470C8	DTS_W_EXTERNALMETADATACOLUMNSOUTOFSYNC	The external metadata column collection is out of synchronization with the data source columns. %1
0x800470C9	DTS_W_EXTERNALMETADATACOLUMNCOLLECTIONNEEDSADDITION	The column " _ " needs to be added to the external metadata column collection.
0x800470CA	DTS_W_EXTERNALMETADATACOLUMNCOLLECTIONNEEDSUPDATE	The column " _ " needs to be updated in the external metadata column collection.
0x800470CB	DTS_W_EXTERNALMETADATACOLUMNCOLLECTIONNEEDSREMOVAL	The " _ " needs to be removed from the external metadata column collection.
0x800470D8	DTS_W_EXPREVALPOTENTIALSTRINGTRUNCATION	The result string for expression " _ " may be truncated if it exceeds the maximum length of _ characters. The expression could have a result value that exceeds the maximum size of a DT_WSTR.
0x800470E9	DTS_W_COMPONENTLEAKPROCESSINPUT	A call to the ProcessInput method for input _ on _ unexpectedly kept a reference to the buffer it was passed. The refcount on that buffer was _ before the call, and _ after the call returned.
0x800470EB	DTS_W_EXPREVALUNREFERENCEDINPUTCOLUMN	The " _ " on " _ " has usage type READONLY, but is not referenced by an expression. Remove the column from the list of available input columns, or reference it in an expression.

Error Code	Symbolic Name	Description
0x8004801E	DTS_W_COULDNOTFINDCURRENTVERSION	Cannot find the "___" value for component ___. The CurrentVersion value for the component cannot be located. This error occurs if the component has not set its registry information to contain a CurrentVersion value in the DTSInfo section. This message occurs during component development, or when the component is used in a package, if the component is not registered properly.
0x8020020F	DTS_W_PARTIALROWFOUNDATENDOFFILE	There is a partial row at the end of the file.
0x8020202B	DTS_W_ENDOFFILEREACHWHILEREADING HEADERROWS	The end of the data file was reached while reading header rows. Make sure the header row delimiter and the number of header rows to skip are correct.
0x80202066	DTS_W_CANTRETRIEVECODEPAGEFROMOLEDB PROVIDER	Cannot retrieve the column code page info from the OLE DB provider. If the component supports the "___" property, the code page from that property will be used. Change the value of the property if the current string code page values are incorrect. If the component does not support the property, the code page from the component's locale ID will be used.
0x802020F7	DTS_W_TXSORTSORTISTHESAME	The data is already sorted as specified so the transform can be removed.
0x8020400D	DTS_W_NOPIPELINEDATATYPEMAPPINGAVAILABLE	The ___ references an external data type that cannot be mapped to a Data Flow task data type. The Data Flow task data type DT_WSTR will be used instead.
0x802070CC	DTS_W_STATICTRUNCATIONINEXPRESSION	The expression "___" will always result in a truncation of data. The expression contains a static truncation (the truncation of a fixed value).
0x8020820C	DTS_W_UNMAPPEDINPUTCOLUMN	The input column "___" with ID ___ at index ___ is unmapped. The lineage ID for the column is zero.
0x80208305	DTS_W_TXFUZZYLOOKUP_DELIMITERS_ DONT_MATCH	The specified delimiters do not match the delimiters used to build the pre-existing match index "___". This error occurs when the delimiters used to tokenize fields do not match. This can have unknown effects on the matching behavior or results.
0x80208308	DTS_W_TXFUZZYLOOKUP_MAXRESULTS_IS_ZERO	The MaxOutputMatchesPerInput property on the Fuzzy Lookup transformation is zero. No results will be produced.
0x80208310	DTS_W_TXFUZZYLOOKUP_NO_FUZZY_JOIN_ COLUMNS	There were no valid input columns with JoinType column property set to Fuzzy. Performance on Exact joins may be improved by using the Lookup transform instead of FuzzyLookup.

Error Code	Symbolic Name	Description
0x8020831C	DTS_W_TXFUZZYLOOKUP_TIMESTAMPCAVEAT	The reference column "___" may be a SQL timestamp column. When the fuzzy match index is built, and a copy of the reference table is made, all reference table timestamps will reflect the current state of the table at the time of the copy. Unexpected behavior may occur if the CopyReferenceTable is set to false.
0x80208321	DTS_W_MATCHINDEXALREADYEXISTS	A table with the name '%1' given for MatchIndexName already exists and DropExistingMatchIndex is set to FALSE. Transform execution will fail unless this table is dropped, a different name is specified, or DropExisitingMatchIndex is set to TRUE.
0x8020832B	DTS_W_TXFUZZYLOOKUP_JOINLENGTHMISMATCH	The length of input column '%1' is not equal to the length of the reference column '%2' that it is being matched against.
0x8020832D	DTS_W_TXFUZZYLOOKUP_CODEPAGE_MISMATCH	The code pages of the DT_STR source column "___" and the DT_STR dest column "___" do not match. This may cause unexpected results.
0x8020832E	DTS_W_FUZZYLOOKUP_TOOMANYEXACTMATCH COLUMNS	There are more than 16 exact match joins, so performance may not be optimal. Reduce the number of exact match joins to improve performance. SQL Server has a limit of 16 columns per index, the inverted index will be used for all lookups.
0x80208350	DTS_W_FUZZYLOOKUP_MEMLIMITAND EXHAUSTIVESPECIFIED	The Exhaustive option requires that the entire reference be loaded into main memory. Since a memory limit has been specified for the MaxMemoryUsage property, it is possible that the entire reference table will not fit within this bound and that the match operation will fail at runtime.
0x80208351	DTS_W_FUZZYLOOKUP_EXACTMATCHCOLUMNS EXCEEDBYTELIMIT	The cumulative lengths of the columns specified in the exact match joins exceeds the 900 byte limit for index keys. Fuzzy Lookup creates an index on the exact match columns to increase lookup performance and there is a possibility that creation of this index may fail and the lookup will fall back to an alternative, possibly slower, method of finding matches. If performance is a problem, try removing some exact match join columns or reduce the maximum lengths of variable length exact match columns.
0x80208352	DTS_W_FUZZYLOOKUP_EXACTMATCH INDEXCREATIONFAILED	Failed to create an index for exact match columns. Reverting to alternative fuzzy lookup method.
0x80208353	DTS_W_FUZZYGROUPINGINTERNALPIPELINE WARNING	The following Fuzzy Grouping internal pipeline warning occurred with warning code 0x___: "___".

Error Code	Symbolic Name	Description
0x80208375	DTS_W_XMLSRCOUTPUTCOLUMNLENGTHSETTO DEFAULT	No maximum length was specified for the __ with external data type __. The SSIS Data Flow Task data type "__" with a length of __ will be used.
0x80208376	DTS_W_XMLSRCOUTPUTCOLUMNDATATYPE MAPPEDTOSTRING	The __ references external data type __, which cannot be mapped to a SSIS Data Flow Task data type. The SSIS Data Flow Task data type DT_WSTR with a length of __ will be used instead.
0x80208385	DTS_W_NOREDIRECTWITHATTACHEDERROR OUTPUTS	No rows will be sent to error output(s). Configure error or truncation dispositions to redirect rows to the error output(s), or delete data flow transformations or destinations that are attached to the error output(s).
0x80208386	DTS_W_REDIRECTWITHNOATTACHEDERROR OUTPUTS	Rows sent to the error output(s) will be lost. Add new data flow transformations or destinations to receive error rows, or reconfigure the component to stop redirecting rows to the error output(s).
0x802090E4	DTS_W_TXLOOKUP_DUPLICATE_KEYS	The Lookup transformation encountered duplicate reference key values when caching reference data. The Lookup transformation found duplicate key values when caching metadata in PreExecute. This error occurs in Full Cache mode only. Either remove the duplicate key values, or change the cache mode to PARTIAL or NO_CACHE.
0x802092A7	DTS_W_POTENTIALTRUNCATIONFROM DATAINSERTION	Truncation may occur due to inserting data from data flow column "__" with a length of __ to database column "__" with a length of __.
0x802092A8	DTS_W_POTENTIALTRUNCATIONFROM DATARETRIEVAL	Truncation may occur due to retrieving data from database column "__" with a length of __ to data flow column "__" with a length of __.
0xC020822C	DTS_W_UNMAPPEDOUTPUTCOLUMN	The __ has no input column mapped to it.

The symbolic names of Integration Services informational messages begin with **DTS_I_**.

Error Code	Symbolic Name	Description
0x4001100A	DTS_I_STARTINGTRANSACTION	Starting distributed transaction for this container.
0x4001100B	DTS_I_COMMITTINGTRANSACTION	Committing distributed transaction started by this container.
0x4001100C	DTS_I_ABORTINGTRANSACTION	Aborting the current distributed transaction.
0x40016019	DTS_I_PACKAGEMIGRATED	The package was successfully migrated from version ___ to version ___. It must be saved to retain migration changes.
0x40016025	DTS_I_FTPRECEIVEFILE	Receiving file "___".
0x40016026	DTS_I_FTPSENDFILE	Sending file "___".
0x40016027	DTS_I_FTPFILEEXISTS	File "___" already exists.
0x40016028	DTS_I_FTPERRORLOADINGMSG	Cannot get extra error information due to an internal error.
0x40016036	DTS_I_FTPDELETEFILE	The attempt to delete file "___" failed. This may occur when the file does not exist, the file name was spelled incorrectly, or you do not have permissions to delete the file.
0x40016037	DTS_I_CONFIGFROMREG	The package is attempting to configure from a registry entry using the registry key "___".
0x40016038	DTS_I_CONFIGFROMENVVAR	The package is attempting to configure from the environment variable "___".
0x40016039	DTS_I_CONFIGFROMINIFILE	The package is attempting to configure from the .ini file "___".
0x40016040	DTS_I_CONFIGFROMSQLSERVER	The package is attempting to configure from SQL Server using the configuration string "___".
0x40016041	DTS_I_CONFIGFROMFILE	The package is attempting to configure from the XML file "___".
0x40016042	DTS_I_CONFIGFROMPARENTVARIABLE	The package is attempting to configure from the parent variable "___".
0x40016043	DTS_I_ATTEMPTINGUPGRADEOFDTS	Attempting an upgrade of SSIS from version "___" to version "___". The package is attempting to upgrade the runtime.
0x40016044	DTS_I_ATTEMPTINGUPGRADEOFANEXTOBJ	Attempting to upgrade "___". The package is attempting to upgrade an extensible object.
0x40016045	DTS_I_SAVECHECKPOINTSTOFILE	The package will be saving checkpoints to file "___" during execution. The package is configured to save checkpoints.
0x40016046	DTS_I_RESTARTFROMCHECKPOINTFILE	The package restarted from checkpoint file "___". The package was configured to restart from checkpoint.
0x40016047	DTS_I_CHECKPOINTSAVEDTOFILE	Checkpoint file "___" was updated to record completion of this container.

Error Code	Symbolic Name	Description
0x40016048	DTS_I_CHECKPOINTFILEDELETED	Checkpoint file "__" was deleted after successful completion of the package.
0x40016049	DTS_I_CHECKPOINTSAVINGTOFILE	Checkpoint file "__" update starting.
0x40016051	DTS_I_CHOSENMAXEXECUTABLES	Based on the system configuration, the maximum concurrent executables are set to __.
0x40016052	DTS_I_MAXEXECUTABLES	Maximum concurrent executables are set to __.
0x40016053	DTS_I_PACKAGESTART	Beginning of package execution.
0x40016054	DTS_I_PACKAGEEND	End of package execution.
0x40029161	DTS_I_FSTASK_DIRECTORYDELETED	Directory "__" was deleted.
0x40029162	DTS_I_FSTASK_FILEDELETED	File or directory "__" was deleted.
0x400292A8	DTS_I_TRANSFERDBTASK_OVERWRITEDB	Overwriting the database "__" on the destination server "__".
0x4002F304	DTS_I_SOMETHINGHAPPENED	"__".
0x4002F323	DTS_I_ERRMSGTASK_SKIPPINGERRORMESSAGEALREADYEXISTS	Skipping error message "__" since it already exists on the destination server.
0x4002F326	DTS_I_ERRMSGTASK_TRANSFEREDNERRORMESSAGES	"__" Error Messages were transferred.
0x4002F351	DTS_I_STOREDPROCTASKS_TRANSFEREDNSPS	The task transferred "__" Stored Procedures.
0x4002F352	DTS_I_TRANSOBJECTSTASK_TRANSFEREDNOBJECTS	Transferred "__" objects.
0x4002F358	DTS_I_TRANSOBJECTSTASK_NOSPSTOTRANSFER	There are no Stored Procedures to transfer.
0x4002F362	DTS_I_TRANSOBJECTSTASK_NORULESTOTRANSFER	There are no Rules to transfer.
0x4002F366	DTS_I_TRANSOBJECTSTASK_NOTABLESTOTRANSFER	There are no Tables to transfer.
0x4002F370	DTS_I_TRANSOBJECTSTASK_NOVIEWSTOTRANSFER	There are no Views to transfer.
0x4002F374	DTS_I_TRANSOBJECTSTASK_NOUDFSTOTRANSFER	There are no User Defined Functions to transfer.
0x4002F378	DTS_I_TRANSOBJECTSTASK_NODEFAULTSTOTRANSFER	There are no Defaults to transfer.
0x4002F382	DTS_I_TRANSOBJECTSTASK_NOUDDTSTOTRANSFER	There are no User Defined Data Types to transfer.
0x4002F386	DTS_I_TRANSOBJECTSTASK_NOPFSTOTRANSFER	There are no Partition Functions to transfer.

Error Code	Symbolic Name	Description
0x4002F390	DTS_I_TRANSOBJECTSTASK_NOPSSTOTRANSFER	There are no Partition Schemes to transfer.
0x4002F394	DTS_I_TRANSOBJECTSTASK_NOSCHEMASTOTRANSFER	There are no Schemas to transfer.
0x4002F398	DTS_I_TRANSOBJECTSTASK_NOSQLASSEMBLIESTOTRANSFER	There are no SqlAssemblys to transfer.
0x4002F402	DTS_I_TRANSOBJECTSTASK_NOAGGREGATESTOTRANSFER	There are no User Defined Aggregates to transfer.
0x4002F406	DTS_I_TRANSOBJECTSTASK_NOTYPESTOTRANSFER	There are no User Defined Types to transfer.
0x4002F410	DTS_I_TRANSOBJECTSTASK_NOXMLSCHEMACOLLECTIONSTOTRANSFER	There are no XmlSchemaCollections to transfer.
0x4002F418	DTS_I_TRANSOBJECTSTASK_NOLOGINSTOTRANSFER	There are no Logins to transfer.
0x4002F41D	DTS_I_TRANSOBJECTSTASK_NOUSERSTOTRANSFER	There are no Users to transfer.
0x4002F41E	DTS_I_TRANSOBJECTSTASK_TRUNCATINGTABLE	Truncating table "__"
0x40043006	DTS_I_EXECUTIONPHASE_PREPAREFOREXECUTE	Prepare for Execute phase is beginning.
0x40043007	DTS_I_EXECUTIONPHASE_PREEXECUTE	Pre-Execute phase is beginning.
0x40043008	DTS_I_EXECUTIONPHASE_POSTEXECUTE	Post Execute phase is beginning.
0x40043009	DTS_I_EXECUTIONPHASE_CLEANUP	Cleanup phase is beginning.
0x4004300A	DTS_I_EXECUTIONPHASE_VALIDATE	Validation phase is beginning.
0x4004300B	DTS_I_ROWS_WRITTEN	"__" wrote __ rows.
0x4004300C	DTS_I_EXECUTIONPHASE_EXECUTE	Execute phase is beginning.
0x4004800C	DTS_I_CANTRELIEVEPRESSURE	The buffer manager detected that the system was low on virtual memory, but was unable to swap out any buffers. __ buffers were considered and __ were locked. Either not enough memory is available to the pipeline because not enough is installed, other processes are using it, or too many buffers are locked.
0x4004800D	DTS_I_CANTALLOCATEMEMORYPRESSURE	The buffer manager failed a memory allocation call for __ bytes, but was unable to swap out any buffers to relieve memory pressure. __ buffers were considered and __ were locked. Either not enough memory is available to the pipeline because not enough are installed, other processes were using it, or too many buffers are locked.

Error Code	Symbolic Name	Description
0x400490F4	DTS_I_TXLOOKUP_CACHE_PROGRESS	__ has cached __ rows.
0x4020206D	DTS_I_RAWSOURCENOCOLUMNS	The raw source adapter opened a file, but the file contains no columns. The adapter will not produce data. This could indicate a damaged file, or that there are zero columns and, therefore, no data.
0x402020DA	DTS_I_OLEDBINFORMATIONALMESSAGE	An OLE DB informational message is available.
0x40208327	DTS_I_TXFUZZYLOOKUP_EXACT_MATCH_PERF_COLLATIONS_DONT_MATCH	Fuzzy match performance can be improved if the exact join FuzzyComparisonFlags on the input column "__" are set to match with the default SQL collation for reference table column "__". It is also necessary that no fold flags are set in FuzzyComparisonFlagsEx.
0x40208328	DTS_I_TXFUZZYLOOKUP_EXACT_MATCH_PERF_INDEX_MISSING	Fuzzy match performance can be improved if an index is created upon the reference table across all of the specified exact match columns.
0x40208387	DTS_I_DISPSNOTREVIEWED	Error and truncation dispositions were not reviewed. Make sure this component is configured to redirect rows to error outputs, if you wish to further transform those rows.
0x402090DA	DTS_I_TXAGG_WORKSPACE_REHASH	The Aggregate transformation has encountered __ key combinations. It has to re-hash data because the number of key combinations is more than expected. The component can be configured to avoid data re-hash by adjusting the Keys, KeyScale, and AutoExtendFactor properties.
0x402090DB	DTS_I_TXAGG_COUNTDISTINCT_REHASH	The Aggregate transformation has encountered __ distinct values while performing a "count distinct" aggregation on "__". The transformation will re-hash data because the number of distinct values is more than expected. The component can be configured to avoid data re-hash by adjusting the CountDistinctKeys, CountDistinctKeyScale, and AutoExtendFactor properties.
0x402090DC	DTS_I_STARTPROCESSINGFILE	The processing of file "__" has started.
0x402090DD	DTS_I_FINISHPROCESSINGFILE	The processing of file "__" has ended.
0x402090DE	DTS_I_TOTALDATAROWSPROCESSEDFORFILE	The total number of data rows processed for file "__" is __.
0x402090DF	DTS_I_FINALCOMMITSTARTED	The final commit for the data insertion has started.
0x402090E0	DTS_I_FINALCOMMITENDED	The final commit for the data insertion has ended.

The symbolic names of Integration Services error messages begin with **DTS_MSG_**.

Error Code	Symbolic Name	Description
0x1	DTS_MSG_CATEGORY_SERVICE_CONTROL	Incorrect function.
0x2	DTS_MSG_CATEGORY_RUNNING_PACKAGE_MANAGEMENT	The system cannot find the file specified.
0x100	DTS_MSG_SERVER_STARTING	Starting Microsoft SSIS Service. Server version %1
0x101	DTS_MSG_SERVER_STARTED	Microsoft SSIS Service started. Server version %1
0x102	DTS_MSG_SERVER_STOPPING	The wait operation timed out.
0x103	DTS_MSG_SERVER_STOPPED	No more data is available.
0x104	DTS_MSG_SERVER_START_FAILED	Microsoft SSIS Service failed to start. Error: %1
0x105	DTS_MSG_SERVER_STOP_ERROR	Error stopping Microsoft SSIS Service. Error: %1
0x110	DTS_MSG_SERVER_MISSING_CONFIG	Microsoft SSIS Service configuration file does not exist. Loading with default settings.
0x111	DTS_MSG_SERVER_BAD_CONFIG	Microsoft SSIS Service configuration file is incorrect. Error reading config file: %1 Loading server with default settings.
0x112	DTS_MSG_SERVER_MISSING_CONFIG_REG	Microsoft SSIS Service: Registry setting specifying configuration file does not exist. Attempting to load default config file.
0x150	DTS_MSG_SERVER_STOPPING_PACKAGE	Microsoft SSIS Service: stopping running package. Package instance ID: %1 Package ID: %2 Package name: %3 Package description: %4 Package started by: __.
0x40013000	DTS_MSG_PACKAGESTART	Package "__" started.
0x40013001	DTS_MSG_PACKAGESUCCESS	Package "__" finished successfully.
0x40013002	DTS_MSG_PACKAGECANCEL	Package "__" has been cancelled.

Error Code	Symbolic Name	Description
0x40013003	DTS_MSG_PACKAGEFAILURE	Package "__" failed.
0x40013004	DTS_MSG_CANTDELAYLOADDLL	Module __ cannot load DLL __ to call entry point __ because of error __. The product requires that DLL to run, but the DLL could not be found on the path.
0x40013005	DTS_MSG_CANTDELAYLOADDLLFUNCTION	Module __ loaded DLL __, but cannot find entry point __ because of error __. The named DLL could not be found on the path, and the product requires that DLL to run.
0x40103100	DTS_MSG_EVENTLOGENTRY	Event Name: %1 Message: %9 Operator: %2 Source Name: %3 Source ID: %4 Execution ID: %5 Start Time: %6 End Time: %7 Data Code: %8
0x40103101	DTS_MSG_EVENTLOGENTRY_PREEXECUTE	Event Name: %1 Message: %9 Operator: %2 Source Name: %3 Source ID: %4 Execution ID: %5 Start Time: %6 End Time: %7 Data Code: %8
0x40103102	DTS_MSG_EVENTLOGENTRY_POSTEXECUTE	Event Name: %1 Message: %9 Operator: %2 Source Name: %3 Source ID: %4 Execution ID: %5 Start Time: %6 End Time: %7 Data Code: %8

Error Code	Symbolic Name	Description
0x40103103	DTS_MSG_EVENTLOGENTRY_PREVALIDATE	Event Name: %1 Message: %9 Operator: %2 Source Name: %3 Source ID: %4 Execution ID: %5 Start Time: %6 End Time: %7 Data Code: %8
0x40103104	DTS_MSG_EVENTLOGENTRY_POSTVALIDATE	Event Name: %1 Message: %9 Operator: %2 Source Name: %3 Source ID: %4 Execution ID: %5 Start Time: %6 End Time: %7 Data Code: %8
0x40103105	DTS_MSG_EVENTLOGENTRY_WARNING	Event Name: %1 Message: %9 Operator: %2 Source Name: %3 Source ID: %4 Execution ID: %5 Start Time: %6 End Time: %7 Data Code: %8

Error Code	Symbolic Name	Description
0x40103106	DTS_MSG_EVENTLOGENTRY_ERROR	Event Name: %1 Message: %9 Operator: %2 Source Name: %3 Source ID: %4 Execution ID: %5 Start Time: %6 End Time: %7 Data Code: %8
0x40103107	DTS_MSG_EVENTLOGENTRY_TASKFAILED	Event Name: %1 Message: %9 Operator: %2 Source Name: %3 Source ID: %4 Execution ID: %5 Start Time: %6 End Time: %7 Data Code: %8
0x40103108	DTS_MSG_EVENTLOGENTRY_PROGRESS	Event Name: %1 Message: %9 Operator: %2 Source Name: %3 Source ID: %4 Execution ID: %5 Start Time: %6 End Time: %7 Data Code: %8

Error Code	Symbolic Name	Description
0x40103109	DTS_MSG_EVENTLOGENTRY_EXECSTATCHANGE	Event Name: %1 Message: %9 Operator: %2 Source Name: %3 Source ID: %4 Execution ID: %5 Start Time: %6 End Time: %7 Data Code: %8
0x4010310A	DTS_MSG_EVENTLOGENTRY_VARVALCHANGE	Event Name: %1 Message: %9 Operator: %2 Source Name: %3 Source ID: %4 Execution ID: %5 Start Time: %6 End Time: %7 Data Code: %8
0x4010310B	DTS_MSG_EVENTLOGENTRY_CUSTOMEVENT	Event Name: %1 Message: %9 Operator: %2 Source Name: %3 Source ID: %4 Execution ID: %5 Start Time: %6 End Time: %7 Data Code: %8

Error Code	Symbolic Name	Description
0x4010310C	DTS_MSG_EVENTLOGENTRY_PACKAGESTART	Event Name: %1 Message: %9 Operator: %2 Source Name: %3 Source ID: %4 Execution ID: %5 Start Time: %6 End Time: %7 Data Code: %8
0x4010310D	DTS_MSG_EVENTLOGENTRY_PACKAGEEND	Event Name: %1 Message: %9 Operator: %2 Source Name: %3 Source ID: %4 Execution ID: %5 Start Time: %6 End Time: %7 Data Code: %8
0x4010310E	DTS_MSG_EVENTLOGENTRY_INFORMATION	Event Name: %1 Message: %9 Operator: %2 Source Name: %3 Source ID: %4 Execution ID: %5 Start Time: %6 End Time: %7 Data Code: %8

The symbolic names of Integration Services success messages begin with **DTS_S_**.

Error Code	Symbolic Name	Description
0x40003	DTS_S_NULLDATA	The value is NULL.
0x40005	DTS_S_TRUNCATED	The string value was truncated. The buffer received a string that was too long for the column, and the string was truncated by the buffer.
0x200001	DTS_S_EXPREVALTRUNCATIONOCCURRED	A truncation occurred during evaluation of the expression. The truncation occurred during evaluation, which may include any point in an intermediate step.

The symbolic names of Integration Services error messages begin with **DTSBC_E_**, where "BC" refers to the native base class from which most Microsoft data flow components are derived.

Error Code	Symbolic Name	Description
0xC8000002	DTSBC_E_INCORRECTEXACTNUMBEROF TOTALOUTPUTS	The total number of outputs and error outputs, ___, is incorrect. There must be exactly ___.
0xC8000003	DTSBC_E_FAILEDTOGETOUTPUTBYINDEX	Cannot retrieve output with index ___.
0xC8000005	DTSBC_E_INCORRECTEXACTNUMBEROFERROR OUTPUTS	The number of error outputs, ___, is incorrect. There must be exactly ___.
0xC8000006	DTSBC_E_INVALIDVALIDATIONSTATUSVALUE	Incorrect validation status value, "___". It must be one of the values found in the DTSValidationStatus enumeration.
0xC8000007	DTSBC_E_INPUTHASNOOUTPUT	The input "___" has no synchronous output.
0xC8000008	DTSBC_E_INPUTHASNOERROROUTPUT	The input "___" has no synchronous error output.
0xC8000009	DTSBC_E_INVALIDHTPIVALUE	The HowToProcessInput value, ___, is not valid. It must be one of the values from the HowToProcessInput enumeration.
0xC800000A	DTSBC_E_FAILEDTOGETCOLINFO	Failed to get information for row "___", column "___" from the buffer. The error code returned was 0x___.
0xC800000B	DTSBC_E_FAILEDTOSETCOLINFO	Failed to set information for row "___", column "___" into the buffer. The error code returned was 0x___.
0xC800000C	DTSBC_E_INVALIDPROPERTY	The property "___" is not valid.
0xC800000D	DTSBC_E_PROPERTYNOTFOUND	The property "___" was not found.
0xC8000010	DTSBC_E_READONLYPROPERTY	Error assigning a value to the read-only property "___".
0xC8000011	DTSBC_E_CANTINSERTOUTPUTCOLUMN	The ___ does not allow the insertion of output columns.

Error Code	Symbolic Name	Description
0xC8000012	DTSBC_E_OUTPUTCOLUMNSMETADATAMISMATCH	The output columns' metadata does not match the associated input columns' metadata. The output columns' metadata will be updated.
0xC8000013	DTSBC_E_OUTPUTCOLUMNSMISSING	There are input columns that do not have associated output columns. The output columns will be added.
0xC8000014	DTSBC_E_TOOMANYOUTPUTCOLUMNS	There are output columns that do not have associated input columns. The output columns will be removed.
0xC8000015	DTSBC_E_OUTPUTCOLUMNSMETADATAMIS MATCHUNMAP	The output columns' metadata does not match the associated input columns' metadata. The input columns will be unmapped.
0xC8000016	DTSBC_E_UNMAPINPUTCOLUMNS	There are input columns that do not have associated output columns. The input columns will be unmapped.
0xC8000017	DTSBC_E_MULTIPLEINCOLSTOOUTCOL	There is an input column associated with an output column, and that output column is already associated with another input column on the same input.
0xC8000018	DTSBC_E_CANTINSERTEXTERNALMETADATA COLUMN	The __ does not allow the insertion of external metadata columns.

Expression Evaluator Reference Sheet

Math Functions

ABS(«numeric_expression»)

CEILING(«numeric_expression»)

EXP(«numeric_expression»)

FLOOR(«numeric_expression»)

LN(«numeric_expression»)

LOG(«numeric_expression»)

POWER(«base», «exponent»)

ROUND(«numeric_expression», «length»)

SIGN(«numeric_expression»)

SQUARE(«numeric_expression»)

SQRT(«numeric_expression»)

String Functions

FINDSTRING(«character_expression», «search_expression», «integer_expression»)

HEX(«integer_expression»)

LEN(«character_expression»)

LOWER(«character_expression»)

LTRIM(«character_expression»)

REPLACE(«character_expression», «search_expression», «replace_expression»)

REPLICATE(«character_expression», «integer_expression»)

RIGHT(«character_expression», «integer_expression»)

RTRIM(«character_expression»)

SUBSTRING(«character_expression», «start», «length»)

TRIM(«character_expression»)

UPPER(«character_expression»)

Date/Time Functions

DATEADD(«datepart», «number», «date»)

DATEDIFF(«datepart», «startdate», «enddate»)

DATEPART(«datepart», «date»)

DAY(«date»)

GETDATE( )

GETUTCDATE( )

MONTH(«date»)

YEAR(«date»)

Operators

+	addition	!=	inequality	&	bitwise AND
+	string concatenation	>	greater than	|	bitwise OR
-	subtraction	<	less than	^	bitwise exclusive OR
*	multiplication	>=	greater than or equal	~	unary bitwise NOT
/	division	<=	less than or equal	!	unary logical NOT
%	modulo	&&	logical AND	-	negative
( )	parentheses	||	logical OR		
==	equality	? :	conditional operator		

Type Casts

(DT_I1)

(DT_I2)

(DT_I4)

(DT_I8)

(DT_UI1)

(DT_UI2)

(DT_UI4)

(DT_UI8)

(DT_R4)

(DT_R8)

(DT_STR, «length», «code_page»)

(DT_WSTR, «length»)

(DT_DATE)

(DT_BOOL)

(DT_NUMERIC, «precision», «scale»)

(DT_DECIMAL, «scale»)

(DT_CY)

(DT_GUID)

(DT_BYTES, «length»)

(DT_DBDATE)

(DT_DBTIME)

(DT_DBTIMESTAMP)

(DT_FILETIME)

(DT_IMAGE)

(DT_TEXT, «code_page»)

(DT_NTEXT)

NULL Functions

ISNULL(«expression»)

NULL(DT_I1)

NULL(DT_I2)

NULL(DT_I4)

NULL(DT_I8)

NULL(DT_UI1)

NULL(DT_UI2)

NULL(DT_UI4)

NULL(DT_UI8)

NULL(DT_R4)

NULL(DT_R8)

NULL(DT_STR, «length», «code_page»)

NULL(DT_WSTR, «length»)

NULL(DT_DATE)

NULL(DT_BOOL)

NULL(DT_NUMERIC, «precision», «scale»)

NULL(DT_DECIMAL, «scale»)

NULL(DT_CY)

NULL(DT_GUID)

NULL(DT_BYTES, «length»)

NULL(DT_DBDATE)

NULL(DT_DBTIME)

NULL(DT_DBTIMESTAMP)

NULL(DT_FILETIME)

NULL(DT_IMAGE)

NULL(DT_TEXT, «code_page»)

NULL(DT_NTEXT)

Index

SYMBOLS

OLEDB, 442

RawFile, 443

Recordset, 486

SQL Server, 486

DSVs, 238, 241

enumerators, 45

environment variable package configurations, 311-313

Excel Connection Manager, 213

Execute DTS 2000 Package Task, 143

embedding option, 145

inner/outer variables, 146

packages, 144

structured storage, 145

Execute Package Task, 173

Execute Process Task, 176

Execute SQL Task, 178-181

File Connection Manager, 215

Flat File Connection Manager, 216

advanced options, 220-221

columns, 218-220

previewing, 221

sourcefile/format, 217-218

Flat File Destination Adapters, 74-75

Foreach loops, 45-46

FTP Connection Manager, 222

FTP Task, 151-153

Fuzzy Grouping transform, 527

advanced settings, 529

connection managers, choosing, 528

householding, 529-530

input columns, 528

Fuzzy Lookup transform, 522

columns, 524

ETI, 522

reference data, 525

similarity threshold, 525

HTTP Connection Manager, 223-224

Integration Services Server, 382

access, 384

diagnostics, 385-386

executing packages, shutting down, 383

folders, 383

header, 383

MSDB Store, 384

restarting, 381

MSMQ Task, 155

Receive Mode, 157-159

Send Mode, 156

MultiFile Connection Manager, 227-228

MultiFlatFile Connection Manager, 228

ODBC Connection Manager, 229-230

OLEDB Connection Manager, 231

OLEDB Sources, 73

output paths, 574

packages. *See* configurations

scope, 117

Send Mail Task, 47-50, 149

SMOServer Connection Manager, 233

SMTP Connection Manager, 233

source adapters

DataReader, 432-433

Excel, 437

Flat File, 439-440

OLEDB, 442

RawFile, 443

XML, 446

surface area, 13-14

How can we make this index more useful? Email us at indexes@samspublishing.com

How can we make this index more useful? Email us at indexes@samspublishing.com

U

How can we make this index more useful? Email us at indexes@samspublishing.com

THIS BOOK IS SAFARI ENABLED

INCLUDES FREE 45-DAY ACCESS TO THE ONLINE EDITION

The Safari® Enabled icon on the cover of your favorite technology book means the book is available through Safari Bookshelf. When you buy this book, you get free access to the online edition for 45 days.

Safari Bookshelf is an electronic reference library that lets you easily search thousands of technical books, find code samples, download chapters, and access technical information whenever and wherever you need it.

TO GAIN 45-DAY SAFARI ENABLED ACCESS TO THIS BOOK:

- Go to **http://www.samspublishing.com/safarienabled**
- Complete the brief registration form
- Enter the coupon code: **LNKN-BEHJ-PEBS-W4JB-ZMTD**

If you have difficulty registering on Safari Bookshelf or accessing the online edition, please e-mail customer-service@safaribooksonline.com.